106

Polling America

Polling America

AN ENCYCLOPEDIA OF PUBLIC OPINION

Volume II (P–Z)

Edited by
Samuel J. Best and Benjamin Radcliff

Greenwood Press
Westport, Connecticut • London

Library of Congress Cataloging-in-Publication Data

Polling America : an encyclopedia of public opinion / edited by Samuel J. Best and
  Benjamin Radcliff.
     p.   cm.
    Includes bibliographical references and index.
    ISBN 0–313–32701–7 ((set) : alk. paper)—ISBN 0–313–32712–2 ((vol. 1) : alk.
  paper)—ISBN 0–313–32713–0 ((vol. 2) : alk. paper) 1. Public opinion—United
  States—Encyclopedias.   2. Public opinion—United States—History—Encyclopedias.   3.
  Public opinion polls—Encyclopedias.   4. Public opinion
  polls—History—Encyclopedias.   I. Best, Samuel J.   II. Radcliff, Benjamin.
  HN90.P8P645   2005
  303.3'8'097303—dc22   2005008245

British Library Cataloguing in Publication Data is available.

Library of Congress Catalog Card Number: 2005008245
ISBN: 0–313–32701–7 (set)
        0–313–32712–2 (vol. I)
        0–313–32713–0 (vol. II)

First published in 2005

Greenwood Press, 88 Post Road West, Westport, CT 06881
An imprint of Greenwood Publishing Group, Inc.
www.greenwood.com

Printed in the United States of America

The paper used in this book complies with the
Permanent Paper Standard issued by the National
Information Standards Organization (Z39.48–1984).

10 9 8 7 6 5 4 3 2 1

To Niki and Amy

Contents

List of Entries

P

Panel Surveys

Panel surveys are used to measure gross changes in the population and to aggregate data for sample members over time. In a panel study, data is collected from the same sample members (i.e., individuals, households) at multiple points in time. Repeated interviewing of the same people at different points in time is the best way to measure changes in the composition or characteristics of a given population of interest.

The design of a panel study is primarily dependent on the research objectives and priorities of the funding agency. For example, the National Longitudinal Surveys (NLS) comprise a set of panel surveys sponsored by the U.S. Bureau of Labor Statistics that follow several groups of men and women, some for more than thirty years, to gather information at multiple points in time on labor market activities and other significant life events. The Medical Expenditure Panel Survey (MEPS) is a panel study sponsored by the Agency for Health Care Research and Quality. MEPS collects data on the specific health services that Americans use, how frequently they use them, the cost of these services, and how they are paid for, as well as data on the cost, scope, and breadth of private health insurance held by and available to the U.S. population. And, the Survey of Income and Program Participation (SIPP), sponsored by the U.S. Census Bureau, is a national panel study designed to provide data about the income and program participation of individuals and households in the United States. The survey collects data on taxes, assets, liabilities, and participation in government transfer programs.

A panel survey design should not to be confused with a **repeated survey** design, which is a series of cross-sectional surveys conducted at different points in time. A good example of a repeated survey is the CAHPS Medicare Fee-for Service Survey that is conducted annually with a probabalistic sample of the

Medicare population. Unlike a true panel survey, no attempt is made to include the same sample members in subsequent rounds of data collection. Collecting repeated measures over time on the same sample members using a panel survey design provides a much more powerful analysis of the social processes underlying a particular event than can be achieved with a cross-sectional or repeated study design.

There are many design issues that need to be considered in the planning of a panel study. First are decisions about how long the panel should be followed, the length of the reference period and the number of waves of data collection. The longer the panel is followed, the richer the data set will be. However, there is a tendency to lose panel members as time passes, which can become a problem for maintaining the representativeness of the sample. The reference period refers to the time period for which a sample member is asked to recall a particular set of events (e.g., over the past six months . . .). In general, memory decays over time so the longer the reference period, the greater the likelihood of incurring some recall error. However, longer reference periods may be suitable if the events in question do not occur with great frequency. For example, a twelve-month reference period may be suitable if the events in question are periods of unemployment. The same twelve-month reference period may not work as well if the events in question are the number of visits to the grocery store or the amount of money spent on all recreational activities.

The decision about the number of waves of data collection is determined by both the length of the panel and the length of the reference period. Too frequent waves of data collection will significantly increase burden on the sample member, which can lead to panel attrition. Decisions also need to be made about how to collect the data—in-person, telephone, Web, mail or with a multimodal design. Varying the mode of data collection can reduce the burden on sample members and help to reduce attrition in studies that required frequent waves of data collection. Finally, a decision needs to be made about the sample design. Clustered samples are often used to reduce the costs associated with in-person interviews. However, for a long-term panel study, the reduced cost benefit quickly disappears as the initial sample moves out of the cluster areas. This is less of an issue with telephone, Web, or mail surveys. These decisions depend to a great extent on the topic of the survey.

Although all surveys are subject to various sources of nonsampling error, there are three unique types of error associated with panel surveys: nonresponse, time-in-sample bias, and the seam effect. Retention of sample members in each wave of a panel study is critical to the success of a longitudinal study. The burden of being asked repeatedly to participate in the study can cause some sample members to refuse to participate in a single wave of the study. This is referred to as "wave nonresponse." Or, the sample member can refuse to participate in any future wave of the study, which is known as "panel nonresponse." Although the nonresponse experienced in the first wave of a panel survey is no different than in a cross-sectional or one-time survey, the nonresponse in a panel survey accumulates with subsequent waves of data collection. As the overall nonresponse rate increases over time, it weakens the power of the analysis to detect long-term effects and threatens the study's internal validity and generalizability.

One of the challenges of managing a panel survey is to reduce or flatten the nonresponse rate by managing panel attrition. The main reasons for panel attrition include the inability to locate sample members and **refusals**. Nonrespondents can be categorized in three ways. Sample members that cannot be located for a particular wave of data collection are referred to as "lost-to-follow-up." Although classified as wave nonrespondents, these sample members are included each time a wave is conducted and inevitably some are found and (others lost). A second type of wave nonrespondent is one who refuses to participate in the current wave but does not rule out future participation. This kind of nonrespondent is also retained in the panel. The third type of nonrespondent is one who refuses to participate in the current wave or any of the future waves of the study. These nonrespondents represent true panel attrition.

Plans for managing panel attrition are implemented with the first wave of data collection. Gaining the cooperation of sample members in a panel study differs from gaining cooperation in a cross-sectional study or one-time study. A panel study requires a higher level of commitment from the sample members than is required of participants in a cross-sectional survey. Inducing compliance to participate a study once is much easier than getting sample members to commit to participate in a long-term study. Careful thought must be given to the use of incentives as a way of inducing compliance in any wave of a panel study. There is a large body of literature in social psychology that has repeatedly shown that large rewards may induce compliance with a single task, but small rewards are more effective in eliciting a change in behavior over the long term. The reasoning is that when people receive a large reward for performing a task, they tend to attribute their participation to an external motivator: the reward. "I completed the survey because it paid me one hundred dollars." When people receive a small reward for completing a task, they tend to attribute their participation to an internal motivator rather than the small reward. "I completed the survey because it was important for me to do so." Careful thought also needs to go into any decision to increase the incentive once the study is fielded. Sample members learn by experience and if sample members who initially refuse are rewarded by an increase in the incentive, then they will be more likely to do so in subsequent waves of the study. This effect has been noted to occur with interviewers as well.

The time-in-sample bias refers to the learning that takes place as sample members participate in subsequent waves of data collection. Some sample members learn that they can influence the administration of the survey by selecting their responses based on previous experience with the survey. For example, some sample members recognize that responding affirmatively to a particular type of question typically leads to follow-up questions. As a result, the sample member learns to respond negatively to avoid follow-up questions. The time-in-sample bias also refers to sample members who, based on previous experience in the panel, begin to prepare for their interviews by tracking information that they think to be relevant.

Many panel surveys ask sample members to report about events in a series of subintervals within the survey's larger response periods. A good example would be a survey that is conducted three times a year in April, August, and December. At each of the interviews, sample members are asked to report their experiences in one-month intervals. For example, the interview in April asks sample members to report about events in January, February, March, and April. When the data for each month are plotted, more change can be noted between the responses given for the "seam" months (those that cross two waves of data collection) than between the responses that are given in months within one wave of data collection. In the example provided, the seams would be between April and May, August and September, and December and January. Thus, the seam effect refers to the finding that there are more changes reported between the seam months than between months when all data was collected within one wave of data collection. This effect is generally attributed to underreporting of changes for periods that occur within one wave of data collection or to over reporting of changes for periods that span two waves of data collection. The effect seems to increase as a function of the demands on recall memory.

Further Reading

Duncan, G. J., and G. Kalton. "Issues of Design and Analysis of Surveys Across Time." *International Statistical Review* 55 (1987): 97–117. A detailed treatment of panel survey designs.

Kalton, G., and M. E. Miller. "The Seam Effect with Social Security Income in the Survey of Income and Program Participation." *Journal of Official Statistics* 7 (1991): 235–45. A discussion of the classic seam effect.

Kasprzyk, Daniel, Greg Duncan, Graham Kalton, and M. P. Singh. *Panel Surveys*. New York: John Wiley, 1989. A complete review of issues related to the conduct of panel studies.

Web Sites

The Web site for the National Longitudinal Surveys (NLS) can be found at http://www.bls.gov/nls/.

The Web site for the Medical Expenditure Panel Study can be found at http://www.meps.ahrq.gov/whatismeps/bulletin.

The Web site for the Survey of Income and Program Participation (SIPP) can be found at http://www.sipp.census.gov/sipp/intro.html.

Linda L. Dimitropoulos

Partial Interviews

Partial interviews (or break-offs) are surveys that are terminated by respondents in-progress and left uncompleted. Partial interviews can occur for many reasons, such as the respondent running out of time or losing interest in the study. There are two types of partial interviews: sufficient and insufficient. Sufficient partial interviews are those in which respondents have completed enough of the instrument for the instrument to be useful for study. Conversely, insufficient partial interviews are not far enough along for the interview to be considered acceptable. Sufficient partials contribute to the overall **response rate**, whereas insufficient partials are included in the refusal rate (*see* **Outcome Rates**).

Despite their importance, partial interviews have not been studied in-depth. Research on survey nonresponse has largely focused on how nonrespondents differ from respondents, item nonresponse, and the use of incentives to increase response rates. Understanding the source of partial interviews and their relationship to refusals and completed interviews is no less vital, and will only enhance the development of strategies for reducing nonresponse in similar surveys.

Fortunately, the issue of partial interviews is of particular importance to the National Health Interview Survey (NHIS). The NHIS is a nationally representative annual household survey of health, often lasting over an hour and often involving two or more respondents. Because of the modular nature of the NHIS, partial interviews often result in whole subject matter sections and supplements not being completed. To combat this phenomenon, the NHIS included questions designed to explore the reasons for breakoffs. Using data from the 2002 NHIS, we report the results of this effort.

The NHIS is conducted annually by the Census Bureau for the National Center for Health Statistics. The NHIS is a representative household survey of the general health of the civilian, noninstitutionalized, household population of the United States. The NHIS has four major modules: the household, family, sample child, and sample adult questionnaires. Each of these modules is made up of various smaller sections. From a knowledgeable adult in the family, the household composition module collects basic demographic information on members of the household and the family module collects general health information. From each family, one sample adult and one sample child (if applicable) are selected randomly, and more detailed health information is collected directly from the sample adult and from a knowledgeable adult for the sample child. Supplemental modules that are placed at the end of a major module or interspersed in the survey are added on a yearly basis. The NHIS often lasts for more than an hour, and involves two or more respondents in 40 percent of interviews.

Because of increases in partially completed interviews in the NHIS in the late 1990s, questions for interviewers were added in the NHIS in 2000 to provide more information about reasons for partial interviews. The first question (PARTIAL variable) asks, "Indicate the main reason why the case cannot be completed" and provides the following response categories: (1) Break-off/Respondent terminated interview, (2) Sample Adult refused or unavailable, (3) Sample Child respondent refused or unavailable, (4) No one home, repeated calls, (5) Language problem, and (6) Other (which the respondent is asked to specify). The second question (BREAKOFF variable) is asked for responses of 1, 2, 3 to the PARTIAL variable, and asks, "Indicate the main reason why the respondent terminated the interview." The following categories are provided: (1) Questions too personal, (2) Interview too long, (3) Respondent didn't have time to complete, (4) Respondent didn't feel well, (5) Abrupt end, respondent didn't give reason, and (6) Other (which the respondent is asked to specify).

In addition to the calculation of overall response rates for 2002, response rates for completed and partially completed interviews were computed based on whether the household respondent and sample adult was the same person. For partially completed interviews, frequencies of PARTIAL and BREAKOFF variables, as well as their accompanying "Other: specify" categories, were calculated.

Open-ended responses from approximately 2000 cases were analyzed using the constant comparative method. The constant comparative method is the process of generating conceptual categories from uncategorized data. This involves comparing each piece of data so that similar pieces of data are labeled

Table 1. Household Response Rates and Partial Rates, 2002 NHIS

Quarter (Sample Size = 36,745)	Response Rate (%)	Partial Rate (%)
Quarter 1	90.1	17.2
Quarter 2	90.4	15.6
Quarter 3	91.0	16.2
Quarter 4	89.7	16.6

Table 2. Percent of NHIS Interviews in Which the Household Respondent and Sample Adult Respondent Were the Same or Different by Outcome of Interview, 2002 NHIS

Outcome of Interview (Sample Size = 36,745)	Household and Sample Adult Respondent Same (%)	Household and Sample Adult Respondent Different (%)	Total (%)
Completed interview	69.0	31.0	100
Partial interview	12.0	88.0	100

and grouped to form categories. Every new piece of data is then compared to this categorical structure, and the structure is reconstructed in an iterative manner until no new piece of data challenges its ability to account for all pieces of data.

Approximately one in six NHIS interviews were partial completions in 2002; this percent was consistent over four quarters of data (see Table 1).

Households where the household respondent was not the sample adult accounted for only 31 percent of completed interviews but 88 percent of partial interviews (see Table 2). Clearly, the need to interview a second respondent is a major factor in interviews not being complete. Analyses of the pre-existing categories reveal that more than half (52 percent) of all partials are due to the sample adult respondent not finishing the interview (see Table 3). One-third of partial cases fell into the "Break-off/Respondent terminated interview" category, and 9 percent ended up in the "Other: specify" category. The categories are somewhat vague and only one category can be chosen, even if multiple reasons for partials apply. Therefore, it is unclear whether the pre-existing categories are capturing a true picture of partial interviews in the field.

Table 4 shows the most common responses listed in the "Other: specify" category for the PARTIAL variable. These are cases for which the interviewer did not select any of the predefined categories. A frequent number of these cases are not complete because the interviewer did not finish with the additional family or roommate. Instrument error is another common reason in the "Other: specify" category. The respondent was busy, not physically able to finish the interview, or unavailable in other cases.

Table 3. Reasons Given by Interviewers for Partial Interviews, 2002 NHIS

Reason (Sample Size = 6,560)	Percent
Break-off/Respondent terminated interview	33.4
Sample adult refused or unavailable	51.6
Sample child respondent refused or unavailable	2.1
No one home, repeated calls	2.9
Language problem	1.2
Other: specify	8.9

Table 4. Other: Specify Categories in the PARTIAL Variable, 2002 NHIS

PARTIAL—Other: specify (Sample Size = 519)	Percent
Second family in household did not respond	22.7
Instrument problem	14.4
Respondent busy	11.0
Respondent not physically able	10.6
Respondent unavailable or out of town	7.3
Immunization section incomplete	6.6
No reason given	5.2
Respondent does not trust government	4.6
Another relative did not allow respondent to participate	3.3
Interviewer ran out of time	3.3
Miscellaneous	11.0

Table 5. Reasons for Break-offs, 2002 NHIS

Reason (Sample Size = 5,713)	Percent
Questions too personal	17.9
Interview too long	20.1
Respondent didn't have time to complete	22.5
Respondent didn't feel well	3.1
Abrupt end, respondent didn't give reason	9.2
Other	27.3

Table 5 shows data from the pre-existing categories of the BREAKOFF variable. It shows that "Questions too personal," "Interview too long," and "Respondent didn't have time to complete" made up 60 percent of the responses, split nearly evenly among the three categories. An additional 27 percent fell into the "Other: specify" category. Because the pre-existing categories are not very

Table 6. "Other: Specify" Categories in the BREAKOFF
Variable, 2002 NHIS

BREAKOFF—Other: Specify (Sample Size = 1,546)	Percent
Respondent unavailable	37.4
Respondent out of town	13.3
No reason given	11.4
Respondent does not trust government	10.7
Respondent busy	6.5
Another relative did not allow respondent to participate	5.1
Respondent not physically able	4.5
Respondent just did not want to participate	3.6
Respondent spoke another language and did not understand English very well	2.0
Instrument problem	1.6
Interviewer ran out of time	0.8
Miscellaneous	3.1

specific, analysis of the "Other: specify" responses may provide more detail that can be used to expand the precodes in subsequent surveys.

Table 6 shows the breakdown of the 27 percent of cases that were not captured in the predefined categories under the BREAKOFF variable. Frequently, the interviews were incomplete because the respondent was either unavailable or out of town. It appears from this and the precoded data that interviewers are facing an extremely busy public, which spends a great deal of time away from home. Additional reasons for break-offs include mistrust of the Federal government, the respondent's spouse, parent, or child counseling them not to participate, instrument problems, and the interviewer running out of time.

Methodologically, this research demonstrates that the analysis of textual data can provide valuable information to redesign precoded questions. By adding additional categories to the precoded questions, we will learn if the categories that emerged from the "Other: specify" are common. By using the open-ended responses to redesign the questions, we will likely gain a more complete and detailed account of reasons for partials and break-offs in the future. Further analysis should focus on demographic characteristics of partial respondents as well as a more thorough analysis of respondent reasoning.

Further Reading

Atrostic, B. K., N. Bates, G. Burt, and A. Silberstein. "Nonresponse in U.S. Government Household Surveys: Consistent Measures, Recent Trends, and New Insights." *Journal of Official Statistics* 17, no. 2 (2001): 209–26. Provides an overview of nonresponse trends and issues in federal household surveys.

Purdon, S., S. Campanelli, and P. Sturgis. "Interviewers' Calling Strategies on Face-to-Face Interview Surveys." *Journal of Official Statistics* 15, no. 2 (1999): 199–216. Separates factors that interviewers can influence from factors that are beyond the interviewer's control.

Howard Riddick, Barbara J. Stussman, and Beth L. Taylor

Partisanship

Most Americans have a partisan affiliation and thus consider themselves to be Republicans or Democrats. Partisanship, often called "party identification" (or party ID), refers to what has been aptly labeled a voter's "standing decision." That is, in the absence of any other information this is the party a voter is inclined to support. While political scientists generally agree that party ID is of central importance in explaining how people vote, they disagree on its fundamental nature. Some argue that partisanship is a deeply ingrained identity, a product of childhood **socialization** that rarely changes over the course of someone's life. Others see party identification as more variable, shifting with the political winds. The fact that decades after the first scholarship on the subject was published there is still an ongoing debate over the nature of party ID puts into sharp relief the continuing relevance of partisanship in American elections. While many observers have predicted that the United States would experience a decline in the relevance of partisanship in determining who wins elective office, party identification is a stronger predictor of the vote than ever.

The American political environment is complicated. American voters regularly confront multiple elections for offices having different responsibilities, while candidates, interest groups, and members of the press exchange charges on an array of issues. Somehow, voters must impose order on the chaos that characterizes contemporary elections. A fundamentally important means of ordering the political world is through one's partisanship, or what political scientists often call party identification. Party ID is generally defined as a long-standing psychological attachment to a party (although, as we will see, the very definition of party ID is itself at the heart of a vigorous debate). The concept of a long-term commitment to a party was a central organizing principle within the seminal research of Angus Campbell and his colleagues in the 1950s, as they founded what came to be known as the Michigan School of political science and published their landmark book, *The American Voter*, in 1960.

In their analysis of the factors explaining the vote, Campbell and his colleagues noted that one of the most reliable indicators of how people cast their ballots is their partisan preference. Significantly, however, while partisan affiliation is an important factor affecting the vote, it is far from definitive. Somewhat ironically, perhaps, party ID is only interesting to political scientists because it does not perfectly predict how someone votes. If it did, party ID would simply be equated with vote choice, leaving us no further along in explaining why people vote the way they do. While in other nations there is typically little difference between party affiliation and the vote, in the United States it is not uncommon to see voters who call themselves Republicans voting for Democratic candidates, and Democrats voting for Republicans. Party ID is thus largely conceived of as an American concept. While some scholars have sought to export the idea abroad, it is of primary interest in the stable yet diverse two-party system of the United States.

Campbell and his colleagues theorized that people develop a psychological attachment to one party, largely as the result of childhood socialization. The choice of terms is significant—voters *identify with*, not necessarily *belong to*, one of the two major parties. While most Americans have a party identification, very, very few are "dues-paying" members of their party. This psychological attachment, therefore, is only a disposition—and not necessarily a commitment—to support candidates of one party over another; it is what V. O. Key aptly described as a voter's "standing decision." Think of party ID as a default position, the party for which voters will cast their ballots unless the short-term conditions of a particular election persuade them otherwise.

Campbell and others of the Michigan School were not the first to note that most Americans are inclined to support one party over another. They were the first, however, to draw on research in psychology to explain the process by which people come to identify with a party. Borrowing from psychological theory in vogue in the 1950s, they likened party identification to membership in a reference group, like one's social class or religion. Religious affiliation is a useful analogy. Just as most people adopt a religious affiliation from their parents while still in their childhood and before fully understanding what their particular religion entails, most people also develop a partisan attachment while they are young, based largely on the views of their parents. As with religion, they come to identify with a party before they are of an age to understand the party's philosophy or policies. As reference group theory has fallen out of favor among psychologists, political scientists today rarely describe party ID using this exact language. Instead, they use the similar term "social identity"—one is a Republican or Democrat in the same way that one identifies with, say, an ethnic group.

In the framework of the Michigan School, then, party ID is a deep-seated psychological attachment rooted in childhood socialization, which in turn acts as a filter through which information about the political environment must pass. People therefore tend to see the political world in a light favorable to their party, which strengthens their partisan allegiance. As people age, party identification is thus self-reinforcing. Consequently, during times of political flux, it is the youngest voters who are the most likely to adopt new partisan attachments. In recent years this has been observed in the Southern United States, which over the last generation has been transformed from a Democratic bastion to a Republican redoubt as Southern white voters have adopted the Republican label. During this period of change, it has been young voters who have been most likely to adopt the Republican label.

While the Michigan School's perspective on party identification set the agenda for a mountain of subsequent research, this is not to say that it has been universally adopted among political scientists. While there is consensus on the fundamental idea that Americans generally favor one party over another, and that this preference is a good—but not perfect—predictor of how they vote, some scholars have objected to the implication that partisan affiliation is essentially hard-wired in one's youth and thus virtually impervious to changes in the political environment. Perhaps the most compelling of these critiques comes from Morris Fiorina, who proposes a "retrospective theory of voting." Fiorina begins with the assumption that voters are rational actors whose evaluations of elected officials constitute a running tally, rewarding incumbent office-holders for positive performance and punishing them when things go awry. When asked to indicate their party ID, voters refer to their tally and identify with whichever one is "ahead." It is not the case, however, that this constant updating of partisan assessments leads to a constant switching between the parties. The baseline of the tally is likely to be in one party's favor, which means that it takes a sustained series of "missteps" by one's preferred party until a voter switches allegiance to the opposing camp. Party identification thus appears relatively static, as voters do not flit back and forth from supporting one party versus another.

The retrospective take on partisanship is both intuitive and supported by empirical evidence, and thus represents a strong challenge to the Michigan model of party ID. Nonetheless, it is easy to overstate the differences between the two perspectives, as they actually share much common ground. Campbell and his colleagues, for example, never said that party ID is immutable, just that it does not easily change. And Fiorina, for his part, acknowledges that voters do not start their running tallies so that both parties are even. Most people are inclined toward one party or the other, leaving socialization in one's youth as a viable explanation for each individual's perception of the two parties.

More recently another challenge to the Michigan School perspective on party ID, similar in kind to the theory of retrospective voting, has come from the study of the electorate in the aggregate: for example, the percentage of Republicans and Democrats in the electorate as a whole. When we narrow our focus to individual voters, we see that their partisan affiliation generally does not change over time. Once a Republican (or Democrat), always a Republican (or Democrat). Expanding our scope to the public as a whole, however, we see a very different picture, as partisanship in the aggregate shows considerable variability. The view of the electorate in the aggregate is known as "macropartisanship," whose proponents argue in the same vein as Fiorina—that voters shift their partisan allegiances in response to political events, such as perceptions of the economy's health or approval of the president's performance.

The literature on macropartisanship has triggered a debate among political scientists that circles back to the long-standing question of the degree to which party identification is malleable. The debate is often highly technical, resting on the statistical methods employed for the analysis. The most prominent critics of the macropartisanship perspective—political scientist Donald Green and his colleagues—argue that the observed variability in party ID is really owing to statistical noise: that is, the errors that inevitably creep into any measurement. They posit that once steps are taken to account for the noisiness of data collected through public opinion surveys, party ID is extremely stable. As with the debate over retrospective voting, however, the proponents and critics of the macropartisanship model actually agree on much. Both camps agree, for example, that shifts in the partisan profile of the electorate as a whole are relatively subtle. The fundamental disagreement is over the substantive importance of such shifts. Any consumer of information about America's political landscape should thus be suspicious of claims that there have been large swings in voters' allegiance to one party over another over a short period of time. Changes in partisanship are more a matter of evolution than revolution.

Because it revolves around seemingly arcane statistical issues, the debate over macropartisanship can seem far removed from politics as it is practiced "on the ground." In reality, though, the implications for practical politics are profound. If the Michigan model is correct and a voter's partisan identification is largely unshakeable, it suggests that political operatives ought not to devote resources to winning new identifiers for their political label and should instead pursue a strategy of mobilizing their fellow partisans. In contrast, if partisanship is pliable then it makes sense to work at conversion, or, winning new converts to one's party.

Scholars studying partisanship not only need to pay attention to the way data on party ID is analyzed; they also need to pay attention to the way partisanship is measured in the first place (*see* **Partisanship Measurement**). While there is no "right way" to measure party preference, it is important to keep in mind that nuances in the questions that are asked affect the answers people give. For example, much of the macropartisanship literature is based on trends in partisanship as measured by the Gallup Poll, which asks respondents their partisan allegiance "*in politics, as of today.*" In contrast, the biennial **National Election Study** (NES) asks a three-part question designed to emphasize a respondent's long-term partisan affiliation. This, it should be noted, is the same question used by Campbell and his colleagues in their original studies of the American electorate, since the NES is the continuation of the data collection undertaken by the early Michigan School researchers. The three-part question follows:

1. Generally speaking, do you usually think of yourself as a Republican, a Democrat, an Independent, or what?

If a partisan affiliation is selected in (1):

2. Would you consider yourself a strong Democrat/Republican or a not very strong Democrat/Republican?

If a partisan affiliation is not selected in (1):

3. Do you think of yourself as closer to the Republican or Democratic Party?

Since the Gallup question primes the respondent to think of the immediate political environment (politics *today*), it is more likely to pick up fluctuations in partisan allegiance than is the NES, which cues people to think "generally" of which partisan allegiance they "usually" think of themselves as having.

The NES question not only encourages people to think generally, it is also designed to minimize the number of people who are classified as political independents. In common parlance, independence is thought to be a political virtue, and so when asked about their partisan allegiance many Americans reflexively indicate that they do not favor a particular party; instead, they say that they are independents. When nudged to indicate whether they are closer to one party rather than another, many of these independents confess that they actually do lean toward a party. Once these faux independents—they are generally referred to as independent "leaners"—are separated from those voters who maintain they are independent from either party, the NES question arrays party ID across a seven-point scale:

1. Strong Republican
2. Weak Republican
3. Independent-leaning Republican
4. Independent
5. Independent-leaning Democrat
6. Weak Democrat
7. Strong Democrat

Figure 1. All Independents (Including Partisan Leaners)

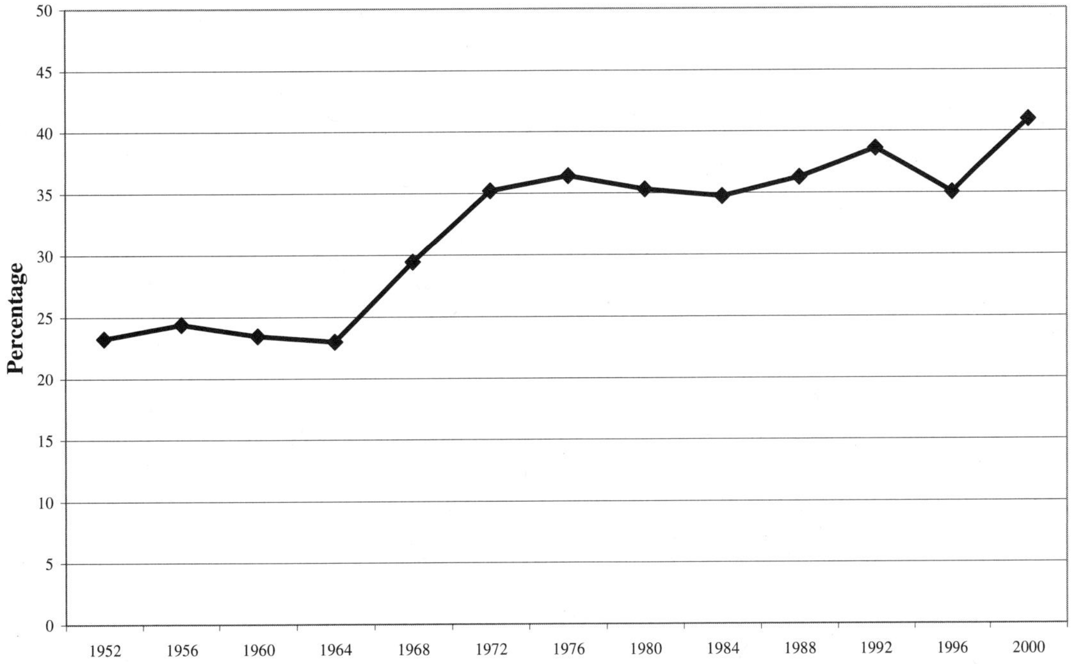

When analyzing American politics, it is extremely important to pay attention to how independent voters are classified, as it turns out that there are sharp differences between a "pure independent" and one who admits leaning toward one party. Independent leaners generally vote in a consistently partisan way, sometimes even more so than weak partisans. For example, in the 2000 presidential election 84 percent of Weak Republicans voted for George W. Bush, compared with 86 percent of Independent-leaning Republicans and only 55 percent of pure independents.

Understanding the covert partisanship behind many voters' self-identified independence helps to explain the political significance of the apparent increase of independent voters in the American electorate. As shown in Figure 1, when all independents are grouped together (based on responses to the first of the NES questions), it appears that the percentage of independents has risen since 1952. This would imply that the United States has undergone a period during which a large segment of the electorate became unmoored from partisan anchors, which indeed is a frequently held misconception.

However, separating out the pure independents from the partisan leaners suggests a different conclusion. Figure 2 demonstrates that although the percentage of pure independents did rise slightly in the mid-1970s, it fell off again in the 1980s and 1990s. But while the percentage of pure independents was falling over the last twenty or so years, the percentage of independent-leaning Democrats and Republicans was rising. What we have, therefore, is not an increasingly in-

Figure 2. Independents

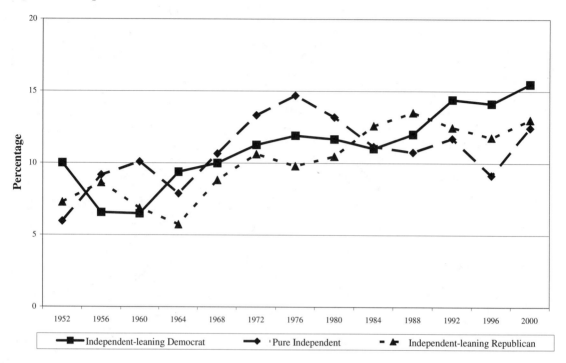

dependent electorate at all, but rather an electorate with more voters who simultaneously claim the mantle of independence while nonetheless voting like partisans when they reach the polling booth.

To complement the display of voters who profess some degree of partisan independence, Figure 3 displays the trends in Americans who overtly identify with a party (either strongly or weakly) over the same period of time. The primary trend is a decline in the proportion of Democratic identifiers in the electorate since 1952, so that by 2000 we see that although the Democrats have maintained their historical edge over the Republicans, the gap has narrowed considerably. The fact that Republican presidents have spent more time in the White House through a period in which there were more Democrats than Republicans within the electorate reminds us that party ID is only one of many factors influencing for whom voters cast their ballots.

It is also illuminating to look at trends in partisanship within different subpopulations of the electorate. While there are myriad factors that can be explored, here we will focus on a few of the most significant changes in party identification over the last fifty or so years. Figure 4 displays what is perhaps the most dramatic change in partisan allegiance among American voters—white southerners' shift toward the Republican party. As with all the remaining figures, Strong, Weak, and Independent-leaning partisans are grouped together in this figure, and pure Independents are excluded. We see that in 1952, only 14 percent of whites in the South identified with the Republican party, while 84 percent were Democrats. From that point on, however, the Republicans steadily

Figure 3. Democrats and Republicans (Strong and Weak)

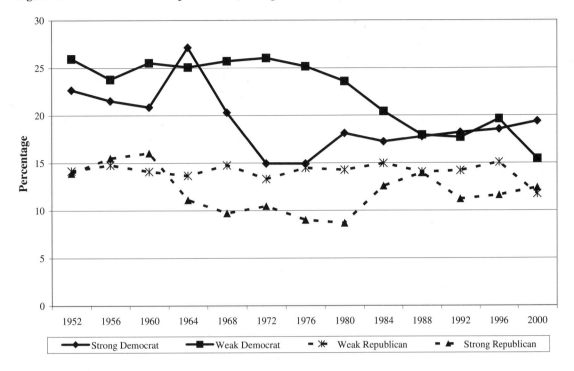

Figure 4. White Southerners

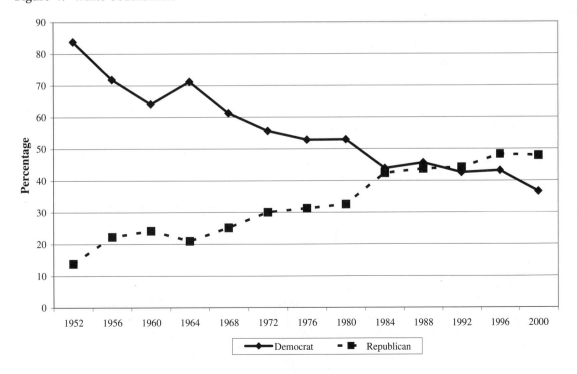

Figure 5. African Americans

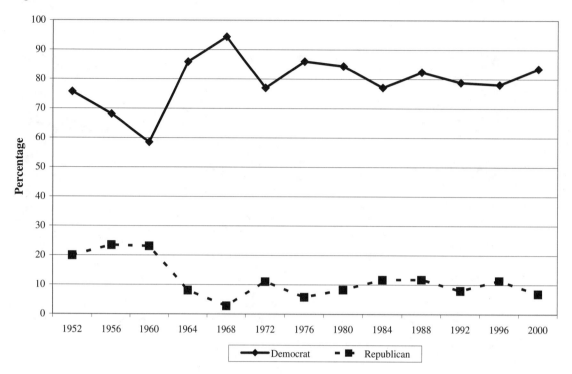

gained identifiers while Democratic identifiers eroded so that by 2000, 48 percent of white southerners identified themselves as Republicans, while only 37 percent were Democrats. Over this same period African Americans, who were predominantly Democratic in the 1950s, became almost monolithically so in the wake of the civil rights reforms enacted under Democratic president Lyndon Johnson in the mid-1960s (Figure 5).

Another significant shift in the partisan landscape over this same period has occurred in the party identification of men versus women, as recent years have seen a "gender gap" develop between the two parties (*see* **Gender Differences in Public Opinion**). As shown in Figures 6 and 7, in the 1950s men and women had essentially the same partisan profile. In the years since, however, a gender gap has opened up. Today, Democrats are more likely to be women (by a margin of about 8 percentage points) while Republicans are more likely to be men (by roughly the same margin).

At the same time that the gender gap has opened up, another once-significant divide has narrowed—the "Protestant-Catholic" gap (*see* **Religious Differences in Public Opinion**). For much of the twentieth century, Catholics were a reliable constituency of the Democratic Party, as shown in Figure 8. Beginning in the early 1980s, however, Catholics became less Democratic, to the advantage of the Republicans. This trend continued through the 1990s so that by 2000, Catholics and Protestants did not differ at all in their partisan allegiances (see Figures 8

Figure 6. Percentage of Democrats by Gender

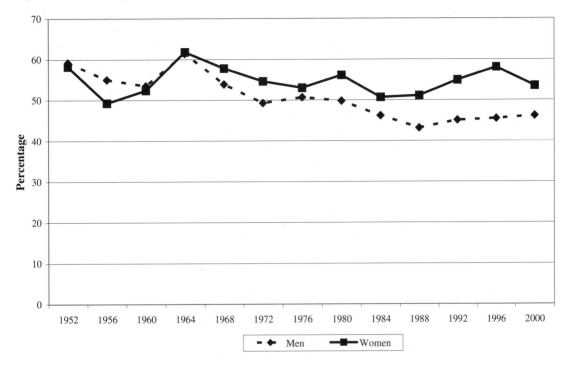

Figure 7. Percentage of Republicans by Gender

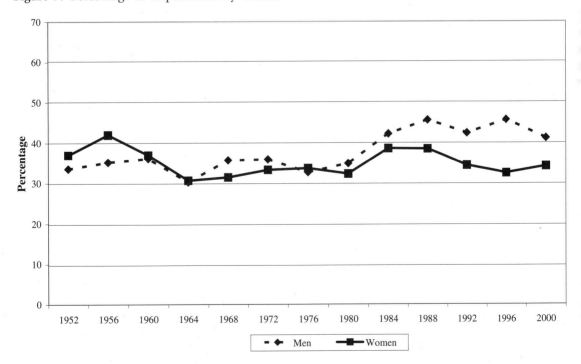

Figure 8. Percentage of Democrats by Religious Affiliation

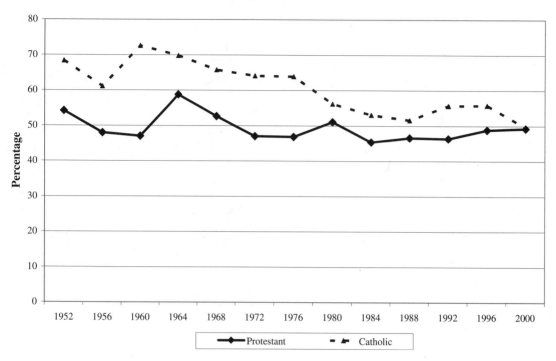

and 9). Meanwhile, significant changes were occurring within Protestantism, as evangelical and fundamentalist (as compared to mainline) Protestants increasingly adopted a Republican identification, particularly among those who attend religious services regularly. As a result of differences between the parties on moral issues, especially abortion, conservative Protestants and devout Catholics have increasingly united under the Republican umbrella. Given the antipathy between these groups on theological grounds it is noteworthy that, politically, they have become brothers and sisters in arms.

In conclusion, it is important to stress that these shifts in the partisan allegiances of various subgroups within the electorate have all occurred against a backdrop of partisanship's increasing relevance as a factor shaping how Americans vote. Far from fading in importance, party ID has become in recent elections a stronger predictor of who votes for whom, even when accounting for numerous other factors known to affect the choices voters make. There are a variety of reasons for the growing significance of partisanship. As we have seen, one is that conservative Southerners were once content to vote for Republicans, particularly at the presidential level, while retaining their Democratic party ID. A new generation of Southerners, however, have reconciled this political schizophrenia by both identifying with and voting for Republicans. Across the entire nation, the parties have also become more ideologically cohesive, meaning that a political conservative who identifies with the Republicans is not likely to find an ideologically acceptable Democratic candidate (and vice versa for liberals who

Figure 9. Percentage of Republicans by Religious Affiliation

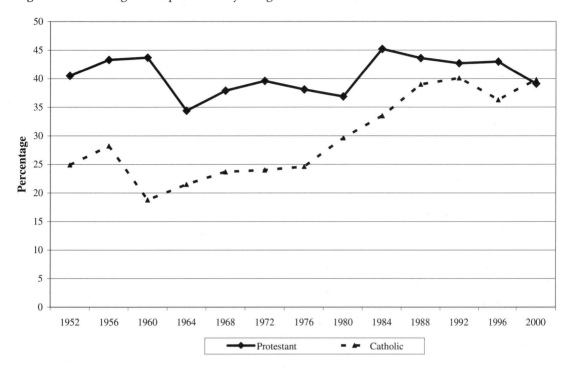

identify with the Democrats). While the Republicans once had a strong liberal wing, and the Democrats a large contingent of conservatives, that is less and less the case. Another reason for the growing importance of partisanship in determining election outcomes is that independents have become less likely to turn out at the polls, giving the electorate—that is, those who actually participate in the election—a stronger partisan flavor.

There is a huge body of research on the venerable subject of party ID, even though it has been decades since the original Michigan School scholarship was published. The fact that political scientists continue to devote much attention to the subject, even to the point of continuing to debate its nature and thus its malleability, underscores that its role in shaping the outcome of American elections is as strong as ever, with all signs suggesting that it is not going to fade away any time soon.

Further Reading

Bartels, Larry M. "Partisanship and Voting Behavior, 1952–1996." *American Journal of Political Science* 44, no. 1 (2000): 35–50.

Campbell, Angus, Philip E. Converse, Warren E. Miller, and Donald E. Stokes. *The American Voter*. New York: John Wiley, 1960.

Erikson, Robert S., Michael B. MacKuen, and James A. Stimson. *The Macro Polity*. New York: Cambridge University Press, 2002.

Fiorina, Morris P. *Retrospective Voting in American National Elections*. New Haven, CT: Yale University Press, 1981.

Green, Donald, Bradley Palmquist, and Eric Shickler. *Partisan Hearts and Minds: Political Parties and the Social Identities of Voters*. New Haven, CT: Yale University Press, 2002.

Keith, Bruce E., David B. Magleby, Candice J. Nelson, Elizabeth Orr, Mark C. Westlye, and Raymond E. Wolfinger. *The Myth of the Independent Voter*. Berkeley: University of California Press, 1992.

Key, V. O. "Secular Realignment and the Party System." *Journal of Politics* 21, no. 2 (1959): 198–210.

Layman, Geoffrey. *The Great Divide: Religious and Cultural Conflict in American Party Politics*. New York: Columbia University Press, 2001.

Miller, Warren E., and J. Merrill Shanks. *The New American Voter*. Cambridge, MA: Harvard University Press, 1996.

David E. Campbell

Partisanship Measurement

Partisanship refers to psychological attachment to a particular political party. Many intriguing nuances lie behind the apparently simple definition that makes partisanship a relatively complex concept. As a result, scholars have toiled for years over how to measure it.

Since the 1950s, measurement of individual partisanship has been fairly consistent although debates exist on the structure of the measure and its true meaning. One of the most widely used surveys of political interests, the **National Election Study**, uses a branching question to measure partisanship. In the first part of the question, respondents are asked "Generally speaking, do you usually think of yourself as a Republican, a Democrat, an Independent, or what?" If they indicate a partisan affiliation to either the Democratic or Republican Party, they are then asked "Would you call yourself a strong Republican/Democrat or not a very strong Republican/Democrat? Those who claim no partisan leaning in the first question are then asked "Do you think of yourself as closer to the Republican or Democratic Party?" Measuring partisanship in this way has allowed scholars to determine an individual's relative degree of partisanship. Respondents are classified as strong Democrats, weak Democrats, Independents who lean Democrat, pure Independents, Independents who lean Republican, weak Republicans, or strong Republicans. Although other surveys, particularly those done by media outlets and polling firms, may use a more simplistic question to attain a measure of individual partisanship, the scale employed by the National Election Study is the most widely used in academic studies.

This common measure of partisanship has some limitations however. One of the key criticisms leveled against it concerns the usefulness of dividing partisanship into so many categories. Some have argued that, given the level of political interest and engagement in the United States, there is little reason to separate the strong partisans from the weak partisans and independents. In fact, certain studies have shown that there are often few differences in the opinions or behaviors of independents and weak partisans. In fact, independents who lean toward a certain party can occasionally act in a more predictable partisan fashion than those who claim weak partisanship. These findings suggest that measuring partisanship in a simpler manner may be advisable as it forces people to make a clear decision about the party they favor most.

A second concern about the National Election Study measure of partisanship deals with the single dimension on which it is gauged. That is, some have argued that partisanship should not be measured on a single dimension running from strong Democrat to strong Republican because adhering to any of the categories is not the polar opposite of another category on the scale. To say that you are a strong Democrat, for example, does not necessarily mean that you are the polar opposite of being a strong Republican. Instead, some have argued that strength of partisanship and independence have their own dimensions and ought to be treated as such.

These and other more technical concerns with this widely used measure of partisanship have prompted alternative measures. One of the alternatives that is included in the National Election Study is to gauge how one feels toward the two major parties rather than directly asking people with whom they identify. Respondents are asked to rate the parties on a feeling thermometer from 0 to 100. That is, people who feel very warmly toward a party would give it a score of 100, those who feel very cool toward the party would give it a 0, and those with less polarized feelings would give the party a thermometer score somewhere in between. The advantage of this form of the question is that it helps determine how nonpartisans feel, which can be difficult to ascertain with the more widely used question. It also provides a measurement for feelings toward the two parties individually. The major drawback is that the thermometer questions do not necessarily cause people to differentiate between their feelings toward the two parties. Even the most consistent and predictable partisan can rate both parties fairly warmly or coolly on the thermometer and thus blur their true preferences between the parties. In addition, the thermometer measures do not tap into the identification aspect of partisanship very well and there is some precision lost by using a scale from 0 to 100.

Another alternative measure of partisanship asks respondents an open-ended question about how they feel toward the parties. Investigators measure party allegiance by totaling the number of positive and negative things that a respondent has to say about each party. While this form of the question allows respondents to say whatever comes to mind, rather than having to decide between strict, predetermined categories, the drawback is that it is highly susceptible to short-term forces. For example, a respondent who has always voted for the Republicans could appear to support the Democrats if he or she is interviewed right after the Republican Party does something objectionable. The objectionable action could be at the top of his or her head and therefore be expressed quite readily when interviewed, making the respondent appear to dislike the party he/she actually identifies with. Another drawback of open-ended form of the question is that responses tend to be subjective and difficult to quantify.

Despite the controversy, the scale from the National Election Study continues to be the most commonly used and has been helpful in studying numerous political phenomena. The debate and discussion around how best to measure partisanship has, however, caused scholars to test alternative measures and cautioned them about interpreting relationships with other political variables.

Further Reading

Campbell, Angus, Philip Converse, Warren Miller, and Donald Stokes. *The American Voter.* Chicago: University of Chicago Press, 1960. A classic study of American voting behavior in which seminal claims are made concerning partisanship as a psychological attachment.

Weisberg, Herbert F. "Political Partisanship" In *Measures of Political Attitudes,* edited by John P. Robinson, Phillip R. Shaver, and Lawrence S. Wrightsman. New York: Academic Press, 1999. This contribution provides a careful and extensive overview of how partisanship has been measured and the debates that have occurred.

Web Sites

The Web site of the American National Election Study, a biannual survey of American citizens conducted during each election since 1952, has a great deal of data on partisanship over time. At the site http://www.umich.edu/~nes click on the "The NES Guide to Public Opinion and Electoral Behavior" and follow the link to "Partisanship and Evaluation of the Political Parties."

Michael Parkin and Joanne M. Miller

Personalization of Politics

It is frequently argued that citizens perceive and evaluate presidents and other political actors primarily on the basis of personality. Characteristically, in his influential book *Home Style: House Members in Their Districts,* Fenno stresses that "most voters vote more on style than they do on issues" (p. 135). "How have you looked to me lately" seems to be a more accurate description of what voters think, than "what have you done for me lately." Similarly, politicians pay significant attention to their style, design the way they speak and look, and carefully shape their image. Because they desire to maximize their chances of being elected, they are motivated to manipulate the way they present themselves. The significance of political image and personal style creates a new political reality captured in the term "the personalization of politics."

The emphasis of political actors on personal style is in line with a parallel phenomenon in the social world. A number of studies in social psychology that focus on impression management provide evidence of the primary role of a social target's image. In their important book published in 1981, titled *Attitudes and Persuasion: Classic and Contemporary Approaches,* Petty and Cacioppo argue that "people are hedonically motivated to convey a positive 'face' to those around them" (p. 155). Apparently, social and political actors are motivated to receive social rewards, such as liking and respect. Our attempts to impress others, whether they are our friends, coworkers, or potential voters, are driven by this desire to attain social approval.

This is especially important in politics, where image is intended to impress an audience. But how do we make sense of others? Social perception studies suggest that when members of a social or a political audience form a judgment of another person, they compose a description. Interestingly, people's descriptions of others are based on similar criteria. Queues such as physical appearance, style and attractiveness are the primary determinants of impressions, and people use them broadly when they describe others. Social scientists have also detected a consistent effort across cultures and epochs to use a "common sense" criterion that would group together individuals with similar dispositions. Apparently, people's maps of how they think about others seem to have some shared, uniform qualities that are conveyed with personality traits.

When we are asked to describe others, whether they are family, strangers, or public figures, trait words are identified as the primary component of our descriptions. We are able to do this from a young age; studies on student populations show that such words as "intelligent," or "easy going," account for about 60 percent of descriptions of others, followed by behavioral descriptions, which account for about 25 percent. The explanation of why traits are so broadly used is because they help to make sense of behaviors, capturing the meaning of an action or standing as an explanation of why people acted as they did. Not only do we use traits very frequently, but we also use a great variety of them. Characteristically, studies indicate that people make use of 18,000 distinct trait terms in their evaluations of others. The use of traits is also documented in every day conversation and discourse, both filled with descriptions of personal qualities.

Early studies in traditional psychology saw traits as "the roots of personality" and since then, traits have been often contrasted with instincts, motives, beliefs, attitudes, desires, and goals. Despite definitional differences, traits are enduring and relatively stable characteristics, used to evaluate behavior. In personality theory, the study of traits generated two different questions: what does personality consist of, and what do people believe about personality.

Explicit personality theories attempt to answer the first question, and they look at personality through the theorists' perspective. They argue that carefully selected samples of behavior can provide measurable evidence for a person's underlying personality traits (for example an honest behavior is an indicator of the trait of honesty). Traits are seen as being stable, and also shaped by social processes. Thus explicit personality studies use traits to understand the observable manifestations of behavior, in other words what people *display* to others. They classify individuals in central trait categories that are assigned a causal potency; they focus on the structure (nature of factors comprising personality), dynamics (how structure leads to behavior), and development (origins and maturation) of personality. This traditional view of traits is used to identify the factors that make individual behavior consistent over time.

To understand how traits are used by individuals as components of social perceptions we turn to implicit personality theories. Implicit personality theories are interested in discovering the ideas about personality that are in people's minds, and use traits to understand what people think about personality, the shared beliefs and everyday theories about others. Here, traits are seen as summarizing concepts serving a descriptive purpose, as for example when we use the words "smart" or "polite" to describe someone we just met.

Traits are also studied by cognitive approaches that see them as components of social impressions, arguing that personality is perceptions. As Fiske and Taylor illustrate in their book *Social Cognition*, traits are used to explain how people integrate information about others in a coherent impression, and traits are defined as summary judgments, stemming from observations of the target's behavior, appearance, and other information. This use of traits as cognitive categories of social and political perceptions is central to political scientists who study the way ordinary people perceive the political world.

Traits as social observations are used very easily and also widely. They can be assigned without much attention or intention, even when people are preoccupied with other tasks. Also, they can be made spontaneously, in the absence of an intention to form a judgment. Adjectives such as hard-working, industrious, compassionate, sociable, popular, intelligent, skillful, determined, sentimental, humorous, naïve, passive are some of the most frequently used traits in personal evaluations.

Personality language is not limited to simple "good-bad" evaluations. While all traits have a good or bad evaluative component, they also have a more specific descriptive aspect. Take two trait words, such as "openhanded" and "extravagant," for example. While they are synonyms in respect to the behavior they describe—the act of giving—the first has a positive evaluative component, while the second has a negative connotation associated with excess.

Recent studies show that when people are asked to identify traits that go together, they seem to organize their trait knowledge in two dimensions: competence and sociability. In studies of perceptions of manipulated person profiles, scholars identified two dimensions: competence and warmth. In studies of how individuals describe people that they know, intellectual desirability and social desirability were recorded as being the two trait dimensions most frequently used. These two ubiquitous classification categories have also been named competence-success and sociability-intimacy, or referred to as expertise and trust in research on source credibility. The two dimensions of competence and warmth were also identified in the way group members perceived others in small group leadership analyses, while in research on interpersonal attraction they form the two dimensions of respect and affection. Similarly, in studies of peer evaluations they appear as competence and affection.

The two dimensions of competence and warmth have also been exported from person perception to perceptions of groups, which identify two recurring types of stereotyped out-groups: the incompetent but warm, and the competent but not warm "others." Similarly, work on gender and racial **stereotypes** draws on competence and warmth to assess stereotype-content. For example, gender stereotypes portray women as warm homebodies, and men as competent breadwinners. Typical male qualifications are competence and rationality, while the typical female characteristics are warmth and expressiveness. The relationship of trait types with power is also interesting. In racial and social stereotypes, the dominant status groups are perceived as competent, such as rich people. In contrast, the dependent groups are perceived as warm, such as people with disabilities.

In the same way that expectations of behaviors and dispositions permit individuals to effortlessly and automatically arrive at judgments about others, voters use an implicit theory, a small set of personality traits, when they think of political candidates. From early on, political science scholars suggested that such qualities as ability, concern, and similarity are what voters are looking for in political candidates. In an influential article published in the *Midwest Journal of Political Science* in 1972, Graber indicated that public images of candidates were more heavily based on a narrow spectrum of personal characteristics than on policy commitments or specialized skills. This research was based on data from a national survey of U.S. voters conducted during the 1968 presidential campaign. Characteristically, while 77 percent of public responses dealt with personality traits, only 20 percent referred to the candidate's party affiliation and respondents' personal feelings toward the candidate, and 3 percent referred to specific policy stands and actions.

Individual-level survey data also indicated that open-ended responses of voters are driven by assessments of performance and character conveyed by key personality traits, such as competence and honesty. In their article titled "Schematic assessments of presidential candidates," published in 1986 in the *American Political Science Review*, Miller, Wattenberg, and Malanchuk show that personal attributes and trait terms make up to 70 percent of the things citizens like and dislike about presidential candidates. In a very influential article titled "Presidential Character Revisited," published the same year, Kinder offered similar findings. Traits were used by more than 90 percent of the respondents in the 1980 **National Election Study** (NES) when rating presidential candidates. In the years that followed more researchers examined the determinants of overall evaluations for presidential candidates, using the NES data. Findings concur that the use of traits is extensive and document candidate-specific variation in the way that traits matter for overall evaluations.

Political science research demonstrates that citizens categorize their judgments of personality into two dimensions: competence and integrity. For analytical purposes, several studies of voter reactions to political candidates separate competence and integrity into finer paired dimensions. Competence is divided into performance-competence and leadership-competence. Integrity is split into honesty-integrity and empathy-warmth. The dimensions of competence and leadership, or honesty and warmth are distinct, but factor analysis demonstrates that they are not completely orthogonal from another. A fifth dimension, personal appearance, is sometimes added, and the trait categories are also classified in affective and cognitive dimensions. Despite the variability in classification preferences, there is general consensus that the two organizing themes of candidate character are the traits of competence and integrity.

The competence dimension of candidate evaluations is identical to the category of competence identified by social psychology studies of person perception. Interestingly, the dimension of sociability and empathy, central in the person perception literature, is a secondary consideration in political perceptions. Warmth is incorporated into the dimension of integrity. This modification in the evaluative theories of citizens is not surprising. People use traits to create meaning out of the social world. In a political context, traits have a similar function. They help citizens manage the flood of information available to them in public affairs. Information that typically defines media agendas includes references to the economy, power in Washington, international peace, policy proposals on major issues, and very frequently political scandals. References to warmth, however, are less relevant in such a setting. Therefore, it is logical that judgments of political actors will be reduced to competence and integrity considerations. An additional concern is important here. As the stakes in choosing political candidates are high, interest in maintenance of high public standards reinforces the significance of the two dimensions. In his 1986 article Kinder argued that in the same way that individuals evaluate the character of friends, they also ask what sort of person is a political candidate. Perhaps this argument requires a slight modification. Citizens seem to evaluate the personality of political candidates not as they evaluate friends, but rather as they evaluate their financial advisers.

Turning now to the characteristics of the primary dimensions of political personality, competence is directly related to performance in office. It indicates the candidate's past or potential abilities and strengths, political experience, adequacy as a statesman, comprehension of political issues, and intelligence. Adjectives indicating competence have been hard-working, knowledgeable, intelligent, smart, informed, qualified, and efficient. Cues referring to competence are found to be one of the most frequently mentioned criteria for candidate evaluations, especially for Senate and House races, and voters appear quite sensitive to them. Getting the job done is what matters, so competence is the most consequential aspect of candidate personality.

The curious reader might wonder about the relationship between competence and job approval, which is the topic of an interesting debate. Some scholars see competence is a direct indicator of job performance and approval, while others use competence as a mere connection between job performance and character arguing that job performance and character are two distinct aspects of public assessments of candidates. While character includes competence, integrity, leadership and empathy, as conceptualized by Kinder, job approval refers to how well "things are going on." From an analytical perspective, the distinction between competence and job approval might seem superfluous, given that competence evaluations stem from performance criteria. However, there might be substantial differences if the determinants of the two judgments are different. Recent studies show that job approval and competence ratings are indeed inferred from actual policy considerations for the most sophisticated voters. However, for most people it is a general liking of the political actor and the economy that drives competence assessments.

The integrity dimension with its components of good moral judgment, sincerity, and honesty refers to the evaluations of candidates with respect to civic norms. Webster defines integrity as "the quality or state of being of sound moral principle, uprightness, honesty and sincerity." It is tapped through words such as decent, moral, sets a good example, responsible, honest. Along with an ability to inspire confidence, integrity is proved to be one of the public's dominant concerns in a presidential election because the public wants a president whose private and public life is exemplary. In such a setting, the importance of morality in politics is clear.

The qualities of a warm and good leader receive less emphasis than the competence and integrity dimensions. In the 1972 Graber study, indicators of charisma rate third in frequency of mentions among voters. Empathy refers to how friendly, sociable or good-natured a candidate is regarded to be, and is captured through words such as down to earth, fair, kind, easy going, and charitable. In two-dimensional models of candidate evaluations, warmth is folded into integrity. It seems that voters see the honesty of a political candidate as an aspect of caring for citizens, although this association might not always be very tight. Finally, leadership qualities are signified though such characterizations as inspiring, decisive, strong, open-minded, committed, enthusiastic. In two-dimensional models of candidate evaluation leadership is folded into competence. Graber argues that leadership qualities are underrated, possibly due to concerns of excess of power among the public and the press.

As Fenno noted, candidates make a particular effort to convey a positive impression to their audience. They try to control public response and acquire political support, and a strategy a large number of candidates adopt when running for office is to establish their positive public image. This image consists of projections of experience, service, and personal style which are promoted in their political advertisements, campaign speeches, public policy statements, or appearances in news programs. By placing more emphasis on some qualities and de-emphasizing others, candidates create distinct public images. For instance, Nixon was the candidate that invested a lot in his coming across with "professional image qualities." Jimmy Carter's strength, in contrast, was his reputation of integrity. Clinton's reputation was based on competence. In August 1998, 77 percent of the respondents of a Gallup poll evaluated Clinton as competent ("could get things done"). However, the candidate did not fare that well in the public's eyes with respect to his integrity. Only 29 percent argued that the candidate was "honest and trustworthy."

Distinct political profiles are not generated by candidates' efforts alone. Naturally, the coverage candidates receive determines their public image. Most people do not experience politics directly, but rather view the political landscape through the eyes of the news media. Media analysis demonstrates the broad use of trait categories in the presentation of political actors. Content analysis of the 1968 campaign-coverage in twenty newspapers throughout the country indicates the heavy emphasis of the press on qualities of candidates, the bulk of which stress personality attributes. In Graber's analysis, qualities referring to personality and image made up 77 percent of news about candidates, whereas professional capacities were mentioned only 23 percent of the time. This pattern is confirmed by later studies that repeatedly show that soft news programs as well as talk shows focus on the personal qualities of political actors.

As a result, voters' perceptions of political actors become heavily personality-oriented. Naturally, frequent media users make judgments about political actors that are mainly based on perceptions of personality. The influence of candidate personality characteristics is evident also in models of vote choice, where traits consistently outweigh issue positions. The importance of traits was recognized by the first political behavior researchers who referred to assessments of personal qualities as the most important predictor of vote swings.

Extensive use of personality traits is also found in stereotypical perceptions of political actors, drawing striking parallels with socially constructed gender stereotypes. As we saw earlier, social stereotypes about males and females have discernable patters. Traits related to warmth are seen as more appropriate for women, and traits related to competence are seen as more appropriate for men. Thus, a typical man is expected to be assertive, tough, and aggressive, while a typical woman should be warm, gentle, and kind. Political science studies offer experimental and survey evidence that female candidates are thought of as more honest, moral, and warm than their male counterparts. Competence and low integrity are seen as characteristic qualities of the typical male politician. Women are seen as warmer, more compassionate, and more honest, while the traits themselves take on a feminine and masculine dimension. Being "intelligent" or a "strong leader" are considered "masculine" traits, while being "warm" and "honest" are associated with a "feminine" personality.

Similar trends are also evident in news media. A content analysis of newspapers covering twenty-six U.S. Senate campaigns from 1982 to 1986 identified gender differences in coverage of politicians, especially incumbents, related to the substance and the means of evaluations of female and male candidates (*see* **Gender and Campaigns**). Differences are also evident in the media coverage of gubernatorial contests. Compassion and integrity, instead of competence, are the personality qualities stressed for female candidates. Research focusing on the impact of scandals on candidate evaluations demonstrates also that gender stereotypes influence perceptions of female and male candidates involved in financial scandals. Men are punished more severely for their involvement in a scandal because it is easier to stereotype them as typical self-serving politicians.

In the social world, perceptions of others are not static but develop over time. Similarly, in the political world, images of politicians are under constant revision and reconsideration, as new information becomes available. As McGraw explains in a recent article titled "Political Impressions: Formation and Management," once voters establish an impression of a political actor, they use it to interpret, evaluate, and incorporate in their cognition further information.

To identify the dynamic change of candidate evaluations, and to tap into what goes on in the minds of the voters when they evaluate political candidates, we turn to impression formation theories. Impression formation theories touch extensively on three elements: thinking, feeling, and motivation. Thinking is the focus of cognitive studies and includes what individuals know about a target. Feeling focuses on emotions, evaluations, moods, and what individuals generally like about a target. Motivation studies the accuracy and directional goals that determine why individuals process information. The above highlight the complexity underlying citizens' reactions as they do not necessarily follow one pattern when they think about political candidates. Rather, depending on the nature of information available to them, they can individuate, bias their judgments, or be influenced by their stereotypical expectations.

Several models try to explain what goes on in the mind of the individuals as they form impressions and respond to social stimuli. Elemental models argue that each piece of information is updated independently in the context of an impression. Associative network models provide more detailed predictions about the way in which specific evaluations of a candidate are updated. They also put forward a mechanism for understanding the existence of cognitive and affective biases in information processing. Motivated reasoning models examine the impact of motivational biases on impressions. Categorization models point to stereotyping as one of the central processes as individuals attempt to fit new information to their preexisting knowledge about politics.

Despite their differences, these models share a common theme: the significance of prior impressions for the evaluation of new information. Clearly, the way people interpret the meaning of new information depends on existing impressions. We saw previously how specific personality information and stereotypic impressions form a reputation. Now we see that this reputation can establish expectations of behavior. This is why general reputations, their detailed ingredients, and the processes at work that determine the character of those ingredients, matter significantly in understanding how the public perceives political candidates.

The broad political significance of reputations has been stressed in a blame avoidance setting. Fenno observed that candidates' reputations can save them from negative results of unpopular or controversial activities, operating as a protective shield. Political actors with a positive image suffer less from implementing the "wrong" policies than do actors with a more negative image. Real-world scenarios provide illustrations of how specific components of reputations—and politicians' attempts to manipulate them—have operated as moderators of scandal harm. For example, during Watergate, Nixon's tape transcripts show clearly the great effort spent to promote honesty as a significant component of Nixon's reputation. Similarly, in 1988, Senator Gary Hart of Colorado was forced to drop out of the presidential race after his reputation of honesty was shattered by evidence that he was lying to the press and the public. Four years later, in 1992, presidential candidate Bill Clinton survived impeachment for lying under oath by being more careful when handling his image and by promoting his image of competence.

Experimental studies examining the way voters perceive and respond to scandal involvement, provide further evidence of the significant role of traits and reputation. For example, studies have examined the independent impact of a candidate's perceived competence and warmth on public evaluations in a scandal setting and find that competence and warmth ratings of the candidate do affect scandal impact and shape overall evaluations. Interestingly, the effects of personality can be conditional on the nature of the scandal, as well as the level of sophistication of the respondents. Several experiments also focus on the specific contribution of competence and integrity as factors of scandal immunity, and examine the effects of party affiliation as a catalyst for favorable reputations in a scandal setting. These studies show that when citizens think of political candidates involved in scandals, they bring to mind the candidates' reputation. Voters' assessments of a candidate's competence, as well as a sense of identification with the candidate based on party affiliation, can minimize the effects of a financial scandal.

The explanatory value of reputations is also appreciated in the study of impression management and account effectiveness. Political accounts are statements made by politicians in an effort to explain to the public unanticipated or very often improper behavior, and are classified in justifications, denials, excuses, and concessions. These public statements that politicians offer to the media, the electorate, and the political elites, affect public judgments of political accountability. However, there is an interesting relationship between what a politician says and who he is. Experimental studies show that reputations can influence the electorate's reactions to the accounts provided, and examine further whether explanations inconsistent with an established impression are politically damaging.

To conclude, political reputations and their trait components are broadly used by political actors, the media, political elites, and the public. The emergence of candidate-centered campaigns and elections, the decline of party power, and the increase in split ticket voting made personality characteristics central to the evaluation of political candidates and political decision making.

In recognition of the significance of traits for evaluations of political figures, indicators of personality have been included in the NES in every election since 1952 and political science research makes frequent references to political reputations. Political psychologists on the other hand, studying how citizens' impressions of political candidates affect their evaluations, prefer the more general term "prior impression" or "existing impression" when referring to a candidate's image. References to "reputations" are rare and when the term is used, it is equated to overall candidate impressions.

It is important to bridge the communication gap created by the discontinuity in the way the term "reputation" has been used in political science and political psychology studies. Reputation, the way citizens see a candidate as a person, is the part of the overall evaluation of a candidate that is generated on the basis of qualification and trust assessments and is used in the later processing of information. Reputation is a middle-range concept, more detailed and specific than an overall impression, more rich than a single-trait attribute, operating as a reflection of a candidate's personality that is not only in the mind of a single perceiver but can also exist as a shared, public entity.

This conceptualization of reputation allows for a better understanding of its specific components and function. We have identified competence and integrity traits as the ingredients of reputation, which operate as positive or negative "priors" that affect how new information about a candidate is processed. Reputations establish expectations, which facilitate the role of traits. Ignoring this element of expectation generated by political reputations, and studying traits in isolation could be a major oversight in understanding how people use personality information in their evaluations of political candidates.

It is fair to argue that the prominent role of reputation, as well as the idiosyncrasies in political profiles, are creations of political reality. Recognizing the importance of reputations goes hand-in-hand with an active political audience. Some scholars argue that managing reputations is identical to manipulating the citizenry. However, citizens are active participants in this process of impression updating. In the end, it is what citizens *know* and *feel* about a political candidate that becomes the vehicle for their judgments. Opinion polls can provide an understanding of the way that citizens perceive a political candidate and can identify the weaknesses and strengths of a candidate's evaluation. Thus, reputation management requires a politician to build a reputation for competence and integrity that can withstand political shocks. Reputations are not built on words alone but require a public record. A solid reputation requires a solid public record. For some political actors, creating desired images might simply be used for political gain; for the rest, the creation of favorable reputations might be one way to inspire and build honest and competent leadership.

Further Reading

Fenno, R. *Home Style: House Members in Their Districts*. New York: HarperCollins, 1978. A detailed description of how Congress works. The author examines the relationship between candidates and their constituents, placing significant attention to the value of political reputations.

Fiske S. T., and S. E. Taylor. *Social Cognition*. 2nd ed. New York: McGraw-Hill, 1991. Provides a critical overview of the theories and methods of social cognition. The authors focus on how people make sense of themselves, of other people, and of the social world in general.

Graber, Dorris A. "Personal Qualities in Presidential Images: The Contribution of the Press." *Midwest Journal of Political Science* 16 (1972): 46–76. Highlights the influence of the mass media in the results of the electoral process, focusing on the "personal" images by which candidates are presented in news stories.

Kinder, D. "Presidential Character Revisited." In *Political Cognition: The 19th Annual Carnegie Symposium on Cognition*, edited by Richard Lau and David Sears. Hillsdale, NJ: Lawrence Erlbaum, 1986. The author's analysis of the American National Election Studies data shows that candidate personality traits offer citizens a familiar way to manage the information available to them. Classifies personality traits in four dimensions: competence, integrity, leadership, and warmth.

McGraw, Kathleen. "Political Impressions: Formation and Management." In *Handbook of Political Psychology*, edited by David Sears, Leonie Huddy, and Robert Jervis. New York: Oxford University Press, 2003. A review article that offers a thorough presentation of impression formation theories and the process of candidate evaluation.

Miller, A., M., Wattenberg, and O. Malanchuk. "Schematic Assessments of Presidential Candidates." *American Political Science Review* 80 (1986): 521–40. Investigates the cues used by voters in their evaluations of political candidates. The authors analyze open-ended ANES responses about candidates showing that references to the personal attributes outnumber references to issues or parties.

Petty, R. E., and J. T. Cacioppo. *Attitudes and Persuasion: Classic and Contemporary Approaches*. Dubuque, IA: W. C. Brown, 1991. Offers a comprehensive review of seven major theoretical approaches on attitude formation, persuasion, and belief change.

Theresa Capelos

Political Alienation

Political alienation may best be thought of as an attitude of estrangement held by citizens toward their politicians and/or their political system. Citizens who exhibit high levels of alienation often feel politically weak and unable to fulfill their duties as citizens. They distrust politicians and believe that government is not responsive to their needs and interests. While at its core alienation involves estrangement toward the polity, attempts to measure it empirically separate it into four interrelated dimensions: powerlessness, meaninglessness, normlessness, and isolation.

Studies measuring alienation focus on one or more of its four dimensions. Political powerlessness refers to attitudes that the actions of government cannot be influenced, that political decisions are made without respect to the concerns, needs, or interests of citizens. It is an attitude that reflects an individual's sense of **political efficacy**. Political meaninglessness tends to shift the blame externally, toward politicians or the political system, as it measures feelings that political choices are of no consequence and that they do not alter social conditions. A third dimension, political normlessness, also reflects attitudes of suspicion about political leaders. It refers to the perception that the rules that should govern politics have broken down and that politicians cannot be trusted to even obey the law let alone respond to the concerns of citizens. A final dimension of political alienation used less frequently than the others is isolation. While normlessness accepts the legitimacy of norms but finds that they are violated by politicians, political isolation goes further to reflect a feeling on the part of the citizen that the entire political community itself is fraudulent.

Alienation is affected by both personal and political characteristics. One's theoretical approach to the study of alienation—whether viewing it as a personal problem related to the self-conceptions of individuals or a political problem related to flaws in the political system—will determine what causes of alienation are identified. In either case, the personal and political factors that influence political alienation are not mutually exclusive, rather they may be viewed as complementary. For example, in particular circumstances (e.g., where political decisions made run counter to public opinion) individuals with particular personal or social characteristics (e.g., poor people) are more likely to be alienated than those with other characteristics. Thus, alienation may best be conceived of as a subjective process (rather than a fixed objective status) that can vary in intensity as well as in how it is expressed.

Over the years research in the United States has identified a variety of social characteristics associated with political alienation. Among those identified as exhibiting high levels of alienation have been women, the elderly, the young, the maritally separated, readers of highly critical newspapers, the post–World War II generation, African Americans, the educated poor, ideological extremists, and those who supported the losers in electoral competition. What's more, some groups have been found to possess higher levels of one dimension of alienation than other dimensions. For example, although men score higher on measures of normlessness than do women, women have scored (perhaps understandably) higher on powerlessness. Still, it would be a mistake to try to associate political alienation with any particular social or economic grouping. Instead, the common link among those who are alienated is that they feel marginalized from politics—they possess feelings of being ignored, that their values run counter to those of others, that political leaders do not care about them, that there is nothing that can be done to change the situation. These feelings will vary temporally and spatially among different groups depending on the actions of political leaders and in response to government policies that have been enacted.

Although particular personal and political characteristics have, from time to time, been associated with high levels of alienation, perhaps more significant is the research that has shown dramatically increased levels of alienation since the mid-1960s in virtually all modern democracies among almost all groups of citizens. Surveys have documented declining confidence in government and politicians as well as increasing distrust and skepticism of each. Conservative and liberal governments alike have been targets of growing alienation. While some have attempted to explain the surge in alienation in the United States to the Vietnam War, to the failure of the Great Society policies, and to political assassinations of the Kennedy brothers and Martin Luther King (among others), the fact that alienation has increased in other nations as well leads one to believe that the root causes of alienation lie deeper. In such countries as the United States, England, Italy, Germany, France, Japan, Canada, and Sweden, dissatisfaction with the political options presented to voters by the parties characterizes the feelings of majorities of citizens. Nonetheless, even while such high levels of alienation are occurring citizens in those countries are still expressing pride in their nationalities. For example, while almost 75 percent of all Americans could be classified as alienated, well over 90 percent say that they are proud to be an American. Similar though less dramatic patterns are present in other Western democracies. Thus, although being frustrated and distrustful with government, citizens are enthusiastic supporters of the political community itself.

No definitive explanation for the alienation crisis that characterizes present-day democracies is available, although a number of explanations have been posited. One explanation is that government policies that deal with fundamental social and economic issues (e.g., poverty) have been ineffective and citizens have concluded that nothing that government does will solve such problems. An alternative explanation focuses on the post–World War II generation (where alienation levels are highest) and suggests that people who have not experienced depression or world war are less concerned with subsistence and security needs and more concerned with quality of life issues (*see* **Post-Materialism**). For numerous reasons governments have been least effective at addressing such post-materialistic issues, thus producing disillusionment, particularly among citizens of that generation.

Another set of explanations focuses less on the behaviors of governments and more on changes that have recently taken place in the political parties and in political communications. One such explanation has focused on the rigidity of political parties, claiming that parties have become dominated by special interests and commitments to traditional policy positions and, therefore, have failed to integrate new, disaffected members of the citizenry into the political culture. Related to this is an explanation that claims that there has been a change in the nature of the structures of political organizations that has produced feelings of powerlessness. Older forms of organization were characterized by face-to-face interactions. These personalized institutions have been replaced by large, impersonal bureaucratic structures that are inherently alienating. In a similar fashion alienation has been traced to changes that have occurred in political communications. People today obtain most of their news through television. Yet, television news tends to be fragmented, sensationalized, and cursory. This makes it difficult for the average viewer to understand what is happening in the world. Unable to understand news events, feelings of helplessness result. What's more, some scholars argue that the media (both print and broadcast) are consistently cynical about politics, thus encouraging distrust. Whatever the explanation, the fact remains that political alienation in modern democracies has become so widespread that it now constitutes the norm rather than the exception in public opinion.

Although salient for all political systems, political alienation is a concept of greatest importance in democracies because ultimately, governments in democracies are based on the support of their citizens. Although political alienation emphasizes personal feelings and individual attitudinal responses it may also be thought of as a concept that threatens the linkage between the individual and the political system. Widespread and persistent alienation ultimately reflects upon the legitimacy of the regime and questions the effectiveness of representation. The representative system works best when the citizenry is modestly skeptical, supportive of the political system, and possesses feelings that their participation can make a difference. Where the relationship between the elected representatives and the citizens is one of trust, representatives are provided with enough flexibility to make decisions that are in the national interest even though those decisions may run counter to short term constituency concerns. If, after being able to reflect upon a representative's behavior, citizens still conclude that his or her actions were inappropriate, they must possess strong enough feelings of political efficacy to be able to act to correct the situation. High levels of distrust and feelings of powerlessness erode the representative relationship by undermining citizen control.

Several different, sometimes contradictory, political behaviors have been theoretically associated with alienation. On the one hand, it has been hypothesized that alienation leads to apathy and withdrawal from politics due to a belief that politicians cannot be trusted and that nothing can be done to change things. On the other hand, it has been argued that alienation leads to aggressive, nontraditional forms of participation such as protesting and even rioting. Even further, it has been suggested that alienation is associated with conformist behavior, while another line of reasoning suggests that the alienated are likely to support reform-oriented movements. Over the years research has shown that there is no simple relationship between political alienation and political behavior.

A popular myth frequently promoted by the news media is that low voter turnout is the result of alienation. This simplistic explanation of nonvoting is inaccurate. When it comes to traditional forms of political participation, such as voting (or any other form of participation related to campaign politics), the alienated and the nonalienated participate at similar rates. However, differences are expressed in other ways. For instance, the politically alienated tend to support minor party candidates or candidates of the major parties who present themselves as opponents of the dominant political establishment (e.g., George Wallace in 1968, George McGovern in 1972, John Anderson in 1980). This occurs, however, only if those voters tend also to possess weak attachments to either of the major parties.

Whether or not political alienation leads to other behaviors—conformity, withdrawal, protesting, rioting—is contingent upon a host of intervening factors. For example, political alienation tends to lead toward support for reform-oriented behavior, but only if there is social support for such behavior and only if there is a clearly defined response to a concrete situation. When large numbers of alienated citizens believe that the government should be responsive to them, the likelihood of reform-oriented action increases. However, lacking that condition, the alienated are no more likely than the nonalienated to participate in reformist behavior. Diffuse feelings of alienation among an isolated citizenry are unlikely to lead to political action. The degree of intensity that the alienated feel also influences their behavior. Where politics is not central to one's belief system—as is the case for most Americans—feelings of alienation fail to determine any particular behavioral response. When politics is salient there is a greater likelihood that individuals will participate in nontraditional forms of political behavior (e.g., protesting, rioting).

In addition to these factors, the object of the attitudes of alienation is of relevance. It is seldom the case that individuals are alienated from all aspects and all levels of government and politics. Citizens distinguish between the different branches of government (e.g., Congress often elicits the highest feelings of alienation) and the different levels of government (federal, state, local). In addition, it is not unusual for citizens to express attitudes of distrust toward particular politicians while indicating support for the political system as a whole. For example, although there is some evidence that rioters in the 1960s were alienated from their local governments, those same people thought that the national government was attempting to be responsive to their concerns. Likewise, distrusting a particular politician is apt to lead to a different behavioral response (e.g., "throw the rascal out") than intense feelings of alienation directed toward the entire political community (e.g., support for changes in the Constitution).

Political alienation stands at one end of an attitudinal continuum whose opposite pole is defined by support or integration. When alienation levels are low, government can act decisively and effectively; when alienation is high, government action becomes difficult and often ineffective. In modern democracies, however, complete integration of the citizenry—total acceptance of political authority—is neither possible nor desirable. Democracy requires a vigilant and skeptical citizenry. Although it is obvious that high levels of alienation directed toward the political community are problematic, in a democracy some distrust of government policies and politicians may be viewed as healthy, a necessary condition for citizen control of the government.

While there is a temptation to think that political alienation is undesirable, that may not always be the case. Certainly extreme forms of alienation are dangerous to democratic government. Where citizens feel estranged from politics, an atmosphere conducive to tyranny may exist. Still, one may make the case that in democratic nations low levels of alienation may actually have beneficial effects both for individual citizens and for the entire political community. Modest levels of distrust and skepticism can lead to an active and critical citizenry, which is essential in a democracy. Furthermore, low levels of detachment from the government encourage citizens to go beyond conformist behavior. Still, for alienation to be healthy rather than debilitating distrust must remain at low levels and political organizations must exist that will allow citizens to respond to the concerns of citizens in a nonviolent fashion.

The alienation crisis of the past several decades has prompted efforts to rebuild civil society (*see* **Social Capital**). In particular, public high schools, colleges, and universities have responded by requiring courses in citizenship and encouraging civic participation through service learning and moral and civic education programs. The belief underlying such educational efforts is that by actively exposing students to their civic and political communities and by building moral character, attitudes of alienation will be reduced as students gain a greater appreciation for their roles as citizens. Results have been mixed. Most civic education programs attempt to improve citizenship by building the moral and civic character of students. While such programs do produce improvements in short-term attitudes toward citizen responsibilities and obligations, long-term changes in attitudes have not been demonstrated. This is most likely due to the fact that the fundamental causes of political alienation are rooted in the actual performance of the government and the behavior of politicians. Lacking changes in these areas, attitudinal changes that result from civic education programs are likely to be modest and transitory.

Political alienation has become so widespread and so common that some polling organizations have stopped measuring it. Academics, unable to establish a firm relationship between alienation and behavior that is dangerous to democracy, have similarly stopped studying it. Politicians, aware of the high levels of alienation, have exploited the feelings of estrangement for short-term electoral gain instead of attempting to address the root causes of the attitudes. These are all indicators of the enigma surrounding political alienation today.

The enigma associated with political alienation concerns the relationship of attitudes to behavior in a democracy. The essence of democratic government lies in the control of the government by the citizenry. A democratic crisis occurs when large segments of the population are so estranged that people believe that they cannot influence politicians or government policies. Not only does such a situation make it difficult for government to function, but also the potential exists for violence to erupt. Although widespread and persistent alienation exists in many modern democracies, the danger of radical regime change in those countries seems unlikely. Attitudes alone do not provide a thorough enough explanation of political behavior. To understand the significance of political alienation we must understand how those attitudes interact with other political attitudes, how psychological predispositions affect those attitudes, and the influence of the political context in which the attitudes exist.

Further Reading

Citrin, Jack, Herbert McClosky, J. Merrill Shanks, and Paul M. Sniderman. "Personal and Political Sources of Political Alienation." *British Journal of Political Science* 5 (January 1975): 1–31. Examines a wide range of variables associated with political alienation.

Finifter, Ada W. "Dimensions of Political Alienation." *American Political Science Review* 64 (June 1970): 389–410. Identifies the range and scope of political alienation.

Freie, John F. "The Effects of Campaign Participation on Political Attitudes." *Political Behavior* 19 (June 1997): 133–56. Analysis of the effects of participation in electoral campaigns on altering attitudes of alienation.

Muller, Edward N. "Behavioral Correlates of Political Support." *American Political Science Review* 71 (June 1977): 454–67. Empirically examines the political behavior associated with alienation.

Web Sites

For an analysis that challenges the myth that low voter turnout is related to nonvoting, see the League of Women Voter's site available at: http://www.org/elibrary/pub/mellman.htm. A list and analysis of political reforms designed to reduce alienation can be found at: http://www.newamerica.net/index.efm?pg=program&ProgID=13.

John F. Freie

Political Debates

Political debates are direct encounters between or among candidates for a political office. Their purpose is to provide potential voters with an opportunity to compare candidates and their positions on issues. Political debates are important in a campaign because they are the only opportunity for the public to view the candidates side-by-side for an extended period of time. In presidential campaigns, they are the single most watched campaign event, outranking convention viewership by as much as 3 or 4 times. For this reason, presidential debates are often thought to provide the most defining moments of the entire campaign.

While debates are an established part of political campaigns, arguments are often made that they should be called something else because the structure and type of questions often preclude serious clashes and comparisons. Some debates, especially with multiple candidates, are run as round table discussions and may not require all candidates to address the same issues. Scholars and academic debate coaches have called them "counterfeit" because of the presence of a moderator or panelists, short response times, and the inability of participants to pose (and follow up on) questions to one another. As a result of these factors, debates are frequently referred to as forums, joint appearances, or joint news conferences instead of actual debates.

Regardless of what they are called, political debates do have three things in common with traditional forms of debate. First, the candidates are on opposing sides of an issue or topic (implicitly, the question is who is better qualified for office?). Political debates follow a series of topics on which candidates compare positions, attack opponents' arguments, and defend their records or positions. Second, they follow a formalized set of rules that include, for example, time limits for speeches, types of questions asked, topics for debate, order of speakers, use of notes, and style of presentation, such as standing behind a podium or sitting around a table. Finally, participants are appealing to a third party (potential voters) for a decision. Thus, the title of "debate" for these encounters is appropriate.

One of the most appealing aspects of debates for voters is that they produce a level of spontaneity that is not present in other forms of campaign communication, such as speeches, television advertisements, and Web sites. Debates are high-risk events for candidates because they contain the element of surprise—from either a question or an opponent's attacks. Even the best-prepared candidates have been caught off guard. Debates enable the public to see how the candidates act under pressure and are considered by viewers to give insights into personality or character.

With an unbroken chain of U.S. presidential debates since 1976, and an increasing prevalence of debates for lower-level offices, political debates are effectively institutionalized as part of campaigns. Since the public expects debates, it is difficult for candidates to avoid them completely. The best a reluctant candidate can often do is to reduce the number of debates or negotiate formats that are perceived as safe.

Most presidential candidates prepare extensively for debates. They usually take a day or two off from the campaign trail to work. Staff members prepare briefing materials on all the possible topics and hold practice sessions. Even at the state and local levels, candidates learn as much as they can about the format, about who is asking the questions, and about what their opponent(s) will argue.

Although there are risks associated with political debates, there are also benefits for the candidates and for the public. Candidates who are not well known have an extended platform. Candidates who are behind can use debates as an opportunity to improve their standings. Incumbents are usually less likely to want to debate if they are ahead, and they often try to negotiate fewer debates than challengers would prefer. For incumbents who are behind in the race, debates provide the potential to answer attacks and to bolster their accomplishments.

One of the major advantages of debates for both the public and candidates is that they serve as focal points for the entire campaign. Debates crystallize the major issues and enable the candidates to emphasize major campaign themes. If someone had not followed a campaign closely prior to the debates, most of what was presented in the prior months is summarized in the course of a few hours. Candidates can explain and clarify comments made during the campaign and can directly respond to attacks or challenges in a way that is not possible through advertising. The debates affect campaign strategies and media coverage of the campaign both positively and negatively.

Even with extensive preparation, candidates do make mistakes or misstatements that require explanation or "spin." In 1976 Gerald Ford, the Republican presidential candidate, remarked in response to a question about Soviet influence in Poland, "There is no Soviet domination of Eastern Europe, and there never will be under a Ford Administration." Since Poland was a satellite of the Soviet Union, the reporter expressed shock at the answer and gave the president an opportunity to correct his mistake. He did not. Polling after the debate was positive for Ford; however, as he stuck to his position in the days immediately after the debate and the media explained the problem with his response, his polling numbers started to slide.

Not all defining moments are gaffes, however. Some are based on a positive response to an important question. For example, in 1984 Republican President Ronald Reagan successfully put the issue of his age to rest when questioned about his ability to meet the demands of a second term, he retorted, "I will not make age an issue of this campaign. I am not going to exploit for political purposes my opponent's youth and inexperience." Everyone, including his opponent, Walter Mondale, laughed, and Reagan went on to say, "I might add that it was Seneca or it was Cicero, I don't know which, that said if it was not for the elders correcting the mistakes of the young, there would be no state." The reporter dropped the line of questioning and went to another issue.

Four years later Democratic candidate Michael Dukakis was caught off guard by the first question of the debate, which asked if he would change his views on capital punishment if his wife were raped and murdered. The question was intended to give Dukakis an opportunity to respond to a nagging concern that he was a "policy wonk" whose lack of emotion would hinder his ability to connect with the public. He showed no emotion in answering the question and gave a policy-based response that did not resonate with voters. It was a mistake from which his campaign never recovered.

While the main impact of debates is to reinforce viewers' predebate choices (and thus perhaps their propensity to actually turn out to vote), the debates also influence undecided voters or those who are leaning toward but are not solidly committed to a candidate. In close elections, debates can thus make a significant difference. Perhaps the best-known example is the election of 1960, where the debates are credited with winning the election for Democrat John Kennedy. Kennedy was not as well known as his opponent Vice President Richard Nixon. Nixon was also known to be an excellent debater. When Kennedy exceeded expectations by demonstrating presidential qualities and a grasp of the issues, there was a demonstrable impact on public attitudes about Kennedy. Survey data confirm the importance of debates to voters. A survey conducted after the 2000 presidential debates as part of the Debate Advisory Standards Project found that nearly two-thirds of the respondents said debates played a role in helping them decide for whom to vote. In state and local contests where candidates are not as well known as presidential candidates, debates can be especially important in defining the candidates and their issues. In **exit polls**, debates come out ahead of all other forms of campaign communication as the single best source of information influencing a person's vote.

Postdebate polling often concentrates on who "won" the debate. While it is a natural question, some political analysts and scholars argue that there are no clear standards for determining a winner and that both candidates and their supporters can often make compelling arguments. Postdebate "spin doctors" often declare a winner based on expectations. If a candidate is not expected to do well and does better than anticipated, that person is often considered to be a winner. When there are high expectations for a candidate who performs well but is not significantly better than the opponent, that person could be said to have lost, even if overall he or she did a better job of answering the questions. Research conducted after presidential debates in 1992, 1996, and 2000 suggests that many viewers determine a winner based on the ability to exhibit leadership potential. This potential is defined as demonstrating a vision for the country, setting broad goals, exhibiting an approach to problem solving that is credible, and exposing the elements of personality that foster trust and generate enthusiasm.

Contemporary political debates occur in both primary and general elections. Primary debates are intra-party debates used to assist voters in selecting the party nominee. Primary debates occur in nonpartisan elections, such as for school board or city council, when there is a large field that needs to be narrowed to a specific number for the general election. In nonpartisan races with large numbers of candidates—usually more than eight—the field may be divided into two separate debates usually held back to back to allow sufficient time for each candidate to participate. While all the candidates do not appear together, comparisons can be made if they are all asked the same questions. General election debates are held between party nominees or the finalists in nonpartisan races. In partisan races, debates may or may not include minor party or independent candidates depending on the ground rules established by the sponsor for debate eligibility. Polling data is often used to make such determinations by setting a minimum, such as 15 percent.

In presidential races in the United States, the sponsor is required to have a publicly announced set of guidelines for determining participation because broadcasters are providing free airtime to the candidates. The equal time provision (Section 315) of the 1934 Federal Communications Act requires that all candidates for an office receive free airtime if one candidate receives it. This provision creates major problems when there are dozens or even hundreds of declared candidates for a position such as president. The Federal Communications Commission (FCC) has revised its interpretation of the law over the years to make it easier for sponsors to limit who is invited. At the state and local levels, the number of minor party candidates is usually small—one or two—and it is common practice among local or statewide broadcasters to include all candidates.

In addition to candidate debates, political debates can also be held on issues. When an issue debate occurs, the leaders of groups advocating one side or the other participate in a debate. One of the most widely publicized issue debates in the United States occurred in 1993 when Vice President Al Gore debated Ross Perot, the 1992 independent candidate for president, on the issue of the North American Free Trade Agreement (NAFTA).

One of the most important considerations in a political debate is the format. There are countless variations on the major elements of format: types of speeches, length of speeches, types of questions, and who is asking questions. The topic(s) for debate are also considered as part of the format. The first few U.S. presidential debates had separate debates to discuss foreign and domestic policies. More recently, each debate has covered both with the time split equally. Nonpresidential debates are often characterized by questions on a theme, such as education, economy and taxes, or the environment. This is especially true if the debate is sponsored by a group with a particular public policy interest. Related to format is the set for the debate—standing behind a podium, sitting at a table with the moderator between or across from the candidates, sitting on stools with or without a podium, and moving around on a stage for a town hall debate that includes citizen questioners seated in front of or around the candidates. Part of context also relates to audience. Presidential debates are always conducted before a live audience and are televised internationally. While some state and local debates are broadcast, a large percentage occur in front of small groups with reporters covering but not broadcasting them. Many local debates are sponsored by the media and take place in a broadcast studio without an audience.

Questioners in debates can be a single moderator, a group of three or four panelists with one acting as moderator, or citizens either selected at random from a pool of undecided voters or selected from the audience. Traditionally, a panel is composed of media representatives such as news anchors, reporters, or columnists. In primary debates or nonpresidential debates, content experts may also be included, especially when debates are focused on a single issue such as the economy. Primary debates and local or state debates may also include questions from citizens submitted online or by mail. Regardless of who is asking questions, there is always a moderator who indicates whose turn it is to speak and who controls the time for each answer or speech.

There are four types of speeches in a political debate: opening, response, rebuttal, and closing. Opening speeches provide the candidates with an opportunity to set the stage for the debate by outlining a general philosophy. Response speeches directly answer a question posed by a moderator or panelist. Rebuttal speeches are given by the opposing candidate after the response. It is possible to have more than one round of rebuttal speeches for each question. The closing speech is the candidate's opportunity to summarize the debate and present major themes of the campaign.

Response and rebuttal speeches are given as answers to questions. There are two types of questions: initial and follow-up. In addition to questions from a moderator, panelists, or citizens, candidates may also question one another. This is referred to as cross-examination.

The citizen or town hall debate is a format that gained popularity as a result of the 1992 U.S. presidential debates. There are several variations on the town hall format. The moderator can call on questioners at random, prescreen before the broadcast and call on the questioners at the appropriate time, or collect written questions and randomly, or through a screening process to avoid duplication, read the questions. Some town hall rules allow the moderator to ask follow-up questions to the citizens' questions and other sets of rules allow the citizens to ask the follow-up. Some town hall rules allow for no follow-up questions. Regardless of who is asking, an opening question is addressed to one candidate or to both. The order of speakers is determined by a coin toss or random selection process prior to the start of the debate.

Candidates alternate answering opening questions. Typically the person who had the first question gets the last question or closing statement. In some debates the opposing candidate is not asked to respond to the same question and is only allowed a rebuttal to the opponent's response. In other debates, each candidate has an opportunity to state a position and offer rebuttal on the same topic. In such a debate, there would be six speeches for a single question: Answer by Candidate A, rebuttal from Candidate B, rebuttal by Candidate A, answer by Candidate B, rebuttal by Candidate A, and rebuttal by Candidate B.

In intra-party or multiple candidate debates, rebuttal opportunities are often limited to include a wider range of questions. Many primary or multicandidate debates for five or more debaters do not provide an opportunity for rebuttal speeches. Everyone has one opportunity to answer, and the first person cannot respond to what any of the other candidates said.

Some formats include a follow-up question after a series is completed. The question can be framed around something one or both candidates said in their speeches or it can be on a similar subject to the first question, but has no relationship to the responses. The former approach to a follow-up question is intended to encourage candidates to expand or clarify something said in an initial response or to elicit more clash. The second approach of a related but unique question is used when an issue is highly complex and needs to be addressed from several perspectives.

Cross-examination adds interest to a debate by generating more direct clash. It has never been used in a general election presidential debate but was an option for candidates in the 1992 vice presidential debate. It is more commonly used in primary, state, and local debates.

There are hundreds of variations of how questioning is conducted in a debate. The most common debate format is a minor variation on the following:

> Opening Statement by Candidate A
>
> Opening Statement by Candidate B
>
> Question to Candidate A
>
> Response by Candidate A (90 seconds)
>
> Rebuttal by Candidate B (2 minutes)
>
> Rebuttal by Candidate A (30 seconds)
>
> Question to Candidate B . . .

The use of candidate debates is not unique to the broadcast era. In the United States, debates began with our nation's first elections. Congressional candidates such as James Madison and James Monroe engaged in debates in 1788. The Lincoln-Douglas Senate debates in Illinois in 1858 are among the best-known of the pre–twentieth century debates. They are still held up as a standard because the candidates focused on the issues of states rights and slavery and confronted one another directly without a moderator intervening. It was also common in the early to mid-nineteenth century for elected officials or party leaders to engage in surrogate debates on behalf of presidential candidates since candidates did not campaign for themselves. Abraham Lincoln honed his debating skills as a surrogate for Whig Party candidates for president.

Debates for offices at all levels continued to occur in the twentieth century with the first broadcast debate in 1948 between Republican Party rivals Harold Stassen and Thomas Dewey. Prior to the Oregon primary, they debated before a national radio audience on the topic, "Resolved: That the communist party should be outlawed in the United States." This debate was structured like an academic debate in which both candidates had opening speeches to construct their arguments and then had a rebuttal speech.

Eight years later, a televised Democratic Party debate between Adlai Stevenson and Estes Kefauver introduced the panelist format that dominated presidential debates until 1992 and is still a common format for primary and state and local debates. Primary debates were also held in 1960 followed by the first-ever general election debates between John F. Kennedy and Richard Nixon.

After a sixteen-year hiatus, presidential debates returned in 1976 and have been held every election cycle since then. The 1976 debates also included the first vice presidential debate between Republican Bob Dole and Democrat Walter Mondale. The 1980 debates provided a unique twist in that three candidates qualified to participate. The major party candidates, Democratic President Jimmy Carter, Republican nominee Ronald Reagan, and independent John Anderson all met the prescribed criteria of having 15 percent in the polls. President Carter refused to debate if Anderson was included. The sponsor, the League of Women Voters, held the debate without him. After the two-way debate between Reagan and Anderson, Anderson's numbers dropped in the polls and Carter agreed to debate Reagan. In 1984 Democratic vice presidential candidate Geraldine Ferraro became the first and only woman, thus far, to participate in either a presidential or vice presidential debate.

In 1988 a new sponsor replaced the League of Women Voters, which had organized the 1976, 1980, and 1984 debates. The Commission on Presidential Debates was established by the heads of the two major parties in 1987 as a nonpartisan organization with the mission of conducting general election presidential debates and providing voter education. In 1988 both the League and the Commission were to host one of the presidential debates, but the League withdrew as a result of a negotiated agreement between the candidates that the League considered unacceptable because of the restrictions placed on the sponsor in producing the debate.

The 1992 debates included a different format for each debate. The town hall, single moderator, and cross-examination were introduced as well as the first three-way debate. In 1996, the Commission announced the end of panelist debates in favor of a single moderator and town hall. The 2000 debates introduced a less formal stage setting for the vice presidential and one presidential debate in which the moderator sat between the two candidates. The questions were more free-flowing with follow-ups coming immediately after the initial response. Requests for direct rebuttal were also common.

It is anticipated that each election cycle will produce further refinement of old formats and introduction of new features. While the perfect format may never be developed, debates are one of the best sources of information for voters and their use as a campaign communication and voter education tool is likely to continue for campaigns at all levels. Political debates have benefits for candidates, the public, and the media that reports on campaigns.

Further Reading

Carlin, Diana B., and Mitchell S. McKinney, eds. *The 1992 Presidential Debates in Focus.* Westport, CT: Praeger, 1994. Summarizes a national *focus group* research project to determine how the debates influence voter learning and decision making.

Faucheux, Ronald A., ed. *The Debate Book: Standards and Guidelines for Sponsoring Political Candidate Debates in Congressional, State and Local Elections.* Washington, DC: Campaigns & Elections Publishing, 2003. A summary of data collected from debate participants and voters about debates and recommendations based on the research for nonpresidential level debates.

Kraus, Sidney. *Televised Presidential Debates and Public Policy*, 2nd ed. Mahwah, NJ: Lawrence Earlbaum, 1999. A comprehensive look at broadcast political debate history and a summary of research conducted since 1960.

The Racine Group (David S. Birdsell; Diana B. Carlin; Edward A. Hinck; Kathleen E. Kendall; Michael Leff; Kathryn M. Olson; Shawn Parry-Giles; Michael Pfau; and David Zarefsky). "White Paper on Televised Political Campaign Debates." *Argumentation & Advocacy* 38 (Summer 2002): 199–218. A summary of the research conducted on political debates with conclusions about their impact on voter learning and election outcomes. Also includes recommendations for future research and improved debates.

Web Sites

CNN has a Web site that was done for the 2000 debates that includes history of pre-broadcast debates and contemporary debates: available at http://www.cnn.com/ELECTION/2000/debates/history/.

The Commission on Presidential Debates Web site also includes history and transcripts and has suggestions for sponsoring a debate and voter education activities: available at http://www.debates.org.

The PBS Web site includes presidential debate history, transcripts of the presidential debates, and excerpts from interviews with presidential debate participants: http://www.pbs.org/newshour/debatingourdestiny/debates_campaigns.html.

Diana B. Carlin

Political Efficacy

Broadly defined, political efficacy denotes an individual's belief that he or she is capable of understanding political matters, competent to participate in the political process, and confident that one's actions can influence political leaders and policy outcomes. Political efficacy has been studied most extensively as one of the key psychological and motivational resources enhancing the likelihood of voting and of a broader set of participatory behaviors. The interactions between participation, political competence (real or perceived), and beliefs in government responsiveness to citizen demands have also been central concerns of both normative and empirical analyses of democracy.

The concept and measurement of political efficacy were developed by the group of scholars at the University of Michigan who pioneered the analysis of elections from a social-psychological perspective based on large sample surveys of American voters. These studies in turn led to the **National Election Studies** (NES). In its original formulation in the early 1950s, political efficacy was designed to reveal differences among individuals in their perceived ability to exert control over public officials and policies. Its main purpose was to account for the variance in the level and scope of citizens' political involvement. The proposed measure of efficacy blended references to making sense of how government works and to making a difference on what government does.

Specifically, survey respondents were asked to agree or disagree (*see* **Agree/ Disagree Question Format**) with four statements:

1. "Sometimes politics and government seem so complicated that a person like me can't really understand what is going on."
2. "People like me don't have any say about what the government does."
3. "I don't think public officials care much what people like me think."
4. "Voting is the only way people like me can have any say about how government runs things."

The highest level of political efficacy was achieved by respondents who disagreed with all four statements; conversely, the lowest score of political efficacy was received by those who agreed with all four statements. Better educated individuals displayed a stronger sense of political efficacy, and people with higher levels of efficacy were more likely to vote and to participate in a number of campaign-related activities.

The same or very similar items were used in the 1950s and 1960s by other scholars to array individuals in terms of political potency, effectiveness, self-confidence, optimism or, reversing polarity, political anomie, incapability, futility, powerlessness, estrangement, and pessimism. These studies dealt primarily with the correlates or causes of several aspects of political involvement, authoritarianism, **political alienation**, political cynicism. In general, they reinforced the original finding that higher levels of efficacy were associated with greater participation in established channels of electoral and partisan politics (e.g., voter turnout, campaigning on behalf of candidates for public office).

These results lent themselves to a straightforward interpretation. The belief that a citizen's political expression is heeded and has an impact on the conduct of government made participation to communicate one's views worthwhile and thus more likely. At the same time, the relationship between efficacy and participation was far from perfect, suggesting that at least some forms of political action undertaken by at least some individuals were also based on considerations other than their perceived instrumental value. Moreover, that same relationship need not be the sole result of efficacy driving participation. It is quite plausible, and indeed it has long been theorized, that attitude and behavior interact with each other, with participation feeding back into the sense of political efficacy.

During the 1970s, a conceptual articulation and empirical refinement of political efficacy was strongly advocated by many scholars and led to the identification of two distinct attitudes, often denoted as internal and external efficacy. These two analytically separate yet empirically related attitudes focus on the individual and the political system, respectively. Thus, internal efficacy typically refers to perceptions about one's effectiveness in dealing with the complexity of, and in taking active part in, politics. External efficacy, in contrast, reflects beliefs about the openness and responsiveness of the political regime, its institutions, and its leaders to the demands of the public. As a result, inefficacy could be either an admission of personal shortcomings regarding one's political grasp and clout or an indictment of a political system indifferent and disconnected from its citizens.

Both attitudes are tied to core values and expectations articulated in democratic theories. The ideal of democratic self-government rests on the premise of competent citizens capable of performing effectively in political roles and discharging civic responsibilities. In particular, proponents of "participatory democracy" argue that active involvement in decision-making processes will hone individuals' political skills, supply expertise, and nurture their competence; as a result, meaningful citizen empowerment and sustained self-rule will become more likely. Political competence, and in particular its unequal distribution among individuals with different social backgrounds and interests, is also an issue raised in recent debates about the functioning and goals of deliberative democracy. In the classic liberal democratic theory, political elites are ultimately accountable to the public; responsiveness to citizen concerns provides both a standard for elite behavior and a criterion for the public evaluation of that behavior. Indeed, a well-known cross-national analysis of political culture by Almond and Verba argues that government responsiveness is generated by the belief shared by both elites and nonelites that citizens are capable of exerting political influence and will act to compel and enforce responsive behaviors if such need arises. Anticipation or desire to prevent the occurrence of such mass mobilization provides leaders with an incentive to be responsive; political confidence-induced responsiveness, in turn, contributes to the legitimacy, support, and stability of the regime. An important and related question is whether the belief about one's efficacy in wielding influence and providing guidance rests on direct experience and an accurate political assessment, or whether it is primarily a resilient and internalized democratic norm somewhat removed and independent from reality.

The conceptual distinction between the two referents (the individual and the political system) and components (the internal and the external) of efficacy is now generally accepted and well established among students of elections, public opinion, political socialization, and participation. Scholars in these fields have alluded to that distinction using such terms or descriptive labels as personal competence and government (institutional) responsiveness, ego construct and system-related construct, personal ability to cope with the political world and responsiveness of the political system, characteristics of the individual effort and characteristics of the agents to be influenced, input efficacy and output efficacy.

It should also be noted that further analytic distinctions can be introduced within the external domain of political efficacy. A perceived lack of responsiveness could be triggered by considerations regarding different aspects of the political system. In principle, a sense that one's voice has been disregarded or diluted could be attributed to the political process (rigged or unfair procedures), its main players (self-serving or unethical incumbents), or its products (policies at odds with one's preferences). Although these and other aspects of public opinion figure more prominently in the debate about the meaning and implications of **trust in government** (or its opposite, political cynicism), they are also relevant in the study of political efficacy. This is particularly the case when an examination moves from the theoretical to the empirical level. There are two types of problems. Attempts to craft measurement instruments that accurately reflect their conceptual referents are always fraught with difficulties; analytic categories of theoretical import that are clear in the abstract may be less salient and more blurred to the public or large sections of it. As a consequence, empirical findings may be open to multiple interpretations.

The main conceptual reformulation, grounded in images of the self as opposed to images of the political system, carries important implications for a better understanding of the plausible roots of efficacy and its placement in theories of political participation and democratic politics. As a measure of personal competence, internal political efficacy is expected to be a facet of a broader sense of confidence in one's skills and ability to exert some control over the surrounding environment—political or otherwise. As such, it may be anchored and shaped by the dynamics of early socialization. In addition, it is thought to be related to levels of formal schooling since education consistently promotes deeper interest, greater information, and more accurate knowledge about political affairs. Yet higher education should also convey stronger feelings of external efficacy as a measure of perceived system responsiveness because school curricula normally enhance exposure to, and absorption of, fundamental democratic norms.

On the other hand, external efficacy should be more closely tied than internal efficacy to trust in government and unfolding political events that affect the appraisal of government performance. Thus, the shift from an internal to an external attitude object is likely to be reflected in a different degree of stability of the two attitudes, most obviously during times of political crisis, scandal, or turbulence. In addition, different combinations of the two attitudes may lead to divergent political behaviors and affect the range of subjectively acceptable participatory venues. For instance, the conjunction of high internal efficacy and low external efficacy may be hypothesized to foster, all else being equal, a sense of both the ability and the necessity to engage in unconventional or disruptive forms of political action to claim the attention of otherwise unresponsive political leaders. However, to the extent that assessments on the two dimensions of efficacy co-vary, the simultaneous occurrence of the two opposing views may be rare and its alleged behavioral manifestation sporadic. In contrast, high levels of both internal and external efficacy may be conducive to conventional and institutionalized forms of participation such as campaigning on behalf of parties or candidates and voting (as has been consistently found). By a similar logic, political apathy may be the predictable result of low levels of both internal and external efficacy—when action appears to be beyond personal reach and without a political point. Finally, internal and external efficacy can show divergent patterns of association with the political content of participation (as separate from its frequency or specific form). Although both may increase the likelihood of voting, external efficacy may also affect voting preferences for insurgents or candidates outside the political mainstream, offering a more appealing alternative to those who do not feel adequately represented. While the connection between low levels of external efficacy and the electoral success of independent candidates is not automatic, citizens who perceive limited government responsiveness may provide both an incentive for independent candidates to run for office and a preferred audience in their campaign.

While the distinction between the two dimensions of efficacy is conceptually clear and easy to draw, social scientists have devoted considerable efforts to devising measures of each meeting validity and reliability criteria. Of course, the development and empirical test of theoretical propositions about the distribution, level, and relationships involving internal and external efficacy hinge on the availability of sound measures of both. Furthermore, the ability to replicate and cumulate findings in support of theories is—and has been—hampered by the lack of consensus on methodological issues. Such problems are relevant to studies conducted within the United States as well as in crosscultural studies comparing efficacy in the United States with efficacy in other countries.

Of the four statements originally proposed to gauge an undifferentiated sense of political efficacy, item 1 has been considered the most appropriate to tap its internal component. Items 2 and 3 have often been used to capture the external component; item 2, however, has also been interpreted as a measure of internal efficacy given that the subject of the statement is the people and not the political leaders—as in item 3. Only these three statements have been included in all NES conducted in presidential election years between 1952 and 2000, constraining tests of longitudinal trends. One of the best-known illustrations of the importance of choosing valid measurement instruments that are also comparable over time is the attempt to account for the decline of reported voter turnout in the United States between 1960 and 1980. Growing doubts about government responsiveness as measured by items 2 and 3 appear to mirror and be partially responsible for the lower level of electoral participation. However, other studies relying upon a mix of internal and external items to capture the effect of political efficacy on turnout find no or little influence.

Over the years, the battery of measures of political efficacy in the NES has undergone several changes as a result of scholars' attempts to improve their quality. New items have been added to the survey questionnaire, while others have been permanently or temporarily dropped. Among the latter, item 4 was last used in 1980; it appeared to suffer from lack of clarity in its wording (whereby either agreement or disagreement could be construed as the efficacious answer) and was only weakly related to the other items. Among the former are four statements often inserted in the NES since 1988 that are intended to improve the measurement of internal efficacy. They are:

5. "I consider myself well-qualified to participate in politics."

6. "I feel that I have a pretty good understanding of the important political issues facing our country."

7. "I feel that I could do as good a job in public office as most other people."

8. "I think that I am better informed about politics and government than most people."

Clearly, the intent is to afford a better assessment of how individuals rate themselves in terms of their performance in a political role: whether as attentive and discerning spectators or as effective and competent actors. Thorough method-ological testing—repeated and expanded recently—has shown that items 5 through 8 meet several desirable criteria, making them the most satisfactory gauge of internal political efficacy to date.

Among the temporary additions to the NES are two items used between 1968 and 1980 ostensibly designed to tap the external component and employed as such along with item 3. Hence, both are worded so as to elicit reactions to the commitment of office incumbents and major institutions to stay in tune with the public. They are:

9. "Generally speaking, those we elect to Congress in Washington lose touch with the people pretty quickly."

10. "Parties are interested only in people's vote, not their opinions."

Other NES questions not usually associated with external efficacy but sharing a common focus on the responsiveness of institutions and office holders are:

11. "Over the years, how much attention do you feel the government pays to what the people think when it decides what to do?" (Introduced in 1964)

12. "How much attention do you think most congressmen pay to who elects them when they decide what to do in Congress?" (Asked between 1964 and 1980)

Select data about several indicators of political efficacy illustrate the time and type of changes in levels of internal and external efficacy in the United States as well as the usefulness of the analytic difference between these two components. These data also emphasize the need to place empirical readings of these indicators in a broader context to reach a more accurate interpretation of their significance.

Figure 1 tracks the percentage of survey respondents who chose, between 1952 and 2000, the efficacious answer in response to the four statements designed or deemed to gauge the sense of external efficacy; two of them cover only 1968 to 1980. The figure also includes the only statement available for the entire period considered to tap internal efficacy (item 1). The evidence indicates that an increase in perceived efficacy (of both types) between 1952 and 1960 was followed by a very sharp decline between 1960 and 1968. Two new measures of external efficacy were introduced at that time. Three of the four external items show a steady continuation through 1980 of the downward trend started in 1960. Moreover, the same tendency is replicated by the distribution of answers to the two questions about institutional and incumbent responsiveness listed above; the percentage of respondents believing that the government and members of Congress pay "a good deal" of attention to what people think when they decide what to do fell, between 1964 and 1980, by 19 and 25 points, respectively. Of course, these were years of great turmoil, encompassing several developments with powerful and negative consequences on the evaluations of the political system and its leadership: military involvement in Vietnam, the growth of a "credibility gap" between the administration's version of the events and their actual unfolding, antiwar demonstrations, urban violence and unrest, the Watergate break-in and

Figure 1. Internal Political Efficacy and External Political Efficacy Indicators: 1952–2000

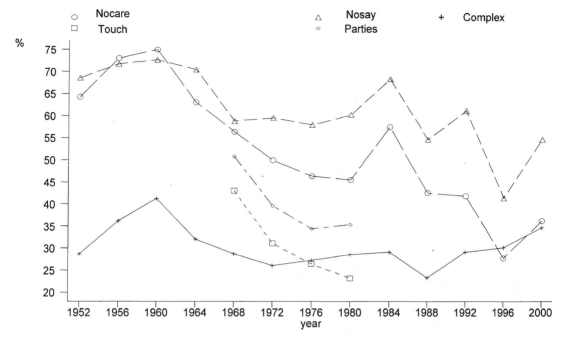

Note: Wording of items is shown in the text, as numbered: Nocare (3); Touch (9); Nosay (2); Parties (10); Complex (1). For all items, "disagree" indicates higher efficacy. Beginning in 1988, answers to Complex, Nosay, and Nocare included the new option "neither agree nor disagree." To preserve comparability with the data collected before 1988, percentages for these three items are based on the sum of agreements and disagreements. (As a result, values for the latter two differ here and in Table 1.)
Source: 1948–2000 National Election Studies, Cumulative Data File.

cover-up, and economic stagnation coupled with inflation. Quite plausibly, these troubling incidents and circumstances triggered a deeper disconnect between the public and the polity, with more people feeling that the government was unable to meet common expectations or fulfill specific aspirations. The two traditional measures of external efficacy have moved in tandem since 1980, and both display much greater variability than internal efficacy. In particular, they show a sharp increase in 1984 and 2000. This upward change may be a reflection, at least in part, of the widespread belief that the country was on the right economic track and the ensuing satisfaction with the job done by the political elites (primarily, the president). Given the obvious and beneficial effects of prosperity, more people were probably inclined to perceive greater responsiveness to public demands and needs. Finally, the data are consistent with the ambiguity regarding the proper classification of item 2 as an indicator of internal or external efficacy; its movement from 1968 through 1980 and between 1988 and 1992 follows a direction shared by item 1 but not item 3.

Table 1 compares levels of internal efficacy, external efficacy, and political trust in surveys conducted before and after the September 11 attacks. The data are

Table 1. Internal Political Efficacy, External Political Efficacy, and Political Trust, 2000–2002

	2000 (percent)	2002 (percent)
Internal Political Efficacy		
I think that I am better informed about politics and government than most people. [Agree]	30.2	27.1
I consider myself well-qualified to participate in politics. [Agree]	33.7	30.0
External Political Efficacy		
People like me don't have any say about what the government does. [Disagree]	49.1	56.9
Public officials don't care much what people like me think. [Disagree]	32.2	45.2
Political Trust		
How much of the time do you think you can trust the government in Washington to do what is right? [Just about always, Most of the time]	43.5	54.9
Do you think that people in government waste a lot of money we pay in taxes, waste some of it, or don't waste very much of it? [Waste some, Don't waste very much]	40.8	52.5
Would you say the government is pretty much run by a few big interests looking out for themselves or that it is run for the benefit of all the people? [Government run for the benefit of all the people]	34.3	49.9
Do you think that quite a few people running the government are crooked, not very many are, or do you think hardly any of them are crooked? [Not very many, hardly any are crooked]	61.3	69.4

Sources: 2000 and 2002 National Election Studies.

based on measures that were available in both years. The actions undertaken by the government to fight terrorism, guarantee national security, protect the homeland, and insure citizen safety find a clear echo in a greater sense of trust and responsiveness. As anticipated, some commonalities between external efficacy and trust appear to underline their change in the same direction. In addition, the parallel increase of external efficacy and trust probably found a fertile ground in a renewed sense of national unity and pride as well as in more subdued and less frequent manifestations of partisan conflict engendered by the presence of an outside threat. To the extent that expressions of cynicism about politics (including the perceived lack of responsiveness of the government) have become a more fashionable posture since the 1960s, the refrain of such a reflexive cliché did not fit the prevailing political mood in the aftermath of the terrorist attack on September 11, 2001. As would be expected, however, there is no apprecia-

Table 2. Internal Political Efficacy, External Political Efficacy, Turnout and Vote for Independent Candidates in 1968 and 1992

	1968		1992	
	Voted (percent)	Voted for Wallace (percent)	Voted (percent)	Voted for Perot (percent)
Internal Political Efficacy				
"Sometimes politics and government seem so complicated that a person like me can't really understand what's going on."				
Strongly Disagree			89.6	19.2
Disagree	76.7	14.1	85.3	18.4
Agree	62.2	25.3	78.4	18.2
Strongly Agree			63.1	20.6
External Political Efficacy				
"Public officials don't care much what people like me think."				
Strongly Disagree			82.9	12.4
Disagree	77.6	12.1	84.3	17.8
Agree	55.7	35.3	75.9	20.2
Strongly Agree			60.8	22.8

Note: Given the distribution of Wallace's support, the 1968 data are based on the eleven former Confederate states. In 1968 respondents were given only the option to agree or disagree with both statements.
Sources: 1968 and 1992 National Election Studies.

ble change in the subjective sense of internal efficacy; if anything, the data show a slight decline perhaps due to the unsettling and novel nature of the danger posed by international networks planning violent actions against Americans on U.S. territory.

Table 2 shows the relationship between the decision to vote in the presidential elections of 1968 and 1992, the choice of independent candidates George Wallace and Ross Perot for the White House, and items 1 and 3—the traditional measures of internal and external efficacy, respectively, available in both years. Wallace and Perot mounted the most successful independent campaigns since 1924. Although their policy platforms were very different, they both adopted strong populist tones that could find resonance among disaffected or alienated voters (and potential voters). In addition, there is no doubt that the values and specific issue positions on racial relations and law and order championed by Wallace fed the sense of disconnect shared by many who in 1968 perceived the government to be unresponsive and unconcerned with their views ("what people like me think"). In contrast, Perot's message in 1992 did not contain extreme or particularly controversial policy recommendations; rather, it delivered a sweeping indictment against the corruption of the political process and the perceived insulation and incompetence of professional politicians. Thus, the conditions and motivations to assert that "public officials don't care much what people like me think" were not the same. As a result, this indicator of external efficacy should be more strongly related to candidate choice in 1968 than in 1992 (and, by extension, in 1980, 1996, and 2000); nevertheless, external efficacy should be more relevant than internal efficacy in shaping voting preferences in both years. The data show that the turnout rate reported in 1992 by the most efficacious respondents was at least 20 percentage points higher than that observed among the least efficacious. However, while the level of support for candidate Perot did not vary according to internal efficacy, it was inversely related, albeit moderately, with feelings of external efficacy. In 1968 the decision to vote was also made more often by the most efficacious, and yet the decision to vote for Wallace was more common among the least efficacious, especially on the external indicator. It is worth noting that in that year support for Nixon and Humphrey was stronger among efficacious voters, as was support for Clinton in 1992 (while support for Bush was unrelated to efficacy).

As anticipated, a sense of personal competence and the belief in authorities' receptivity to citizen input are positively linked to engagement in conventional forms of participation. Perceptions of responsiveness, however, are negatively tied to preferences for particular candidates challenging the normal two-party choice. Voters who think public officials do not care about their opinions may be more readily inclined to bypass candidates of the major parties controlling the government in favor of proponents of a political outlook insufficiently represented by national policies or self-declared anti-establishment newcomers.

Further Reading

Almond, Gabriel A., and Sidney Verba. *The Civic Culture*. Princeton, NJ: Princeton University Press, 1963.

Morrell, Michael E. "Survey and Experimental Evidence for a Reliable and Valid Measure." *Public Opinion Quarterly* 67 (2003).

Niemi, Richard G., Stephen C. Craig, and Franco Mattei. "Measuring Internal Political Efficacy in the 1988 National Election Study." *American Political Science Review* 85 (1991): 1407–13.

Reef, Mary Jo, and David Knoke. "Political Alienation and Efficacy." In *Measures of Political Attitudes*, edited by John P. Robinson, Phillip R. Shaver, and Lawrence S. Wrightsman. San Diego: Academic Press, 1999.

Web Sites

The Web site of the National Election Studies is available at http://www.umich.edu/~nes/nesguide/nesguide.htm. It features a guide to public opinion and electoral behavior, allowing direct access to data about several attitudes regarding politics and the political system.

Franco Mattei and Richard G. Niemi

Political Efficacy Measures

Political efficacy measures are survey questions designed to assess not only citizens' beliefs about their capacity to understand and participate in politics but also their perceptions of how responsive political institutions are to themselves and their fellow citizens. **Political efficacy** has contributed to our understanding of many theoretical and empirical issues, including democracy, citizenship, and political participation. Although political efficacy was one of the earliest social-psychological attitudes that political scientists developed to study political behavior, researchers are still working on developing conceptually clear and statistically reliable and valid measures of this important concept.

Researchers at the University of Michigan's Survey Research Center initially developed and defined efficacy as the "feeling that individual political action does have, or can have, an impact upon the political process, i.e., that it is worthwhile to perform one's civic duties" (Campbell, Gurin, and Miller 1954, p. 187). They conceived of political efficacy as a unidimensional concept and measured it with a cumulative scale constructed from respondents' answers to four agree-disagree items:

1. "People like me don't have any say about what the government does."

2. "Sometimes politics and government seem so complicated that a person like me can't really understand what's going on."

3. "Voting is the only way that people like me can have any say about how the government runs things."

4. "I don't think public officials care much what people like me think."

Since all of these statements are constructed negatively ("don't have any say," "can't really understand," "only way," and "don't think"), Campbell, Gurin, and Miller classified subjects who disagreed with all four statements as having the highest political efficacy and those who agreed with all four statements as the least politically efficacious (1954, p. 189). The initial work of the University of Michigan Survey Research Center eventually developed into a series of studies of elections in the United States known as the **National Election Studies** (NES), and items gauging political efficacy have appeared in most of these studies from 1952 to the present.

For most of the 1950s and 1960s, the NES questionnaire simply asked citizens if they agreed or disagreed with the original four statements, and social scientists measured political efficacy by summing disagree responses. One exception was in 1966 when the NES included a test of a five-point response scale ranging from "strongly agree" to "strongly disagree"; this approach to response categories, however, did not resurface again until 1988. It was not until the 1968 NES questionnaire that there was any attempted change in how we calculate political efficacy. This instrument included two new statements as indicators of political efficacy: "Generally speaking, those we elect to Congress in Washington lose touch with the people pretty quickly," and "Parties are interested only in people's vote, not their opinions." Along with the four original items, these items appeared in every NES study from 1968 through 1980.

The exploration of the two new statements resulted from theoretical and empirical concerns during this period that persuaded researchers to conclude that political efficacy actually had two dimensions: internal efficacy and external efficacy (see Balch 1974). Internal political efficacy refers to citizens' sense of their own ability to comprehend and effectively take part in politics, while external political efficacy focuses on citizens' perceptions of the responsiveness of political bodies and actors to citizens' demands. Researchers used these items as indicators of external efficacy; when they added them to the four original items, the researchers attempted to derive two separate measures: one for internal and one for external political efficacy (see Acock, Clarke, and Stewart 1985). These six statements appeared on all NES studies from 1968 to 1980, but continuing debate surrounding the measurement of efficacy appears to have resulted in the inclusion of a limited number of the items from 1982 to 1986 (see Table 1).

Concerns that the existing six items were not reliably or validly capturing the bidimensional conception of efficacy led the NES to test new questions in a 1987 pilot study (Craig, Niemi, and Silver 1990). In addition to several of the original items, the pilot study included hypothesized new measures of internal efficacy and two hypothesized forms of external efficacy: regime-based and incumbent-based. The study also expanded the response categories for all the questions from the original dichotomous agree/disagree format to a five-point scale (agree strongly, agree somewhat, neither agree nor disagree, disagree somewhat, and disagree strongly). The four new items that proved to be reliable and valid indicators of internal efficacy are:

1. "I consider myself well-qualified to participate in politics."
2. "I feel that I have a pretty good understanding of the important political issues facing our country."
3. "I feel that I could do as good a job in public office as most other people."
4. "I think that I am as well-informed about politics and government as most people."

Unlike the original indicators, each of these is worded positively; thus researchers created an internal political efficacy scale by summing responses to these four items and categorizing respondents who agree strongly with all four statements as the most efficacious and those who disagree strongly with all four as the least efficacious. Further empirical examination has confirmed these four items are reliable and valid indicators of internal political efficacy (see Niemi, Craig, and Mattei 1991; Morrell 2003).

Results regarding external efficacy have not been as clear. The data indicate that two of the original items—"People like me don't have any say about what the government does" and "I don't think public officials care much what people like me think"—primarily tap into external efficacy, though researchers have not yet developed clear measures to differentiate between regime-based and incumbent-based variants of this concept. The other older item that remains in use—"Sometimes politics and government seem so complicated that a person like me can't really understand what's going on"—appears to capture parts of both internal and external efficacy. These three original items, along with the four new internal efficacy statements, appeared on the 1988, 1992, and 2000 NES instruments.

The 1990, 1994, 1996, and 1998 NES questionnaires only included the three remaining original items, and the 2002 instrument contained a hybrid of two

Table 1. Political Efficacy Measures in the National Election Studies'
Time Series

Year(s)	Measures	Response Categories
1952, 1956, 1960, 1964	NOSAY; NOCARE; COMPLEX; VOTING	Agree / Disagree
1966	NOSAY; NOCARE; COMPLEX; VOTING	Strongly Agree / Agree / Not Sure, It Depends / Disagree / Strongly Disagree
1968, 1970, 1972, 1974, 1976, 1978, 1980	NOSAY; NOCARE; COMPLEX; VOTING; LOSETOUCH; PARTIES	Agree / Disagree
1982	NOSAY; NOCARE	Agree / Disagree
1984	NOSAY; NOCARE; COMPLEX	Agree / Disagree
1986	NOCARE	Agree / Disagree
1988, 1992, 2000	NOSAY; NOCARE; COMPLEX; SELFQUAL; UNDRSTND; PUBOFF; INFORMD	Agree Strongly / Agree Somewhat / Neither Agree Nor Disagree / Disagree Somewhat / Disagree Strongly
1990, 1994, 1996, 1998	NOSAY; NOCARE; COMPLEX	Agree Strongly / Agree Somewhat / Neither Agree Nor Disagree / Disagree Somewhat / Disagree Strongly
2002	NOSAY; NOCARE; SELFQUAL; INFORMD	Agree / Neither Agree Nor Disagree / Disagree

NOSAY: "People like me don't have any say about what the government does."
NOCARE: "I don't think public officials care much what people like me think."
COMPLEX: "Sometimes politics and government seem so complicated that a person like me can't really understand what's going on."
VOTING: "Voting is the only way that people like me can have any say about how the government runs things."
LOSETOUCH: "Generally speaking, those we elect to Congress in Washington lose touch with the people pretty quickly."
PARTIES: "Parties are interested only in people's vote, not their opinions."
SELFQUAL: "I consider myself well-qualified to participate in politics."
UNDRSTND: "I feel that I have a pretty good understanding of the important political issues facing our country."
PUBOFF: "I feel that I could do as good a job in public office as most other people."
INFORMD: "I think that I am as well-informed about politics and government as most people."

original statements ("People like me don't have any say . . ." and "Public officials don't care much . . .") and two newer ones ("I think that I am as well-informed . . ." and "I consider myself well-qualified . . ."). Thus, even after the development of valid and reliable indicators of internal political efficacy, the political efficacy measures have not consistently appeared on the NES surveys. This has hampered social scientists' ability to compare the development of political efficacy across time, but in every presidential election year in the United States there has been at least one indicator of one of the dimensions of political efficacy in the NES studies (see Table 1). One consistent approach the NES has taken since 1988 is that the response categories for all the questions have been on a five-point scale ranging from agree strongly to disagree strongly. This has increased both the range of the scales measuring political efficacy and our ability to further discriminate between citizens having the highest and lowest levels of political efficacy.

Though the NES studies have been the primary source for our measures of political efficacy, social scientists have used many of these items in contexts outside of national elections in the United States. Sometimes adapted to fit the population under investigation, the items have appeared in studies of other countries, such as China and Russia; in more local contexts in the United States; and even in experimental research. In 1976 the NES itself included three political efficacy items asking respondents how they perceive their local political contexts. Recent research indicates that these adaptations are more than likely reliable and valid, especially with regard to the new internal efficacy scale (see Morrell 2003). This indicates that investigators can utilize these items across research projects and methodologies, thus increasing our cumulative knowledge of this important political concept. Further conceptual and empirical exploration of our measurements of political efficacy is still necessary, especially regarding external efficacy and its various possible dimensions.

Further Reading

Acock, Alan C., Harold D. Clarke, and Marianne C. Stewart. "A New Model for Old Measures: A Covariance Structure Analysis of Political Efficacy." *Journal of Politics* 47 (1985): 1061–84.

Balch, George I. "Multiple Indicators in Survey Research: The Concept 'Sense of Political Efficacy.'" *Political Methodology* 1 (1974): 1–43.

Campbell, Angus, Gerald Gurin, and Warren E. Miller. *The Voter Decides*. Evanston, IL: Row, Peterson, 1954.

Craig, Stephen C., Richard G. Niemi, and Glenn E. Silver. "Political Efficacy and Trust: A Report on the NES Pilot Study Items." *Political Behavior* 12 (1990): 289–314.

Morrell, Michael E. "Survey and Experimental Evidence for a Reliable and Valid Measure." *Public Opinion Quarterly* 67 (2003): 589–602.

Niemi, Richard G., Stephen C. Craig, and Franco Mattei. "Measuring Internal Political Efficacy in the 1988 National Election Study." *American Political Science Review* 85 (1991): 1407–13.

Web Sites

The Web site of the National Election Studies, available at http://www.umich.edu/~nes/nesguide/nesguide.htm, features a guide to public opinion and electoral behavior, allowing direct access to data about several attitudes regarding politics and the political system.

Michael E. Morrell

Political Knowledge

Political knowledge is the body of information that citizens have regarding political institutions, actors, and developments. Political scientists also have referred to this concept as "citizen knowledge" and "political information." Although citizens possess knowledge on topics ranging from domestic policy to political geography, for it to exert a meaningful impact on a person's attitudes and behavior it must exist in the person's long-term memory and be available for retrieval. Citizen knowledge typically is measured by survey respondents' ability to recall the correct answer to objective knowledge questions (e.g., "Which party is in control of Congress?").

If information is a vital resource for citizens in a democracy, how well equipped is the average American? The answer depends on what question is being asked. According to professors Michael Delli Carpini and Scott Keeter, authors of one of the most comprehensive studies of citizen knowledge, there is a wide array of facts about which substantial percentages of the public are aware. Large majorities of citizens know that the U.S. Constitution can be amended; identify visible political actors, such as the president; and demonstrate familiarity with important social indicators like the minimum wage. Overall, however, there is a tremendous amount of variation in levels of citizen knowledge across different topics.

Citizen knowledge about the institutions and processes of politics is higher than knowledge about political actors and policies. This difference is attributed to the fact that the institutions and processes of politics are fairly stable and therefore require less monitoring of the political landscape. Across all categories, however, citizens display greater knowledge about objects that are more visible. For instance, a 1989 poll showed that 89 percent of the public could define a presidential veto; only 20 percent could name two of the First Amendment rights. Similarly, research has shown that nearly all citizens can identify the president of the United States, while far fewer can identify their representative in Congress, leaders of other countries, or even their own state representative.

Figure 1 displays a similar level of variation in citizen's knowledge about two important domestic policies: Medicare and Social Security. These data come from two surveys administered in February and April of 1999 by Princeton Survey Research Associates. In the February survey, citizens were asked if they could identify proposals to reform Medicare and Social Security that had been mentioned in then-President Clinton's **State of the Union Address**. In the April survey, citizens were queried about recent trustees' reports regarding the future financial condition of both of these programs. The bars in Figure 1 show the percentage of people correctly answering these questions. Citizens demonstrate greater levels of knowledge about Social Security and Medicare when the president is talking about them in a visible context (i.e., a nationally televised address). They show much lower levels of knowledge about these same programs when the source of the information are the boards of trustees overseeing them. Other surveys administered by Princeton Survey Research Associates in the late 1990s show that citizens had higher levels of knowledge about visible policies. Seventy-five percent of the public knew about then-President Clinton's "Don't Ask, Don't Tell" policy regarding gays in the military while only 25 percent could identify aspects of the settlement between the tobacco industry and the states.

On the whole, Delli Carpini and Keeter's evidence shows that a majority of citizens can provide correct answers to about half the questions in a comprehensive political information survey, with very few citizens at either extreme (i.e., answering all the questions correctly or incorrectly). A few caveats to this general finding are worth noting. First, recent research has shown that the misin-

Figure 1. Citizen Knowledge about Social Security and Medicare, by Source of Information

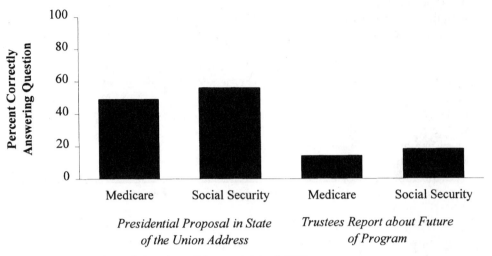

Source: Princeton Survey Research Associates, February and April 1999.

formed—or those who provide incorrect answers to objective knowledge questions—tend to be the most confident in their answers and therefore the most difficult to correct. In addition to those who are providing incorrect responses to political knowledge questions, a large number of individuals give a "don't know" response (*see* **No-Opinion Response Options**). Finally, some scholars insist that measuring levels of general political knowledge is less preferable than measuring the public's level of knowledge about specific policy problems, such as **crime** or the **environment**. These scholars note that people who have high levels of general political knowledge may nonetheless be ignorant of policy-specific information that might alter their judgments about those policies.

Why do some citizens know a lot about politics while others know relatively little? In an attempt to answer this question, many researchers have focused on individual-level factors, such as social and economic status. The dominant conclusion from empirical studies of socioeconomic status is that traditionally disadvantaged groups tend to know less about politics. For example, women, low-income, and younger citizens are less informed than men, wealthy, and older citizens. It is also the case that people with higher levels of education and Caucasians know more about politics. Combinations of these traits prove to be particularly powerful predictors of political knowledge. Using data from the late-1980s, Delli Carpini and Keeter have shown that older males whose family income exceeded $50,000 correctly answered 66 to 75 percent of the factual questions on two nationally representative surveys. These scores were more than two and a half times higher than those of the least informed group in their sample: black women whose family income was less than $20,000 per year.

Although they are powerful determinants of knowledge, demographic and social characteristics change slowly if at all. As a result, scholars also have investigated the behavioral causes of knowledge. Of the many possible sources of motivation to learn and retain political facts, interest in politics is among the most important. Those who care about and seek out political information tend to know more. However, it is also the case that previously learned knowledge increases the likelihood of exposure to and reception of additional facts.

Attention to political issues or the news media only increases knowledge to the extent that the environment supplies factual information. Studies have shown that citizen knowledge is driven by the importance of a particular subject in the news and the amount of coverage it receives in the media. When there have been gains in knowledge on a subject over time, scholars have attributed those gains to increased media coverage. Over a five-year period in the mid-1980s, for example, citizen knowledge about U.S. policy in Nicaragua increased by more than 25 percentage points. The increase was likely due to heavy media coverage of the congressional debate over aid to the Contras. Thus, one important conclusion arising from research in this area is that levels of knowledge ebb and flow with the supply of information about a particular subject (*see* **Agenda Setting**).

Construed broadly, the information environment on any given topic varies considerably. On some issues, such as outbreaks of the West Nile virus in the United States, the news media provide a substantial amount of coverage and expert testimony. On other issues, such as changes in health insurance coverage costs, televised and print news sources provide only minimal treatment. The quality of coverage is also a concern. When the news media disseminate inaccurate or misleading information, there may be lower levels of citizen knowledge. Historical examples include inaccurate public perceptions of the missile gap between the United States and the Soviet Union during the Cold War. A more recent illustration might be the alarmist rhetoric surrounding the financial health of the Social Security system. Studies have shown that citizens overestimate the financial problems of this program, making errors that likely stem from the content of media coverage on this issue. Although political information often originates from media sources, it spreads indirectly via informal political discussion networks. As citizens discuss and deliberate about politics, they tend to learn and know more.

Finally, scholars are beginning to understand that how they measure political knowledge may affect their conclusions. Citizens often are classified as informed, misinformed, or uninformed. Those who are classified as informed provide the correct response to a factual question about politics; the misinformed provide incorrect responses; while the uninformed do not provide any response, right or wrong. Most studies of political knowledge focus on the informed group, but recent studies have shown that "don't know" or "refuse to answer" responses are not distributed randomly. In particular, scholars have shown that personality characteristics lead members of some sub-groups, such as women, to appear as though they are uniformed even when they might be able to guess the correct answer. In short, some respondents are risk takers who guess even when they might not know the answer while others play it safe by not guessing. The implications are that some respondents may appear uninformed due to survey methods that discourage guessing rather than a lack of substantive knowledge.

For decades scholars have debated whether people need extensive knowledge on political issues to make good decisions. Although it can be argued that citi-

Figure 2. Actual Opinion versus Simulated Estimates of Fully Informed Opinion

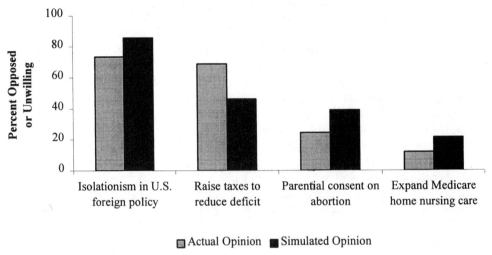

Source: Althaus (1998).

zens who rely on cognitive shortcuts can make reasonable decisions, in many cases knowledge has no substitute. The best evidence on this score comes from studies that show that collective choices would differ were the public's level of political information greater.

According to research by Professor Scott Althaus, the preferences of a hypothetical fully informed citizenry would look much different. Some of these knowledge-based differences in public opinion are shown in Figure 2. Using the **National Election Studies** data from 1988 and 1992, Althaus has shown that Americans would have been 12 percentage points more likely to oppose isolationism in U.S. foreign policy, 23 percentage points more willing to raise taxes to offset the federal deficit, 15 percentage points more opposed to parental consent for minors seeking an **abortion,** and 10 percentage points more likely to oppose expanding Medicare to include a home nursing care benefit. While many of these movements are in a liberal direction, simulating opinion to produce fully informed citizens does not yield reliably liberal or conservative judgments (*see* **Liberalism and Conservatism**).

Not only do attitudes differ, but opinions are also more stable when citizens are knowledgeable. In other words, when asked for their views on the same question at two or more time points, those who know the most are typically the most consistent over time. Knowledge also helps citizens translate their political predispositions into the most logical or appropriate policy preferences.

In addition to its effects on opinions, political information promotes civic virtues, such as tolerance. Those who know more are more willing to permit the expression of ideas or interests even if they conflict with a person's own values. People who are knowledgeable also participate in politics more than those who do not know much. According to one analysis of an election study in 1988, respondents who were highly knowledgeable were 20 percentage points more likely to vote than respondents at the low end of the scale, even after controlling for a variety of demographic and attitudinal factors. Not only does knowledge structure the decision to vote, it also affects vote choice. According to one study, a hypothetical fully informed electorate is less likely to vote for incumbent presidents.

Scholars are expected to develop an even better understanding of how the broader information environment affects citizen knowledge. As existing research has shown, exposing citizens to more information tends to increase their knowledge about politics. However, given most citizens' limited appetite for news about politics, there likely is a declining marginal effect for increasing amounts of political information. We also know relatively little about the precise features of the information environment that increase citizen knowledge, and whether knowledge varies according to the source of the information, the quality of the news coverage, or the particular issue being covered. We anticipate that scholars will answer these and related questions in the coming years.

Further Reading

Althaus, Scott L. "Information Effects and Collective Preferences." *American Political Science Review* 92, no. 2 (1998): 545–58. A statistical analysis of the effect of citizen knowledge on aggregate-level public opinion.

Bartels, Larry M. "Uninformed Votes: Information Effects in Presidential Elections." *American Journal of Political Science* 40, no. 1 (1996): 194–230. A simulation of how citizens would have voted in six past presidential elections if they had been fully informed.

Delli Carpini, Michael X., and Scott Keeter. *What Americans Know About Politics and Why It Matters.* New Haven, CT: Yale University Press, 1996. A comprehensive study of citizen knowledge in America, with data spanning multiple decades.

Mondak, Jeffery J., and Mary R. Anderson. "A Knowledge Gap or a Guessing Game." *The Public Perspective* 14, no. 2 (2003): 6–9. A discussion of gender-based differences in "don't know" responses on survey questions.

Web Sites

A number of organizations disseminate data about public opinion and citizen knowledge on their Web sites. Three useful references are: The Gallup Organization (http://www.gallup.com/); the University of California, Berkeley's Survey Documentation and Analysis Web site (http://sda.berkeley.edu/); and the **Roper Center for Public Opinion Research** Web site (http://www.ropercenter.uconn.edu/).

Jennifer Jerit and Jason Barabas

Political Talk Radio

Talk radio refers to the ubiquitous trend in radio programming in which a host talks directly to an audience, with or without guests, and takes call-in questions, statements, or comments. As a great deal of such programming is explicitly political in content, scholars have begun to consider the role of political talk radio in shaping public opinion. That talk radio does influence opinion is beyond doubt. However, the how's, why's, and "so what's" implied are neither simple nor straightforward.

Although most studies concerning political talk radio and its role in society have been published within the past decade, research predates the 1990s. The past thirty-five years encompassed major changes in the regulatory structures of political radio broadcasting that led to the development of mass, national audiences for political talk shows. As the nature of the audiences changed the nature of the medium also changed, ushering in highly talented, extremely flamboyant entertainers who could engage large audiences and sell political slogans in ways that resemble electronic evangelicals. These changes paralleled a trend in mainstream news media to become more popular and thereby bolster ratings by injecting elements of entertainment in programming that is nominally "news" or "public affairs." The period also encompassed major changes in theories of media effects that shifted scholars' concerns from a presumption that media, including talk radio, had "minimal effects" (*see* **Campaign Effects**) to a paradigm that drew heavily on communication theory and enlarged the range and nature of effects that media may have.

Early studies of the characteristics of the audience for and content of political talk radio tended, with some exceptions, to be alarmist. The portrait that emerged was one of lonely and isolated listeners who were fed a diet of hostile information that was viewed by some as ominous and threatening. During this early period, survey studies found political talk audiences to be older, less affluent, and less educated than nonlisteners. Listeners were more likely than nonlisteners to be socially isolated—living alone, single or widowed, retired, elderly—and to spend large amounts of time in the home. One speculation was that political talk audiences used the programs as a surrogate companion to overcome their loneliness. It was also reported that entertainment, information seeking, escapism, convenience, relaxation, and passing time were motives for listening to political talk. The content of programming also gave many commentators pause. Liberal journalists in particular were troubled by what they saw as the outrageous and biased messages that they saw in much of the programming hosted by conservatives. There was, however, little evidence that exposure to talk radio had more than "minimal effects" on people's attitudes or behaviors.

More recent studies suggest very different conclusions about talk radio. This may reflect more sophisticated research designs, but it also doubtless reflects objective changes in telecommunications. The political talk radio audiences changed markedly with the removal of the fairness doctrine (which essentially required that stations give equal time to competing points of view) from FCC rules in 1985, the emergence of high-quality satellite transmission of AM programming that could be broadcast nationally, the development of 1-800 numbers for call-ins, and the proliferation of car phones. Highly segmented local audiences became large national audiences, and talented if controversial national hosts, such as Rush Limbaugh, became household personalities across the land. It is clear that the changing nature of program content and audiences and the rise of flamboyant, dominant radio personalities changed the relationships between exposure to political talk radio and its audiences.

In a study of the American political talk audience during the Republican primaries in 1993–1995, a team of researchers reported that regular listeners (those who regularly listened two or more times per week) constituted 18 percent of the adult population and that 11 percent listened to Limbaugh. They found that listeners were more likely to monitor other news media (except for television news) to be more knowledgeable about politics, and to be more involved in politics. Another study found listeners tended to be male, more Republican, and conservative. Callers were more likely than others to be Republican (though it remains unclear if that is self-selection by listeners or screening by program staff). Looking at Limbaugh listeners per se, they were more likely than others to respond positively to Republican leaders and negatively to President Clinton, to oppose government regulation, to have positive views of big corporations, to be critical of mainstream news media, and to distrust government.

Many social scientists have reported that exposure to political talk radio is associated with heightened **political efficacy** and increased levels of political participation. In another study, political talk exposure in Madison, Wisconsin, was found to be associated with positive views of Congress and negative views of other political institutions, including courts, schools, and news media; it was not associated with views of the (senior Bush) presidency. Another team reported that those more highly involved in political talk radio were more likely to participate socially and politically than the less involved. Talk audiences were found to be higher in social status, more socially integrated into the broader society, and more attentive to political issues.

Listeners construct political reality from the messages that they hear on talk radio by extrapolating from what they see or hear. These constructions may result in gaining a variety of factually true and false images, especially from exposure to highly charged and psychologically engaging partisan talk content, even when hosts are technically not making false assertions. Data from a San Diego survey demonstrated that active listening was associated with higher levels of information regardless of the ideological bent of the host, but that exposure to conservative talk radio was also associated with greater levels of misinformation. People listening to conservative hosts gained both information and more misinformation (a fact that remained true even when controlling statistically for a wide variety of other factors, such as **partisanship**, age, gender, etc.).

A number of studies have examined the impact of talk radio on the evaluations of candidates and elections. Studies concluded that the listening audience was more disposed to dislike Clinton and that talk radio served as a reinforcing mechanism. Another study found that political talk radio plays a major role in Republican Presidential Primary elections. Yet another demonstrated that audience explanations for the outcome of the 1996 presidential election differed depending on which talk radio program they listened to, with Limbaugh listeners most likely to disregard "substantive" reasons for why Clinton won.

Contrary to other studies, one that examined the perceptions of Pat Buchanan during the 1996 Republican primaries found that "the members of Limbaugh's audience were no more likely to harbor negative feelings toward Buchanan than were nonlisteners," despite Limbaugh's portrayal of Buchanan as a "liberal in disguise." Utilizing the "Gamson Hypothesis," which states that people with high efficacy and low levels of political trust are the optimal targets for mobilization, one analyst reported that talk radio and the Gamson typology (alienated, subordinate, dissident, assured) was better suited for describing the behavior of conservatives, but not liberals. This may explain, in part, why talk radio may potentially affect the behavior of conservatives more than that of liberals.

Analysts examined the attitudes of political talk radio listeners toward the leaders of both the Democratic and Republican parties. The authors reported that listeners' agreement with hosts increases as exposure increases. Interestingly, Democrats and Independents who listen to conservative talk radio tended to start agreeing with the message as exposure increased and vice versa (conservatives and independents who listen to liberal/moderate talk radio).

Another important study made use of data from **panel surveys** from the **National Election Studies** (1992 through 1997) to examine the continuity of talk radio's audience in the latter half of the 1990s; it concluded that the number of listeners dropped significantly from 1992 to 1997 (57.0 to 39.3 percent). Importantly, the decline was not general: "quitters" tended to be female, liberal, nonwhite, more tolerant of other people's views, and more trusting of the mainstream media. Overall, it should be noted, the national audience for talk radio in general, and for Limbaugh in particular, has remained relatively constant, suggesting that "quitting" is again not a general phenomenon.

Beyond its role in affecting individual behavior, talk radio also has important consequences for the public sphere. One analyst examined the motives behind political talk radio activity and identified four reasons why callers use the medium: advice seeking, to transmit opinions, dialogue engagement, and "policing" the public sphere. Call-in talk radio, she concluded, offers the greatest potential for citizens to engage in a mass dialogue and to convey their emotions and opinions—something that other vehicles of communication (e.g., public opinion polls) cannot provide. Another analyst demonstrated the role of black political talk radio in Chicago in sustaining and integrating a community of interest among African American listeners to facilitate collective action to solve problems and to develop group identity. Yet another provided evidence that exposure to Limbaugh programming tends to build a community of like-minded persons among conservatives by enhancing their sense of self-efficacy and emboldening them to participate in dialog. It has a deleterious effect on efficacy and participation among liberals.

The nomination of Zoe Baird for Attorney General offered a hint of the power and utility of political talk radio in creating a public among average citizens. Social scientists found that the traditional, "elite" media supported the nomination even after a controversy concerning the hiring of undocumented immigrants was aired. Citizen outrage, mobilized largely through call-in radio, led to a barrage of calls to senators' offices that ultimately produced withdrawal of the nomination. A community of interest in the public sphere was formed in the process, one that resulted in the exercise of political power. This demonstrates the potential, noted by scholars, for political talk radio to mobilize opinion when large numbers of people distrust traditional media and when they feel that the media and political elites are unresponsive to their views.

The perceptions of others in the political talk audience may bolster building a public sphere in the political talk radio audience. In particular, those who perceive political talk programs to be more interactive and who are more psychologically involved in programming are more likely to perceive callers as like themselves, more likely to conclude that callers know what they are talking about, and more likely to gain new ideas from the programming. The statistical relationships are present after controlling for exposure to political talk programming, political interest, partisanship, ideology, age, education, and gender. These perceptions may be the building blocks for public spheres linked to political talk.

Future research is likely to follow a number of trends. First, students of the role of political talk radio in contemporary society should not be constrained within the boundaries of a single discipline. The field has already begun to benefit from the application of both political science and communication studies approaches. Empirically, researches should continue to examine specific situations and events as natural **experiments** to garner evidence of the influence that political talk has on public opinion and behavior. Although this path is not as exciting as grand theorizing, the accumulation of knowledge under varying situations and about different political issues using improved measurement schemes is the way toward theory building.

Theory is indeed an area in which more work is required. A great deal of "data mining" has been done with large national surveys; instead, smaller, more innovative, theoretically informed experimental studies are needed. What types of issues and situations are most conducive to the efficacy of political talk as a change mechanism? What types of talk messages combine with which individual dispositions to produce change? What is the role of emotional factors in the talk radio experience? To answer these questions we need better theories and better experiments.

The medium has transformed itself several times in recent history and may transform itself again, especially if its popularity during the past decade constitutes but a passing fad in the long term. At the micro level of individual behavior, research focusing on information processing theories has proven useful in the past, and scholars will find it productive to continue asking questions in this vein. But what are the consequences if audience interest should decline? What are the characteristics of political talk groupies who are no longer listeners? Will audiences become more homogenous? What about possible connections between talk radio and the use of the **Internet**?

We also have much to learn about how political talk radio is involved in building and maintaining public spheres at both macro and micro levels of analysis. How do communities inspired by political talk radio evolve? How stable are they? To what extent do they encourage hostility and divisiveness? What are the conditions under which such communities make a significant difference in the larger political system?

Further Reading

Barker, David C. *Rushed to Judgment: Talk Radio, Persuasion, and American Political Behavior*. New York: Columbia University Press, 2002.

Cappella, John E., Joseph N. Turow, Kathleen Hall Jamieson. *Call-In Political Talk Radio Background, Content, Audiences, Portrayal in Mainstream Media*. A report from the Annenberg Public Policy Center of the University of Pennsylvania. Philadelphia: Annenberg Public Policy Center, University of Pennsylvania, 1996.

Crittenden, John. "Democratic Functions of the Open Mike Forum." *Public Opinion Quarterly* 35 (1971): 200–210.

Davis, Richard, and Diana Owen. *New Media and American Politics*. New York: Oxford University Press, 1998.

Hofstetter, C. Richard, Mark C. Donovan, Melville R. Klauber, Alexandra Cole, Carolyn Huie, and Toshiyuki Yuasa. "Political Talk Radio: A Stereotype Reconsidered." *Political Research Quarterly* 47 (1994): 467–79.

C. Richard Hofstetter and Neil Baer

Political Tolerance

In the study of American public opinion, political tolerance refers to the willingness of citizens to allow disliked groups or individuals to practice a variety of democratic rights and freedoms. The study of political tolerance has typically focused on attitudes toward groups that may be disliked for their political beliefs (e.g., communists, racists, or atheists) or social behaviors (e.g., gays and lesbians—*see* **Gay Rights**). What we know about the levels of political tolerance, changes in tolerance over time, and the sources of more or less tolerant attitudes depends, in part, on how we measure tolerance and, in part, on what types of tolerance targets and activities we focus. More recently, some analyses of political tolerance have focused on attitudes toward individuals associated with unpopular political groups rather than groups as a whole.

The earliest significant study of political tolerance was published in 1955, at the time of a national witch hunt directed at communists and other groups on the left end of the political spectrum. Samuel Stouffer, the sociologist behind the study, measured tolerance with a series of questions asking about survey respondents' willingness to allow communists, socialists, and atheists to practice different citizenship rights (e.g., making a speech in the respondent's community, teaching in high schools or colleges, or working as a clerk in a store). In addition to surveying ordinary citizens, Stouffer conducted an examination of political activists' support for the three groups' rights and freedoms. Based on the two surveys, Stouffer demonstrated widespread political intolerance in the United States—although he showed that political activists were considerably more tolerant than were ordinary citizens. For example, more than 66 percent of ordinary citizens were unwilling to allow a communist to make a speech in their community or to have a book in the public library collection and almost all favored firing a communist from a college teaching position. While Stouffer found alarmingly low levels of tolerance, he was nonetheless optimistic about the future of political minority groups. He predicted that tolerance would increase over time as a result, in part, of steadily rising levels of education and the decline in authoritarian child-rearing practices.

Numerous investigations of political tolerance have since revolved around several controversies concerning Americans' attitudes toward political minorities. One question that has stimulated considerable discussion is whether Stouffer's prophecy about increases in tolerance over time has been fulfilled. The answer to that question depends, in part, on how tolerance is defined and measured, as well as on what types of targets and activities one focuses. Two principal approaches to measuring tolerance have emerged in the literature, one of them based on Stouffer's original study. The **General Social Surveys** (GSS), one of the principal sources of public opinion data available to social scientists, have included a modified set of Stouffer tolerance questions since 1972. The GSS asks questions about five groups (communists, atheists, racists, militarists, and homosexuals) and three activities to be performed by each group (speaking in the respondents' community, teaching in a college or university, and allowing a book written by a member of each group to remain in the public library).

The second major approach to measuring tolerance was developed in the 1970s by political scientist John Sullivan and his colleagues. They criticized any approaches to measuring tolerance (including the original Stouffer approach and the modified GSS approach) based on querying respondents about targets preselected by the researchers. Sullivan and his colleagues proposed that tolerance involves putting up with objectionable targets; approaches based on asking respondents about targets that the researcher selected are thus flawed because they fail to establish in the first place whether respondents dislike the groups about which they are asked. According to this view, tolerance is not measured when respondents who do not dislike communists are asked about extending citizenship rights to communists; tolerance is measured only when respondents who dislike communists are asked about their readiness to allow communists to exercise their citizenship rights. To measure tolerance, Sullivan and others use a "least-liked" methodology—asking respondents to identify their least-like group(s) first and, only subsequently, to indicate how much they are prepared to tolerate those groups.

To summarize so far, the GSS approach to measuring tolerance is based on asking survey respondents about targets of researchers' choice. In spite of the limitations of this approach (i.e., targets chosen by the researcher may not be disliked by the respondents), some researchers have argued that GSS questions are valuable because they ask about widely, albeit not universally, disliked groups. In addition, GSS questions have been asked consistently over time and thus make it possible to study changes in Americans' attitudes over time toward political dissenters. The "least-liked" methodology, in contrast, essentially personalizes tolerance questions for each respondent. Only respondents who identify communists, for example, as one of their least-liked groups are asked about their readiness to extend various citizenship rights to communists. Respondents who identify a different group as one of their least-liked are asked about that group's rights instead.

What we can conclude about changes in Americans' tolerance over time depends on whether we rely on the GSS or the Sullivan approach to measuring tolerance. Keeping the criticisms and countercriticisms of the GSS questions in mind, I rely on the GSS data to chart the picture of attitudes toward atheists, communists, racists, militarists, and homosexuals. To streamline the picture of changes in attitudes toward these five political minorities, Table 1 reports attitudes toward each group and activity at approximately four-year intervals between 1976, the year in which questions about all five groups were asked for the first time, and the most recent year for which the GSS data are available (2000). This presentation does not capture all the minor shifts in public opinion toward political dissenters that took place during this time period, but it nonetheless depicts the broad changes in tolerance of the five groups and three activities that took place over an almost thirty-year period.

The data reported in Table 1 suggest that, with the exception of attitudes toward racists, willingness to tolerate all groups (particularly communists and homosexuals) has steadily gone up over time. The attitudes toward racists, in

Table 1. Changes in Attitudes Over Time Toward Atheists, Communists, Racists, Militarists, and Homosexuals

GSS year	1976	1980	1984	1988	1993[1]	1996	2000
Allowing atheists to:							
Speak	64.7	66.7	68.6	70.9	72.5	74.5	75.4
Teach	42.2	46.9	47.4	46.8	54.2	58.0	58.9
Have a book in the library	61.1	63.3	65.3	65.3	70.1	70.5	70.6
Allowing communists to:							
Speak	55.8	56.6	60.8	61.7	70.5	65.8	67.5
Teach	43.6	43.2	48.3	50.4	60.6	60.4	60.7
Have a book in the library	58.2	59.5	61.6	61.3	69.7	67.5	68.2
Allowing homosexuals to:							
Speak	64.0	68.0	70.6	72.6	80.8	82.7	83.0
Teach	53.9	56.8	61.3	59.5	71.7	77.3	79.3
Have a book in the library	57.5	59.5	61.3	62.7	69.5	71.2	73.5
Allowing militarists to:							
Speak	55.3	58.1	57.9	57.6	66.1	64.2	64.6
Teach	38.4	41.1	42.4	38.6	49.8	50.7	50.3
Have a book in the library	58.2	60.1	60.4	59.0	69.7	66.7	66.3
Allowing racists to:							
Speak	62.0	63.3	58.7	62.6	62.0	62.0	61.3
Teach	42.0	45.0	42.2	43.0	45.2	47.7	48.1
Have a book in the library	62.1	66.3	65.1	63.8	67.1	66.3	65.4

1. The General Social Survey was not administered in 1992.

contrast, have been remarkably stable over time. Another qualification is that the degree of tolerance of the five groups has depended on the activity they have been asked to tolerate. In general, GSS respondents have been more hesitant to allow a member of each group to teach in a college or university; they have been more willing to allow a speech by a minority group member and to oppose removing from the public library a book written by the group member.

While GSS-based examinations of tolerance suggest that Americans have grown generally more tolerant over time, Sullivan and his collaborators' conceptualization of tolerance implies that such a conclusion is not necessarily warranted. Sullivan and his colleagues' work suggests that it may not be entirely appropriate to use GSS questions to study patterns in tolerance over time because the levels of tolerance may not have changed—the groups asked about in the GSS questions may simply have become more liked over time. Because GSS questions are asked about targets preselected by the researchers, it is possible that they capture not only tolerance (among respondents who dislike the targets) but also simple liking for the group (among respondents who happen to like them). Sullivan and his colleagues' own analysis of attitudes toward political dissenters (and later replications of their original work) in fact shows that intolerance, generally speaking, is widespread—albeit attitudes toward communists and their "fellow travelers" may have become marginally more positive.

While the Stouffer/GSS and Sullivan approaches represent two dominant methods for measuring tolerance, some scholars have been urging that we pay attention to another issue when measuring tolerance and its sources. We should not only ensure that we are asking survey respondents about groups they dislike but also consider whether and to what extent attitudes toward disliked groups may, in part, reflect attitudes toward disliked *acts*. Thus, people may be reluctant to tolerate flag burning regardless of what group wants to burn the flag (this has been labeled "generic intolerance," or, reluctance to allow a particular act regardless of the identity of the group which wants to perform it). Alternatively, they may be willing to allow flag burning by one group but not another (this has been labeled "discriminatory intolerance," or, unwillingness to allow a particular act only when it is performed by a disliked group). Once this distinction between discriminatory and generic intolerance is made and captured in measurement, studies show that discriminatory intolerance (examined in virtually all studies of political tolerance) is typically overestimated once its levels are adjusted for generic intolerance. In short, this argument suggests that the levels of American intolerance, whether based on the GSS or least-liked methodologies, may have been overestimated in most studies to date.

Students of tolerance have also been trying to identify the factors associated with more or less favorable attitudes toward political dissenters. Generally speaking, most investigations have focused on long-term influences (i.e., factors that are stable over time) on political tolerance. More recently, studies of political tolerance have also started exploring the linkages between short-term factors (i.e., factors that vary from one civil liberties controversy to another) and support for the rights of political dissenters. Three types of long-term factors typically are considered in examinations of the sources of tolerance: sociodemographic (e.g., education), political (e.g., commitment to general democratic norms), and psychological (e.g., dogmatism). Short-term factors that have so far received research attention include, among other things, the nature of the group's behavior (peaceful vs. belligerent), media interpretations of the essence of the civil liberties dispute (as primarily about free speech or primarily about a possible disruption to public order), and whether members of the political majority pay attention to their thoughts or feelings.

Education, age, religiosity, and gender have been considered some of the more important sociodemographic influences on tolerance. Though there has been some controversy concerning the influence of education on political tolerance, most studies identify education as the most important sociodemographic influence on political tolerance. The well-educated tend to be more tolerant than the poorly educated, in part because of their higher cognitive sophistication (and resultant ability to apply general democratic norms to specific situations) and in part because of their higher endorsement of values associated with greater openness to diversity. Religious individuals, or those who practice their religion with greater ardor, are less tolerant than individuals who are less religious or non-religious. Younger people, all else being equal, are more likely to support political dissenters' rights than are their older counterparts. Studies going back to Stouffer's original work on the subject also demonstrate that women tend to be more reluctant than men to extend citizenship rights and freedoms to members of unpopular political groups. Women tend to be less tolerant in part because they evidence a lower commitment to general democratic norms (such as free speech for everyone without regard to their political beliefs), in part because they perceive more threat from their political enemies, in part because they are higher in moral traditionalism, and in part because they are less likely to be political experts (or interested and knowledgeable about politics) than men (*see also* **Gender Differences in Public Opinion**).

Among political influences on tolerance two stand out: threat perceptions from the group and respondents' commitment to abstract democratic norms. Individual differences in political expertise (composed of political interest and **political knowledge**) are also influential. Typically threat perceptions have been defined to include threat to the respondent herself/himself and threat to the society as a whole. The latter form of threat has significantly more impact on tolerance than does the former form of threat, with individuals perceiving their political foes as a threat to the American way of life evincing less tolerance than those who do not think their political enemies pose such a threat. Americans expressing weak support for abstract democratic values or principles (e.g., minority rights, majority rule, equality under the law, and free speech for everyone) are similarly less supportive of extending democratic rights and freedoms to groups they dislike than those who profess a stronger commitment to general democratic norms. Political experts (or individuals highly interested in and knowledgeable about politics), finally, tend to be more willing to extend citizenship rights to their disliked groups than are political novices (or individuals evincing little or no interest in and knowledge about politics).

In addition to investigating the influence of political background characteristics and attitudes on tolerance, researchers have been trying to establish whether and how political activism affects attitudes toward political nonconformists. This is a significant question to address because some democratic theorists suggest that tolerance of ordinary citizens is not necessary for democracies to flourish. Rather, theorists espousing this view argue, the rights of political dissenters can be guaranteed even in the presence of widespread public intolerance as long as the "carriers of the creed" (or political elites) are ready and willing to protect them. In a partial test of this assumption, several studies have compared and contrasted tolerance of political elites (typically community leaders, public officials, legal elites, or political activists) and the general public. Most of these studies have established that political elites are more tolerant than ordinary citizens. A common explanation for the generally greater elite tolerance focuses on elites' characteristics, and particularly their greater education, intellectual ability, or political sophistication. A supplementary argument for the greater tolerance of elites emphasizes the formative nature of political socialization that the politically active experience.

Important psychological influences on tolerance, finally, include such personality dimensions as dogmatism, interpersonal trust (*see* **Social Capital**), neuroticism, extroversion, and openness to experience. Generally speaking, highly dogmatic individuals (or rigid thinkers) are less tolerant than individuals who are low in dogmatism (or more flexible thinkers). Individuals high in interpersonal trust exhibit more supportive attitudes toward their political enemies than do individuals who do not have very much trust in other people. Those high in neuroticism (worrying, nervous, emotional, and insecure) are less tolerant than those low in neuroticism. People high in extraversion (sociable, active, talkative, person-oriented, fun-loving, and affectionate) tend to be somewhat less tolerant than those who are more introverted. Finally, people who are high in openness to experience (curious, creative, original, imaginative, and nontraditional) tend to be significantly more tolerant of political minorities than those who are low in openness to experience.

A variety of short-term influences, or factors specific to a given civil liberties controversy, have been shown to make a difference in more or less tolerant responses to the same disliked group. The study of short-term influences on political tolerance has been significantly advanced by political scientists George Marcus, John Sullivan, and their colleagues. In a groundbreaking study of how people make civil liberties judgments, Marcus and colleagues argue for the importance of "contemporary information," or information available in the context of a particular civil liberties controversy in understanding how people make political tolerance judgments. In line with their predictions, Marcus and colleagues demonstrate that the nature of contemporary information can result in more or less tolerant responses to the same group. When an unpopular group violates the norms of peaceful, orderly behavior, for example, it receives less tolerance than when it complies with the norms by acting peacefully. When people pay attention to their feelings in the midst of a given civil liberties controversy, in addition, they respond with greater intolerance than when they pay attention to their thoughts. How commentators or activists interpret democratic principles in a particular situation also makes a difference. Individuals exposed to a positive interpretation of democratic principles (e.g., exhorting people to be tolerant) express more tolerance than individuals exposed to a negative interpretation of those principles (e.g., warning of the dangers extremist groups can pose to a democracy).

Other studies similarly demonstrate the importance of context-specific information in understanding why people respond more or less tolerantly to extremist political groups. One analysis shows that media interpretations of civil liberties disputes can influence the extent of tolerance the public is willing to accord unpopular groups. Drawing on actual civil liberties controversies involving the Ku Klux Klan (KKK), this study shows that the KKK rallies are tolerated more when the media interpret them as essentially about free speech; the same rallies are tolerated less, in contrast, when the media instead emphasize possible disruptions of public order. Another study shows less tolerance for the same group's activities when they impinge on respondents' personal space to a greater degree (e.g., when a disliked group's member is seeking to teach in a school attended by the respondents' niece or nephew) and more tolerance when the same activity does not threaten their personal space as much (e.g., when a disliked group's member is seeking to teach in a school without a personal connection to the respondents' life).

A small subset of the literature on tolerance of groups, finally, seeks to investigate the political consequences of political intolerance. One question addressed in this work is whether intolerance of ordinary citizens leads to repressive public policies. Some research demonstrates that repressive public policies during the McCarthy Red Scare and the Vietnam War eras did not stem from mass political intolerance but rather the strategic behavior of elites, suggesting that it is the intolerance of elites rather than ordinary citizens that drives governmental repression. Other research shows that widespread political intolerance matters politically because it constrains individual citizens' liberty. More specifically, ordinary citizens perceive more political freedom for themselves when they live in tolerant communities than do citizens who reside in relatively intolerant communities.

While the bulk of analyses on political tolerance has focused on "group-targeted" tolerance, or the question of whether Americans are willing to extend democratic protections to fringe groups as groups, some recent research instead examines support for citizenship rights of individuals affiliated with unpopular groups. Since our major civil liberties controversies have historically focused on the violations of group rights and since group rights have been at the center of many community disputes, studying tolerance of groups as a whole has been important. Because individual group members are typically tried in American courts, may be fired from their jobs, have their books censored, get their rental applications turned down, run into the invisible barriers of intolerance in political campaigns, or are targets of hate crimes, it is also important to consider how the broad principles of political tolerance are applied to and molded when individual members of unpopular minorities are involved. Based on research in psychology, there is reason to expect that individuals may not always be evaluated on the basis of the same considerations as groups of which they are members; they therefore may be tolerated more or less than groups as a whole.

Recent work draws attention to this previously neglected notion of "individual-targeted" tolerance, or public readiness to allow individual members of politically unpopular groups to exercise their rights and freedoms. Focusing on gay men and racists, this research demonstrates that how much individual gay men and racists are tolerated depends in part on whether their traits match or contradict their respective groups' **stereotypes**. Both individual gay men and racists receive more tolerance when their attributes are inconsistent with their group's stereotype (e.g., when gay men are described as assertive and sexually monogamous and racists are described as college graduates and coming from a wealthy family) than when their attributes match their group's stereotypes (e.g., when gay men are described as unassertive and sexually promiscuous and racists are described as high school dropouts and having few social ties).

In addition to demonstrating a link between group stereotypes and political tolerance judgments concerning individuals affiliated with unpopular groups, research on individual-targeted tolerance explores the implications of a concealable nature of membership in political minorities. Since one cannot tell "with a naked eye" whether an individual is a gay man or a racist, to elaborate, the question addressed in this research is whether individuals affiliated with unpopular groups are awarded more or less tolerance depending on when they disclose their group membership. Focusing on racists, this research shows that individual racists are tolerated more when they are upfront about their racism than when they delay its disclosure until after they have first disclosed other information about themselves. Linking the work on stereotypes and timing of group membership disclosure, finally, research on individual-targeted tolerance shows that the effect of group stereotypes on tolerance in part depends on the timing of group membership disclosure and how greatly a group is disliked. Stereotypes influence judgments of gay men, a moderately disliked group, more when their group membership is disclosed first; they affect judgments of individual racists, a strongly disliked group, more when their group membership is disclosed after other information.

Almost five decades of systematic research on attitudes toward the rights of political dissenters has greatly informed our knowledge about the extent, changes, and sources of political tolerance in the United States. Much more research on the subject, though, remains to be done. One question that would benefit from research attention is how malleable Americans' intolerant and tolerant attitudes are. Marcus and colleagues' work cited earlier is an important step in that direction, but many more questions remain about the types of contemporary information that may lead to more or less tolerant judgments. Another area deserving research attention is that of individual-targeted tolerance. Investigations of the dynamics of individual-targeted tolerance are few and thus raise at least as many questions as they answer. More research is necessary, finally, on the linkages between tolerance of groups and tolerance of individuals. One question here is whether tolerance of individual group members translates into greater tolerance of the group as a whole and, conversely, whether unwillingness to put up with a specific individual's exercise of democratic freedoms may translate into greater intolerance of the group to which that person belongs.

Further Reading

Golebiowska, E. A. "Individual-Targeted Tolerance and Timing of Group Membership Disclosure." *Journal of Politics* 63, no. 4 (2001): 1017–40. Shows that tolerance judgments of individual members of disliked and concealable groups are, in part, dependent on whether people learn about their group membership before or after receiving other information about them.

———. "The 'Pictures in Our Heads' and Individual-Targeted Tolerance." *Journal of Politics* 58, no. 4 (1996): 1010–34. Suggests a distinction between group- and individual-targeted tolerance and showing how group stereotypes and information inconsistent with them affect tolerance toward gay men.

Hurwitz, J., and J. J. Mondak. "Democratic Principles, Discrimination and Political Intolerance." *British Journal of Political Science* 32 (2002): 93–118. Puts forth a distinction between generic (intolerance of an expressive act independent of the group performing the act) and discriminatory intolerance (intolerance of an expressive act that in part depends on what group is performing the act).

Marcus, G. E., J. L. Sullivan, E. Theiss-Morse, and S. L. Wood. *With Malice Toward Some: How People Make Civil Liberties Judgments.* Cambridge: Cambridge University Press, 1995. A comprehensive study of civil liberties judgments, including attention to the role of long-standing factors (predispositions) in tolerance judgments as well as factors specific to a civil liberties controversy (contemporary information).

Stouffer, S. *Communism, Conformity, and Civil Liberties.* New York: Doubleday, 1955. A classic study of tolerance at the height of the Red Scare Era.

Sullivan, J. L., J. Pierson, and G. E. Marcus. *Political Tolerance and American Democracy.* Chicago: University of Chicago Press, 1982. An important book criticizing

the Stouffer approach to measuring tolerance and proposing an alternative measurement approach (the least-liked or content-controlled method).

Web Sites

A data archive including the General Social Surveys and other sources is available at
http://sda.berkeley.edu:7502/archive.htm.

Ewa A. Golebiowska

Polling and Voting

Public opinion polls, of course, are most often thought of as tools to help measure the public's views on any number of issues, most often relating to public
figures, public policies, or upcoming elections. The availability of such information to the public, however, carries with it the possibility of helping to shape
both the views and the actions of individuals. In most cases, we are left to guess
what the public at large believes, and those guesses are often formed by pro-
jecting our own beliefs or those of our relatively small circle of friends and ac-
quaintances on the population as a whole. Polling information, however,
provides a more objective measure of what our fellow citizens actually think,
which can lead people to reevaluate their preconceptions. Scholars who study
the effects of public opinion on voting behavior tend to focus on three specific
influences that this information can have on individuals: providing guidance
about which candidates to prefer in an election; shaping expectations about the
outcome of elections, which in turn can affect the desire to participate in that
election; and affecting strategic decisions about whom to support in multicandidate elections.

The growth in the number of polls conducted and reported by the media over
the past seventy years has been amazing. While early political polls were done
by a small number of organizations such as Gallup and Roper, almost all major
media outlets now are involved in polling, along with a growing number of independent polling organizations. The frequency with which these organizations
conduct polls has also increased. While the Gallup organization called the Truman versus Dewey election in September of 1948 and felt confident enough (incorrectly, as it turned out) to stop asking the question at that point, modern
presidential electorates are subject to an almost constant probing about their
opinions. During the 2000 presidential election campaign, one Web site alone
(http://www.pollingreport.com) reported the results of 298 separate tracking
polls from thirty-four organizations or combinations of organizations between
August and November, for an average of more than three a day. Media coverage of these polls has also increased accordingly. It is difficult to go more than
a day, even outside of election season, without hearing the results of a poll on
the evening news. During election years, this trend is even more pronounced. In
fact, many observers have become very critical of the media's emphasis on **horse
race journalism.**

For polling results to affect the public, however, individuals have to be exposed to them and find them credible. The little research that has been done on
the public's opinion about public opinion polls seems to indicate that people tend

to view polls themselves rather favorably, both as accurately representing the views of their fellow citizens, and as being useful for public officials to take into account when making decisions. Additionally, the information contained in polls seems to be getting through. Perhaps the best way to measure the public's ability to remember the results of polls comes from the ability of potential voters to correctly predict the winner of an upcoming presidential election. Since tracking polls make an explicit prediction about the outcome of an election and are widely available, the results of those polls should affect people's expectations. An examination of such predictions by nationally representative samples from the past ten presidential elections indicates that, in almost all cases, the ability of average citizens to predict the winner of an election varies with the closeness of the race (see Table 1). The largest percentage of respondents were able to predict the winners in 1964, 1972, 1984, and 1996, years in which one candidate led by a considerable margin from the outset and never seemed to be in any danger of losing the election. Respondents had the most difficult time predicting the winner in 1976, 1980, and 2000, years in which the polls themselves did not provide a clear or consistent expectation about the state of the race. In each of these years, both candidates spent some time as the leader in the polls, and the final Gallup Poll was within the margin of error. It would seem, therefore, that individuals are paying some attention to reports about the opinions of their peers.

Perhaps the most interesting and important way that polls can affect individuals is to influence their decisions about for whom to vote in a presidential election. While we might prefer that voters put a significant amount of time and effort into comparing the candidates' positions on relevant issues and reviewing their qualifications for office before making a decision, relatively few voters actually act that way. Most voters, in fact, use some sort of information shortcut to choose between the two major candidates in a race—most often, for example, party identification, group affiliations (see **Religious Differences in Public Opinion, Gender Differences in Public Opinion**), and positions on a single issue, such as **abortion**. Polls can provide such a shortcut. After all, if a majority of our fellow citizens have decided that one candidate is better than the other, then that candidate must be doing something right. Since most Americans know that they are not themselves paying close attention to the race, they are likely to assume that the people who have chosen to support the leading candidate have probably put more time and effort into the decision than they have. Some researchers have found evidence to suggest that just this type of bandwagon effect does occur. It is most noticeable when the least is known about the candidates, either because it is still early in the campaign, when the public is still just becoming aware of the candidates running for an office, or because the race is for a lower office that receives less media coverage and in which the candidates have less money to spend on political advertising (see also **Campaign Effects**). This provides an additional obstacle to candidates with less name recognition and less money than their rivals. Not only do they need to persuade voters that they are the better choice in the election, but they also need to overcome the perception that few people like or support them. Not all voters react the same way to this information, however. When a candidate enjoys a large lead, some voters react in just the opposite fashion, deciding to support the underdog, either because they sym-

Table 1. Percentage of Respondents Correctly
Predicting the Winner in Presidential Elections,
by Year

Year	Percent Predicting Correct Winner	Actual Margin of Victory (%)
1964	92.1	22.5
1968	69.2	0.7
1972	92.4	23.2
1976	50.7	2.1
1980	44.9	9.7
1984	87.2	18.2
1988	73.5	7.8
1992	64.7	5.6
1996	90.0	8.0
2000	48.0	0.5
Total	70.6	

Source: Taken from the American National Election Studies databases for each of the years listed, conducted by the University of
Michigan Center for Political Studies.

pathize with the trailing candidate, or because of a basic concern that a candidate who is too popular may no longer need to worry about the will of the public.

A second area in which polls can influence voters is in the decision of whether
or not to participate in an election. Polls provide a prediction about the outcome
of elections, often completely removing the suspense of potential voters on Election Day. If it is already clear weeks ahead of time who the winner of an election is going to be, individuals have a much smaller incentive to vote. After all,
voting can be an inconvenience. It may mean taking time off work, driving to
an unfamiliar polling location, and waiting in line for a significant period of time.
While many citizens feel a sense of duty or get satisfaction just from participating in the process, and thus will vote regardless of the circumstances, other citizens are naturally less inclined to go to the polls. Therefore, if the most
important reason to vote—trying to help particular candidates get elected—no
longer seems relevant because the outcome appears to be predetermined, it is
hardly surprising that some people are not willing to put in the time and effort
to show up on election day.

The polls do not affect everyone equally, though. Although anyone can come
across the results of polls, they are not equally likely to accept them as accurate.
People who support the candidate leading in the polls, and thus are pleased by
the results of the poll, as well as those who do not have any strong preference
for either of the candidates, are more likely to believe the polls and allow this
new information to shape their expectations. In other words, if an individual
likes what the polls tell her, then she will most likely assume that they must be
correct. A supporter of the candidate trailing in the polls is much more likely to
doubt their accuracy. If the polls are correct, then the person that he wants to

Table 2. Electoral Prediction of ANES Respondents, by Year and Pre-Interview Candidate Preference

	Respondents Who Prefer the Leader (%)			
	Trailing Candidate in a Landslide	Trailing Candidate in a Close Race	Leading Candidate in a Close Race	Leading Candidate in a Landslide
1964	0.5	1.6	42.6	55.3
1968	0.2	5.2	62.2	32.5
1972	0.1	0.3	27.1	72.5
1976	2.5	15.1	65.9	16.5
1980	2.2	17.9	65.1	14.8
1984	0.4	0.8	34.5	64.3
1988	1.0	4.9	59.6	34.6
1992	1.5	12.1	63.3	23.2
1996	1.1	0.0	98.9	0.0
2000	1.6	14.0	73.4	11.0
Total	1.1	6.7	57.0	35.3

	Respondents Who Prefer the Trailer (%)			
	Trailing Candidate in a Landslide	Trailing Candidate in a Close Race	Leading Candidate in a Close Race	Leading Candidate in a Landslide
1964	5.0	27.3	42.2	25.5
1968	8.2	54.8	26.7	10.3
1972	3.1	21.7	32.8	42.4
1976	13.5	68.3	16.0	2.2
1980	16.5	70.7	12.0	0.7
1984	3.6	26.5	42.1	27.8
1988	8.8	42.4	37.6	11.2
1992	7.3	62.5	25.1	5.1
1996	26.9	0.0	73.1	0.0
2000	11.5	71.0	15.4	2.1
Total	11.0	48.9	29.1	11.0

Source: Taken from the American National Election Studies databases for each of the years listed, conducted by the University of Michigan Center for Political Studies.

win will lose. Since this is both unpleasant and, for most individuals, will be contrary to their original expectations, the natural tendency is to resist the information. Table 2 illustrates this phenomenon. While the predictions that individuals made about the election certainly varied in a logical fashion with the actual results of the polls, the preferences of the respondents clearly makes a difference in how much this information shapes their expectations. In every case, more respondents who prefer the leading candidate predict a landslide victory for that candidate than do the respondents who prefer the trailing candidate. The reverse is true for predictions of a landslide for the trailing candidate. While there are never more than 20.1 percent of those who prefer the leading candidate predicting a victory for the opposition, there are never fewer than 24.8 percent of those who prefer the trailing candidate predicting victory for the underdog, and it is usually a significantly higher percentage. Therefore, when an election outcome seems certain in the days leading up to election day, people who prefer the leader are actually more likely to expect that the race is already decided than are the people who prefer the underdog, and thus are more likely to decide that it is not worth the cost to go vote.

Finally, polls can be used by voters to help them make strategic decisions about which candidate to support in an election. While the earlier discussion focused on which candidate a voter would prefer to win the election, the literature on strategic voting separates the decision about which candidate an individual prefers from the decision about which candidate to vote for. These strategic decisions only occur in multicandidate elections. When there are only two candidates in a race, there is no incentive to attempt to vote strategically. However, when there are more than two candidates running for the same office, a voter may decide to vote based on expectations about the most likely outcome, rather than based on policy or partisan preferences. In essence, supporters of a candidate who is in third place or below in a presidential election often have to consider whether it is better to express support for the candidate they like the most, or instead to vote for the major party candidate whom they dislike the least, in an attempt to try and prevent their least preferred candidate from winning. In the 2000 presidential election, for example, supporters of Ralph Nader, the Green Party candidate, faced such a decision. In a tight election in which their most preferred candidate had no realistic chance to become president, it seems that many potential Nader voters became nervous as Election Day neared about the possible effects of voting for him, rather than for Al Gore. By supporting Nader instead of Gore, they could in effect help George W. Bush, who it seems safe to assume, few Green Party supporters would favor over Gore, win the election. In fact, Nader's support, which was consistently around five percent three to four weeks before the election, began to evaporate at the end of October, as polls indicated that Bush enjoyed a very narrow lead in the race. This type of voting has been found to occur in many different contexts. Research indicates that voters who support minor party candidates become increasingly likely to vote strategically as the gap between the two major party candidates narrows, and as support for their own candidate dwindles. Obviously, if one candidate has an insurmountable lead in the election, there is no point in abandoning the candidate you prefer the most. Similarly, if a third party candidate has enough support to be competitive, it also would make no sense for his supporters to vote for anyone else. In these cases, of course, it is the availability of information about the state of the race through public opinion polls that allow voters to make these strategic decisions.

The effects of polls on voting behavior have generally prompted concern by scholars of American elections. The fact that some individuals may be influenced to support a particular candidate for office because of his or her popularity may be understandable, but it is hardly encouraging. The fact that the constant reporting of poll results may rob some citizens of the incentive to show up at the voting booth is also clearly something to worry about, especially because elections that are too close to call in the weeks leading up to election day are the exception, rather than the rule. Anything that tends to drive down political participation is certainly worth noting. The tendency of polling information to lead to strategic voting, however, tends to be of much less concern. Strategic voting illustrates that at least some voters are acting in a very politically sophisticated fashion, weighing not just their own preferences, but the possible impact of their actions on public policy. Regardless of any concerns, however, these effects are unlikely to disappear, and in fact may even intensify in the future. Media coverage of polls has only been increasing in recent years, and with the greater emphasis on polls in the coverage of elections, some citizens are likely to continue to rely on them when making important decisions about whether or not to vote, and for whom to vote.

Further Reading

Cain, Bruce E. "Strategic Voting in Britain." *American Journal of Political Science* 22 (Fall 1978): 639–55. An analysis of strategic voting in Great Britain, where there are more frequent and meaningful opportunities to support more than two parties, and thus more incentive to act strategically.

Gimpel, James G., and Diane Hollern Harvey. "Forecasts and Preferences in the 1992 General Election." *Political Behavior* 19 (Summer 1997): 157–75. An example of the research being done on how polls affect voters' preferences in an election.

Mutz, Diana C. *Impersonal Influence: How Perceptions of Mass Collectives Affect Political Attitudes.* New York: Cambridge University Press, 1998. A thorough investigation of how individuals react to information about the opinions of the public.

Joseph D. Giammo

Post-Materialism

Post-materialism refers to a set of value orientations that emphasize non-economic quality of life human needs, such as personal self-fulfillment, concern for the protection of others, aesthetics, social equality, and human freedom. In contrast, materialist values focus on physical safety, physiological needs, and economic security. Post-materialists are more likely than materialists to favor social change, and consequently, are also thought more likely to participate in both conventional social movements and other more disruptive forms of political protest. Environmental protection in advanced industrial societies is perhaps the archetypical example of a post-materialist issue. People with post-materialist values are more likely to be concerned about environmental issues, be willing to make financial sacrifices to help protect the environment, and be members of environmental groups than people with materialist values; most significantly, they are more likely to see the protection of the environment as more important than fostering economic growth (*see* **environment, animal rights**).

Following World War II, people in many industrial countries, including the United States, entered a period of affluence and began to experience a gradual shift away from materialist values and toward post-materialist values. By the 1960s, many argue, there had begun a significant value change in many Western countries. This trend continued into the 1990s. For example, if we take the percentage of individuals categorized (using survey data on their political and social attitudes) by political scientists Ronald Inglehart and Paul Abramson as post-materialists minus the percentage they see as materialists we find that the United States has a score of −24 in 1980 that increased to +6 by 1990. This suggests not only a massive 30 percent net increase in post-materialists, but also, of course, that post-materialists had become a comfortable majority of adult citizens. Other countries experienced similar changes. Italy underwent the most significant net increase in post-materialists, from an index score of −39 in the early 1980s survey to a score of 7 in 1990. North Ireland, Spain, the Netherlands, West Germany, Canada, Sweden, France, and Belgium also experienced significant net increases in the percentage difference index, ranging from net shifts of 38 to 18. Only two countries surveyed, South Africa and Iceland, underwent net decreases in the percentages of post-materialists.

Naturally, scholars have looked to the reasons for these shifts in value orientations. Led by Inglehart, the leading figure in this area of study, students of public opinion have produced an extensive body of literature examining why this shift in value orientations occurred. Studies have focused on two main explanations: economic conditions and **education**.

According to several scholars, the concurrent timing of post-war affluence and post-materialism is not a coincidence. They suggest that the new emphasis on post-materialism can be explained by the economic security enjoyed by many people following World War II. Inglehart and others have suggested that Abraham Maslow's famous "hierarchy of needs" can help explain the connection between the economic condition and the contemporary shift to post-materialism. Maslow asserts that post-materialist values take a backseat to physiological needs related to human survival, but that after individuals meet their basic material physical and economic needs, they can turn their attention to other, less-need or survival oriented values. These we label "post-materialist." Inglehart built on Maslow's theory by developing a scarcity hypothesis, which suggests that people value those things that are scarce to them and place less emphasis on those things that are not. Essentially, the argument is that if people cannot afford to buy groceries, obtain adequate medical care, or pay their mortgage bills, they do not have the luxury of being concerned about the environment, social justice, or similar post-materialist issues. In short, there is a positive relationship between people's economic prosperity and their support for post-materialist values; post-materialist value orientations can be explained by secure and prosperous economic conditions.

Much of the recent academic literature on the connection between economic conditions and post-materialism has focused on the question of whether the value change is one of immediate adjustment to improved economic conditions or whether people's values reflect the economic conditions of their formative pre-adult years. The **socialization** hypothesis suggests that because individuals' value systems are formed early in life, people who are socialized during times of economic prosperity and security will possess long-term post-materialist values rather than materialist values. In other words, the economic conditions of different generations' childhood and early adolescent periods will produce different cohort attitudes regarding post-materialist issues. These values orientations should remain largely intact as a person experiences various life events. Thus, it is not so much one's personal level of economic affluence, which predicts how post-materialist they tend to be, but rather the social level of affluence in their formative years. The socialization hypothesis helps explain why some people who experienced poverty in their pre-adult years but prosperity during their adult years continue to live well below their income level; such people were socialized during times of economic instability and those values stayed with them throughout their lives.

According to the socialization hypothesis, a public's shift from materialist to post-materialist values happens gradually as younger generations of people who were socialized during periods of economic security reach adulthood and replace older generations of people whose formative years took place during periods of economic instability, causing a lag between economic change and signs of post-materialism. Changes in a nation's economic condition should produce corresponding intergenerational value changes across age groups. Post-materialist value change should be expected in countries that have experienced significant economic growth such that older generations of people were significantly less economically secure than younger generations of people. In countries that have not experienced sufficient economic growth, intergenerational value changes should not be expected.

On a global scale, there should be cross-national differences in post-materialism value changes depending on individual nations' changing economic conditions. Following this argument, the gradual value change to post-materialism that occurred in Western nations is the result of younger generations of people who were brought up during years of economic prosperity in those countries following World War II replacing older generations of people in society and political offices who grew up in times of economic insecurity, such as the Great Depression in the United States. Several empirical studies have found evidence supporting the socialization hypothesis.

Whereas the socialization hypothesis suggests that there should be a relationship between the economic conditions of individuals' youth and their value orientations, some scholars reject this notion. They are instead that there is a connection between people's current economic conditions and their post-materialist or materialist values. These scholars find little to no evidence that economic conditions during people's formative, pre-adult years have lasting and long-term effects on their values. Instead, they find that post-materialism is influenced by contemporary economic conditions, such as the current level of inflation or unemployment. In contrast to the socialization hypothesis, they argue that economic security at different points in people's lives affect their post-materialism values, not economic security at one fixed point in their pre-adult years.

The former communist regimes of Eastern Europe and the Soviet Union are interesting cases. These countries tend to show surprisingly high levels of post-materialism, which might be thought to be a significant challenges to the socialization hypothesis. Yet, because these communist regimes provided job security, basic food, medical care, and education to their citizens, these examples may actually support the socialization hypothesis: despite their recent history of economic instability and hardship, citizens are much more post-materialist than one might expect because they were raised under regimes which (whatever their other failings) provided exactly the kind of economic security that fosters post-materialist orientations. Further, the scarcity and socialization hypotheses themselves suggest that people will experience short-term fluctuations in post-materialism due to changing economic conditions, although long-term values formed during the pre-adult formative years will eventually prevail. For example, a recession will likely result in a short-term shift away from post-materialism as economic insecurity increases. Yet, when economic recovery occurs, the long-term trend toward post-materialist value changes will resume. Overall, post-materialist value change results from long-term generational replacement over the course of several decades, not short-term economic fluctuations. Enduring and long-term generational changes in value orientations cast doubt on the hypothesis that post-materialism is solely an immediate reaction to economic changes and is not related to the economic condition of people's pre-adult years.

Some scholars suggest that education, not pre-adult economic socialization, is the most significant factor in post-materialism value orientations. Past studies have found that people who support democratic, post-materialist values tend to be highly educated. For example, research on environmentalism has found that education is positively related to environmental concern, and past research on the animal protection movement, another post-materialist issue, has found that people who support animal protection measures are more likely to have college degrees than the general public. The explanation for why education is linked with post-materialism is straightforward. Education, it is suggested, introduces and reinforces traditional liberal values. As people are educated about concepts such as individual liberties and equality, they become enlightened about those issues, appreciate their value, and adopt post-materialist beliefs regarding them. Research certainly shows that there is a positive relationship between education and support for post-materialist values. But saying that because there is a positive relationship between education and post-materialism is obviously not to prove that it is education, not pre-adult economic socialization, that is the more important influence on post-materialism. In addition to measuring people's exposure to post-materialist issues, education can also be an indicator of people's economic security during their formative years. People who are highly educated tend to come from educated families, who in turn tend to be more economically secure families. Thus, people's educational levels not only reflect their exposure to and acceptance of liberal (in this context, post-materialist) values but can also reflect the economic security of their youth.

Today post-materialist values are a major component of global attitudes and lifestyles. It seems certain that a gradual shift to post-materialism in recent years has transformed what many people seek in their daily lives. Instead of being concerned about day-to-day survival, they focus their attention on quality of life issues. It is likely that both industrialized and developing countries will continue to experience growth in post-materialism as global economic development continues and as generation after generation of people continue to grow up during relatively more prosperous times than predecessors.

In the future, research should focus on several related issues. One is the connection between the conventional class-oriented interpretation of politics (predicated upon political conflict generated on class differences) and the implications of post-materialism (implying a partial displacement of that dimension of conflict). More generally, we need to know more about the public policy implications of moving toward a greater post-materialist public. It is interesting as well to ponder, in the age of globalization and the increasing opposition to it in developing countries, whether and in what ways we will see a genuinely global shift to post-materialism. In the West, at least, the antiglobalization movement is itself a product of post-materialism. We thus face the fascinating dynamic of possible opposition to economic liberalization and globalization brought by capitalism itself. On a more purely theoretical level, future research should also examine what factors other than economic socialization affect post-materialism. Although Inglehart's position is that economic affluence during individuals' formative years is an important influence on post-materialism, it does not suggest that it is the only factor. More systematic study of other factors is needed. Similarly, post-materialism is obviously not the only factor influencing contemporary social movements such as the environmental movement. More research on the relative importance of post-materialism compared with other influences on social movements is needed. Finally, researchers should undertake more tests on the micro, individual level. Recent research on the individual level has found that although the post-materialism value change theory performs well with attitudes concerning some participatory norms, it does not perform well with other attitudes, including views regarding **civil rights** and civil liberties, environmentalism, and **political knowledge**.

Further Reading

Abramson, Paul R., and Ronald Inglehart. "Education, Security, and Postmaterialism: A Comment on Duch and Taylor's 'Postmaterialism and the Economic Condition.'" *American Journal of Political Science* 38 (1994): 797–814. In this article, Abramson and Inglehart react to Duch and Taylor's 1993 rejection of the socialization hypothesis and reassert that economic conditions during people's formative, pre-adult years influence their attitudes regarding post-materialism.

Davis, Darren W. "Individual Level Examination of Postmaterialism in the U.S.: Political Tolerance, Racial Attitudes, Environmentalism, and Participatory Norms." *Political Research Quarterly* 53 (2000): 455–75. In this article, Davis tests Inglehart's theory of post-materialist value change by examining individual, micro-level behavior and challenges many of Inglehart's macro-level findings.

Duch, Raymond M., and Michaell A. Taylor. "Postmaterialism and the Economic Condition." *American Journal of Political Science* 37 (1993): 747–79. These authors challenge Inglehart's socialization hypothesis and find that contemporary economic conditions and education are better explanations of post-materialist value orientations.

Inglehart, Ronald. "Post-Materialism in an Environment of Insecurity." *American Political Science Review* 75 (1981): 880–900. Inglehart tests his socialization hypothesis that economic prosperity in Western countries following World War II led to generational changes in post-materialism.

———. "Public Support for Environmental Protection: Objective Problems and Subjective Values in 43 Societies." *PS: Political Science and Politics* 43 (1995): 57–72. In this article, Inglehart examines whether post-materialism can help account for increased environmentalism.

Inglehart, Ronald, and Paul R. Abramson. "Economic Security and Value Change." *American Political Science Review* 88 (1994): 336–54. Using a time series analysis, Inglehart and Abramson demonstrate that there is a long-term trend toward post-materialism and that intergenerational post-materialist differences tended to be found in countries that experienced significant changes in economic growth.

Maslow, Abraham. *Motivation and Personality*. New York: Harper & Row, 1954. A classic work developing the theory of the hierarchy of needs and its implications for human psychology.

Mahalley D. Allen

Prenotification Letters

Prenotification letters are letters sent by a polling organization to potential survey respondents prior to attempting to contact them. A prenotification letter alerts potential respondents that they may be contacted to participate in a survey and may provide additional information about the survey, such as the sponsoring organization, the topic of the survey, or the reason for conducting the survey. Polling organizations send prenotification letters to improve the **response rate** for a survey. Nonresponse is a major problem for survey research because it can bias even the most carefully selected sample (in an unknown direction and magnitude) and lowers confidence in inferences made from the data. By improving the response rate prenotification letters help address this problem, although they cannot entirely eliminate it. Prenotification letters are most commonly sent before face-to-face interview surveys, less frequently before **mail surveys,** and only occasionally before telephone surveys (*see* **Computer Assisted Telephone Interviewing**).

A useful metaphor for prenotification letters is the introduction at the beginning of a conversation between strangers. Like a proper introduction in a conversation, a prenotification letter establishes identity, sets the topic and purpose, and defines the rules for the interaction between the survey researcher and the respondent.

Researchers expect that prenotification letters increase response rates for a number of theoretical reasons. First, they communicate the legitimacy of the survey and the authority of the survey organization. Second, a potential respondent may be more likely to agree to be surveyed if he or she has a positive association with the organization sending the letter, or feels the organization is acting in some way that is beneficial to him or her. Third, providing advance warning for the visit, telephone call, or mailed questionnaire establishes a norm of politeness and can draw out reciprocal politeness from potential respondents in the form of cooperation in completing the survey. Fourth, prenotification letters can identify the purpose of the survey (e.g., gathering data to inform public policy decisions), which may encourage potential respondents to think of the survey as civic participation. Fifth, prenotification letters can enhance the social validity of the survey by noting that others are cooperating in completing the survey. Sixth, if potential respondents are interested in the topic of the survey, informing them of the topic in the prenotification letter may increase response rates.

The current practice of using prenotification letters is somewhat different for the three main types of surveys: face-to-face, mail, and telephone. The use of prenotification letters is most common in face-to-face interviews because the prior notice that a stranger will be knocking on the potential respondent's door to conduct an interview has proven to significantly increase the response rate. First, potential respondents are more likely to open their doors and talk to the interviewer, so the contact rate is higher. This is particularly true for seniors and others with heightened concerns about personal security. Second, the advance notification makes potential respondents less likely to refuse to complete the interview, so the cooperation rate among those who are contacted is higher than if no letter is sent. The prenotification letter alerts potential respondents that the person knocking on their door is nonthreatening, not trying to sell products, and not evangelizing for a cause, but is instead a representative of an identified, known, and polite organization.

Many mail surveys also send a prenotification letter before mailing the actual questionnaire to potential respondents. A number of meta-analyses of mail surveys have concluded that such prenotification letters consistently increase response rates. However unlike for face-to-face surveys, prenotification letters may not be a highly efficient way to address the problem of nonresponse bias. Some researchers have found that follow-up contacts, especially reminder letters with replacement questionnaires, provide a greater increase in the response rate at a lower overall cost. Therefore if funds are limited, a survey researcher is likely to get better results if these funds are used to ensure adequate follow-up contacts, rather than spending them on prenotification letters. When survey researchers need the maximum possible response rate for a mail survey, they often use prenotification letters as well as follow-up contacts.

Prenotification letters are used only rarely in telephone surveys because so many current telephone surveys use **random digit dialing** (RDD) to generate the sample. RDD samples do not allow researchers to know the addresses of their potential (or actual) respondents. Research on prenotification letters in telephone surveys has been conducted using either samples drawn from lists that include addresses and phone numbers (especially voter registration records) or by matching RDD-generated phone numbers to phone company records to capture addresses of potential respondents. This research has focused on whether the letter will increase the cooperation rate. The findings in these studies have been mixed: some experiments find no statistically significant effect while others find a positive effect on cooperation rates (usually in the range of 3 to 5 percentage points). Although it is unlikely that a prenotification letter would cause potential respondents to sit around waiting for the phone to ring, the increasing use of Caller ID has made contacting respondents more than simply a matter of catching them at home. Recent research suggests that prenotification letters increase the contact rate as well as the cooperation rate for telephone surveys (*see* **Outcome Rates**).

For face-to-face, mail, and telephone surveys, prenotification letters differ from the **financial incentives** that are sometimes used by polling organizations to improve response rates because nothing of material value is provided to the potential respondents. Past studies have shown that prepaid financial incentives have a desirable effect on response rates and data quality for face-to-face, phone, and mail surveys. Prenotification letters have been shown to have similar effects at a lower cost, but the circumstances in which prenotification letters that offer no financial incentives will be effective are much narrower. To increase cooperation with the survey, prenotification letters rely on tapping into the internal motivations of a potential respondent, not an external financial incentive. (These internal motivations rely upon the theoretical principles underlying the use of prenotification letters described above: they include the respondent's interest in the topic of the survey, his or her sense of the value of the purpose of the survey, his or her respect for the survey sponsor, and the norm of civic participation.) In the absence of internal motivations, prenotification letters will not be effective at increasing response rates.

Prenotification letters are used with the expectation that higher response rates will lead to a survey sample that is more representative of the target population. However, studies of efforts to improve response rates (including the use of prenotification letters) have not shown significant improvements in the representativeness of the sample that cooperates in completing a survey. Since prenotification letters depend on internal factors that vary between demographic groups, the effects of prenotification letters can vary significantly between demographic groups. For example, analyses of prenotification letters in pre-election polls suggest that most age groups are more likely to cooperate after receiving a prenotification letter, but registered voters between the ages of eighteen and twenty-four are more likely to avoid completing a survey after being sent a prenotification letter. As a result of differences between demographic groups, the use of prenotification letters may introduce new biases to the survey results that can exacerbate, neutralize, or reverse the bias from nonresponse.

As might be expected, the effect of prenotification letters on response rates declines as the baseline response rate without a prenotification letter increases because prenotification letters are unlikely to have much of an impact on the response rate of a survey that many people are likely to respond to without prenotification. This pattern suggests that researchers should consider the expected response rate when deciding if prenotification letters will be cost-effective. For example, the evidence from nonresponse in mail surveys suggests that prenotification letters for mail surveys increase response rates when the baseline response rate is below 50 percent but appear to have no effect when the baseline response rate is above 50 percent.

Thus the effect of prenotification letters is likely to be greatest among demographic groups with low baseline response rates: that is, the groups that may otherwise tend to be underrepresented in a survey. With sufficient prior demographic information available about potential respondents, prenotification letters can be used selectively to target demographic groups with lower expected response rates. Although the effectiveness of this technique depends on how effective prenotification letters are with the various targeted groups, selective targeting may be useful to survey researchers to achieve the desired demographic distribution of their sample. For example, if people in highly educated or affluent areas respond at higher rates than those who live in areas with low educational attainment or low median income, then letters could be sent only to less-educated or less-affluent areas to even out the response rates and to achieve the distribution of respondents that the researcher desires.

One of the primary pieces of information conveyed by a prenotification letter is the topic of the survey. The topic of the survey is also often communicated in the introduction to the survey provided by the interviewer (in face-to-face or telephone surveys) or the cover letter to a mail survey. However, providing the topic in a prenotification letter may increase the contact rate by interesting potential respondents in picking up the phone, opening the door to apparent strangers, or opening the subsequently mailed questionnaire.

Furthermore, the more interest potential respondents have in the topic of the survey the more likely they are to cooperate in completing the survey. A prenotification letter that announces the topic can alert potential respondents who are interested in the topic, making them more likely to complete the survey; of course the letter will have less effect on those not interested in the topic. If the survey is seeking to be representative of both people who are interested in the topic and people who are not interested in the topic, then this divergence will exacerbate an existing bias. However, if the survey is seeking to be representative of only those who are likely to take some action related to the topic, this pattern can be quite helpful. For example, election surveys that seek to forecast the vote outcome are looking for the opinions of likely voters. If the letter states that the upcoming survey concerns politics or the election, potential respondents who are interested in politics will be more likely to cooperate. Since potential respondents who are interested in politics are also more likely to vote, the effect of the letter can be quite helpful in gathering a sample of likely voters.

Another piece of information that prenotification letters can communicate to potential respondents is the sponsor of the survey. The sponsoring organization usually sends the letter, so its name is among the first pieces of information the reader sees on the envelope or letterhead. The prenotification letter also provides an opportunity for sponsors to explain who they are, what their mission is, and why they are conducting the survey. This explanation can be especially important to organizations that are not immediately recognizable to potential respondents.

The attitude of potential respondents toward the sponsoring organization plays a significant part in determining cooperation. Well-known public institutions, such as universities and government agencies, usually achieve a far higher response rate than commercial researchers on otherwise equivalent surveys. An extreme example of this phenomenon was a study in 1969, which found that among potential respondents sent a prenotification letter on a university letterhead the cooperation rate increased by 30 percentage points, while an identical prenotification letter from a commercial firm for the same survey decreased the cooperation rate by 6 percentage points. Nonetheless, even for well-known public institutions response rates will vary by demographic group depending on whether the respondent perceives that the sponsor is doing something beneficial for them.

Using prenotification letters to identify the sponsor to potential respondents carries an important risk: desire to please, fear of reprisal, or other motivations can cause respondents to alter their answers from their true response. Thus the letters may skew the distribution of responses to survey questions. This problem can affect even ostensibly neutral sponsors if potential respondents perceive the "neutral" sponsor as having an agenda. For example, potential respondents may see surveys that are sponsored by government agencies as actually intended for the political party that controls the government. Unfortunately, unscrupulous survey researchers can use the likely effect of revealing the sponsor to push the results in a desired direction without resorting to more obvious techniques.

The design of the letter also makes a difference in the effectiveness of prenotification letters. Prenotification letters that do not exceed one page in length usually increase response rates, but longer letters for the same survey have been found to have no effect on response rates. The decline in effect for the longer letters may be due to a decline in the number of people who read the letter. For surveys that require more than one page of introductory material, the best practice appears to be a concise one-page letter followed by supplementary pages that provide more detailed information in the form of Frequently Asked Questions or descriptive brochures. In crafting the text of the letter, past research suggests that informal letters are more effective than formal or complex letters. Sentences should be short and use simple, direct wording. The tone of the letter should be personal, not formal, bureaucratic, or businesslike.

The personalization of prenotification letters may also increase their effectiveness. Most surveys (especially face-to-face and telephone surveys) randomize at the household level. As a result, prenotification letters are often sent to the household with no assurance that the person who completes the survey is the same one who read the prenotification letter; if these people are different, the effect of the letter is lost. This problem can be corrected when prenotification letters are sent using samples drawn from a list including name, address, and, for telephone surveys, phone number. A wide array of databases is available from which samples can be drawn: voter registration lists are useful for election surveys; subscription lists or organization membership lists are often useful when specific populations are of interest. In addition to increasing the chance that the selected potential respondent actually handles the letter, the personalization of the letter conveys a degree of seriousness and intentionality, which may enhance the effect of a prenotification letter. The evidence from past studies that have asked for respondents by name shows no effect on response rates or data quality compared with traditional anonymous random selection of respondents.

The timing of the letter is another key to ensuring that prenotification letters have maximum effect with potential respondents. The closer the letter arrives to the date the potential respondent is contacted (face-to-face or via telephone) to complete the survey, the more effective the letter will be at increasing cooperation.

Of course, much of the effectiveness of prenotification letters depends upon the addressee (whether individual or household) actually reading, responding positively to, and remembering the letter. The prenotification letter is unsolicited mail, so it may never be opened. Even if it is opened, it may not be read in full. Even if it is read in full, the letter may reduce the response rate if a potential respondent finds the topic especially uninteresting or the sponsor undesirable. Moreover, although the letter may communicate the topic, the sponsor, and other information in a timely fashion, even those respondents who have actually read the letter may not recall this information when they are contacted. Therefore, some of this information may be appropriate to repeat in the introduction to the survey to increase the cooperation rate.

Despite these uncertainties, prenotification letters have proven their value in increasing the response rates for face-to-face and mail surveys and show promise in counteracting the general trend of declining response to telephone surveys. The variation across demographic groups in the effects of sending advance notice means that there is a need to study the effects of prenotification letters across a wide variety of settings, topics, and sponsors to improve our understanding of when and how they maximize survey response rates.

Further Reading

Fox, Richard J., Melvin R. Crask, and Jonghoon Kim. "Mail Survey Response Rate: A Meta-Analysis of Selected Techniques for Inducing Response." *Public Opinion Quarterly* 52, no. 4 (1988): 467–91. A thorough review of techniques for reducing nonresponse in mail surveys, including a discussion and empirical analysis of past research on the effects of prenotification letters.

Goldstein, Kenneth M., and M. Kent Jennings. "The Effect of Advance Letters on Cooperation in a List Sample Telephone Survey." *Public Opinion Quarterly* 66, no. 4 (2002): 608–17. A review of the research on prenotification letters for telephone surveys, and results from a recent experiment for pre-election surveys.

Lynn, Peter, Rachel Turner, and Patten Smith. "Assessing the Effects of an Advance Letter for a Personal Interview Survey." *Journal of the Market Research Society* 40, no. 3 (1998): 265–72. Discusses the considerations important in designing a prenotification letter and provides the results of an experiment on letter design.

Mann, Christopher B. *Getting Pre-Election Surveys Right: The Effects of Advance Letters on Pre-election Forecasting.* Forthcoming. Results from a series of recent experiments on prenotification letters in pre-election surveys, including discussion of the representativeness of the sample, accuracy of results, and ways to use empirically known biases from prenotification letters to a researcher's advantage.

Web Sites

"Advance Letters: An ABS Approach" (2002)—a discussion of the Australian Bureau of Statistics' use and development of advance letters—is available at http://www.sch.abs. gov.au/SCH/A1610103.NSF/0/9778176ba336237fca256cc300106b85/$FILE/ ASC%2016%20-%20Advance%20Letters_24-7-2002.pdf.

Christopher B. Mann

Presidential Approval

Presidential approval refers to the degree to which the American public as a whole approves of the way the president is performing his responsibilities as the nation's leader. Essentially, presidential approval is the percentage of citizens who respond positively to a particular survey question asking whether they approve or disapprove of the president's performance.

The staple question in research on presidential approval is based on responses to the Gallup Poll question: "Do you approve or disapprove of the way _____ is handling his job as president?" Gallup has posed this question in national surveys conducted since 1937. Between 1937 and 1952, the number of months in which Gallup asked the question varied widely, with the average being 6.6 months per year. However, starting in 1953, the question became a regular feature of Gallup's monthly surveys. Subsequently, approval questions have appeared in other opinion polls, such as those conducted by CBS News/*New York Times*, ABC/*Washington Post*, and NBC News/*Wall Street Journal*. A presidential approval question has also been asked in the American **National Election Studies** since 1980.

Interest in the dynamics of presidential approval is understandable. An American president is the preeminent political figure in the country, and incumbent presidents are subjects of intense scrutiny by press and public alike. Presidents are virtually always in the news, and public reactions to them matter enormously. High approval ratings are crucial to presidents and their parties for the obvious reason that public support is key to retaining control of the Oval Office. A popular president can help to attract support for his party's candidates for Congress and other important electoral offices. In addition, presidents with strong approval ratings have political currency that they can spend to influence the outcomes of their domestic legislation and foreign policy initiatives.

The foundational study of presidential approval is Mueller's 1970 article in the *American Political Science Review*. Subsequent research has produced a large body of research characterized by disagreements over measurement, model specification, and statistical techniques. Regarding measurement, most researchers have relied on the Gallup question cited above. Although many analysts are content with this measure, others argue that it has two flaws. One is ambiguity: that is, words such as "(dis)approve" or even "the president" may have different meanings for different people. Another is dimensionality: that is, a single-indicator approach may capture only a limited view of how people evaluate presidents.

From Mueller onward, scholars have demonstrated an abiding interest in determining how economic conditions affect presidential approval. Accordingly, many studies have utilized a political economy theoretical framework to guide their analyses. The fundamental assumption is that people believe that government generally, and the president in particular, influences their individual and collective economic well-being. As a result, people assess national and personal economic conditions, and these assessments inform evaluations of how well the president is performing. The political economy framework subsumes numerous specific models of presidential approval, the best known of which is the "reward-punishment" model. This model is straightforward—people praise or blame incumbent presidents for the state of the economy and/or their personal economic situations. A president receives high approval ratings when the economy is booming, inflation and unemployment are low, and people have money in their pocketbooks. Conversely, if prices are increasing, jobs are hard to find, and wallets are empty, a president's approval numbers are in jeopardy.

Reward-punish models have the virtue of great simplicity. However, they ignore the possibility of disagreements among parties over economic (and other) policy priorities. According to an issue priority model, parties develop distinctive policy agendas that they use to structure public debate, and they establish track records for dealing more or less effectively with various issues than their rivals do. Over time, parties claim "ownership" of particular issues, and they build policy reputations that are widely recognized by voters. Counterintuitively, the model implies that an incumbent president may not suffer a decline in approval when certain issues become salient because the public will judge that the president and the president's party are best suited (more competent, more responsive) to deal with those issues. For example, an issue priority model suggests that people concerned about rising unemployment will not punish a Democratic president—although they will punish a Republican one—whereas those who accord priority to inflation will not punish a Republican incumbent when prices are increasing—although they will punish a Democratic one.

Given the strong political economy emphasis in theorizing about the determinants of presidential approval, "usual suspect" predictor variables have been measures of the state of the national economy, and measures of the public's subjective assessments of national and personal economic condition (see **Economy**). Early studies focused exclusively on objective economic conditions, most notably inflation and unemployment rates. Subsequently, subjective economic evaluations have received a great deal of attention, with responses to survey questions being used to tap evaluations of personal (egocentric) and national (sociotropic) economic conditions over past (retrospective) and future (prospective) time horizons. Egocentric evaluations fit well with neoclassical microeconomic theory concerning how self-interested, utility-maximizing individuals behave. Sociotropic evaluations fit less easily with this theory, because of the possibility that people making sociotropic-based economic judgments are concerned about a stream of benefits that flow to society rather than to themselves.

The retrospective-prospective distinction in large part pivots on assumptions about what kinds of information are credible. Since judgments about past performance make use of "concrete facts," many analysts have argued that it makes sense for the public to rely on retrospective evaluations. However, the problem is that rational individuals have no interest in rewarding or punishing a president for what has already happened. Rather, they wish to maximize their utilities and, thus, rely on expectations about future economic conditions when deciding whether a president merits approval now. In the empirical literature on presidential approval, numerous analysts have argued that assessments of the performance of the national economy in the recent past are what matter. Others stoutly maintain that people are forward-looking "bankers" whose economic expectations inform their presidential (dis)approval judgments.

Although there has been a strong emphasis on mapping economic effects, most researchers have not treated "politics" as irrelevant. Rather, beginning with Mueller, analysts have acknowledged the importance of political variables, including "rally 'round the flag" events, such as international crises and wars; transitions from one presidential administration to another; "honeymoon" periods following the election of a new president; off-year congressional elections; and scandals, such as Watergate, Iran Contra, or the Lewinsky affair. Another variable used in several studies is a cumulative count of wartime casualties—a proxy measure for growing public opposition to that protracted conflict. Again following Mueller, some studies have used "time counters" to measure hypothesized trends in approval, typically downward movements said to be caused by growing coalitions of aggrieved or disappointed groups.

A major area of controversy in the presidential approval literature concerns methodological issues. Many models of presidential approval have been specified as simple linear additive functions:

$$Y_t = B_0 + \Sigma B_{1-k} X_{1-k,t-i} + \varepsilon_t \qquad (1)$$

where: Y_t = presidential approval at time t; $X_{1-k,t-i}$ = predictor variables operating either contemporaneously (time t), or with a lag (t − i, with i > 0); ε_t a stochastic error term, $\sim N(0,\sigma^2)$. Model parameters are estimated using ordinary least squares (OLS) regression. Beginning with Mueller's early studies, many presidential approval researchers have failed to address the threats to inference posed by regression analyses of time series models such as (1). The key difficulty is the "spurious regressions" problem that arises when X and Y are nonstationary, that is, they lack constant means and (co)variances. Time series variables often manifest nonstationarity, and, as econometricians have demonstrated, regression analyses of such variables often yield misleading results.

Presidential approval scholars concerned about this threat to inference have reacted in various ways. Often they have interpreted the problem as just another regression analysis "nuisance"—a technical violation of the familiar OLS "no autocorrelation" assumption. Analysts reacting this way typically use a Durbin-Watson test to determine if the residuals from their regression suffer from (first-order) autocorrelation. If autocorrelation in the residuals is detected, analysts infer autocorrelation in the *errors*, that is, $\varepsilon_t = \rho\varepsilon_{t-1} + v_t$, where ρ is the correlation between errors at time t and time t–1 and v_t is assumed $\sim N(0,\sigma^2)$. The traditional "cure" has been to perform a Cochrane-Orcutt transformation, thereby producing the following:

$$(1 - \rho L)Y_t = (1 - \rho L)B_0 + B_1(1 - \rho L) X_t + v_t \tag{2}$$

where L is the lag operator, that is, $(1 - \rho L)Y_t = Y_t - \rho Y_{t-1}$. Since, by assumption, v_t is a Gaussian error term, (2) can be estimated by OLS if ρ is known. However, since ρ is unknown, it must be estimated. Various methods exist for doing this and, because ρ can be estimated, the resulting statistical procedures are called "feasible generalized least squares" (FGLS).

Equation (2) is a variant of an autoregressive distributed lag (ADL) model: that is, (2) may be rearranged with ρY_{t-1} on the right-hand side. This means that the analyst's presidential approval model is no longer a static regression where X (e.g., unemployment) at time t affects Y (approval) at time t. Rather, in (2), the effects of *all* of the predictor variables (e.g., economic conditions, rally events, honeymoons, scandals) on presidential approval are *distributed over time* and *decay at exactly the same rate ρ*. The long-run effect of any predictor (X_k) is $B_k/(1 - \rho)$. These are very strong theoretical assumptions, and they remain implicit because dynamic features of such a presidential approval model are "hidden" in the error process. In addition, a model like (2) has a common factor restriction: that is, $(1 - \rho L)$ is applied to all variables, including the error process. Researchers do not provide a theoretical justification for the restriction, and they fail to determine if it is empirically warranted. Most importantly, approval analyses of FGLS models like (2) continue to be premised on the assumption that the data are stationary.

Starting in the early 1980s, a number of presidential approval researchers began implicitly to relax the common factor restriction by specifying dynamic effects for predictor variables directly. They do this by including a lagged endogenous variable, i.e., approval at time t–1, on the right-hand side of a model, that is,

$$Y_t = B_0 + B_1 Y_{t-1} + B_2 X_{t-i} + \varepsilon_t \tag{3}$$

Perhaps the most influential example of this type of specification is the "Bankers and Peasants" model proposed by MacKuen, Erikson, and Stimson. Like model

(2), (3) is an autoregressive distributed lag (ADL) specification, and the effects of all predictor variables are (at least implicitly) assumed to have the same dynamics, evolving at a rate determined by the value of B_1, the coefficient for the lagged endogenous variable. And, like (2), (3) does not address the possibility that inferences will be confounded because variables are nonstationary.

Although approval models such as (3) continue to enjoy widespread popularity, approval researchers concerned about the "spurious regressions" threat have specified their models in other ways. When nonstationarity is suspected, the simplest approach has been to assume that it is produced by a stochastic trend process. The most familiar such process is the random walk: that is, $Y_t = Y_{t-1} + \varepsilon_t$ where Y at time t equals the full value of Y at time t–1 plus ε_t, a stationary Gaussian error process. If the data-generating processes for the dependent and independent variables are random walks, then (first) differencing them will yield the following:

$$(1 - L)Y_t = B_0 ++ B_1 (1 - L)X_t + \varepsilon_t \tag{4}$$

In (4), the first-differenced Y (approval) is regressed on the first-differenced X (e.g., unemployment), both of which have been rendered stationary by differencing.

A more sophisticated version of this method of dealing with nonstationarity is based on the autoregressive integrated moving average (ARIMA) forecasting models. These models have been used in a number of presidential approval analyses. In addition to differencing nonstationary variables, ARIMA analysts may specify autoregressive ($\Phi(L)$) and moving average $\theta(L)$ components to ensure that model residuals are "white noise." With independent (X) variables included, the resulting ARIMAX approval model is:

$$(1 - L)Y_t = \omega_0 + \omega_1(1 - L)/(1 - \delta_i L)X_{t-i} + \theta(L)/\Phi(L)\varepsilon_t \tag{5}$$

where: the ω's are effect parameters, and the $\Phi(L)$ are autoregressive and $\theta(L)$ are moving average parameters. All effects may be specified to operate at various (and multiple) lags. The term $(1 - \delta_i L)$ allows the effect of any predictor variable to be distributed over time. The rate at which such an effect accumulates (in the case of a permanent effect) or decays (in the case of a temporary effect) is governed by the magnitude of δ. ARIMAX models permit one to specify different δ's for different predictor variables, thereby relaxing the strong assumption of FGLS and ADL models (see above) that "one-dynamic fits all."

ARIMAX models have one significant theoretical drawback, namely the failure to consider the possibility that approval and key predictor variables move together in the long run. For example, if the trajectory of the economy is fundamental for the dynamics of any president's approval ratings, the need to investigate the long-term co-movements in approval and economic variables is clear. A class of "error correction" models that facilitate such analyses has been developed as part of econometric work on cointegration. Several approval scholars have employed error correction models, such as the following:

$$(1 - L)Y_t = B_0 + B_1(1 - L)X_t - \alpha(Y_{t-1} - \lambda X_{t-1}) + B_2 Z_t + \varepsilon_t \tag{6}$$

In (6), Y_t (approval) and X_t (e.g., an economic evaluation) are nonstationary variables that have been rendered stationary by first differencing, B_1 measures the short-run effect of X on Y, $(Y_{t-1} - \lambda X_{t-1})$ is the error correction mechanism, and α measures the strength of the effect of the error correction mechanism.

When specifying a model like (6), an approval researcher is hypothesizing that X and Y *cointegrate*—they tend to "travel together" through time. Cointegration, a stationary linear combination of two or more variables, must be demonstrated empirically, rather than simply assumed. The α parameter measures the rate at which various shocks to the approval system—for example, those associated with Z—are eroded by the cointegrating relationship between X and Y. In a model like (6), the dynamic effects of all of the Z's are subject to the force of the long-run cointegrating relationship between X and Y. However, unlike the simple ADL models, this cointegrating relationship provides a *theoretically motivated* rationale for these dynamics. Error correction models also avoid the spurious regressions problem. All variables in a model like (7) are stationary, and parameters can be estimated using OLS two-step or NLLS (nonlinear least squares) one-step methods.

Not everyone is a fan of error correction models of presidential approval. Such models have been criticized on the grounds that approval cannot ultimately be a nonstationary variable in the classic sense. As measured in public opinion polls, approval is a percentage and thus bounded between 0 and 100. Moreover, even if approval were measured differently, it is implausible to believe that it would increase or decrease forever. In addition, some critics of error correction models (and other aggregate time series models) of presidential approval do not think it is sensible to believe that factors such as rallies or scandals that occur when a given president is in office will affect a successor. This latter point is contentious, however. Major events, such as the Watergate scandal, may affect not only how the public judges an incumbent president, but also how it evaluates politicians more generally. These effects may eventually dissipate, but they do not necessarily terminate abruptly just because a particular "rascal" has been thrown out.

Recently, some researchers have reacted to these criticisms by embracing the concept of "fractional integration." This concept is theoretically attractive because it allows one to think of presidential approval as a "long-memoried" process that can wander away from its central tendency for long periods but is ultimately mean reverting. Methodologically, the concept of long memory enables analysts to assess the dynamics of presidential approval and related variables, such as macropartisanship (*see* **Partisanship**), using ARFIMA models that generalize the familiar Box-Jenkins ARIMA models. The key idea in an ARFIMA model is "fractional differencing." Consider the following:

$$(1 - L)^{\delta 1}Y_t = \theta(L)/\Phi(L)\varepsilon_t \tag{7}$$

In (7), the $(1 - L)^\delta$ differencing operator $(1 - L)$ has a parameter, δ, that assumes values in the range $-.5$–1.0. Values greater than 0.0 indicate that the series has "long memory," values greater than $+.5$ indicate that it is nonstationary, although ultimately mean reverting. As in normal ARIMA models, the short-run dynamics of the system are captured via autoregressive ($\Phi(L)$) and moving average ($\theta(L)$) parameters. By adding suitable (fractionally) differenced regressors, the result is a ARFIMAX model. And, going a step further, one can specify a fractional error correction (FEC) model:

$$(1 - L)^{\delta 1}Y_t = B_0 + B_1(1 - L)^{\delta 2}X_t - \alpha(Y_{t-1} - \lambda X_{t-1})^{\delta 3} + \varepsilon_t \qquad (8)$$

where: δ's are fractional differencing parameters and $\delta 3 < \delta 1$ and $\delta 2$.

ARFIMAX and FEC models presently are leading-edge statistical methods for the analysis of time series models, and approval analysts are just beginning to use them in their applied work. These models would appear to have considerable utility of studying presidential approval, with the concept of "long memory" addressing the above-mentioned criticism that approval cannot be nonstationary in the classic sense. Studies using these techniques likely will appear in journals in the near future.

Finally, it should be noted that scholars have begun to study *volatility* in presidential approval. To this end, some analyses have employed heteroskedastic probit models of individual-level NES data. Others have used ARCH (autoregressive conditional heteroskedasticity) models developed for studying volatility in financial time series to investigate factors that affect variability in aggregate approval. These latter analyses are potentially interesting because they may enhance understanding of how volatility in presidential approval evolves in reaction to such variables as economic uncertainty, threat levels in international affairs, and trends in the strength and stability of partisanship in the electorate.

In retrospect, it is clear that research on presidential approval has benefited from two methodological developments. The first concerns advances in econometrics. Concepts such as cointegration and error correction that were unknown in the 1970s and the 1980s have played major roles in approval modeling since being introduced to political scientists in the early 1990s. These concepts have invigorated both theories about the determinants of presidential approval and statistical analyses of models informed by such theories. Current work on fractional cointegration and fractional error correction promises to have a similar impact over the next few years.

The second important methodological development concerns data availability. Here, the major advance has been access to the University of Michigan's Surveys of Consumers (SC) economic evaluation data. These data have enabled analysts to address controversies regarding the objects and time horizons of politically relevant economic judgments. And recently, some researchers have begun to use the individual-level (SC) data to build group-specific time series of economic evaluations to address interesting questions about the extent and nature of group heterogeneity in the dynamics of presidential approval. Although more work is needed, there are two problems. One is that the *individual-level* SC data available for secondary analysis from the ICPSR data archive currently extends only to December 1997. A more fundamental problem concerns the size of population sub-groups in the SC surveys. Since the surveys are relatively small (typically 500–700 respondents), N's for politically significant groups such as African Americans, Asian Americans, and Latino/as are very small. Time series data generated by such small samples will be too noisy to be useful.

The situation is even worse for those wishing to do group-level analyses of presidential approval, when groups defined in terms of important concepts in political psychology, such as information availability, cognitive capacity, and political interest. Proxy variables for some of these concepts may be generated from available survey data (e.g., using formal education to proxy cognitive capacity), but these proxies may be too rough to be useful. Again, aggregation for time series analytic purposes may have to be done using very small samples.

A preferable long-range solution to these problems is for students of presidential approval to begin to gather their own data. For nearly forty years, researchers have relied exclusively on data gathered by other groups for other purposes. A large-scale, ongoing survey research project gathering time series data on the variables competing theories tell us are central for understanding the dynamics of American political attitudes and behavior is long overdue. Such a project would be expensive, but the costs need not be exorbitant. This is particularly the case when such costs are compared with a project such as a national election study that absorbs millions of dollars every presidential election cycle and produces only one or two widely spaced data points for many key variables.

It might be objected that a traditional national election study can produce high-quality data on presidential approval and numerous other variables. Moreover, the N can be large enough so that group-level analyses can be done with confidence. And, individual-level analyses are crucial for individual-level inferences. These points are valid, but they do not address the need for finely aggregated *temporal variation* in the data. We may not know what the ideal level of temporal aggregation is for studying the dynamics of presidential approval, but surely it is not four, or even two, years. Typically, interesting, politically consequential dynamics are much more quickly paced.

The simple observation that the American public's perceptions of the president are consequential and can change—sometimes quite quickly—motivated the pioneers in presidential approval research to use readily available monthly Gallup Poll data to capture these dynamics. It also motivated the adoption of political economy, rather than social psychology, as an overarching theoretical framework. The faster-paced dynamics of the former, as compared with the latter, were (and remain) readily apparent. If it could have been assumed that the only explanatory variables needed were monthly macroeconomic series and a few dummy variables to capture rallies and other politically influential events, and that one model fits all, very impressive progress in understanding presidential approval, if not assured, would have been quite likely. However, circa 1990, political scientists recognized such data were not adequate to address their theoretical concerns. Unfortunately, well over a decade later, the situation is largely unchanged. Marshaling the SC data to address the theoretical interests of students of presidential approval has been an important step, but it is not enough. Long-standing theoretical debates remain unresolved, and understanding of the causes and consequences of the dynamics of presidential approval for the entire electorate and important segments thereof remains limited. To be sure, it will require patience (several years' worth) to assemble the new time series database advocated here. But, the sooner the project is initiated, the sooner the requisite data will be available for use by presidential approval researchers and other students of public opinion.

Further Reading

Clarke, Harold D., and Marianne C. Stewart. "Prospections, Retrospections and Rationality: The 'Bankers' Model of Presidential Approval Reconsidered." *American*

Journal of Political Science 38 (1994): 1104–23. This article uses an error correction model to analyze the impact of economic evaluations on presidential approval. The authors criticize MacKuen, Erikson, and Stimson's (1992) claim that the electorate uses rational expectations when assessing presidential performance.

Clarke, Harold D., Marianne C. Stewart, Michael Ault, and Euel Elliott. "Men, Women and the Dynamics of Presidential Approval." *British Journal of Political Science* 34 (2004). This article uses monthly SC survey data for the 1978–1997 period to compare the explanatory power of rival models of presidential approval among men and women.

Gronke, Paul W., and Paul Newman. "FDR to Clinton, Mueller? Regarding Presidential Approval." *Political Research Quarterly* 56 (2003): 501–12. Gronke and Newman conduct a detailed review of the literature, focusing on theoretical and conceptual developments.

Hibbs, Douglas A., Jr., R. Douglas Rivers, and Nicholas Vasilatos. "The Dynamics of Political Support for American Presidents Among Occupational and Partisan Groups." *American Journal of Political Science* 26 (1982): 312–32. Analyzes heterogeneity in presidential approval among social classes. The article is a classic example of the use of objective economic indicators in approval models.

MacKuen, Michael B., Robert S. Erikson, and James A. Stimson. "Peasants or Bankers? The American Electorate and the U.S. Economy." *American Political Science Review* 86 (1992): 308–25. The authors use SC economic evaluation data and argue that the electorate behaves as rational "bankers" when judging presidential performance.

Mueller, John E. "Presidential Popularity from Truman to Johnson." *American Political Science Review* 64 (1970): 18–34. This path-breaking article initiated the field of presidential approval research. Several hypotheses articulated by Mueller continue to guide inquiry today.

Norpoth, Helmut. "Presidents and the Prospective Voter." *Journal of Politics* 58 (1996): 776–92. Norpoth criticizes MacKuen, Erikson, and Stimson (1992) and argues that national retrospective economic evaluations are what matter for presidential approval.

Harold D. Clarke, Marianne C. Stewart, and Chris Rodgers

Presidential Debates. *See* Political Debates

Presidential Use of Public Opinion Polling

The presidency remains the only indirectly elected branch of government. Despite the continued presence of the Electoral College, the president's relationship with the public represents a critical source of power, as the president is the only person who can, and does, claim to represent the nation as a whole. The unique link between the president and the citizenry leads the White House to gather information about the public from a variety of sources: the media, the party, other elites, the presidential mail bag, and of course, public opinion polls. Presidents tried to sample public opinion early in American history, with institutions like straw polls and canvassing that have existed longer than the Republic itself. However, it was the recognition that the public offered a valuable strategic tool for the president that increased presidential interest in gathering and utilizing public opinion over time. Those efforts, of course, became more feasible with the advent of polling.

The first efforts to employ public opinion polling data began as Presidents Hoover and Roosevelt sought quantitative representations of the public's attitudes. Roosevelt's efforts represent the embryonic form of what scholars term the "presidential polling apparatus." However, due to costs and logistics, no White House could consistently make use of public opinion polling until the Nixon Administration. In the 1970s, public opinion became a crucial element of presidential public relations, in particular efforts to manage the president's constituents. Polling has become so ubiquitous that presidents even turn to "the data" for help with crisis management. By the end of the twentieth century, critics routinely charged that the use of polling by the presidency went so far as to create a "permanent campaign" in the White House.

The framers of the U.S. Constitution intentionally created distance between the office of the president and ordinary citizens. The public's wants, needs, and desires were to be the purview of the House of Representatives. The function of the president was not representation, but implementation of the law. The president is thus indeed our "chief executive." However, the framers could not foresee the creation of the political party, the technological changes sweeping over the nineteenth and twentieth centuries, or the increasing global role for the United States. These changes combined to increase the power of the president and to increase the connections between the president and the public.

At the start of the nineteenth century, presidents did appeal to the public but did so via the party and the partisan newspaper. The political party served to document and channel citizen feedback. However, the direction of power within the presidential-party relationship changed in the twentieth century. Changing voting patterns and independent citizen attitudes compounded the separation forming between the president and his party. As presidents established identities apart from their role as head of the party, the attitudes and needs of the national voting audience began to matter more. Presidents wanted and needed a mechanism, a reliable mechanism, to identify supporters. Applying social science techniques, President Hoover's staff produced the first crude effort to sample opinion of the day. Without the benefit of statistics, Hoover had his White House staff do a relatively sophisticated content analysis of the editorial pages of newspapers. In effect, Hoover attempted to sample elite opinion. Nevertheless, it was in the 1930s that the first presidential effort to employ public opinion emerged.

Franklin Delano Roosevelt was the first president to seek out public attitudes via public opinion polls. Pollster Hadley Cantril informally and secretly provided Roosevelt and his staff with polling data. The data provided the administration with evidence of changing attitudes toward the prospect of war as early as 1940. Cantril supplied the White House with public opinion supporting aiding the British months before Roosevelt advocated his lend-lease program. Roosevelt used the polls to determine the depth of support across different constituencies and to test potential policy options. For example, would American Catholics support the war if Rome were bombed? Should the United States create temporary refugee camps for those the Nazis persecuted? Moreover, Roosevelt's executive branch departments, such as the Department of Agriculture, the Works Progress Administration, and the Social Security Administration, all sought to understand public attitudes to evaluate policy making. Robert Eisinger argues that Roosevelt used public opinion polls to trump Congress's representational role.

Moreover, the secret connection between Roosevelt and public opinion increased his ability to set the nation's agenda independently, separate both from Congress and from his own party.

The Truman and Eisenhower administrations continued to receive public opinion polls, but substantially less frequently than the FDR administration. President Truman openly disdained the practice of predicting with the polls, most likely because of the infamous erroneous prediction of a Thomas Dewey victory, by George Gallup in the 1948 presidential election. However, the Truman Administration did continue the practice of collecting polling data from Gallup, as well as polls reported in newspapers and by university public opinion research groups. The Truman Administration also used public opinion polling to evaluate presidential actions and decisions and to connect demographics to attitudes. For example, in 1951 members of the Truman Administration noted that support for the president's firing of General MacArthur decreased with the amount of formal education of the respondent. Truman's staff also used Gallup polls to evaluate presidential speeches, although the quality of the polling questions and analysis troubled the staff.

Unlike President Truman, President Eisenhower was comfortable with public opinion polling. Key members of the Eisenhower Administration received public opinion polls from varied sources, but primarily relied on public polls. The polls continued to cover key issues and policies, in particular military involvement in Southeast Asia. The State Department, which began polling under the Truman Administration in 1944, also continued to query the public for its support for foreign policy actions.

However, access to opinion data, even for the president, was limited by cost and by technology. Polling was expensive and could not be paid for by the White House budget, as it was a political activity. Nevertheless, the Johnson Administration greatly expanded the use of public opinion in governing due to the effectiveness of polls used during the campaigns of 1960 and 1964. There were sixteen nonelection polls commissioned during President Kennedy's three years in office; in contrast, the Johnson Administration commissioned eighty-three in its three years. The cost to the White House for private public opinion polling was relatively minimal since these White Houses still primarily "piggybacked" presidential questions onto surveys for other clients.

The Nixon Administration commissioned over two hundred polls, however more than half were for Nixon's re-election effort. More importantly, Nixon ceased "piggybacking" and began purchasing private surveys designed specifically for the White House. Thus, a fundamental shift occurs between the Kennedy Administration and the Nixon Administration regarding the use of presidential public opinion polling. While in the White House, President Nixon spent more than $5 million (in current inflation-adjusted dollars) on polling to receive access to the best surveys available. By purchasing the complete survey, the Nixon White House received control over the timing, frequency, and locale of the surveys as well as the content. The ability to poll on specific presidential issues or events, whenever the White House needed the information, revolutionized the use of public opinion polling for the presidency. As a result, the amount of money presidents spent on polling increased dramatically. Pollster Patrick Caddell received more than $1.3 million between 1977 and 1979 while polling for President Carter. In 1981 alone, Pollster Richard Wirthlin received $820,000 polling for Ronald Reagan. The George H. Bush polling budget was $650,000 in 1989 for quarterly national surveys from Robert Teeter. By 1998 President Clinton spent over $15 million on weekly, sometimes daily, public opinion polls.

The development of a "public opinion polling apparatus," however, was not without risk. Most presidents feared that relying on polling and public relations appeared weak, slick, or lacking in leadership. The contrast between the desire to employ the public via the polls and the need to appear above politics haunted administrations. After blatant attempts to disseminate favorable public opinion data failed, President Johnson suspended his relationship with his pollster due to "overexposure." The taint from the poll usage, which stained President Johnson, continued for two administrations. Nixon's Chief of Staff, H. R. Haldeman, noted in his diary that Nixon wanted to avoid LBJ's boasting of positive poll results. President Ford's staff urged him not to make any direct reference to a private poll like LBJ did.

The hesitance to admit interest in public opinion, let alone usage of it, continued through the Carter, Reagan, G. H. Bush, and G. W. Bush Administrations. However, the Clinton Administration deviated from this pattern. Not only was President Clinton himself skilled in reading and interpreting polls, but he and his staffers made no secret of their interest in, and attention to, the American public's attitudes. Critics even accused the Clintons of planning their Martha's Vineyard vacations and choosing the name of their dog based on polling numbers. The Clinton Administration so overtly referenced public opinion that George W. Bush highlighted an antipolling stance in his campaign for the White House. At the 2000 Republican National Convention, George W. Bush asserted, "I believe great decisions are made with care, made with conviction, not made with polls." Bush continued, "I do not need to take your pulse before I know my own mind." Repeatedly and publicly, the Bush campaign staffers and White House staffers insisted that Bush would not subscribe to Clinton's poll-driven presidency.

Most presidents since Nixon were aware of, interested in, and active in using the White House poll apparatus. George W. Bush's frequent censorious statements and his disdain for a decision-making process that included public opinion superficially appears to make him the exception to the rule. Nevertheless, the Bush White House staffing arrangements deliberately included staffers highly experienced with public opinion polling. More importantly, and certainly more telling, the Bush presidential rhetoric did not translate into a lack of spending on polling data or even attention to public opinion. Where the Bush White House is truly different from its predecessors is in relying on polling while simultaneously attempting to sell the perception that opinion polling is bad, suggests lack of leadership, and is not to be tolerated. Disparaging polling has not translated into any significant lessening of its use, in part due to the influence of Senior Adviser Karl Rove.

Karl Rove represents yet another evolution for incorporating public opinion into White House processes. Traditionally, the president's public opinion pollster works for the national committee of the president's party and funnels the poll data to particular staffers who in turn disseminate the information to the president and to the rest of the staff. During the first G. W. Bush Administration outside pollsters, like Jan van Lohuizen, continued to report to Matthew Dowd at the Republican National Committee (RNC). For a public opinion polling apparatus to flourish, the White House requires staffers comfortable with public opinion and a trustworthy polling consultant. From the Nixon Administration through the Clinton Administration, no White House combined the staff function with the outside pollster's role. Patrick Caddell (Carter), Richard Wirthlin (Reagan), Lee Atwater (G. H. Bush), and Richard Morris (Clinton) were presidential strategists, pollsters, and all-around advisers, but none officially worked inside the White House. Rove changed this pattern by more closely connecting polling to decision making than did the previous White Houses. Moreover, with Rove on staff, the information gleaned from the polls is, in a sense, laundered. Sheltered from the president, politics and polling data seep stealthily into policy as Rove and others do not mention poll data explicitly to the president (much less the press), preferring instead to work the information into their arguments obliquely. The Rove staffing arrangement underscored the need of the presidency for public opinion, regardless of the attitudes of an individual president.

The modern White House spends considerable amounts of money to produce a consistent supply of public opinion data because of the inherent value of the information. Scholarly, media, and pundit attention to **presidential approval** ratings suggest that presidents primarily poll to discern whether the public "approves of the job the president is doing?" Presidents, especially Nixon and Reagan, were very aware of their approval ratings and often designated a staff member to chart fluctuations. However, while scholars can determine, with ever-increasing accuracy, the factors that influenced observed fluctuations in presidential approval, the ratings are not effective means for designing future strategy. It is useful to learn that after a presidential speech, public approval of the job the president was doing fell 4 percentage points. However, without determining the cause for the falling approval ratings, the knowledge is not strategically significant. Unless the very ability to measure approval fluctuations produces a dependence on the ratings, what scholars term a "follower presidency." In this hypothetical scenario, the White House's preeminent presidential goal becomes the achievement of high approval ratings. The goal of popularity then infuses behavior. In reality, however, monitoring approval ratings is not the focal point of the presidential polling apparatus.

The media, pundit, and scholarly focus on approval ratings misses the relationship between the president and the public as it ignores the origins of that relationship—the campaign trail. During any campaign, the media constantly informs the candidate and the public who is ahead, who is behind, and who is showing improvement. Information from **horserace journalism** is clearly not enough information about public attitudes for candidates. Presidential candidates spend millions of dollars on public opinion polls to disaggregate supporters and opponents and to explain why individuals support one candidate over another. Attitudes toward candidates are morasses of issues opinions, personality evaluations, partisanship, and other socioeconomic factors. These pieces of information are critical to successful campaigns because campaign strategy emerges from attitudes and reactions gleaned from the polling analysis. Winning candidates, as president, bring the campaign interest and dependency on the polls to the White House. Presidents learn well the value of public opinion polling from their campaigns for office. Moreover, poll data is a crucial tool accessible to most members of the campaign staff. After victory, many members of the campaign staff follow the president-elect to the White House. Consequently, most key members of the White House staff are comfortable using polls and consider them a relevant part of decision making.

Presidents and their staffs use polls in two distinct areas of White House activity: public relations and preparing for re-election. In both areas, the White House seeks information beyond mere evaluations of performance and turns instead to evaluations of the public's agenda, issues, and events. The White House relies on public opinion heavily during the first two years of the four-year term. This time frame is generally when the president is most productive legislatively. Using the poll apparatus, the White House determines if its issues dovetail with the public's agenda and determines how it wants the public to become involved. For example, poll questions may ask Americans either to prioritize or to choose amongst alternative means of issue response. For prioritizing, poll respondents answer the open-ended most-important-problem question. For choosing, respondents indicate support for a proposed response to a policy problem, or select among options.

The most common use of the poll apparatus emerges from efforts to communicate to the public. Poll data influence message design via phrasing, speeches, and event evaluation. Presidential staff hone presidential rhetoric by testing phrases for unwanted reactions (e.g., was "law and order" a code for "racism" in the 1960s and 1970s). In addition to testing for inflammatory rhetoric, presidents have also polled for understanding and for clarifying terminology (e.g., using Star Wars instead of Strategic Defense Initiative to explain a satellite missile defense program). The White House also used the polls to determine when to give speeches. Troubling **political alienation** and **political knowledge** indicators prompted pollster Patrick Caddell to advise President Carter to give an invigorating, mood-enhancing speech. Unfortunately, the speech, dubbed the Crisis of Confidence Speech, did not serve its designed purpose and instead became a symbol of the failure of the Carter Administration.

One of the more interesting uses of public opinion, under the guise of public relations, came during the two impeachment crises of the twentieth century. In March 1973, as questions regarding Watergate relentlessly played in the press, the Nixon White House watched the polls. Nixon's Chief of Staff, H. R. Haldeman, informed the president that their pollster that "Oliver Quayle says nobody gives a damn about the Watergate." However, by the end of April 1973 support for the president and belief that his version is the truth declined in the polls. The decline in support evident in the poll numbers forced the resignation of Nixon's two top aides. In May of 1973, 77 percent of Americans believed the president should not resign. Public opinion data became a lifeline and a justification for the president. President Nixon took comfort in the polls and used them to bolster his desire to fight the charges. When public approval of the president dropped to a low of 20 percent, Nixon resigned.

During President Clinton's impeachment crisis, public opinion helped determine not when to leave, but instead revealed a strategy of how to remain in office. In January 1998, as the White House learned that President Clinton's relationship with a White House intern would be made public, Clinton and his pollster put a survey into the field. The Independent Counsel's investigation of President Clinton made the details of that survey public. The polls distinguished the depth and degree to which the public would forgive the president. The public was most concerned about obstruction of justice and subornation of perjury, and not whether Clinton had simply engaged in a sexual affair outside his marriage. Dick Morris, President Clinton's pollster, warned the president, "they're willing to forgive you for adultery, but not for perjury or obstruction of justice or the various other things. They're even willing to forgive the conduct. They're not willing to forgive the word. In other words, if in fact you told Monica Lewinsky to lie, they can forgive that, but if you committed subornation of perjury, they won't." Thus, the poll data clearly offered the president a survival strategy—do not admit to obstructing justice and suborning perjury. Clinton's remarkably stable approval rating during the impeachment crisis suggests the strategy was effective.

In addition to public relations, during crises and normal governing times, the re-election efforts of the White House greatly influence presidential polling usage. The poll apparatus is extremely effective for identifying, tracking, and employing opinion data from the president's electoral coalition. The White House uses public opinion polls to classify and categorize individuals. The component at the heart of the presidential classification effort is not voter mobilization but rather identification of support for the president and his policies. Using the poll apparatus, presidents define their unique presidential constituency, separate from their political party. The hunt for the presidential coalition begins with traditional demographic questions (e.g., party identification and socioeconomic variables). Over time, the White House increasingly segments the presidential constituency by issues and ultimately categorizes presidential supporters by nontraditional socioeconomic factors, like home ownership or identification as a "soccer mom" or "Nascar dad."

The massive White House efforts to appeal to the public using public opinion lead critics to suggest that politicians either pander to public whims or manipulate the public via advertising campaigns. Charges condemning the presence of a permanent campaign contend that the presence of polling dilutes or even prevents legitimate governing and leadership. Supporting permanent campaign charges is the fact that the consecutive administrations from Richard Nixon to George W. Bush have employed former campaign workers and have capitalized on their capabilities to interpret and use public opinion. The White House poll operation influences presidential messages and responses to events and crises. Moreover, the poll data enables the production of presidency-centered constituency strategies, linking the president's initial electoral coalition to a viable re-election coalition. Thus, presidential use of polling alters the target and framework of presidential persuasion toward an increasingly segmented and adversarial conception of the president's supporters. However, the public's input generally waxes and wanes during a presidential term often flourishing in the first two years and within crises but languishing at other times and across a multitude of issues. Consequently, a model of leadership built upon the permanent campaign has not subsumed traditionally styled governing behavior. The presidential use of polling exists alongside traditional governing strategies and approaches.

Further Reading

Brace, Paul, and Barbara Hinckley. *Follow the Leader: Opinion Polls and Modern Presidents*. New York: Basic Books, 1992. Explores the connection between presidential awareness of approval ratings and presidential behavior.

Eisinger, Robert M. *The Evolution of Presidential Polling.* New York: Cambridge University Press, 2003. Explores the evolution of public opinion polling in the White House from Hoover to the present.

Heith, Diane J. *Polling to Govern: Public Opinion and Presidential Leadership.* Stanford, CA: Stanford University Press, 2003. Argues that the presence of public opinion polling within the White House does not translate into campaign behavior dominating governing and leadership.

Jacobs, Lawrence, and Robert Shapiro. *Politicians Don't Pander: Political Manipulation and the Loss of Democratic Responsiveness.* Chicago: University of Chicago Press, 2000. Elites ignore the public's policy preferences. The constant presence of public opinion exists to help craft presentations not to alter stances.

———. "The Rise of Presidential Polling: The Nixon White House in Historical Perspective." *Public Opinion Quarterly* 59 (1995): 163–95. Details how the Nixon use of polls represents a turning point in White House attention to public opinion.

Diane J. Heith

Pretesting

Pretesting is the systematic evaluation of a survey's quality before it is used for actual data collection. It identifies flaws in a questionnaire that may lead to errors in the **response process**. Based on such information, efforts can be taken to improve the survey before it is administered to the full sample.

The process of answering a question is called the response process. In general, four major components are distinguished in this process: comprehension, retrieval, judgment, and reporting (Figure 1). In the first stage, the comprehension stage, someone who has to answer a question in a questionnaire (the respondent) has to interpret the question. In the ideal situation the question is interpreted in the same way as intended by the researcher. However, ambiguous, unclear, or difficult words in the question may lead to deviant interpretations. Also it may not be obvious to the respondent what he is expected to do: that is, the response task is not clear. Once the respondent has understood the question or thinks that the question is understood correctly, he has to retrieve relevant information from memory or other sources to answer the question. Here, problems may arise because of difficulties in retrieving the correct information: information may be forgotten, or the question asks for specific information that is not immediately available. The third step is the formulation of an answer by integrating and evaluating the retrieved information. With some questions this step is trivial, but in others a complicated calculation has to be carried out. The respondent may also decide not to report the true answer but to provide a socially desirable response. After an answer is formulated, the answer has to be reported. In closed questions the judgment answer has to be mapped onto the predefined response options. Choosing the appropriate answer may be difficult because of ambiguous wording in the options, overlapping, or missing options. This description of the response process has become the theoretical basis for pretesting questionnaires.

In other words, pretesting identifies flaws in a survey by detecting systematic errors in the response process. It assesses whether respondents (1) understand the questions and their response tasks as intended, (2) retrieve relevant infor-

Figure 1. The Response Process

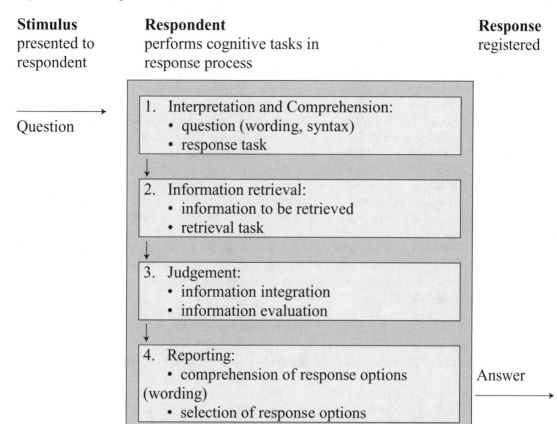

| **Stimulus**
presented to
to respondent | **Respondent**
performs cognitive tasks in
response process | **Response**
registered |

Question →

1. Interpretation and Comprehension:
   • question (wording, syntax)
   • response task

2. Information retrieval:
   • information to be retrieved
   • retrieval task

3. Judgement:
   • information integration
   • information evaluation

4. Reporting:
   • comprehension of response options (wording)
   • selection of response options

Answer →

mation quickly and accurately, (3) process the information appropriately, and (4) report the information easily and truthfully. If and when problems are identified, actions can be taken to improve the questionnaire. The adapted questionnaire can then be used for the actual data collection. Preferably, however, an adapted questionnaire is tested again to investigate whether the changes reduce or eliminate the identified problems. This results in an iterative process in which prototypes of questionnaires are pretested, improved, and pretested again. Even when the researcher is unable to adapt the questionnaire because of time constraints or the need for longitudinal data, pretesting is worthwhile. Pretesting gives researchers insight into the quality of the data and provides clues for the causes of unexpected conclusions.

Several methods can be used to pretest questionnaires. The most frequently used methods are expert appraisal, **focus groups, cognitive interviewing, behavior coding,** debriefing, and pilot studies. Regardless of the method employed, the researcher who has developed the questionnaire should not be involved in pretesting it.

In an expert appraisal, a questionnaire is reviewed by a number of survey specialists. These specialists consider the design of the questionnaire and its administration from both a conceptual and an operational perspective. They use a coding scheme (with precoded design errors) to organize their review. Typically, coding schemes are structured according to the stages of the response process. To assess comprehension, experts can check whether questions contain difficult or unclear words, whether the questions are double-barrelled, or whether there is a mismatch between the question and predefined response options. To gauge retrieval and judgment, experts can check whether it is difficult to retrieve all relevant information, because it requires the respondent to look too far back in time. To assess response formulation, experts can check whether difficult calculations need to be carried out or whether sensitive questions might produce socially desirable answers. As for the last stage, reporting, experts can check whether the predefined response options are confusing, overlapping, or incomplete.

Expert appraisals possess several shortcomings. Since this method is based on the number and the experience of the experts, it can yield subjective results. Therefore, at least three experts typically review the questionnaire and discuss their views on the questionnaire in a panel discussion, to get a general view. Second, it does not consult any eligible respondents, meaning experts must project their own reactions, leaving them vulnerable to missing significant problems in the questionnaire.

Another method for assessing the quality of a survey is focus groups. Focus groups are open discussions among a small number of individuals eligible for the study. Focus group participants are carefully selected with regard to background characteristics to ensure a variety of perspectives are included (*see* **Focus Group Assembly**). Preferably, they do not know each other. A moderator leads the discussion, using a list of selected topics (*see* **Focus Group Moderating**). During the discussion, the participants are stimulated to deliberate the topics with each other and to generate new ideas, suggestions, and recommendations. Dialogue and behaviors are recorded and later analyzed (*see* **Focus Group Reporting**).

Focus groups can be used at any stage of the design process. The groups can provide information relevant to the development of the questionnaire when one is not yet available: for example, the topics of research interest, the different aspects that go together with these topics, the information that has to be collected, the way it should be asked, the order of topics in the questionnaire, the sensitivity of these topics. Once a draft questionnaire is developed, it can be administered to a focus group. The group then can discuss the content, appearance, and functioning of the questionnaire.

Focus groups possess several drawbacks. They can be costly to facilitate, requiring recruitment incentives, space, and time. Second, if focus group participants are not sampled probabilistically, the information collected will not necessarily reflect the opinions of the target population. Lastly, focus group discussion can become easily sidetracked or dominated by a few voices, providing insufficient information to warrant their cost.

More detailed information on the response process can be collected by cognitive interviewing. A cognitive interview is an open interview in which a questionnaire is tested in a laboratory setting with one respondent and an interviewer. Typically, a small number of interviews (fifteen to twenty-five) are sufficient to collect enough information to make judgments about the response process.

Cognitive interviewing is a method to evaluate the questionnaire directly with respondents. It entails the face-to-face administration of a survey instrument to a small number of eligible participants (usually fifteen to twenty-five) by a set of skilled interviewers. Respondents are carefully selected to ensure variation in relevant background characteristics—such as age, gender, education level—and in predispositions germane to the questionnaire. Typically, they are invited to come to a laboratory setting at a central location where the in-depth interviews are conducted. Researchers either take notes from behind a one-way mirror or analyze videotapes or audio recordings of the interview after it is completed.

The most common techniques employed in cognitive interviews are thinking aloud in combination with follow-up probing. Thinking aloud involves asking respondents to express their thoughts while answering a question. To stimulate respondents to keep thinking aloud when they are silent for a long time, in-depth interviewers can use probes, like "Go on, I'm listening" or "What are you thinking now?" Moreover, they can employ follow-up probes to ask for additional information and to go into more detail: for example, "I don't understand what you mean," "Could you explain that to me?", or "How did you come to that answer?" Apart from these probes, which are used by interviewers whenever they feel it is necessary to probe, pre-scripted follow-up probes can also be used. These probes focus on particular aspects of the response process that the researcher wants to know more about. For example, cognitive interviewers can ask for the interpretation of a particular term or ask for how the respondent got to his answer. To make sure that all in-depth interviewers conduct the interviews in the same way, the procedure for conducting in-depth interviews is defined in an interviewing protocol.

Like other pretesting techniques, cognitive interviews have some drawbacks. Cognitive interviewing is more time-consuming than other methods. Getting respondents to think aloud is often difficult, requiring skilled interviewers. And probing can influence the response process, so interviewers have to take care to collect facts rather than artifacts.

Another method that can be used for pretesting questionnaires is behavior coding. Behavior coding is the systematic classification of respondent and interviewer behavior in a one-on-one interview. Interviews with a fully drafted questionnaire can be coded concurrently (observing an interview from behind a one-way mirror) or afterward using videotapes or audiotapes. For each question in the interview, respondent and interviewer behavior is coded. The codes focus on how the interviewer asks the questions and how the respondent reacts. Codes for the interviewer include whether a question has been read aloud exactly as printed or whether there are minor or major changes made to the wording. Respondent codes tap the reaction of the respondent, such as whether the respondent requests that questions be repeated, asks for clarification, expresses confusion about predefined response options, gives an answer that does not fit in the list of response options, or changes his answer. These codes are then related to the components of the response process.

This method is directed at identifying questions that are troublesome to interviewers and respondents. However, it is not considered to be a sensitive enough tool to identify the exact source of problems it uncovers. For example, a respondent requesting repetition or clarification indicates that the question may be unclear, contain undefined terms, be too long, have poor syntax, or be influenced by previous questions. Without additional information, it is not clear, however, what the exact source of the problem is.

Debriefing respondents and interviewers afterward can provide additional information about the quality of the instrument. After an interview has been completed, each question showing difficulties is discussed with the respondent (or interviewer), using the registered codes as guidance for the discussion. Also the taped interview can be played back as a way to help the respondent to refresh his memory. Behavior coding can also be the starting point for a topic list to be used in a focus group discussion. Behavior coding in itself does not identify as many problems in a questionnaire as do other techniques; however, it does provide quick results.

Although the aforementioned methods can often identify the worst flaws in the questionnaire, they all suffer from the fact that they are administered in a laboratory setting. Pilot studies avoid this problem by evaluating the questionnaire under actual field conditions. Pilot studies not only enable the instrument to be tested, but also permit administration procedures (e.g., contacting procedures, mode functioning, etc.) to be evaluated.

In a pilot study a relatively large number of questionnaires will be completed according to the procedures of the social or market research that is being prepared. To find out how well the questionnaire works, the collected data are analyzed with regard to item nonresponse and the answer distribution of specific questions. A question showing a high rate of item nonresponse means that a lot of respondents did not answer the question. This might indicate that flaws are still present in the questionnaire. The answer distribution of questions germane to the research can be analyzed to find out whether the data collected show strange patterns. Again, this may point to a poorly designed questionnaire.

Pilot studies, however, also possess drawbacks. They are costly to conduct, consuming scarce resources, valuable field time, and limited sample. Moreover, they do not provide much insight into the source of identified problems. For that, laboratory methods such as in-depth interviewing or focus groups are better suited.

In sum, pretesting is a critical component of survey design, enabling researchers to assess the quality of a questionnaire and its associated field protocols. Ideally, pretesting methods should be used in combination, since each method does not identify the same flaws or provide the same level of detail. For example, expert appraisals or behavior coding could precede in-depth interviews, or focus groups could be followed by pilot tests. Moreover, these methods should be used in an iterative process of prestesting and adapting the questionnaire—thus, improving the questionnaire step by step.

Further Reading

Presser, S., J. Rothgeb, M. Couper, J. Lessler, E. Martin, J. Martin, and E. Singer, eds. *Methods for Testing and Evaluating Survey Questions.* New York: John Wiley, 2004. In this monograph the latest developments in prestesting are discussed.

Snijkers, Ger. *Cognitive Laboratory Experiences: On Pre-testing Computerised Questionnaires and Data Quality.* Utrecht: Utrecht University, and Heerlen: Statistics Netherlands, 2002. A systematic overview of pretest methods; focuses on the application of setting up and carrying out pretest research, analyzing the data, and presenting the results. Includes several case studies as illustration.

Sudman, Seymour, Norman M. Bradburn, and Norbert Schwarz. *Thinking about Answers; The Application of Cognitive Processes to Survey Methodology.* San Francisco: Jossey-Bass, 1996. Presents an overview of pretest methods and their results.

Tourangeau, Roger, Lance J. Rips, and Kenneth Rasinski. *The Psychology of Survey Response.* Cambridge: Cambridge University Press, 2000. This book examines the response process in great detail.

Ger J.M.E. Snijkers

Priming

Priming is the process through which individuals change their opinion not because they alter their beliefs or evaluation of the object in question, but because they alter the relative weight they give to the various considerations that they use to determine their evaluation of the object. Through priming, an individual's opinion of a policy or candidate can be changed without changing the individual's opinion on the merits of the object, but merely through changing his/her evaluation of what is important to consider when judging the policy or candidate. For example, a voter could be persuaded to give the president a higher approval rating without changing any of their judgments of the president if the voter had been primed to think of her positive evaluation of the president's foreign policy performance and not primed to recall her negative evaluation of the president's domestic policy performance. When a consideration is "primed," it is given more importance in the ultimate decision. Priming is thus a combination of **agenda setting** and persuasion. The more attention a subject receives in the media, the greater its weight is likely to be in subsequent judgments. Beginning in the mid-1980s, a great deal of political science, psychology, and communications research found evidence of priming, both in analysis of surveys and in small group experiments.

The priming hypothesis rests on three assumptions. First, people have incomplete information on most questions and do not take into consideration all available information when making judgments. Second, the information they do consider is that which is most easily available to them. Third, what is available to them is powerfully shaped by television news. When individuals are asked, "Do you think we should go to war in Iraq?" they may have a variety of swirling and contradictory considerations swimming in their heads. John Zaller has shown that because individuals usually have competing and contradictory considerations on political questions and rarely have well-defined opinions, when called upon to make a judgment, their opinion responses will be constructed by what comes to mind. Opinion instability on a whole range of questions can be understood as shifts in which considerations come to mind (priming), rather than shifts in underlying attitudes (persuasion). This line of reasoning is consistent with other research on opinion formation that has shown that people understand politics by resorting to cognitive shortcuts and the use of heuristics; thus, judgments are often based on those constructs that are accessible.

A great deal of political science and communications research from the 1940s through the 1980s found little evidence of direct persuasion through the mass media. It was rare for individuals to say, "I used to support abortion rights but now I oppose them." Despite the lack of evidence for media persuasion, a great deal of evidence emerged for the agenda-setting hypothesis, summarized in the aphorism that "the media can't tell people what to think, but it can tell them what to think about." The assumption of those interested in priming takes the agenda-setting logic one step further: presumably, if the media can influence what people think about, it can influence which considerations people bring to bear when making a decision about what to think. It can influence which elements of political life are salient, which in the end can in fact get people to change their minds.

As an extension of the literature about agenda setting, Iyengar and Kinder introduced the concept of priming into the political science literature. Since then, many studies have confirmed that the media can prime. Iyengar and Kinder found evidence that when news stories are framed (*see* **Issue Framing**) in terms of an individual—when a particular politician is given responsibility for a policy—viewers are primed to base their judgments of the policy on their evaluations of the individual. Keeter also found that increased exposure to television during the 1960s and 1970s primed leadership as a more important component of individuals' voting decisions. Because the media tend to frame stories in more personalized—or "episodic" terms—it has been shown that citizens more exposed to television news are more likely to attribute responsibility to individuals rather than to broader societal forces.

Most research on priming has focused on issues of character and leadership—in particular, on how exposure to dramatic events can alter the criteria used to judge leaders, especially the criteria used to assess presidential performance. For example, evaluations of how presidents were doing on foreign policy (as opposed to domestic policy) became more important in the approval ratings of President Reagan during the Iran-Contra controversy and President George H. Bush during the first Persian Gulf War. The high approval ratings for President Bush in the immediate aftermath of the war proved to become poor predictors of voters' eventual judgments because his performance on the war became a less important factor influencing vote decisions as domestic issues rose in prominence in the news media during 1991 and 1992.

Electoral strategists take the question of priming seriously. Often, an election campaign is a communications battle to shape the "ballot question." That is, what question are voters answering when they mark their ballot? "Do I like this guy?" "How has the economy been going?" "Who shares my values?" "Is it time for a change?" Imagine that one candidate is widely liked personally by voters but has a policy platform that is inconsistent with most voters' preferences. Which of these two considerations—personal attributes or policy considerations—will be more important when voters mark their ballot? Presumably, the hypothetical candidate will have an interest in making the election a choice of leadership, while opposing candidates will have an interest in making the election a choice of policies. A voter may go back and forth on their vote intention without ever changing their opinion of the candidate's character or the issues. If the election is framed in the media as a choice of leadership, candidate factors may be primed in voters' minds; if the election is framed instead as a choice of opposing platforms, issue considerations may be primed instead. During the formation of campaign strategy, pollsters and communications specialists work very closely to identify the issues on which their candidate is currently strong and then attempt to make those issues more important to voters. Likewise, they identify the issues on which their opponent is weakest and try and prime those.

The priming hypothesis has been aptly demonstrated in study after study. New research on priming is interested in more subtle questions, such as which groups of voters are most likely to be primed, under what circumstances is priming most likely to occur, when does it not occur and why. On these questions, there is as yet no consensus.

Further Reading

Iyengar, Shanto, and Donald R. Kinder. *News that Matters: Television and American Opinion.* Chicago: University of Chicago Press, 1987.

Iyengar, Shanto, and Adam Simon. "News Coverage of the Gulf Crisis and Public Opinion: A Study of Agenda Setting, Priming, and Framing." *Communication Research* 20 (1993): 365–83.

Keeter, Scott. "The Illusion of Intimacy: Television and the Role of Candidate Personal Qualities in Voter Choice." *Public Opinion Quarterly* 51 (1987): 344–58.

Krosnick, Jon, and L. A. Brannon. "The Impact of the Gulf War on the Ingredients of Presidential Evaluations: Multidimensional Effects of Political Involvement." *American Political Science Review* 87 (1993): 963–75.

Krosnick, Jon, and Donald R. Kinder. "Altering the Foundations of Support for the President Through Priming." *American Political Science Review* 84 (1990): 497–512.

Zaller, John. *The Nature and Origins of Mass Opinion.* Cambridge: Cambridge University Press, 1992.

Matthew Mendelsohn

Prospect Theory

Prospect theory is an account of individual decision making under conditions of risk or uncertainty. Because most political decisions, such as for whom to vote or what policies to favor, are indeed characterized by uncertainty, the applicability of this approach to public opinion is apparent. At its core, prospect theory has two main components. The first is the realization is that people make decisions in different "frames." The frame in which a decision maker perceives himself or herself to be thus affects his or her decision calculus. In particular, decisions may differ depending on which of the three principle frames (implied by the context of risk) are employed: those of gain, loss, or remaining even. The second component is that people do not take probabilities at face value but rather subjectively place more weight on low probability events and less weight on high probability events.

Prospect theory was developed by Daniel Kahneman and Amos Tversky in response to a number of empirical findings suggesting that people often act contrary to the coldly rational or "expected value" calculations that an economist would predict. As such, prospect theory has often been viewed as a competitor to rational-choice theory. The main idea of prospect theory is that when a person makes a decision, he or she attempts to avoid risk in the presence of gains and to take risks in the face of losses. Only in the (relatively rare) even frame would a decision maker be risk neutral and act according to strict expected value calculations. Thus, a decision maker's risk propensity depends upon his or her perception of currently being in a losses or gains frame (as in being ahead or down when gambling).

Risk taking or avoidance is a natural part of our common understanding of decision making. On one level, we each see ourselves as either more of a risk taker or more of a risk avoider. Those of us who participate in skydiving, for instance, can reasonably be labeled risk takers, while those of us too cautious for such sport may be conceived of as risk avoiders. The primary insight of prospect theory is that our risk propensity is situation specific. The person who is willing to take some risk in skydiving may be entirely unwilling to engage in dubious investing for his or her retirement account; the prudent individual who avoids dare-devil sports may lose his or her house due to gambling. Risk propensity in one context does not directly carry over to other contexts.

Consider a trip to a casino. After spending some time gambling, it is easier to leave the casino if you have won some money than if you have lost some money. The prospect theory explanation for this is that as you win money, you move into the gains frame. If you continue to win money, your risk aversion also increases. In essence, you become increasingly afraid that you will lose what you have already won. However, if you lose money, you move into the losses frame. If you continue to lose money, your risk acceptance also increases. Now, you become increasingly desperate to regain what you have lost and take greater risks in your desperation.

Rational-choice theorists have known for a long time how risk aversion or risk acceptance would affect a decision maker's choice between a "sure thing" and a chance (or "lottery")—between something better than the sure thing and something worse than the sure thing. One can find the odds in the lottery where a risk-neutral decision maker would value the chance of winning the prize and the cost of the ticket equally. For example, at some arts fairs there is the option of buying a quilt (the sure thing) or buying a raffle ticket for a quilt of equal value (the lottery). If the quilt costs $100 and the raffle ticket costs $1, a risk-neutral decision maker would value the chance of winning the quilt and the cost of paying for the ticket equally if the chance of winning the quilt were one in a hundred. A risk-neutral decision maker would be making a rational choice whether or not he or she would buy a raffle ticket with this chance of winning. Given the same chance of winning the quilt, a risk-averse decision maker would not be expected to buy a raffle ticket while a risk-acceptant decision maker would be expected to buy a raffle ticket.

Economists have known for even longer that a person values a $100 increase in wealth differently depending on how much wealth the person had to begin with. In particular, a wealthier person values the increase less than a poorer person. Beyond this standard use in economics, risk aversion and risk acceptance are not generally used in rational-choice models.

Prospect theory has gained currency across many disciplines. There are more than 3,200 citations in scholarly journals alone to Kahneman and Tversky's initial article outlining its principles. These range across all disciplines of the social sciences and include citations in business, biology, and medical journals. As one would imagine for so broadly applicable an idea, prospect theory has several things to say regarding public opinion. First, inflating low probability events gives insights into particular **question-wording effects** (*see also* **Issue Framing**). Imagine two questions that are substantively identical: "Would you be willing to adopt a proposed policy if it has a ninety-five percent chance of succeeding?" and "Would you be willing to adopt a proposed policy if it has a five percent chance of failing?" Given that the two statements ask exactly the same question, we might expect identical answers. However, prospect theory tells us that we should expect a higher affirmative response rate to the first question than to the second. While the policy is likely to succeed, respondents inflate its chances of failing when presented with the second formulation and, therefore, subjectively reduce its chances of succeeding. Thus, respondents presented with the second way of wording the question are more likely to say no to adopting the policy.

Changing the frame also affects decisions. Given two more questions of "Would you be willing to adopt a policy if it has a ninety-five percent chance of failing?" and ". . . if it has a five percent chance of succeeding?," we expect a lower affirmative **response rate** to the first than to second. Because the policy is more likely to fail, we are placing the respondent into a losses frame. Again, respondents inflate the small probability in the second phrasing, but this now means that they subjectively reduce the policy's chances of failing. Thus, more respondents would say yes to the second way of wording the question.

The second insight of prospect theory for public opinion is that it also helps us make sense of how individual-level economic circumstances affect opinion. If a respondent's economic circumstances have deteriorated over the previous year, he or she is in a losses frame. Being in a losses frame, the respondent is more likely to show support for a change in policy or incumbent compared with a respondent whose economic circumstances have improved over the previous year. This second respondent is in a gains frame and is more likely to support an incumbent in an election and less likely to support major changes to existing policy.

The third insight is that the flexibility of politicians is partially constrained by mass public opinion. Following from the second point above, if there is an economic downturn, the bulk of the public will be in a losses frame and more amenable to policy change. This gives politicians an opportunity to change a policy that under better economic times may have been untouchable. Reversing the usual adage, the public demands that "if you fix it, it had better be broke." Further, a leader who does not try some policy change when times are bad will likely find himself or herself out of a job. This circumstance prompts risky behavior on the part of leaders that they might not otherwise attempt; maintaining the status quo is no longer an option. Thus, the frames of both the public and the leadership are based on economic circumstances. This affects a leader's willingness to adopt a potentially harsh policy and the public's willingness to give the leader's policy time to work.

This last insight helps explain the defeat of Herbert Hoover by Franklin Delano Roosevelt in the 1932 presidential election. Given the collapse of the stock market in October 1929 that precipitated the massive unemployment of the Great Depression, the vast majority of the American public was thrown into a losses frame. In response to this, prospect theory predicts a greater tolerance by the public for untested policies and a greater likelihood that leaders will try risky policies. Indeed, Hoover did start the process of expanding the role of the national government by convincing Congress to fund public works projects. The bulk of the public, however, did not perceive benefits from Hoover's new policies and, so, remained in a losses frame by the time of the presidential election. Roosevelt's victory was thus partially a result of Hoover not being daring enough in his attempts to pull the country out of the Depression.

Prospect theory also helps explain the difference between Roosevelt's energetic economic reforms and his dearth of reform in **civil rights**. In terms of the economy, Roosevelt showed the daring that Hoover did not. This included attempting some policies that either failed (such as the National Recovery Administration) or met too much political resistance to be implemented. With respect to civil rights, Roosevelt benefited too much from the support of Southern Democrats. Thus, Roosevelt himself was in a gains frame along the civil-rights issue while African Americans were in a losses frame. Because African Americans were only a fraction of Roosevelt's coalition, he felt no compulsion to push for "risky" civil-rights legislation that would only serve to break his winning coalition.

The interaction between public perceptions and leader reactions suggests that prospect theory may be useful beyond the level of the individual decision. A growing body of literature in international relations examines foreign policy decision making from a prospect theory perspective. This has included reconstructing the frame of a national leader and the leader's closest advisers from historical evidence for a particular foreign policy decision. The frame is reconstructed to account for public opinion reactions, the level of threat perceived by the decision makers from the foreign adversary, and the chances of success (objectively and subjectively weighted) of alternative policies that were discussed by the group. The reconstructed frame—now in terms of gains or losses—is then used to understand why the group chose the policy that it did.

The collective decision making of a group has also been studied experimentally in which the group decision is how risky a gamble to take. These experiments vary the number of people in the group who are in each frame and then have them vote on which gamble to take. Generally, the more people who are in a losses frame, the riskier the collective decision ends up being. As one might expect, if those in a losses frame are in a minority while those in a gains frame are in the majority, the risk-taking propensity of the minority tends to be overridden by the more conservative (risk averse) majority.

Further Reading

Berejikian, Jeffrey D. "A Cognitive Theory of Deterrence." *Journal of Peace Research* 39 (March 2002): 165–83. The beginnings of a strategic theory incorporating key concepts of Prospect theory.

Farnham, Barbara, ed. *Avoiding Losses/Taking Risks: Prospect Theory and International Conflict*. Ann Arbor: University of Michigan Press, 1994. A collection of articles applying Prospect theory to foreign policy decision making.

Kahneman, Daniel, and Amos Tversky. "Prospect Theory: An Analysis of Decision under Risk." *Econometrica* 47 (March 1979): 263–91. The original exposition of Prospect theory, including a summary of experimental problems and results on which the theory is based.

Levy, Jack S. "Prospect Theory, Rational Choice, and International Relations." *International Studies Quarterly* 41 (March 1997): 87–112. A critical review of the absence of Prospect theory concepts in the rationalist literature in international relations, emphasizing the potential for synergy between Prospect theory and game theory.

Weyland, Kurt Gerhard. *The Politics of Market Reform in Fragile Democracies: Argentina, Brazil, Peru, and Venezuela.* Princeton, NJ: Princeton University Press, 2002. Presents the argument, backed by case-study evidence, that leaders sometimes make risky policy choices that they otherwise would not when confronted with an economic downturn.

Christopher K. Butler

Proxy Respondent

A proxy respondent is someone who is not the requested target but answers the survey on behalf of that person. For example, when an interviewer calls for John Smith, Sue Smith answers the phone and John Smith is not available. The interviewer might ask questions of Sue Smith about John Smith. This makes Sue Smith the proxy respondent for John Smith. Proxy responses are most often accepted when the target subject is incompetent or unavailable for the survey interview. By allowing proxy responses, survey organizations may reduce the cost of data collection and achieve better **response rates**.

There are two types of proxy respondents. The first type of proxy respondent is a household informant—any responsible adult member of a household who provides answers about all the eligible members of the household (including himself or herself). This can be found in the Current Population Survey in the United States and the Labor Force Survey in the United Kingdom. The second type is "standard proxy" respondents (Moore 1988). These are the people who answer only for the target subjects, because the targets are unable (e.g., hospitalized patients) or incompetent to respond for themselves (e.g., seven-year-old children). Standard proxy respondents are also commonly used in surveys, such as National Health Interview Survey, National Immunization Survey, and National Crime Victimization Survey in the United States.

One way to explain the differences between self- and proxy responses is to examine the cognitive processes involved in answering survey questions (*see* **Response Process**). There are possible differences in each of the five cognitive components: encoding, comprehension, retrieval, judgment, and communication. Survey respondents appear to take systematically different routes when they are answering for other people.

First, prior to the survey, respondents need to have encoded the relevant information. The information that self- and proxy respondents encode is different in terms of the amount and type. Self-respondents typically have abundant and detailed first-hand information coming directly from their own experience. By contrast, unless the experience is shared, proxy respondents are privy only to partial, second-hand information. This generally leads proxies to rely on inferences and uneducated guesses when answering questions about other people. One common exception may be a mother who is primarily engaged in the children's health care; she is likely to have a greater amount of information about her child's health status than her child may.

Schwarz and Wellens (1997) argue that self- and proxy respondents use systematically different types of information to form responses. Self-respondents have detailed information about their own actions/behaviors and are able to recall them directly. This information is very specific and situational, which makes it flexible and dynamic. Proxy respondents simply use information from observable attributes of the target subjects because the targets' actions are not the focus of the proxy's attention unless the action is jointly taken. Proxies often estimate or make inferences about the target's actions from their dispositional characteristics. Thus, proxy reports tend to be stable over time and predictable. However, this stability does not necessarily result in higher information quality because self-reporters are much more able to take into account the dynamic states that cannot be easily observed, such as internal health conditions and personal beliefs.

The second step in responding to a survey is question comprehension. Self-respondents understand the question in one way as they are evaluating only themselves. However, proxy respondents may comprehend the same question in their own various ways with different intentions. For example, the educational attainment in "what is the highest educational attainment of your husband?" may be interpreted differently than in "what is your highest educational attainment?" and in "what is the highest educational attainment of your mother-in-law?" It is impossible to know how comprehension will be influenced in proxy responses as we often do not know in advance who will answer for the subject.

Third, self- and proxy respondents retrieve memories or knowledge relevant to the question differently. A self-respondent's own state or viewpoint is more salient than that of another. Due to the limited amount of information available, proxies are much more likely than self-respondents to experience difficulties in retrieving appropriate information from which to make a judgment about the target person's state or view. In addition, motivational differences between self- and proxy respondents may exist. Because they have less information available, proxy respondents use estimation much more frequently than do self-respondents; estimation requires less effort than do judgments based on action-led recall. Survey respondents are viewed as cognitive misers, as they are unwilling to make a full cognitive effort in survey interviews and provide only **satisficing** answers. When they have to answer for someone else, this trend is likely to be higher, as they are less motivated. Proxy respondents, therefore, may provide quick and easy answers simply to satisfy the request.

The fourth stage is the formulation of the judgment called for in the question. As proxy respondents are more likely to exert only minimal effort to meet the survey requirements, answers from proxy respondents will be more affected by easy-to-use heuristics than are answers from self-respondents.

The last component, communication of the answer, often involves filtering as a way of editing the judgment. Social desirability plays a role in this step. Survey respondents may be hesitant about giving a true answer that might embarrass them. This supports the use of proxy respondents; proxy informants may experience less self-presentation pressure and, thus, be more willing to reveal sensitive attributes of the target subjects.

The differences in the cognitive processes of self- and proxy respondents in surveys can be summarized in two ways. On the one hand, proxy respondents are expected to produce lower quality information than self-respondents. This is because (1) proxies, in general, have less information than self-respondents; (2) self- and proxy respondents rely on different information when carrying out the cognitive tasks required for survey interviews; proxies' information is from rather stable and observable traits, whereas self-respondents' information is from dynamic and specific information; and (3) proxies may not be as willing to perform intensive thought processes as are self-respondents and thus may provide heuristic-based or satisficing answers. Therefore, the use of proxy responses may weaken survey measurement. On the other hand, the prevalent tacit belief that the self-responses provide true values and that the differences between self- and proxy reports are proxy errors may be misleading. This belief may have been induced as researchers did not consider what was measured in surveys when examining proxy responses. In fact, surveys may achieve higher or equivalent information quality by interviewing proxy respondents than self-respondents, because (1) proxies are less subject to social desirability bias; (2) proxies have better knowledge about stable and observable attributes; and (3) the use of "knowledgeable experts" as proxies may yield more accurate answers than do self-respondents. For example, with long-term physical health conditions, care providers are more likely to provide less socially desirable, more stable, and more knowledgeable answers than are the targets themselves. Depending on the survey topics and the relative capabilities of the proxies, surveys may benefit from collecting data from proxy respondents.

The consistency of responses is often used as a measure of response quality. Reporting consistency is found to be stronger in proxy responses compared with self-responses, because proxy responses change less over time. This occurs because proxies retrieve information from stable and general traits of the target persons. It should be noted that the higher internal consistency of proxy responses does not mean higher data quality or greater accuracy of proxy respondents' memory; it merely indicates proxy respondents' reliance on the general and stable characteristics of the target. This may imply needs for some other measures than response consistency to assess response quality.

Past research comparing proxy and self-responses has been inconclusive. This failure to show a substantial difference between self- and proxy responses has been regarded as encouraging evidence for surveys that collect proxy responses. However, the failure to document self-proxy differences may stem from examining proxy respondents in an aggregate. Not all proxies are equivalent. The depth and breadth of shared information and viewpoints between the target and proxy are likely to vary dramatically depending on their social relationship, depending on whether the proxies are spouses, direct family members, relatives, roommates, care givers, or neighbors. In addition, the characteristics of the individual proxies, such as memory capability, affect the response quality.

The quality of proxy responses may vary in particular by social relationship between the proxy and target person. The degree of familiarity between the proxy and target may affect the accuracy of the answer. The closer the relationship is, the more accurate and consistent the information should be. For example, joint participation in some behaviors and frequent discussion about some issues may affect the convergence of self/proxy responses positively. Also, the difference between self- and proxy reports may be related to the relationship between the proxy and the target subject. It is likely that spouse proxies would give answers consistent with those of self-respondents. This may indirectly imply that other proxies do not have any information to rely on when making a judgment about the target's states. Likewise, the length of relationship can be another measure of the familiarity between a proxy and a target. The number of years living together, for example, appears to have a positive effect on the convergence of self- and proxy reports.

Memory capability of a respondent is also found to have an effect on the quality of reports. A common measure of the memory capability is the respondent's age. Age is negatively related to the proxy respondent's ability to recall and recognize. Elderly respondents are less able to retrieve memories and less likely to stay on the topic than younger respondents. However, one needs to be cautious because the effects of respondent age may be offset by the duration of the relationship. As respondents are older, the memory capability decreases, producing a lower response consistency; the length of relationship is likely to increase, producing a higher response consistency.

Proxies arrive at their answers differently from self-reporters. This is because, when answering surveys on behalf of someone else, proxies rely on less information and the information they use is likely to be more general. Proxies may also have less motivation to respond carefully than self-reporters. However, proxy responses may be less susceptible to social desirability biases and more accurate when the proxies are more knowledgeable about the subject matter than the targets. This calls into question the common assumption that self-respondents are always more accurate. Proxies themselves differ depending on their social relationship with the survey targets, their memory capacity, and possibly their demographic characteristics. Proxy responses are not homogeneous. The quality of proxy responses depends on the characteristics of information a survey seeks, the capability of the proxies, and the relationship between the proxies and targets.

Further Reading

Blair, J., G. Menon, and B. Bickart. "Measurement Effects in Self vs. Proxy Responses to Survey Questions: An Information-Processing Perspective." In *Measurement Errors in Survey*, edited by Biemer et al. New York: John Wiley, 1991.

Moore, J. C. "Self/Proxy Status and Survey Response Quality." *Journal of Official Statistics* 4 (1988): 155–72.

Schwarz, N., and T. Wellens. "Cognitive Dynamics of Proxy Responding: The Diverging Perspectives of Actors and Observers." *Journal of Official Statistics* 13 (1997): 159–79.

Sunghee Lee

Public Opinion. *See* Gender Differences in Public Opinion; Opinion Formation; Public Opinion and Public Policy; Racial Differences in Public Opinion; Religious Differences in Public Opinion

Psychology of Survey Response

The psychology of survey response refers to the cognitive processes involved in answering survey questions. From its beginnings, survey research has drawn on the work of psychologists, especially those who pioneered in the development of techniques for measuring attitudes (such as Louis Guttman and L. L. Thurstone). In addition, many well-known survey researchers (including George Gallup) were originally trained as psychologists. But over the past twenty-five years, the relationship between survey research and psychology has become even closer, as both psychologists and survey methodologists have attempted to apply concepts and methods from cognitive psychology and related disciplines to understand and address problems of survey methods. This intensified interdisciplinary collaboration grew out of a series of conferences beginning with one in England in 1979 that examined retrospective data in surveys and including one held in the United States entitled "Cognitive Aspects of Survey Methodology" that gave the movement its name (CASM). Several book-length treatments summarize the work carried out under the CASM banner and present detailed cognitive analyses of survey methods issues. Thus, the psychology of survey response has become a hot topic for survey methodologists over the past few decades.

Some classic papers in the literature of survey methods helped pave the way for this development. One was an article by Neter and Waksberg that examined reporting in a survey on household expenditures. Neter and Waksberg designed an experiment to tease apart the effects of several distinct sources of error in reports about home repair jobs. (The design of the experiment and the topic of the question were modeled on real questions and procedures used in the Consumer Expenditure Survey, a survey carried out by the U.S. Bureau of Labor Statistics.) They proposed a sophisticated model that distinguished three sources of errors in reports about the number and costs of home repair jobs. First, respondents could completely forget about repair jobs, leading to omission errors. Second, they could report jobs that were actually completed before the beginning of the period covered by the survey questions (the reference period), a type of error called telescoping. Finally, respondents might fail to mention jobs to avoid answering detailed follow-up questions about them and thus to reduce their overall level of response burden. Neter and Waksberg referred to this third problem as conditioning. Their experiment enabled them to assess the impact of each of these processes on the survey reports. They estimated, for example, that about 40 percent of the expenditures reported in the survey were reported in error due to telescoping. Subsequent methodological investigations by Bradburn, Cannell, Sudman, and others built on this pioneering work and examined the multiple sources of errors affecting reports about behaviors and other factual matters, such as consumer purchases and hospital stays.

With the advent of the CASM movement, psychologists and survey researchers began to develop more systematic theories about how people answer questions and, more specifically, how survey respondents formulate answers to questions in surveys. One influential model, originally proposed by Tourangeau and building on earlier work by Cannell and his colleagues, posits four main components of the survey **response process**:

1. Comprehension (interpretation of the question);
2. Retrieval (recall of relevant information from memory);
3. Judgment and estimation (use of material from memory to make the judgment or estimate called for in the question); and

    4. Reporting (formatting and editing the answer to fit the require-
       ments of the survey question).

In addition, it is often useful to take into account the processes through which
respondents interpret and store their experiences in memory—that is, their encoding of information. Each of these components can be further analyzed into
more detailed processes. For example, comprehension involves such processes as
identifying the focus and presupposition of the question, retrieving the meaning
of key terms, and understanding the intent of the question.

    Although it is natural to suppose that these components are generally carried
out in order (with people first encoding relevant experiences, then, having been
asked a question about them, interpreting the question, retrieving relevant facts,
combining these into a judgment or using them to make an estimate, and finally
reporting their answers), it is likely that components are often carried out simultaneously, that individual components may be short-circuited or omitted entirely,
or that respondents may backtrack to an "earlier" component after beginning a
"later" one.

    The cognitive analysis of **survey response behaviors** has proven useful because
it provides a coherent framework for understanding a large body of methodological findings, leads to new insights into survey measurement problems, and
has inspired some practical methods for reducing such problems. Researchers in
this area have done work on several methodological topics—including question
order effects, reports about behavioral frequencies, and response sets—that illustrate some of these benefits.

    Question-order effects refer to changes in the pattern of the answers because
of differences in the order of the questions. In one well-known example, respondents are less likely to endorse an item asking about **abortion** when the
women "is married and does not want any more children" when that item comes
immediately after one that asks about abortion when "there is a strong chance
of serious defect in the baby." Question order can alter the overall direction of
answers to a question (as with the abortion item), or it can affect the relationship between two items, heightening or lowering the correlation between them.
Similar phenomena are apparent in the literature on judgment, in which judgments of earlier stimuli can affects judgments of later ones. The cognitive analysis suggests that prior items in a survey questionnaire can affect how a later item
is interpreted, what specific memories it brings to mind, how respondents evaluate these memories, and how they map their judgments onto the answer categories. The literature on question order effects includes examples of each of these
mechanisms.

    Telescoping is a second topic where the cognitive perspective has helped shed
light on a long-standing methodological problem. As Neter and Waksberg noted,
telescoping involves errors in placing events in time and it can lead to substantial reporting errors. Researchers have proposed two main accounts for telescoping. According to one theory, telescoping is a product of a systematic
distortion in the perception and encoding of the passage of time. Perceived time
is distorted so that events generally appear more recent than they really are. Relative to the objective time line, subjective time is compressed. (The "psychophysical" functions relating objective stimulus dimensions to subjective

impressions of them often show such distortions.) The other major theory argues that memory for the timing of an event, like memory for other event details, simply becomes worse over time. As a result, the timing of the event becomes progressively more uncertain. Because of the greater uncertainty associated with the timing of events that happened near the beginning of the reference period, respondents are more prone to place such events incorrectly in time, judging some that occurred before the reference period to fall into the reference period. Because events that are incorrectly recalled as having occurred prior to the reference period will go unreported, the net direction of telescoping errors tends to be forward in time. Although both theories have some merit, the latter theory (sometimes referred to as the "variance" theory) seems to account for more of the evidence.

A third focus of CASM research has been reports about behavioral frequencies, questions that ask how often the respondent has used an Automated Teller Machine (ATM), visited the doctor, or eaten particular food items during a specified time period. This research indicates that respondents use several distinct routes in arriving at their answers. One strategy, called recall-and-count (or sometimes episodic enumeration), involves remembering individual episodes and then counting them up. A variation on this strategy involves making separate counts by different domains (visits to the family physician versus visits to other doctors). Another common strategy is called rate-based estimation. When people do something frequently and on a regular schedule, it may be easier for them to remember the pattern, including the typical rate, than the individual episodes. They can use the typical rate to estimate the total number of episodes during the reference period ("I visit the ATM every Wednesday and Saturday, or twice a week. For the past month, that would mean about eight times."). Two other strategies are to recall an exact tally of relevant events or to hazard a guess based on a vague impression ("Oh yeah, I do that pretty often—let's say, six times."). Researchers have examined what determines which strategy respondents use and how the strategy they choose affects the accuracy of their answers.

A final topic for research on the psychology of survey response has been response sets, the tendency for respondents to agree with every statement (acquiescence) or to give the same answer to every question (nondifferentiation). Krosnick has argued that these and other response problems reflect **satisficing**. Satisficing refers to the various shortcuts survey respondents take to produce answers that are just good enough to get through the questionnaire rather than answers that reflect their best efforts. Respondents may engage in strong forms of satisficing, in which they do not engage in retrieval of relevant information at all, or weaker forms, in which they carry out all four components of the response process but in a sloppy way. When respondents select the first acceptable answer they consider (rather than carefully weighing each possible response option), it is an example of weak satisficing and can produce response order effects. Picking the same answer category for every question in a battery of similar items is an example of strong satisficing.

The psychology of survey response remains a lively area for research. Recently, investigators have begun exploring new issues, such as the impact of visual presentation of the questions (in **mail surveys** and **Internet survey methods**), the processes governing the interplay between respondents and interviewers, and methods for getting respondents to pay more attention to the definitions and other instructions that often accompany survey questions. The cognitive perspective has had particular impact on the development and testing of survey questionnaires; survey researchers often carry out "cognitive" tests of draft survey questionnaires, which include special probes designed to reveal the cognitive processes involved in answering the questions. For the foreseeable future, this strand of methodological research is likely to continue to have a major impact on survey practice.

Further Reading

Krosnick, Jon. "Survey Research." *Annual Review of Psychology* 50 (1999): 537–67. Examines "satisficing" and response sets.

Sudman, Seymour, Norman Bradburn, and Norbert Schwarz. *Thinking about Answers: The Application of Cognitive Processes to Survey Methodology.* San Francisco: Jossey-Bass, 1996. A more introductory treatment.

Tourangeau, Roger, Lance J. Rips, and Kenneth Rasinski. *The Psychology of Survey Response.* Cambridge: Cambridge University Press, 2000. A thorough but advanced discussion of the topic.

Web Sites

The National Academy of Sciences Press has on online version of the report from the original "CASM" conference, available at http://books.nap.edu/books/POD234/html/index.html.

Roger Tourangeau

Public Opinion and Public Policy

The question of how much the preferences of the mass public influence the policy decisions of government is a crucial one for the study of public opinion and for democratic theory. This essay summarizes the principal methods and substantive findings to emerge from the extensive scholarly literature on the extent of correspondence between public opinion and public policy.

Attempts to measure the opinion-to-policy correspondence can be divided roughly into dyadic and collective. Dyadic studies are those in which the behavior of an individual decision maker (almost always a legislator) is correlated with some kind of measure of public preference in his or her constituency. The results of this research program strongly suggest that the key variable in responsiveness to constituency is the salience of the issue. Put differently, the more important an issue is to a legislator's constituency, the greater the relationship between constituency opinion and the legislator's decisions.

While dyadic analyses are important to our understanding of legislative behavior, they are inevitably limited in their ability to measure the actual extent of correspondence between public opinion and public policy for two reasons. First of all, legislators' individual votes on bills do not equal policy. It is quite possible that even if most representatives do what a majority of their constituents would wish, the resulting outcomes would not be what most of the public as a whole would wish. This is particularly possible in the complex world of American national politics with divided partisan control of government, powerful congressional committees, filibusters, presidential vetoes, equal representation of states in the Senate, and decisions made by judges and bureaucrats who lack identifiable elective or geographic constituencies. Second, dyadic analysis as usually conducted is sensitive only to those issues where mass preferences vary between constituencies. If public opinion is roughly the same in most districts (as is often the case), it can have little explanatory power for legislative behavior. Therefore, dyadic studies can tell us little about the extent of correspondence of mass opinion with actual policy.

Collective analyses of the relationship between public opinion and policy use actual policy decisions (e.g., laws passed) in comparison to measures of opinion. This has been done in several different ways. The first is similar to the dyadic approach in that it compares different parts of a larger system: for example, states within the United States. This has been done both by disaggregating national surveys to the state level and by using a simulation technique to make estimates of the distribution of public opinion for states or other units from national survey data. When studies such as these compare their public opinion measures with policy decisions, they generally find a positive relationship—though one that varies with the type of issue and other variables. While the results of this kind of collective analysis are of considerable relevance to the subject of public opinion as it relates to public policy, its utility for direct comparison is constrained by the limited number of issues that can be studied this way and by the need for geographic variation that faces dyadic analyses.

A rather straightforward method for measuring the correspondence between public opinion and public policy is to select a number of issues on which national survey data is available to determine the distribution of preferences. This can then be compared to the actual decisions, if any, of government to see what the relationship is. While this approach has been used on a small scale by a number of researchers, the major investigations at the U.S. national level have been performed principally by Alan Monroe.

Table 1 reports Monroe's overall findings, both for the whole period of 1960 through 1999 and for three temporal subsets. For simplicity, issues have been divided into those where the public majority favored a proposed change in public policy versus those where the majority favored maintenance of the status quo. The same categories were also used for the actual policy outcomes: that is, was the status quo maintained or did the proposed policy change occur. For each portion of Table 1 a percentage of "consistent" is reported; this is the proportion of cases in the table in which both the majority preference and the policy outcome were status quo or in which both were change. This figure therefore yields a direct measure of how much of the time public policy decisions were consistent with the preferences of the majority of opinion holders.

Overall, the finding is that policy decisions were consistent with public opinion on 56 percent of the issues. Before 1980 consistency was 63 percent, declining to 55 percent and 53 percent in the two decades following. Interestingly, opinion-to-policy consistency was noticeably higher for cases of foreign policy and defense, including the Vietnam War. Consistency was lowest for those cases involving questions of political reform. As is also apparent from the percentages in all of the parts in Table 1, there is a marked bias against change: that is, policy decisions are more likely to be consistent with majority preference on those issues where the public favors the status quo than when it wants a policy change.

Table 1. Majority Preference and Policy Outcomes

A. All Cases (1960–1999)

Policy Outcome	Majority Preference		
	Status Quo	Change	
Status Quo	76%	57%	Consistent = 56%
Change	24	43	
	100%	100%	
	N =537	843	

B. 1960–1979

Policy Outcome	Majority Preference		
	Status Quo	Change	
Status Quo	82%	49%	Consistent = 63%
Change	18	51	
	100%	100%	
	N = 125	202	

C. 1980–1991

Policy Outcome	Majority Preference		
	Status Quo	Change	
Status Quo	70%	55%	Consistent = 55%
Change	30	45	
	100%	100%	
	N = 230	336	

D. 1992–1999

Policy Outcome	Majority Preference		
	Status Quo	Change	
Status Quo	80%	64%	Consistent = 53%
Change	20	36	
	100%	100%	
	N = 182	305	

Source: Alan D. Monroe, "Public Opinion and Public Policy 1960–1999." Prepared for delivery to the American Political Science Association, San Francisco, August 30–September 2, 2001.

Since the public is usually more likely to favor the change alternative (in 61 percent of the cases overall), opinion-to-policy consistency is necessarily constrained. Analysis of this phenomenon within types of policy reveals that where the bias is the greatest (political reform), consistency is the lowest, while where bias is lower (such as foreign policy), consistency is higher. This pattern, as well as the history of particular cases, suggests that a major reason why government in the United States does not act more frequently in agreement with public preferences is the difficulty in making major policy changes, even when those proposals have the support of both political leaders and the mass public. Among the other findings of this research is that opinion-to-policy consistency is somewhat higher for those issues that are more salient to the public and that consistency was higher when the public favored an ideologically liberal position. Also, of course, the larger the size of the majority, the more likely that policy was to be consistent with it.

The other method for investigating the relationship between mass preferences and national policy decisions for a large number of specific issues looks at whether the direction of change in public opinion is the same as the direction of change in public policy. This requires the availability of survey items that ask exactly the same policy question at two or more points in time. While this method has been used by several researchers, the most important investigation has been that by Benjamin Page and Robert Shapiro, who found more than 600 such issues from 1935 through 1979, though only 357 displayed significant enough change in public opinion to be used in the analysis. They found that policy changed in the same direction as public opinion only 43 percent of the time. However, this was due, in part, to the fact that frequently there was no change in policy and sometimes policy was already in agreement with public opinion. When the analysis was limited to those instances where there was policy change, the change in policy was congruent with the change in public opinion on 66 percent of the issues. When these data were analyzed in the majoritarian fashion used by Monroe, consistency between public opinion and public policy was 68 percent.

Among Page and Shapiro's other findings is that congruence between opinion and policy changes is greater on more salient issues. However, there was no significant difference in congruence between domestic and foreign policy questions. They also found that congruence was greater when the change in public opinion was in a liberal, rather than a conservative, direction (*see* **Liberalism and Conservatism**). Finally, the greater the magnitude of the change in public preference, the greater the likelihood of congruent opinion change.

A final method of analysis called "dynamic representation" uses a measure of the relative liberalism of the public mood over time as a measure of public preference. The most important use of this approach has been by Robert Erikson, Michael MacKuen, and James Stimson, who investigated the relationship between the ideological "mood" of the U.S. public and a number of summary measures of public policy over four decades. They found impressive evidence of correlation between shifts in public opinion and policy not only overall but also for actions taken by the president, both house of Congress, and the Supreme Court. It must be noted, of course, that this method does not yield findings about opinions or policy decisions on specific issues.

All of the research discussed above and almost all of the many smaller studies show that there is some relationship between public opinion and public policy, though a far from perfect one. It is less clear that public opinion is the causal variable in this relationship, though the evidence seems to be that it usually is. About the only variable that might affect the relationship for which there is general evidence is salience: that is, the more salient an issue is to the public, the more likely policy is to be in agreement with public preferences.

As to future research, it appears that no single research strategy can provide a complete answer to the question of how much public opinion influences public policy. But as the several methodological approaches are expanded in their coverage of time, geography, and issues, the picture should become clearer. More attention is needed to the role of linkage variables, particularly interest groups. There are few studies of the opinion-to-policy relationship outside the United States, but given the greater availability of reliable survey data around the world in recent years, it may be possible to make cross-national analyses, thus allowing for the role of political system variables.

Further Reading

Burstein, Paul. "The Impact of Public Opinion on Policy: A Review and an Agenda." *Political Research Quarterly* 56 (March 2003): 29–40. An extensive review and analysis of opinion-to-policy research in the United States and other nations.

Erikson, Robert S., Michael B. MacKuen, and James A. Stimson. *The Macro Polity.* Cambridge: Cambridge University Press, 2002. The most complete presentation of the dynamic representation approach.

Monroe, Alan D. "Public Opinion and Public Policy, 1980–1999." *Public Opinion Quarterly* 62 (Spring 1998): 6–28. The largest study of consistency between public opinion and public policy.

Page, Benjamin I., and Robert Y. Shapiro. "Effects of Public Opinion on Policy." *American Political Science Review* 77 (March 1983): 175–90. The major study of congruence between change in public opinion and public policy.

Alan D. Monroe

Public Opinion Polling. *See* **Presidential Use of Public Opinion Polling**

Public Policy. *See* Public Opinion and Public Policy

Push Poll

A push poll is a telemarketing technique in which respondents are presented with offensive or damaging statements about political candidates or issues under the guise of assessing how such information affects preferences. They are not designed to measure opinions, but to boost the prospects of a competing candidate or policy by creating a negative impression of their counterparts. In the process, though, such unethical tactics undermine the public's faith in legitimate polling and promote cynical views about politics.

Push polls do not take a single form, but typically possesses certain features. Push polls are usually short, taking no more than five minutes to complete. The interviewer rarely identifies the sponsor of the poll or any other identifying information. The questions typically contain extremely one-sided or loaded statements. The survey does not solicit demographic information about the respondents, such as their age, race, income, and education, that might be used to understand their choices.

Most push polls are conducted in the last two weeks of a campaign, when they will have the greatest impact. Late in a campaign, candidates are the most vulnerable to negative revelations about them because they have little time to explain or refute the charges.

An example of a push poll appeared in a column entitled "Progress in Campaign Reform," by Waldo Proffitt for the *Sarasota Herald Tribune* on February 23, 1997:

> Caller: Are you planning to vote in the Smith-Jones race for senate?
> You: Yes
> Caller: And whom do you plan to vote for?
> You: Jones
> Caller: Tell me if your vote would be affected definitely, possibly or not at all if you knew that Jones had been charged with passing bad checks?
> You: Uh, possibly
> Caller: And, if you knew that Jones had been arrested for drunken driving? Would that affect your vote definitely, possibly or not at all?
> You: Oh, definitely
> Caller: Thank you very much. We appreciate you taking the time to help us.

For those who indicated they were voting for Smith, they would not have received the questions. Instead, the caller would have thanked the respondent and hung up. Typically, calling of this nature would continue until the news media or someone supporting the targeted candidate exposed the activity, thereby generating negative publicity for the sponsor and forcing the sponsor to cease and desist.

As this example suggests, though, it is often difficult to determine if a question is a push poll or an honest effort to assess candidate preferences. There is a fine line between the two. Many media polling organizations use questions to get at whether a candidate's belief about an issue or a candidate's behavior will make them more or less likely to vote for that candidate. Take for example a February 2002 *Los Angeles Times* poll. During the campaign leading up to the California primary for governor, the committee to support the Democratic incumbent governor, Gray Davis, ran a television ad showing that Richard Riordan, one of the Republican candidates, said that abortion is murder. To test public reaction to this negative advertisement, the *Los Angeles Times* poll asked the following question about Riordan's position on abortion:

> As you may know, Gray Davis' campaign has been running ads showing Richard Riordan being interviewed by a reporter in the early 1990's about his views on abortion. In the ad, Riordan says that he considers abortion to be murder. However, in spite of his beliefs about abortion, Riordan says he strongly believes in a woman's right to choose. Based on what you just heard, does that make you more likely

to vote for Riordan for governor, or less likely, or does that not affect your vote one way or the other?

The results showed that more than half of the voters said they were not affected by this ad, 13 percent were more likely to vote for Riordan for governor, while 25 percent said less likely. Even though the question contains negative statements, it is not a push poll question. It gives the voters both sides of the story, claiming that Riordan said abortion was murder, while asserting that he still believes in a woman's right to choose. It does not single out Riordan but was part of a series of questions about all the candidates running for governor. The interviewer, moreover, was upfront about the source of the poll, identifying the sponsor (the *Los Angeles Times*) at the outset.

Allegations of push polling have become increasingly common during recent election campaigns for all levels of public office in the United States, including the presidency, Congress, state legislatures, and state initiative campaigns. For instance, Bob Dole and Steve Forbes accused each other of financing push polls during the 1996 Republican presidential primary campaign. Dole was charged with calling voters in Iowa and New Hampshire asking if they would be more or less likely to support Forbes if they knew that Forbes was pro-choice and backed President Clinton's decision to allow gays in the military (which was untrue). Meanwhile, the Forbes campaign allegedly contacted voters in competitive areas asking questions regarding Dole's vote to fund a $6.4 million ski resort in Idaho and an $18.4 million subway for senators to get from their offices to the Capitol.

Charges of push polling have been made in numerous other high profile races, including the 2000 Republican primaries between candidates George W. Bush and John McCain, the 2000 New York senate race between Hillary Clinton and Rick Lazio (and before him Rudy Giuliani), the 2001 New York mayoral campaign between Michael Bloomberg and Herman Badillo, and the 2001 special election in Massachusetts' 9th congressional district to replace longtime Congressman Joseph Moakley—just to name a few. In each case, the candidates accused of conducting push polling adamantly denied any wrongdoing.

Push polling is problematic for a number of reasons. First, push polling damages the electoral process. It harms candidates and their chances by affecting the decision calculus of voters. If the press publishes the results, or even the accusations of push polls, it can provide a flawed or biased picture of the race, changing the nature of the campaign.

Second, push polling adversely affects the tenor and character of election campaigns and adds to the rampant negativism of modern politics. One charge typically invites another, and before long accusations, rather than issues, dominate a campaign.

Finally, push polling calls into question legitimate polling. The public often cannot distinguish between them, which potentially leads to an aversion to participate in polling altogether. Scholars have speculated that pushing polling has contributed to declining **response rates**.

In light of such problems, many state legislatures have tried to pass legislation banning or at least limiting the use of push polls. Currently, West Virginia is the only state that completely restricts push polls. Unfortunately, the law is difficult to enforce because it lacks standards for determining the intent of a poll's sponsor. Push polling is not illegal as long as there is some truth to the questions or they avoid actually declaring such charges are true. In the aforementioned example, the interviewer does not say that Jones was charged with passing bad checks or was even arrested for drunk driving. It was a hypothetical question but was clearly intended to leave the impression that Jones actually performed these acts.

As a result of this difficulty, several other states have passed legislation to try to deal directly or indirectly with features of push polling. For example, Florida passed legislation that requires anyone making a telephone call in favor of or against a candidate or issue to identify the sponsor of the call. Such measures, though, are difficult to prosecute swiftly, leaving ample time for thousands of individuals to be contacted.

Further Reading

Fox, Jonathan S. "Push Polling: The Art of Political Persuasion." *Florida Law Review* (1996): 563–628.

Sabato, Larry J., and Glenn R. Simpson. *Dirty Little Secrets: The Persistence of Corruption in American Politics*. New York: Random House, 1996.

Streb, Matthew J., and Susan H. Pinkus. "When Push Comes to Shove: Push Polling and the Manipulation of Public Opinion." In *Polls and Politics: The Dilemmas of Democracy*, edited by Michael A. Genovese and Matthew J. Streb. New York: SUNY Press, 2004.

Traugott, Michael W., and Mee-Eun Kang. "Push Polls as Negative Persuasive Strategies." In *Election Polls, the New Media, and Democracy*, edited by Paul J. Lavrakas and Michael W. Traugott. New York: Chatham House, 2000.

Susan H. Pinkus

Q

Question-Answer Sequence

A question-answer sequence is the series of all verbal utterances by interviewer and respondent in a face-to-face or telephone survey interview, starting with a scripted question and ending with the next one. Generally, a distinction is made between paradigmatic and nonparadigmatic sequences. A paradigmatic sequence (also called a straightforward sequence) consists of the interviewer posing the question as worded in the questionnaire, followed by an adequate answer of the respondent. The interviewer may close the sequence with repeating the answer or saying something like okay. Nonparadigmatic sequences deviate in one or another respect from the paradigmatic one; the question posed may deviate from the scripted one, the answer may not be adequate, the respondent may ask for repetitions or clarifications, and so on. The study of question-answer sequences is usually confined to standardized survey interviews. In open interviews it does not make much sense to talk about deviations or paradigmatic sequences.

The study of question-answer sequences serves a number of purposes. First, deviations from paradigmatic sequences indicate how the question design can be improved. For example, if the interviewer often deviates from the scripted question, this may signify that the question is not very well formulated (*see* **Question-Wording Effects**). Frequent requests by the respondent to elucidate a question suggest that particular concepts used in the question are ambiguous. Inadequate answers (e.g., the respondent gives an answer that does not belong to the set of response alternatives) can be used to improve the formulation of the alternatives. Second, nonparadigmatic sequences inform the researcher about the quality of the eventual data. For example, if an answer is inadequate, the interviewer may probe in a suggestive way or even fill in a score based on the inadequate answer. Third, the study of question-answer sequences yields information about how interviewer training can be improved.

Consider the following question-answer sequence from a telephone interview ("I" means interviewer, "R" respondent):

> I: And what is your age, if I may ask?
> R: I'm retired.
> I: Okay.

Actually the interviewer typed "sixty-five" on her computer. First, the question-answer sequence suggests that a better question might be to ask for the year of birth of the respondent, for the very simple reason that an inadequate answer to such a question is less likely. Second, it is quite likely that the eventual score ("sixty-five") is an invalid one. Third, the sequence clearly shows that much can be gained from better interviewer training or interviewer instructions: interviewers should be taught how to recognize inadequate answers and how to correct them. Analyses of question-answer sequences show that more than 50 percent of the question-answer sequences are nonparadigmatic, whereas in 25 to 40 percent of the cases, the eventual score is at least doubtful.

The study of question-answer sequences can take either a more quantitative or a more qualitative approach. The quantitative approach essentially means that all utterances are coded, that is, assigned to a particular category. In the example above, the three utterances might be categorized and coded as: adequate question (AQ), inadequate answer (IA), and interviewer closes sequence (CS), respectively, thus yielding the coded sequence AQ, IA, CS. Given a large number of question-answer sequences coded this way, the occurrence of particular codes can be related to preceding codes, and/or characteristics of questions, interviewers, etcetera.

The quantitative approach originated in the late 1960s from the study of interviewer behavior to monitor interviewer performance: e.g., how often interviewers deviate from the scripted question or how often they probe in a suggestive manner (*see* **Interviewer Performance Measures**). Elaborate coding schemes were developed to account for various kinds of such deviations. These schemes were soon complemented with various codes for respondent behavior, as it soon became apparent that respondent behavior could equally affect the quality of the eventual data. The next step, starting in the 1980s, was studying the dependencies between interviewer and respondent behavior. To this end, use is made of sequential analyses, based on the transition probabilities between successive codes. A typical analysis is a so-called interaction tree: given a particular utterance of the interviewer (e.g., a question posed as scripted), what kind of action by the respondent occurs next (an adequate answer, an inadequate answer, a request for elucidation); what kind of interviewer behavior occurs next; and so forth. As an example, Figure 1 shows an interaction tree, with transition probabilities of a particular utterance, given the preceding path.

For reasons of intelligibility, short descriptions of the utterances are used instead of codes. For example, given that the question is read as scripted and the respondent gives an inadequate answer, chances are 17 percent that the interviewer probes adequately, but 43 percent that she probes in a suggestive manner (figures are fictitious). In addition, one can calculate whether such percentages occur above or below chance expectations. The study of such de-

Figure 1. Example of an Interaction Tree

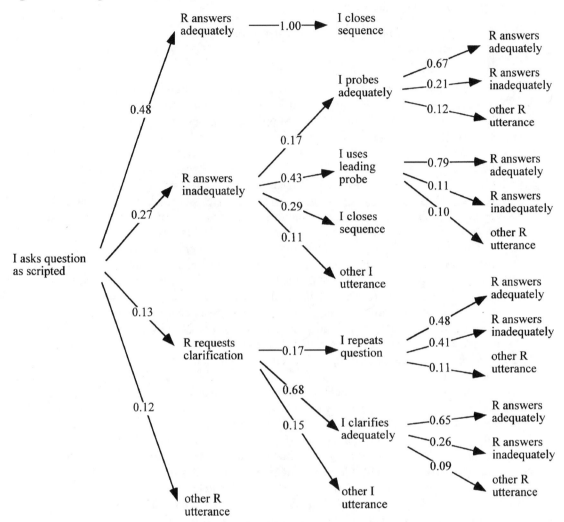

pendencies shows that most interviewer deviations are caused by respondent deviations. For example, suggestive probing by the interviewer is typically preceded by an inadequate answer of the respondent.

   To obtain coded question-answer sequences, a number of different strategies are used. First, utterances can be coded directly during the interview, usually by an observer, but sometimes even by the interviewer herself. A prerequisite is that the coding scheme consists of only a very limited number of categories. Second, interviews can be taped and then coded by listening to the tapes afterward. Third, taped interviews can be transcribed first, with the transcription coded subsequently. A main drawback of the quantitative approach is that to generalize findings, quite a lot of question-answer sequences have to be coded—concerning different interviewers, different questions, and different surveys—and coding is a very tedious and time-consuming job.

The qualitative approach, or conversation analysis, usually analyzes a limited number of question-answer sequences. The goal is not so much to generalize findings, but rather to understand the complexity of the interaction, the different roles interviewer and respondent can take and how this affects the eventual responses. A key concept is the frame of reference of interviewer and respondent, both with respect to their respective roles and with respect to the meaning of particular questions. The interviewer may adopt the frame of reference of the researcher by asking a number of standardized questions and expecting standardized answers, like selecting one of the proposed response alternatives. The respondent, however, may expect to become engaged in a kind of common conversation and is not very inclined to confine himself or herself to just give standardized answers. Careful study of transcribed question-answer sequences can reveal the nature of such differences in the frame of reference. In the example given above about the respondent's age, the respondent's answer "I'm retired" clearly shows differences in the frame of reference between the respondent and the researcher, whereas the interviewer apparently both adapts to the frame of reference of the respondent (because she does not probe for an adequate answer) and the researcher (because she types "sixty-five" according to the format required by the researcher). Although the amount of question-answer sequences in the qualitative approach is usually much less than in the quantitative approach, it is often quite time consuming too—because question-answer sequences are usually fully transcribed, according to the conventions of conversation analysis, to account for a host of paralinguistic speech characteristics, like pauses, stutters, interruptions, and so on. Such paralinguistic speech characteristics (e.g., the time a respondent takes before giving an answer) are viewed essential for a correct interpretation of the interaction process. Here is an example of the way a question-answer sequence is transcribed using these conventions (where hh is an inbreath, (0.4) is the timed silence in seconds, : is a stretched word, and (gh) is gutturalness):

> I: hh (0.4) a:(gh)::nd what's your age if I may ask?
> R: m::: i'm retired
> I: hh_oh kay (gh)

The quantitative and qualitative approaches are certainly complementary. First, to develop meaningful coding schemes one should start with a qualitative analysis of question-answer sequences. Second, having established dependencies between codes, it is necessary to go back to the original transcripts to obtain insight about the underlying processes of such dependencies. The quantitative study of question-answer sequences is no longer solely directed toward detecting interviewer misbehavior. Conversation analysis has clearly showed that the eventual response is the result of a complex interaction between interviewer and respondent. Due to this insight, the quantitative analysis has moved from just counting deviations, to sequential analyses of successive coded utterances to disentangle these intricacies.

Further Reading

Bakeman, R., and J. M. Gottman. *Observing Interaction: An Introduction to Sequential Analysis*. Cambridge: Cambridge University Press, 1997. A must read for everyone who wants to perform more elaborate quantitative analyses.

Dijkstra, W. "A New Method for Studying Verbal Interactions in Survey-Interviews." *Journal of Official Statistics* 15 (1999): 67–85. Describes coding of question-answer sequences.

Houtkoop-Steenstra, H. *Interaction and the Standardized Survey Interview: The Living Questionnaire*. Cambridge: Cambridge University Press, 2001. Detailed analysis of interaction between interviewers and respondents in standardized survey interviews, applying techniques of conversation analysis.

Maynard, D., H. Houtkoop-Steenstra, N. C. Schaeffer, and J. van der Zouwen, eds. *Standardization and Tacit Knowledge: Interaction and Practice in the Survey Interview*. New York: John Wiley, 2002. Covers both quantitative and qualitative approaches and provides an excellent overview of the field.

Wil Dijkstra

Question Interpretation

Question interpretation is one of several stages of cognitive processing during the course of answering a survey question (*see* **Response Process**). The stages included in most psychological models are question interpretation, memory retrieval, judgment, and response selection. Question interpretation is the process of comprehending what the question means. Memory retrieval is the process of accessing relevant information from memory that furnishes content to be included in the answer. Judgment processes evaluate and compare ideas during the course of converging on an answer. Response selection is the process of choosing an answer from a set of alternative options. The stage of question interpretation is particularly critical because the fidelity of all processing stages hinges on the correct interpretation of the question. Therefore, the task of revising questions to minimize interpretation problems is an important strategy for reducing measurement error.

Given that question interpretation is so critical, how do survey methodologists identify questions that are difficult for respondents to comprehend? There are several methods. One method is to have experts prescreen the items and identify particular problems with questions. There are checklists, rating scales, and other systematic analytical schemes for an experienced survey methodologist to use to spot potential problems with questions. A second approach is to conduct a pretest (*see* **Pretesting**) that collects verbal protocols from respondents as they answer questions. The content of these verbal protocols often exposes potential problems of question interpretation. For example, respondents might "think aloud," saying whatever comes to mind, while interpreting and answering a question. Alternatively, the survey expert might probe the respondent with specific questions, such as "What words, if any, are difficult for you?" "What parts of this question do you have trouble understanding?" or "Why is this question being asked on this survey?" Some problems with questions can be articulated by respondents in words, but other problems are invisible or are difficult to put into words for most people.

A third approach to identifying interpretation difficulties is to observe behaviors of the respondent that suggest the respondent is struggling with particular questions. For example, pauses, frowns, or requests for clarification ("Could you restate the question?" "What does that word mean?" or "Does part-time work count as employment?") are diagnostic signals that a respondent is having trouble understanding a question (*see* **Question-Answer Sequence**). A fourth approach is to develop a computer program that automatically identifies problems with questions according to theoretical models or empirical research. For example, there is a Web facility called QUAID (Question Understanding Aid) that critiques questions on potential comprehension problems that many respondents may encounter.

It is important to take stock of the different classes of question interpretation problems that frequently arise in surveys. One or more of the problems described below might arise and threaten the validity, reliability, or efficiency of a survey.

One frequent problem with questions is that there is a word that poses comprehension difficulties. Some words are technical terms that are unfamiliar to the respondent. For example, consider a patient who is completing an intake questionnaire for a dentist and encounters the question "Have you ever had a myocardial infarction?" Most respondents would not be aware that this is a type of heart condition, so the answer would have a high likelihood of being skipped or being answered incorrectly. Respondents are fairly good at identifying unfamiliar technical terms so most of these words can be detected during a pretest when a sample of participants provide think-aloud protocols.

Aside from unfamiliar technical words, there are many types of problematic words that most respondents do not identify as being difficult: for example, a word may be ambiguous, vague, or imprecise. An ambiguous word has two or more meanings. The word "bank" might refer to an institution that manages money or to the land alongside a body of water. Pronouns are often ambiguous, particularly the pronoun "it." Vague words are very common on surveys. A word is vague when it is not obvious to a respondent what referents (e.g., instances, cases, examples) fall under the umbrella of the word's intended meaning. Vagueness often results in a misalignment between the referents inferred by the respondent and the referents intended by the designer of the survey. For example, consider the question "How many members of your household work?" This question has several vague words, most of which would be missed by the vast majority of respondents. It could be argued that members, household, and work are all vague words. Who counts as being a member of the household? Does a grandparent who lives at the home only four months a year count? Does a live-in maid count? What falls under the category of household? Does a nanny living in the attic count? Do an uncle and aunt living in the garage apartment count? What if there are two homes? What counts as someone working? Does a part-time job count? If so, what if the person works only one hour per week? What if a person is not paid for the work they do? What if the person works but does not make Social Security payments? Vagueness is ubiquitous in most survey questions.

Relative terms that are imprecise present comprehension difficulties. The values of an imprecise relative term are not specified on an underlying quantitative continuum. Adverbs such as rarely or frequently are good examples. How frequent is "frequently"? How rare is "rarely"? It depends on the context of the question. The value of 10 would be considered frequent when it comes to consuming alcoholic drinks per day but rare when considering alcoholic drinks per year. Many adjectives are imprecise relative terms, such as large, happy, and attractive. Imprecise relative terms can be anchored by the survey designer to reduce the uncertainty. For example, in a survey of the consumption of alcoholic beverages the terms never, rarely, occasionally, and frequently could have values of 0, 1, 2 to 10, and 11 or more drinks per week.

A question has complex syntax if its grammatical composition is dense, has embedded phrases, is structurally ambiguous, or is not well-formed syntactically. A noun-phrase is syntactically dense if the main noun is modified by many adjectives and adverbs, such as "the regular monthly mortgage payment." The main noun is "payment," whereas the three modifiers are "regular," "monthly," "mortgage." A clause or sentence is dense if the set of words has many underlying ideas, propositions, qualifiers, or assumptions, such as "Approximately how many miles was it one way to the place you hunted small game most often in this state?" The syntactic composition is highly embedded when there are many clauses, prepositional phrases, and qualifiers before the main verb of the main clause occurs in the question. An example of embedded composition is: "At any time during the past 12 months, were you or any member of this household enrolled in . . . ?" The respondent has to hold sixteen words in short-term memory before the main verb (enrolled) is received.

Ambiguous syntactic structures occur when two or more syntactic structures can be assigned to a question: for example, "Is this house or apartment owned by you or someone in this household with a mortgage or loan?" It is ambiguous what "with a mortgage or loan" modifies. Does it modify owned or someone? In the case of garden-path questions, the respondent starts reading a question and assumes it has a certain syntactic structure but eventually realizes the structure is wrong and has to re-read the question from the beginning with a different syntactic structure. Consider the question "Did you know the owner of the apartment sold the property?" Most respondents start out interpreting this question as "Do you know the person who owns the apartment?" By the end of the sentence, the respondents realize that they were mistaken and reinterpret the question as "Did you know about the event of the property being sold?" This syntactic ambiguity could have been prevented by inserting the word "that," as in "Did you know that the owner of the apartment sold the property?"

Working memory is the immediate memory (or short-term memory) that holds information while the respondent is actively comprehending the question. Working memory is limited in capacity so it may be overloaded if the question requires the respondent to hold too much information in mind at the same time. Question interpretation suffers if the question imposes an overload on working memory. Dense and embedded syntax imposes a high load on working memory, as described in the previous question. Other sources of working-memory overload are extremely long sentences, sentences with many logical operators—or, and, not, if-then—and quantifiers.

Disjunctive expressions (which have or's) impose a high load on working memory because the respondent needs to keep track of different options and possibilities. When an "or" appears twice in a question, a two-dimensional mental table of possibilities needs to be constructed. The following sentence requires the respondent to keep track of six cells in a mental table: "During the past 12 months, how many times have you seen a doctor or other health care professional about your own health at a doctor's office, a clinic, or some other place?" When there are three or more or's in a question, there may be a combinatory explosion problem that severely overloads working memory.

Questions with quantifiers place a load on working memory because they require mental computations or the construction of precise referents. Mathematical computations are normally accomplished with the aid of pencil and paper or with some technological device, not in working memory. Mental mathematics taxes working memory, as in the question "Counting all jobs, how many hours did you usually work per week in 2000?"

Every question has a number of nouns and prepositions that constitute "presupposed" information. Presuppositions are assumed to be true or to exist; they are taken as "given." For example, the question "What year did you graduate from high school?" presupposes that the respondent did in fact graduate from high school. If the respondent never graduated from high school, it would be impossible to supply information about when the graduation occurred. Presuppositions can refer to people, places, entities, events, actions, and states. The question "What are the annual real estate taxes on this property?" presupposes that there are taxes. The question "What is the main reason you left this job?" presupposes the person left the job. It is appropriate to break down the questions into two or more questions when there are presupposition problems. The two questions would be "Did you leave this job?" and "If YES, why did you leave this job?"

Sometimes it is difficult for the respondent to ascertain what type of question is being asked. This occurs when the focus of the question is camouflaged in the item. For example, the following question appears on the 1040 Income Tax Form of the Internal Revenue Service: "_____ Qualifying widow(er) with dependent child (year spouse died _____)." This question functionally is two different questions: "Are you a qualifying widow(er) with a dependent child?" and "If you are, what year did your spouse die?" Another example question that appeared on a clinic intake form is "When was your last trip to the doctor and why did you visit?"—an amalgamation of two questions that should have been segregated. These amalgamated questions periodically occur on surveys in the real world even though they would normally be detected by a survey methodologist.

A more common problem is the respondent not understanding the purpose of the question. The respondent may not know why the question is asked. The question might appear out of the blue because the words and ideas in the question are not related to the previous questions on the survey. For example, one of the questions on the 1040 Income Tax Form of the Internal Revenue Service is: "Presidential Election Campaign Fund. Do you want $1 to go to this fund? _____ YES _____ No." A respondent might be confused about the purpose of the question because presidential campaigns are allegedly unrelated to paying taxes.

Sometimes the respondent infers motives behind the survey question that in truth has no correspondence to the actual goals of the survey. For example, the following question has appeared in some women's health clinics: "Did you have any unwanted sexual experiences over the past year?" The original purpose might be to track sexually transmitted diseases or spouse abuse in a community, whereas some respondents might incorrectly infer that the purpose of the questionnaire is to identify and prosecute prostitutes.

Sometimes the purpose of the question is unclear because the respondent would have little likelihood of having access to an answer. This occurs frequently when patients visit a clinic for the first time and are expected to fill out forms. Some of the questions are targeted for the patient, others for the receptionist, others for the insurance company, and yet others for the doctor. However, the patient has minimal knowledge of the purpose of the questions and who is the appropriate respondent. A cooperative receptionist might highlight the relevant questions for the patient in yellow, but there is no guarantee that the patient will be lucky enough to have a receptionist who is on the ball.

According to analyses of questionnaires designed by the U.S. Census Bureau, approximately one out of five questions suffer from one or more of the interpretation problems described above. The rate of problematic questions is substantially higher for surveys, forms, and questionnaires that are not prepared by the professional staffs of government agencies. Moreover, problems with question interpretation are much more prevalent in a multicultural and multilingual society, such as the United States. These challenges intensify the need for survey methodologists to prescreen, pretest, revise, and field test the questions that appear in surveys throughout our society.

Further Reading

Graesser, Arthur C., Katja Wiemer-Hastings, Roger Kreuz, Peter Wiemer-Hastings, and Kent Marquis. "QUAID: A Questionnaire Evaluation Aid for Survey Methodologists." *Behavior Research Methods, Instruments, and Computers* 32 (2000): 254–62. A computer facility on the Web that critiques questions on potential difficulties respondents might have interpreting the questions.

Schober, Michael F., and Fred G. Conrad. "Does Conversational Interviewing Reduce Survey Measurement Error?" *Public Opinion Quarterly* 60 (1997): 576–602. Evidence that clarifying the meaning of questions through conversation can improve the validity of the respondents' answers.

Schwarz, Norbert, and Seymour Sudman, eds. *Answering Questions: Methodology for Determining Cognitive and Communicative Processes in Survey Research.* San Francisco: Jossey-Bass, 1996. The chapters in this edited volume provide a comprehensive overview of the cognitive and social aspects of survey methodology.

Web Sites

The Web site of QUAID (Question Understanding Aid), a computer facility that critiques questions on potential difficulties that respondents will have interpreting the questions, available at http://www.psyc.memphis.edu/quaid.html.

Arthur C. Graesser

Question-Order Effects

Question-order effects refer to the tendency for responses to survey questions to be influenced by the context of the larger questionnaire in which they are asked. In most of the well-documented cases researchers have shown that responses to a given question can be significantly affected not merely by the actual content of a prior question, but more precisely by the respondent's answer to an immediately preceding question that is closely related in subject matter and has direct psychological implications for how the following question should be answered. Other well-controlled experiments have demonstrated that question-order effects can occur even when such closely related and affected questions are widely separated in the survey questionnaire as a preventive practice. Furthermore, we now know that question-order effects have occurred in self-administered **mail surveys** in which respondents have looked ahead at later questions in the questionnaire as a context for understanding and answering earlier questions, thus reversing the typical sequence for such effects. So the problem does not lend itself to easy practical solutions.

A classic example of a question-order effect documented and replicated extensively by Howard Schuman and his associates at the University of Michigan's Survey Research Center consisted of responses to the following pair of questions that were first experimented with at the dawn of the anticommunist era in the United States during the late 1940s:

1. Do you think the United States should let Communist newspaper reporters from other countries come in here and send back to their papers the news as they see it?

2. Do you think a Communist country like Russia should let American newspaper reporters come in and send back to America the news as they see it?

When the questions were asked in this sequence respondents were much more likely to say no to letting communist reporters into the United States to describe America to audiences in their home countries than when the questions were asked in the reverse sequence. Conversely, respondents were significantly more likely to say, yes to the idea of a country like Russia letting American reporters in to tell it as they see it back home when this was asked as the first question in the sequence.

This well-demonstrated order effect appears to be the result of several social-psychological elements. When the letting-in-the-communist reporters question is asked first, most U.S. respondents seem to answer no based on their general attitudes toward communism, which were predominantly negative at the time of the original experiments. Similarly when the letting-in-the-American reporters question comes first in the interview, most U.S. respondents appear to answer it in terms of their generally positive attitude toward freedom of the press and are more likely to say, yes to the idea. But when they are asked the second question, a norm of reciprocity kicks in and respondents therefore feel obligated, so the interpretation goes, to treat the American and communist reporters fairly and evenhandedly. Respondents thus become significantly more likely to say it is okay for the communist reporters to come over here and tell it like it is when they have just said in response to the previous question that it is okay for the American reporters to go over there and report back freely as they see it. Vice versa, they are significantly more likely to say no to letting the American reporters go over there if they have just said no to letting the communist reporters come in here in response to the prior question. An implicit be-consistent principle seems to rule the responses.

An example of a rather different type of question-order effect, involving contrast rather than consistency between responses to survey questions, shows up when respondents have been asked about their opinions on approving abortion under different circumstances: what has become known as the "abortion context effect." First discovered serendipitously by Howard Schuman and his associates at the University of Michigan and replicated numerous times since then, it arises when respondents are asked the following two questions in either this or the reverse order:

1. Do you think it should be possible for a pregnant woman to obtain a legal abortion if she is married and does not want any more children?

2. Do you think it should be possible for a pregnant woman to obtain a legal abortion if there is a strong chance of serious defect in the baby?

When the question about the married woman who does not want any more children is asked first, respondents are significantly more likely to say yes to an abortion—typically 10–15 percent more likely—than when it is asked after the question about abortion in the case of a serious birth defect. Responses to the birth defect question, however, do not appear to be affected by the sequence of the questions.

The bulk of the evidence to date suggests that this contrast effect in responses to the question about the married woman who does not want any more children occurs largely because this does not seem to be as good a reason compared with the far more traumatic circumstances of a woman facing the strong chance of a serious defect in the baby. The implicit negative-comparison hypothesis would appear to explain why this well-demonstrated order effect occurs among both those who approve of an abortion in the case of a birth defect and those who disapprove of it when asked about this situation as the first question in the sequence.

More prototypical examples of question-order effects in public opinion polls arise when respondents are asked ambiguous and vague questions about such things as their general happiness, their overall confidence in societal institutions, their overall approval of the president, and their general interest in politics (*see* **Question Interpretation**). A telling example comes from the work of the author and his associates at the University of Cincinnati triggered by the discovery of an unexplained drop in the public's attention to politics in the late 1970s as measured by trend data from the American National Election Studies (ANES). Suspecting that the drop was due to a change in the context in which the interest in politics question had previously been asked, the researchers simulated what happened by designing an experiment that varied the order of the following ANES questions:

1. Now, some people seem to follow what's going on in government and public affairs most of the time whether there's an election going on or not. Others aren't that interested. Would you say you

follow what's going on in government and public affairs most of the time, some of the time, only now and then, or hardly at all?

2. Do you happen to remember anything special that your U.S. representative has done for your district or for the people in the district while he has been in congress? (IF YES): What was that?

3. Is there any legislative bill that has come up in the House of Representatives on which you remember how your congressman has voted in the last couple of years? (IF YES): What bill was that?

When the questions were asked in this sequence respondents were noticeably more likely to say they followed what is going on in government and public affairs "most of the time" than when the sequence was reversed. When the difficult questions about congressional knowledge (typically 80–85 percent of respondents cannot answer them), were asked first, many respondents seemed to interpret the meaning of following government and public affairs more narrowly to mean following the activities of their congressman and their congressional district; this understanding lowered their estimate of how much attention they paid to it—replicating exactly what had happened accidentally in the ANES time series of the late 1970s. Even more troubling for the polling practitioner, the researchers also discovered that simply separating the question about attention to government and public affairs from the congressional-knowledge items by interspersing questions about unrelated subjects could not eliminate this context effect. It lasted throughout the entire interview.

Question order can thus complicate the task of making reliable and valid generalizations not only about the distribution of public opinion at any given point in time but more importantly about changes in public opinion over time. **Experiments** by Schuman and his colleagues have also shown that, even if the context of the questions is compulsively maintained as is, the researcher will not necessarily reach the same conclusions about a given trend—because the meaning of the context-generating question can itself change over time. Most pollsters, of course, are usually quite sensitive to the importance of keeping the wording of the questions they ask constant over time because they want to be sure that any trends they observe in public opinion are not the artificial result of a change in wording. But keeping the entire questionnaire and sequence of questions constant over time is quite rare and often impractical as new political and social issues continually emerge leading to frequent changes in the content and context of the questions. Many unknown question-order effects are probably "hidden" in the polling data archives maintained by such organizations as the **Roper Center for Public Opinion Research** at the University of Connecticut and by the Inter-University Consortium for Political and Social Research (ICPSR) at the University of Michigan. Furthermore, since questions about related subject matter are typically grouped together in a "block" for practical reasons, many such effects continue to go undetected if the pollster does not vary the order of the questions and analyze the results for potential effects. Though many practitioners today do rotate the order of at least some of their questions randomly or systematically, they generally assume that such rotations eliminate the problem as if it were all just a matter of random error. But this is simply wrongheaded because question-order effects produce systematic errors in the results and no amount of randomization or averaging of the data can eliminate such biases. The effects have to be rigorously assessed—and controlled for—in the analysis and reporting of the poll results.

Not surprisingly, explaining and predicting question-order effects in public opinion polls has turned out to be quite difficult. Initial attempts by Schuman and his associates focused on developing conceptual classifications of the various types of order effects that had been observed. The question-order effects produced by varying the sequence of questions about communist and American reporters were classified as an example of a "part-part" consistency effect. Such effects involve questions that are at the same level of specificity (communist and American reporters) and arise whenever respondents attempt to make responses to a subsequent question consistent with responses given to a previous question closely related in subject matter. The order effect generated by the sequencing of the abortion questions illustrate what Schuman and his associates called a "part-whole" contrast effect, which involves two or more questions, one of which is more general (e.g., abortion for a married woman who does not want any more children) and either subsumes or implies responses to the more specific question (e.g., abortion in the case of a potential birth defect). In this situation respondents appear to deliberately contrast their responses on the specific question to those given to the more general question whenever the specific-general sequence is used, but not when the reverse sequence is used. More recently, Tom Smith at NORC, has elaborated the classification of order effects into different types of causes and effects and categorized the various question-answering steps identified by cognitive social psychologists in recent years to understand the processes by which such effects occur: how respondents interpret questions, how they retrieve information from memory to answer the question, how they put all this information together to form a judgment, and how they fit or map their judgments onto the response categories provided by the questionnaire or interviewer to produce what pollsters call an opinion—and which when aggregated across a sample of individuals, generates what we typically call public opinion (*see* **Response Process**).

Promising as these theoretical developments have been, however, they have yet to produce much guidance for the practical pollster. Does knowing about such causes and effects, for example, cause one to design a questionnaire or interview schedule any differently than before knowing about them—or do any more redesign than simply varying the order of questions that seem closely related in subject matter and then analyze the possible consequences? The author's sense of all this research is that question-order effects arise largely, if not entirely, because of the general vagueness and ambiguity of the questions that are commonly asked in public opinion polls. As a consequence the order in which the questions are asked in a given questionnaire or interview often helps respondents interpret the meaning of such vague questions as well as the psychological intent of the questioner. It is this reduction in ambiguity that probably generates many, if not most, of the reported question-order effects. The practical implication here is that public opinion pollsters must get in the habit of writing and asking questions that are much more specific and concrete (e.g., abortion in the specific case of a birth defect) if they are to minimize the likelihood of unknown and unwanted question-order effects. This will often mean asking several more specific questions rather than one broad question. But like most other choices in designing public opinion surveys, there is always a trade-off between minimizing error—in this case measurement error—and the cost of data collection. No free lunch here either.

Further Reading

Schuman, Howard, and Stanley Presser. *Questions and Answers in Attitude Surveys*. New York: Academic Press, 1981. Chapter 2. Classic experiments on question form, wording, and context effects in public opinion surveys.

Schwarz, Norbert, and Seymour Sudman, eds. *Context Effects in Social and Psychological Research*. New York: Springer-Verlag, 1992. Multidisciplinary perspectives of question-order and context effects in surveys by social scientists and cognitive social psychologists.

Sudman, Seymour, Norman M. Bradburn, and Norbert Schwarz, eds. *Thinking About Answers*. San Francisco: Jossey-Bass, 1996. Chapters 4–5. Synthesis of cognitive social-psychological perspectives of the question-and-answer process in public opinion surveys.

Tourangeau, Roger, Lance J. Rips, and Kenneth Rasinski. *The Psychology of Survey Response*. New York: Cambridge University Press, 2000. Chapter 7. Psychological models of the question-and-answer process based on more than a decade of empirical research.

Web Sites

The Web site of the annual NORC General Social Survey includes a list of GSS methodological reports on question effects in surveys, including experiments on question order. At the Web site, http://www.icpsr.umich.edu/gss, click on "Reports." Also click on "Bibliography" to locate published studies of question-order and context effects.

George Bishop

Question-Wording Effects

Question-wording effects are differences in survey responses to the same concept due to minor variations in the phrasing of the question. They are capable of producing misleading conclusions about respondents' (and by extension, the target population's) actual positions. A variety of question types are particularly vulnerable to wording effects. Fortunately, techniques are available to identify them and to diminish their impact.

The Impact of Wording. Questions are measurement tools designed to capture respondents' true opinions, attitudes, or values. Although the choice of vocabulary is used to express the question, the meaning of the words may go well beyond it. Meaning may be derived from the inflection in the interviewer's voice, the education level of the respondent, the cultural or situational context surrounding the interview, or even recent idiosyncratic experiences of the respondent. Thus, the wording of a survey question may be the same for two respondents, but the meaning they derive may be quite different (*see* **Question Interpretation**).

Conversely, words may be different but convey the same meaning. For example, the questions "How old are you?" and "What is your age?" do not share a single word but the interpretation of the two questions is typically the same for everyone. The difficulty is identifying when wording variations may be conveying different meanings and when they do not.

Ideally, question wording would accomplish two tasks. First, the question wording would assess the concept it was designed to measure. In other words, a policy question would tap positions toward an initiative and not attitudes toward the president who introduced it or the symbolism potentially tied to its name. Moreover, everyone reading the question wording would interpret it uniformly. The meaning would be the same regardless of the characteristics of the respondents.

Sources of Question-Wording Effects. Previous research has identified a variety of question types particularly vulnerable to question-wording effects. Probably the most well known are questions that use symbolic language. Such questions contain value-laden words that provoke an affective reaction, which may be inconsistent with subjects' actual positions on the topic. For example, the term "welfare" has come to take on negative connotations in the United States, implying, for instance, programs designed to support individuals with a poor work ethic. Studies have shown that the public generally opposes welfare in general but tends to be highly supportive of programs that could justifiably be included under the rubric of welfare (e.g., government spending on assistance to the poor).

Second, wording effects have been demonstrated to occur with questions containing a normatively correct response. Certain questions tap behaviors or attitudes that possess response options that are widely frowned upon. Rather than choosing a response that might make them look bad, some people simply offer the socially acceptable response. Notable examples include "Did you vote?" or "Have you used illegal drugs?" Sometimes socially desirable responses are far more subtle. For instance, most Americans are uncomfortable with the outright banning of anything. A classic study showed that a proposed social policy that asked whether the United States should "forbid" a certain act received less support than a policy that did "not allow" that same act. "Forbid" evidently evoked a stronger emotional reaction (which some respondents could not tolerate) than did its less emotionally charged synonymous phrase "not allow."

Third, questions not specific enough can generate error. Vague questions can lead to alternative interpretations, rather than possessing a uniform meaning: for example, the question "How often do you exercise?" Some people may consider exercise to mean going to a health club or having a regular routine, such as running for thirty minutes, three times a week. This may be an enduring belief they picked up as a child or a temporary state of mind because they had just finished talking to a friend who maintains such a routine. They may answer "not very often" if they do not engage in these activities, even if they walk briskly to school or work every weekday and go bowling or ride their bicycles on most weekends. Others may answer "frequently" because they consider their walk from the car to their office during the week and their golf game on the weekend exercise. Different individuals give different meaning to the word "exercise." Without clarification of the meaning of the word (e.g., "by exercise, we mean engaging in an activity for at least 20 minutes where you are sweating, breathing heavily, or your heart rate is above 120 beats per minute") it is difficult to interpret the response.

Even seemingly straightforward questions can be vulnerable to alternative interpretations. For example, "What was your income for the calendar year 2002?" may not be interpreted uniformly because respondents with multiple sources of income may not know which to report or may not define certain sources of income, such as revenue from investment or profit from the sale of a house, as income. As with the question about exercise, if the target concept is open to interpretation, examples will help to narrow the interpretation in the direction most useful to the investigator.

Fourth, **agree/disagree question formats**, where respondents are presented a series of statements and asked their level of agreement/disagreement with them, are also problematic. Respondents have a tendency to agree with statements regardless of their content, a phenomenon known as the "acquiescence effect"—more prevalent when respondents are uninformed about a topic or the topic possesses a socially desirable response. Moreover, agree/disagree statements typically can affect results when they do not provide reasons for disagreeing. For example, asking questions such as "I want taxes cut" or "I want more police on the streets" will yield high levels of agreement, without these responses offering any insight on budget priorities.

Fifth, wording effects can result when questions provide too much background. Questions that offer extensive information tend to prime respondents to think about the question in terms of the information provided rather than more generally. As a result, they are vulnerable to skewing responses in a direction consistent with the information. This problem is especially acute in polls commissioned by candidates in a political campaign (*see* **Push Poll**). For example, prior to the 1974 Ohio Democratic gubernatorial primary between incumbent Attorney General William Brown and former Mayor of Cincinnati Jerry Springer, voters were asked the following question in a poll conducted by the Brown campaign:

> As you may know, in 1974, Jerry Springer, who had gotten married 6 months earlier, was arrested on a bad morals charge with three women in a hotel room. He also used a bad check to pay for the women's services, and subsequently resigned as mayor of his city. Does this make you much more likely, somewhat less likely, or much less likely to support Jerry Springer for governor this year?

Not surprisingly, the results were different from those generated by a typical vote choice question.

Sixth, questions that include prestige names can skew the distribution of responses. Prestige names, such as Reagan, Clinton, or Ashcroft, produce affective reactions regardless of the content of the question. Research has shown that including them in a question can influence not only the direction of responses but also the frequency of "Don't Know" responses. A classic question-wording experiment demonstrated that differential responses were received when individuals were asked "Do you favor or oppose President Reagan's tax proposal?" as opposed to "Do you favor or oppose the 1986 Tax Reform bill?"

Seventh, double-barreled questions produce measurement error. Double-barreled questions are those in which more than one question is being asked.

For example, consider the question "Did you have eggs and toast for breakfast?" There are four, not two, positions on the question. Respondents may have had both eggs and toast for breakfast or neither. Alternatively, respondents may have had eggs but not toast, or toast but not eggs. As a result, it is not clear what yes or no means for this question; hence, response variation may occur, even though the distribution of actual behaviors remains unchanged.

Eighth, wording effects can stem from questions with answers posed in an unbalanced way. For example, take a question querying support for a government policy, which includes reasons for supporting and opposing it. Research has demonstrated that if more positive reasons than negative ones are given, or vice versa, responses tend to gravitate in the direction with the greatest number of justifications. To avoid such problems, the number of choices offered to respondents must be balanced. There should be the same number of categories on the scale representing both directions of opinion for the given question.

Lastly, questions without a middle position can affect the distribution of responses (a similar effect occurs when a "Don't Know" option is omitted; *see* **No Opinion Response Options**). The proportions supporting directional positions are significantly less when a middle position is offered than when one is not. For example, ideological self-identifications garner different results if the question asks whether respondents are "on the liberal side or the conservative side of most political issues" as opposed to asking whether respondents are "on the liberal side, on the conservative side, or in middle of the road on most political issues." Some researchers believe middle of the road respondents actually prefer one of the directional positions, albeit weakly; whereas, other researchers believe they do not, and the omission of a middle position artificially inflates the proportions taking the directional positions.

Identifying Question-Wording Effects. Although researchers can exercise considerable care in crafting their questions, they still do not know for sure whether wording differences produce variations in responses. Fortunately, methods are available to assess whether wording differences change response distributions. Researchers can employ split ballot **experiments, cognitive interviewing,** or Rasch analysis.

Split ballot experiments divide the sample into groups (typically two) and administer different versions of a question to each group. If respondents are randomly assigned to each group, statistical techniques (e.g., analysis of variance) can be used to test whether the frequency distributions are the same or whether the concept relates to other variables, such as **education** or **partisanship**. If the tests reveal no differences, researchers can be confident that the wording differences do not change the meaning. Alternatively, if the tests reveal differences in the response distributions of the questions, researchers need to consider which question version better captures the concept under consideration.

Alternatively, researchers could use cognitive interviews to gauge whether a question worded in a particular way conveys the intended meaning. Cognitive interviewing involves directly questioning respondents about the meaning of particularly worded questions. Typically it is done with small numbers of people who are similar in characteristics to the target population. A cognitive interviewer administers the question to a respondent in a face-to-face setting and, rather than focusing on responses, asks about meaning and how they came to it. Using this technique, the researcher can assess whether the wording in various questions is being interpreted both as intended and consistently across subjects.

Sometimes researchers have to administer a survey without the benefit of pretesting. In this case, they can employ a measurement technique called Rasch modeling to estimate the relative difficulty or endorsability of questions administered in two different randomly selected surveys. If the endorsability of a question is different between two surveys, it suggests the presence of a wording effect. Although it is possible that the differences are due to contextual changes (such as the time period), researchers should be cautious about their interpretation of the result, reconsidering the concept allegedly being measured.

Avoiding Question-Wording Effects. Considering the dangers implicit in wording decisions and the challenges in identifying when certain questions are vulnerable, researchers often adopt measurement approaches designed to diminish or eliminate question-wording effects altogether.

One approach is to use multi-item scales to tap attitudes or behaviors if resources permit. Multi-item scales are typically created by crafting a set of questions (with identical response sets) that capture different attributes of an attitude or behavior, weighting them in importance (most often equally), and then summing the responses to these questions together. Such scales are not only easily interpreted, but they also generally do a better job of tapping the underlying concept. To ensure that a multi-item scale is a reliable measure of the concept, researchers can compute an Item Reliability Index or a Cronbachs alpha. An Item Reliability Index is the correlation between the score on the item and the score on the test as a whole multiplied by the standard deviation of that item. Items with correlations less than .3 are usually excluded from the questionnaire. Cronbach's alpha measures how well a set of items measure a latent concept. It is a function of the number of questions and the average inter-correlations among them. Typically, it should be .8 or more and the deletion of any item should not affect this value too much.

A second approach to avoiding wording effects is to adopt the identical question wording used in other studies. If questions tapping similar concepts are available, this has several benefits. There may be some published information about the question's reliability and validity. Second, researchers can compare responses to other surveys using the same question wording. Third, it enables researchers to assess changes in attitudes or behaviors in a particular population over time. If they adopt different wording, changes in the results may be a function of question-wording effects rather than actual changes.

Further Reading

Bond, Trevor G., and Christine M. Fox. *Applying the Rasch Model: Fundamental Measurement in the Human Sciences.* Mahwah, NJ: Lawrence Erlbaum, 2001. Illustrates the use of the Rasch measurement model in analyzing questions and constructing scales.

Schuman, Howard, and Stanley Presser. *Questions and Answers in Attitude Surveys: Experiments on Question Form, Wording, and Context.* London: Sage Publications, 1996. Examines many questionnaire issues in the design of attitude surveys.

Sudman, Seymour, and Norman M. Bradburn. *Asking Questions: A Practical Guide to*

Questionnaire Design. San Francisco: Jossey-Bass, 1982. Discusses the elements necessary to construct a questionnaire, including wording of questions.

Kenneth A. Rasinski, Michelle Ernst, and Catherine Haggerty

Questionnaire Covers

A questionnaire cover is the topmost page of a **mail survey**. Occasionally this is simply the first page of the questionnaire, but usually it is a separate front that sits atop the instrument and requires specific design decisions. Intuitively, an attractive cover design should enhance the response to a mail survey, but beyond this there is little guidance available to researchers about what constitutes a "good" questionnaire cover. Attempts have been made, but with little success, to develop a theory of questionnaire cover design. However, there is some evidence that the more that respondents like a questionnaire cover, the more effective it will be.

There are no fixed rules of questionnaire cover design. Most designers think carefully about the target audience for the questionnaire and choose imagery, typefaces, and paper stock they believe will appeal to the target audience. The general assumption is that the typeface and imagery chosen will communicate on several different levels and that "reading" a cover design is a complex operation involving conscious and subconscious processes.

On one level, designers seek literal legibility—respondents have to be able to read a questionnaire cover and understand what it is—but on another level they seek to create associations between a respondent (the "reader") and a range of emotions, feelings, and ideas. Through these associations, designers hope that respondents will become interested in the survey and encouraged to open the questionnaire and complete it.

The idea of using graphic design to enhance mail survey response rates is not new. As early as 1978 Don Dillman suggested that prominent graphic designs on questionnaire covers encourage their recipients to respond. This view was supported in a small exploratory study that concluded that subjects were overwhelmingly drawn to a cover page containing a picture (in this case, an icon of an apple sitting on a pile of books). In another **experiment**, a questionnaire with a graphic of a child by a fountain of water and the title "The Effects of Fluoridation on Children's Health" produced a higher response rate than the same questionnaire with a young girl in a dentist's chair and captioned "At What Cost, Dental Care." However, the most extensive test of the use of graphics in questionnaire cover design was conducted by the U.S. Census Bureau.

In 1990 the U.S. decennial census suffered a 10 percent decrease in its mailback response rate. Prompted by this decline, Congress requested the Census Bureau to evaluate a "public information design" approach to questionnaire and mailing package design as part of its U.S. 2000 Census Test. The Census Bureau commissioned a commercial contractor to design two prototype mailing packages, using color, informational icons (symbols to replace words), and graphics to design a questionnaire and accompanying envelopes that would "allow the Federal Government to present itself with style—a style that was patriotic, contemporary, and good-looking." The predominant color of the two packages was gold, compared with the official government approach of green questionnaires mailed in plain white envelopes.

The rationale behind this test was that using marketing tools in the form of color and graphic design (and a coordinated slogan, "Count me in!") would produce a mail package that would be more appealing to the general public (i.e., more likeable). This in turn, it was assumed, would enhance the response rate achieved.

This comparison of a marketing-oriented approach, consistent with that used in private sector direct mail campaigns, and an official government approach to questionnaire and mail package design was part of a larger experiment that also included tests of questionnaire length, subject content, and specific question wording, format, and sequencing of items. The test was conducted in February and March 1996.

Response rates for the two questionnaires using the public information design approach were 5 percent and 9 percent lower than for the official government approach control. However, it is impossible to draw inferences about the questionnaires themselves from this test, since the evaluation applies to the complete set of features used in the two questionnaire design approaches. For example, one explanation for the higher response rates for the official government approach is that the outgoing envelope portrayed more prominently that a response was required by law. It is possible that the response rates for the public information design questionnaires would have been higher if they had been mailed in the official government envelopes.

Thus the U.S. Census 2000 test illustrates the difficulty, first, of operationalizing a concept, such as "appeal," and, second, of isolating the specific effect of questionnaire cover design on the response rates of mail surveys. Nevertheless, the fact is that some questionnaire cover designs produce better response rates in self-completion surveys than others. Thus it is not surprising that researchers have tried to develop an explanation for this phenomenon.

In a 1988 mail survey of Dutch biotechnologists, Anton Nederhof found that a questionnaire with a largely black contrastive front cover produced an 11 percent higher response rate than an alternative version of the same cover that was predominantly white and barely contrastive. Nederhof's explanation for this result was that the black questionnaire was more distinctive and visually complex, and, consequently, more memorable. He argued that potential respondents who had set the questionnaire aside after receiving it would recall it more easily when prompted by a reminder, because of its enhanced longer-term cognitive accessibility. This, in turn, would increase the likelihood that the questionnaire will ultimately be completed and returned.

The significance of this enhanced cognitive accessibility was supported by the fact that the white covers performed at least as well as the black covers early in the survey, but did significantly worse after the fourth wave when reminder techniques (postcards and telephone calls) that did not include a copy of the questionnaire were used. However, several tests of Nederhof's theory—that a more distinctive, complex questionnaire cover design is more effective than a simple one—failed to replicate the results on which this theory was based (Dillman and Gendall 1996). One of these tests did, however, suggest that photographs should be avoided on questionnaire covers because they have the potential to create unpredictable, and sometimes undesirable, images in the minds of respondents.

One possible explanation for this failure to reproduce Nederhof's results using different cover designs is that the phenomenon he studied was contrast rather than complexity. The visual elements of design perceived by the eye are brightness (or contrast) and color, shape, and location; when Nederhof used the word "complex" it appears that he was actually describing a high degree of contrast.

However, two studies by the author designed to test the proposition that contrast, rather than complexity, is the key determinant of an effective mail survey cover design provided only weak support for this interpretation of Nederhof's theory. In one study, where a questionnaire accompanied each wave of the survey, questionnaire cover design had no effect on response rate. In the other study, a highly contrastive cover design was 4 percent more effective than a barely contrastive design, in the absence of an accompanying questionnaire. Despite this, the most effective strategy for increasing survey response was to include a questionnaire with every wave of the survey.

These attempts to develop a theory, or explanation, of what constitutes an effective questionnaire cover design are based on the assumption that such a goal is ultimately attainable. A different approach is to accept that this may not be possible. In other words, though we may know a "good" cover design when we see one, we may not be able to explain how to achieve this. Thus, rather than attempt to solve the problem of how to design an effective questionnaire cover, researchers can instead draw on the experience of advertising, which has a similar problem but also has a solution: likeability. Regardless of how advertisements are created, there is some evidence that more likeable advertisements are more effective than less likeable ones.

The suggestion that likeability, a predictor of advertising effectiveness, might also predict the effectiveness of questionnaire cover design in a mail survey was weakly supported in a series of experiments by the author. These experiments measured the likeability of alternative questionnaire cover designs using the question "How much do you like this cover" and a seven-point semantic differential scale ranging from "Don't like it at all" to "Like it very much." Response to the covers was determined in several surveys of the general public in New Zealand conducted between 1994 and 2001. Further evidence of the relationship between cover design likeability and mail survey response rate was also inferred from two previous studies reported by Don Dillman.

In five out of six studies of questionnaire covers involving graphic designs (rather than designs involving photographs), the more likeable covers produced an average increase in response rate of approximately 2 percent. The individual-effect sizes ranged from zero to 3.5 percent, though none was statistically significant. Thus, while a more likeable questionnaire cover may enhance the response to a mail survey, the increase is likely to be relatively small and is not guaranteed. However, questionnaire cover design likeability is easy to measure and produces relative likeability scores that appear to have face validity. Consequently, researchers can use likeability to choose between alternative graphic cover designs, even if they cannot be sure that they have created the most effective design.

When testing the likeability of questionnaire cover designs it is better to use representative samples of the survey population than convenience samples. For surveys of the general public, a representative mall-intercept sample would be appropriate. It is also important to include a "no design" alternative among the covers tested—to allow for the possibility that this may be the most likeable cover and to randomize or rotate the order of cover design presentation, thus addressing the problem of item-order effect.

If questionnaire cover design does influence mail survey response rates in a predictable way, compelling evidence for this remains elusive. Overall, it appears that the effect of questionnaire cover design on response rate will be marginal in a well-conducted mail survey. Nevertheless, the appearance of the questionnaire inevitably contributes to the impression created by any survey package, thus it would be wrong to ignore the issue of questionnaire cover design simply because researchers have not yet been able to determine reliably how to create a better questionnaire cover. Until this happens, the best advice for mail survey practitioners is to use a simple, well-balanced cover, including a relevant, neutral graphic design, and to avoid photos.

It seems unlikely that questionnaire cover design will prove to be a major determinant of response rates in mail surveys of the general public. Certainly none of the cover design studies that have attempted to reproduce Nederhof's 11 percent difference have found differences approaching this order. But the survey population for these studies has been members of the general public contacted in their homes, whereas Nederhof surveyed biotechnologists at their workplaces. It is possible that something about the people Nederhof surveyed or their environment explains the results of his study. Perhaps professionals whose jobs involve considerable paperwork are more likely to be influenced by the cover design of a questionnaire than are members of the public in their daily lives. This is one area in which further research on questionnaire cover designs may be productive.

Further Reading

Dillman, Don A. *Mail and Internet Surveys: The Tailored Design Method.* New York: John Wiley, 2000. Discusses all aspects of mail survey questionnaire design, including designing the cover page.

Gendall, Philip J. "The Effect of Contrasting Cover Designs on the Response to a Mail Survey." *Australasian Journal of Marketing Research* 7, no. 1 (1999): 3–12. Discusses an experiment designed to test the proposition that, if mail survey reminders are not accompanied by another copy of the questionnaire, the response rate will be increased by a highly contrastive cover design.

———. "The Effect of Likeable Questionnaire Cover Designs on Mail Survey Response Rates." *Proceedings of the ANZMAC Conference, Melbourne, Australia* (2002): 3331–36. Reports the findings of a series of experiments testing whether more likeable questionnaires produce higher mail survey response rates.

———. "The Effect of Questionnaire Cover Design in Mail Surveys." *Marketing Bulletin* 7 (1996): 30–38. Reports the results of a study testing six different questionnaire cover designs, varying in terms of complexity of graphic design and the presence or absence of graphics.

Hedersof, Anton J. "Effects of a Final Telephone Reminder and Questionnaire Cover Design in Mail Surveys." *Social Science Research* 17 (1988): 352–61. The first author to provide an explanation for the differential effect of different questionnaire covers.

Philip Gendall

R

Racial Differences in Public Opinion

The "racial divide" in the political attitudes of African Americans and whites has been studied extensively over the past decade. Table 1, using data from the 2000 American **National Election Study** (NES) and the "Race and Crime" survey conducted by Mark Peffley and Jon Hurwitz, displays racial differences across a wide range of political evaluations. As is evident, the racial divide is often quite large. The largest differences in public opinion across race are found in support for policies that bear directly on race. For example, African Americans show substantially greater support than white Americans for school desegregation, equal employment opportunity, programs that assist blacks, and affirmative action in both hiring and college admittance. Looking at the first few rows showing percent of support for three explicitly "racial policies," we see that African Americans report substantially greater support for affirmative action, government aid to blacks, and government help in school integration than do whites. While such large racial divergence in support for these explicitly racial policies may be anticipated, substantial differences across race exist in numerous other areas.

As seen in the second set of rows in Table 1, racial differences in support for spending on social welfare policies and other issues that have been characterized as "implicitly racial" are also quite substantial. African Americans report considerably greater support than whites for spending on **welfare**, food stamps, aid to the poor, public schools, and government-guaranteed jobs. In some cases (e.g., support for food stamps and guaranteed jobs) racial differences in support for implicitly racial policies are just as large as those observed for explicitly racial policies.

Attitudes toward the criminal justice system may also be seen as implicitly racial (*see* **Crime**) and are characterized by substantial interracial differences. For

Table 1. The Extent of Racial Differences in Public Opinion

Selected Issues	Percent Support	
	Whites	African Americans
Race Policy		
Affirmative Action	46	83
Government Aid to Blacks	25	68
Government Help in School Integration	45	77
Social Spending and Implicitly Racial Issues		
Increase Spending on Welfare	14	30
Increase Spending on Food Stamps	22	61
Increase Spending on Aid to Poor	56	81
Increase Spending on Public Schools	73	87
Support Government Guaranteed Jobs	22	61
Criminal Justice Issues		
Support Death Penalty	76	52
Justice System Is Fair	74	44
Courts Are Fair	61	26
Social/Moral Issues		
Ban Partial Birth Abortion	75	68
Protecting the Environment over Increasing Jobs	65	69
Support Homosexual in Military	22	35
Support Tougher Gun Control Laws	57	62
Support School Vouchers	55	59
Woman's Place Is in the Home	5	11
Trust in Government		
Trust Government Some of the Time or Never	54	67
Government Wastes a Lot of Taxes	60	59
Government Run by Big Interests	65	68
Quite a Few in Government Are Crooked	35	46

Source: Data on perceptions of fairness in the justice system and courts are from Hurwitz and Peffley (2002). All other data were obtained from the 2000 American National Election Study.

example, African Americans have significantly more negative assessments of the police than do whites. Likewise, looking at the third set of rows in Table 1, we see that blacks express less support for the death penalty than do whites and are more likely to believe that the courts and criminal justice system are unfair. Overall, attitudes toward the criminal justice system, similar to support for implicitly racial policies, are characterized by sharp racial differences.

Much more parity is found in support for policies related to moral or social issues that are not linked to race. For example, while it was previously thought that African Americans were not as concerned with the **environment**, recent research has demonstrated that African Americans are as committed to environmental issues as are whites. Similarly, early research concluded that African Americans were less supportive of legal **abortion** than whites, though recent research suggests little difference in support across race. Looking at the third set of rows in Table 1, we see that African Americans report somewhat less support for banning partial birth abortions, while showing slightly greater support for protection of the environment over increasing jobs, allowing homosexuals in the military, tougher laws for **gun control**, school vouchers, and the belief that the woman's place is in the home. So, when it comes to abortion, the environment, **gay rights**, gun control, and school vouchers, blacks take a slightly more liberal position than whites (*see* **Liberalism and Conservatism**). Blacks, however, appear more conservative on gender issues. On the whole, racial differences in opinion on social and moral issues, while still important, are much smaller than those found when considering issues related to race.

The last set of opinions we consider are related to **trust in government,** where again we observe important racial differences, though again, they are not as dramatic as differences in support for policies related to race. The last set of rows in Table 1 show that, while not the case for all indicators of trust, African Americans tended to be less trusting of government than whites in 2000. Small and insignificant differences are found in the belief that government wastes a lot of taxes and is run by big interests. However, African Americans are more likely than whites to believe that the federal government can be trusted to do what is right only some of the time or never and are more likely to deem quite a few in government to be crooked. Indeed, when looking at aggregate levels of political trust in the NES measured every two years from 1958 through 2000, we find that African Americans are less trusting of government than whites more than 50 percent of the time and never achieve levels of trust that are significantly higher than those of whites.

The findings of numerous studies, as well as those reported in Table 1, suggest white and black Americans differ substantially in their opinions over a large gamut of policies. For issues directly and indirectly related to race, sizeable racial differences are observed. When it comes to preferences toward social or moral issues, racial differences are not as large—but, with some exceptions, blacks tend to be more liberal than whites. Finally, blacks also appear somewhat less trusting of government than whites.

The often large differences in public opinion found across race have prompted some analysts to suggest a need for separate explanatory models of political behavior and public opinion for blacks and whites. For example, Michael Dawson, in his book *Behind the Mule*, argues that the legacy of black politics in the United States has led to the development of different heuristics, institutional frameworks, leadership styles, and behavioral patterns across races. While racial differences in opinion span a large range of different policy areas, the bulk of the literature focuses on the often enormous racial differences in support for policies related to race. Examined here are the most prominent explanations for why whites and African Americans hold such divergent opinions on implicitly and explicitly racial issues—along with a review of the research examining racial differences in the sources of political trust, a topic largely ignored until recently.

There exist three general explanations for racial differences in attitudes toward issues related explicitly or implicitly to race: material interest, principles and politics, and racial attitudes. The first explanation, focused on conflict over material interests, has been described as both an economic approach and a sociological approach to explaining public opinion in this area. Under either label, material interest explanations argue that citizens support policies that advance their material self- or group interests and oppose policies that are in conflict with these interests. Under this explanation, attitudes toward policies related to race follow from either realistic or perceived conflict over interests. Consequently, racial differences in support for policies related to race may follow from racial differences in the interests of African Americans and whites. For example, we might expect racial differences in socioeconomic status to help explain racial differences in support for policies related to race because a much larger portion of African Americans, relative to whites, fall among the poor and working class. Hence, class difference found across race may help explain why whites are less supportive of social welfare policies.

Some evidence exists supporting the material interest model in the case of implicitly racial issues. For example, socioeconomic status, measured as family income or education, strongly influences African Americans' support for social welfare policy, with those among the lower status showing strong support for such policies. However, support for social welfare policy among whites is also influenced by socioeconomic status, with whites in higher income brackets showing greater opposition to increased social welfare spending. Less support, however, is found for the influence of material self-interest on support for explicitly racial issues. Some evidence, however, exists suggesting that both whites and African Americans' perceptions of group interests do influence support for racial policies.

The other two most prominent explanations for racial differences in support for implicit and explicit racial policy—principles and politics; and racial attitudes—are the subject of considerable debate, especially in regard to whites' attitudes toward explicitly racial policies, such as preferential hiring and affirmative action in college admissions.

The principles and politics position in this debate argues that opposition to social welfare and racial policies is founded on such principles as individualism, support for democracy, or dispositions that are fundamentally political: for example, political ideology and opposition to big government. Therefore, from the principles and politics perspective, racial differences in support for social welfare policy, other types of implicitly racial policies, as well as support for explicitly racial policy should follow from racial differences in political ideology and principles or values.

The racial attitudes explanation, in contrast, argues that support for these policies follows primarily from negative racial attitudes among whites and strong racial identification among African Americans. In the case of whites' opposition to racial policies, researchers adopting this view argue that while very little overt, or "old fashion," racism remains within the American public, there are still many whites who believe African Americans do not try hard enough and take what they have not earned. This "racial resentment" or "symbolic racism," some argue, is at the heart of opposition to racial policy among whites (see **Symbolic Politics**). However, under the racial attitudes explanation African Americans' support for implicitly or explicitly racial policy follows from their belief that they share a common fate with other black Americans, rather than resentment toward whites.

Evidence in support of the principles and politics versus racial attitudes explanations for whites' support for explicitly racial policy is decidedly mixed. Many find a significant relationship between racial resentment and opposition to affirmative action in both hiring and college admissions. However, others argue that, while attitudes toward blacks do have an effect on attitudes toward racial policy (e.g., affirmative action), the effect is weak and complicated. For example, Paul Sniderman and Edward Carmines's book *Reaching Beyond Race* argues that conservatives, who are most likely to have negative attitudes toward blacks, do not oppose racial policy because of anti-black attitudes, but because of conservative ideals that are in conflict with affirmative action programs. In fact, they argue that it is anti-black attitudes of liberals that have the largest impact on attitudes toward affirmative action.

The origin of whites' support for implicitly racial policy is less controversial. Studies findings that both racial attitudes and principles and politics are important in understanding whites' support for social welfare policy and more stringent criminal justice policy. However, the influence of whites' racial attitudes is often found to depend on context: when black welfare recipients or criminal suspects do not fit the common stereotypes that whites hold (e.g., lazy or violent), racial considerations do not have a significant impact on whites' evaluations.

Racial identification, rather than negative attitudes toward whites, has been found to influence blacks' support for explicitly and implicitly racial policies. For example, perceptions of a linked fate with other African Americans (one indicator of racial identification) as well as a perceived decline in black economic status leads to stronger support for policies of economic redistribution and explicitly racial policies. However, studies have also found that, after controlling for the influence of racial identification, African Americans identifying with a conservative ideology are less supportive of both explicitly and implicitly racial policies. Hence, while racial identification (as well as group interests) may be the dominant predictors of African Americans' support for these policies, politics may have some influence also.

The comparison of racial differences in support for explicitly and implicitly racial policies is made difficult by the fact that most studies concentrate on explaining opinion among either whites or African Americans, rarely comparing the two. Donald Kinder and Nicolas Winter's article "Exploring the Racial Divide: Blacks, Whites, and Opinion on National Policy," published in the *American Journal of Political Science*, is an exception. Lending support to the material interests hypothesis, they find that the elimination of class differences between African Americans and whites would lead to important reductions in the racial divide on support for federal assistance to the unemployed, government health insurance, and the belief that the federal government is responsible for providing jobs and an adequate standard of living. However, they also find that if blacks were equal to whites in education, income, and wealth they would still show substantially greater support for explicitly racial policies than do whites. So, while material interests may help explain why whites and African Americans have such sharp differences in support for social welfare policies, this explanation may not be as helpful in understanding support for policies like affirmative action.

Regarding the principles and politics versus racial attitudes explanations, Kinder and Winter find that principles—specifically, support for equal opportunity and limited government—play an important role in explaining racial differences in support for both explicitly and implicitly racial policies. That is, if African Americans and whites did not differ on these principles, racial differences in support for social welfare policies as well as racial policies like affirmative action would narrow dramatically. Kinder and Winter also find some support for the racial attitudes explanation in the case of explicitly racial issues, though no influence is found for its influence on implicitly racial issues (i.e., social welfare policies).

Overall, and not surprisingly, the evidence suggests that racial consideration influences support for explicitly racial policy, though it has a more moderate or conditional effect on policies implicitly related to race. Beyond racial considerations, the material interests and principles and politics explanations have also found support, though for the former, it appears that *group* material interests, as opposed to self-interest, have the largest impact.

Racial differences in public opinion are not limited to evaluations of policies related to race. Previously, we identified smaller, though important, racial differences in political trust. However, as opposed to attitudes toward racial policies, research seeking to explain these differences has been practically nonexistent until recently.

Numerous studies, examining political trust using largely white samples, have demonstrated the importance of several key political factors that influence citizens' trust in government. Among these prominent explanations are evaluations of incumbent authority like the president, evaluations of Congress, and evaluations of the policy outputs and outcomes they produce. However, little support is found for the influence of political factors on trust among blacks. Instead, distrust among blacks follows more from racial group consciousness, which encompasses political beliefs about the status of one's own racial group and its relationship among other racial groups. African Americans who have a strong sense of shared fate with other blacks and perceive continued racial discrimination, inequality, and underrepresentation in government are less trusting of government than others.

The aggregate differences in levels of political trust found across race do not appear to be the product of racial differences in political evaluations. That is, the political factors that influence political trust among whites do not play a large role explaining trust among blacks. Instead, the foundations of political trust among blacks appear to be tied closer to blacks' racial group consciousness.

As we have seen, substantial racial differences exist in support for policies implicitly and explicitly related to race. Whether looking at support for affirmative action programs, support for social welfare policies, or attitudes toward the criminal justice system, African Americans are considerably more liberal than whites. Research has identified several factors that explain racial differences in policies linked to race, either explicitly or implicitly: material interests, principles and politics, and racial attitudes. Though controversy regarding the relative influence of each remains, credible support has been found for each explanation. However, the influence of racial attitudes on support for racial policies is quite different across race. Among whites, attitudes toward African Americans (i.e., "racial resentment" or negative racial **stereotypes**) influence support for racial policy, while among blacks racial identification (e.g., perceptions of linked fate), rather than attitudes toward whites, influences opinion. That is, there appears to be important inter-racial differences in how black and white Americans use racial attitudes to inform opinion.

While the differences are not as dramatic, compared with whites, blacks are often more liberal on social and moral issues that are not linked to race. Likewise, blacks often report lower levels of trust in government than whites. While little work has sought to explain racial differences in attitudes toward the former, we have reviewed research suggesting important racial differences in the sources of political trust. Race appears to matter in explaining blacks' trust in government, where those with stronger racial group consciousness are less trusting of government. Whites, in contrast, rely more on political factors, including satisfaction with the president, Congress, and the policies they produce.

While numerous studies have documented important racial differences in support for various policies and attitudes toward politics and government, our understanding of inter-racial differences in explanations for these aggregate differences is lacking in many respects. That is, while we can often identify various different explanations for blacks' and whites' opinions on policies by comparing studies examining opinion among whites with those examining opinion among blacks, strict interracial comparisons of the influence of various predictors of opinion are more difficult to make. For example, while we know that racial identification is important in understanding blacks' support for many different policies we know little about the influence of racial identification among whites. Likewise, while volumes of work have studied the influence of whites' negative attitudes toward blacks on policy preferences, very little work considers the potential influence of blacks' attitudes toward whites.

Perhaps the primary reason strict inter-racial differences in public opinion are hard to come by is the lack of surveys that include large samples of both whites and African Americans. The bulk of survey data available, including the NES, have relatively small samples of African Americans and often do not include questions taping dispositions known to be important in understanding opinion among blacks (e.g., racial identification). Hence, studies using the NES to examine explanations for racial differences in public opinion are limited significantly. Likewise, while the surveys of African Americans conducted over the past couple decades have added to our knowledge of public opinion among blacks, they too do not allow for strict interracial comparisons (for example, the 1996 National Black Election Study). One option is to combine a primarily white sample with an African American sample taken around the same time, thus making interracial comparisons. However, differences in question wording and questions asked across surveys among whites and blacks (e.g., the 1996 National Black Election Study and the 1996 NES) continue to make interracial comparisons difficult. Considering these difficulties in examining interracial differences in the sources of public opinion, future research would benefit from surveys drawing large, representative samples of both whites and African Americans.

Further Reading

Dawson, Michael C. *Behind the Mule: Race and Class in African-American Politics*. Princeton, NJ: Princeton University Press, 1994. Offers an extensive examination of the comparative role of racial identification versus social class as explanations for African Americans' political attitudes and behavior.

Kinder, Donald R., and Lynn M. Sanders. *Divided by Color: Racial Politics and Democratic Ideals*. Chicago: University of Chicago Press, 1996. Provides an examination of interracial differences in support for implicitly and explicitly racial policies.

Kinder, Donald R., and Nicholas Winter. "Exploring the Racial Divide: Blacks, Whites, and Opinion on National Policy." *American Journal of Political Science* 45 (2001): 439–53. Presents a thorough examination of the racial divide in political attitudes in America.

Sears, David O., Jim Sidanius, and Lawrence Bobo, eds. *Racialized Politics*. Chicago: Chicago University Press, 2000. Provides a review of competing explanations for whites' attitudes toward explicitly racial policy.

James M. Avery

Racial Messages in Political Campaigns

Given the long and troubled history of racism in America, it should come as no surprise that racial messages have a similarly long history of finding their way into election campaigns. Even in the twenty-first century—150 years after the end of slavery and 50 years after the prohibition of Jim Crow laws—racial messages often play an important role in affecting public opinion and thus how individuals vote.

Some scholars have noted that media messages—not just those about elections or candidates for office—tend to present stereotypical depictions of racial minorities (*see* **Stereotypes**). This includes associating minorities with criminal behavior (especially in television news), painting nonwhites as simpleminded caricatures, or depicting minorities as violent and threatening. Other research has demonstrated that whites' perceptions of black political candidates approximate many of those stereotypes found to be present in media messages. For example, in a national survey studying white and black perceptions of black politicians' electability, one study found that most whites attributed characteristics such as "intelligent," "a strong leader," "knowledgeable," "hard-working," "gets things done," "experienced," and "trustworthy" more often to white candidates than black candidates. Another found that whites, particularly those who harbor some racial prejudice, tend to evaluate black candidates more negatively than white candidates. The author further concluded that a black candidate's skin color had a significant effect on the evaluation of his or her competence, with the darker-skinned candidate evaluated more harshly.

It is important to note, however, that these sorts of conclusions are partially contradicted by other research. For instance, Sigelman and his coauthors suggest that despite the correlation between espoused stereotypes and perception or evaluation of candidates, a minority candidate's race is not necessarily the most salient predictor of his or her negative evaluations. They found that an individual's previously held ideologies and beliefs about what a minority candidate should "look like" politically is a significant factor in overall evaluations of mi-

nority candidates. This view is, at least on the surface, inconsistent with the notion that race itself (or a "racist" attitude) is the primary factor in white voters'
assessment of minority candidates. But such findings, in fact, lead us to a more
sophisticated understanding of how racial messages operate in the context of a
political campaign.

All this research has led political communication scholars to conduct further
work on the way racial messages are used in campaigns and the potential effect
that such messages may have on voting decisions. The effect of media messages
on political attitudes and behaviors was once thought to be direct. That is, it
was theorized that if a person was exposed to a certain type of message long
enough, he or she was likely to embrace, or at least accept, that message. Over
time, however, researchers began to appreciate the complex, interactive nature
of communication. The so-called "hypodermic model" of media effects has been
abandoned for a more sophisticated approach rooted in cognitive psychology
(*see* **Opinion Formation**).

Working from the **priming** hypothesis, some have argued that the way citizens
psychologically process racially tinged media (or campaign) messages is at the
root of the potential effect of such messages. Priming may explain the way white
candidates use racial appeals to gain an advantage over minority opponents by
using largely implicit messages to prime racial predispositions. This priming may
translate into voters' negative perceptions of a minority candidate and may result in a decision not to vote for him or her. The most thorough research on the
effects of racial priming in political campaign communication is Tali Mendelberg's 2001 book, *The Race Card*.

Working within an American context, Mendelberg points out that there is now
a social stigma attached to racism. That is, even if a person is overtly prejudiced
against racial minorities, he or she is not generally comfortable expressing that
idea publicly. Because of this, candidates cannot (and generally do not) convey
explicit racist messages in campaign communication. That does not mean, however, that racial messages are not used in campaigns. In fact, Mendelberg argues
that implicit racial messages are used, and the effect is potentially much greater
because such messages are not perceived to violate the social norm of racial
equality.

Mendelberg's assertion that such implicit appeals are more easily communicated through visual images increases the potential power of televised political
advertising to affect attitudinal change based on racial cues. Other research concerning the differential effect of media forms seems to bear this out. For instance,
it has been found that television advertising may be a stronger primer of attitudes given the fact that they, rather than messages from news media, are intentional. That is, while a candidate's message may be framed and communicated
to the public in a particular manner by the media, a candidate's own advertising communicates directly and precisely what is intended. Further, television advertisements may have a greater effect on voters' knowledge of campaign issues,
their evaluation of candidates and their likelihood to vote than news stories.
Given this, implicitly racial messages—those that have the potential to elicit the
greatest degree of negative racial attitudes—will most likely "work" in the
medium of television advertising.

To illustrate this point, consider two examples of how racial messages were
used in actual campaigns. In 1990 and 1996, incumbent U.S. Senator Jesse Helms

(Republican from North Carolina) ran for re-election against Harvey Gantt, the former mayor of Charlotte. Helms had a history of working against **civil rights** and opposing programs that were designed to alleviate racial inequality. Gantt is a black man whose platform was, in part, geared toward supporting such programs. In 1990 Helms ran a television campaign advertisement (*see* **Campaign Advertising**) that came to be known as "the hands ad." The visual image is a close up of a white man's hands (wedding ring and flannel shirt visible) holding a piece of mail at what appears to be a kitchen table. A few seconds into the ad, the man crumples the letter, as the narrator says: "You needed that job, and you were the best qualified. But they had to give it to a minority because of a racial quota. Is that really fair? Harvey Gantt says it is." A still photograph of Gantt is then shown next to a similar photograph of Senator Edward Kennedy (Democrat of Massachusetts) as the announcer says, "Gantt supports Ted Kennedy's racial quota law that makes the color of your skin more important than your qualifications." The ad ends with a still photo of Gantt beside a still of Jesse Helms. The announcer's voice says, "You'll vote on this issue next Tuesday. *For* racial quotas: Harvey Gantt. *Against* racial quotas: Jesse Helms." This is an example of an explicit racial appeal. The target is clearly white voters who may fear that their own status will be jeopardized if affirmative action programs become commonplace. There are no code words or ambiguously racial images. It is quite obvious that this message is about race, and it is clearly intended to favor white interests.

Conversely, Vice President George H. Bush ran an ad against Michael Dukakis in the 1988 presidential race that has come to serve as an example of an implicit racial message. The topic was crime. With still pictures of both candidates on the screen, the narrator says, "Bush and Dukakis on crime." Moving to a single still photograph of Bush, the narrator continues: "Bush supports the death penalty for first degree murderers." The image then shifts to a still photograph of Dukakis. The narrator refers to Massachusetts's furlough program while Dukakis was governor: "Dukakis not only opposes the death penalty, he allowed first degree murderers to have weekend passes from prison." At this point, we see a mug shot of Willie Horton, a black man who wore a slight Afro hairstyle and a bushy beard. His name appears below his picture. The narrator says, "One was Willie Horton, who murdered a boy in a robbery, stabbing him nineteen times." The image shifts to another photograph of Horton: "Despite a life sentence, Horton received ten weekend passes from prison. Horton fled, kidnapping a young couple, stabbing the man and repeatedly raping his girlfriend." Finally, we see a still image of Dukakis, while the narrator says, "Weekend prison passes. Dukakis on crime." Whereas the Jesse Helms spot mentioned above made no attempt to disguise the racial message, this spot used an image of Willie Horton (his mug shot) to invoke latent fears and stereotypical prejudices among potential voters. Horton's race was never mentioned, but the existence of his picture (which is unnecessary to convey the intended message) likely primed negative racial stereotypes in the minds of voters who would have otherwise rejected the message as racist if it were more explicit.

As noted above, the importance of this line of research has to do with the implications for representation and democracy. If one is working from the assumption that groups need to be represented by members of their own groups, there must be concern about the use and effectiveness of racial appeals priming anti-minority attitudes, and effectively harming minority candidates' chances of winning.

The premise of Mendelberg's theory is that racial appeals are most often used by whites to gain advantages over nonwhites. This is logical given the history of racial discrimination and prejudice in America. This is only part of the picture, though. The Project on Race in Political Advertising seeks to explain the various ways that racial messages are used in political campaigns. Indeed, early work on this Project reveals that both black and white candidates use racial appeals, but for different reasons.

There is an important difference between "racist" appeals and "racial" appeals. Because of institutionalized power differentials, many scholars believe it a mischaracterization to refer to a member of a racial minority group as being "racist," though certainly anyone can be prejudiced or bigoted. Given this distinction, racist appeals are conceptualized as those fears, prejudices, and resentments that some whites continue to hold against nonwhites. Racial messages, in contrast, are not necessarily built on, and do not necessarily appeal to, individual or institutionally reinforced attitudes of racial superiority. The "white hands" ad by Jesse Helms that we previously described would be an example of a racist message because it appeals to the deeply held institutional favoritism of whites over blacks and other minorities, but racial messages do not necessarily appeal to any institutionalized belief in the superiority of one race over another.

With this distinction in mind, we may specify five ways that racial messages can be used in political campaigns. First, black candidates may use racial messages in campaigns against white candidates to mitigate the effects of racially stereotypical messages employed by the white candidate to negatively affect the perception of the black candidate. An example of this is Harvey Gant's response to the aforementioned "white hands" ad by Jesse Helms. In the response ad, Gantt claimed that Helms was using his (Gantt's) race to scare people. The ad is therefore racial in nature, but it is clear that the strategy behind it is to counter the effect of Helms's ad, not to use race to gain some advantage over Helms.

Second, black candidates may employ racial messages to separate themselves from stereotypical images of their racial group. That is, they may do so to invoke a color-blind message to appeal to white voters. This scenario, which is generally the case when black candidates are running in districts where a large portion of the voting population is white, often leads black candidates to make a "preemptive strike," to eliminate the possibility that some white voters might view him or her as seeking to represent only black interests. Former Congressmen Alan Wheat, of Missouri, and Gary Franks, of Connecticut, for instance, both used such strategies in their bids for the U.S. Senate. In each of their respective ads, they repeatedly claimed they had "worked hard and played by the rules" to get to where they are. In one Wheat ad, a white, rural father and son are shown as a voiceover discusses Wheat's desire to make the "American Dream" become real for all Missourians. Viewers do not see until the last few seconds of the ad that the person speaking is, in fact, Alan Wheat, who is black. In each of these cases the intent is to counter or anticipate stereotypes that these successful figures attained their position through some kind of "racial preference." The Wheat ad works to counteract the stereotype that a black man would only be interested in representing the interests of black people.

Third, white candidates may use racial messages to rehabilitate an existing racist image, not necessarily to appeal to and gain minority votes, but to mitigate the risks of appearing to violate the norm of racial equality held by white voters. For instance, if the former Ku Klux Klan leader David Duke were to run for office in an area where a notable percentage of the population was African American, he may produce an ad that shows him shaking hands with an African American man or kissing an African American child. Though this show of affiliation with this community may not be enough to undue a hardened racist image, the intent would be to soften that perception.

Fourth, minority candidates may employ racial messages when facing other minority candidates. This form of message generally rests on appeals to racial authenticity. In races in which both candidates are nonwhite, these forms of appeal are not intended to draw on voters' attitudes on race per se, but on ideological beliefs about appropriate political strategy used to further minority interests. In this way, the conflict is not between upholding or violating norms of equality, but between either side of the debate over within-group solidarity or assimilation. An excellent example of this was the 2002 Democrat primary contest between challenger Arthur Davis and longtime incumbent Congressman Earl Hilliard in a majority-black district in Alabama. The difference between the two candidates—Davis, who was a young, Harvard-educated attorney, and Hilliard, an old-school politician, entrenched in the party machine—led many of the messages of the race to center on claims about who is "really" black, or who is more black than the other.

The fifth proposition is that minority candidates running in majority-minority districts may use racial messages to prime anti-white sentiment to appeal to and mobilize minority constituencies or whites who adhere to egalitarian norms. In keeping with the David Duke example above, if a black candidate were running in the same race, he or she might decide to produce an ad that asks the people of the community to "remember who David Duke really is"—in hopes that by highlighting his racist past, blacks will mobilize against Duke and in support of the black candidate.

The research discussed here focuses on cultural as well as political issues. The importance in continuing to pursue such research is therefore vitally important to us, both culturally and politically. The more we understand about racial attitudes—how they are shaped, drawn upon, and communicated—the better we can effect positive change in our culture more broadly to be consistent with the "norm" of racial equality discussed earlier. If we allow such an understanding to permeate the political realm, drastic changes in public policy are also likely to change—from what our priorities are as a country made up of diverse citizens to how we talk about issues long associated with race. If we believe that the voices of this diverse group of citizens should be represented at every level of government, our further understanding of how racial messages affect public opinion are vitally important to this outcome.

Further Reading

Entman, R. M., and A. Rojecki. *The Black Image in the White Mind: Media and Race in America*. Chicago: University of Chicago Press, 2000. The authors argue that the images of African Americans in the media—from television sitcoms to news—are

largely negative and inconsistent with the goal of racial justice and building inter-
racial community.

Guinier, L. *The Tyranny of the Majority: Fundamental Fairness in Representative Democracy*. New York: Free Press, 1994. Guinier argues that because minority interests can and are consistently blocked by the majority of members of
representative office, proactive efforts need to be made to help ensure the representative parity of racial minorities in elected bodies.

Mendelberg, T. *The Race Card: Campaign Strategy, Implicit Messages, and the Norm of
Equality*. Princeton, NJ: Princeton University Press, 2001. Mendelberg develops a
theory of how racial appeals are used in political campaigns. She argues that implicit racial messages are likely to be more effective than explicit racial messages.

Reeves, K. *Voting Hopes or Fears? White Voters, Black Candidates and Racial Politics
in America*. New York: Oxford University Press, 1997. This work provides much
of the foundational work for many of Mendelerg's arguments. Reeves argues that
although efforts have been made over the past thirty years to redress previous
wrongs against, and counter negative perceptions of, African Americans, many
whites continue to oppose the election of minorities to political office. This is
largely the case, he argues, because white candidates often appeal to the fears and
resentments of whites voters who rely on such to make voting decisions.

Sigelman, C. K., L. Sigelman, B. J. Walkosz, and M. Nitz. "Black Candidates, White Voters: Understanding Racial Bias in Political Perceptions." *American Journal of Political Science* 39 (1995): 243–65. These authors challenge the notion that white
racism is the primary factor in negative evaluations of blacks as officeholders.

Terkildsen, N. "When White Voters Evaluate Black Candidates: The Processing Implications of Candidate Skin Color, Prejudice, and Self-Monitoring." *American Journal
of Political Science* 37 (1993): 1032–53. This study reveals that skin color differences in black candidates were found to affect white respondents' cognitive processing.

Web Sites

The Joint Center for Political and Economic Studies (http://www.jointcenter.org/) is an
international nonprofit institution that conducts research on public policy issues of special concern to black Americans and other minorities.

The Project on Race in Political Advertising (http://race-project.org) seeks to explore
and explain the ways racial messages are used in political campaigns—specifically in television advertisements. The Project contains both qualitative and quantitative empirical
analyses, using experimental and descriptive research methods to cast light on the historical and current uses of racial messages.

The Congressional Black Caucus Foundation (http://www.cbcfinc.org/) serves as the
nonpartisan policy-oriented catalyst that educates future leaders and promotes collaboration among legislators, business leaders, minority-focused organizational leaders, and
organized labor to effect positive and sustainable change in the African American community.

The Congressional Hispanic Caucus Institute (http://www.chci.org) works to develop
the next generation of Latino leaders. The CHCI sponsors programs designed to increase
the participation of young Hispanics in both public and private sectors and to foster a
network of young Hispanic leaders in government-related areas.

Stephen Maynard Caliendo and Charlton D. McIlwain

Racial Stereotypes

Political scientists have identified race as a powerfully divisive element in
American politics. Few would reject the proposition that racial attitudes are part

of the foundation and justification of many whites' stands on racial issues. Indeed, racial attitudes have been found to influence voting behavior and support for various public policies ranging from explicitly racial issues, such as affirmative action, to "implicitly racial" issues, such as social **welfare**. In such studies, racial attitudes have been measured in various ways: for example, racial **stereotypes.**

Social stereotypes are commonly defined as "cognitive structures that contain the perceiver's knowledge, beliefs, and expectations about human groups." As **Walter Lippmann** observed in his classic study *Public Opinion*, stereotypes are "pictures in the head," which allow cognitive misers with limited motivation and mental capacities to process information more efficiently in an uncertain political world. However, stereotypes must be viewed not only as cognitive shortcuts but also as a source of ethnocentric bias. That is, social stereotypes tend to be quite negative, suggesting that they are not only used to simplify the social world but also to justify discrimination and hostility toward the out-group. Indeed, early work in social psychology implicated stereotypes as a major source of prejudice and discrimination. More recent research in social psychology has also explored the ways stereotypes bias information processing (*see* **Opinion Formation**) and thus affect such phenomena as racism and discrimination.

We must consider the prevalence of racial stereotypes. A majority of whites now reject traditional racist beliefs about the genetic inferiority of blacks. However, more than thirty years after the **civil rights** movement and the passage of historical civil rights legislation, racial stereotypes of African Americans remain pervasive among many whites. A 1991 national survey found that a substantial percentage of whites rated "most blacks" negatively, describing them as "lazy" (31 percent), "lacking discipline" (60 percent), and "aggressive or violent" (50 percent).

The more recent 2000 **National Election Study** (NES) suggests little change in whites' stereotypes of blacks since 1991. For example, only 7 percent of whites rate "whites in general" as lazy, while 32 percent rate "blacks in general" as lazy. Similar discrepancies exist for ratings of "unintelligent" and "untrustworthy."

The findings of both surveys show that negative stereotypes of African Americans remain strong among a consequential number of whites. Furthermore, due to changes in the social acceptability of holding negative racial attitudes, it is safe to assume that there may be a slight tendency for whites to underreport negative sentiments toward African Americans, leading to an underestimation of the actual number of whites holding negative racial stereotypes.

What types of individuals are more likely to subscribe to negative stereotypes of blacks and what social, political, and psychological antecedents help to explain the dynamics of racial stereotyping? Demographic explanations offer very little explanation of racial stereotyping. Demographic variables (i.e., formal education, age, gender, region) collectively explain no more than about 5 percent of the variance in various racial stereotype measures. Core beliefs and values, however, prove to be more important. While economic values like individualism are essentially unrelated to racial stereotypes, social values such as generalized ethnocentrism, reminiscent of authoritarianism, are much more important. Accordingly, such constructs as social intolerance (or an unwillingness to "put up with" different values, appearances, and behaviors), conformity (a desire for an orderly and structured world in which people obey authority and adhere to convention and externally imposed rules), social dominance orientation (a rejection of egalitarian values and desire to establish ingroup dominance over outgroups), and anti-Semitism appear to go a long way toward predicting who accepts, and who rejects, negative characterizations of African Americans.

To more fully understand the sources of racial stereotypes we must look beyond personal factors and consider the sources of stereotypes in the political information environment. Two elements in the information environment that may influence racial stereotypes have received increased attention from political scientists. The first of these is the use of racially "coded" political rhetoric. A number of studies have examined the use of racially coded political rhetoric by politicians who engage such issues as welfare and crime to exploit whites' racial prejudice and activate racial thinking without explicitly playing the "race card." The use of such political rhetoric is exemplified by the infamous "Willie Horton" and "Turnstyle" television ads created by supporters of George H. Bush in 1988, which paired nonracial narratives with racial imagery to produce an "implicitly" racial message (see **Racial Messages in Political Campaigns**). Not only were the ads effective in portraying Bush's opponent, Michael Dukakis, as weak on crime, but news about the ads primed racial attitudes in opinions about various policies. Indeed, political ads with *implicit* racial messages (e.g., a nonracial narrative about government spending paired with images of undeserving blacks) are much more effective than *explicit* racial messages (e.g., the same narrative with positive images of whites alongside negative images of blacks) in priming racial attitudes and, consequently, augmenting support for George W. Bush over Al Gore in 2000.

A second line of research explores the influence of the mass media on the activation of racial stereotypes. Of particular importance are recent studies that examine the way news portrayals of welfare and crime tend to link such issues with African Americans. Based on content analysis of news coverage of welfare, analysts find that the news media tend to "racialize" welfare policy by disproportionately using images of African Americans to accompany negative news stories on poverty. Similarly, **crime** stories in local news broadcasts tend to overrepresent violent crimes where the perpetrator is black in such a manner that highly exaggerates the involvement of African Americans in criminal activities.

Moreover, research indicates that such biases in media coverage of both welfare and crime have important political consequences. By creating the inaccurate impression that a majority of welfare recipients is black, public support for welfare is diminished and negative stereotypes of African Americans as the "undeserving poor" are reinforced. Moreover, time-series studies find that news coverage of racial issues affects whites' racial attitudes over time. Public support for more liberal racial policies increases when media coverage focuses on egalitarianism, while support wanes when the media frames issues to highlight individualistic values.

Crime attitudes are similarly affected. Experimental evidence suggests that even a brief visual image of a black male in a typical local news story on crime is powerful and sufficiently familiar to activate viewers' negative stereotypes of blacks, producing racially biased evaluations of black criminal suspects. In their innovative experimental studies manipulating only the skin color of a male perpetrator in local news broadcast, Franklin Gilliam and Shanto Iyengar and their associates convincingly demonstrate that when the perpetrator was African American, more adult subjects endorsed punitive crime policies and negative racial attitudes after watching the news broadcast. When no perpetrator was depicted, subjects—both white and black—were much more likely to recall the perpetrator as being African American. However, this relationship appears to be dependent on the social context. When exposed to racial stereotypes in the news, whites living in homogeneous neighborhoods endorse more punitive policies to address crime, express more negative stereotypic evaluations of blacks, and feel more distant from blacks as a group. However, whites from heterogeneous neighborhoods are more willing to endorse less punitive crime policies, less negative stereotypes, and feel closer to blacks as a group as a result of exposure to stereotypic coverage.

We now turn to a more exhaustive discussion of the consequences of racial stereotypes for political judgments and behavior. Indeed, for many, the most important question regarding racial stereotypes is whether they have demonstrable political consequences. Specifically, to what degree and under what circumstances do racial stereotypes influence whites' political responses toward African Americans and policies that affect blacks? Considering the prevalence of negative racial stereotypes held by many white Americans and the political information environment that often serves to activate and reinforce such stereotypes, the suspicion is that stereotypes will have a substantial influence on political attitudes and behavior. For example, it seems fair to hypothesize that whites endorsing negative stereotypes of African Americans will express greater opposition to welfare if it is perceived to benefit blacks, or prefer white to black political candidates when in the privacy of the voting both. Early research on the connection between whites' attitudes toward blacks and their support for policies designed to assist them predicted that preferences on such issues would tend to boil down to the same simple question of one's feeling toward blacks. However, a great deal of research has shown that the connection between racial stereotypes and racial issues is far more complicated than this early formulation suggested. Racial stereotypes appear to have strong influence on support for "implicitly racial" issues like social welfare policy and the criminal justice system, while they exert relatively little influence on policies explicitly related to race like affirmative action and other types of government aid directed at African Americans. For example, research has found that social welfare issues are strongly tied to racial stereotypes but opposition to affirmative action is essentially disconnected from such beliefs. These findings are consistent with the more general finding showing racial attitudes to have a stronger influence when race is cued implicitly or subconsciously than when race is made explicit.

The influence of racial stereotypes is not only conditioned by the issue being evaluated (explicitly vs. implicitly racial issues), but even among implicitly racial issues, where we do see an influence, the use of stereotypes are dependent on the context in which the evaluation is being made. To be sure, the empirical relationship between racial stereotypes and political judgments is characterized by striking inconsistencies, appearing in some settings but not at all (or only weakly) in others. One solution to this puzzle lies in the simple recognition that people are not prisoners to their prior beliefs; rather, stereotypes guild judgments only when the stereotype "fits" the judgment at hand.

When stereotypes do fit, they are powerfully consequential. Based on a series of survey experiments where the race and other characteristics of the target (e.g., welfare recipients and criminal suspects) were manipulated, we consistently find that whites who regard African Americans as "lazy" and lacking in a strong work ethic are much more negative in their assessments of welfare policy, particularly when they believe that most welfare recipients are black. By the same token, whites who perceive African Americans to be "violent," "short-tempered," and the like are more supportive of harsh and punitive anti-crime policies.

There are, however, numerous "disconnects," or instances in which racial stereotypes play little role in driving individuals' attitudes toward welfare or crime policy. Even among whites who see "most blacks" as violent, for example, such stereotypes do not seem to translate into more punitive policy attitudes when blacks have been described as committing white collar crimes, such as embezzlement (rather than the more racially stereotypic crimes such as car jacking). In such instances, the crime itself does not comport with the African American stereotype, and, as such, the stereotype makes far less difference.

Even more important for understanding the impact of stereotypes are instances when individuals are supplied with individuating, or counter-stereotypical, information—that is, information about *individuals* that conflicts with the stereotypes of the larger group. In our earlier work, we investigated how two groups of whites—those with negative and those with positive views of blacks—react to welfare mothers and criminal suspects where the race and work histories of the targets are randomly varied. For example, in the welfare mother experiment, respondents were asked whether they would favor a welfare program where the recipients are either black or white (i.e., immigrants from Europe) and were described as either "people who have trouble hanging onto a job" or "people who have shown that they want to work."

In these experiments, we found that whites with positive views of black were, for the most part, remarkably consistent in their responses to black targets, regardless of their described work histories. Thus, they did not abandon their positive view of blacks when confronted with black welfare recipients who were stigmatized in some way. Whites who stereotyped blacks as lazy, however, tended to evaluate the black welfare recipient more harshly than similarly described white recipients, and they did so both in the case of the black recipient who fit their expectations (dropped out of high school, had trouble hanging onto a job) and when the recipient was mildly discrepant from their expectations (had completed high school). However, in the welfare policy experiment, when information about the target is *strongly* discrepant from the stereotype—that is, when whites who think blacks are lazy are asked about welfare for blacks who want to work—these whites tend to "bend over backwards" in supporting welfare for African Americans who have characteristics that are clearly contrary to their stereotypes of most blacks.

The conditional impact of stereotypes is also very much in evidence in studies of voting behavior. In her experimental analysis, Nadya Terkildsen asked some 350 participants (selected randomly from jury pools in Jefferson County/Louisville,

Kentucky) whether they would vote for a fictitious gubernatorial candidate after reading campaign materials that included a photograph of the candidate (former Republican Senator Edward Brookes from Massachusetts) in which the candidate's skin color was varied to depict either a light-skinned or a dark-skinned black male. As expected, whites with negative stereotypes of African Americans were more likely to vote for the lighter than for the darker-complected candidate, but only among individual who were low self-monitors (individuals who tend to act on their own beliefs rather than on situational cues). High self-monitors, in contrast, due to their greater propensity to offer environmentally "appropriate" responses, disingenuously reported being more likely to vote for the dark- than the light-skinned candidate. This pattern of results helps to explain the tendency among whites to report an increased willingness to vote for African American candidates in national surveys, while at the same time displaying a marked unwillingness to vote for blacks in the privacy of the voting booth, especially African American candidates with darker skin.

Other research has demonstrated different consequences of stereotypes on vote choice. For example, when voters have only general or incomplete information about candidates, candidate demographics provide them with stereotypical information that can help them in their vote choice. In the case of African American candidates, voters appear to use their stereotypes of blacks as more liberal and willing to help the poor to make inferences about candidates' positions on issues, which then influence voting decisions. In this case, racial stereotypes of both traits (wanting to help the poor) and beliefs (being liberal) are used as information shortcuts to make inferences about both the character and the policy preferences of black candidates.

Where does this leave us? While a majority of whites in the United States now reject traditionally racist attitudes and beliefs (e.g., segregation and white supremacy), recent national surveys make plain that a substantial number of whites continue to endorse decidedly negative beliefs about African Americans, nearly four decades after the peak of the civil rights movement. Between 25 and 30 percent of whites continue to rate African Americans as more violent and hostile, more lazy and preferring to live on welfare, and less trustworthy than whites.

The studies reviewed here have sought to uncover the antecedents as well as the consequences of racial stereotypes in the American polity. Research has identified several important sources of racial stereotypes. Values, like ethnocentrism, social dominance orientation, and anti-Semitism, are strongly related to racial stereotypes. Likewise, research has identified important sources within the mass media that appear to cue and reinforce racial stereotypes. Research examining media coverage of social welfare policy and crime are noteworthy.

Likewise, and perhaps most important, research has identified important political consequences of racial stereotypes. Whites who regard blacks as "lazy" and lacking in work ethic are much more negative in their assessments of welfare policy, while whites who perceive blacks to be "violent" or "short-tempered" are more supportive of harsh and punitive anti-crime policies. Similarly, whites holding negative racial stereotypes are less likely to vote for an African American candidate for office. However, research has also found that whites holding negative racial stereotypes do not use these stereotypes in evaluating policy when the situation does not fit. For example, when confronted with counter-stereotypical individuating information, whites who believe that blacks are lazy tend to support welfare for African Americans who clearly do not fit their stereotypes of most blacks as lazy.

One important implication of these findings is that counter-stereotypic information may be used to short-circuit stereotypic thinking among whites. By framing policies such as welfare in terms of exemplars that are contrary to the stereotype, such as the hard-working black welfare mother, it is possible to sever the connection between negative stereotypes and policy views. Similarly, by portraying positive images of African Americans in political ads, racial stereotypes are not activated and therefore racial thinking does not influence voting intentions after watching a televised political ad.

While the ability of counter-stereotypic information to eliminate stereotypic thinking may be possible, such information has been presented in survey experiments and is not necessarily available in political and social discourse. In fact, the research on the prevalence of racial stereotypes in the mass media and political rhetoric reviewed above suggests that whites are rarely presented with counter-stereotypic information. Indeed, African Americans are overrepresented in negative media coverage of welfare as well as media coverage of violent crime, making it unlikely that many whites will be exposed to counter-stereotypic situations. After all, a story about violent crime containing no picture or no other reference to race is seen by many to involve a black male. This being the case, it is likely that when primed to think of welfare or crime, most people holding negative stereotypes will use them in making policy evaluations.

Despite the recent advances in research on racial stereotypes, opportunities abound for future studies in the area. In particular, more research is needed to extend our understanding of the stereotypes of other minorities such as Hispanics, Asians, and Native Americans, as well as how stereotypes about black and other minorities fit into the wider constellation of prejudice and ethnocentrism in the United States. Moreover, while some studies have examined blacks' perceptions of whites' stereotypes of blacks, there are few studies of the social stereotypes African Americans hold. So while a growing literature has examined the political attitudes and behavior of blacks, little work has examined their contrasting images of whites and other groups.

Another important omission in the studies of public opinion in how racial stereotypes translate, if at all, into actual behavior in the political arena. While some studies reviewed above are obvious exceptions in this area, many question remain unanswered. Are African American candidates able to campaign in a manner that overcomes negative racial stereotypes? And are African American women candidates subject to a double-barreled form of discrimination?

More work is also needed on the role of the mass media in cultivating, activating, and reinforcing negative racial stereotypes in American politics. More attention to the various ways that biases in media coverage of issues like welfare and crime may lead to a more detailed understanding of how race-neutral issues (e.g., welfare and crime) often become racially charged. Finally, there must be a more concerted effort to think about the causal direction of stereotypes and policy attitudes. Some research suggests that programs like affirmative action, which are opposed by many whites, may actually engender negative stereotypes of blacks. More generally, stereotypes may serve as beliefs (or ideologies) to rationalize (or legitimize) discrimination and opposition to programs designed to assist blacks.

While it is always easier to generate a larger number of questions than answers about a topic as rich and important as racial stereotyping, if the research reviewed here is an indication, social science research can make an important contribution to understanding and documenting racial prejudice in the United States. Though we are constantly reminded in the United States that there is no guarantee that improved understanding leads to improved relations across the racial divide.

Further Reading

Gilens, Martin. *Why Americans Hate Welfare*. Chicago: University of Chicago Press, 1999. Presents a thorough examination of the large impact of whites' stereotypes of blacks on opposition to welfare, as well as the sources of such stereotypes in news coverage of poverty.

Gilliam, Franklin D., Jr., and Shanto Iyengar. "Prime Suspects: The Corrosive Influence of Local Television News on the View Public." *American Journal of Political Science* 44 (2000): 560–74. Uses experiments to demonstrate the power of televised news coverage of violent crime to shape negative views of African Americans and support for punitive crime policies.

Hurwitz, Jon, and Mark Peffley. *Perception and Prejudice: Race and Politics in the United States*. New Haven, CT: Yale University Press, 1998. Presents a thorough examination of whites' racial attitudes, including how whites' stereotypes of blacks influences attitudes toward welfare and criminal justice attitudes.

Sniderman, Paul M., and Edward G. Carmines. *Reaching Beyond Race*. Cambridge, MA: Harvard University Press, 1997. Examines the smaller role that whites' stereotypes of blacks play in shaping opinions on attitudes toward affirmative action, as well as ways to assess racial attitudes unobtrusively.

James M. Avery, Mark Peffley, and Jon Hurwitz

Random Digit Dialing (RDD)

Random digit dialing (RDD) is a group of techniques for selecting telephone numbers randomly from a **sample frame** of all possible telephone numbers. It overcomes the problems posed by unlisted or unpublished telephone numbers, generating representative samples that offer an equal probability of reaching any household with telephone access. In recent years, it has become complicated by the growing role of mobile telephones, which do not possess the same features as household telephones.

Surveys by telephone began in the 1920s and 1930s as soon as telephone directories were published. However, early surveys were local in scope, and the **sample frame** was typically the local telephone directory. The standardized U.S. telephone number system (3-digit area code and 7-digit number) was established in 1947, but it was not until 1961 that the telephone system supported full direct distance dialing (national dialing without operator assistance). This development made the ideal of selecting a random sample of all telephone numbers, and surveying them, a practical possibility. Prior to that time, telephone surveys were dependent on printed telephone directories and were usually local in scope; there are about five thousand telephone directories nationally.

In 1972 random digit dialing was proposed as a method of telephone sampling by Glasser and Metzger in the *Journal of Marketing Research*. In 1977 Thomas Danbury set up Survey Sampling Inc., the first major vendor of probability samples of telephone numbers. The first RDD studies selected numbers at random (usually a systematic random sample) from the universe of possible numbers defined by amalgamating data on all area codes (ACs) and central office codes (later known as prefixes) that were in use. However, in the 1970s the hit rate (i.e., the proportion of such numbers that were working household numbers) for this process was only 20 percent, leading to high costs for survey organizations in calling and screening nonworking numbers.

The first breakthrough came with the development (by Joseph Waksberg and Warren Mitofsky) of a method that increased the hit rate from 20 percent to about 50 percent through a two-phase sampling method now known as the Mitofsky-Waksberg method. A random sample of telephone numbers from the universe determined by working AC/prefixes would first be selected; these numbers defined a set of 100-block, eight-digit numbers (AC/prefix combinations followed by two random digits). If the selected number was a working household number, then numbers within that 100 block would be called until k (usually a number between four and eight) working household numbers were selected from that block. If the number was not a working household number, another 100 block would be selected. Through a clever application of probability proportional to size sampling, this procedure generates an equal probability sample of working household numbers from the universe, but with a much higher hit rate. However, the method had a number of practical difficulties related to problems with sparsely populated 100 blocks and lack of predictability of the required number of telephone numbers to be called.

The practical problems of the Mitofsky-Waksberg (M-W) method led to the exploration and introduction of a new RDD methodology in the 1980s called list-assisted sampling. There are two basic differences between list-assisted and M-W sampling. First, in list-assisted sampling, the universe of (potentially) eligible numbers is defined through detailed analyses of the universe of listed numbers. Second, list-assisted sampling is a one-phase rather than a two-phase sampling method, and control of the initial sample size is considerably greater. The objective is still to be able to select an equal probability sample of working telephone numbers in the United States. List-assisted sampling is now the dominant procedure for selecting RDD samples.

Mechanism and Specifications. Today, there are an estimated 100 million-plus telephone households in the United States. The ability to represent all households in a telephone sample is complicated by two main factors: some households are unlisted by choice, and others are unlisted by circumstance (particularly mobile phones). Approximately 30 percent of telephone households in the United States have unlisted numbers, and these are disproportionately distributed across the country. Statewide, unlisted rates range anywhere from 11 to 46 percent, and rates are even higher in some urban areas. In addition, each year, about 20 percent of American households move, so that 12 to 15 percent of the residential numbers in a typical directory are disconnected. Samples drawn entirely from directories and "plus-one" techniques, in which a directory-listed number is incremented by one in an attempt to incorporate some unlisted numbers, often significantly underrepresent unlisted households.

Creating a Frame for Random Digit Selection. Most RDD samples are generated using a database of "working blocks." A *block* (also known as a *100-bank* or a *bank*) is a set of 100 contiguous numbers identified by the first eight digits of a telephone number. For example, in the telephone number 312-749-5512, "31274955" is the block containing that phone number, and includes the set of all numbers between 312-749-5500 and 312-749-5599. Blocks are merged with the database of all directory-listed households in the country and are determined to be *working* if at least one listed telephone number is found in that block. Once the working blocks are identified, the RDD frame is stratified (e.g., by county). The number of working blocks in an exchange is multiplied by 100 (the number of possible 10-digit telephone numbers in a block) to calculate the total number of possible phone numbers.

Sample Selection. Samples are typically drawn systematically from the frame. EPSEM (equal probability of selection method) samples are single stage, equal probability samples of all possible ten-digit telephone numbers in blocks with one or more listed telephone numbers (i.e., working blocks). The Working Residential Number (WRN) rate for an EPSEM sample is on average about 50 percent.

Selection Options. Samples can be ordered from geographic areas as large as the entire United States and as small as census tracts or exchanges. The exact geography from which the sample is to be selected must be specified to the vendor. Some common geographic selections include states, counties, zip codes, area code/exchange combinations, and groups of census tracts. Currently, vendors will not provide samples ordered by census block or block group due to the instability of data from census geographies being applied to telephone geographies at this detailed level.

Several demographic selection options are also available for RDD and listed samples. Samples can be ordered to target racial or ethnic groups, particular income brackets, urban, suburban, or rural areas, and age groups. The information used to target these groups is based on census data. For example, racial groups are targeted based on their density in the population using census data, which are typically available down to tract level. RDD samples have the option of being targeted based on race, income, and urban status. Listed samples can also be targeted based on ethnicity and age group.

Sample Screening. Often, there are particular types of numbers that researchers would like to exclude from a sample. For example, in a survey targeting households, it is useful to remove known businesses from the sample before beginning data collection to reduce the number of calls made to ineligible lines. In most surveys, known disconnected lines are removed before data collection. This process of *screening* for particular types of phone numbers usually involves creating a *flag,* or identifying variable, to label each sampled number with a particular disposition (e.g., disconnected, business, fax). The flag can later be used to remove unwanted numbers, such as disconnects, from the sample. Screening can be accomplished using various methods, including automated tone detection, database matching, and manual identification.

Automated tone detection is a method by which sampled telephone numbers are called by a machine that identifies special tones the instant a connection is made (usually before the phone even rings on the receiving end). Some tones signify nonworking (disconnected) numbers; others, fax or modem lines. Database matching involves comparing sampled numbers to a database to identify particular numbers for possible removal from (or inclusion in) the sample. One common instance of this involves matching sampled numbers to a database of known businesses. Finally, manual identification involves a human being calling each sampled number to determine whether it is a nonworking (disconnected), business, fax, modem, or household line.

Coverage and Hit Rate. If a target population is defined by a geographic area, coverage and hit rate become additional factors important in the design and selection of a RDD sample. Because telephone geographies do not coincide with physical geographies, it is necessary to find an appropriate balance between how well the targeted geography will be covered by a telephone sample, and how efficient the telephone sample will be in terms of incidence. Coverage refers to the proportion of numbers in the targeted geographic area that are included among the frame of telephone numbers from which the sample is selected. Incidence, or *hit rate*, refers to the proportion of numbers in the frame that are actually in the targeted geographic area. Generally there are trade-offs between the two, and both must be considered when specifying the sample. For all RDD samples, telephone sampling vendors translate the targeted geography into a set of telephone exchanges before selecting the sample. They can then provide an analysis of how well these exchanges line up with the specified geographic boundaries. Based on this analysis, one can select the set of exchanges that represent the coverage level and geographic incidence most appropriate for the study.

Mobile Phones. Of particular concern with respect to RDD coverage and sampling is mobile phone usage. The FCC indicates that more than 60 percent of U.S. households have at least one mobile phone, and estimates of households with only cellular service range from 2 to 3 percent and are steadily increasing. Because wireless-only users tend to be younger, urban, single, renters, and in one-person households, noncoverage of this group in RDD surveys could severely underrepresent particular sub-groups in the population.

The pricing structure in the United States is such that mobile phone owners pay for all outgoing *and* incoming calls. As a result, legal restrictions for calling mobile phones have been imposed, and cell phone sampling frames are not publicly available. Another issue that complicates the sampling of cell phones relates to the idea of the sampling unit. In most RDD surveys, the household is the primary sampling unit from which household members may be selected. However, with mobile phones, which are more likely for personal or business use rather than for an entire household, the mobile phone user is the primary and final sampling unit.

Because of the increasing usage of mobile phones, it will be necessary to overcome the barriers to sampling mobile phone users (*see* **Cellular Telephone Survey Methods**). If the pricing structure were changed such that incoming calls were not charged to the mobile phone owner, the ethical difficulties and legal restrictions would likely be eased. In the meantime, free anytime minutes or other monetary incentives could be offered to offset the cost of the call, or a toll-free number to be used as a mobile phone equivalent to an 800 number could be created. A group was formed to work with the U.S. Census Bureau to include a short sequence of questions in the February, 2004, Current Population Survey. This should provide the first set of reliable, nationwide estimates relating to mobile-only households. Extensive future research is expected in this field.

Further Reading

Biemer, Paul, and Don Akin. "The Efficiency of List-Assisted Random Digit Dialing Sampling Schemes for Single and Dual Frame Surveys." *Proceedings of the American Statistical Association, Survey Research Methods Section* (1994). Available at http://www.amstat.org/sections/srms/Proceedings/papers/1994_001.pdf.

Murphy, Whitney, Colm O'Muircheartaigh, and Carol-Ann Emmons, with Steven Pedlow and Rachel Harter. "Optimizing Call Strategies in RDD: Differential Nonresponse Bias and Costs in REACH 2010." *Proceedings of the American Statistical Association, Survey Research Methods Section* (2003).

Whitney Murphy and Colm O'Muircheartaigh

Rare Event Measures

Rare event measures are questions specially designed to elicit the odds of an infrequent event occurring. Ample research has shown that the probability of rare events tends to be overestimated. Such biases in risk judgments have been attributed to the influence of context effects, like the salience, or lack thereof, of the event. They can have harmful implications when new policies are implemented on the basis of biased risk estimates. Rare event measures that minimize context effects are thus important to identify.

Judgments of rare events can be assessed in a variety of ways. Figure 1 provides examples of the different approaches that have been used to assess perceived risk in quantitative terms. They include linear approaches like open response formats (see Figure 1a) and scales with constant (equal) intervals (see Figure 1b), as well as nonlinear (e.g., logarithmic) rating scales (see Figure 1c). In general, open response formats have been found to lead to substantial overestimation of the probability of rare events and low correlations with actual risk factors. Equal interval scales usually perform slightly better than open response formats, resulting in somewhat less overestimation and somewhat higher correlations with relevant risk factors. As one reason for their limited measurement performance it has been pointed out that equal interval scales constrain respondents in expressing low probabilities precisely (e.g., in Figure 1b they would either be expected to give values of 0 percent or 10 percent for expressing a low probability). Consequently, the precision of the estimates and chances to detect meaningful relationships in the data are also restricted.

The nonlinear rating scale shown in Figure 1c can be conceived as a variation of the three-step hierarchical probability assessment procedure developed by Linville, Fischer, and Fischhoff. They asked people to estimate the probability of getting infected with HIV during the next three years as the result of sexual activity. Participants were directed to a general order of magnitude location by asking them to provide a whole percent if they think that their chances of getting infected with HIV are between 1 and 100 percent. If they thought their chances of getting infected were less than 1 percent they were given options from 0.1

Figure 1. Different Approaches to Assessing Probability Judgments

Linear Scales

(a) Open response format: _____ %

(b) Equal interval rating scale:

☐ ☐ ☐ ☐ ☐ ☐ ☐ ☐ ☐ ☐ ☐
0% 10% 20% 30% 40% 50% 60% 70% 80% 90% 100%

Nonlinear Scales

(c) Odds scale (Diefenbach et al. 1993, Study 2):

☐   ☐   ☐   ☐   ☐
no   1 chance   1 chance   1 chance   certain
chance   in 1000   in 100   in 10   (100%)
            (0.1%)   (1%)   (10%)

(d) Magnifying Glass Scale (Woloshin et al. 2000):

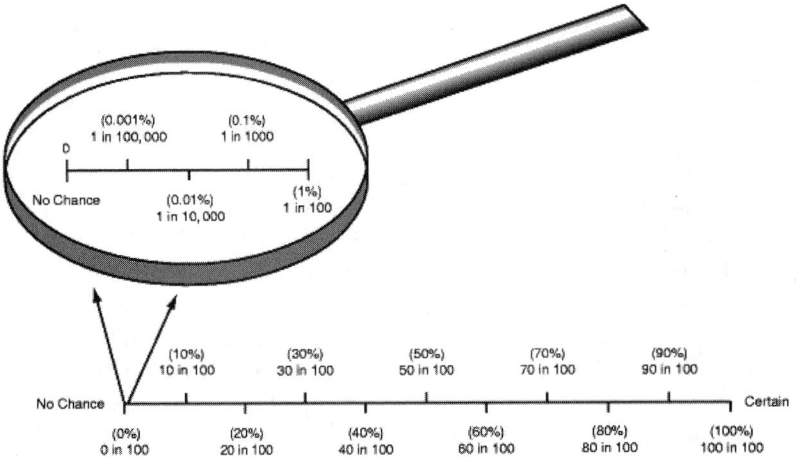

(e) Simplified nonlinear scale ("stretched scale"):

☐ ☐ ☐ ☐ ☐ ☐ ☐ ☐ ☐ ☐ ☐ ☐ ☐ ☐ ☐ ☐
0% 0.1% 0.2% 0.3% 0.4% 0.5% 1.0% 2.0% 5% 10% 20% 30% 40% 60% 80% 100%

percent (or one in a thousand) to 1 percent (or ten in a thousand) in 0.1 percent intervals. Those who thought that their chances of getting infected are still smaller (less than one in a thousand) were given options between 0.01 percent (or one in ten thousand) and 0.1 percent (or ten in ten thousand). Using this approach, Linville, Fischer, and Fischhoff substantially increased the accuracy of probability judgments for various rare events when compared with actual risk statistics. A drawback of this method is that it is rather complicated to administer, particularly in self-administered surveys.

Several researchers therefore developed other versions of nonlinear rating scales for the assessment of small probabilities, particularly "odds scales" as the one shown in Figure 1c. These, "one in x" scales, though, have been found to not work well in terms of test-retest reliability, accuracy, validity, and rated usability. Apparently it confuses respondents that smaller chances are expressed with larger numbers in the denominator (e.g., one in two hundred vs. one in five hundred) and that "x" decreases from left to right while the percentage values with which the odds are coupled increase. Thus, while a "one in x" format might be useful for risk communication, as has been suggested by various researchers, it might not be useful for assessing perceived risk.

To alleviate these problems, Woloshin and his colleagues (2000) introduced a new rating scale (see Figure 1d). This scale combines a linear with a nonlinear approach. Building on the earlier work by Linville, Fischer, and Fischhoff others, their "magnifying glass scale" has a linear portion for larger probabilities and a nonlinear, logarithmic portion for small probabilities. The picture of a magnifying glass is used to represent the logarithmic part with probabilities between 0 and 1 percent. That is, the portion of the scale that corresponds with the actual statistical probability of the event is "magnified." Respondents are asked to place a mark in either the magnifying glass or the linear portion of the scale. Woloshin and his colleagues found that risk estimates for rare events (e.g., becoming the parent of sextuplets sometime in the next ten years) were orders of magnitude lower, and thereby more accurate, when this scale was used than when a linear scale was used (median perceived chance of 10^{-5} vs. 10^{-2}). Also, the scale performed equally well as a linear scale in terms of test-retest reliability and usability, and it performed better in terms of user satisfaction and the perceived ability to represent small chances. Using direct rankings of the probability of events as the gold standard, estimates gathered with this scale were also found to be equally valid as estimates gathered with a linear scale.

Recently, an improved nonlinear rating scale was introduced (see Figure 1e). It builds on previous nonlinear approaches described above but avoids some of their disadvantages in terms of clarity and ease of use. First, unlike the logarithmic scales in Figure 1c and the magnifier scale, the new stretched scale is a pure percentage scale. The use of the "one in x" format was completely avoided because it appears to confuse respondents. Second, the scale does not display a magnifying glass, thereby stressing the continuity of the scale and rendering it easier to administer in surveys and questionnaires.

In two experiments the new stretched scale was tested in terms of accuracy and validity by Knäuper and her colleagues. Participants were either asked to estimate the percentage of Germans currently infected with HIV or to estimate the percentage of Germans who will develop skin cancer at some point in their lives. To examine whether the stretched scale results in more accurate probability judgments the probability estimates were assessed with different types of scales, namely an open response format, an equal interval scale, or a stretched scale. The obtained probability estimates were compared with official statistics for the events. As expected, the results showed that the medians of the estimated risks were closest to the public health statistics when the stretched rating scale was used.

To examine whether the stretched scale results in more valid risk assessments than ordinary rating scales, predictive validity was evaluated in a second study by examining the relationship between the perceived probability of developing a specific disease and self-reported protective behaviors and behavioral intentions, respectively, for the disease. Participants were randomly assigned to either an equal interval scale or a stretched scale condition and their perceived risk of personally developing skin cancer in their lifetime was assessed in each group. The results show that the perceived risk of developing skin cancer, together with past protection behaviors, was a significant predictor of behavioral intentions when the stretched scale was used, but not when the equal interval scale was used. The results of this study thus demonstrated predictive power of the perceived risk variable for health behavior intentions when it was assessed with the stretched scale, but not when it was assessed with an ordinary equal interval rating scale. This suggests that risk assessments using stretched scales may result in more statistical power to uncover existing relationships between relevant variables.

Woloshin and his colleagues explained the increased accuracy achieved with the magnifier scale simply with the fact that it allows people to choose precise small values at the low end of the continuum whereas equal interval scales do not allow such precision. For example, on the equal interval scale in Figure 1b people are restricted to either choose 0 or 10 percent to express a low probability. Respondents would be hesitant to select 0 percent, which would indicate no chance of it happening, but could then only choose 10 percent as the next possible value for expressing a small probability. This would result in inflated estimates if they really wanted to express a smaller likelihood. Thus, nonlinear scales such as the magnifier scale allow distinguishing between small differences in risk perception of rare events. In other words, they are more precise measurement tools for rare events.

It was recently suggested, however, that the pure opportunity to express small probabilities cannot be the only reason for the increased accuracy and validity of the magnifier scale. Specifically, open response formats (and to a certain extent equal interval scales) also allow respondents to express small and very small probabilities. Nevertheless, estimates given in an open response format or on an equal interval scale show little convergence with individual risk factors and are usually highly inflated for rare events. For example, in a recent study, by Knäuper and Kornik, college students were asked in an open response format to estimate the probability that a woman would contract HIV in one encounter of unprotected vaginal intercourse with an infected male. The median estimate was 75 percent while the actual epidemiologic estimate is 0.1 percent. The range and variance of the judgments was huge (range: 0.05 percent to 100 percent; standard deviation: 33.89 percent).

Thus, the pure opportunity to express small probabilities cannot be the only reason why "stretched scales" like the magnifier scale fare better in terms of accuracy and validity. Two additional explanations have been proposed. First, nonlinear scales may result in more accurate judgments because they give respondents "hints" that a small probability value is the correct response to the question. That is, the small values in the scale may simply have demand character such that they suggest to respondents to use these values for a response, resulting in higher correlations with official statistics if the researcher chose values that match the official statistics. The second explanation entails that the nonlinear scales lead to more *thoughtful*, and thereby more accurate and valid, responses. Specifically, by providing cues about the reasonable probability range of the target event respondents may retrieve relevant knowledge about the event from memory and their judgments may be less affected by unrelated context information. This is in contrast to open response formats and equal interval scales which implicitly suggest that the entire range from 0 percent to 100 percent qualifies as correct responses, thus leading respondents to base their judgment on irrelevant context influences such as the salience, perceived threat or media coverage of the event.

Preliminary support for the second explanation is provided by evidence from a study conducted by Woloshin and his colleagues, showing that response distributions are only shifted toward the lower numeric values for rare events, not for common events. Furthermore, the study found that judgments seem to become not just more accurate (i.e., closer to official statistics) but also more valid (i.e., higher correlations with direct rankings of different events and better prediction of behavioral intentions).

More research is needed to examine whether such nonlinear scales merely provide cues as to the correct range of probability of the target event or indeed lead to more thoughtful and thereby more valid responses. Furthermore, the external validity of risk assessments elicited with stretched rating scales needs investigation: Stretched scales, compared with other approaches, may maximize the input of the reasoning and knowledge and minimize the influence of other, temporary context influences. However, it is as yet unknown whether judgments on such scales better reflect the perceived risk that mediates decision making in real life.

Further Reading

Diefenbach, M. A., N. D. Weinstein, and J. O'Reilly. "Scales for Assessing Perceptions of Health Hazard Susceptibility." *Health Education Research: Theory and Practice* 8 (1993): 181–92. Introduction of a nine-point logarithmic scale, which performed very poorly in comparison to seven other numerical and verbal scales, and open-response scales.

Knäuper, B., and R. Kornik. "Perceived Transmissibility of Sexually Transmitted Infections: Lack of Differentiation Between HIV and Chlamydia." *Sexually Transmitted Infections* (2004). Shows that assessing probabilities in an open response format can result in flat distributions (large range and variance), rendering it meaningless to calculate and report averages.

Linville, P. W., G. W. Fischer, and B. Fischhoff. "AIDS Risk Perceptions and Decision Biases." In *The Social Psychology of HIV Infection*, edited by J. B. Pryor and G. D. Reeder. Hillsdale, NJ: Lawrence Erlbaum, 1993, pp. 5–38. Development of a three-step hierarchical probability assessment procedure that can be seen as a precursor of the later developed nonlinear rating scales.

Woloshin, S., L. M. Schwartz, S. Byram, B. Fischhoff, and H. G. Welch. "A New Scale for Assessing Perceptions of Chance: A Validation Study." *Medical Decision Making* 20 (2000): 298–307. Introduction of a nonlinear rating scale, the magnifying glass scale, which is differentiated into very low probabilities at the extreme lower end of the scale. The studies demonstrate improved reliability and validity of low-risk estimates as compared with ordinary assessment approaches.

Christine Stich and Bärbel Knäuper

RBS. *See* Registration-Based Sampling

RDD. *See* Random Digit Dialing

Referendum. *See* Initiative and Referendum Voting, Public Opinion on

Refusal

A refusal occurs either when a sample household chooses not to participate in a survey—through the person who is the first point of contact refusing to cooperate, or by the selected respondent refusing to participate—or when a respondent breaks off an interview while in process. Refusals are important to the field of public opinion as they are widely assumed to impact survey quality. The American Association for Public Opinion Research's "Best Practices" guidelines state: "[F]ailure to follow up nonrespondents and refusals, in particular, can severely undermine an otherwise well-designed survey." But while survey refusals are on the rise, and evidence exists that the types of people who are reluctant to participate in surveys are different from those who cooperate easily, there is conflicting evidence on whether they impact the aggregate results, or accuracy, of surveys.

Respondents refuse to cooperate with survey interviewers for a variety of reasons, some situational, and some general. Perhaps the foremost situational reason is inconvenience. In a telephone survey, for example, the specific time an interviewer calls may be inconvenient for the respondent or the household, resulting in a refusal. In addition, the length of the survey may be inconvenient for the respondent—the longer a survey is, the greater the likelihood of refusals. Although disclosing the length of the survey during the introduction results in fewer refusals overall, even for longer surveys.

Other situational factors that influence cooperation include the topic of the survey—whether it is interesting to the respondent, for example—and the mode of the survey. Face-to-face interviewing generally results in fewer refusals than does telephone interviewing. In addition, telephone surveys based on lists (in which the interviewer is asking for a specific person) generate fewer refusals than do **random digit dialing** surveys.

Some potential respondents also have a general reluctance to participate in surveys. Recent increases in telephone sales (telemarketing) are believed to negatively affect respondents' willingness to engage with unsolicited callers in telephone surveys. In addition, some potential respondents have privacy concerns—doubting that their answers, specifically their personal information, will be kept confidential.

Most telephone refusals occur early in the call, specifically before the introduction. Fewer occur once the survey is in process, although again, the longer the survey, the greater the likelihood that respondents will break off the call while the survey is under way. As with refusals in general, in-person interviews result in fewer break-offs than do telephone surveys.

In general, the survey research industry has seen a steady rise in the rate of survey refusals over time. Recent findings by the Council for Marketing and

Opinion Research (CMOR) place the average telephone refusal rate at 33 percent (defined as the total number of refusals/break-offs divided by the total number of contacts; *see* **Outcome Rates**). There is no doubt that increasing rates of refusal should be of concern to the industry, but there is conflicting evidence about whether current levels pose a danger to survey accuracy.

Little is, or can be, known about respondents who continually refuse to participate in surveys—if they are never successfully interviewed, their attributes or attitudes can never be known. It is possible, however, to look at differences between those who initially refuse to participate, but are convinced at a later date to cooperate, and those who are initially cooperative to provide some clues to the differences between the types of people who refuse and the types who do not. In other words, the question of what effects that reducing refusal rates has on surveys can be answered, but the question of what effects that completely eliminating refusals might have, cannot.

Potential respondents who initially refuse to participate in a survey differ demographically from those who readily accept. Table 1 illustrates some of the well-documented differences. The table contains basic demographic data from respondents to CBS News and CBS News/*New York Times* surveys in the year 2000. The first column contains those respondents who accepted survey participation from the start, and the second contains those respondents who initially refused participation, but were later convinced to take part. As previous studies have shown, refusers tend to be older, less educated, and more likely to earn mid- or low-level household incomes than respondents who initially cooperate with survey interviewers (and are more likely to refuse to give income information). In addition, women are more likely to initially refuse to participate in surveys than men are.

Evidence also exists of some attitudinal differences, although it is mixed. Refusers are less likely to be politically engaged than are cooperative respondents, which may also be an explanation for why they have less interest in participating in public opinion surveys. In addition, pundits have argued that surveys typically underrepresent political conservatives as they are reluctant to cooperate with media polls. While there is some evidence that increased response rates (and thereby fewer refusals) do yield more conservative respondent pools, there is also evidence to the contrary—that increased response rates have no effect on the partisan or ideological predispositions of the respondent pool as a whole.

An even bigger question than whether refusers are different from acceptors is whether these individual differences translate into overall differences in survey results. In one of the few studies of its kind, Keeter and his co-authors (2000) conducted two surveys in the summer of 1997—one was a typical five-day survey while the other (their "rigorous" study) was conducted over the course of eight weeks using a much more exhaustive effort to contact respondents and gain their cooperation. While greatly increasing their response rate, and decreasing their refusal rate, by taking significantly more time to complete a survey, Keeter and his colleagues found few differences in the surveys' overall results. When specifically analyzing the differences between "amenable households" and "reluctant households" they found significant differences on only five of eighty-eight demographic and attitudinal measures: a rate commensurate with chance. This indicates that those more reluctant to participate in surveys are little different

Table 1. Unweighted Demographics for Initial Acceptors and Initial Refusers in CBS News and CBS News/*New York Times* National Surveys, 2000

Demographics	Initial Acceptors	Initial Refusers
Age	*(percent)*	*(percent)*
18–29	17	13
30–44	32	24
45–64	33	33
65+	18	30
Education		
< High school	9	12
High school grad	30	34
Some college	27	25
College grad +	35	29
Gender		
Male	44	38
Female	57	62
Race		
White	83	86
Nonwhite	16	13
Income		
<$15,000	10	13
$15K–$30K	21	21
$30K–$50K	28	25
$50K–$75K	17	14
$75,000+	18	17
Refused	7	10
Number of Cases	16,966	643

from those who cooperate easily. On the issue of whether any existing differences affect survey results overall, in comparing their rigorous survey with their standard survey, they found there were few aggregate differences. On political and social opinion questions differences between the two surveys were rarely more than a few percentage points in the modal category.

While refusals do not currently appear to affect overall survey results, the question of survey accuracy remains. If all surveys are underrepresenting certain groups—specifically, consistent refusers—then their accuracy remains in question. Unfortunately, there are few ways to measure survey accuracy, as there is typically no objective measure of public opinion with which to compare it. The one exception is pre-election surveys, which can be directly compared to actual election results to determine their accuracy. While these surveys are also subject to other influences on their accuracy—such as determining likely voters—on the aggregate there are differences among surveys based on their likelihood of containing reluctant respondents. Specifically, studies have found that pre-election polls by organizations that follow more rigorous methods in their surveys, such as consistent refusal conversion attempts, are more likely to yield accurate pre-election predictions. This indicates that survey accuracy may be affected by the inclusion or exclusion of refusers. But whether these differences in accuracy are due solely to refusal conversion or to a host of survey method differences—organizations that follow rigorous refusal conversion policies are also likely to differ on other survey method techniques from firms that do not—has yet to be demonstrated.

Further Reading

Brehm, John. *The Phantom Respondents: Opinion Surveys and Political Representation.* Ann Arbor: University of Michigan Press, 1993.

Crespi, Irving. *Sources of Accuracy and Error in Pre-Election Polling.* New York: Russell Sage Foundation, 1988.

DeMaio, Theresa J. "Refusals: Who, Where and Why?" *Public Opinion Quarterly* 44 (1980): 223–33.

Keeter, Scott, Carolyn Miller, Andrew Kohut, Robert M. Groves, and Stanley Presser. "Consequences of Reducing Nonresponse in a National Telephone Survey." *Public Opinion Quarterly* 64 (2000): 125–48.

Monika L. McDermott

Registration-Based Sampling (RBS)

Registration-based sampling (RBS) is a telephone sampling technique used by survey researchers conducting pre-election surveys. It is a special case of list-based sampling, where the list in question is a registration list or, more precisely, a list of registered voters with known phone numbers. In contrast, **random digit dialing** (RDD), the first and most widely used telephone sampling method, involves calling randomly chosen phone numbers and, upon contacting a residence, selecting a randomly chosen member of the household who is eligible to vote.

The core principle behind registration-based sampling is that voter registration lists provide important clues about who will vote on Election Day. Registration lists, which are typically available from commercial list vendors and local government offices, contain background information such as age, precinct, and turnout in past elections. The quality of this background information varies from one jurisdiction to the next, but even minimal information such as age and data of registration can be helpful in distinguishing likely voters from unlikely voters.

Background predictors of voter turnout are used to shape the sampling weights assigned to different segments of the registration list (*see* **Weighting**). Intuition suggests that any survey of the voting electorate should place special emphasis on the opinions of citizens with a high ex ante probability of voting. Consider the limiting case in which members of the population come in two types, those who are certain to vote and those who are certain to abstain. There would be no point in interviewing any members of the latter group. By this logic, constructing an optimal sample—that is, a sample that gives the smallest prediction errors when forecasting the actual election outcome—should take notice of prior voting history because it predicts whether someone will vote in the upcoming election.

When building a weighted sample, each person on the registration list is assigned a probability of voting in the next election, based on such factors as registration date and past voting history. These probabilities enable the researcher to create a profile of those who will actually cast ballots. A random sample is drawn from this expected electorate (*see* **Simple Random Sampling**). The procedure of constructing a weighted sample involves the following steps. First, one breaks the registration list into strata. For purposes of illustration, suppose one divides a registration list into three strata: those who were not registered prior to the last election, those who were registered but did not vote, and those who voted. Second, one estimates the rate at which each stratum is expected to vote (more about how to do this in a moment). Third, one multiplies the voting rates times the number of people in each stratum to find the size of the anticipated electorate and what fraction of the electorate each stratum constitutes. These fractions then become the sampling weights for the RBS survey.

For example, suppose that the three strata consist of 100,000 new registrants, 400,000 past abstainers, and 500,000 past voters. Suppose that voting rates among the three strata are 50, 20, and 90 percent. The expected electorate therefore consists of 50,000 new registrants (8.6 percent), 80,000 past abstainers (13.8 percent), and 450,000 past voters (77.6 percent). When drawing a sample from the registration list to be interviewed, 8.6 percent of the sample should be new registrants, 13.8 percent past abstainers, and 77.6 percent past voters.

In practice, voting rates within each stratum are not known beforehand. It is therefore handy to know how voting history has predicted subsequent turnout in recent elections. This forecasting exercise is best conducted using registration lists from prior elections. For example, the extent to which voting in 2004 predicts voting in 2006 may be inferred from the corresponding relationship between 2000 and 2002 voting. This approach may break down, however, if the current election has no close parallels in the past.

The mechanics of an RDD survey are shaped by the fact that phone calls are placed to people whose identities and addresses are unknown. The RDD survey relies on the respondent to furnish all of the key pieces of information needed to interpret the survey results. The respondent must help the interviewer select a randomly chosen member of the household for questioning, who in turn must furnish information about whether they are currently registered to vote and whether they intend to vote in the upcoming election.

The mechanics of an RBS survey are much more straightforward. Since the identity of the respondent is known to the interviewer, the caller may ask for the respondent by name. No further enumeration of the household is necessary. The survey is shortened not only by the absence of enumeration procedures at the start of the survey but also by the information available to the researcher from the registration list. There is no need to quiz respondents about their age, whether they are registered to vote, or whether they happened to vote in the last election. In terms of gaining the cooperation of respondents, one advantage of RBS is that it enables survey organizations to send out a letter ahead of time explaining the purpose of the survey, inviting participation, and perhaps offering some incentive.

An even greater drawback of RDD is the necessity of conducting interviews whose sole purpose is to screen out nonvoters. Because the aim of pre-election polling is to describe the opinions of the voting public, a great many respondents are excused during the interview process. Unregistered voters receive a polite thank you, and their interviews are terminated early on. Respondents who make it past this screen are cross-examined about their proclivity to vote in the upcoming election. Those who express uncertainty about whether they will cast a ballot or who report having skipped elections in the past are discreetly removed from the sample afterwards. Those who remain constitute the sample of "likely voters" whose opinions become the poll's official results. Whether this procedure provides a reliable means for forecasting election outcomes depends in part on whether the interviewer accurately discerns which respondents will vote. In many, if not most elections, voters and nonvoters have different candidate preferences; mistaking a nonvoter for a voter in these instances will bias the survey results.

The sampling principle underlying RBS is that respondents are selected in proportion to their share of the expected electorate. Background information is used to identify likely voters and give them greater prominence in the sample. By design, some of the RBS will be conducted with low propensity voters, whose opinions will be weighted according to their (small) share of the expected electorate. But none of the interviews are discarded, as is the case with RDD surveys.

The cost advantages of RBS are magnified when pollsters attempt to study specialized populations. In most states, where absentee voters constitute a small but important fraction of the electorate, it is prohibitively expensive to conduct an RDD survey of absentee voters. If, for example, 50 percent of the adults in a state vote in federal mid-term elections, and only 20 percent of all voters cast absentee ballots, RDD must plow through approximately ten screening interviews to reach a single absentee voter. Similar arguments apply to surveys of young voters, minority voters, or voters who have recently switched parties. RBS seems particularly valuable for journalists or political marketers intent upon studying small segments of the electorate.

A similar point holds for populations defined by geographic boundaries that do not coincide with telephone exchanges. Consider, for example, the case of polling recently redrawn congressional districts. One may not wish to depend on RDD respondents to report accurately whether they reside in the newly drawn district. Even if respondents can be trusted to reliably identify their congressional district, the RDD poll will have incurred additional costs when screening ineligible respondents.

Matching addresses and phone numbers is the point at which slippage occurs in the RBS sampling process. The availability of listed numbers varies widely by region. Iowa is very good; California is very bad. In some cases the matching rate can be improved by sending registration lists out to multiple vendors, who draw their phone numbers from different sources.

Nothing prevents the pollster from falling back on RDD in cases where the phone match is particularly poor. It should be stressed, however, that the forecasting accuracy of RBS compared with RDD is an empirical question, for as we note below, RBS may have certain advantages in terms of reducing nonresponse. If RDD phone surveys are enlisting the cooperation of less than half of the households they contact, it is by no means clear ex ante which source of bias is more problematic. The only way to assess the relative accuracy of RDD and RBS is to do both and see what happens. As experience with RBS accumulates, pollsters may develop hybrid approaches that use weighted averages of both RBS and RDD results.

Although knowing the names of potential respondents alleviates some of the clumsiness of RDD enumeration procedures, it may have some drawbacks. It appears that respondents to RBS surveys may need extra assurances about confidentiality. One subtle but nonetheless noteworthy difference between RBS and RDD respondents is that the former seem to show more reluctance to disclose their vote intentions. A possible solution to this problem involves sending prospective RBS respondents a letter in advance of the survey encouraging them to participate. This letter, however, can be costly to print and mail. Worse yet, if the election suddenly becomes uninteresting, as occurs when one of the major candidate drops out of the race, the advance letter becomes a deadweight loss.

RBS is at present a promising but relatively untested technique. In terms of forecasting accuracy, RBS has performed well in a handful of head-to-head competitions with RDD. Not only has RBS done a better job of anticipating the actual election outcomes, it has done so at substantially lower cost. Nevertheless, questions remain. Can RBS be used successfully in elections in which voters can register at the polls? To what extent do interregional differences in the quality of registration and phone lists bias RBS election forecasts? How should RBS survey analysts make use of the stated vote intentions of RBS respondents?

One of the constraints limiting the growth of RBS is the absence of a national **sample frame.** Even a nationally representative clustered sample currently remains beyond the reach of pollsters seeking to forecast presidential elections. Federal legislation mandating the standardization of state voting lists will help to improve the quality of national lists, but the future development of RBS hinges on market forces. Will list vendors find it profitable to develop high quality clustered samples? Will pollsters find RBS sufficiently attractive to bear the costs of these more expensive sampling frames?

Further Reading

Green, Donald P., and Alan S. Gerber. "Enough Already with Random Digit Dialing: Using Registration-Based Sampling to Improve Pre-Election Polling." Paper presented at the 58th meeting of the American Association for Public Opinion Research, Nashville, Tennessee, and the Gallup Conference on Improving the Accuracy of Polling, May 2–4, 2002, Washington, DC, 2003. Available on the Internet at http://www.vcsnet.com/pdf/RegistrationBasedSampling.pdf.

Mann, Christopher. "Improving Pre-Election Forecasts from Registration Based Sampling: Using Voter Registration Data to Predict Partisan Vote Intention and to Allocate Undecided Voters." Paper presented at the Annual Meeting of the American Political Science Association, Philadelphia, Pennsylvania, 2003. Available on the Internet at http://www.vcsnet.com/pdf/Mann-APSA_2003.

Schwartz, Doug, and Clay F. Richards. "The Big East Two: A Comparison of RBS and RDD Polls in the 2002 Elections in New York and Pennsylvania." Paper presented at the Annual Meeting of the American Political Science Association, Philadelphia, Pennsylvania, 2003. Available on the Internet at http://www.vcsnet.com/pdf/ Schwartz-Richards-APSA_2003.

Donald P. Green

Religious Differences in Public Opinion

Religious faith plays a role in structuring differences in public opinion. It distinguishes issue positions, value orientations, and voting patterns. Considered here are the seven major traditions: mainline and evangelical Protestants, black Christians, white Catholics, Hispanic Christians, Jews, and Seculars. Mainline Protestants are descended from the early leaders of American society—the Puritans and the Congregationalists, the Episcopalians, and the Presbyterians. As the center of religious and political gravity moved westward and ethnic groups were assimilated, these expanded to include the Methodists and the Evangelical Lutheran Church of America. Generally people of social position, economic means, and higher education, the mainline Protestants often formed the power elites of Middle American towns and cities. Although Episcopalian and some Lutheran churches had hierarchical church polities, most mainline Protestants practiced consultative or democratic decision making and effectively taught civic skills to the laity. Generally the laity thought of themselves as social transformationists. Capitalism, as a liberal economic system, was good, but enlightened capitalism, which used government to assure equality of access to those less privileged was better, because it expanded opportunity and dignity to a broader proportion of people, who after all, were created in the image of God. About a third of mainliners are biblical literalists or claim a born-again conversion experience, in contrast to evangelicals who have twice these proportions. While not denying the divinity of Christ, they pay more attention to the principles of social justice that Christ taught.

Both Max Weber and Alexis de Tocqueville saw in this style of religion that placed less emphasis on sacramental, literalistic, or priestly authority, the roots of American democracy and capitalism. Affiliation carried a notion of individual "membership," of passing muster for righteousness. With church membership one knew whom to trust in economic transactions and political office. Religious historian Martin Marty characterized it not as a believer's religion but a behaver's religion. Over the past half-century, mainline Protestants have evolved from the core of the Republican Party to somewhat unreliable coalition partners. In part, that is because they have lost on many issues that defined the earlier GOP: the role of the government as engine for furthering **civil rights** and racial equality, **feminism** and **abortion** rights, a progressive tax structure and the state provision of **welfare,** and multilateralism in foreign policy. Analyzing American **National Election Study** data from the past half century, Leege and his associates have shown that those mainline Protestants who left the GOP did so in direct proportion to the GOP's conservative message aimed at attracting evangelical Protestants. Throughout the later half of the twentieth century, defections increased whenever the party made heavy use of racial codewords that suggested negative judgments about African Americans, preached restrictive practices on abortion, and adopted a more bellicose posture during the Cold War. In fact in 2000 for the first time, Democratic identifications and loyalty among mainline Protestants had grown so high that their actual partisan advantage in turnout and preference shifted in favor of the Democrats.

On specific issue domains, slightly less than half of mainline Protestants take the most permissive position on the availability of abortion—less than seculars and Jews, but twice as many as evangelical Protestants. They are generally more conservative on economic policies than on social issues, but approximate the positions of evangelical Protestants, Roman Catholics, and seculars on a bundle of issues thought to tap economic conservatism. Only Jews and black Christians tip in the economically liberal direction (*see* **Liberalism and Conservatism; Racial Differences in Public Opinion**). Still, it is important to remember that within each tradition there may be great diversity of viewpoints.

For white evangelical Protestants, however, the movement of the past half-century has been all in the same direction: Republican. Only the presence of Southern Democrats with evangelical roots—Johnson, Carter in his first run, and Clinton in his first run—slowed their realignment. Actually, when party identification, defection, and turnout enter the same equation, the Democratic presidential candidate has carried them only once in the past half century: Johnson in 1964. Otherwise defection to Republicans was so high and turnout of Democrats so low that Republicans carried them, often handily as in 1972 and ever since 1984. Leege and his associates show that realignment occurred, first in the 1960s largely due to racial issues, and then continuously since 1984 on a combination of racial and family values issues. In 1964, two thirds of all white evangelical Protestants called themselves Democrats; in 2000, only one-third survived. In 1960, only 30 percent of white evangelical Protestants were Republican; now over half are. More importantly, the turnout and party loyalty of evangelical Republicans grew to the point where there are now twice as many loyal voting Republicans as loyal voting Democrats. That transformation from apolitical Democrats to highly activist Republicans is what has thrust evangelicals into the political limelight.

Scholars usually include within the evangelical Protestant tradition evangelicals, fundamentalists, and pentecostals. These range from Southern Baptists, holiness sects, Bible Baptists, Assemblies of God, and a variety of pentecostalists, to conservative nondenominational mega-churches. What unite them are a literal view of Scripture, the born-again experience, and the obligation to evangelize and witness for the faith. While mainliners often regard biblical norms as prescriptions for the godly life, evangelicals typically treat biblical norms as proscriptions, injunctions against behaviors that must be avoided at pain of eternal damnation. Both many mainline bodies and Roman Catholics place great confidence in the sacraments and foster early exposure to them as manifestations of God's grace. Evangelical bodies, on the other hand, are more likely to stress willful conversion, adult baptism, spirit baptism (e.g., speaking in tongues), healing, and other gifts of the Holy Spirit. Scholars have argued that some mainliners and Catholics place more emphasis on what God has done; evangelicals, on what I must do. While such characterizations miss many nuances, certainly evangelicals consider personal transformation as the key to social transformation. Society will never change unless its individual members accept Christ and live according to God's rules. Generally fundamentalists are more likely than other evangelicals to stress the need for rigid personal adherence to biblical norms for behavior. Pentecostals are open to spiritual seizure and enthusiastic reception of special gifts from the Spirit. Holiness sects speak of an inner light that transforms the believer into a new person, impervious to sin. Sometimes these different religious emphasis spill over into political conflict, such as the Rev. Jerry Falwell, a fundamentalist, refusing to endorse the Rev. Pat Robertson, a pentecostal in his bid for the presidency in 1968. For Falwell, Robertson lacked the religious discipline of a true Christian political leader.

In earlier times, some evangelical bodies eschewed politics in favor of a singular emphasis on salvation and world withdrawal. Nowadays, however, politically active evangelicals embrace politics as a curb on the power of the devil in this world. Premillenial dispensationalists view the American state as a necessary actor in hastening the return of Christ to earth for the thousand-year rule and the end of all time. For them, American support of Israel and aggressive anti-Muslim policies become necessary components of God's plan of salvation. Some argue that a devout evangelical, President George W. Bush, has become a chosen instrument of God's will. For some evangelicals, presidential politics has taken on religious urgency.

In the 1920s evangelicals were characterized as ill-educated Southern country bumpkins. This was never accurate. Several of the mainline bodies grew from evangelical roots before liberalizing and assimilating. Early in the twentieth century, evangelicals already had developed a widespread network of colleges, Bible schools, publishing houses, fortnightly and other publication media in Northern urban areas. While evangelicals were disproportionately Southern, the heavy migrations northward after the Great Depression planted many evangelical, fundamentalist, and pentecostal churches in the Northern cities, suburbs, and small towns. In the past two decades, the greatest religious growth has occurred in the independent, nondenominational Protestant mega-churches of the suburbs and small cities. Ministering especially to apostate Baby Boomers who had tried many things to excess, these churches have carried a strict message of religious transformation along with pop cultural forms of worship that provide both controlled enthusiasm and an anchor of meaning to lives formerly spinning out of control. They also carry an evangelical political message that sometimes scapegoats other religious and secular groups for being responsible for the moral decay of America. President George W. Bush, himself a Baby Boomer who experienced binge drinking and entrepreneurial failure prior to giving his life to a Higher Power, has become something of a prodigal role model for these converts.

Like all religious traditions, evangelicals have climbed the education and income ladders. At one time many supported the social welfare policies of the New Deal and the Great Society. Now they regard social programs as impediments that create dependency on the government; they advocate reducing governmental bureaucracies to the functions of maintaining order and fending off threat—the justice system, police, and military. Thus both economic conservatism and social conservatism are now joined. Many preach that economic rewards are God's promise to those who convert. Dependency is the curse of those who continue unrighteous behavior. Christian schools and home schooling, preferably with tax support from school vouchers, have become the preferred option to public schools. Public schools are perceived to be controlled by teachers' unions (often led by Jewish women and minorities) and teach value relativism.

Some social issues—particularly abortion and the civil rights of gays—have become anathema to evangelical Protestants. On both matters, opinion polls show them to be far more restrictive than Roman Catholics or mainline Protestants. They see liberal government as having given legal sanction to sexual behaviors that God's law has forbidden. They see other churches as celebrating gay marital unions or ordaining gay clergy; worst of all, while service in the military would be a badge of honor to any American, it has been besmirched by President Clinton's "don't ask, don't tell" policy that allows gays and lesbians to serve without challenge. For many evangelicals those are nonnegotiable zero-sum issues. The consequence of getting it wrong is punishment like "God rained on Sodom and Gomorrah"—a point made by televangelists and Republican religious leaders Jerry Falwell and Pat Robertson in the wake of the 9/11 attacks by terrorists.

Televangelism and pervasive religious broadcasting networks have created a parallel media culture so that evangelical Protestants are no longer at the mercy of the "liberal press." Evangelical churches have many opportunities for worship and interaction among the faithful. Not only weekly attendance on Sundays but midweek worship has become the norm. The consequence of regular interaction with coreligionists under the sanction of the group is not only strong leadership cues but also behavioral contagion among the laity. Studies of religious right political organizations have shown their consummatory nature: decreased contact with those outside the group and greater expectations that the Republican Party will be the Christian political party. Clearly evangelical Protestant bodies display the highest attendance at religious services, replacing Catholics in that category, greater interaction with coreligionists in friendship networks, fewer cross-pressures from conflicting points of view, and more political cue giving by religious leaders, a legitimate activity according to the laity. Before elections, scorecards rating the candidates are widely distributed. All contribute to a more coherent, constrained worldview or political ideology, and offer clear signals for the immediate elections.

In certain respects, evangelical Protestants today are where Roman Catholics were organizationally and culturally prior to World War II. While Catholics in America came from many different ethnic groups, lived in bounded neighborhoods, and worshiped in ethnic parishes, they shared a common religious ideology, sense of persecution by the external society, zeal for developing their own institutions that would carry the true message, and reinforcing social networks. One major difference was that party preference was based more on economic advancement and social security concerns than it was on righteous policy. Although there had been a long history of social encyclicals that prescribed "just" economic and international behavior, these were not common currency among the Catholic laity the way proscriptive injunctions from the Bible are for evangelical laity. For Catholics in a Protestant land, the gulf that separated Church from state was much wider. This less directive approach is currently evident in studies that show far fewer attempts by Catholic clergy to influence laity on political matters, beyond abortion, than is common in evangelical churches, and far less legitimacy ascribed to church statements by Catholic laity. Catholics are in the middle of the American spectrum, wooed by both political parties and forming reliable bases in each.

Roman Catholics constitute simply too large a church, at over a quarter of the adult population of the United States, to be considered a political bloc. Arriving in the United States from many distinct Western and Eastern European countries, and infused periodically by Latin American and Asian immigrants and black converts, Catholics have had far different national and ethnic histories and patterns of assimilation among themselves. Catholics are often described as an urban church that suburbanized with rising educational and economic achievement following World War II. Yet about one-third of all Catholics live in small towns, villages, farms, and exurban locations. That is a number larger than the four largest Protestant bodies combined. In some places they became Republican early and in others they were Democrats from the start. Catholic affinity with the Democrats peaked with the Al Smith election and the two FDR elections following, and again with JFK and the single Johnson election. Absent these, Catholic party identification has followed the general alignment patterns of the nation but has stayed about 6 percent more Democratic than has Protestant Party identification. Further, unlike Protestants, where greater salience of religion has come to be associated with Republican identification, deeply devout Catholics are as likely to be Democratic as Republican. There are, however, significant generational and gender differences that affect Catholic politics.

The dissolution of the Catholic component of the coalition that elected Kennedy gained steam with the civil rights legislation and the urban riots of the 1960s. Many urban white ethnic Catholics were union members in "closed" industries (access to jobs through unions could be controlled by generations of workers), and others did not like the fragmentation of their neighborhoods through the urban planning designs of governmental elites. Suburban Catholics were not even a generation removed from the old ethnic neighborhood. Communication networks remained tight; empathy with one's own kind was reinforced by church-related institutions: for example, sodalities, burial societies, ethnic betterment organizations, real estate agencies, and even precinct committees. Thus, racial issues and the role of government in ensuring equal opportunity and access festered. In the Nixon-Humphrey-Wallace contest of 1968, realignment of Catholic men as Republicans reached its highest level of the second half of the twentieth century, a net shift of 38 points. Furthermore, 18 percent of Democrats defected to Wallace or Nixon. In 1972 the new partisan alignments stayed stable but 42 percent more Catholic Democrats crossed over to Nixon, and 19 percent failed to vote. The central issue for white Catholic male defectors was race, according to Leege and associates. Furthermore from 1968 to 1992, racial policies were the principal reason Catholic Democratic men defected to the Republican Party. During the Nixon and Reagan years, an effective system of racial codewords was developed to communicate the slowdown of the government in fostering change. When later generations of Catholic males entered the active electorate during the Reagan years and after, they aligned disproportionately with the Republican Party. Only the accumulating economic problems of the Bush term caused them to defect in the 1990s.

White Catholic women, in contrast, were considerably slower to realign Republican. Although a steady trend through the last decades, Republican identification was broken abruptly in the 1990s by Baby Boom and post-Baby Boom Catholic women, showing huge net shifts in partisan identification of over sixty points in the Democratic direction. An important demographic change had occurred among generations of Catholic women. Historically, Catholic women who had larger families than Protestants still worked outside the home in greater proportions; economic necessity took them into blue-collar and pink-collar jobs. By the late 1970s, however, Catholic women were having fewer children than Protestant women, even with race and ethnicity controlled. In the smaller Catholic families, parents had the same business and professional aspirations for their daughter as for their son. By the 1990s, young college-educated Catholic women had entered the business and professional ranks and saw Democratic policies as more friendly to both their economic advancement and to their compassion for the less fortunate. Many perceived a harsh edge to Republican policies that they took to be inconsistent with Catholic social teaching. They were more likely to attend mass regularly than were the younger Catholic men and to be exposed to social teaching. Neither young men nor women were as restrictive on abortion and women's roles as their parents' generation.

Some Catholic political entrepreneurs have argued that the Catholic shift toward Republicans occurred during the Reagan years in response to his "family values" or moral restoration agenda. When NES data are estimated through controlled multivariate models rather than bivariate inspection throughout the time series, however, it is clear that much of the movement preceded Reagan and was based on racial opportunity policies. Further, when Republican family values positions finally did attract Catholics, it tended to be among middle-aged and older regular-attending Catholic women after several years of the Clintons. Younger Catholic women, however, found these rhetorical positions and policies less attractive, and wanted to see more evidence of policies consistent with social justice teaching.

Most people think of the Catholic church as a hierarchical body with tight clerical control, and clear norms about daily life emanating from the pope and bishops through the clergy. The reality, however, is somewhat different. American Catholic dioceses answer to a distant pope through their bishops; efforts to develop a common American consensus often are frustrated by this decentralized structure. The average Catholic parish is six times the size of the average Protestant church. Size, along with post-Vatican II teaching that encourages lay responsibility for parish and civic leadership, has developed cadres of highly active and politically skilled laity. When controlled comparisons are made of Protestant and Catholic blacks and Protestant and Catholic Latinos, for example, the Catholics from each tradition show higher levels of political participation and civic skills. More importantly, those more active in parish and civic leadership show deeper levels of identification with the church and its social teaching. Yet they may split, some supporting the human life agenda (e.g., abortion) more than the social justice agenda (e.g., social welfare), and others reversing the order. Detractors call this "cafeteria-style Catholicism," but others claim it reflects a "loyal opposition." The "seamless garment" position formulated by influential Joseph Cardinal Bernardin of Chicago expects both, but has the support of a minority of Catholics; nevertheless seamless garment Catholics are always a leaven, an electoral threat to hold over either political party. Again it may explain why President George W. Bush seemingly ignored other religious leaders but consulted with Catholics before his controversial decisions on embryonic stem-cell research and mobilizing for war in Iraq.

In addition to the substantial body of Catholic social teaching, the American bishops will offer episodic pastoral letters. Studies show that the laity expect such teaching, but may or may not let it guide their political decisions. In a general way, Catholics are more tolerant of minorities and more socially compassionate, but recent electoral history shows that significant numbers will respond to appeals that do not manifestly serve such purposes. Catholics also remain remarkably loyal to the church hierarchy, even in the face of such failures as the response to the pedophilia scandal. Some observers claim that oft-stressed notions of sin and grace, along with respect for human dignity, account for the persistence of tolerant attitudes. At the same time, a strong fundamentalist movement has always sought to capture the soul of the church.

Finally, the early and extensive development of Catholic institutions—schools and universities, hospitals, welfare services, economic betterment societies, publishing houses, and communications outlets—has resulted in vigorous institutional interests in public policy. Chaves's studies show that Catholic parishes far outstrip other churches in emphasis on interest articulation, lobbying, and organized demonstrations. The public square is seldom devoid of Catholic public opinion.

Black Protestants, or black Christians generally, have also constituted a vigorous public presence. Many observers trace the unique emphases of black Christianity to the experience with slavery. White slave owners Christianized them, the script goes, in part because it was "right," in part because it would keep them obedient. As part of that legacy, black religiosity has tended to be socially conservative and revivalist. African mysticism and notions of the spirit world fused with Old Testament themes of oppression and deliverance and dominated songs and preaching. Early on, black religion had elements of world withdrawal and seizure by religious rapture. In time, separate African Methodist Episcopal and black Baptist churches were founded. The later civil rights movement harnessed this communitarian and spirit-filled energy while organizing sit-ins, freedom rides, and demonstrations. The Rev. Dr. Martin Luther King adapted Gandhi's principles of civil disobedience and nonviolent resistance. This transformation of the black church as the base for a powerful social movement became one of the defining events in the partisan realignments of the 1960s and 1970s and of current campaign strategies.

Attendance at services, private devotionalism, and religious salience are higher among black Christians than among any of the predominantly white traditions. Because of the nature of black-white relationships and neighborhood settlement patterns, contact has been largely within-group and the church formed a consummatory loyalty system. As desegregation came in the sixties, seventies, and eighties, some black professionals entered other social networks and some politically active blacks sought to jettison the church and its leaders as the engine for black interest articulation. Yet their policy interests remained the same: opportunities for economic betterment, improvements in the quality of education, equal treatment by police and the justice system, retention of a welfare safety net, social respect, and often representation of blacks by blacks.

Blacks are a powerful base in the Democratic Party, sometimes constituting 20–25 percent of their votes, although only about half that size in the population. Although Republicans had been the party of racial progress from the time of Lincoln and the Emancipation Proclamation, as blacks left the South for jobs in Northern cities, economic interests had moved them into the orbit of the New Deal party. Northern Democratic politicians saw them as a potential new member of the party coalition, and had felt uncomfortable anyway with Southern Democratic segregationists. The social welfare party became the social justice party. In reaction, the Republican Party vigorously pursued the former segregationists. The combination of these factors moved black Christians into both heavy political mobilization and Democratic identification. By 1968, 90 percent of all blacks claimed to be Democrats and the figure has never dropped below 80 percent. More black Republicans defect to the Democratic Party than remain loyal Republicans. The biggest difficulty is turnout, with black Democrats having the weakest record of going to the polls.

In part because of the mobilization problem, black Protestant and Catholic churches are twice as likely as white Catholic parishes and nine times as likely as other Protestant churches to sponsor registration drives. They are also eight times more likely than either to offer candidates the opportunity to speak at the church. They are almost twice as likely as other Protestants to encourage political activity, and even more likely than white evangelicals to distribute voter guides. The link between religion and American politics is most clearly seen and practiced in the black churches.

We have used "black" rather than "African American" purposely. This is because increasing migration of black Caribbeans to American cities has contributed to a population less-centered in the common experience of slavery, the Jim Crow period following the end of Reconstruction, and the civil rights movement. Yet white educational and social service administrators and law enforcement officers, as well as ordinary citizens tend to use the same racial construct for categorizing African Americans and blacks of other national histories. In time, census classifications may assist with differentiation. Certainly churches that minister to different "black" populations find rather different cultural patterns. For example, black bourgeoisie in Baltimore's African American Catholic parishes expect a far different style of worship than in upper Manhattan's Dominican parishes.

Jews also share a religious emphasis on themes of oppression and deliverance. Like blacks, their theology and religious folkways are communitarian rather than individualistic: God acts on and through the group, "God's people," rather than simply on the individual. Although their average educational attainment and level of affluence far outstrip black Christians, Jews' concerns with social justice, social welfare, and protection from persecution are somewhat similar. In politics Jews are liberal and Democratic. Though the smallest of the religious traditions, they are in the reliable core of the party.

High education levels, financial achievement, and civic skills among Jews contribute to the highest turnout of any religious tradition. Jews are organized not only by houses of worship but more so by eleemosynary and political institutions. Their financial resources and prominence in the mass media of communication, entertainment, and educational institutions make them subject to political courtship beyond their numbers.

Another important category that scholars analyze is called "seculars." These are people who report no religious affiliation and appear in the lowest rungs of religious practice and religious salience. Their proportion of the eligible electorate appears to have grown over the last two decades. When NES modified question wording so that it appeared to be as socially acceptable to report no religious values as it was to express values, the number of seculars nearly doubled. With pun intended, this is removal of a "halo effect," a social desirability response bias that overestimates religious activity among Americans. Unfortunately, prominent telephone polls have not followed NES's lead and still suffer from many kinds of overreporting of religious commitment.

At one time seculars were among the more socially isolated sectors of the American public. Now, however, there is considerable growth of seculars within the more highly educated and professional sectors. Earlier, as social isolates, they were far less likely to vote or engage in other political activities. Now they are increasingly likely to vote when a party offers a favorable candidate or, even more likely, a party offers a candidate who advocates policies that are perceived to be inimical to seculars' policy positions. Thus, for example, Democrats could maximize secular turnout by charging that a Republican victory on both ends of Pennsylvania Avenue would lead to theocratic rule, would bring the government into our bedrooms, or would reverse *Roe v. Wade*. Seculars have generally embraced the opposite end of the spectrum from Republican family values policies during the past two decades. At the same time, many seculars are deeply committed to total economic freedom, to encouraging entrepreneurial activity, and to diminishing regulation. Thus, in the choice between Reagan and evangelical Carter, the majority of seculars voted Republican, an irony since many analysts have claimed that Reagan attracted the more devout voters. Yet, when Republicans stress moral restorationist themes (antiabortion, antigay rights, etc.), seculars either realign Democratic, defect, or, most likely among the 40 percent of seculars who are Republican, do not vote. Libertarians are typically seculars. Thus, the libertarian wing of the Republican Party is often at odds with the evangelical Religious Right.

Many people who report a religious affiliation seldom participate in religious exercises. About 30 percent of Catholics, for example, are essentially apostate. Among those with weak involvement with their religious community, public opinion among seldom-attending Catholics is most like seculars and weakly involved Jews. Seldom-attending mainline Protestants more closely approximate the opinions and political activities of more regular attenders, rather than seculars. Even seldom-attending evangelical Protestants are acting politically more like regular attenders than seculars. This suggests that for Protestants, factors other than moral restorationist policies may be involved in current political cleavages, such as economic policy, social standing, and "our kind" group identification.

In future decades, increasing attention will be paid to Hispanic Christians. It is typical to think of Hispanics as being both ethnically homogenous and almost uniformly Catholic. Neither is quite accurate. Based on a variety of surveys, we can conclude that somewhere between sixty and seventy percent of Hispanics are Catholic. There is also great ethnic diversity among Hispanics, based upon country of origin, with Mexico, Puerto Rica, and Cuba, to take just the most obvious examples, all having different cultural and immigration experiences.

Partisan political behavior differs by national and local history. About two-thirds of Mexican Americans are Democrats, but turnout is quite low for many reasons: franchise eligibility, voter intimidation, mobility, language, economic factors, and a frame of reference that treats their stay in the United States as temporary. In some states, such as Texas when George W. Bush was governor, Mexican Americans were courted by Republicans and are a growing presence in the party. Ambitious politicians learned to speak Spanish, appeared on Spanish-language television, radio programs, and the Mexican state-owned network, appointed Mexican American officials, and consulted with Mexican American officials, leaders, and bishops. In California and some other Southwestern states, on the other hand, Republicans decided to stereotype, scapegoat, and intimidate Mexican Americans, and now Mexican Americans are a rapidly mobilizing presence in the state Democratic Party. Hispanic Catholic parishes, in particular, have developed citizen training and voter registration programs across the country; Hispanic lay deacons assist Anglo priests on matters of church and society. Puerto Ricans have historically been about 60 percent Democratic. The strong minority Republican presence can be traced to organizational efforts during the Eisenhower years concerning the politics of statehood. Largely because of Republican policy toward Fidel Castro and the early migration of affluent professionals and business leaders, Cuban Americans have been heavily Republican in Florida, where they are concentrated. Yet in recent years, less affluent Cubans have tended Democratic, pushing the vote into a toss-up situation by election 2000.

Where is the current political action as a result of these religious differences in public opinion? Some scholars, politicians, and publicists have talked about a "culture war" or a "great divide" between the religiously devout, particularly evangelicals, and seculars. They claim that the middle has given way to the extremes. Some support for this argument can be found in Table 1. Out of all presidential elections in the past half-century, it shows three elections at sixteen-year intervals that represent the trends. The entries, drawn from American National Election Study data, are arranged by religious traditions. The first entry is the proportion of all adults claiming affiliation with that ethnoreligious tradition. The second entry is the proportion of all U.S. voters who are within this religious tradition and who claim weekly attendance (and thus are exposed to group cues regularly). The third entry is the Democratic partisan advantage among those in the designated religious tradition who actually voted.

Table 1 supports a number of conclusions: mainline Protestants are likely to have declining influence within the parties because fewer people are mainline Protestants and their proportion of regular attenders who voted has declined. A similar conclusion can be drawn for Roman Catholics. Although the figures for evangelical Protestants remain stable, their relative position has increased, thus providing the basis for increased influence in the parties. Jews and black Christians have experienced ever so slight a decline. Hispanic Christians and seculars show substantial increases, although the actual vote of regular attending Hispanics remains no higher than Jews. Perhaps the key stories are in the declining electoral basis for white mainline Protestant and white Catholic influence, and the growing basis for evangelical Protestant (relative), Hispanic Christian, and secular influence (absolute). Since religious activists are often the ones who make the case for their positions within the party, and they will point to the electorate as a resource, it should come as no surprise that evangelicals have risen in the

Table 1. The Changing Strength of the Religious Electorate

	1964	1980	1996
Mainline Protestants (white, non-Hispanic)	39	30	24
	16	6	5
	2	−16	−5
Evangelical Protestants (white, non-Hispanic)	21	20	20
	8	6	7
	22	−3	−11
Roman Catholics (white, non-Hispanic)	21	20	20
	16	9	6
	41	5	6
Black Christians	10	10	13
	5	4	3
	58	59	51
Hispanic Christians	n.a.	3	8
	n.a.	1	2
	n.a.	24	n.a.
Jews	3	3	2
	3*	4*	2*
	71	42	61
Seculars	4	10	13
	3*	9*	8*
	16	4	n.a.

Top entry = Percent of all adults claiming affiliation with designated ethnoreligious tradition.
Middle entry = Percent of all voters who are in designated ethnoreligious tradition, and report weekly attendance.
Bottom entry = Democratic partisan advantage among voters within the ethnoreligious tradition.
* Since attendance is inappropriate measure for Jews and seculars, this figure reports only the proportion of U.S. voters within each category.
Source: American National Election Studies.

structure of the Republican Party, that Roman Catholics have diminished slightly within Democratic councils, and seculars have mounted a stronger case there.

Elections are contested by elites but are still won and lost among the rank-and-file. When one adds together the middle entries each election year and considers the actual proportion of the electorate who voted (declining from 60 to a little over 50 percent), one can quickly see that a winning coalition will have to include appeals to a lot of people who have religious affiliations, may or may not retain group loyalties, but are not so regularly exposed to group cues. That is one point where the culture wars thesis breaks down. Religious (or nonreligious) activists and political elites may structure conflict in dichotomous ways, but candidates cannot win without the middle. The electoral standoff in 2000 is a curious case in point. In the postelection reviews, Religious Right figures argued that the 50 percent of the country who were religiously devout and supported righteousness in the White House defeated the 50 percent who had deserted godliness and thought only of their pocketbooks. But the composition of the (almost) winning coalition of George W. Bush tells a quite different story: while three-fifths of Bush's coalition was composed of regularly observant white Christians, led by evangelical Protestants, a majority of less observant white Protestants also voted for him and fully one quarter of his coalition consisted of voters from minority religious faiths and seculars. Vice President Gore's support came heavily from traditional Democratic sources: 96 percent of devout black Christians, 77 percent of Jews, 76 percent of devout Hispanic Catholics and Protestants, and interestingly, a more modest 65 percent of seculars. While religious differences in public opinion have developed into notable dimensions of conflict, they have hardly set the country into such peaked partisan war that voters cannot support either party. Just as the psalmist claimed that God sends rain on the just and the unjust, Republican and Democratic candidates will take their support where they can get it out of a complex mosaic of public opinion.

Further Reading

Chaves, Mark. *Congregations in America*. Cambridge, MA: Harvard University Press, 2003. An important empirical study of the range of activities nurtured by American congregations, including civic engagement and politics.

Green, John C., James L. Guth, Corwin E. Smidt, and Lyman A. Kellstedt. *Religion and the Culture Wars: Dispatches from the Front*. Lanham, MD: Rowman & Littlefield, 1996. A significant collection of essays demonstrating that religion matters in American voter choice, that is particularly strong in its understanding of evangelical politics.

Leege, David C., Kenneth D. Wald, Brian S. Krueger, and Paul D. Mueller. *The Politics of Cultural Differences: Social Change and Voter Mobilization Strategies in the Post-New Deal Period*. Princeton, NJ: Princeton University Press, 2002. Develops a theory of cultural politics and attempts to explain the effects of campaign themes about patriotism, race, gender, and religion on partisan alignment, loyalty and defection, and turnout.

Verba, Sidney, Kay Lehman Schlozman, and Henry E. Brady. *Voice and Equality: Civic Voluntarism in American Politics*. Cambridge, MA: Harvard University Press, 1995. The major contemporary work tracing the effects of a variety of factors, including several dimensions of religious life, on political participation.

Wald, Kenneth D. *Religion and Politics in the United States*. 4th ed. Lanham, MD: Rowman & Littlefield, 2003. The pioneering text that introduces factors either enhancing or diminishing the connection between religion and American politics.

Web Sites

The survey of record for understanding American voting and public opinion over the past half century is the National Election Studies, available at http://www.umich.edu/~nes. Specialized surveys can be accessed through the American Religion Data Archive at http://thearda.org.

David C. Leege

Repeated Surveys

Repeated surveys pose the same questions to different samples of people. **Panel surveys,** by contrast, reinterview the same individuals over time. Although repeated surveys and panel surveys both enable researchers to study change over time, they are designed for different purposes. Panel surveys track how individuals change over time—for example, whether an individual changes political parties—whereas repeated surveys track aggregate change over time—for example, change in percentage of the American electorate who identify themselves as Democrats.

Repeated surveys have become a staple of social science research. Perhaps the best known repeated survey in the United States is the **General Social Survey** (GSS), an omnibus survey of attitude change since 1972. From 1972 to 1993 the survey was done annually; since 1994 the survey has been done every other year. To monitor attitudinal change in the United States, the GSS selects a fresh sample for each new survey. This is important because if the GSS followed the same individuals over time it would become increasingly unrepresentative of the U.S. adult population and thus would lose its value for tracking change in U.S. society. The youngest respondents in the original GSS sample were eighteen years old in 1972, so by 2002 those respondents were forty-eight years old. If the GSS were based on the original 1972 sample, then, the 2002 GSS would consist only of individuals age forty-eight and older, and our sample for 2002 would be representative only of the U.S. population age forty-eight and older, not of the U.S. adult population in general.

There are two major reasons why national attitudes, beliefs, and values change over time. The first is that individuals themselves change—in other words, a conversion effect. In discussing the underlying causes of some observed change in American society, commentators often assume that conversion is the underlying cause. For example, popular discussions of the 1980s rise in the percentage of Republicans often centered on the question "Why are people switching to the Republican Party?" Because of population turnover, however, the percentage of Republicans could be rising when no one is switching to the Republican Party. The composition of the U.S. electorate changes over time as older birth-cohorts gradually die off and are replaced by younger birth-cohorts. This population turnover can lead to societal change. Specifically, societal change occurs when the attitudes and beliefs of the cohorts entering the electorate differ from the attitudes and beliefs of the cohorts that are dying off. This is called a cohort replacement or cohort succession effect, and scholars discovered that cohort replacement in fact accounted for a large part of the 1980s rise in Republicanism, as cohorts entering the electorate in the 1980s tended to be more Republican than the older cohorts they were replacing.

One of the common goals in analyzing repeated surveys is to separate the conversion effect from the population turnover effect. Strictly speaking, the population turnover effect consists of more than just cohort replacement effects, since populations can change because of migration as well as birth and death. In most instances, however, it is the cohort succession process that accounts for virtually all the population turnover effect, so studies generally focus on separating cohort replacement from conversion effects.

Repeated surveys are well suited for decomposing societal change into its cohort replacement and conversion components, whereas panel surveys are not. The first step in decomposing overall societal change is to separate within-cohort change from across-cohort change. Within-cohort change bears on conversion effects and across-cohort change bears on cohort replacement effects. Suppose we find that political party percentages remain the same over time within cohorts. Then we know that there is no net conversion effect: to the extent that there is party-switching, the switching is having no net effect, since the changes are cancelling each other out within each cohort.

If there is no net change in the percentage Republican within cohorts as they age over time, then any societal change in the percentage Republican must arise from cohort replacement. Cohort replacement results in societal change when and only when the entering cohorts differ (on the variable of interest, for example, the percentage Republican) from the cohorts they are succeeding. In other words, cohort replacement effects depend on across-cohort change. In the instance of linear within-cohort and across-cohort change, societal change can be decomposed into its conversion and cohort replacement components with a simple regression model where the variable of interest is regressed on year of survey and respondent's year of birth.

In short, repeated surveys are useful for monitoring overall societal change and decomposing that change into its conversion and cohort replacement components. Decomposition studies have found that cohort replacement is the primary engine driving social change in some instances, whereas individuals' change (conversion) is the primary engine in other instances. For example, increasing tolerance of interracial marriage in the United States has been driven primarily by cohort replacement—reflecting generational change—whereas changes in other racial attitudes have arisen largely from individuals' changing attitudes (see Racial Differences in Public Opinion).

Repeated surveys are useful for addressing other questions as well. One question is whether different groups in America are changing their views in the same direction and at the same rate over time. Given the concern over the quality of public education in the United States, for example, we might want to know whether public support for spending on public schools is changing the same way for retirees as it is for paid workers. Similarly, it would be interesting to know if views about spending on Social Security are changing in the same way for retirees and those who are in the labor force. Repeated surveys permit researchers to answer such questions by employing models where the variable of interest is regressed on survey year (to get the overall trend) and on interaction terms of the form survey-year times subpopulation (e.g., retirees, paid workers). A statistically significant interaction term indicates that the trend for the subpopulation differs from the trend for the reference group.

In addition to detecting differences in political and social trends across groups in the United States, repeated surveys are well-suited for studying whether the effects of variables are changing over time. It is well known, for example, that voting is correlated with race in the United States, with African Americans much more likely (than other groups) to vote for Democratic Party candidates. Given the rise of a black middle class in the United States, one might wonder whether the effect of race on voting has diminished. Such questions are readily addressed with repeated surveys, again using interaction terms. In this instance, however, the interaction terms multiply the independent variable of interest (here, race) by time to see if the effect is changing over time. Using the GSS to investigate the changing relationship between race and Democratic Party identification from 1974 to 1994, we find that African Americans were significantly *more* likely to identify themselves as strong Democrats in 1994 than they were in 1974.

Finally, repeated surveys are useful for determining how political and social change in a nation arises from change in both the level and effects of other variables. To illustrate, we know that education tends to increase tolerance, at least with respect to some groups and certain types of activities. If we observe increasing **political tolerance** in a society—say toward homosexuality—we might want to know how much of that increase is associated with a general increase in the society's educational level. Decomposition methods are available for using repeated survey data to estimate the contributions of change in the levels and effects of independent variables on societal change in some other variable. Those decomposition methods are also useful for trying to solve puzzles where societal change is moving contrary to what we would expect, given other trends. We know, for example, that the educational level is rising in America, and that more educated people are more likely to vote. Yet voter turnout has not been rising in recent decades in the United States as we would expect given the rising educational level of the electorate. Decomposition methods applied to repeated surveys can provide the sort of leverage political scientists need to shed light on such puzzles.

Further Reading

Davis, James A. "Changeable Weather in a Cooling Climate Atop the Liberal Plateau: Conversion and Replacement in Forty-Two General Social Survey Items, 1972–1989." *Public Opinion Quarterly* 56 (1992): 261–306. Classic article illustrating how repeated surveys can be used to study and decompose social trends.

Firebaugh, Glenn. *Analyzing Repeated Surveys.* Sage University Paper Series on Quantitative Applications in the Social Sciences, no. 07–115. Thousand Oaks, CA: Sage, 1997. Explains in depth how to do the analyses described here.

Norpoth, Helmut. "Under Way and Here to Stay: Party Realignment in the 1980s?" *Public Opinion Quarterly* 51 (1987): 376–91. Concludes that cohort replacement accounts for most of the rise in Republican Party strength in the 1980s.

Glenn Firebaugh

Respondent Debriefing

Respondent debriefing involves incorporating follow-up questions (in the context of **standardized interviewing**) during a field test to gain a better understanding of how respondents interpret questions asked of them. Debriefing questions are used to accomplish several goals: (1) to identify words, terms or concepts that respondents do not understand, interpret consistently, or interpret as the researcher intends; (2) to identify questions that respondents cannot answer accurately; (3) to assess close-ended response choices; (4) to assess question and/or respondent sensitivity; and (5) to obtain suggestions for revising questions and/or questionnaires. Respondent debriefing can be included as part of a survey **pretest** to identify problems to be corrected prior to the administration of the survey or it can be included in the actual survey to provide supplemental information for the data or for the next administration of a survey.

A similar method to respondent debriefing, called the "question testing" method, was first used by William Belson. In this method, specially trained interviewers visited respondents the day after they completed a questionnaire. They were then asked a series of questions focusing on specific questions from the previous questionnaire. More recent methods place the "debriefing questions" at the end of an interview. This particular method has gained in popularity over the years and has also been referred to in the literature as special probes or frame of reference probing.

Unlike **cognitive interviewing** or expert review, respondent debriefing is typically utilized at a later stage in the questionnaire design or evaluation process. These questions are generally included in a field test or in the survey itself. Typically, they are administered to far more individuals than cognitive interviews, in which only a very small number of purposively chosen respondents are interviewed. They are advantageous in that they enable researchers to talk with a more representative sample of respondents, and produce quantitative assessments of questionnaire performance. Respondent debriefing questions can also be used to evaluate the effectiveness of questionnaire changes based on cognitive interviews, and to assess whether findings from cognitive interview research are replicated when the questions are fielded in the survey setting. In research conducted by Hughes and DeMaio, respondent debriefing questions were used to evaluate cognitive interview results.

A major strength of respondent debriefing, compared to other pretesting techniques, is that it can provide insights into the nature of the problem and, in many situations, suggestions for dealing with the problem. Because they can be administered to a large and representative sample, respondent debriefing questions are an important "back-end" supplement to the one-on-one interviews used in the early phases of development.

The limitations involve how much follow-up questioning and probing can be accomplished without unduly burdening respondents. Only a subset of the questions can be probed with any one respondent. To evaluate the entire questionnaire, the questions are usually grouped by topic and random sub-samples of respondents are asked follow-up probes for only one or a few groups of questions. The exception is for questions that apply to only a small proportion of the respondents; then, all respondents are asked the follow-up probes.

To get the most out of using this technique, researchers need to develop good debriefing questions that will shed light on sources of error. These may be based on hypotheses about question problems developed from analysis of previous implementations of the questions, insights from cognitive interviews or other research on the topic.

Several different variations of collecting respondent debriefing information exist. These methods can easily be used with interviewer and self-administered including both paper and automated versions of the questionnaires. It is much easier to administer for automated instruments because the computer can display appropriate debriefing questions based on a respondent's previous response given earlier in the interview. Typically, in a paper instrument, the interviewer uses a protocol to direct the respondent's attention back to specific questionnaire items and then probes for specific information. In either instance, the most common approach is to conduct a pretest and ask the debriefing or follow-up probes at the end of each interview.

Probes can be either open-ended or closed-ended. In using open-ended probes, respondents can be asked how they developed their response to the target question (e.g., what did they include or exclude when formulating their response). For example, Fowler and Roman conducted a pretest to examine various methods of question evaluation. Respondent debriefing questions were asked to gather more in-depth information about four specific survey questions. One of those questions asked respondents about "reading novels, stories, and other works of fiction." To find out the kinds of books respondents were including in each category, they were asked a series of questions. Results showed that there was a major misunderstanding with the way respondents interpreted what was considered a novel (i.e., many of the books named were not works of fiction). Without the debriefing questions, this error would have never been identified.

With closed-ended probes, structured questions can include specific concepts or interpretations that respondents might have used, and ask which was the one they used. For example, respondents can be offered various reference periods and asked which they used in formulating their response to determine if the intended reference period is the one being used. Hughes and DeMaio asked a series of respondent debriefing questions to find out what computers (i.e., computers at home, work, libraries, or schools) respondents were including when asked how many computers they had access to. By doing this, it was also possible to tell whether the respondents were interpreting the term "access" narrowly, by including only computers in the home, or widely, by including all computers that the respondent could potentially use.

The follow-up probes discussed above typically refer to a specific situation and how it applies directly to the respondent. In many cases, the situation of interest may be rare, so only a small number of respondents would be administered the debriefing questions. One way to collect information in rare situations or a wide variety of situations rather than the respondent's own is through the vignette. Vignettes are brief narratives, generally no more than one or two sentences long, which contain hypothetical elements of social situations and actions in which the researcher is interested. For example, researchers at the U.S. Census Bureau used vignettes to evaluate a respondent's understanding of residence rules. In this case, the vignettes allowed the researcher to ask respondents if they thought an individual in a particular situation (e.g., college students, people who live one place during the week and live somewhere else on the weekends) should be listed on the census roster and to explore the reasons why they were included or excluded. Vignettes have also been used to evaluate respondents' understanding of terms used in particular survey questions, such as the concept of "work" in the Current Population Survey.

The possibilities for future research in this area are virtually limitless. As with all methods of questionnaire design, there is always room for evaluation and improvement. In reviewing the literature, it seems as though debriefing questions have typically been used alone as a "back end" supplement to determine comprehension of a question or parts of a question. Instead of using respondent debriefing questions as an individual tool, for example, respondent debriefing questions could be used to evaluate the effectiveness of questionnaire changes based on cognitive interviews, and to assess whether findings from cognitive interview research replicate when the questions are fielded in the survey setting.

The use of respondent debriefing questions to evaluate cognitive interview results or other "front end" methods, such as the expert review, might provide new insights about the role that respondent debriefing questions can play in evaluating and improving questions.

Further Reading

Belson, W. *The Design and Understanding of Survey Questions.* Aldershot, England: Gower, 1981.

DeMaio, T., ed. *Approaches to Developing Questionnaires.* Statistical Policy Working Paper 10. Washington, DC: Office of Management and Budget, 1983.

DeMaio, Theresa J., and Jennifer M. Rothgeb. "Cognitive Interviewing Techniques in the Lab and in the Field." In *Answering Questions: Methodology for Determining Cognitive and Communicative Processes in Survey Research*, edited by Norbert Schwartz and Seymour Sudman. San Francisco: Jossey-Bass, 1996.

Fowler, F., and T. Roman. "A Study of the Approaches to Survey Question Evaluation." Center for Survey Research, University of Massachusetts, 1992.

Gerber, E., T. Wellens, and C. Keeley. "Who Lives Here? The Use of Vignettes in Household Roster Research." *Proceedings of the Survey Research Methods Section, American Statistical Association*, 1996, pp. 962–67.

Hess, J., and E. Singer. "The Role of Respondent Debriefing Questions in Questionnaire Development." *Proceedings of the Section on Survey Research Methods, American Statistical Association*, 1995, pp. 1075–80.

Hughes, K., and T. DeMaio. "Does This Question Work? Evaluating Cognitive Interview Results Using Respondent Debriefing Questions." *Proceedings of the American Statistical Association, Section on Survey Research Methods* [CD-ROM]. Alexandria, VA: American Statistical Association, 2001.

Martin, E. A., P. C. Campanelli, and R. E. Fay. "An Application of Research Analysis to Questionnaire Design: Using Vignettes to Study the Meaning of 'Work' in the Current Population Survey." *Statistician* 40 (1991): 265–76.

Kristen Hughes

Respondent-Generated Intervals (RGI)

The Respondent-Generated Intervals (RGI) protocol for asking questions in sample surveys involves asking respondents for a basic answer to a recall-type question, as well as the smallest value his/her true answer could be, and the largest value his/her true answer could be (referred to here as the lower and upper bounds or brackets provided). The result of the RGI protocol is that the respondents themselves generate the intervals in which their true beliefs lie, instead of having their quantitative beliefs forced into intervals pre-assigned by the survey designer. Other survey protocols sometimes provide pre-assigned intervals for the response, and the respondent must choose one of the intervals.

Interval-Response Surveys. Survey protocols that permit the respondent to give answers in intervals—self-determined, or pre-assigned by the survey designer— are often preferred by respondents for sensitive questions because the respondent need not be specific about the exact value being requested. Interval response protocols are also often preferred by respondents for questions for which the answers are not very well known. By responding in intervals for such questions, respondents need not be precise about the exact answer. Respondents prefer the RGI technique because it allows them to have control over their disclosures, and

RGI allows respondents to feel confident about the accuracy of the information they provide. The intervals RGI respondents provide tend to be narrower than predefined intervals.

Genesis of RGI. The RGI protocol for questionnaire design has its origins in Bayesian assessment procedures. In that context, for a specific individual, we might assess an entire prior distribution about an unknown parameter. That prior distribution represents the individual's degrees of uncertainty about that unknown parameter. In certain contexts, we might assess many points on the individual's subjective probability distribution for that parameter by means of a sequence of elicitation questions, and then connect those points by a smooth curve that represents the underlying distribution.

For example, using some purely hypothetical numbers, suppose an individual has a normal subjective probability distribution representing "θ_0", the true (but unknown) change in the number of doctor visits he/she believes he/she made last year, compared with the previous year, so that $\theta_0 \sim N(4,1)$. In such a case, the individual believes that it is most likely that he/she visited a doctor 4 more times last year than the previous year, with a standard deviation of 1. So this individual equivalently believes that there is a 99.7 percent chance that he/she visited a doctor between 1 and 7 more times last year, or that there is really almost no chance that the true number of excess times was less than 1 or greater than 7. This probability distribution is subjective, in that it represents a specific individual's degrees of belief about his/her uncertainty about the underlying quantity, in the case of this example, the individual's uncertainty about how many more visits he/she believes he/she truly made to the doctor last year compared with the previous year.

We postulate that in a factual survey each respondent has a distinctive recall distribution, and in an attitude or opinion survey he/she has an underlying probability distribution for his/her opinion or attitude about some issue. In the case of a recall-type question, we assume that the respondent knew the true value at some point (or had enough information to construct it) but because of imperfect recall, he/she is not certain of the true value. He/she may feel confident that he/she knows the true value (but may be wrong in spite of high confidence), or he/she may be quite uncertain of the true value (and conceivably could be correct about the true value, but not realize it). We furthermore assume that the respondent is not purposely trying to deceive. In the case of opinion or attitude questions, the respondent may have a very fuzzy idea of his/her attitude about an issue or may feel quite strongly and specifically about it.

Benefits of RGI to the Survey Administrator. The RGI survey protocol has several benefits for the survey administrator. There are issues of (1) **response rate**, (2) measurement of range-of-belief, and (3) accuracy of estimating the population mean (in the case of factual questions). We treat these issues in turn.

1. *Response Rate.* Interval protocol methods tend to reduce item non-response in that such techniques present a viable method for obtaining *some* information from respondents who might otherwise provide none.

2. *Measurement of Range-of-Belief.* Suppose a_i, b_i denote the lower and upper bounds, respectively, for respondent i, $i = 1, \ldots, n$, where n denotes the number of respondents in the sample. Then,

if, $a_0 \equiv \min_i (a_i)$, and $b_0 \equiv \max_i (b_i)$, a measure of range of belief for the sampled respondents is given by: $(b_0 - a_0)$.

3. *Accuracy.* Data collected from a factual RGI survey can be used to generate an estimate of the population mean that has smaller nonsampling error (bias) than that associated with estimators obtained from more conventional surveys. The proposed estimator is model-based and is Bayesian. To obtain an estimate of the mean in a population, we typically just form the simple average of the opinions or attitudes or recalled values from individuals who may have very different abilities to carry out the task required for a response. But such a simple average may not necessarily account well for typical unevenness in assessment of opinion or attitude, or in recall ability. The RGI protocol can be used to improve upon more traditional population estimates by its ability to learn more about the different abilities respondents have to quantify their fuzziness about their beliefs, and then take that fuzziness into account in the estimation process. Ideally, we would ask the respondents many additional questions about their beliefs. That would permit us to assess many fractile points on each of their underlying opinion or attitude or recall distributions. Owing to the respondent burden of a long questionnaire, the sometimes heavy cost limitations of adding questions to a survey, the cost of added interviewer time, and so on, there may sometimes be a heavy penalty imposed for each additional question posed in the survey questionnaire. In such cases, RGI might be used for just a few questions. The RGI protocol obtains three points on each respondent's underlying distribution. A hierarchical Bayesian procedure is suggested below for using the collection of triples of points from the respondents for estimating the population mean. The resulting RGI estimator can often improve upon the accuracy of the usual sample mean.

Let the triple (y_i, a_i, b_i) denote the basic response, and, as above, the lower bound response, and the upper bound response, respectively, for respondent i, $i = 1, \ldots, n$. Suppose that the y_i's are all normally distributed $N(\theta_i, \sigma_i^2)$, that the θ_i's are exchangeable, and $\theta_i \sim N(\theta_0, \tau^2)$. θ_i denotes the true (factual, or opinion, or attitude) value for respondent i. It has been shown using a hierarchical Bayesian model that in such a situation, the conditional posterior distribution of the population mean, θ_0, is normal, and is given by:

$$(\theta_0 | \text{ data}, \sigma_i^2, \tau^2) \sim N(\tilde{\theta}, \omega^2), \tag{1}$$

where the posterior mean, $\tilde{\theta}$, conditional on the data and (σ_i^2, τ^2), is expressible as a weighted average of the usage quantities, the y_i's, and the weights are expressible approximately as simple algebraic functions of the bounds. The conditional posterior variance, ω^2, drives the credibility (Bayesian confidence) interval, and is discussed below.

We assess values for the σ_i^2 parameters from $k_1 \sigma_i = b_i - a_i \equiv r_i$, the respondent interval lengths. Analogously, we assess a value for τ^2 from $k_2 \tau = \bar{b} - \bar{a}$, the average respondent interval length. For normally distributed data it is commonly assumed that lower and upper bounds that represent extreme possible values for the respondents can be associated with 2 standard deviations below, and above, the mean, respectively. We will generally assume, therefore, that $k_1 = k_2 = k = 4$ (corresponding to standard deviations above and below the mean).

The conditional posterior mean was shown to be given by:

$$\tilde{\theta} = \sum_1^n \lambda_i y_i,$$ (2)

where the λ_i's are weights depending upon the interval lengths that are given approximately by:

$$\lambda_i = \frac{\left(\dfrac{1}{r_i^2 + (\bar{b} - \bar{a})^2}\right)}{\displaystyle\sum_1^n \left(\dfrac{1}{r_i^2 + (\bar{b} - \bar{a})^2}\right)}.$$ (3)

We note the following characteristics of this RGI (weighted average) estimator:

1. The weighted average is simple and quick to calculate, without requiring any computer-intensive sampling techniques.

2. It will be seen in the examples that follow that if the respondents who give short intervals are also the more accurate ones, the RGI estimator will tend to give an estimate of the population mean that has smaller bias than does the sample mean. In the special case in which the interval lengths are all the same, the weighted average reduces to the sample mean, $\bar{y}$, where the weights all equal $(1/n)$. In any case, the lambda weights are all positive (although some may be extremely small), and must sum to one.

3. The longer the interval a respondent gives, the less weight is applied to that respondent's usage quantity in the weighted average. The length of respondent i's interval is a measure of his/her degree of confidence in the basic response he/she gives, so that the shorter the interval, the greater degree of confidence that respondent has in the basic response he/she reports. Of course, a high degree of confidence does not necessarily imply an answer close to the true value.

4. If we define the precision of a distribution as its reciprocal variance, the quantity $\{[r_i^2 + (\bar{b} - \bar{a})^2]/(4)^2\}$ may be seen to be the conditional variance in the posterior distribution corresponding to respondent i, and therefore, its reciprocal represents the conditional precision corresponding to respondent i. Summing over all respondents' precisions gives:

$$\text{total conditional posterior variance} = \omega^2 = \cfrac{1}{\sum_1^n \left(\cfrac{16}{r_i^2 + (\overline{b} - \overline{a})^2} \right)}. \tag{4}$$

The number "16" is the square of the 4 that arises from $4\sigma_i = b_i - a_i \equiv r_i$, and $4\tau = \overline{b} - \overline{a}$.

So another interpretation of λ_i in equations (2) and (3) is that it is the proportion of the total conditional posterior precision in the data attributable to respondent i.

The variance of the conditional posterior distribution is given in equation (4). The posterior variance is the reciprocal of the posterior total precision. Because the posterior distribution of the population mean, θ_0, is normal, it is straightforward to find credibility intervals for θ_0. For example, a 95 percent credibility interval for θ_0 is given by:

$$(\tilde{\theta} - 1.96\omega, \tilde{\theta} + 1.96\omega). \tag{5}$$

That is,

$$P\{(\tilde{\theta} - 1.96\omega \leq \theta_0 \leq \tilde{\theta} + 1.96\omega)|data\} = 95\%. \tag{6}$$

An alternative interval estimate of the population mean that is more likely than the credibility interval to cover the true population value is the Average Respondent-Generated Interval, $ARGI \equiv \overline{b} - \overline{a}$. The range-of-belief for the sample of respondents is $b_0 - a_0$.

Examples

We next present some numerical "theoretical examples" of the use of RGI estimates.

Example for Recall Questions. We examine an artificial extreme case. Suppose we have a sample survey of size $n = 100$ in which the RGI protocol has been used. Suppose also that the true population mean of interest that we are trying to estimate is given by $\theta_0 = 1000$. In this example we fix both the basic response quantities and the respondents' bounds, (a_i, b_i), $r_i = b_i - a_i$, $i = 1, \ldots, n$, artificially.

Assume that the respondents have been ordered so that the first 30 respondents all have excellent memories, are quite accurate, and have individual truths of 900. Suppose the intervals these accurate respondents give are:

$$(a_1, b_1), \ldots, (a_{30}, b_{30}) = (975,975), \ldots, (975,975). \tag{7}$$

That is not only are they all pretty accurate, but they all believe that they are accurate, so they respond to the bounds questions with degenerate intervals whose lower and upper bounds are the same. Accordingly, these accurate respondents all report intervals of length $r_i = 0$, and usages of equal amounts, $y_i = 975$ (compared with the true population value of 1000).

In addition, suppose the next 20 respondents also are quite accurate, but their individual truths are above 1000, say 1100. Suppose the intervals these respondents give are:

$$(a_{31}, b_{31}), \ldots, (a_{50}, b_{50}) = (1125, 1125), \ldots, (1125, 1125). \tag{8}$$

Next suppose that the last 50 respondents all have poor memories and are inaccurate. They report the intervals:

$$(a_{51}, b_{51}), \ldots, (a_{100}, b_{100}) = (500, 1500), \ldots, (500, 1500), \tag{9}$$

that have lengths of $r_i = 1000$, and they report unequal basic response quantities of 550, for the first 30, and 1450 for the last 20. We now find: $\bar{a} = 767.5$, and $\bar{b} = 1267.5$, so $\bar{b} - \bar{a} = 500$. We may now calculate that the weights are given by:

$$\lambda_i = \begin{cases} .0167, & i = 1, \ldots, 50 \\ .0033, & i = 51, \ldots, 100 \end{cases} \tag{10}$$

It is easy to check that: $\sum_{1}^{100} \lambda_i = 1$. We may now readily find that the conditional posterior mean RGI estimator of the population mean, θ_0, is given by:

$$\tilde{\theta} = \sum_{i=1}^{100} \lambda_i y_i = 1014.17. \tag{11}$$

The corresponding sample mean is given by:

$$\bar{y} = 972.5. \tag{12}$$

The numerical error (bias) of the posterior mean is given by:

$$|\tilde{\theta} - 1000| = |1014.17 - 1000| = 14.17. \tag{13}$$

The numerical error (bias) of the sample mean is given by:

$$|\bar{y} - 1000| = |972.5 - 1000| = 27.5. \tag{14}$$

The RGI estimator has reduced the bias error by

$$27.5 - 14.17 = 13.33, \text{ or about } 48\%, \tag{15}$$

compared with the error of the sample mean.

It is also interesting to compare interval estimates of the population mean by comparing the standard error of $\bar{y}$, with ω, the standard deviation of the coditional posterior distribution of $\tilde{\theta}$. These estimates give rise to the correspoding confidence and credibility intervals for θ_0, respectively.

We may readily find that for the data in our theoretical example, $\omega = 16.14$. It is also easy to check that, for our data, the standard deviation of the data is 323.80. So the standard error for a sample of size 100 is $323.80/10 = 32.38$. Thus, the RGI estimate of standard deviation is about half the standard error of the sample mean. Correspondingly, the length of the 95 percent credibility interval $2(1.96)(\omega) = 63.27$, while the length of the 95 percent confidence interval is $2(1.96)(32.38) = 126.93$. The 95 percent confidence interval is about twice as long as the 95 percent credibility interval. The 95 percent credibility interval is given by: (982.53, 1045.80). The 95 percent confidence interval is given by: (909.04, 1035.96).

We note in this theoretical example that:

1. Both the RGI credibility interval and the confidence interval cover the true value of 1000, but the credibility interval is smaller.

2. We expect to find many situations for which the bias error of the RGI estimator is smaller than that of the sample mean; however, the differences may be more, or less, dramatic compared with their values in this example.

3. In large samples, we expect that both the sample mean and the RGI estimator will converge to one another, and to the true population mean.

4. We also note that the success of the theoretical example depends on the fact that the accurate respondents give short intervals and so have heavier weights than the inaccurate respondents who give longer intervals. In order to help assure that such conditions hold in operational studies, we can ask respondents a preliminary question concerning their confidence in their accuracy and use their confidence weightings to moderate their responses.

Example for Opinions and Attitudes. Suppose there is a population of opinions about some issue, say, "Issue A." Perhaps the analyst would like to establish the mean of the opinions of all people living in the city of New York about Issue A. This is "truth." But it is not an absolute truth. It is a relative truth—a truth at this time and under current circumstances. It is not an absolute truth that will have the same value next month, or next year, as would be the case for a factual or recall-type question. The analyst would like to estimate that relative truth. Relative true values are generally different for each person in a sample, as is generally the case in a recall question. But accuracy in an opinion or attitude context has no meaning, other than with respect to sampling error, although respondents with fuzzy attitudes or opinions who give intervals as well as point values provide additional information with which their views may be sharpened. There is no "correct" answer for an opinion or for an attitude for a given respondent, as there would be for a person answering a recall-type question. Similarly, response bias does not have the same meaning as in recall. (With a recall-type question, one of the reasons for response bias arises out of faulty memory.)

When using RGI for attitudes or opinions, we can find both point and interval estimators, although we cannot really say much about accuracy per se. But we can speak about the RGI point estimator coming closer to second-guessing the opinions of New Yorkers in the above example than a mere sample mean that includes some people with very fuzzy opinions and some people who have very firm opinions. RGI can provide a measure of average opinion strength, as measured by the average range supplied by all respondents, $(\bar{b} - \bar{a})$. It can also supply a credibility interval measure of belief; a confidence interval can also supply an interval measure of belief. The confidence interval, however, only reflects sampling uncertainty, whereas the RGI credibility interval also reflects fuzziness of opinion. The range-of-belief also available with RGI, $(b_0 - a_0)$, is somewhat different.

Optimally efficient RGI used with factual questions requires that respondents who give narrow intervals also be the more accurate ones, and that respondents who give wide intervals also be the more inaccurate ones. When RGI is used with opinion or attitude questions, firm and fuzzy opinions or attitudes should be analogously categorized. Future research with RGI should involve developing meta-cognitive procedures that will achieve these objectives.

Further Reading

Chu, LiPing, S. James Press, and Judith M. Tanur. "Confidence Eliciation and Anchoring in the Respondent-Generated Intervals Protocol." *Journal of Modern Applied Statistical Methods* 3, no. 2 (2004): 417–31.

Press, S. James. "Respondent-Generated Intervals (RGI) for Recall in Sample Surveys." *Journal of Modern Applied Statistical Methods* 3, no. 1 (May 2004): 104–16.

Press, S. James, and Kent H. Marquis. "Bayesian Estimation in a U.S. Government Survey of Income Recall using Respondent-Generated Intervals." *Proceedings of the Conference of the International Society of Bayesian Analysis.* Eurostat: Crete, 2002. Available at http://www.statistics.ucr.edu/press.htm.

Press, S. James, and Judith M. Tanur. "Experimenting with Respondent-Generated Intervals in Sample Surveys," with discussions. In *Survey Research at the Intersection of Statistics and Cognitive Psychology*, Working Paper Series #28, edited by Monroe G. Sirken. National Center for Health Statistics, Center for Disease Control and Prevention, pp. 1–18. Available at http://www.statistics.ucr.edu/press.htm.

———. "An Overview of the Respondent-Generated Intervals (RGI) Approach to Sample Surveys." *Journal of Modern Applied Statistical Methods* 3, no. 2 (2004): 288–304.

———. "Relating Respondent-Generated Intervals Questionnaire Design to Survey Accuracy and Response Rate." *Journal of Official Statistics, Statistics Sweden* 20, no. 2 (2004): 265–87. Special issue on questionnaire development, evaluation, and testing methods.

———. "The Respondent-Generated Intervals Approach to Sample Surveys: From Theory to Experiment." In *New Developments on Psychometrics*, edited by Haruo Yanai, Akinori Okada, Kazuo Shigemasu, Yutaka Kano, and Jacqueline J. Meulman. Tokyo: Springer-Verlag, 2003.

S. James Press and Judith M. Tanur

Response Latency

Response latency refers to the measurement of reaction time from the onset of a stimulus to the offset of a response. Survey researchers typically start measuring at the offset of a question until the onset of a definite, valid answer, because the speed with which interviewers verbally present questions (i.e., stimuli) to respondents tends to differ. Reaction times in surveys interviews have been used increasingly to understand question comprehension and attitude accessibility.

Response latency was first measured in surveys by market researchers assessing paired comparisons. They believed that the faster a choice was made between two brands, the stronger the preference for the chosen brand. Subsequent research on response latencies revealed that they could also serve as indicators of question difficulty, attitude stability, and actual behavior.

Researchers have demonstrated orderliness in the latencies of various types of questions, ranging from very brief latencies for simple factual questions to long ones for complex attitudinal ones. More complex questions, especially ones flawed in construction, frequently take more time to answer. Similarly, longer latencies are more often found for incorrect and non-substantive answers than for correct answers.

Response latencies have also been used to study the stability of attitudes. Respondents who hold stable attitudes tend to react faster to questions than respondents with unstable, noncrystallized attitudes. It is also believed that the more stable an attitude or the stronger a preference is, the less difficult a question concerning the attitude or preference will be, and the more certainty a respondent will have about the correctness of a selected answer. Likewise, the difficulty of a question may express itself in a state of uncertainty, which in turn causes a longer response latency.

Finally, response latencies have been used as a predictor of actual behavior. Slower response times typically suggest that the respondent is unsure or confused about participating in an activity. For example, response latency is a better predictor of discrepancies between voting intentions and actual voting behavior than a verbal measure of "certainty" (e.g., a question about the finality of the voter's intentions).

Although response latency can be a useful indicator of question difficulty and attitude strength, measuring it is fraught with challenges. Typically, researchers assess response latency by having interviewers employ a computer clock during survey administration. At the completion of a question, interviewers press a computer key, thereby starting a computer clock. A voice key is triggered when the respondent emits a sound, providing an initial timing. The interviewer also presses a key when the respondent is judged to have given an answer, resulting in a second timing. Finally, the interviewer codes the validity of the two clock readings. The end result is a series of response latencies measured in milliseconds.

In practice, computer clock measurement is far less seamless than it sounds. It is almost impossible for an interviewer to determine precisely when respondents initiate (or ends) an adequate answer to a question. Second, interviewers typically code the offset time of answers, rather than the onset time, artificially inflating latencies as the duration of the response increases. Third, inadvertent noises may trigger the voice key. Background sounds, like television or radio sounds, or "hemming sounds" from respondents filling time as they think about their answer can result in shorter timed latencies than is actually the case. Couple these problems with the increase in interviewer burden from having to record times as well as responses, and the response latencies generated by interviewer timings are likely to be unreliable and/or invalid and may compromise the quality of the interview data.

Alternatively, coders can assign response latencies after the telephone interviews have actually taken place. This requires that the interviews are taped and even digitized. Although such procedures may result in a more reliable measurement, they require considerable more time and effort to conduct.

Future research is aimed at identifying and perfecting new methods for measuring response latency. With the growth of **Internet survey methods**, techniques and protocols must be established for assessing reactions times. Moreover, technological advances in telephone surveys (e.g., touch-tone entry) raise new questions about the meaning of latency and its computation.

Further Reading

Bassili, John N. "The How and Why of Response Latency Measurement in Telephone Surveys." In *Answering questions*, edited by N. Schwarz and S. Sudman. San Francisco: Jossey-Bass, 1996. Describes the history and technical procedures of response latency methodology.

Bassili, John N., and Joseph F. Fletcher. "Response-Time Measurement in Survey Research: A Method for CATI and a New Look at Nonattitudes." *Public Opinion Quarterly* 55 (1991): 331–46. Develops a methodology for measuring accurately the time it takes respondents to answer questions in computer-assisted telephone surveys.

Fazio, Russ, H. "A Practical Guide to the Use of Response Latency in Social Psychological Research." In *Research Methods in Personality and Social Psychology*, edited by C. Hendrick and M. S. Clark. Newbury Park, CA: Sage, 1990. A good presentation of the challenges associated with measuring response latency.

Stasja Draisma

Response Process

Response process is the cognitive tasks undertaken by survey participants to formulate an answer to a question. It requires that respondents (1) interpret the question to understand what is meant and (2) retrieve relevant information from memory to (3) form a judgment. In most cases, they cannot report their judgment in their own words but (4) need to map it onto a set of response alternatives provided by the researcher. Finally, respondents may wish to (5) "edit" their answer before they communicate it to the interviewer for reasons of social desirability and self-presentation. Respondents' performance of each of these tasks is context dependent and profoundly influenced by characteristics of the questionnaire, including its administration mode.

Question Comprehension. The response process begins with the interpretation of the question. Understanding the literal meaning of a question is not sufficient to provide an informative answer. When asked, "What have you done today?", respondents certainly understand the words, but they still need to determine what kind of activities the researcher is interested in. Should they report, for example, that they took a shower? Providing an informative answer requires inferences about the questioner's communicative intention to determine the pragmatic meaning of the question. To infer the pragmatic meaning, respondents draw on contextual information, including the content of adjacent questions and the nature of the response alternatives. Their use of this information is licensed by the tacit assumptions that govern the conduct of conversation in daily life, which respondents apply to the research interview.

Response options also shape understanding of the question. They clarify the intent of a question and shape the alternatives to be considered. Closed-answer formats present a list of alternatives for respondents to choose from, whereas open-answer formats do not provide any guidance for respondents. Not surprisingly, any given opinion is less likely to be reported in an open-answer format than as part of a list in a closed-answer format. Moreover, any opinion not included in the list is likely to go unreported, even if an "other" option is offered.

Going beyond the content of response alternatives, respondents pay close attention to apparently "formal" features of the response scale. Suppose respondents have to report how successful they have been in life along an 11-point rating scale, ranging from "not at all successful" to "extremely successful." Does "not at all successful" refer to the absence of outstanding success or to the presence of failure? Respondents resolve this ambiguity by attending to contextual information, including the numeric values of the rating scale. When these values range from 0 (not at all successful) to 10 (extremely successful) they infer that "not at all successful" refers to the absence of success, yet when the values range from −5 (not at all successful) to +5 (extremely successful) they infer that "not at all successful" refers to the opposite of success, namely failure. As a result of this differential interpretation, 34 percent endorsed a value below the midpoint of the 0 to 10 scale, whereas only 13 percent endorsed one of the formally equivalent values on the −5 to +5 scale. In general, rating scales that use only positive numeric values suggest that the researcher has a unipolar dimension in mind (pertaining to the presence of a single attribute, e.g., success), whereas a combination of negative and positive numeric values suggests that the researcher has a bipolar dimension in mind (pertaining to the presence of a given attribute or its opposite, e.g., success vs. failure).

Findings like these demonstrate that respondents use the response alternatives in interpreting the meaning of a question. In doing so, they proceed on the tacit assumption that every contribution is relevant to the aims of the ongoing conversation. In the survey interview, these contributions include apparently formal features of questionnaire design, such as the numeric values given on a rating scale. Hence, identically worded questions may acquire different meanings, depending on the response alternatives by which they are accompanied.

Respondents' interpretation of a question's intended meaning is further influenced by the context in which the question is presented. This influence is more pronounced, the more ambiguous the question wording is. As an extreme case, consider research in which respondents are asked to report their opinion about a highly obscure (or completely fictitious) issue, such as the "Agricultural Trade Act of 1978." Empirically, about 30 percent of a sample typically provides answers to fictitious issues, apparently confirming skeptics' nightmares. From a conversational point of view, however, their answers may be more meaningful than assumed. The sheer fact that a question about some issue is asked presupposes that the issue exists—or else asking a question about it would violate norms of cooperative conversational conduct. Given that respondents have no reason to assume that the researcher would ask meaningless questions, they will try to make sense of it. Hence, they turn to the context of the ambiguous question to infer a plausible meaning, much as they would be expected to do in daily conversations, where the use of contextual knowledge is a key feature of cooperative communication. For example, German students inferred that a question about the introduction of a fictitious "educational contribution" pertained to receiving money when it followed a question about fellowships for students, but to paying money when it followed a question about tuition. Not surprisingly, they supported the introduction of an "educational contribution" in the former case, but opposed it in the latter.

As these examples illustrate, question comprehension is not primarily an issue of understanding the literal meaning of an utterance. Rather, question comprehension involves extensive inferences about the speaker's intentions to determine the pragmatic meaning of the question. To make these inferences, respondents draw on the nature of preceding questions, the response alternatives, the researcher's institutional affiliation, and similar variables. Accordingly, survey methodologists' traditional focus on using the "right words" in question writing needs to be complemented by a consideration of the cognitive and communicative processes involved in question answering.

Recalling Information and Computing a Judgment. Once respondents determine what the researcher is interested in, they need to recall relevant information from memory. Researchers usually hope that this information is a previously formed opinion, available in memory. In most cases, however, respondents will not find an appropriate answer readily stored in memory and will need to recall information to compute a judgment on the spot. In doing so, they never retrieve all information that may be relevant to the topic but truncate the search process once enough information has come to mind to form a judgment. Accordingly, their judgment is based on the subset of relevant information that most easily comes to mind, which is often information brought to mind by preceding questions. To understand how this information influences their judgment, we need to understand the nature of mental construal processes.

All evaluative judgments require a representation of the target (i.e., the object of judgment), as well as a representation of some standard against which the target is evaluated. Both representations are context dependent and include information that is chronically accessible as well as information that is only temporarily accessible, for example, because it was used to answer a preceding question. How accessible information influences the judgment depends on how it is used. Information that is included in the temporary representation that respondents form of the target results in assimilation effects; that is, the judgment is more positive (negative) when positive (negative) information comes to mind. The size of assimilation effects increases with the amount and extremity of temporarily accessible information and decreases with the amount and extremity of chronically accessible information included in the representation of the target.

Suppose, for example, that respondents are asked to report their marital satisfaction and their general life-satisfaction in different question orders. In one study, the answers to these questions correlated r = .32 in the life-marriage order, but r = .67 in the marriage-life order. This increase in correlation reflects that respondents can draw on a wide range of information to evaluate their lives and are more likely to consider their marriage it has just been brought to mind by the question. Accordingly, happily married respondents reported higher, and unhappily married respondents lower, mean life-satisfaction in the marriage-life than in the life-marriage order. This increase in correlation was attenuated (r = .43) when questions about three different life-domains (job, leisure time, and marriage) preceded the general question, thus bringing a more diverse range of information to mind.

However, the same piece of accessible information that may elicit an assimilation effect may also result in a contrast effect, that is, a more negative (positive) judgment when positive (negative) information is brought to mind. This is the case when the information is excluded from, rather than included in, the cognitive representation formed of the target. As a first possibility, suppose that a given piece of information with positive (negative) implications is excluded from the representation of the target category. If so, the representation will contain less positive (negative) information, resulting in less positive (negative) judgments. This possibility is referred to as a subtraction based contrast effect. Specifically, rules of conversational conduct request speakers to provide information that is new to the recipient, rather than to reiterate information that has already been given. Applying this rule to the survey interview, respondents may interpret a subsequent question as a request for new information, thus inducing them to disregard information that they have already provided. In the above study of marital satisfaction and life-satisfaction, both questions correlated r = .67 in the marriage-life order. However, this correlation dropped to r = .18 in the same question order when both question where introduced by a joint lead-in that read, "We now have two questions about your life. The first pertains to your marriage and the second to your life as a whole." Increasing the conversational relatedness of the questions in this way induced respondents to interpret the general life-satisfaction question as if it were worded, "Aside from your marriage, which you already told us about, how satisfied are you with other aspects of your life?" Consistent with this assumption, a condition in which this reworded general question was presented resulted in a highly similar correlation of $\underline{r}$ = .20. Once they disregarded their marriage under these conditions, happily married respondents reported lower, and unhappily married respondents higher, general life-satisfaction than without the lead-in. Such subtraction based contrast effects are limited to the specific target (here, "my life") from whose representation a given piece of information is subtracted. The size of subtraction based contrast effects increases with the amount and extremity of the temporarily accessible information that is excluded from the representation of the target, and decreases with the amount and extremity of the information that remains in the representation of the target.

As a second possibility, respondents may not only exclude accessible information from the representation formed of the target, but may also use this information in constructing a standard of comparison. If the implications of the temporarily accessible positive (negative) information are more extreme than the implications of the chronically accessible information used in constructing a standard, they result in a more positive (negative) standard, relative to which the target is evaluated less positively (negatively). The size of comparison based contrast effects increases with the extremity and amount of temporarily accessible information used in constructing the standard, and decreases with the amount and extremity of chronically accessible information used in making this construction. In contrast to subtraction based comparison effects, which are limited to a specific target, comparison based contrast effects may generalize to all targets to which the standard is applicable.

As an example, consider the impact of political scandals on assessments of the trustworthiness of politicians. Not surprisingly, thinking about a politician who was involved in a scandal, say Richard Nixon, decreases trust in politicians in general. In theoretical terms, the exemplar (Nixon) is included in the representation formed of the superordinate category (American politicians), which now includes a highly accessible untrustworthy exemplar. If the trustworthiness question pertains to a specific other politician, however, say George W. Bush, the primed exemplar cannot be included in the representation formed of the target—after all, Bush is not Nixon. In this case, Nixon serves as a standard of comparison, relative to which Bush is evaluated as more trustworthy than would otherwise be the case. An experiment with German exemplars confirmed these predictions: Thinking about a politician who was involved in a scandal decreased the trustworthiness of politicians in general, but increased the trustworthiness of all specific individual politicians assessed. In general, the same information is likely to result in assimilation effects in evaluations of superordinate target categories (which allow for inclusion), but in contrast effects in evaluations of lateral target categories (which force exclusion). These judgmental processes are reflected in a wide range of discrepancies between general and specific judgments in public opinion research. For example, Americans distrust Congress in general but trust their own representative; they support capital punishment in general but are less likely to apply it in any specific case. Moreover, members of minority groups consistently report high levels of discrimination against their group yet also report that they personally have experienced much less of it. In each case, these patterns are to be expected when we take into account that recalling extreme and vivid instances drives the general and the specific judgments in opposite directions, as predicted on theoretical grounds.

Numerous variables can influence whether information is used in forming a representation of the target, resulting in assimilation effects, or a representation of the standard, resulting in contrast effects. Sudman and his colleagues provide a detailed discussion and present a model that predicts the emergence, direction, and size of **question-order effects**. Reflecting the crucial role of information accessibility in question-order effects, older respondents are less likely to be influenced by earlier questions, due to age-related declines in memory.

Similar processes contribute to the emergence of response order effects, which are particularly pronounced when several response alternative are similarly plausible. Suppose, for example, that respondents are asked, (A) "Should divorce be easier to get or more difficult to get?" versus (B) "Should divorce be more difficult to get or easier to get?" When these questions are presented in writing, many respondents will initially think about the first response alternative presented to them ("easier" in form A, "more difficult" in form B). In either case, some supporting thoughts are likely to come to mind on this issue. Consistent with the principle of truncated information search, respondents are likely to rely on these initial thoughts and may endorse the first alternative with limited consideration of the second one, resulting in a primacy effect. But when the same questions are read to them, respondents are likely to think first about the alternative they heard last ("more difficult" in form A, "easier" in form B). Finding agreeing thoughts, they are again likely to endorse it, resulting in a recency effect. Hence, primacy effects are more likely under visual, and recency effects under auditory, presentation formats. In both cases, the effect can be traced to the influence of response order on the mental representation that respondents form of the attitude object. Response order effects are more pronounced of older respondents, whose limited working memory capacity makes it more difficult to consider several response alternatives and to compare their relative advantages.

Survey researchers have long assumed that attitudes vary in their degree of strength, centrality, or crystallization and that context effects are limited to attitudes that are weak and not (yet) crystallized. The data bearing on this proposition are mixed. Self-reports of **attitude strength** (in the form of importance or centrality) are usually unrelated to the emergence of context effects. In the most comprehensive test, based on more than a dozen experiments and different self-report measures of attitude strength, Krosnick and Schuman found no support for the assumption that context effects decrease with attitude strength, except for the not surprising finding that respondents with a weak attitude are more likely to choose a middle alternative. Other studies, however, used respondents' reaction time as an indicator of attitude strength, based on the assumption that more central beliefs should be more accessible in memory (*see* **Response Latency**). These studies found that respondents with short reaction times provide more consistent answers and may be less influenced by preceding questions, an observation that is compatible with the construal processes discussed earlier.

Formatting the Response. Having formed a judgment, respondents can usually not report it in their own words, but need to format it according to the response alternatives provided by the researcher. From a theoretical point of view, the influence of response alternatives is not limited to the formatting stage and response alternatives are likely to influence other steps of the question answering sequence as well, as already seen in the section on question comprehension.

The only effects that occur unequivocally at the formatting stage pertain to the anchoring of rating scales. As numerous studies demonstrate, respondents use the most extreme stimuli to anchor the endpoints of a rating scale. As a result, a given stimulus will be rated as less extreme if presented in the context of a more extreme one, than if presented in the context of a less extreme one. In Parducci's range-frequency model, this impact of the range of stimuli is referred to as the "range effect." In addition, if the number of stimuli to be rated is sufficiently large, respondents attempt to use all categories of the rating scale about equally often to be maximally informative. Accordingly, the specific ratings given also depend on the frequency distribution of the presented stimuli, an effect that is referred to as the "frequency effect."

Editing the Response. Finally, respondents may want to edit their response before they communicate it, reflecting considerations of social desirability and self-presentation. Not surprisingly, editing on the basis of social desirability is particularly likely in response to threatening questions and is more pronounced in face-to-face interviews than in self-administered questionnaires, which provide a higher degree of confidentiality. Methods that increase the privacy of respondents' answers usually attenuate response editing.

Further Reading

Payne, Stanley. *The Art of Asking Questions.* Princeton, NJ: Princeton University Press, 1951. A classic and still useful volume that documents early research into response effects.

Schuman, Howard, and Stanley Presser. *Questions and Answers in Attitude Surveys.* San

Diego: Academic Press, 1981. A highly influential volume that sets the agenda for research into context effects.

Schwarz, Norbert. "Self-Reports: How the Questions Shape the Answers." *American Psychologist* 54 (1999): 93–105. A short review of the cognitive and communicative processes involved in answering survey questions.

Sirken, Monroe G., Douglas J. Herrmann, Susan Schechter, Norbert Schwarz, Judith M. Tanur, and Roger Tourangeau, eds. *Cognition and Survey Research*. New York: John Wiley, 1999. Different perspectives on the question-answering process, including advice on pretesting questionnaires and reviews of key research areas.

Sudman, Seymour, Norman M. Bradburn, and Norbert Schwarz. *Thinking About Answers: The Application of Cognitive Processes to Survey Methodology*. San Francisco: Jossey-Bass, 1996. A comprehensive introduction to the cognitive and communicative processes underlying survey responding.

Tourangeau, Roger, Lance J. Rips, and Kenneth Rasinski. *The Psychology of Survey Response*. New York: Cambridge University Press, 2000. A comprehensive introduction to the cognitive and communicative processes underlying survey responding.

Norbert Schwarz

Response Rate

The response rate is the ratio of completed interviews to the number of eligible units in the **sample frame**. Several different formulas have been developed to calculate response rates, varying by the criteria used to determine a completed interview and an eligible unit. Response rates are often used as a measure of survey quality, because surveys will yield misleading results if those completing them are systematically different from those who did not. Considerable debate, though, has arisen over the minimum acceptable threshold for response rates.

Importance of Response Rate. Probabilistic sampling methods, such as **simple random sampling, stratified sampling**, or **cluster sampling**, ensure that sample statistics can be inferred to the population they were drawn from *if* everyone chosen from the **sample frame** completes the survey. When eligible respondents fail to participate, the sample statistics are susceptible to bias. If the participants are systematically different from the eligible members of the sampling frame who failed to respond on measures germane to the study then the results will be skewed, and misleading conclusions may be propagated.

Unfortunately, rarely does everyone in the sample frame participate. Take, for example, telephone surveys. Dialed numbers often result in busy signals, answering machines, or no answers altogether. Sometimes these numbers are invalid, belonging to a business, an ineligible respondent, or a nonworking exchange. Other times, those contacted are unavailable or unwilling to answer (i.e., screen their calls). Even if an eligible respondent answers, they may refuse to participate or only partially complete the survey.

Calculating Response Rate. The American Association of Public Opinion Research (AAPOR) recognizes six different methods for calculating response rates, varying by how respondents of unknown eligibility or only partially complete the survey are treated. Response Rate 1 computes the ratio of completed interviews to the sum of completed interviews, partial interviews, refusals, noncontacts with known eligible participants, and unknown cases (i.e., efforts that do not reveal whether the contact information corresponds to an eligible respondent, such as no answer).

$$\text{Response Rate 1} = \text{Completes} / ((\text{Completes} + \text{Partials}) + (\text{Refusals} + \text{Non-contacts}) + (\text{All Unknown Cases}))$$

Response Rate 2 calculates responses rates in the same way as Response Rate 1, except that partially completed interviews are treated as completed ones in the designation of the numerator.

$$\text{Response Rate 2} = (\text{Completes} + \text{Partials}) / ((\text{Completes} + \text{Partials}) + (\text{Refusals} + \text{Non-contacts}) + (\text{All Unknown Cases}))$$

Response Rate 3 does not assume that all unknown cases correspond with eligible respondents. Instead, it assumes that some contact information will be linked to businesses, fax machines, or individuals outside the target population. The estimated number of eligible respondents among the unknown cases is used in the denominator rather than the overall total. Researchers are expected to provide documentation about how they arrived at this figure.

$$\text{Response Rate 3} = \text{Completes} / ((\text{Completes} + \text{Partials}) + (\text{Refusals} + \text{Non-contacts}) + (\text{Unknown Cases Estimated to Be Eligible}))$$

Response Rate 4 calculates responses rates in the same way as Response Rate 3, except that partially completed interviews are treated as completed ones in the designation of the numerator.

$$\text{Response Rate 4} = (\text{Completes} + \text{Partials}) / ((\text{Completes} + \text{Partials}) + (\text{Refusals} + \text{Non-contacts}) + (\text{Unknown Cases Estimated to Be Eligible}))$$

Response Rate 5 assumes that none of the unknown cases correspond to eligible respondents, omitting these cases from the denominator entirely. Researchers are expected to provide some basis for this assumption.

$$\text{Response Rate 5} = \text{Completes} / ((\text{Completes} + \text{Partials}) + (\text{Refusals} + \text{Non-contacts}))$$

Response Rate 6 calculates responses rates in the same way as Response Rate 5, except that partially completed interviews are treated as completed ones in the designation of the numerator.

$$\text{Response Rate 6} = (\text{Completes} + \text{Partials}) / ((\text{Completes} + \text{Partials}) + (\text{Refusals} + \text{Non-contacts}))$$

Minimal Response Rates. There is considerable debate about the minimum response rates needed to achieve quality surveys. The American Association of Public Opinion Research provides little guidance, advising practitioners to maximize response rates within ethical limits. Implicit in this advice is the assumption that the closer the response rate comes to 100 percent, the less threat nonresponse error poses to the data. This assumption, though, is not necessarily true. Nonresponse bias depends both on the level of nonresponse and on whether there are systematic differences between responders and nonresponders. These differences may occur with both low response rates and high response rates. Because researchers rarely know the differences between responders and nonresponders on substantive survey questions, it is difficult to identify under what conditions they threaten to undermine data quality. As a result, researchers may be justified in adopting the conventional scientific protocol that the null hypothesis—in this case, that a low response rate does not suffer from nonresponse error—is true until proven otherwise.

A number of high-profile studies have demonstrated that lower response rates do not necessarily pose a threat to data quality. For example, Richard Curtin, Stanley Presser, and Eleanor Singer at the University of Michigan analyzed the results of seventeen years of monthly surveys of 500 individuals. Respondents who required more than five calls to complete were compared with those who required more than two calls to complete and those who required refusal conversions to complete. The researchers found no effect of excluding any of these respondent groups on cross-sectional estimates of the Index of Consumer Satisfaction.

Example. Let us assume that we conduct a survey by calling numbers from a **random digit dialing** (RDD) list. We want to predict the outcome of a ballot alternative in a statewide issue election. We need to speak to registered voters who say they are certain to vote in the next election, so once a person answers, we need to determine how many such persons there are in the household and, if there is a qualified potential respondent, speak to him or her and ask the question; if there is more than one such person, we need to randomly select one as a designated respondent and attempt to ask him or her the question.

If the interviewer gets no answer or a busy signal, those responses are considered nonresponses under the most conservative AAPOR response rate calculations (RR1 and RR2). Clearly identified residential call answering machines or privacy managers are nonresponses. If a person answers and refuses to provide information about who is in the household, that is a nonresponse; if there is an eligible respondent in the household who refuses the interview, that too is a nonresponse. So the person who screens his calls and does not answer unless the caller is known to him personally, the person who lives alone and works during the survey's calling hours, and the person who refuses to participate without monetary compensation are all nonrespondents who are assumed to be systematically different from the respondents.

In this example, we are not particularly interested in predicting the exact number of voters choosing either alternative, just the outcome. We shall consider four factors in developing our measure of confidence: the size of the sample, the size of the plurality, the response rate, and the sampling error.

Of these, sampling error may be the most familiar to casual observers of polls, and also the least understood. The formula for sampling error is the square root of $(.9604 (N-n) / (nN-n))$, where n is the size of the sample and N is the size of the population. Let's say we have a sample size of 400 and a target population of 1,000. The formula will deliver a sampling error of 3.8 percent. With the same **sample size** but a target population of 10,000, the sampling error goes up to 4.8 percent, which makes sense—we are trying to use the same size sample, but instead of 40 percent of the population, we now are working with a sample of 4 percent of the population. If we go up to a target population of 100,000, the sampling error increases again, but only to 4.9 percent—and it stays at that figure if we go to 1 million or 1 billion. In other words, for target populations

Table 1. Likelihood of Neutralizing the Result with a 55 Percent Plurality and a 40 Percent Response Rate

Element	Value	Explanation
Total eligible sample	2500	
Percent choosing A	55%	
Percent choosing B	45%	
Response rate	40%	
Total number of respondents	1000	
Respondents choosing A	550	
Respondents choosing B	450	
Converted respondents	750	One-half of all nonrespondents
Converts needed to choose B	425	Number of converts needed to produce an even split
Even split after conversion	875	(Respondents + (Nonrespondents / 2)) / 2
Magnitude needed for negation	−12%	(% Choosing B) − ((Converts needed to choose B) / (Converted respondents))
Sampling error	3.1%	Square root of (.9604(N−n) / (nN−n))
Odds against negation = 1	3.8	Absolute value of magnitude / sampling error

above 10,000, sampling error is just a way of translating sample size; if we increase our sample size to 4,000, our sampling error is 1.5 percent for any target population above 100,000. Note that a sample size of 4,000 produces a sampling error of 1.5 percent totally independent of the response rate.

Researchers typically calculate the response rate using AAPOR definition 1, which boils down to the number of completes divided by the number of eligible respondents. To achieve a high response rate using this definition, one must try to reduce the number of unknown cases (no answers, answering machines, etc.) to zero. The plurality is simply the percentage who favor the more popular alternative, that is, any number from 51 to 99 percent. In this example, we have specified that the total eligible sample was 2,500 individuals, of whom 1,000 answered the question, choosing alternative "A" over "B" (also known as ~A) 55 percent of the time.

Now, suppose that we could sample half of the nonrespondents and get them to respond (through intensive refusal conversion, multiple attempts at contacting, etc.). How likely would it be for the result to be neutralized? Simple arithmetic tells us that, since we had 550 respondents who chose A in the initial sample, in order to neutralize the result, we would need a total of 875 B votes in the final sample of 1,750, which means that we need 425 of the 750 "converted" nonrespondents to choose "B." What we need to estimate is the likelihood of neutralizing a result, that is, producing an even split after sampling one-half of the nonrespondents. Table 1 demonstrates how we can generate this estimate.

Table 2. Likelihood of Neutralizing the Result with a 55 Percent Plurality and a 70 Percent Response Rate

Element	Value	Explanation
Total eligible sample	2500	
Percent choosing A	55%	
Percent choosing B	45%	
Response rate	70%	
Total number of respondents	1000	
Respondents choosing A	550	
Respondents choosing B	450	
Converted respondents	214	One-half of all nonrespondents
Converts needed to choose B	157	Number of converts needed to produce an even split
Even split after conversion	607.14	(Respondents + (Nonrespondents / 2)) / 2
Magnitude needed for negation	−28%	(% Choosing B) − ((Converts needed to choose B) / (Converted respondents))
Sampling error	3.1%	Square root of (.96004(N−n) / (nN−n))
Odds against negation = 1	9.1	Absolute value of magnitude / sampling error

Table 1 shows that the neutralization magnitude is −12 percent. This is computed by subtracting the percentage of converted nonrespondents who must vote for B from 100 percent (i.e., the percentage of voters negating A) and subtracting the number of A voters in the sample. The calculated sampling error is 3.1 percent from the formula given earlier. If we divide the neutralization magnitude by the sampling error, we arrive at the Figure 3.8, which is an estimate of the odds against neutralizing the result. In other words, the chances are 3.8:1 that "A" is the choice of the population, given this sample.

Now, suppose that we alter only the response rate, moving it up from 40 percent to 70 percent. Table 2 shows the effect of neutralizing the result.

Multiplying the response rate by 1.75 raises the odds against negation from 3.8 to 9.1, a factor of 2.4. However, if we went back to the 40 percent response rate, kept the respondents at 1,000, but had obtained a plurality of 75 percent instead of 55 percent, the odds that the result would be stable go up to 18.7:1 (see Table 3).

We can calculate the credibility of a research finding by combining response rate, sampling error, and plurality. The formula used here, neutralization magnitude divided by sampling error, is suggested as a way of estimating the likelihood of nonreversal if it were possible to sample half of the nonrespondents. So, if we could accept as a level of credibility an odds ratio of 5:1, and as virtually "true" an odds ratio of 10:1, we might find Figures 1 and 2 useful.

Table 3. Likelihood of Neutralizing the Result with a 75 Percent Plurality and a 40 Percent Response Rate

Element	Value	Explanation
Total eligible sample	2500	
Percent choosing A	75%	
Percent choosing B	25%	
Response rate	40%	
Total number of respondents	1000	
Respondents choosing A	750	
Respondents choosing B	250	
Converted respondents	750	One-half of all nonrespondents
Converts needed to choose B	625	Number of converts needed to produce an even split
Even split after conversion	875	(Respondents + (Nonrespondents / 2)) / 2
Magnitude needed for negation	−58%	(% Choosing B) − ((Converts needed to choose B) / (Converted respondents))
Sampling error	3.1%	Square root of (.9604(N−n) / (nN−n))
Odds against negation = 1	18.7	Absolute value of magnitude / sampling error

Figure 1. 10:1 and 5:1 Ratios with 55 Percent Plurality

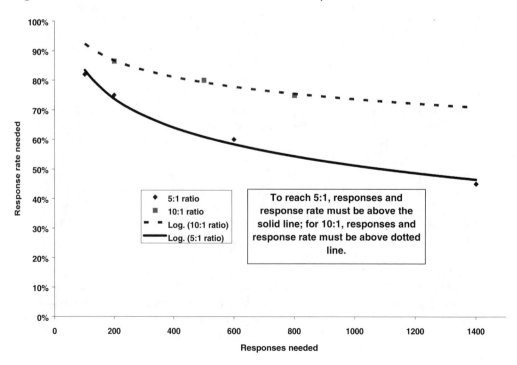

Figure 2. 10:1 and 5:1 Ratios with 75 Percent Plurality

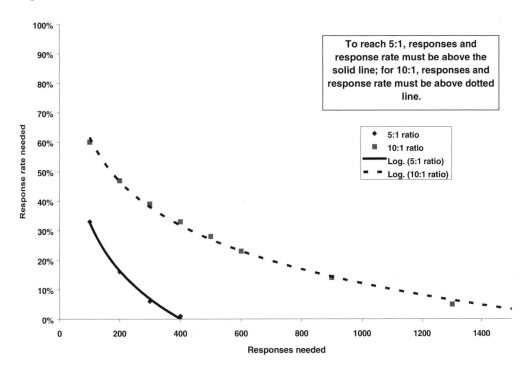

Figure 1 shows the response rate needed to achieve 5:1 and 10:1 ratios with a 55 percent plurality for sample sizes ranging from 100 to 1,500. The chart was generated using a logarithmic trendline as a best-fit match for the calculated ratios. Note that, in order to generate a 5:1 ratio with a 55–45 split, one would need a response rate of 75 percent with 200 respondents. Collect seven times as many respondents, and the response rate needed is still 45 percent. To achieve a 10:1 ratio with 200 respondents, one needs a response rate of 87 percent; going to 1,400 responses still requires a 68 percent response rate.

Figure 2 shows needed response rates for a plurality of 75 percent. With a 75/25 split in preference, all that is required for a 5:1 ratio with 100 respondents is a 33 percent response rate; and a 75/25 split with 400 or more respondents is virtually immune to negation.

There are many other implications that can be drawn from these charts, but the most important for this discussion is the fact that both sample size and plurality are more influential than response rate. Maximizing the response rate does nothing but ensure that greater and greater resources will be used to achieve results that can be obtained and validated by simply increasing sample size, at a far lower cost.

Further Reading

American Association for Public Opinion Research. *Standard Definitions: Final Dispositions of Case Codes and Outcome Rates for Surveys.* Lenexa, KS: American Association for Public Opinion Research, 2000.

Curtin, Richard, Stanley Presser, and Eleanor Singer. "The Effects of Response Rate Changes on the Index of Consumer Sentiment." *Public Opinion Quarterly* 64 (2002): 413–28.

Groves, Robert M. *Survey Errors and Survey Costs*. New York: John Wiley, 1989.

Nathaniel Ehrlich

Restricted Access Buildings

Restricted access buildings are multiple-unit housing structures that deny entrance to nonresidents. Although these structures take many forms, they typically feature a full-time gatekeeper, such as a doorman or security guard, who screens all requests for access to the building. A variation of restricted access buildings can also be found in suburban environments, where restricted access, or gated, communities and subdivisions that also deny physical access to outsiders are becoming more common.

Restricted access buildings often inhibit respondent accessibility in face-to-face surveys, posing challenges for measuring **unit nonresponse**. First, without the cooperation of the building gatekeeper, it often is not possible to enumerate the precise number of occupied housing units within the structure, making the calculation of sampling probabilities, weights (*see* **Weighting**), and **response rates** difficult, if not impossible.

Second, because a single individual may refuse survey participation on behalf of dozens, if not hundreds, of individual housing units, the random selection of a restricted access building as part (or whole) of a primary sampling unit (PSU) can often have a dramatic negative effect on a survey's response rate.

Third, failure to include restricted access housing units that are selected during the preliminary stages of sample designs may introduce serious **coverage error** into sample surveys, as available evidence suggests that the demographic composition of restricted access building households may vary systematically from other urban residents.

Although there is little documentation available, there are several strategies known to sometimes be successful for increasing contact with respondents in these buildings and for reporting survey results when these buildings are a substantial part of the sample. One approach is to contact building managers and condominium and renters' associations and present them with an overview of the study. A second is to enlist the help of the gatekeeper in gaining cooperation. A third is to use reverse directories to find phone numbers by which to contact the respondents or send them advance letters.

With respect to reporting survey results, approaches that have been used by researchers include (1) dispositioning them as any other household in which an informant or respondent cannot be contacted, (2) redefining the **sample frame** to exclude them, and (3) reporting multiple sets of response rates, with the restricted buildings both included and excluded, to document the effects of these buildings on survey quality.

Contacting building managers and associations can be successful in some situations, but not others. For example, an organization like the U.S. Census Bureau may have more success in contacting building managers because they have a legal mandate to fulfill. All residents of the United States are required by law to complete their census forms. For other organizations, this approach is dependent on the individual building manager and whether that person is willing to cooperate. In many cases, building managers are not cooperative. Some will refuse to listen to an interviewer's explanation of the study, and those that do listen typically do not provide assistance.

Enlisting the help of gatekeepers involves some of the same issues as above. Many of them are uncooperative. In addition, it is ethically questionable to solicit the help of a doorman or security guard, either with or without a payment of incentive, when they are being paid by the building manager specifically to keep nonresidents out. Typically, the best information one can obtain from gatekeepers is information about the number of units in the building, how many are occupied, how many are residential, and so on. Although this does not help with gaining cooperation, it does help with the calculation of sampling probabilities and determining a final disposition for the units in the building.

Using reverse directories to obtain telephone numbers for the residents of restricted access buildings, then calling them to either interview by phone or set up appointments for face-to-face interviews is another common method for addressing problems of limited access. Although this strategy does result in some completed interviews, there are several shortcomings to this approach. First, a substantial number of phone numbers are often unlisted, limiting the number of housing units that can be contacted. Second, those that are listed do not typically include a unit number. Therefore, without actually contacting a cooperative informant or respondent, it is impossible to know how to disposition each individual unit in the building. Finally, reverse directories only help increase the contact rate but do not provide enough information to help interviewers and listers enumerate the units in the building. Without a complete listing of the number of units in the building, one cannot calculate probabilities of selection, weights, or response rates.

Although advance letters can explain to respondents the purpose of a study and provide phone numbers by which the respondents can contact the surveying organization, they are of limited usefulness in restricted access buildings. Assuming one has a list of all units in the building, a letter can be sent to each unit. However, in some buildings, mail will not be delivered to a specific unit without a name but will instead be dumped in a pile in the foyer. Residents are unlikely to pay much attention to these types of mailings. The only way to determine names to place on the envelopes is by looking up the address in a reverse directory—whose limitations have been discussed above. At best, only a subset of respondents will receive the advance letters. However, even if the letters result in only a handful of interviews, this is more information than one would have without them and may well be worth the effort and cost.

With respect to reporting the correct disposition code, the most methodologically sound suggestion is to treat these housing units like any other household in which a screener cannot be conducted (*see* **Outcome Rates**). In other words, if a doorman refuses on behalf of all of the units in a 200-unit building, then all 200 units should be treated as non-contacts. Without solid evidence to the contrary, some percentage of these units should also be treated as eligible. The most conservative treatment is to assume all are eligible. A less conservative, yet reasonable, treatment is to assume that they are eligible to the same degree as housing units for which eligibility can be determined. In a face-to-face study in which most households are eligible, this means that the vast majority of units in restricted access buildings will be eligible and will therefore have a substantial and negative impact on the response rate.

Another tactic is to redefine the sampling frame to exclude theses units. However, eliminating these housing units simply increases response bias. Based on what little data are available on the subject, we know that the demographic composition of residents of restricted access buildings differs from that of people who live in other types of housing units. To eliminate them altogether from the sampling frame is to bias the sample and restrict survey generalizability. More importantly, this suggestion violates the integrity of survey research by manipulating the sampling frame in whatever manner necessary to maximize response rates. In spirit, it is no different from eliminating respondents who do not cooperate from the sampling frame. As a result, the sample becomes a convenience sample.

Finally, the suggestion to report multiple sets of response rates is beneficial in showing the impact of these buildings on the data collection efforts. However, it does nothing to address the response bias that results from failing to conduct interviews within these types of buildings.

In short, although no perfect solution currently exists to the problem of respondent access in restricted buildings, several strategies for reducing the negative impact of these buildings on survey quality are available. First, the field staff should attempt to negotiate with building representatives and/or homeowners' and renters' associations. These negotiations may result in the attainment of more information about the units and people in the building or something as simple as field staff being allowed to post a flyer about the study in the foyer of the building. Second, the addresses should be matched to a reverse directory, and telephone calls should be made to all listed residences in the buildings. Third, advance letters should be sent to all residents, informing them of the nature of the study and providing a toll-free number they can call to learn more about the study or set up an appointment for an interview.

In spite of these strategies, the response rates in these buildings will almost certainly be substantially lower than among other types of dwellings. Nevertheless, even a small number of completed interviews can provide the investigators with some information about the residents of these buildings, which may then allow them to make statistical adjustments to compensate for the nonresponse.

Further Reading

Abraham, S. Y. "Field Techniques for Coping with Nonresponse in Major Urban Centers." Paper presented at the annual meeting of the American Association for Public Opinion Research, Lancaster, Pennsylvania, 1990.

Groves, R. M., and M. P. Couper. *Nonresponse in Household Interview Surveys*. New York: John Wiley, 1998.

Kennedy, J. M., R. B. Parks, and L. F. Hecht. "A Demographic Analysis of the Impact of Presurvey Letters on Cooperation Rates in Urban Neighborhoods." Paper presented at the annual meeting of the American Association for Public Opinion Research, Danvers, Massachusetts, 1994.

Owens, L. K., T. P. Johnson, K. F. Retzer, and M. Fendrich. "The Impact of Restricted Access Buildings on Face-to-Face Response Rates." Paper presented at the annual meeting of the American Association for Public Opinion Research, St. Pete Beach, Florida, 2002.

Linda K. Owens and Timothy P. Johnson

RGI. *See* Respondent-Generated Intervals

Roper Center for Public Opinion Research

The Roper Center for Public Opinion Research maintains and disseminates the world's largest archives of data and supporting documentation from public opinion surveys conducted by other organizations. Founded in 1946 at Williams College and now a part of the University of Connecticut, the center's holdings represent the work of more than 150 polling firms in the United States. These firms have contributed data from about 7,500 surveys and more than 500,000 discrete questions that have been asked of the American people since 1935. There are extensive holdings from other nations as well. In addition to providing archival and data access services, the center operates educational and outreach programs around the nation.

The existence of the Roper Center depends upon a unique aspect of public opinion polling: the professional obligation to make such data publicly available. The founders of public opinion polling in the United States began their careers by eagerly giving away the questions and methods for any of their polls that had seen the light of day through publication (i.e., entered the public domain). Soon, they even began giving away the anonymous individual-level data that those polls had collected so that others could analyze the data for themselves. With these data, anyone could catch the pollsters in errors or, worse, in falsification. Why did the pollsters do this? Why would most of their successors have continued this practice of making their core products freely available for public scrutiny and criticism?

With the erratic exception of the financial securities industry, no other industry has built itself upon a similar foundation of full openness to external and sometimes hostile inspection. The pharmaceutical industry, for example, reveals its research primarily at the behest of laws and regulations, even though undisclosed research could influence medical decisions about people's health and lives. Indeed, much of American industry relies upon claims to proprietary information, enforced by webs of patents, trademarks, and licensing agreements. Why has the polling industry been so different in voluntarily exposing itself to criticism and competition? Why, in fact, has most of the polling industry come to believe that the data become more valuable to the firms when they are given away?

One of the earliest published reasons appears in a series of pamphlets from the Historical Services Board of the American Historical Association. These "GI Roundtable" pamphlets, prepared under contract with the Division of Information and Education of the U.S. Army during World War II, sought "to increase the effectiveness of the soldiers and officers as fighters during the war and as citizens after the war." The redoubtable and visionary Frederick Henry Osborn— a strong proponent of social science research and a member of New York City's merchant elite—headed the division and probably conceived of the series. (The division, once known as the Morale Branch, was also responsible for a pioneering survey effort of the 1940s, the classic studies known as "The American Soldier." Considerable credit is due to that series for the methodological advances of survey research during the 1940s and 1950s.)

Among the almost fifty GI Roundtable pamphlets that survive in full or fragmentary form was one titled "Are Opinion Polls Useful?" The answer to that straightforward question was not obvious to everyone in the early 1940s; it is perhaps not obvious to everyone even at this writing. The big media of the day—newspapers and monthly magazines—had started commissioning polls on a wide range of topics, as also had academic research centers, commercial firms, and government agencies. Polls had been prominent in the public consciousness since at least 1936, when the scientific polls had the great and publicly unexpected success of correctly forecasting the Roosevelt win over Landon. The polls used scientific samples that were tiny in comparison to the "convenience samples" of more than 2.5 million persons who were employed in the previously successful *Literary Digest* Poll. While chairman of the Democratic Party in 1932, James Farley had proclaimed, "Any sane person cannot escape the implication of such a gigantic sampling of popular opinion as is embraced in The Literary Digest straw vote. . . . It is a Poll fairly and correctly conducted." The scientific polls and Roosevelt won, while the *Digest* forecast a Landon landslide and soon died.

Nevertheless, there remained large questions about the trustworthiness of the polls among both ordinary citizens and public leaders. Why should anyone believe that Archibald Crossley, George Gallup, and Elmo Roper were even telling the truth about their findings, much less that they were using valid research methods? How could what the GI Roundtable pamphlets called a "miniature population" of just 1,000 or 2,000 persons produce results that could be generalized to what was then a national population of almost 130 million? How large a sample would keep the random error contributed by sampling within acceptable limits? Did it matter just how this sample of the population was selected, and if so, what constituted good sampling procedures? (The pamphlet pointed out that a chef need taste only a spoonful of soup, provided that it is well-stirred. What was the polling counterpart of stirring the soup well?)

There were also doubts about questions and field procedures. Biased questions would surely produce biased results. Would it be possible to discern biased, bogus, or meaningless questions from neutral and clear questions? On what kinds of topics might people have opinions that could be explored by the polls? As the pamphlet pointed out, "Complicated and technical questions, or those dealing with subjects on which they [the public] have little information, may yield meaningless answers." What could prevent interviewers from inserting their own views and judgments into the process? Critics of the polling industry in its infancy raised these questions (among others) and continue to do so today.

The unnamed authors of "Are Opinion Polls Useful?" gave the timeless, definitive answer: "The pollsters are willing to explain their system. The ABC's of their methods are widely known and are not hard to understand." The first of the pamphlet's guidelines for telling "the difference between reliable and unreliable polls" was "Does the polling organization explain its procedures to the public so that anyone can determine whether it follows reliable practices? Is the organization willing to submit its data to impartial analysis?" The pamphlet baldly asserted that the credibility of the polls rested upon pollsters' openness to public scrutiny, even to the extent of the pollsters' allowing anyone to redo a supposedly impartial analysis that had come under question. While such openness was expected in the scientific world, it was unusual (or anathema) in the commercial world. The early pollsters were of the latter world, but their behavior was that of leaders of science.

By the end of the war, the polling industry had exposed its data to "impartial analysis" in the fullest possible way. While performing his own wartime duties for the U.S. government, Elmo Roper finalized plans for what became the Roper Center for Public Opinion Research. It was in this new research facility that Roper was to archive for public use the "raw data" that resulted from his polls. Here grew the resource that would allow anyone to redo any analysis, whether in the weeks following publication of a contested news article or for generations afterwards. The materials that Roper archived went far beyond newspaper articles and internal statistical reports; they included questionnaires, some information about sampling and field procedures, and, most importantly, the anonymous respondent-level data. Users of the archives had the same access to the data that Roper and his staff had enjoyed. A parallel in the securities industry would be for a firm to publish all of the information used by its analysts to make buy or sell recommendations.

These raw data would soon prove invaluable in ways that Roper perhaps only dimly foresaw: the archives enabled researchers to go far beyond what his staff had done and were thus more than a tool for replication. New kinds of research problems could be studied with novel combinations of questions, perhaps concerning issues that had never occurred to the original pollsters. Collections of polls that repeated essentially the same questions over time could be collated into synthetic "time series" for the study of trends in American society. Researchers could apply newly developed analytical methods, often extending analyses beyond the simple frequency tables and cross-tabulations that are now familiar to consumers of the polls. Moreover, as the pamphlet had foretold, any errors, distortions, or misreporting of polling results could eventually be exposed.

Gallup and Crossley soon joined Roper in archiving their data at the center. The center's resources became an unparalleled scholarly and public resource, soon encompassing thousands of polls, spanning many areas of research and public interest, and representing the work and differing methods of a growing number of pollsters. Perhaps first acting out of self-interest, Elmo Roper had founded the premier archives of polling data in the world and had established a model for other nations.

The American polling industry had thus taken the essential step toward establishing the credibility of its polls. It did so none too soon. When the polls infamously failed in the "Dewey Defeats Truman" election of 1948, the industry's willingness to expose its methods served, in the end, to restore credibility to the polls. That openness enabled the Social Science Research Council's advisers to explain the causes of the erroneous forecasts and to improve future polling methods. The chief lesson of 1948: do not stop polling too early, especially when the electorate is volatile and the candidate who is behind seems to be gaining momentum.

The principle of exposing one's methods and one's data to public scrutiny soon became the norm of the polling industry, summarized in written form in the "Statement of Disclosure" of the **National Council on Public Polls**. The preface of that Statement offers the rationale that standards of disclosure are "designed to insure that consumers of survey results that enter the public domain have an adequate basis for judging the reliability and validity of the results reported." Among the chief "consumers" of survey results have been the pollsters themselves, who evaluate each other's work as heavily on whether the pollster is forthcoming about methods as on whether or not they believe the specific results.

Pollsters soon found that the archives served additional purposes for them. First, the Roper Center was established on a solid basis of archival principles, meaning that the center was explicitly designed to preserve the data and documentation in usable form for the distant future. As digital preservation was not part of the charter of any polling firm, the firms came to rely upon the Roper Center for access to their own data. Second, the center constructed a body of finding tools that spanned the industry, foremost among them a database of questions, responses, frequencies, and survey details. By the beginning of 2004, this database (iPOLL) encompassed over half a million questions that had been asked of the American public since 1935 by about 150 different polling organizations. This database is used throughout the polling industry to construct questions for new surveys, to anticipate the kinds of results that might be expected from a battery of questions, and to create synthetic time series. Third, the center sought to educate the industry and its consumers by publishing examples of excellent usage of polling data, including many articles in *Public Perspective* (1989–2003) (see past issues at http://www.ropercenter.uconn.edu/pp_prev.html).

Although commercial interests predominated, the founders of polling in the United States did not act solely out of self-interest. Concurring with James Madison, they saw public opinion as fundamental to American democracy. In 1791 Madison had observed, "Public opinion sets bounds to every government, and is the real sovereign in every free one." However, Madison despaired, as did Lord James Bryce a century after him, of there ever being a reliable way of gauging public opinion in a country that was constantly growing larger. Madison went on to write: "The larger a country, the less easy for its real opinion to be ascertained, and the less difficult to be counterfeited." Manipulation of perceptions of public opinion could threaten democracy. By the 1930s, however, the founders of American polling had provided what Madison and Bryce had sought: a "mechanism" for reliably gauging public opinion and confronting those who would counterfeit it.

The authors of the GI Roundtable pamphlets, thinking forward to when soldiers would again resume their roles as citizens, saw the new scientific polls as remedies against sweeping, unsubstantiated, and possibly false claims about what "the American public insists" or "the farmers demand." Without "reasonably accurate means . . . to find out what the public's opinion on current issues [is]," almost anyone could "set himself up as an expert on public opinion." Indeed, many had done so until the polls set a higher standard for making such claims about public opinion. It became more difficult for someone with an ax to grind to claim public support without solid polling evidence.

Since 1946 the Roper Center has been the indispensable foundation for studying public opinion and for challenging those who would distort it. Over the years, the partnership between the center and the polling industry has been based upon their shared interests in both the credibility of the polls and the workings of the oldest democracy. The importance of maintaining pollsters' credibility has usually trumped the value of any plausible commercial value of the data that might remain after publication of basic reports and press releases. Even when the data had been collected for private clients and had never resulted in public reports or press releases, the private clients often saw value in having others examine the data. Clients also must be able to trust the polling firms that they hire.

Today's public opinion polls have become Bryce's trustworthy instruments for regularly and clearly giving voice to the whole people. Through the partnership of the center and the polling industry, the honesty of the polling industry's reporting of the voice of the people stands assured.

Web Sites

The best general source of information about the center and its constantly evolving roster of services and products is available at the center's Web site http://www.ropercenter.uconn.edu/.

The complete archive catalog of the center is available at http://roperweb.ropercenter.uconn.edu/Catalog40/StartQuery.html.

The iPOLL database discussed above is available at http://www.ropercenter.uconn.edu/ipoll.html.

Past issues of *Public Perspective* (1989–2003) are available at http://www.ropercenter.uconn.edu/pp_prev.html.

Richard Rockwell

S

Sample Frame

A sample frame represents the list of elements or units from which a sample is drawn. Although a complete list of elements can be used as a sample frame, the term sample frame also more generally includes specified methods that can be used to generate a list of sample records—even if not all records are enumerated. For example, a telephone survey might begin with lists of telephone exchanges rather than a list of all telephone numbers, a household survey might begin with a set of maps rather than a list of households, and a survey of schoolchildren might begin with a list of schools.

The sample frame is most appropriately viewed as a physical tool for operationalizing the target population of a survey. The statistical theory that permits sample error to be calculated assumes that random samples are drawn from complete sample lists. Although the sample error statistics that are commonly reported in polls and research reports are often interpreted as the possible variation of a survey measure from the true value of that measure in the target population, it is more accurate to note that, at best, sample error refers to elements in the sample frame, or frame population.

Relationships Between Sample Frames and Target Populations

In an ideal situation, there is a one-to-one correspondence between members of the sample frame and members of the target population. For example, in surveys of very well defined and clearly identified populations, accurate lists may be available which contain all population members. A survey of members of Congress is an example where this situation is likely to apply, and other similar lists may be available for similar populations.

It is more common, however, to find discrepancies between the sample frame and the target population. Succinct categorizations of these discrepancies have been provided by Kish (1965). The four principal discrepancies between the ideal one-to-one correspondence between the sample frame and the target population are: (1) missing elements, where some members of the target population are missing in the frame population; (2) clusters, or cases where multiple elements of the target population correspond to a single element of the frame population; (3) blanks or foreign elements, where some members of the frame population do not correspond to the target population; and (4) duplicate listings, or cases where multiple members of the frame population correspond to single members of the target population. In practice, almost all sample frames contain several of these discrepancies.

Missing elements, or sample frames where some members of the target population are missing from the frame population, represent the most serious threat to the quality of survey data among these frame concerns because this undercoverage or noncoverage cannot be easily corrected in survey analysis. This commonly occurs when incomplete list or frame data are unavailable, when a sample frame is designed to poorly correspond to a target population, or when decisions are made to restrict the scope of a sample frame for cost savings or operational efficiency.

Kalton (1983) distinguishes between inadequate sample frames and incomplete sample frames. Inadequate frames are not designed to cover the target population while incomplete frames exclude some elements that should be included in the frame. For example, the use of a residential telephone sample frame for general population surveys is inadequate, by this definition, because the frame is not designed to include individuals who do not have residential telephone service. It should be noted that this sample frame would be adequate, by this definition, for a survey of telephone households. In contrast, a telephone sample frame that excluded a small number of telephone households in newly assigned exchanges would be incomplete, because these households fall in the intended target population of telephone households. In surveys where relatively thorough population lists are available, sample frames are sometimes incomplete when attempts to match population lists to addresses or telephone numbers produce imperfect results.

Inadequate sample frames can be seen as typically referring to an asymmetry between the nature of the sample frame and the nature of the target population. Incomplete sample frames usually occur when lists are out-of-date, or where practical concerns prohibit obtaining a complete enumeration of all list members. It should also be noted that the extent of the bias caused by either incomplete or inadequate sample frames is determined by both the magnitude of undercoverage and the differences between those included in the sample frame and those excluded from it on the statistics that are being measured. The magnitude of this bias is not necessarily associated with the nature of the undercoverage. For example, one survey with an inadequate sample frame may produce perfectly acceptable research results, while another survey with an adequate but incomplete frame might produce results with significant bias.

Clusters occur when multiple elements of the target population correspond to single elements of the frame. Although this is typically found in multistage cluster sampling, it is also a common problem in surveys of individuals that use household level sample frames. For example, most contemporary public opinion surveys initially contact households by telephone or in person to conduct an interview. Households that contain more than one member of the target population will have clustering. Public opinion polls and other surveys of individuals typically select one member of sampled household to be interviewed. In this case, respondents have different probabilities of being selected based on the size of their household. For example, if households are selected with equal probability, a respondent in a single-person household will have twice the probability of being selected as a respondent in a household with two eligible inhabitants. This matter can be adjusted by using simple probability weights, where each respondent is weighted by the inverse of their probability of being selected. In cases where the number of eligible respondents for a sample record can be known or estimated prior to data collection, respondents can be selected from frame elements in Probability-Proportionate-to-Size (PPS) sample methods. Another option is to interview all members of the household. This is rarely used in public opinion surveys, in part, because of the difficulty of obtaining independent interviews among multiple members of the same household.

Blanks are where some members of the frame population do not contain eligible members of the target population. They represent problems with incidence, or the proportion of the sample that are eligible for inclusion in the survey. In this case, some of the elements of the sample frame are not useful to the researcher and will not yield useful interviews. If the ineligible records can be accurately determined through data processing or the interviewing process, there is no threat to the quality of the survey data.

In some cases, ineligible frame elements can be removed prior to a survey being fielded based on information contained in or available about the sample frame. However, determining eligibility often requires interviewers to establish contact and actively screen for eligibility. For example, a researcher interested in interviewing people who have viewed a specific political advertisement might need to conduct a short general population survey to identify the specific individuals he is interested in interviewing. In cases such as this, where incidence is likely to be low, the costs of scientific survey with adequate coverage can often be astronomical compared to the costs of a similar survey without a significant number of foreign elements in the sample frame.

Duplicate listings, or cases where multiple members of the frame population represent single members of the target population, often come about when sample frames are derived from multiple sources or where the subject of a survey is different from the way an element is measured in a sample frame. Cases such as these can be accounted for during the preparation of the actual sample, during survey screening, or by appropriate postsurvey adjustments.

Duplicate entries may occur when a sample frame is taken from a source that is compiled from multiple sources or entries. For example, a survey of campaign donors may contain multiple entries for individuals who have donated to multiple campaigns, or who have made multiple donations to single campaigns. A survey of customer satisfaction may include customers who have purchased multiple products or had multiple contacts with a company. In many cases, these duplicates can be eliminated through appropriate screening of the sample frame or sample file. In other cases, survey questionnaires and screeners should be constructed to determine if the respondent may have been included in the sample frame multiple times.

In cases where survey analysis uses both survey responses and supplementary information from the sample frame, it is important that the sample records used for the survey or frame records used for analysis be adjusted to account for the purging of duplicates. Alternatively, or as a supplement to this data manipulation, a survey instrument can be designed to ensure that respondents are responding concerning the specific event or reason they were included in the database. A customer satisfaction survey that intends to use sample information to compare satisfaction across different sites, for example, might include questions to verify that the respondent is answering about the specific visit or interaction that is recorded in the sample.

Single respondents being contained in multiple sample frame records can also occur when the sample frame is measured differently than the respondent. A typical example of this is a general population survey that uses a telephone sample frame. Respondents who live in households with multiple telephone lines may be selected by more than one element of the sample frame. These respondents will have a greater probability of being selected than those who correspond to single frame elements. These cases can be weighted to adjust for this differential probability of selection.

Considerations for Sample Frames in Public Opinion Polls. Most public opinion polls are designed to study some type of general population, using either in-person or telephone methods. **Mail surveys** are also occasionally used for public opinion surveys, and opinion polls via the **Internet** are becoming increasingly used, though with much criticism when applied to general populations. Although social and market surveys often draw samples of specialized populations using specialized frames, these are only occasionally used in public opinion research.

In-person surveys are becoming increasingly rare in public opinion research, especially in the United States, due to relatively high costs, long field periods, and the relatively low costs of telephone surveys. In countries with low telephone penetration, these surveys are more common. Sample designs for in-person surveys are typically multistage cluster samples. Primary sampling units (PSUs) are selected from a frame of all cities, counties, municipalities, and so forth, and several households are selected within these units. Detailed information is typically available for these PSUs in most countries. In many countries, detailed residential listings are available for use as a sample frame in the second stage of the sample, although in other places cruder maps provide the frame for this stage of the in-person sample.

Telephone surveys represent the predominant method of public opinion research in the United States. Since over 95 percent of all U.S. households are estimated to have residential telephones, the bias due to noncoverage in a general telephone sample frame is minimal for most research purposes. For general population telephone samples, **random digit dialing** (RDD) methodologies generate ten-digit telephone numbers based telephone exchanges consisting of a three-digit area code, and a three-digit exchange. Sampling is typically done from a frame containing all or almost-all telephone exchanges believed to contain residential household telephone numbers. Since all possible telephone numbers in these exchanges are eligible for the sample, these frames typically contain a high percentage of nonworking or nonhousehold telephone numbers.

When telephone samples are designed to target specific geographies, telephone exchanges must be further selected to create a sample frame to target these geographies. Commercial sampling suppliers maintain databases of telephone exchanges that contain geographic identifiers. However, many telephone exchanges serve households in several cities, municipalities, towns, or congressional districts. In cases such as these, a number of possible sample frames can be used, with different degrees of incidence and geographic coverage. Researchers typically select a sample frame designed to balance geographic coverage and geographic incidence.

Demographically targeted RDD telephone sample frames are also used in surveys designed to interview individuals with particular demographic characteristics, such as race, age, or marital status. Commercial vendors produce estimates of the demographic composition of different telephone exchanges, and sample frames can be developed to include only exchanges with relatively high incidence of the desired demographic characteristic. These sample frames present similar considerations to geographically targeted exchanges. Researchers who use these frames must attempt to balance coverage and incidence considerations.

Other telephone sample frames sometimes used in public opinion research include lists of registered voters and households listed in telephone directories. Public lists are occasionally used for surveys of registered voters, and are available from a variety of commercial vendors. The quality of these lists varies among states. Researchers should note, however, that that these lists often have incomplete coverage of registered voters due to difficulties obtaining telephone numbers and individuals who register to vote after the list is compiled. Directory listed telephone samples provide a high degree of efficiency, but with both inadequate and incomplete coverage for telephone surveys. These lists exclude telephone households who request to be omitted from public telephone directories, and they omit households with newly assigned telephone numbers.

Internet survey methodologies represent several hurdles in terms of sample frame development for general population surveys. As long as only a portion of the population uses Internet services, Internet sample frames will be inadequate for general population coverage. Internet samples can, at best, be generalized to a sample frame of Internet users. However, even among the population of Internet users, sample frames are incomplete and difficult to obtain. Since the number of possible e-mail addresses or other identifiers for computer users is nearly infinite, generating a workable sample frame of all Internet users is virtually impossible. Current solutions to develop Internet sample frames have typically focused on developing panels of respondents who agree to complete multiple surveys. Since most of these panels are self-selecting, the sample frames consist of Internet users who agree to participate in these panels.

As an alternative, an Internet sample frame might be generated using other survey methodologies, such as RDD telephone surveys. For example, an RDD or in-person survey that identified Internet users and asked them to complete an online survey could be seen as using a sample frame of all Internet users with telephone service. One commercial firm, Knowledge Networks, maintains an Internet panel of participants who are recruited using RDD telephone methodologies. Since the Knowledge Networks panel respondents are provided with Internet services, this sample frame can be seen as a special case of a general population sample frame.

Future Directions. For several decades, from roughly the mid 1970s through the end of the twentieth century, sample frames of residential telephone numbers have provided a consistent source of samples for public opinion research with high levels of population coverage with manageable costs. New telephone-related technologies and policies, however, have the potential to reduce the level of coverage for these frames while subsequently increasing costs.

Policies that permit a telephone subscriber to maintain a current telephone number after moving across a wide geographic area reduce the ability of sample frames to accurately target local geographies. Additionally, increasing numbers of telephone subscribers who maintain cellular telephones and not regular household telephones reduces the coverage of traditional residential telephone household samples. Researchers need to understand the implications of this increasing noncoverage for their data, and need to develop new methodologies to improve population coverage in this era of technological change. Possible solutions to these changes may include the use of multiple sample frames to target different types of sample frames, more sophisticated statistical or analytic methods to adjust for this prospective undercoverage, or in some cases a change in survey mode. In any event, it seems clear that the researchers will need to pay more attention to the level of coverage in their sample frame and the prospective differences in results between respondents contained in the sample frame versus those excluded.

Further Reading

Kalton, Graham. *Introduction to Survey Sampling.* Beverly Hills, CA: Sage Publications, 1983.

Kish, Leslie. *Survey Sampling.* New York: John Wiley, 1965.

Chase H. Harrison

Sample Size

Sample size indicates the total number of respondents interviewed for a survey. It is represented by the letter N in statistical presentations of survey data. Decisions about its value are often the most important and challenging in the entire survey process.

Typically, surveys are not completed by all members of a population of interest or even all the members of the associated **sample frame**, but rather are completed by a subset of individuals from the sample frame. The optimal sample size is determined by a number of factors, the most critical of which are the preferred level of sampling error, the need for subgroup analysis, and the resources available to conduct the survey.

The size of the sample directly affects the sampling error of the population estimate. When random samples are used to determine levels of public opinion rather than a census of the population, the results from the sample are likely to vary by chance from the actual opinions of the population. This sampling error shrinks as the sample size grows, although the relationship between the two is not linear. For example, researchers can be 95 percent confident that the sampling error for a question with two evenly split response options administered to 500 people from the U.S. population would be 4.4 percent, whereas the same question administered to 1,000 people would be 3.1 percent, and 2.5 percent when administered to 1,500 people.

Another common determinate of sample size is the number and nature of subgroups of interest. For example, if the researcher is only interested in finding out whether Americans as a whole approve of the president's job performance the sample size can be much smaller than if the researcher is interested in gender or geographical differences in presidential approval. While there are no clear-cut rules about the minimum sample size necessary to perform sub-group analysis, the sampling error changes dramatically as the sample size increases up to 200 cases before the rate of decrease in sampling error begins to flatten out.

The final major influence on sample size is the resources available to complete the survey. Obviously a census of all the members of the group of interest would be the ideal way of measuring public opinion and a very large sample size of 10,000 would be more accurate than a sample of 1,000 (all other things equal), but the cost and time necessary to do these types of surveys are often outside the means of survey researchers. Therefore, they must weigh the level of accuracy they wish to have against the resources they have at their disposal.

Further Reading

Fowler, Floyd J. *Survey Research Methods*. 2nd ed. Newbury Park, CA: Sage, 1993. An overview of survey methodology, including decisions related to sample size.

Henry, Gary T. *Practical Sampling*, Newbury Park, CA: Sage, 1990. The basics of everything you need to know about sampling, including issues related to sample sizes.

Web Site

A sample-size calculator from a commercial firm is available at http://www.survey system.com/sscalc.htm.

Leo Simonetta

Sampling Process

The sampling process is the means of identifying, selecting, and contacting a group of individuals from a population of interest who can provide information about research questions under investigation. It unfolds in five distinct stages. Researchers must: (1) specify the target population, (2) develop a **sample frame**, (3) choose a sampling method, (4) determine the size of the sample, and (5) implement contacting procedures. Decisions made during each of these stages not only determines the subjects to be studied but also dictates the nature of the findings and, in some cases, the substantive conclusions derived.

Specifying the Target Population. The sampling process commences with the identification of a target population that the study aims to approximate. Theoretically, the target population could be the public at-large, a demographic group, or the members of an organization. While the choice should be primarily informed by the objectives of the study, researchers must also be mindful of the communication mode being used to sample prospective participants. Each communication mode—be it telephony, postal mail, or the Internet—offers access to a unique set of individuals, thereby restricting the populations appropriate for study. If researchers incorrectly define the target population from which the sample is chosen, they are vulnerable to propagating misleading conclusions when those excluded from the population definition possess different characteristics than those who were included.

Developing a Sample Frame. After specifying the target population, researchers must develop a sample frame from which the members of the target population will be selected. The sample frame provides the means of identifying and locating eligible participants. Since those not covered by the sample frame cannot be contacted, the sample frame operationally defines the target population. Excluded population members can bias sample estimates to the extent that they are systematically different from those included in the sampling frame.

Developing sample frames is more difficult for some communication modes than others. Generally speaking, the communication devices used in traditional mediums possess a fixed address assigned to a particular individual or group by a centrally administered organization that compiles them in a comprehensive directory. For instance, each telephone possesses a single fixed number that is generally contracted to a specific household. Such an arrangement enables particular individuals to be easily identified and contacted. Thus, sampling occurs in most traditional mediums by the selection of a specifically assigned number or affiliated individual.

In contrast, the **Internet** is primarily arranged around its services and their associated content, rather than the clients of those services. Individual computers are often assigned a temporary IP (Internet Protocol) address when they connect to the Internet from a pool of available addresses managed by their ISP (Internet Service Provider), or local area network. For example, the IP address of a subscriber to America Online varies each time the subscriber logs on to the Internet because the pool of addresses administered by the service is far smaller than the pool of subscribers. Consequently, specific computers or their users cannot be identified or located in advance. The specific procedures for isolating individuals on the Internet depend on the nature of the service.

Choosing a Sampling Method. In the next stage of the sampling process, researchers must determine how members of the sample frame will be chosen. There are two basic approaches to sampling—probabilistic and nonprobabilistic—each serving different objectives. If the purpose of the study is to make inferences to or predictions about the target population, then a probabilistic sampling method is required. However, if the study is intended only to describe the group of individuals under observation for the purpose of theory building or illustration, then nonprobabilistic sampling methods can be used.

Probabilistic sampling methods ensure that each member of the sampling frame possesses a known, non-zero chance of being selected. Assuming the sampling frame matches the target population, they have the advantage that when samples of a given size are drawn repeatedly using them, corresponding estimates will form distributions from which the true population parameters can be derived. By exploiting the statistical properties of these distributions, researchers can generate confidence intervals within which population parameters possess some statistical likelihood of being found. In other words, probability sampling enables researchers to make statistically based inferences, calculating with a degree of certainty how much sample estimates deviate from the true population parameters.

The accessibility of the communication mode and the availability of its users restrict the conditions under which probabilistic sampling methods can be used. Probabilistic sampling methods can be employed only when the target population is restricted to a group of users that can be fully identified and contacted. For example, the Internet cannot be used to draw probabilistic samples of the general public or individuals accessing the Internet. Any efforts to do so will systematically ignore both non-users and inaccessible users (e.g., those without a publicly available e-mail address), leaving researchers vulnerable to making false inferences about the target population if germane statistics of these groups happen to be distinctive.

The four most commonly used forms of probabilistic sampling are **simple random sampling**, **systematic sampling**, **stratified sampling**, and **cluster sampling**. Simple random sampling generates a sample by selecting individuals from the sampling frame that ensures every individual has an equal and independent chance of being selected. Whereas simple random sampling is akin to picking cases out of a hat, systematic sampling randomly selects a starting value and then chooses every Nth record until a sufficient sample size has been reached. Stratified sampling divides the target population into a number of sub-populations based on a predetermined characteristic and then randomly select a certain number of individuals from each sub-population. Cluster sampling also divides the target population in sub-populations, but it selects from among sub-populations before sampling within them. Determining the optimal method is typically a function of resource and time constraints and the characteristics of the target population.

Nonprobabilistic sampling methods draw samples arbitrarily without a specific probability structure in mind. Individuals are selected because of their availability, geographical proximity, or willingness to participate. Since everyone in the target population does not possess an opportunity of being selected, nonprobabilistic samples cannot be used to compute confidence intervals around the sample estimates that possess some statistical likelihood of containing the true population values. Without such assurances, researchers will be unable to know how well the sample represents the target population. As a result, generalizations beyond the cases studies are no different than educated guesses about the nature of the population.

Nonetheless, nonprobabilistic sampling methods can serve other objectives. They can be used to develop hypotheses or refine theories. They can serve to test various instrument designs. When participants are randomly assigned, they can also be used for experimental manipulations to demonstrate the potential effects of particular stimuli.

The most commonly used forms of nonprobabilistic sampling are convenience sampling, self-selected sampling, snowball sampling, and quota sampling. In convenience sampling (*see* **Intercept Interviewing**), the researcher selects individuals based on their accessibility, such as individuals passing a certain street corner or attending an event. In self-selected samples, individuals volunteer to participate at their convenience. Snowball sampling uses referrals from individuals who initially agree to participate in a study to generate additional subjects. Quota sampling identifies characteristics germane to the study, such as race, gender, party identification, and then selects available individuals until these goals are reached. As with probabilistic sampling, the choice of technique is based on resource availability and population characteristics.

While most scholars acknowledge the threats to generalizability posed by nonprobability samples, some believe measures can be taken to reduce or eliminate them. To this end, researchers have adopted techniques designed to minimize the impact that distinctive characteristics may have on sample statistics. The methods most widely applied to nonprobability samples are poststratification **weighting** and propensity scoring. However, without accurate, reliable information about the individuals who are unreachable with Internet sampling methods, such efforts offer no greater assurances than if they were not adopted at all.

Poststratification weighting attempts to obtain more accurate population estimates by weighting respondents according to the incidence of known characteristics in the target population. The underlying logic is that if the measures of interest vary among certain groups in the population for which the distribution is known, then by correcting the distribution of these groups within the sample, more accurate estimates of the measures of interest can be obtained. For example, if a particular issue preference is highly correlated with age, then matching the age distribution of the sample with the general population will result in a preference distribution more representative of the population. The correct population proportions, however, are only known for certain groups. For example, most weighting variables are based on some combination of demographics measured by the census, such as age, gender, education, race, or income. Unfortunately, if the matching variables are not highly correlated with the key variables then weighting will not improve the data. Thus, the effectiveness of poststratification rests on how strongly the measures of interest are related to the weighting variables.

An alternative method used by researchers to improve the generalizability of survey results is propensity scoring. The propensity scoring approach estimates the likelihood of each participant being in a sample based on a set of covariates that would predict such recruitment and then weights the responses for each individual by their score. For example, in the case of Internet samples, this usually involves adjusting online results to match the results derived from a more representative sampling technique such as those produced by **random digit dialing** telephone recruitment. Propensity scores are estimated by fitting a probabilistic model to a measure indicating the chance of being selected online. Predictors often comprise traditional demographics as well as a number of mode-specific measures, such as in the example of Internet access availability and online usage patterns. The estimates generated in this analysis are then used to create an index that indicates each sample member's propensity for being online. This index is applied to the online sample, and individual subjects are weighted accordingly.

Regardless of which approach is undertaken there are no assurances that the inaccuracies due to **coverage error** will be eliminated. Both methods make two questionable assumptions. They assume that the variables used for adjustment are the only variables related to the variables of interest. This is unlikely considering that each method relies on a limited set of demographics. Experiences, beliefs, or attitudes, for example, could underlie the variables of interest. If the weighting variables are flawed, the quality of the measures will not only fail to improve it may actually worsen.

Moreover, poststratification weighting and propensity scoring assume that respondents within the samples generate opinions in the same manner as those not in the sample. If the causal mechanisms generating the variables of interest do vary from sample respondents to the population, then efforts to improve the representativeness of the samples will be undermined. In other words, it is not simply the relationship between the variables of interest that matters, but the relationship between the variables of interest within the sample and those outside the sample. Poststratification improves the accuracy of estimates only if the relationship between the weighting variables and the variables of interest is equivalent between those who are in the online sample and those who are not. Similarly, propensity scoring reasons that the multivariate model uncovered in the probability samples holds in the nonprobabilitic sample. If the relative importance of the weighting variables is adjusted without correcting for the differences in the relationships, then the distribution of preferences in the sample is likely to remain at odds with the distribution of preferences in the population. Prior research, for example, suggests that the decision-making processes of Internet respondents are likely to vary systematically from others in the U.S. populace across an array of issues. Internet users obtain information from different sources than non-users, participate in different social activities, and socialize in different ways. The only way to reliably estimate differences in the relationships is to draw a probability sample of the U.S. population, which, of course, is not currently possible in the online environment.

Determining the Size of the Sample. After establishing the sample frame and the sampling method, researchers must determine the number of members to solicit for participation in the study. The **sample size** is a function of the desired number of cases, the estimated incidence of the target population in the sample frame, the extent of invalid contact information, and the projected level of respondent cooperation.

Initially, researchers must determine the number of completed instruments necessary to evaluate the hypotheses under investigation. The main factors that should be considered in determining the number of cases are the desired precision of the sample estimates, the number of variables, and the amount of group comparisons. The importance of precision for judgments of sample size depends on whether probabilistic or nonprobabilistic sampling methods are employed. In probabilistic samples, the more confident that researchers wish to be that a population parameter falls within a given confidence interval, the larger the sample required. Since nonprobabilistic samples cannot be used for population inferences, the number of cases has no effect on the precision of the population estimates generated. Both sampling methods, though, are sensitive to the number of variables and group comparisons. As the quantity of each increases, the number of cases needed to differentiate their effects grows.

The sample size is also influenced by the estimated incidence of the target population in the sample frame. Ideally, the sample frame would constitute the entire population, meaning every member is eligible to participate in the study.

However, in many cases the best available sample frame may not contain adequate information to identify whether sample frame members are part of the population. Although screening or validation questions can be used to identify actual members of the population of interest in these cases, the incidence of eligibility can only be estimated. As this incidence drops, the requisite sample size increases.

Another consideration when calculating sample size is the quality of the contact information. Inoperable or outdated information will not yield responses. Thus, the more invalid contact information that exists in the sampling frame, the larger the sample required.

Finally, the sample size is a function of the level of cooperation among subjects. Many of the individuals sampled will not be interviewed because they are either inaccessible during the interviewing period or refuse to participate in the survey. Even if efforts are taken to increase participation, researchers must anticipate a certain extent of non-cooperation, the degree to which largely depends on the nature of the request, the makeup of the subject pool, and the perceived importance of the study.

Implementing Contacting Procedures. The final stage of the sampling process involves implementing procedures capable of contacting members of the sample and soliciting their participation. Researchers can employ a number of techniques to encourage eligible subjects to participate in the study. They can personalize introductions, issue **prenotifications**, and/or offer **financial incentives**. Ultimately the choice should depend upon the objectives of the study and the resources available.

Personalized introductions emphasize how important individual subjects are to researchers and attempt to convey a relationship between them that will spark the desire to interact. They are limited to samples in which personal information can be acquired in advance of the study. If personalized introductions are used, it is imperative that researchers inform subjects how they acquired their name and contact information to avoid resentment or retribution. Existing research finds evidence that personalized messages positively relate to response rates, even after controlling for such competing factors as prenotifications and incentives.

Another approach for inducing participation is to prenotify prospective subjects about forthcoming instruments. Prenotifications attempt to build anticipation, increasing the possibility that subjects will recognize instruments when they arrive and more strongly consider undertaking them. They, too, require advance personal information about subjects and how to reach them.

Prenotifications are transmitted directly to subjects in the days preceding commencement of the study. Generally speaking, the messages should contain four primary elements: (1) an explanation of how subjects were identified and why they are needed, (2) a description of the objectives of the study and the backgrounds of the researchers, (3) assurances of confidentiality, and (4) appeals for participation. This information, though, should be brief and to the point. Studies have found that subjects who received prenotifications were significantly more likely to participate than those who did not.

A final option for inducing participation is to offer a financial incentive either at the time subjects agree to participate or once they have completed the instrument. Financial incentives have the benefit of being an eye-catching enticement as well as emphasizing the importance of the endeavor. Conversely, they can also appear heavyhanded, attract a particular type of participant, and/or bias subjects' responses. Financial incentives have long been successful, though, in promoting participation in studies administered by telephone, postal mail, or face-to-face interaction.

The sampling process concludes with contacting and recruiting eligible participants. Researchers can then begin administering a survey to them. If they have been sufficiently mindful of the threats to sample quality, then they should be able to proceed with the survey for their intended objectives.

Further Reading

Kalton, Graham. *Introduction to Survey Sampling*. Thousand Oaks, CA: Sage Publications, 1983. An introductory monograph to the sampling process.

Kish, Leslie. *Survey Sampling*. New York: John Wiley, 1995. A classic text on sampling techniques.

Levy, Paul S., and Stanley Lemeshow. *Sampling of Populations: Methods and Applications*. New York: John Wiley, 1999. An accessible guide to sampling methods that offers extensive coverage of probabilistic sampling.

Samuel J. Best

Satisficing

Satisficing is providing a sufficient, although not optimal, response to a survey question. This occurs because respondents are not always motivated or capable enough to provide a thorough answer to every survey question. There are many different ways in which respondents can satisfice during a survey as well as many ways that researchers can minimize satisficing.

The best way to define satisficing is to understand optimizing, the opposite of satisficing. When respondents are optimizing, they are responding to surveys in the way that researchers find ideal. Optimizing respondents perform four steps: they fully comprehend the question asked, diligently search for the information required to respond, integrate the information that they find into a summary judgment, and communicate that information to the researcher, using the scale provided, in a way that accurately portrays the summary judgment (*see* **Response Process**). For example, if we ask a question such as, "In the past year, how many times have you, yourself, attended a political rally? Have you attended zero, one, two, or three or more times?" we assume that the respondent listens and understands the meaning of the terms used in the question (in this case "political rally"), thinks about his or her activities within the past year, searches all memories of political rallies, sums up the number, and answers within the framework of the responses given. When respondents do not perform these four steps as thoroughly as they possibly can, they are said to be satisficing. In the example above, if respondents elect to respond that they "don't know" instead of completely searching their memories to recall the political rallies that they attended and when they took place, they would be satisficing. The goal of the satisficing respondent is to provide satisfactory answers that are good enough to complete the questionnaire task without exerting much mental effort.

There are two types of satisficing: weak and strong. Weak satisficers complete all four steps, but not as thoroughly as optimizers. Strong satisficers skip one or more of the steps altogether. The two specific forms of weak satisficing are selecting the first option that seems reasonable and acquiescing, or, agreeing with a statement provided by the researcher. There are four types of strong satisficing: endorsing the status quo, nondifferentiating responses to a series of questions with the same response options, answering with a "don't know" response, and randomly choosing an answer. Both weak and strong satisficing, which are elaborated in more detail below, can occur within the same questionnaire by one respondent.

Weak Satisficing. Respondents might select the first option that seems reasonable to them as a way to make the survey task easier. Thus, they might still be completing all four steps, but instead of fully completing them, they are choosing a reasonable answer that is convenient, without considering all of the options carefully. For instance, if asked the question, "What do you, yourself, think is the most important problem facing the nation today? Is it crime, education, terrorism, or poverty?" satisficing respondents are likely to focus on the first alternative that seems reasonable. Optimizing respondents would compare each possible set of alternatives (Is crime more or less important than poverty? Is terrorism more or less important than crime?). Having too many response options for respondents to remember may particularly promote selection of the most convenient reasonable response option given. Evidence that this type of weak satisficing might be occurring is if an unusual number of respondents choose the first or last response in a set of answers. To balance this problem, survey researchers will randomize the order of the responses.

Another example of weak satisficing is a tendency to agree with a statement from the researcher, also called acquiescence. For example, if given a list of statements and asked whether they agree or disagree, respondents might just agree with all of the statements without completing the requisite processing. Acquiescence cuts down on the amount of processing necessary for the respondent, making it an example of weak satisficing. If response patterns indicate an agreement to a long list of items, this might be evidence of acquiescence. However, this response pattern could also occur if optimizing respondents happen to agree with all of the statements. To help with this problem, researchers will use positively and negatively valenced items within the same list to identify if a respondent is acquiescing. For instance, if a respondent agrees to the statement "I like to think about complex problems" and agrees with the statement "I prefer simple problems," this may be evidence that the respondent is acquiescing.

Strong Satisficing. One type of strong satisficing is selecting the "status quo" response option. That is, when asked whether or not there should be more, less, or the same spending on a certain issue, it is cognitively simpler for respondents to answer to keep things as they are. Thus, respondents may understand the question, but instead of searching for the information required to answer the question (whether or not the respondent prefers more or less spending) will skip this step. An answer is given that requires less cognitive effort—that is, preserving the current order.

Second, when respondents are given a series of questions that use the same response scale, satisficing respondents are likely to not differentiate between the items. For example, if given a list of candidates to rate on the same several dimensions, respondents will avoid optimizing and choose to answer all of the questions using the same response category. Respondents who do this are skipping the steps of thoroughly evaluating the object and accurately mapping it onto the scale provided. Researchers can identify this problem by examining within one respondent if that respondent uses the same response category on a long list. Researchers can also examine this on an aggregate level to see if respondents as a whole stick with the same response category throughout the rating task.

Third, strong satisficers can avoid the cognitive requirements of the survey task by responding that they "don't know" the answer to one or more of the questions. This makes it easier for respondents because they do not have to go through the four steps required to optimize their response, but it can result in a missing data problem for the researcher. An unusual number of "don't know" responses to a single question might be an indication that many respondents are satisficing on that particular question. Also, an unusual number of "don't know" responses from one respondent might be evidence that the respondent is satisficing.

Finally, strong satisficers may choose a response option at random (also known as "mental coinflipping"). Although both randomly responding and answering "don't know" are forms of satisficing, randomly choosing an answer might be more tempting because respondents still appear to be completing the task of the survey. A random response is more socially desirable. Again, respondents are skipping out on the four steps altogether. This form of satisficing is the most difficult, if not impossible, to identify.

The Problem of Satisficing. To sum up the previous section, different types of weak and strong satisficing may produce answers to questions that are not optimal. Satisficing may be identified by looking at responses to questions within an individual. An individual who only chooses the first or last option on a question, acquiesces, maintains the status quo, fails to differentiate, or has a large number of "don't know" responses, *might* be satisficing. Satisficing may also be identified on certain questions by examining the responses to the questions in the aggregate. When there are a large number of responses favoring the status quo, responses that do not differentiate, "don't know" responses, responses that are the first or last choice or responses that agree with the researcher's statement, this *might* be evidence of satisficing.

From a measurement standpoint, satisficing can be seen as adding random or systematic error, or both, to the variables of interest. If some respondents are satisficing by choosing a random response alternative, then the error will be randomly distributed. However, if a large number of respondents are acquiescing, this error could be seen as bias, or systematic error. Thus, if respondents are satisficing, the additional measurement error could alter the strength of the relationships between variables. Predicted relationships might be attenuated or made stronger by the additional measurement error in the variables. Because satisficing is both difficult to identify and impossible to change after data collection, it is most important to understand the reasons why respondents satisfice to minimize it at the questionnaire design phase.

Why Do Respondents Satisfice? A respondent might switch between weak and strong satisficing and optimizing within the same questionnaire. In addition, there might be individual questions on which respondents might be more likely to satisfice. Thus, the problem of satisficing is both a problem with respondent motivation and with questionnaire design. Three main factors affect respondent satisficing: task or question difficulty, respondent ability, and respondent motivation.

For respondents to optimally answer the question posed, they must carefully complete the four steps described above. If at any point in this process of interpreting the question, retrieving the information, summarizing, and reporting, the task itself causes difficulty, respondents will be more likely to satisfice. For instance, respondents might have more difficulty retrieving a piece of information when it is far in the past, as opposed to a short time ago. Respondents might also have difficulty summarizing information into one overall judgment. For example, if respondents must compare and contrast several political candidates at the same time, the task will be too overwhelming for them to complete. Finally, questions that are poorly written, difficult to understand, or ask several questions at the same time will be difficult for a respondent to answer (*see* **Question Interpretation**). Researchers must consider their questions carefully to make sure that their language is clear and that they are asking for one judgment at a time. A question that asks respondents "Do you like George W. Bush and his foreign policy positions?" is inappropriate because it asks respondents to evaluate Bush *and* his foreign policy positions at the same time. A question like this would increase the likelihood that respondents will satisfice.

Respondent ability also has an effect on the likelihood of satisficing. That is, respondents with a high level of cognitive sophistication are more likely to optimize. They are better able to quickly and effectively search their memories for relevant information and are better able to map their summary judgments onto the response options given. In addition, respondents who have thought about a topic more might have an easier time with the cognitive demands of the survey research task. For instance, respondents who are highly engaged in politics might have an easier time comparing and contrasting several candidates at once than a respondent who has not had much experience reading about political candidates. If respondents have preexisting strong views on a particular topic, it will be easier for them to retrieve and express these opinions. A respondent who has a vehement stance on a polarizing issue like abortion, for instance, would be less likely to satisfice on a question about abortion compared with someone without strong views on the subject.

Finally, respondents who have higher motivation to complete the survey task should be less likely to satisfice. There are many reasons why a respondent might be highly motivated. Some respondents have a high need for cognition, which is a general tendency to enjoy thinking and to prefer cognitively complex tasks. Respondents might be more motivated by questions that are interesting and relevant to them and their lives. The interviewer can also influence motivation by making expectations clear. In addition, respondents might be more motivated if they believe that they might later have to justify their responses, or if they are made aware of the importance of the survey. A final consideration of respondent motivation is the fact that motivation might decrease as the interview progresses. Respondents may be particularly likely to lose motivation and to satisfice more as they get tired of the survey task.

Minimizing Satisficing. To minimize satisficing, the surveyor is required to give some thought to the conditions that promote satisficing and to make an attempt to change those conditions. Although respondent ability cannot be changed, making the tasks easier and more relevant can make the respondents more likely to optimize. There are many studies that explore how researchers can ask good, clear questions to communicate effectively with respondents (*see* **Question-Wording Effects**). Surveyors can be sure to make all the questions as clear as possible so that respondents understand what is being asked of them.

Moreover, survey researchers can take into account the typically low motivation of respondents and try to increase motivation whenever possible. This can be done by making the tasks within the survey interesting. Having the respondent complete a variety of simple tasks might make the survey more pleasant to complete. Importantly, the mode of the survey might make a difference in fostering or reducing satisficing. Recent research has shown that telephone interviews make it easier for respondents to satisfice when compared with face-to-face interviews. In face-to-face interviews, interviewers can increase respondent motivation by their enthusiasm and by emphasizing the importance of the survey and of taking the task seriously. Respondents are more motivated to please an interviewer who is right in front of them.

The success of survey research is dependent on the quality of the responses given by survey participants. Thus, the continued research program of understanding how respondents deal with the survey research task is crucial to evaluating the quality of the data. Understanding how and why respondents might optimize or satisfice throughout a survey can help us understand how to minimize weak and strong satisficing and increase the overall quality of survey research.

Further Reading

Crano, William, and Marilynn B. Brewer. *Principles and Methods of Social Research.* Mahwah, NJ: Lawrence Erlbaum, 2002. See especially chapter 3.

Krosnick, Jon A. "Response Strategies for Coping with the Cognitive Demands of Attitude Measures in Surveys." *Applied Cognitive Psychology* 5 (1991): 213–36.

Narayan, Sowmya, and Jon A. Krosnick. "Education Moderates Some Response Effects in Attitude Measurement." *Public Opinion Quarterly* 60 (1996): 58–88.

Tourangeau, Roger, Lance J. Rips, and Kenneth Rasinski. *The Psychology of Survey Response.* Cambridge, MA: Cambridge University Press, 2000. See especially chapter 1.

Monica C. Schneider and Joanne M. Miller

School Choice

School choice refers to the ability of parents to select the school their child attends, rather than the traditional method wherein students are assigned a specific public school based on place of residency. School choice in this context refers to both choice among different public schools and to the potential use of vouchers that would allow public money to be spent to send a child to a private school.

Public opinion on school choice is difficult to assess. It depends, to some degree, upon the type of school choice under consideration. Moreover, question wording and framing techniques can shape attitudes toward these alternatives. Nonetheless, public opinion on school choice is an important question. Politicians frequently tout school choice alternatives as solutions for ailing school systems, and such alternatives have been the focus of a number of state referenda in recent years.

While school choice based on choosing a residential location (and thus an assigned school district) has long been a feature—perhaps even the dominant feature—of American public schooling, other choices, such as magnet schools, open enrollment plans, and transfer options, expanded in the 1960s. Generally, these choices tend to be viewed fairly favorably by most citizens, especially as they allow flexibility, with minimal downside. More recently, however, and far more controversially, choice has included charter schools and voucher programs. Charter schools are public schools that are free from many of the bureaucratic constraints governing public schools; parents choose to send their child to the charter school, and the district's funding follows the child to the school. Charter schools are popular with parents, and many have long waiting lists. Voucher programs allow parents to use some portion of public education funds to enroll their child in any school they choose, including private schools.

Supporters of school choice believe that it will inject competition into public education, giving low-income families options similar to those long held by middle- and upper-income families through residential location mobility, and that choice will force all schools to compete harder for their students. While the original supporters were generally Catholics and free-market conservatives like Milton Friedman, who is credited with originating the idea of vouchers in 1955, the school choice movement has recently attracted more minorities and parents of children attending failing inner-city schools. Rather than advocating universal voucher programs for all students, today's movement is generally targeted to students in failing schools in low-income neighborhoods.

Opponents of school choice, who include many traditional liberals, the American Civil Liberties Union (ACLU), and teachers' unions, argue that (a) it will sap needed funds from the public schools, (b) it is mainly designed to strengthen private, religious-based education, and (c) it is intended to reduce the political power of groups like teachers' unions. Instead, opponents support reforms like better-trained teachers and smaller classroom sizes to improve public education.

Charter schools have been the most rapidly growing segment of the school choice spectrum. Some forty states have laws governing charter schools, and there are nearly 3,000 charter schools serving over 680,000 students, or about 1 percent of American K–12 students. While there are some controversies around charter schools, their rapid growth, support by some teachers' unions and liberal groups, and the fact that forty state legislatures and governors have approved them, all suggest that public opinion is generally favorable. Indeed, most opinion polls have shown support for public school choice programs at over 70 percent.

Controversy about Vouchers. Vouchers provide parents with publicly funded tuition certificates that can be used to pay tuition for their children at any approved public or private school. Voucher programs can be structured in a variety of ways; for example, policy decisions include whether to include religious schools, the amount of the voucher, eligibility requirements (e.g., only low-income families, students from failing schools), school selection mechanisms of eligible students, and accountability standards. Opinion varies somewhat depending on the specific features incorporated.

First, many voucher surveys have been performed by groups actively supporting or opposing the idea. In addition to this potential source of bias, most polls that ask about vouchers also cover a number of topics and have only one or two questions designed to measure public opinion about vouchers. These results are often questionable. Second, the design of vouchers is complicated, but the questions posed are often relatively simplistic. Real opinion may vary greatly depending upon whether religious schools are included, whether schools can select students, the amount of the voucher, and other design features. Third, many Americans may not yet have formed real opinions about vouchers and other school choice options. In a 1995 study, Moe found that two-thirds of those surveyed said they had never heard of vouchers. A 1999 Kaiser poll found that one-third felt insufficiently informed to support or oppose vouchers.

The annual Phi Delta Kappa/Gallup Poll is one of the longest established surveys reporting public opinion about school choice. Since 1996 it has asked respondents whether they "favor or oppose allowing students and parents to choose a private school to attend at public expense." The results of the 2003 poll indicated that 38 percent of respondents supported school vouchers and 60 percent were opposed. This reflected a drop in support from the 2002 survey, which indicated that 46 percent of respondents supported school choice. Since the institution of the question in 1996, the poll results have fluctuated between 34 and 46 percent in favor and between 52 and 62 percent opposed.

The Center for Education Reform (CER), however, argues that the positive responses are artificially low due to the biased wording of the questions—particularly the phrase "at public expense." As a result of perceived "biased wording, prejudicial phrasing, and contextual ambiguity" of surveys undertaken by organizations like Phi Delta Kappa, the CER has instituted its own annual survey measuring public opinion on school choice. CER claims that its findings are more reliable than those of other polls because it has reduced the bias of question wording by removing "loaded phrases" and words with "strong negative connotations." CER's question is phrased as follows: "How much are you in favor of or against allowing poor parents to be given the tax dollars allotted for their child's education and permitting them to use those dollars in the form of a scholarship to attend a private, public, or parochial school of their choosing?" With this wording, the poll found 63 percent of all respondents in favor of choice.

A 2002 Associated Press poll on school vouchers found that 51 percent of respondents would support "providing parents in low-income families with tax money in the form of school vouchers to help pay for their children to attend private or religious schools." Forty-five percent of respondents said if vouchers were available to send their children to private school, they would take them. Also in 2002, an ABC News.com poll found that 50 percent of respondents supported helping low-income parents pay private or religious school tuition, and that the support was at 57 percent among "low-income" groups.

These sorts of disparities in support for vouchers—ranging from 38 percent to 63 percent support among the general public—are frustrating to politicians and other observers. To address these concerns and to overcome the problems identified with other studies, Moe dedicated a large national survey of 4,700 adults to studying public opinion on vouchers. Moe criticized other surveys for being misleading, for failing to look at underlying explanations for public opinion, and for not taking into account that a large majority of the public is not properly informed on the issues. In general, Moe found that Americans are supportive of the voucher movement: "They think vouchers will help improve the schools, promote social equity, and enhance racial balance." Moe's survey also asked respondents about their opinion on specific aspects of proposed voucher programs. He found that a majority of Americans think that voucher systems, if adopted, should include religious education as well as secular private schools. In addition, most Americans believe that private schools participating in voucher programs should have accountability standards and a focus on equity. Although such requirements shift the original notion of vouchers as a "free-market" reform to one including "regulations for accountability and equity," they also increase the political viability of the program.

Since the emerging form of vouchers is targeted mainly to low-income minority groups, observers and politicians are particularly interested in how blacks and Hispanics regard voucher proposals. Again, there is controversy here.

There is some evidence that minorities favor vouchers at higher rates than does the American public as a whole. A 2002 survey by the Center for Education Reform, conducted by Zogby, indicated that 72 percent of African Americans and 64 percent of Hispanics were "strongly/somewhat" in favor of vouchers for "poor parents." The Black America's Political Action Committee survey of 2002 found that 63 percent of African Americans stated they would place their children in either private or charter schools if that option was offered to them, as 56 percent of African Americans rated their schools "C" or below. Annual polls by the Joint Center for Political and Economic Studies have indicated that African Americans are more supportive of vouchers than the general adult population. Although African American support for vouchers fluctuated from 48 percent to 60 percent from 1996 until 2002, the African American figures were higher than those for the general population every year.

Despite showing a majority of respondents opposed to vouchers, the 2002 Phi Delta Kappa/Gallup Poll found that 63 percent of minorities supported allowing parents to send their school-age children to any public, private, or church-related school they choose even when the government would pay for all or part of the tuition. Still, that was slightly below their 1998 survey, which showed 68 percent of minorities in support of vouchers.

While more attention has focused on black support or opposition, the 2000 National Annenberg Election Survey found that 58 percent of Hispanics favored school vouchers. In addition, the Joint Center for Political and Economic Studies added a sample of Hispanics to its National Opinion Poll in 2002 and found that 61 percent of Hispanics supported school vouchers, a percentage higher than both the general adult population (52 percent) and African Americans (57 percent). Thus, minorities, for whom the current set of existing and proposed voucher programs are designed, demonstrate a higher level of support, in most surveys, than all Americans.

While surveys show mixed public opinion, actual state referendum votes have demonstrated clear opposition to vouchers, at least to those programs that are not limited to low-income, failing school districts. Since 1992, four states—Colorado (1992), California (1993, 2000), Washington (1996), and Michigan (2000)—have placed voucher initiatives/referenda on their ballots. All were defeated handily, and in all cases but Washington, voters defeated voucher proposals by more than two to one.

In each of these cases, the initiative was a broad-based proposal that was not limited to low-income families. Only one of the five initiatives (Michigan) specified the use of vouchers for schools with low graduation rates, and only one (Washington) excluded religious schools. As such, the initiatives probably appealed primarily to more extreme supporters of vouchers. Moderate supporters may have approved a more limited initiative, focused on assisting low-income children in failing school districts, but were unwilling to approve the risk of a relatively extensive initiative.

These defeats occurred despite the fact that wealthy supporters backed the voucher referenda in all cases. Moe tries to explain these defeats by arguing that, in most states, the teachers' unions have the financial and electoral power to block vouchers. Moe argues that these votes are not fair reflections of the reality of public opinion. Others might say voters have spoken, and that votes are more meaningful expressions of opinion than are survey questions answered over the telephone at dinner.

The question of the constitutionality of voucher programs that employ religious-based schools has been perceived as a major potential obstacle to the expansion of vouchers. This is a major issue since nearly two-thirds of private schools are religious-affiliated. In June 2002, however, in the Zelman case, the U.S. Supreme Court upheld the constitutionality of the Cleveland, Ohio, voucher program—a major victory for voucher proponents. Still, about half the state constitutions have explicit language opposing the use of public funds for private religious education (the so-called Blaine Amendments), so, depending on further state and federal court decisions, that may still limit the spread of vouchers, regardless of public opinion or popularity.

Despite limitations of survey data and a lack of complete information, public opinion in support of the various forms of school choice appears to be growing. As public awareness and understanding of voucher programs and charter schools grow, perhaps so too will the accuracy of surveys designed to measure public opinion on the issues. As evidenced by recent public opinion polls, the public appears to be open to the idea of school choice and the use of pilot programs—particularly those targeted at failing, low-income schools—as a potential means to improve the public school system. Still, although there is agreement that schools need improvement, disagreement remains about whether school choice is the cure. Above all, it should be noted that the most meaningful form of public opinion expression—voting—has not been kind to vouchers.

Further Reading

Hochschild, Jennifer, and Bridget Scott. "The Polls—Trends." *Public Opinion Quarterly* 62 (1998): 79–120. Provides an overview of public opinion polls concerning governance and education, including question wording and trend data.

Moe, Terry M. *Schools, Vouchers, and the American Public.* Washington, DC: Brookings Institution Press, 2001. Presents the results of an in-depth 1995 study on public opinion and school vouchers.

Rose, Lowell C., and Alec M. Gallup. "The 35th Annual Phi Delta Kappa/Gallup Poll of the Public's Attitudes Toward the Public Schools." *Phi Delta Kappan* (September 2003): 41–56. Reports the results of the organization's 2003 poll, which focuses on the No Child Left Behind Act, and includes trend data for many of the questions.

Teixeira, Ruy, "Myth #4: American Public Is Clamoring for Vouchers." In *Public School Choice vs. Private School Vouchers*, edited by Richard Kahlenberg. New York: Century Foundation. Reports the liberal perspective on opinion about school choice.

Web Sites

The Web site of the Center for Education Reform (www.edreform.com) contains a number of relevant publications, including "Poll Finds 63% of Americans Favor School Choice: Other Surveys Find Growing Support" (2002) and "2002 PDK/Gallup Poll: Skewed Questions Continue to Dictate Responses" (2002).

The Web site of the Joint Center for Political and Economic Studies (www.jointcenter. org) contains information on school choice, including the publication of its annual national opinion poll, covering a wide range of topics, including education.

The Web site of the People for the American Way (www.pfaw.org) provides information about liberal perspectives on school choice and votes against vouchers.

Aimee Williamson and Paul Teske

Self-Censorship

Self-censorship is the conscious choice to censor one's expression of an opinion because of the belief that the audience will disagree with that opinion. Self-censorship is a real phenomenon, and one that public opinion pollsters must be aware of when collecting and interpreting public opinion information.

Self-censorship is conceptually similar to and easily confused with two related concepts: socially desirable responding and conformity. Whereas self-censorship is the withholding of the expression of one's opinion in an environment perceived to be hostile to that opinion, socially desirable responding is the expression of opinions (or admitting to behaviors) to make oneself appear to be a good person or to avoid social disapproval. Thus, socially desirable responding is the untruthful reporting of socially desirable attitudes or behaviors or the underreporting of socially undesirable ones. To be sure, self-censorship can result from worries about social disapproval. But self-censorship, unlike socially desirable responding, is not necessarily motivated by self-presentational concerns. For example, we might not tell a boss that we disagree with his or her decision because of the risks of professional sanction. Or we might refrain from letting a friend know that we do not agree with him or her on some topic of mutual interest to avoid interpersonal conflict or harm to the relationship.

Conformity, in contrast, is the expression of an opinion held by a majority as if it were one's own when in fact it is not. Conformity is a form that self-censorship can take, but self-censorship is not necessarily conformity. A conforming response is an option available to someone who chooses to self-censor, but it is not the only option available. The self-censorer may choose instead to dodge the question about his opinion by refusing to answer it or by answering

"I don't know" or "undecided." Thus, self-censoring responses can take several forms in a public opinion poll.

Harrisson (1940) conceptualized public opinion as "what you will say out loud to anyone" and distinguished it from private opinion, which is what public opinion pollsters are ultimately seeking. If a pollster wants to know what a collection of people think about some topic ("private opinion"), it is important for the pollster to remember that what people actually think and what they say they think may not be the same thing. Self-censorship can occur in a poll because public opinion polling is often (although not necessarily, depending on how the poll is administered) a social interaction. As such, polling can be affected by anything that affects any kind of social interaction. A pollster who asks the opinion of a stranger over the phone or in person is making a bold request indeed. What we believe reflects what we value, the things that are important to us, and how we define ourselves (the value expressive function of attitudes). What incentive does a person have to reveal such personal information about the self to a stranger? Why should the pollster expect a more forthcoming response than anyone who accosts a person on the street and starts asking all kinds of personal questions? Fortunately, little incentive is typically necessary. The pollster has more perceived authority to ask questions than does any random person on the street, and people who agree to be interviewed typically do speak some modicum of truth. Nevertheless, at least the short-term costs of such self-disclosure are potentially high. It is reasonable for a respondent to infer that if most people disagree with his or her opinion, the pollster is probably more likely than not to also disagree. People generally do not like to appear deviant or unusual, even in the eyes of a stranger, but admitting to a belief that is uncommon carries just that risk. So the incentive for "misreporting" (or outright lying) is potentially high, perhaps even higher than the incentive for telling the truth.

What can happen if people who believe their opinions are not widely shared are less willing to truthfully declare their opinions to a pollster? Noelle-Neumann described the insidious nature of self-censorship when she argued that viewpoints that are not publicly expressed will, in time, disappear from the public landscape. Given that the media are a major source of information about public opinion and that the media are major publishers of public opinion polls, it is clear that self-censorship has the potential to affect perceptions of the opinion landscape. Consumers of public opinion polls will perceive that minority viewpoints are even less common then they appear, further discouraging minority opinions from being voiced by their adherents. To the extent that a person's action, such as how he or she votes in an election, is guided in part by information about public opinion, self-censorship could change collective behavior—such as the outcome of an election. Although in some contexts self-censorship can have beneficial outcomes, in the area of opinion polling, it is hard to imagine how self-censorship could ever be construed as desirable.

By Noelle-Neumann's account of self-censorship and the process that produces it, everyone is susceptible to social pressures to self-censor. However, research suggests it is closer to the truth that, rather than being a social constant, people actually vary in their susceptibility to social pressures and their use of information about the opinion climate when deciding whether or not to voice their opinion publicly. Some people will say what they think regardless of the beliefs of the audience and the possible consequences. Others deliberate more carefully on the pros and cons of expressing their opinions openly around a hostile audience before choosing whether or not to do so. Hayes, Glynn, Shanahan, and Uldall constructed the Willingness to Self-Censor scale to measure this individual difference. Respondents to the measure answer a series of questions using a Likert-type response format, such as "It is difficult for me to express my opinion if I think others won't agree with what I say" and "There have been many times when I thought others around me were wrong but I didn't let them know." The more strongly a person endorses statements worded to reflect a tendency to self-censor, the higher that person's willingness to self-censor.

Research using this measure has painted what can be construed as a rather unflattering picture of the self-censorer. Studies of college students have shown that people who score high on the self-censorship index tend to be relatively more shy, more anxious in social situations, lower in self-esteem, more worried about what other people think of them, more likely to look to others for guidance on how to act, and experience negative emotions more frequently and positive emotions less frequently in day to day life compared with low scorers. Studies of the demographic correlates of self-censorship using **random digit dialing** samples of various communities suggest that self-censorers tend to be older, more conservative, and less educated than people who are less willing to censor their own opinion expression. Although the validation of a measure is an ongoing process, initial studies of this instrument are encouraging in that it has good reliability and shows evidence of convergent validity. Hayes and his colleagues provide many possible applications of this measure as a research tool for public opinion scholars interested in such areas as political participation, public opinion perception, group dynamics, and media effects.

Given that self-censorship is an undesirable phenomenon from a pollster's perspective, what can be done about it? How can pollsters enhance the likelihood that minority opinions will be expressed openly? Research on socially desirable response biases and the reporting of sensitive information may provide a clue. Public opinion researchers have studied methodological approaches to bridging the gap between public and private opinion. This research has almost exclusively focused on peoples' willingness to disclose sensitive, personal information as a function of the mode of survey administration. Although the research is conflicting, it does suggest that the methods of data collection that either (a) reduce the social nature of the interaction between pollster and respondent or (b) increase the distance between a respondent's answers and the audience or potential audiences of the respondent tend to increase the reporting of at least some kinds of sensitive information. Self-administered data collection methods such as audio computer assisted self-interviewing (ACASI), **interactive voice response** (IVR), and other forms of self-administered polls, reduce or completely eliminate the interaction between the pollster and the respondent; this can sometimes enhance the respondent's willingness to disclose sensitive information. The distance between a respondent's answers and the audience can be increased by any method where the respondent's answers cannot easily be known to others, such as response anonymity, randomized response methods, self-administration of the questions, and assurances of confidentiality (although even such assurances do not eliminate the fact that at least the interviewer will know the respondent's answers). Thus, there is reason to believe that how a poll is conducted can affect what people will say in response to the questions. But whether such methods would specifically enhance a person's willingness to disclose opinions perceived to be unpopular is uninvestigated and worthy of future research.

Little is known about self-censorship, its forms, its consequences, and who is most likely to self-censor, and there is much research waiting to be done. How predominant of a response is self-censorship in public opinion polls? What factors affect the likelihood that a person will self-censor? What effects does self-censorship have on the accuracy and predictive validity of opinion polls? Are there regional variations in willingness to self-censor, perhaps in response to differences in socialization or the cultural values that distinguish certain regions of the country from others? If so, this suggests that polls of certain areas of the country may be less accurate than they are of others. Does mode of poll administration have different effects on people as a function of their willingness to self-censor? And what forms does self-censorship take? There are other forms of opinion expression than vocalizing one's opinion to a pollster, such as participation in political activities like protesting, volunteering for a campaign, or writing to elected officials. Do people self-censor by refraining from certain forms of political expression if the opinion climate is hostile to that expression? To what extent do people keep their objections to acts of government to themselves if they perceive that others do not agree with their objections? And how can self-censorship be reduced, thereby enhancing the visibility of minority viewpoints that must and should be acknowledged and discussed in democratic societies?

Further Reading

Harrisson, Tom. "What Is Public Opinion?" *Political Quarterly* 11 (1940): 368–83. Presages the spiral-of-silence theory by presenting the important distinction between public and private opinion.

Hayes, Andrew F., Carroll J. Glynn, James Shanahan, and Brian Uldall. "Individual Differences in Willingness to Self-Censor." Paper presented at the Annual Meeting of the American Association for Public Opinion Research, Nashville, Tennessee, May 2003 (see Web sites, below). Describes the development and validation of the Willingness to Self-Censor scale.

Noelle-Neumann, Elizabeth. *Spiral of Silence: Public Opinion—Our Social Skin.* 2nd ed. Chicago: University of Chicago Press, 1993. One of the more important works in public opinion theory in how it describes public opinion as a social process.

Richman, Wendy L., Sara Kiesler, Suzanne Weisband, and Fritz Drasgow. "A Meta-Analytic Study of Social Desirability Distortion in Computer-Administered Questionnaires, Traditional Questionnaires, and Interviews." *Journal of Applied Psychology* 84 (1999): 754–75. A concise quantitative review of mode-of-administration effects.

Web Sites

For information about the Willingness to Self-Censor scale, past research on the construct, and the exact items in the measure, see http://www.jcomm.ohio-state.edu/ahayes/WTSC.htm.

Andrew F. Hayes

Self-Interest and Altruism

A long tradition of political and economic thought from Thomas Hobbes in the seventeenth century to Karl Marx in the nineteenth century and Anthony Downs in the twentieth has led researchers to believe in the power of self-interest as the guiding force in the social universe. When put to the empirical test, however, self-interest appears to exert but "minimal effects" in politics. These minimal findings have inspired empirical research into "other-directedness" and "altruism" in politics. Discussed here are a number of definitions of self-interest and altruism, along with important conceptual problems posed by them.

Loosely defined, political self-interest refers to the expression of beliefs and attitudes, voting behavior, or other participatory behavior that serves the maximization of someone's own utility. Conversely, political altruism can be defined as political behavior maximizing someone else's utility. (The term "altruism" was derived in 1830 by the French philosopher Auguste Comte from *alter*, Latin for "other.") This definition does not take into account the costs that may accrue to the self or to others from the respective behavior. For example, it is possible to maximize one's own utility while not hurting someone else, or even maximizing someone else's utility at the same time. However, if a person improves his or her own position while also improving the position of someone else, this behavior would not necessarily be called "self-interested" in the everyday understanding of the term, but neither could it be called "altruistic." Thus, a more strict definition of self-interest and altruism can be formulated by taking costs into consideration in addition to benefits. Political self-interest could thus be defined as a behavior that is likely to benefit the self at the risk of a disadvantage to someone else. Conversely, altruism is defined as a behavior that is likely to benefit someone else at the risk of a disadvantage to the self.

It is important to distinguish rationality and self-interest (*see also* **Prospect Theory**). This notion of expectation and risk is introduced into the definition to address another important distinction, that between rationality and self-interest. The self-interest–based theory of human nature developed by Thomas Hobbes in 1651 is frequently referred to as *homo economicus* and hypothesizes the human decision maker to be a rational acting maximizer of individual self-interest. While the utility function of an individual is assumed to be linked to the self, an individual may go about pursuing this goal in either rational or irrational ways. Under the assumptions of the Hobbesian *homo economicus* altruistic behavior would only be possible as irrational pursuit of self-interest, not as a rational pursuit of other-regarding goals. Contemporary criticism of the *homo economicus* has largely centered around the assumption of perfect rationality. Nobel Laureate Herbert Simon proposed to replace the assumption of perfect rationality by a notion of rationality that takes into account human limitations in memory and computational capabilities (bounded rationality). Note, however, that this notion does not change expectations about altruistic behavior. Rather than being a sign of irrationality, altruism is now possible as a symptom of computational limitations. The focus on the question of rationality has frequently distracted attention from the more fundamental question of self-interest versus altruism. Even proponents of the Hobbesian *homo economicus* in the public choice literature acknowledge that self-interest is too narrow a concept to account for the variety of human behavior. It is widely agreed, for instance, that people often do what appears to be irrational for them as individuals because they believe it to be socially rational.

We must also distinguish "sociotropic" politics from political altruism. The term sociotropic politics has been introduced to denote this form of social rationality. Political Scientists Stanley Feldman and Marco R. Steenbergen write: "people's behaviors and orientations . . . may originate from considerations of the self in isolation from its social context or from considerations of the self as embedded in this context. For instance, as the discussion of pocketbook and sociotropic voting illustrates . . . a voter may evaluate candidates on the basis of what they have done for him or her personally or on the basis of what they have done for the community as a whole." Empirically, voters appear to respond to the state of the overall economy (*see* **Economy**) much more frequently than to their own individual economic circumstances (sociotropic voting). It is important, again, to distinguish sociotropic from altruistic political behavior. Sociotropic behavior is designed to benefit the collective as a whole, thus benefiting both the self and others since both are members of the collective. In contrast, politically altruistic behavior is designed to benefit others while not benefiting the self (according to the loose definition) or hurting it (according to the strict one). However, if self-interest and altruism refer not to the collective as a whole but to groups within that collective that either contain the self as a member or not, a group-level definition of self-interest and altruism can be formulated.

Altruism and self-interest also involve both individual and collective aspects: According to an individual-level definition, individual-level self-interest describes behavior likely to benefit one distinct individual at the risk of a disadvantage to another individual. Conversely, individual-level altruism describes behavior likely to benefit one distinct other individual at the risk of a disadvantage to the self. While individual-level self-interest and altruism may be relevant to the behavior of individual political leaders, it is the group-level notion that appears to be more relevant to the analysis of public opinion. A group-level definition can be formulated by comparing ingroups (groups the self belongs to as a member) and outgroups (groups the self does not belong to). Group-level self-interest can be defined as a behavior likely to benefit an individual's own group (ingroup) at the expense of a group the individual does not belong to (outgroup). Conversely, group-level altruism can be defined as a behavior likely to benefit a group the individual does not belong to at the expense of the ingroup. Note that the group-level definition does not distinguish between self-interested and altruistic behavior within an individual's own group. For example, a retired member of a racial or ethnic minority may be willing to pay higher taxes in support of affirmative action policies designed to help young minority members in their search for high-quality employment. This behavior would constitute individual-level altruism (a retiree willing to pay higher taxes to benefit a young job applicant), while on the group level representing self-interested behavior (increasing job chances for own membership group [minorities] at the expense of job chances for a nonmembership group [non-minorities]).

While important to distinguish the two levels conceptually, empirically it is often hard to distinguish between the individual and group levels, since each individual possesses a distinct set of group memberships while at the same time each group is made up of a distinct set of individuals. This gives ample opportunity for many confusing interactions. For example a white American man and an African American man share the same demographic group membership with respect to gender but different group memberships with respect to race or ethnicity. Since affirmative action policies refer to both gender and race/ethnicity at the same time, cross-cutting group memberships can lead to confusion with respect to individual and group utility self-interest and altruism. It should be noted, however, that this ambiguity is not necessarily a conceptual weakness due to the definitions provided here; it can be viewed as a property of the social world itself.

An important objection against a conceptualization of altruism that takes behavior as an indication of motivation is raised by the psychologist C. Daniel Bateson. He insists that only altruistic behaviors that are driven by altruistic motives should deserve the label "altruistic" while other forms of altruistic behavior should be labeled "pseudoaltruistic." He writes: "If altruism is equated with helping behavior, then it obviously exists. But the question remains whether this behavior is ever, in any degree, directed toward benefiting the other as an ultimate goal." The problem of underlying motivation, however, is symmetrical, and the concept of self-interest suffers from the same shortcoming, since underlying self-serving goals are usually assumed rather than empirically established. A worker who schemes to gain promotion over her colleagues, for example, may do so out of self-interest as the desire to enhance her own position vis-à-vis that of her coworkers. Alternatively, however, she may do so believing that she would be a better boss than any of her colleagues and that she will be able to provide a better work environment for them than anyone else. Alternatively, she may be motivated by other-directed goals, such as providing for her children or simply living up to social expectations of competitiveness and success. If self-interested motives are assumed to underlie observed self-interested behavior, then altruistic motives should be assumed to underlie observed altruistic behavior. However, if empirical evidence of altruistic motivation is required to make the case for altruism, then evidence of self-interested motivation should be provided for self-interested behavior.

We must also consider the short term versus long term. With respect to self-interest, short-term motivation is sometimes assumed to result from hedonic needs, and sometimes it is assumed to result from self-preservational goals. While hedonic needs require instant gratification, self-preservation requires a long-term perspective. Short-term hedonic needs can be in harmony with long-term self-preservation, for example, when a hungry person satisfies his or her appetite by eating, but the two goals can also be in conflict, such as when an obese person with a high risk of heart disease satisfies his or her appetite by impulsive eating. Problems of addiction and high-risk sexual practices routinely pit short-term hedonic needs against long-term self-preservational goals. In the political arena, such conflicts can arise when special economic interest groups lobby for short-term benefits at the expense of long-term economic development, or when economically weak regions demand their political independence from economically stronger federations.

The distinction between behavior and motivation leads to a number of mixed forms combining self-interest and altruism. For example, Bateson distinguishes several "pseudoaltruistic approaches" that describe altruistic behavior as a function of self-interested motivation. For example, helping behavior may be motivated by external rewards (material compensation or praise), by internal rewards (feeling good about oneself), or by the reduction of empathic distress (a desire to avoid feeling bad for someone else). Since the reward in each case accrues to the helping individual rather than the recipient of help, this form of altruistic behavior can be interpreted as self-interested. Economic theory describes a related form of pseudoaltruism where the external rewards are not immediate but expected to accrue sometime in the future. This form of pseudoaltruism is referred to as "reciprocal altruism," because the recipient of the helping behavior is expected to reciprocate it at a later point in time.

Some conceptualizations of self-interest in economic theory allow individual utility functions to contain altruistic goals. By maximizing such utility functions altruistic actors are said to act in a self-interested fashion because the altruistic goals are held by the self. This approach could be referred to as pseudo–self-interest, since the self-interested behavior it describes is motivated by genuinely altruistic, rather than self-serving, goals. Self-interest defined in this way could refer to any conceivable behavior and thus defies empirical falsification. It comes closer to an article of faith than to an empirically testable theory of human nature.

Another mixed form of self-interest and altruism is described in sociobiology where self-sacrificing behavior benefits close relatives. Based on the self-interest assumption underlying Darwin's theory of evolution by natural selection an interesting paradox arises: The more similar two individual organisms are in terms of the resources on which they thrive, the fiercer the competition between them should be. This individual-level mechanism should lead to the most intense struggle for survival to rage between members of the same species, especially if they are closely related. It should be especially fierce between parents and their offspring, making infanticide the expected behavioral norm rather than a rare exception. Group selection theory was developed to solve this theoretical paradox. It holds that natural selection acts not only on individuals but also on groups. Since altruistic behavior toward ingroup members may enhance the survival chances of the group as a whole, some altruistic behavior may be favored by natural selection. One problem arises with this explanation, however, namely that individual competition within a successfully selected altruistic group should once again favor the most self-interested individual group members, thus neutralizing the effect of group selection. Only if altruism is directed toward genetically closely related kin (parents, children, or siblings), could an "altruistic gene" be selected for and survive, if such a gene (or combination of genes) should actually exist. Since "kin altruism" is altruistic on the individual level yet self-interested on the group level, it represents a truly mixed form of behavior. It does not represent pseudoaltruism according to Bateson's use of the term, since it does not require a mismatch between behavior and motivation. A parent, for example, may not only behave altruistically toward a child but also be genuinely motivated by the child's welfare.

Much debate centers on the symmetry between self-interest and altruism in human nature. Modern political thought is strongly influenced by the assumption of self-interest first formulated by Thomas Hobbes in 1651. Under this assumption, self-interested behavior has come to be viewed as the behavioral norm while altruism is viewed as an anomaly requiring explanation. This asymmetrical treatment of the issue leads researchers to interpret even the most mundane political behaviors (expressing an opinion or casting a ballot) as motivated by self-interest while only the most exceptional and spectacular acts of self-sacrifice are labeled altruistic. As a result, evidence of motivation is required only for altruistic behavior while the claim of self-interest is usually accepted at face value. It should be noted, however, that the idea of human nature as selfish is fairly modern. For several millennia prior to Hobbes's invention of the *Homo economicus*, political philosophers viewed the political actor as a being shaped, defined, and motivated by society. Greek antiquity referred to this model of human nature as *zoon politicon*, and Roman antiquity referred to it as *Homo politicus*. The model of the *Homo politicus* differs in two respects from Hobbes's *Homo economicus*. First, humans are viewed as group-beings rather than individuals; second, they are viewed as motivated by prosocial concerns rather than by self-interest. Even after Hobbes's philosophical innovation, political philosophers continued to disagree about the fundamentals of human nature. Jean-Jacques Rousseau, for example, accepted Hobbes's assumption of individualism but returned to the antique assumption of prosocial motivation. Karl Marx, in contrast, accepted Hobbes's assumption of self-interest but revived the antique idea of the human as a social animal acting as a class member rather than as an individual. The disunity among political philosophers regarding the basics of human nature suggests that neither self-interest nor altruism should be taken as a given and that a more symmetrical and evenhanded conceptualization may be desirable.

The traditional usage of the term "altruism" brings to mind dramatic images of self-sacrificing heroes, be they rescue workers at the World Trade Center on September 11, 2001, or rescuers of Jews from German Nazis during World War II. Although these behaviors definitely qualify as altruistic, a more symmetrical conceptualization of political altruism may include much less spectacular acts. It may provide for the possibility that people can choose a candidate or support a particular policy in a politically altruistic fashion. At the other extreme, however, if only self-sacrificial helping behavior is accepted as an indication of altruism, then evidence of self-interest should involve the sacrifice of others for selfish reasons.

Kristen Renwick Monroe has proposed to treat self-interest and altruism as a continuum rather than discrete concepts with only two alternatives. She writes: "The conceptual continuum allows us to view self-interest and altruism as the two poles between which human behavior oscillates . . . [w]ith self-interested actors located on the left of the continuum, altruists on the right, and individuals . . . of mixed type distributed in between." Her conceptualization is based on the view that self-interest and altruism represent personality characteristics that can be classified into several archetypes along the self-interested to altruistic continuum (entrepreneurs, philanthropists, heroes, rescuers).

While Monroe's archetypes are based on the idea of an altruistic personality, Bateson views altruism as a situational characteristic. The same individual may sometimes act more self-interested and sometimes more altruistic depending on the context. Empirical research presented in the following section provides evidence for both situational and personality characteristics. Feldman and Steenbergen point out that some measurement methods may be more likely to support a personality interpretation (e.g., Monroe's in-depth interviews) while others may be more likely to support a situational interpretation (e.g., Bateson's work using **experiments**). Since the two views are not mutually exclusive, a combination of personality characteristics and situational factors may describe political behavior better than either one or the other alone.

In a broad review of the public opinion literature covering issues as diverse as affirmative action, taxation, and **gender differences in public opinion**, among many others, Sears and Funk find only "minimal effects" of self-interest. They consistently find that "symbolic predispositions" (*see* **Symbolic Politics**), such as **partisanship**, ideological self-placement, or racial resentments exert much stronger influence than do indicators of personal self-interest. In this body of work, self-interest is operationalized as the researchers assessment of whether or not an individual respondent is likely to be personally affected by a given policy. For example, for a white respondent to be personally affected by busing, he or she must have a child, that child must be in a public school, and the family must live in a district in which busing is planned or implemented. If parents and nonparents show the same level of opposition, perhaps due to either their ideology or negative feelings toward African Americans, no effect of self-interest is registered. Thus, the definition of political altruism applied in their work is an individual-level rather than a group-level notion. The possibility that white parents and nonparents may express white group self-interest in their opposition to busing is purposefully excluded by the authors. As Sears and Funk put it: "we rule out group interest, i.e., interests that affect the well-being of the individual's group but not necessarily that of the specific individual. For example, we would not describe as 'self-interested' the support given by wealthy Jews to Jewish welfare agencies. It is not part of everyday understanding, we believe, to identify such generous aid to others as 'selfishness.'" Of course, it is possible that minimal findings of self-interest could be due to the fact that, especially in politics, groups may be more relevant to individual respondents than their own personal circumstances. Another possible problem could be seen in the fact that in some instances a loose definition of self-interest is applied. With respect to women's issues (job-discrimination, pay equity, sexual harassment, **abortion**, and child care), Sears and Funk find few gender differences (*see again* **Gender Differences in Public Opinion**). This could be due to the fact that these policies do not necessarily hurt men. Men may benefit less from these policies, but they may still benefit. Pay equity for women does not necessarily lead to pay inequity for men, and abortion rights, as well as child care may make the lives of both parents, not just of the mother, easier.

In a series of computer-based experiments I applied a group-level notion of political self-interest and altruism according to the strict definition where benefits for one group are pitted against potential costs for another. In these experiments, a computer program recorded demographic information of each individual experimental participant and custom tailored hypothetical candidates whose political positions were either in the interest of the participant's own demographic group or in the interest of a group to which the participant did not belong. This enabled the computer program to isolate effects of political ingroup and outgroup support in the participant's vote choice. The issues included local taxes and employment programs, affirmative action, U.N. peacekeeping operations, and environmental policies. Two studies were based on college student samples in the United States and in Germany, and one study was based on a national stratified nonprobability sample of adult Americans. The results significantly deviate from the predictions based on the assumption of exclusive group self-interest. On a percentage scale of political altruism on which 0 percent represents exclusive group self-interest and 100 percent exclusive altruism, the average score across all three studies (N = 424) was 52.73 percent with a standard deviation of 18.163. Measures were taken to prevent social desirability effects from influencing the data and the effectiveness of these steps was measured separately. The results significantly differed from one political scenario to the next, whereby greater self-interest of one group was usually counterbalanced by greater political altruism of another. The general balance between ingroup and outgroup support was evident in both the German and American samples, and it occurred irrespective of gender, race, age, or educational attainment. Further, it was replicated in an experiment on individual consumer choice. Demographic group size emerged as a powerful context factor predicting political self-interest (ingroup support) and altruism (outgroup support). Respondents were inclined to benefit larger demographic groups at the expense of smaller ones regardless of whether the individual respondent was a member of the benefiting group or not. These findings on the group level are in line with the "minimal-effects" findings regarding political self-interest on the individual level.

Scholars have identified a small number of conditions under which self-interest effects can be observed. When the policy involves large stakes (e.g., large tax cuts), with costs and benefits clearly stated and well publicized, and when the benefits of the policy can be expected with some degree of certainty, self-interest indicators exert significant influence on policy preference even after controlling for other factors. In other words, if people are told to maximize their self-interest, they will, on occasion, do so, especially in the area of tax policies. Interestingly, economic laboratory experiments that maximize the self-interest enhancing conditions of clarity and certainty and where the financial rewards directly benefit the individual participant, evidence of prosocial and even altruistic behavior is consistently identified.

In an important study, James Andreoni investigates whether this prosocial behavior in public goods experiments is due to kindness or confusion about the rules of the game. Andreoni's notion of kindness includes both genuine altruism (caring directly about the payoffs of other subjects) and warm glow (feeling good about being nice to one another). Andreoni concludes that "on average about 75 percent of the subjects are cooperative, and about half of these are confused about incentives, while about half understand free-riding but choose to cooperate out of some form of kindness. . . . It is important to note that laboratory experiments are designed to be neutral and to minimize social effects like kindness. Hence, regular public-goods experiments may already be eliminating a large amount of subjects' natural tendency to be cooperative. In the real world a much larger fraction of people may naturally be cooperative."

Jane Allyn Piliavin and Hong-Wen Charng review research on a wide range of prosocial acts, including the rescue of Jews in Nazi Germany, the willingness to enter a bone marrow donation pool, donating blood, charitable giving, and helping behavior in staged emergencies. They identify both personality characteristics and situational factors for altruistic behavior. There are indications that attribution of responsibility to the self rather than society at large encourages helping behavior, as well as a general trust in people (*see* **Social Capital**). Blood donors, according to their review, were more likely to be risk takers and adventure seekers than nondonors. Further, a gender difference was observed with respect to helping behavior in staged emergencies. Whereas men and women were equally likely to help in situations with a high level of harm, women were more likely to help in situations with low levels of harm, due to a lower threshold to perceived need in others.

These examples take us to the idea of empathy. It has been treated both as a personality characteristic and as a situationally induced mental state. In both cases, the individual steps into the shoes of someone else and tries to feel what they feel; in both cases, activities result that alleviate the suffering. One form of empathy leads to the alleviation of the other's suffering ("sympathy") and hence to altruistic helping behavior, while the other leads to the alleviation of personal distress felt by the individual him- or herself and hence to an escape from the situation where such an escape is possible. Bateson investigates these possibilities experimentally by creating staged emergencies with and without easy escape opportunities. The degree to which people are willing to help despite being offered an easy escape from the situation can be interpreted as evidence of genuine altruism (i.e., altruism motivated by sympathy for the victim's distress, rather than one's own).

In staged emergencies, situational factors play an important role, most notably the so-called bystander effect. As on the political group level, group size appears to play an important role, but this time as an inhibitor rather than a facilitator of altruistic behavior. The larger the group of potential helpers, the lower the willingness of the individual to help. In staged emergencies, the gender of the victim also emerged as an important situational factor with female victims being more likely to receive help than male ones. Another very important situational factor is the effect of personal requests for help. According to Piliavin and Charng, personal requests played a significant motivating role not only for rescuers of Jews in Nazi Europe, but also for potential kidney or blood donors and in the area of charitable giving. Studying rescuers of Jews in Nazi Europe Monroe emphasizes the importance of another effect that she views as independent of any of the aforementioned factors. She writes: "Altruists have a particular perspective in which all mankind is connected through a common humanity." According to her analysis, gentile rescuers of Jews in Nazi Europe shared this view, a perspective that allowed them to view Jewish people as fellow humans deserving of help despite dehumanizing Nazi propaganda. Others may have been unable to recognize the need to help due to the contrasting view of humankind as an assortment of unconnected groups.

In summary, loose and strict definitions of self-interest and altruism should be distinguished both on the individual and on the group level. It should be specified whether behavior is considered alone, or whether motivation is taken into consideration. In the latter case it should also be specified whether motivation is treated as a short-term or long-term phenomenon. It may be useful to treat self-interest and altruism as symmetrical, comparing spectacular altruistic acts (self-sacrifice) with spectacular self-interested ones (sacrifice of others), and self-interested mundane activities with equally mundane altruistic ones (e.g., supporting ingroups or outgroups in electoral politics). To adequately account for mixed forms of self-interest and altruism it may further be useful to place gradations of self-interested and altruistic behaviors along a conceptual continuum. Ultimately, self-interest may not play the fundamental role assigned to it by the theory of the Hobbesian *Homo economicus*. According to classical economic theory, political decision makers are perfectly rational maximizers of individual self-interest. A wide array of empirical evidence from different fields, however, suggests that people may be more adequately described as fairly rational maximizers of socially balanced utility. They appear to act according to the old scientific intuition of the *zoon politicon* as social animals. They do not appear to behave machinelike, typifying the idea of a model human. Instead they appear to respond to questions about public opinion in a highly context sensitive fashion and may be influenced more by group size than by group membership. Further, they may be induced to support others if need is perceived and successfully communicated.

Further Reading

Andreoni, James. "Cooperation in Public-Goods Experiments: Kindness or Confusion?" *American Economic Review* 85 (1995): 891–904. An experimental investigation of economic self-interest and altruism or warm glow.

Bateson, C. Daniel. "The Altruism Question: Toward a Social-Psychological Answer." Hillsdale, NJ: Lawrence Erlbaum, 1991. A conceptual and experimental study on the psychological factors underlying altruistic behavior.

Feldman, Stanley, and Marco R. Steenbergen. "Beyond Self-Interest, Toward Other-Directedness: Prosocial Orientations and Political Behavior." *Research in Micropolitics* 5 (1996): 61–93. A review of empirical work on prosocial political behavior.

Monroe, Kristen Renwick. *The Heart of Altruism. Perceptions of a Common Humanity*. Princeton, NJ: Princeton University Press, 1996. In-depth interviews with entrepreneurs, philanthropists, heroes, and rescuers of Jews in Nazi Europe.

Piliavin, Jane Allyn, and Hong-Wen Charng. "Altruism: A Review of Recent Theory and Research." *Annual Review of Sociology* 16 (1990): 27–65. A review of sociological studies on altruism.

Sears, David O., and Carolyn L. Funk. "The Role of Self-Interest in Social and Political Attitudes." *Advances in Experimental Psychology* 24 (1991): 1–91. Review of a large number of studies on individual-level political self-interest using public opinion data.

Thomas Craemer

SEM. *See* Structural Equation Modeling

Sensitive Questions

Sensitive questions are survey items that require respondents to give information that may reveal behavior that is illegal, socially frowned upon, or personally embarrassing. Examples include items tapping drug use, extramarital behaviors, or sexual practices. Sensitive questions place a heavy burden on respondents, who could suffer adverse consequences from public exposure of their answers. As a result, they are prone to item nonresponse and inaccuracy.

Nonresponse. While sensitive survey items rarely discourage a potential respondent from taking a survey, they tend to increase item nonresponse. Respondents are more likely to omit answers to sensitive questions than to innocuous ones. Item nonresponse of this sort can be especially troublesome when the sensitive topics themselves are the main purpose of the survey.

A notable example of a sensitive question that yields considerable nonresponse is income. Many survey researchers have been baffled by respondents' willingness to share intimate details about sexually transmitted diseases and sinister illegalities, only to rebuff queries about their income. Recent changes in society, such as the profound increase in credit card offers, have made many people more suspicious of providing financial data to any source, reputable or otherwise.

Inaccuracy. Even when respondents provide answers to sensitive survey topics, the question of data accuracy remains. Assessing the accuracy of any type of survey data is difficult, as answers to most questions cannot be verified through outside means. Nonetheless, research has attempted to measure the degree of accuracy in respondents' answers to sensitive survey items. As one might expect, this research has generally concluded that even when respondents do choose to answer a sensitive survey item, their answers tend to be less accurate than when answering innocuous survey items.

A classic example evidencing this tendency is found when comparing male and female self-reported histories of sexual partners. Among heterosexual persons, males tend to report much larger numbers of sexual partners than do females. Other research approaches have suggested that the numbers are far more similar than the polls suggest.

In most cases, inaccurate data from sensitive survey topics results from perceived social pressures. Respondents sense that others will judge them harshly possibly even sanctioning them if their true opinions or behavior are learned, so they offer more socially acceptable responses. For example, women are chastised for having large numbers of sexual partners, whereas men are glorified for such behavior, so they modify their answers in light of such perceptions.

Methods for Reducing Nonresponse and Inaccuracy. There are a host of methodological strategies designed not only to make the respondent feel more comfortable providing sensitive information, but also to ensure that the information provided is accurate (*see also* **Sensitive Survey Item Administration**). Respondent self-administration using such techniques as **mail surveys** or **Internet survey methods** diminishes the sense of interviewer presence, reducing the likelihood that respondents will provide a response calculated to please the interviewer. Confidentiality assurances at the beginning of a survey can help respondents feel more secure about the security of their responses. **Financial incentives**, such as money or coupons, can often legitimize a survey to respondents, although they rarely encourage people to provide information they otherwise would not feel comfortable sharing. Validation checks within a survey, such as incorporating two items designed to yield identical responses, can help to assess the accuracy of responses. Regardless of which measure is employed, researchers must continue to be wary about the nonresponse and inaccuracies that sensitive survey questions can produce.

Further Reading

Tourangeau, Roger, and Tom W. Smith. "Asking Sensitive Questions: The Impact of Data Collection Mode, Question Format, and Question Context." *Public Opinion Quarterly* 60 (Summer 1996): 275–304. This article supplies an overview of asking sensitive survey questions and how the method of question delivery can impact respondents' answers.

Alex R. Trouteaud

Sensitive Survey Item Administration

Sensitive survey item administration comprises the set of procedures developed by researchers for maximizing quality and minimizing nonresponse to questions of a deeply personal nature. **Sensitive questions** raise concerns in respondents' minds about potential negative consequences, such as embarrassment, disapproval from others, or legal sanctions, which lead some to provide inaccurate responses that cast them in a more favorable light or to refuse to respond altogether. To cope with these problems, survey researchers have developed protocols designed to diminish their impact.

Sensitive Item Protocol. First, survey researchers typically offer explicit assurances to respondents that their answers will remain completely confidential (*see* **Survey Introductions**). When the topic of the survey is sensitive, these assurances have been shown to exert small but reliable effects, slightly reducing nonresponse and improving response quality. When the topic of the survey is mundane, however, extensive assurances of confidentiality can backfire, actually inducing apprehension among respondents and reducing data quality.

Second, sensitive questions are typically asked late in the survey. This provides an opportunity for the interviewer to establish rapport with the respondent and for the respondent to become comfortable with the interview process. The establishment of rapport may improve interviewers' ability to effectively reassure respondents of the confidentiality of their responses, and it may enhance their ability to convey to respondents the legitimacy of the research enterprise and the importance of honest, accurate answers.

Third, sensitive questions are typically placed in the context of other, related questions so that they do not seem to come abruptly out of the blue. Some survey researchers preface particularly sensitive questions with an explicit acknowledgment of the sensitive nature of the question and an emphasis of the importance of the information for the research.

In addition, survey researchers usually try to phrase sensitive questions in ways that "normalize" all responses in an effort to reduce the discomfort of providing socially undesirable answers. For example, to assess voting behavior, the **National Election Studies** postelection surveys pose the following question to respondents:

> In talking to people about elections, we often find that a lot of people were not able to vote because they weren't registered, they were sick, or they just didn't have time. How about you—did you vote in the elections this November?

The aim is to alleviate some of the normative pressure that respondents experience, increasing the likelihood that people who did not participate in the election will feel comfortable saying so.

Finally, a great deal of research on surveying sensitive topics has focused on the mode by which survey data are collected. Perhaps not surprisingly, survey mode does appear to have implications for responses to sensitive questions. At the most basic level, there is fairly clear evidence that the presence or absence of an interviewer has an impact on responses to sensitive questions. People are more likely to report socially undesirable behaviors or express extreme or unpopular opinions in self-administered surveys (e.g., paper-and-pencil questionnaires) than they are to report those same behaviors or opinions to an interviewer (e.g., in a face-to-face or telephone survey). They are also less likely to overreport socially desirable behaviors (e.g., voting, exercising regularly) in self-administered questionnaires than in interviews.

New Developments. Historically, procedures for improving the quality of sensitive survey data have primarily involved efforts to allay respondents' privacy concerns, thereby reducing the barriers to accurate responding. Attention has shifted more recently, though, toward strategies for increasing participants' motivation to provide candid, accurate responses to sensitive questions.

Typically, goals are conceptualized as desired outcomes of which individuals are consciously aware and deliberately strive toward. But recent evidence has suggested that goals can also be activated unconsciously, and that once activated can motivate and direct behavior in the very same ways that consciously activated goals do. For example, John Bargh and his colleagues demonstrated in a series of experiments that simply exposing people to words associated with a particular goal is capable of activating that goal without their awareness and leading them to engage in goal-related behavior.

For example, research participants have been presented with simple language games (e.g., word-search puzzles, sentence unscramble tasks). For some participants, the games contain some neutral words and some words that are associated with the goal of achievement (e.g., strive, achieve, succeed), whereas for other participants all of the words are neutral. Later, when presented with a difficult, ostensibly unrelated language task, participants who have been exposed to the achievement-related words perform substantially better than do participants exposed to neutral words. They have also been shown to persist longer on the task, continuing to work on it even when they have been told to stop and choosing to continue working on it even when invited to switch to an easier and inherently more enjoyable task. Interestingly, follow-up questions with these participants have revealed that they are entirely unaware of the goal-activation manipulation—when asked if they noticed a "theme" in the words that were included in the initial language game, participants invariably say no.

In our own research, we have explored the practical implications of nonconscious goal activation for survey research. Survey researchers have always sought to motivate respondents to provide thoughtful, accurate answers. Typically, these efforts have involved impressing upon respondents the importance of the current survey and the value of their responses to the research enterprise, as well as direct requests for candid, considered answers. In our research, we have explored the possibility that the goal of providing honest, accurate answers can be activated unconsciously, improving data quality.

To do so, we have adapted procedures used in previous laboratory experiments for use in surveys. As in the laboratory studies, the manipulation involves incidental exposure to words associated with the goal of being honest and straightforward. Specifically, in the context of a self-administered questionnaire, we presented undergraduate participants with an initial vocabulary task. Participants were presented with a word, followed by three other words similar in meaning to the first word. They were asked to indicate which of the three words

Figure 1. Average Number of Sensitive Behaviors Reported by Participants in Neutral Versus Honesty Prime Conditions

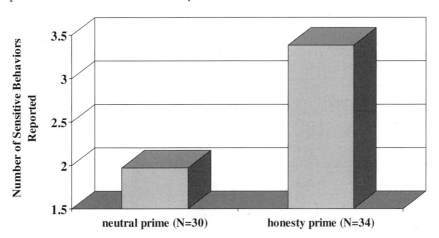

seemed to them most similar to the first word. The instructions assured participants that there were no right or wrong answers—all of the three words would be similar to the first word—and that their task was simply to indicate which of those words seems most similar to them.

In the experimental condition, participants were presented with six target words, four of which were related to the goal of being honest (e.g., honest, genuine). After each word, they were presented with three synonyms of the target word. For example, participants were presented with the word "honest," followed by the words "open," "sincere," and "truthful" and asked which of the latter words was most similar to the first. Participants in a control condition were presented with six target words that were unrelated to the goal of honest responding (e.g., avid, blend, common), along with three synonyms for each word.

After participants completed the vocabulary task they proceeded to the main survey, which included questions about a number of behaviors identified through **pretesting** as sensitive in nature. For example, participants were asked if they had ever drunk so much alcohol that they had difficulty remembering the things they did while intoxicated, if they had ever cheated in their courses, and whether they had ever driven an automobile after drinking two or more alcoholic beverages. Responses to seven sensitive items were combined into a composite index.

The results show that participants who had been exposed to words related to honesty admitted having performed significantly more sensitive behaviors than participants exposed to neutral words (see Figure 1). For example, 57 percent of participants in the neutral condition conceded that they had engaged in "binge drinking" (defined as four or more alcoholic beverages in a single sitting for females, five or more beverages for males), whereas 82 percent of participants in the honesty condition admitted to having done so (see Figure 2). Whereas only 8 percent of participants in the neutral condition said that they had drunk so much alcohol that they had difficulty remembering the things they did while intoxicated, fully 71 percent of participants in the honesty prime condition said they had done so. Remarkably, these differences emerged despite the fact that

Figure 2. Proportion of Participants Reporting Sensitive Behavior by Experimental Condition

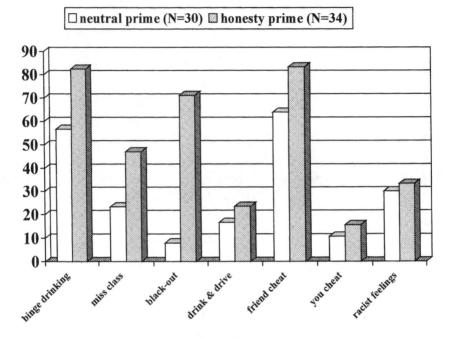

participants had been assured of the confidentiality of their responses and were given an opportunity to complete the self-administered questionnaire in private.

These findings chart a new course for survey researchers concerned about the accuracy of sensitive survey questions. Rather than focusing exclusively on efforts to lower the impediments to honest responding, survey researches should consider techniques for increasing respondents' motivation to provide candid reports. It appears that a very simple and easy to implement priming task can dramatically improve respondents' willingness to accurately report socially undesirable behaviors.

Further Reading

Bargh, J. A., P. M. Gollwitzer, A. Lee-Chai, K. Barndollar, and R. Troetschel. "The Automated Will: Nonconscious Activation and Pursuit of Behavioral Goals." *Journal of Personality and Social Psychology* 81 (2001): 1014–27.

Tourangeau, R., L. Rips, and K. A. Rasinski. *The Psychology of Survey Responding.* Cambridge: Cambridge University Press, 2000.

Penny S. Visser, Kenneth A. Rasinski, and Maria Zagatsky

Simple Random Sampling

Simple random sampling is a sampling procedure that ensures that each person in the population being surveyed has an equal chance at being selected. Because populations tend to be large and resources and time available for studies limited, it is usually not possible to study each elementary unit comprising a population. Simple random sampling is a probabilistic sampling methodology (*see* **cluster sampling, stratified sampling,** and **systematic sampling** for other probabilistic sampling methods) for selecting a representative subset that can be used to make unbiased estimates of the entire population.

The population contains all of the elements or elementary units we are interested in examining. Sampling units refer to nonoverlapping groups of elementary units (sometimes sampling units are the elementary units themselves). The **sample frame** is the entire list of sampling units. For example, suppose a researcher wants to study junior high and high school students in a particular school district to determine their attitudes toward the school district's decision to remove all vending machines in the schools. In this example, the population is the entire group of junior high and high school students. The sample frame could be the list of all homeroom classes (nonoverlapping groups of students), and the elementary units would be the individual students.

Figure 1 presents a diagram of a population of N enumeration units. The proportion of these enumeration units that possess some characteristic, Y, is denoted P, the mean level of some characteristic, X, over all N enumeration units is denoted μ, and the variance of the N values of X is denoted σ^2. Because N may be very large or the time or budget available to carry out the survey very limited, a sample of size n of the original N enumeration units in the population must be selected. To select a simple random sample it is necessary to first construct a sample frame containing the N elementary units. Then, using a random process (e.g., a random number table or a computer), generate n numbers, between 1 and N. These n random numbers identify the n individuals in the sample.

Note that there are $\binom{N}{n}$ possible samples that can be selected from this population [where $\binom{N}{n} = \dfrac{N!}{n!(N-n)!}$ and $a! = a \times (a-1) \times (a-2) \times L \times 1$. For example, if $N = 25$ and a sample of size $n = 5$ is to be selected, there are $\binom{25}{5} = 53{,}130$ possible samples. A simple random sample is formally defined as a sample whereby each of the $\binom{N}{n}$ possible samples has the same probability of being selected and this is equal to $1 \Big/ \binom{N}{n}$. From the n selected enumeration units in the sample, the population proportion, mean and variance may be estimated by p, x, and s^2. If this sample is selected at random from the population, these estimates will be unbiased. That is,

$$\begin{aligned} E(p) &= P \\ E(\overline{x}) &= \mu \\ E(s^2) &= \sigma^2 \end{aligned} \tag{1}$$

Unbiased means that if many random samples (denoted as k samples) were selected from this population, and if p, $\overline{x}$, and s^2 were computed for each of these samples, the average of the k sample proportions would equal the population proportion, P, the average of the k sample means would equal μ and the aver-

Figure 1. Schematic Representation of Population and Sample

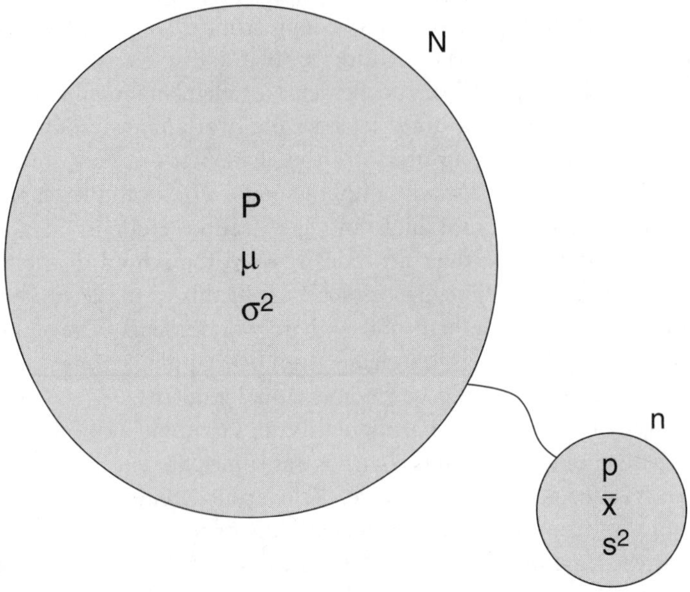

age of the k sample variances would be σ^2. Thus, the concept of unbiasedness relates to repeated sampling and the corresponding averaging process. Unbiasedness is a desirable statistical property since it ensures that the sample values will, on average, provide correct estimates. However, it must be stressed that an estimate computed from any one particular sample may be quite different from the population parameter.

The estimates for a proportion and mean and their standard errors from simple random sampling are computed using the following calculations:

$$p = \frac{\sum_{i=1}^{n} y_i}{n} \qquad \hat{SE}(p) = \sqrt{\frac{N-n}{N}} \sqrt{\frac{p(1-p)}{n-1}} \qquad (2)$$

$$\bar{x} = \frac{\sum_{i=1}^{n} x_i}{n} \qquad \hat{SE}(\bar{x}) = \sqrt{\frac{N-n}{N}} \left(\frac{s}{\sqrt{n}}\right) \qquad (3)$$

In these formulae, x_i is the value of x for subject i, y_i is the value of variable y for subject i (where $y_i = 1$ if present and 0 if absent) and s is the sample standard deviation. The term $(N-n)/N$ is called the *finite population correction factor*. It serves to adjust the standard error as the fraction n/N increases. If a large proportion of the population is contained in the sample, then the finite population correction will be less than 1, which will lead to a smaller standard error. If n is small relative to N, then the finite population correction factor will be close to one. Hence, the usual form of the standard error, $s/\sqrt{n}$, results.

Simple random sampling is easy to conceptualize. Therefore, it provides the probabilistic foundation of much of sampling theory. Furthermore, it provides a baseline to which other methods can be compared. One major disadvantage of simple random sampling is that all N elementary units in the population must be identified and labeled prior to sampling. This process is potentially so expensive and time consuming that it becomes unrealistic to implement in practice. The expense is largely due to the fact that sampled individuals may be highly dispersed, which could make travel costs for an in-person interview prohibitive. Another disadvantage is that certain subgroups in the population may, by chance, be totally overlooked in the sample. Because of these disadvantages, alternatives to simple random sampling are often employed in actual surveys of human populations. The alternative methods may provide more precise estimates (i.e., narrower confidence intervals) for the same cost.

Example. Suppose a Health Maintenance Organization (HMO) is interested in conducting a survey to determine satisfaction among its members. How would the HMO obtain a simple random sample of members? The solution is to take a sample of members directly from the computerized list of members. Many statistical packages have a sampling function that will result in a random sample of size n from the list of N units in the population.

Now, suppose the HMO collects data on 1,000 members (out of 7,500 total) and finds that 750 are satisfied overall with the services it provides. What is the estimated proportion of satisfied members and what is the standard error of this estimate? The solutions is to calculate the point estimate and standard errors as follows:

$$p = \frac{\sum_{i=1}^{n} y_i}{n} = \frac{750}{1,000} = 0.75 \tag{4}$$

$$\hat{S}E(p) = \sqrt{\frac{N-n}{N}} \sqrt{\frac{p(1-p)}{n-1}} = \sqrt{\frac{6,500}{7,500}} \sqrt{\frac{0.75(0.25)}{999}} = 0.013 \tag{5}$$

Further Reading

Levy, Paul S., and Stanley Lemeshow. *Sampling of Populations: Methods and Applications.* New York: John Wiley, 1999. An accessible guide to sampling methods that offers extensive coverage of systematic sampling.

Stanley Lemeshow and Amy Ferketich

Social Capital

Social capital is defined as the features of a social organization, such as networks, norms, and social trust, that facilitate coordination and cooperation for mutual benefit. Thus, social capital is concerned with the connectedness of people, the **social networks** that permit efficient connections, and the norms that tell people how these connections are to be used for the common good or other purposes. On an individual level, social capital may be viewed as a reciprocal relationship between civic engagement and trust. Civic engagement appears to inspire trust and trust tends to increase civic engagement, creating a "virtuous circle" that results in the expansion of social capital. At the social level, high levels of social capital imply high levels of interpersonal trust, coupled wide spread acceptance of norms of reciprocity and cooperativeness. These norms in turn are conceived of as emerging out of social interactions.

Alexis de Tocqueville's *Democracy in America* pointed out the importance of associational life in American democracy. Observing that "Americans form associations for the smallest undertakings," Tocqueville noted that such groups are necessary to the kind of collective action required in a vibrant democracy. In his influential book *Bowling Alone*, Robert Putnam traced a decline in associational life in the United States dating from the 1970s. Associational membership in turn is correlated with political participation, neighborliness, and social trust. Contributing causes to the decline may be the advent of television, which has made communities "wider and shallower," lower real wages, fewer marriages and more divorces, fewer children, suburbanization, and the replacement of community-based shopping with regional and electronic alternatives.

The decline of social capital is seen in a variety of ways: the well documented decline in voter turnout in recent decades; a fall in attendance at public meetings by over a third in the course of twenty years; and a decline in direct participation in community affairs including churches, labor unions, parent-teacher associations, and civic and fraternal organizations. Hence the title of Putnam's book is summary of associational decline: although bowling continues to be a popular sport in the United States, more Americans are bowling alone than in bowling leagues. This trend is significant because solitary bowlers are not learning the norms of trust and reciprocity or creating the networks of friendships that comprise social capital. Presumably, this loss of social capital will result in less cooperation and coordination in solving community problems for public benefit.

The concept of social capital is important because it is believed to affect the public's capacity to cooperate in solving shared problems and to participate in democratic decision making. According to Putnam, social capital predicts certain social goods, including economic development, orderly neighborhoods, responsive government, good schools, and quality of life in general. Thus, the decline of social capital has a deleterious effect on many variables important to public life.

Different types of social capital may be distinguished, each with its own distinct characteristics and implications. First, the distinction between "bonding" and "bridging" associations is an important one. Bridging creates networks across groups, such as race and class, to form more heterogeneous groups. For example, a community fair that results in cooperation across race, class, and neighborhood lines would both build social capital but also contribute to bridging social divides. Bonding activities, on the other hand, link people with others like themselves. An ethnically distinct neighborhood might enjoy a high level of bonding social capital, but have few ties that form bridges to the wider community. While strong bonding capital would allow problems within the boundaries of the neighborhood to be resolved with some ease, the lack of bridging capital would make it more difficult to resolve problems beyond those boundaries. Bonding capital is relatively easy to create because of the homogeneity of the group that forms it; individuals who are alike find bonding to be relatively easy. Bridging capital, while more difficult to form, is essential to societal health in a diverse society. How can bonding and bridging social capital be distinguished? The key is whether networks, norms of reciprocity, mutual aid, and trust extend beyond the boundaries of a specified group.

Second, social capital may be public-regarding or private-regarding. Public-regarding social capital concerns itself with public issues; it is associated with norms that value the public interest. Networks and norms that foster cooperative efforts to improve local schools would be an example of public-regarding social capital. In contrast, private-regarding social capital concerns itself primarily with social relationships. A bowling league is an example of private-regarding social capital. Clearly, many of the same norms and networks characteristic of private-regarding social capital can also be used for the public benefit, suggesting that the positive effects of social capital developed in the private sphere may extend into the public domain.

Third, social capital may exist within formal or informal groups. The cultural context of social capital is important, particularly with respect to how social capital may be measured. Less-developed countries and perhaps low-income neighborhoods will generally have fewer formal organizations and more informal organizations and one-to-one interactions. Thus, a survey of associational memberships in an African village may turn up little evidence of formal networks and thus score low on traditional social capital measures. Measures of informal networks and ties, however, would reveal a rich web of cooperative activity. Therefore, cultural context must be considered when choosing valid indicators of social capital in a given setting.

Fourth, not all social networks are alike in terms of strength. Some networks create deep, rich ties; these are generally forged by multiple contacts within a small group. Thus, a group of volunteers who work together once a week over a period of years would produce strong ties that indicate strong social capital. In contrast, weak ties are created by brief encounters, such as a one-time meeting at the local library to discuss a local matter.

Fifth, multi-stranded ties produce a different quality of social capital than do single-stranded ties. Multi-stranded ties are created by overlapping networks and create strong social capital. For example, if one meets the same person at the ball park, the PTA, the local coffee shop, and the library, the multi-stranded tie that develops permits problem solving and collective decision making across several networks within a community. In other words, multi-stranded ties make bridging social capital possible. Single-stranded ties, however, are limited to one network and may be more likely to produce bonding.

Two kinds of metrics are used to assess the level of social capital: measures of associational networks and measures of norms, such as trust and reciprocity that underlie the concept of social capital. Measurement concepts associated with the presence of networks include the number of associational memberships, the heterogeneity and range of activities, association density, newspaper readership, electoral turnout and other kinds of political participation, voluntary and charitable work, entertaining friends and relatives, and civic leadership. Measurement concepts for measuring norms relating to social capital include trust, public spiritedness, and solidarity. As an interesting aside, note that support groups (e.g.,

Alcoholics Anonymous) are not evidence of social capital, according to Putnam, as they fail to engage members in projects to promote the public good and are self-regarding as opposed to public-regarding organizations.

Social capital is generally measured by using survey data that measure norms of social trust and reciprocity and associational ties that indicate the presence of social networks. What is measured matters in terms of whether one sees social capital as declining or simply shifting into new forms. Some researchers suggest that civic activity may have simply shifted to forms that are less easily tracked using Putnam's methods. For instance, people may be less likely to join PTAs and the League of Women Voters but more likely to be active in a child's soccer league. Thus if participation in formal organizations but not informal organizations is studied, an incomplete picture of social capital decline can be formed.

Survey instruments commonly used include the **National Election Studies** (measures trust and civic engagement), the **General Social Survey** (measures membership in civic and political organizations, trust, confidence in government, frequency of spending the evening with friends, spending the evening with neighbors, spending the evening with relatives), and the DDB Life Style Survey (measures frequency of entertaining, volunteering, family activities, etc.). The Kennedy School of Government at Harvard University has also developed the Social Capital Community Benchmark Survey (SCCBS) specifically to measure social capital. The survey measures nine dimensions of social capital, including social trust, inter-racial trust, electoral political participation, other forms of political participation, civic leadership, associational involvement, giving and volunteering, faith-based engagement, and informal social ties.

Critics of social capital point to a variety of problems with the conception of social capital, how it is measured, and its predictive value. One criticism is that the definition of social capital presents a basic conceptual problem because it is a teleological argument from design. Thus Putnam designs his definition of social capital and then infers its existence using elements of social capital as proof. It has proven to be difficult to distinguish what is an indicator of social capital and what is social capital.

In addition, it has been difficult to separate the concept of social capital from its effects. Does social capital cause trust, or is trust an element of social capital? Is voting an indicator or an outcome of social capital? It is important to operationally define social capital and say precisely what it predicts.

A second criticism of the current research on social capital relates to the choice of the unit of analysis. Social capital is more likely to thrive in small settings—neighborhoods and smaller communities—that are characterized by face-to-face interactions on a regular basis. Thus, the group level or the small community level is the appropriate unit of analysis for most purposes. Generalizing from individual level data to the community, state, or national level presents certain methodological difficulties. For example, Putnam created a state-level social capital index based on national survey data from a representative sample of individual responses. Consider the problem of generalizing individual responses within in a single community where social capital is unevenly distributed. The existence of social capital might be very great within churches, for instance, but poor in the civic arena. Therefore, civic cooperation might be absent, while social cooperation within the boundaries of any individual religious institution might be very great. In this case, it would be impossible to say that the locality as a whole possesses high social capital, despite what the aggregation of individual survey data might suggest. As the ecological fallacy would suggest, measurements of social capital that involve individual surveys do not allow one to make generalizations on other levels absent a way of addressing this problem methodologically (*see* **Ecological Inference**).

Another area of concern is the cultural specificity of much of the survey research done to date. It is unlikely that the same measures of social capital are valid across all cultures because the norms and the various kinds of social networks that form the basis of social capital are dependent on cultural context. Therefore, variables affecting social capital and the indicators used to measure them probably vary across cultures as well.

Theda Skocpol has offered two main critiques of the social capital research. First, she takes issue with Putnam's failure to address the extent to which state-level social capital is tied to economic inequality. In theory, access to resources should correlate with an individual's ability to contribute to his or her community. Those with limited financial and personal resources may be much less likely to contribute to social capital in their community. Second, she points out that social capital is not measured consistently throughout Putnam's work. She argues that Putnam's failure to include church membership and participation in his state-level social capital index ignores a kind of social capital that has traditionally been very strong in the United States. She notes that this type of participation has been on the rise, especially in the Southern United States.

Everett Carll Ladd argues that social capital has not declined at all but rather Putnam's measurements do not reveal the full sweep of associational membership in the United States. His work questions the types of measurement used in the social capital debate. He contends that the United States is not experiencing a decline in social capital at all, but only a "churning," that is, people continue to join associations in great numbers, but they are not the traditional organizations that Putnam measures. To use Ladd's example, memberships in traditionally strong associations such as the Elks or Masons are declining, but membership in other associations, such as the Sierra Club, are increasing. If one understands associations to exist in a "group marketplace," then it stands to reason that groups competing for membership will experience shifts in membership as groups constantly strive to redefine themselves to accommodate the changing needs of their members. Ladd also suggests that high levels of individual volunteerism and Americans' consistently strong sense of trust in the future are indicators that social capital is not declining, but shifting to new venues. As a result, researchers must constantly reassess how to best measure levels of social capital under changing conditions.

Robert Wuthnow's critique points out that Putnam's perceived decline in social capital is not without qualifications. If one is to assume that social capital in the United States is on the decline, Wuthnow argues that the decline should be put into comparative context. He points out that the United States has traditionally enjoyed much higher levels of social capital than other Western nations. Therefore, if the United States has experienced a decline, it is still the case that its degree of state-level social capital remains strong relative to that of other nations. Wuthnow joins with Skocpol in suggesting further research in the area of economic inequality. He argues that social capital as commonly measured shows a greater decline among the marginalized. Commonly used measurements do not account for the unique ways in which the marginalized may become involved in their communities, particularly through informal interactions.

Further Reading

Brehm, John, and Wendy Rahn. "Individual Level Evidence for the Causes and Consequences of Social Capital." *American Journal of Political Science* 41 (July 1997): 999–1023. Uses secondary analysis of General Social Survey data from 1972 to 1994 to define the relationship between civic engagement and interpersonal trust.

Krishna, Anirudh. *Active Social Capital: Tracing the Roots of Development and Democracy*. New York: Columbia University Press, 2002. See especially chapter 4 on measuring social capital, which is helpful in identifying concepts and empirical measures of social capital.

Ladd, Everett Carll. *The Ladd Report*. New York: Free Press, 1999. An argument, with copious evidence, against Putnam's thesis of social capital decline.

Paxton, Pamela. "Is Social Capital Declining in the US?" *American Journal of Sociology* 105 (1999): 88–127. A theoretical model of social capital.

Putnam, Robert D. *Bowling Alone: The Collapse and Revival of American Community*. New York: Simon and Schuster, 2000. Putnam's famous treatment of the decline in social capital.

Web Sites

Robert Putnam's Web site about *Bowling Alone* is available at http://www.bowling alone.org; it contains data sets, survey questions, and links to related sites as well as material about Putnam's book. It also contains links to the DDB data referred to above.

The Social Capital Community Benchmark Survey can be found at http://www. ksg.harvard.edu/saguaro/primer.htm. This Web site includes a primer on social capital, including definitions, measurement tools, research links, and a bibliography.

Elizabeth Theiss Smith and Jeremy Zell

Social Distance

Social distance refers to the preferred level of contact, interaction, and intimacy between people or among groups of people. In practice, social distance has two related meanings. Conceptually, it represents the desire for closeness as opposed to distance, which stands for the nature of relations among members of groups, the representation of social status and hierarchy, and the nature of relations among different social groups. Empirically, it refers to a class of measurement tools that can compare individuals to each other, array groups in terms of status and likeability, and map out the presumed friendliness and pleasantness of interaction among different social groups. Social distance is also an operationalization of social intimacy—the more intimate the relations, the lower the level of social distance. It has been an especially helpful construct in public opinion research by focusing attention on social intimacy and social relationships more generally as the primary indicators of prejudice and intergroup relations.

The conception of social distance is usually identified in the social sciences with Emory Bogardus's work from the 1920s. Indeed, social distance is the oldest commonly used measure of social attitudes in all of social science. By the early 1950s, Donald Campbell could write that the social distance scale "is probably the most used single test of social attitudes with a popularity that shows no signs of waning." Social distance measures did in fact not wan. They remain in frequent use today, as illustrated by recent searches of Sociological Abstracts and "PsycInfo" illustrate. From 1993 to 2002, "social distance" averaged more than 34 listings a year in abstracts compiled in Sociological Abstracts (a total of 342 articles), and it averaged more than 27 times a year in abstracts compiled in PsycInfo (a total of 263 articles).

The first significant use of social distance measures was to measure American attitudes and prejudice toward immigrants. Social distance measures form the quantitative background of Bogardus's seminal *Immigration and Race Attitudes.* One of the first empirical studies of prejudice and discrimination, it pointed out the fundamental importance of perceived similarity in liking and social acceptance. This original social distance scale has been adapted into many forms and versions, which are largely interchangeable, although the different content and wording of the items prohibits direct comparison among the scales. Still, the majority of research in social distance uses measures that are very similar to the original Bogardus scale, first published in 1925.

Social distance focuses on the personal and interpersonal in relations among groups. As such, it elevates face-to-face interaction, friendship, marriage, and so on as the primary dependent variable of researchers' interest in studying intergroup relations, prejudice, and stigma. This conception makes sense, as it is certainly a main component of prejudice and intergroup attitudes. At the same time, it tends to downplay the economic, political, historical, and other dimensions of intergroup relations that affect employment, housing, immigration, marriage, and so forth.

The original conception of social distance is that it reflects cultural rules about social hierarchy. Bogardus was less interested in individual differences in social distance as a reflection of prejudice levels than he was about uncovering which groups were rejected, and the social context that created that rejection. Research has shown that different groups agree on the relative preferred social distance among various target groups. Even minority groups and low status groups tend to create social distance preferences that mimic the preferences of dominant groups in a society (with the typical exception of their own group). These findings are consistent with the notion that prejudice is embedded in social groups, social history, and cultural values—an approach that is in the mainstream of not only sociology and anthropology but also the more individualistic social psychology.

Social and personality psychologists have also treated social distance as a dependent variable worthy of explanation. The scales can be treated as individual difference variables, and there is a large literature on the correlation of social distance scores with, for example, authoritarianism, education, attachment and parenting, and political conservatism. The personal and attitudinal variables that predict prejudice and discrimination also predict higher levels of preferred social distance.

As noted previously, the first, and perhaps still best, measure of social distance is the Bogardus scale, which is reproduced here in its entirety:

According to my first feeling reactions, I would willingly admit members of each race (as a class, and not the best I have known nor the worst members) to one or more of the classifications under which I have placed a cross:

1. To close kinship by marriage.
2. To my club as personal chums.
3. To my street as neighbors.
4. To employment in my occupation.
5. To citizenship in my country.
6. As visitors only to my country.
7. Would exclude from my country.

These seven items were listed across the top of the page in columns, followed by rows for rating a large number of ethnic and nationality groups.

The social distance scale was originally designed as a unidimensional scale, with each level of increasing intimacy entailing all of the lesser intimacies. Bogardus and later Triandis and Triandis developed other scales based on a much longer list of items, using the psychophysical method of equal appearing intervals. However, these "improvements" have since been largely discarded.

One of the strongest components of the measurement strategy of the social distance scale is its ability to be applied to an infinite number of groups or people. Because the scale makes no particular reference to social groups, and does not rely on specific issues, stereotypes, concerns, or areas of conflict, the same items can be used almost universally. Social distance measures have been used to study social acceptance and rejection in race, gender, religion, social class, occupation, sexual orientation, the stigma of mental illness and physical illnesses, intergroup relations, deviance and delinquency, among many others. It has been used on all of the populated continents and in dozens of languages. It has been administered as a written test to literate and educated groups (e.g., American college students), and in face-to-face interviews with nonliterate rural societies (e.g., East African tribal groups) with equal methodological success.

One of the problems with measures of racial attitudes in particular, and attitude scales in general, is that the items go out of date. Racial attitudes often revolve around current social issues, and so employment and affirmative action in education may be useful items now—in the way that housing, busing, and desegregation were 20 years ago, and immigration and religious freedom were more than 100 years ago. But the meaning of these items cannot persist across time or cultures; the issues of social intimacy are likely to continue long into the future as a central concern in intergroup attitudes.

As a result, measures of social distance are simply the best available way of comparing disparate groups on the same variables. To compare the relative social status of, say, black Americans and fat Americans, one may not compare scores on the Modern Racism scale to the Anti-Fat Attitudes scale, but one may compare relative scores on social distance measures. Because the items tend to measure social relations that are likely to persist, social distance measures also can compare across time periods with some reliability.

The most important value of the concept of social distance is that it lends itself to a very good measurement strategy. This typically is instantiated as a social distance scale that measures the willingness to interact with a hypothetical member of a social group. However, the scale does not compare the measurement of *professed willingness to interact* with people and *actual contact and intimacy*. People's actual daily interaction patterns are very unlikely to map perfectly onto social distance scores, because of their work and housing patterns, familial contacts, and so on. Social distance remains an attitude-like measure, which does not take into account structural variables, such as segregation, density of minority group members, and peer approval. Social distance is often conceived as a behavioral marker of an attitude, and the hope is that social distance measures represent the readiness to interact, if not the actual frequency and course of intergroup interaction. People may indicate willingness without actual interaction or experience, in large part because they often have little easy opportunity to interact with a large number of groups in their everyday lives.

The major finding from research in social distance is that similarity is the key dimension to social distance, whether in terms of language, skin color, religion, social class, values, or interests. The groups lowest in social distance (i.e., closest to one) are people who are most like the raters—for white middle-class Americans this typically means Canadians or British. The presence of differences in, for example, social class, race, religion, and employment (presumed or real) increase desired levels of social distance.

The original Bogardus conception of social distance defines it as a component of culture and society, not characteristic of individuals. The overall levels of social distance uncovered in research was thought to represent the cultural values and social hierarchies of the group studied. Nothing in the measurement, however, implies this conception; social distance scores can be interpreted as individual differences, social norms, or evidence of cultural organization. In practice, research has looked both at cultural values and individual differences. Still, to properly test *cultural* hypotheses, one must not only look at the overall levels of social distance, which describe the average value of a group across a sample, but also look at agreement rates within populations (that is, they should look at standard deviations as well as mean differences). Low levels of variability around the mean indicate higher levels of cultural agreement about preferred levels of social distance.

Overall, measures of social distance are among the most important tools in the study of intergroup attitudes and prejudice. Their history is now eighty years old, and their continued use is virtually assured. No other method of intergroup attitude is so well designed to measure across groups, across individuals, across categories, and across time as social distance measures. They are conceptually and empirically healthy and likely to be used as an important tool for the foreseeable future.

Further Reading

Biernat, M., and C. S. Crandall. "Racial Attitudes." In *Measures of Political Attitudes*, 2nd ed., edited by J. Robinson, P. Shaver, and L. Wrightsman. New York: Academic Press, 1999.

Bogardus, E. S. *Immigration and Race Attitudes*. Boston: D. S. Heath, 1928.

———. "Measuring Social Distances." *Journal of Applied Sociology* 9 (1925): 299–308.

Campbell, D. T. "The Bogardus Social Distance Scale." *Sociology and Social Research* 37 (1953): 323–26.

Crandall, C. S., A. Eshleman, and L. T. O'Brien. "Social Norms and the Expression and Suppression of Prejudice: The Struggle for Internalization." *Journal of Personality and Social Psychology* 82 (2002): 359–78.

Triandis, H. C., and L. M. Triandis. "Race, Social Class, Religion and Nationality as Determinants of Social Distance." *Journal of Abnormal and Social Psychology* 61 (1960): 110–18.

Christian S. Crandall and Ruth Warner

Social Networks

Social network theories of public opinion are predicated on the assertion that individual opinions take on meaning in the context of the communication and persuasion processes that occur among citizens. In this view, political opinions—the opinions concerning politics that are held by individual citizens—do not arise as the necessary, inevitable, or automatic consequence of individual characteristics, national crises, or even news media coverage. Rather, public opinion must be informed, and much of the information that produces public opinion is communicated through systematic processes of communication and persuasion that occur within complex networks of social communication occurring among interdependent citizens.

Some of the earliest and most influential treatments of public opinion (e.g., the 1954 classic *Voting*) addressed the issue of social interdependence relative to the communication and persuasion that occur among and between citizens. At the same time, these early lessons are easily and frequently forgotten, particularly in the face of the dominant data collection technologies used to measure public opinion. Telephone surveys, in-person interviews, **Internet surveys methods**, and **mail surveys** produce information on individuals. Creative designs used in the **sampling process** make it possible to aggregate individual survey responses at the level of meaningful geographic units, thereby producing measures of central tendency and dispersion for opinions that are geographically organized. But neither the individual measures nor their associated aggregate versions address the problem of communication and persuasion among the individuals who make up the aggregates. In short, typically conducted surveys of individuals are, by their very nature, poorly equipped to address problems and processes that are driven by individual interdependence.

What difference does this make? Ignoring individual interdependence creates the potential for fundamental misspecifications of the individual and aggregate factors that underlie public opinion. Networks of social communication carry the potential to create individual likelihoods of holding particular opinions that vary across units of aggregation, even when individual level characteristics are taken into account; ignoring these networks runs the risk of creating ecological fallacies in the analysis of aggregate opinion distributions. The corollary individualistic fallacy is just as important: treating individually interdependent opinion holders as if they were independent runs the risk of mistakenly specifying the relationships between individual characteristics and individual opinions.

How are individual interdependence, social interaction, and political networks measured within the context of public opinion research? A long tradition of political research has focused on individuals within the context of particular aggregate settings. The early studies of Paul Lazarsfeld and his colleagues focused attention on political campaigns as they unfolded within Elmira and Erie County, New York, not only as a matter of convenience, but also as a way to isolate and identify the community structures that produced patterns of interdependence among citizens. These studies gave rise to a tradition of contextual research, a tradition in which individual opinion was considered not only as a consequence of individual characteristics and predispositions but also as a consequence of the social context. The social context, in turn, was defined in terms of population composition, and the implicitly or explicitly defined mechanism of influence was typically some form of social interaction. For example, if an individual was located within a community full of Democrats, it was assumed that the individual was more likely to interact with Democrats and be exposed to Democratic viewpoints and opinions. In short, to the extent that the social network was conceived as the mechanism of influence, the network was typically treated as an unmeasured and unspecified intermediating variable.

Subsequent efforts measured the properties of networks directly by employing egocentric name generators. The particular form and wording of these name generators vary across different efforts, but a respondent to a survey might typically be asked to identify the first names of the people with whom she discussed the events of the past election campaign. After identifying some number of names, the interviewer asks the respondent a battery of questions about each of the identified discussant: the nature of the relationship between the respondent and the discussant, the frequency with which the respondent interacts with each discussant, the frequency with which they discuss politics, the relationships among the discussants, the respondents' perceptions regarding the discussants' opinions and viewpoints, as well as the respondents' perceptions regarding the frequency of disagreement with each of the discussants.

In some studies, a snowball component is added to the sampling design in which interviews are conducted with the discussion partners who have been identified by the main respondents to the initial survey. These second-stage (or snowball) surveys are useful for several purposes. First, they provide verification for the main respondents' judgments regarding discussant preferences—the extent to which the main respondents are able to identify the discussants' preferences accurately. In general, the main respondents are quite accurate, but systematic biases regularly appear in the main respondents' judgments. Most importantly, main respondents are better able to recognize preferences accurately if they share the preferences. One explanation for this false consensus bias is cognitive dissonance: people find disagreement to be disturbing, and they misinterpret the messages sent by the discussant. Another explanation is conflict avoidance: individuals avoid conflictive conversations, thereby obscuring the communication of disagreement.

Neither of these explanations is entirely satisfying for several reasons. First, main respondents are also less likely to perceive a discussant's viewpoints accurately if they believe that other individuals in the network do not hold the discussant's self-reported preference. Hence, it would appear that, in making a judgment about another individual's preference, individuals may be generalizing on the basis of their own immediate circumstances. For example, if the main respondent is voting Democratic, and she believes that all her other associates are voting Democratic, she may miss the fact that one of them is actually voting Republican. In this context, it is important for political scientists to remember that relatively few citizens wear their preferences as lapel pins; hence, preferences are frequently ambiguous, even in networks explicitly identified to be political.

Moreover, while the accuracy of respondent perceptions is compromised by disagreement, either between the respondent and the discussant or the particular discussant and the more generalized network, these same forms of disagreement do not compromise the confidence of the respondent either in his perceptions of the discussant's preferences or in the accessibility of these perceptions, measured in terms of response latencies (response times). In short, there is little evidence in the research literature to suggest that individuals are uncomfortable or unwilling in their capacity to acknowledge the existence of disagreement.

In short, snowball surveys of the main respondents' self-identified political networks provide laboratories for the investigation of political persuasion and communication processes among and between citizens. For example, based on the two-stage interviews, it becomes clear that discussants with stronger opinions are more likely to have their preferences recognized accurately by the main respondents. Other analyses show that discussants are more influential if their preferences are widely shared within the larger networks. In other words, an individual who communicates a widely shared preference is both more likely to be correctly understood and more likely to be influential. In this way, the realization of influence and persuasion within dyads is itself autoregressive, depending on the distribution of opinion within the larger network of which the dyad is only one part.

In addition to providing descriptively adequate characterizations regarding the distribution of public opinion, as well as a laboratory for studying communication and influence among interdependent individuals, what insights do social networks offer with respect to the study of public opinion? First, social networks provide a very direct and appropriate means to incorporate **social capital** within the study of public opinion. A primary benefit that derives from social capital relates to the information that people access through networks of social relationships. These informational benefits are directly related to public opinion because citizens are able to rely on one another for information and guidance in politics. Absent social networks, individuals would be forced to bear the acquisition and processing costs of political information on their own. In this way, the social capital that is accessed through networks of communication produces important efficiencies in the creation of informed public opinion.

Second, ignoring the informational potential of socially communicated information has contributed to an underestimation in the knowledge, information, and sophistication that underlie public opinion—in terms of both individual and aggregate opinion holding. The inescapable fact is that individuals often perform quite poorly in providing adequate responses to survey questions regarding basic political knowledge, in providing well thought out rationales for their preferences and opinions, and even in providing thoughtful and stable responses to questions that solicit their opinions. At the same time, individuals report more frequent political discussion with other individuals whom they believe know more about politics. Just as important, the descriptive adequacy of their judgments regarding the political expertise of others is well documented and verified. Hence, political interdependence among citizens helps to explain why public opinion in the aggregate is more sophisticated than the opinions held by the average citizen. Quite simply, the aggregate level of expertise within interdependent democratic electorates is greater than the mean expertise level among citizens considered individually.

Third, identifying networks of political communication provides the opportunity to assess the heterogeneity of preferences surrounding individual citizens. A long-standing assumption of public opinion and communications research is that individuals tend to be located in politically homogeneous surroundings, thereby rendering the experience of political disagreement as a rare event. More recent analyses call this assumption into question—a minority of Bush and Gore voters in the 2000 National Election Study reported that the majority of their discussants supported their own preferred candidate. This is not to say that political influence is absent within these communication networks, but rather that patterns of both agreement and disagreement must be understood within the context of complex networks of communication.

Fourth, political heterogeneity is more likely to persist within larger, more extensive communication networks. Network size, in turn, is predicted by some of the same factors that predict political involvement and engagement. Individuals with higher levels of education and more extensive organizational involvements are more likely to be located in larger communication networks. Hence, the same individuals who are able to draw on larger reserves of social capital are also more likely to be politically active and engaged; they are also more likely to experience a more diverse mixture of political opinions and viewpoints within their networks of political communication. While there is nothing here to suggest that political disagreement and the experience of political diversity produce higher levels of political activation, these patterns of relationships would seem to call into question the politically disabling consequences that are frequently imputed to the experience of political disagreement. At the very least, the consequences of political heterogeneity within communication networks is worthy of further examination.

In summary, social networks provide an opportunity for political scientists to rediscover one part of the group basis of politics—to rethink and reconceptualize the role of groups in mass politics and public opinion. At the end of World War II, when survey research and the empirical study of public opinion were in their infancies, nominal membership in many groups carried enormous political meaning. To say that a voter was an Italian American, or a Polish American, or a German American, or a white southerner, or a union member indicated a great deal about the voter's politics. The political meaning attached to many of these groups has disappeared or been transformed, while other new groups (e.g., Christian fundamentalists) have emerged. Why? What did it mean to say that Polish Americans tended to be Democrats, and why is this no longer the case?

The meaning of group membership has always been anchored in patterns of association and interaction—in the networks within which individuals are embedded. To say that a group is no longer politically meaningful is really to say that a nominal group no longer serves to define and demarcate patterns of social interaction and communication, because it is through these networks that communication and persuasion occurs. In this way, studying public opinion within the context of communication networks creates an opportunity to reintroduce the importance of groups to political analysis, where the groups are defined on the idiosyncratic basis of individual reports.

Further Reading

Achen, Christopher H., and W. Phillips Shively. *Cross Level Inference.* Chicago: University of Chicago Press, 1995.

Berelson, Bernard R., Paul F. Lazarsfeld, and William N. McPhee. *Voting.* Chicago: University of Chicago Press, 1954.

Coleman, James S. "Social Capital in the Creation of Human Capital." *American Journal of Sociology* 94 (1988): S95–S120.

Huckfeldt, Robert, Paul Johnson, and John Sprague. *Political Disagreement.* New York: Cambridge University Press, 2004.

Huckfeldt, Robert, and John Sprague. *Citizens, Politics, and Social Communication.* New York: Cambridge University Press, 1995.

King, Gary. *A Solution to the Ecological Inference Problem.* Princeton, NJ: Princeton University Press, 1997.

Knoke, David. *Political Networks: The Structural Perspective.* New York: Cambridge University Press, 1990.

Wasserman, Stanley, and Katherine Faust, eds. *Social Network Analysis.* New York: Cambridge University Press, 1994.

Web Sites

A number of different studies that incorporate data on public opinion and social networks are available via the Web. One of these data sets—the 2000 National Election Study—is available at Web site of the **National Election Studies**, available at http://www.umich.edu/~nes. To see the network battery, first click on Questions Asked in Network Surveys, then click on the 2000 study, and then search on v001699. Three other studies are available through the Interuniversity Consortium for Political and Social Research (http://www.icpsr.umich.edu) the 1984 South Bend Study (study no. 6522), the 1992 American survey that was part of the Cross-National Election Project (study no. 6541), and the 1996 Indianapolis-St. Louis Study (study no. 2962).

Robert Huckfeldt

Socialization

Political socialization can be defined as the process by which citizens acquire political values, beliefs, and attitudes. Put another way, it is the transmission of political information from one generation to the next by a variety of agents. Commonly noted agents of socialization include family, schools, peers, the media, and religious institutions.

While most research on political socialization has been focused on early childhood development and adolescence, it is important to note that the socialization process continues into adulthood. Changing jobs, moving to a new part of the world, the country, the state, or even a new neighborhood can all lead to political learning for an adult. It helps to think about socialization as a process that does not necessarily involve indoctrination. Explaining the variety of ways in which political learning takes place requires a broad conceptualization of the phenomenon.

Researchers differentiate between four concepts that are often confused or conflated: political learning, political socialization, political education, and civic education. "Political learning" is a broad concept that refers to any transmission of political information, whether intentional or unintentional, and whether or not it promotes support for the existing political system. Learning happens all the time. Imagine that a toddler is riding in the back of the car with her uncle, who is driving faster than the speed limit. As the car rounds a bend, the driver spots a police officer in a car at the side of the road. The dad verbally indicates that he hopes that the officer does not pull him over. When he sees through his rear-view mirror that the police car is not pulling away from the curb, he expresses his pleasure of not getting caught speeding. Certainly there was no intent to transmit any political information in this scenario, neither was this message particularly supportive or hostile toward the existing political structure. Nonetheless, the toddler was involved in learning about ways to perceive authority figures. In this case, the message might be interpreted as breaking the rules is okay, so long as one does not get caught.

"Political socialization" in the most narrow sense refers to the transmission of only that information that promotes support for the existing political system. This transmission does not have to be intentional. For instance, a parent may be in the habit of watching prime-time presidential addresses when they are aired on television. Assuming that there is no commentary by the parent, the very act of prioritizing one's schedule to pay attention to the president sends a message to children that the president is important. This tacitly supports the existing political structure by acknowledging the relevance of its chief executive. As in the example above, this transmission of knowledge is not intentional. The learning would fit the description of civic education (below) if the parent decided to call the children around the television set to encourage them to watch. In that case, there is an intentional transmission of information that is supportive of the existing political structure.

"Political education" is most accurately used to indicate intentional political learning, irrespective of content (that is, whether or not it promotes support for the existing political structure or regime). The same parent mentioned above might use that television experience to provide an opportunity to talk with his or her children about the inequalities and power differential that exist in a capitalist economic system. Or, a teacher might bring a video recording of the speech to class the next day to make similar points. These would be examples of political education. Alternately, the parent or teacher could actively engage the children or students in a supportive learning environment, pointing out, for example, constitutional provisions that allow the president to have the power to do what is being proposed in the televised address. These are all examples of political education because there is intentional dissemination of knowledge and/or attitudes.

Finally, "civic education" is the direct transmission of information that not only serves (as political socialization might) but is specifically designed to support the existing political system or regime. In authoritarian regimes, this type of learning is clearly identified by the requirement of children and adults to salute, pledge, pay homage to, or otherwise indicate respect and support for the nation, a regime, or its rulers. It is also an example of civic education, though, when children in a democratic state are required to recite the Pledge of Allegiance in public schools or when the Boy Scouts of America distribute pocket-sized versions of the U.S. Constitution. It is also a type of civic education when adults are expected (and socially pressured, if not officially required) to stand during the playing of a national anthem before a public event. The transmission of the message is intentional, and it is supportive of the existing political structure.

Supporting an existing political structure does not necessarily mean lending support to specific leaders or political parties. One's political socialization has a lot to do with the way he or she perceives (and, consequently, supports) a given governmental system, a political party or interest, or individual rulers. David Easton wrote at length about the notion of "diffuse support" for existing political structures, as differentiated from specific support for the policy outputs or actions of the people who inhabit offices in that structure. In other words, it is possible to be supportive of republican democracy, of capitalism, of the United States, or even of the U.S. Congress, without liking the policies that the Congress has adopted and passed. There may be a historical component to this line of thinking (for instance, one could like what the Congress did under control of the Democrats, yet dislike what the Republicans have done), but there does not need to be. In the abstract, it is entirely possible to support the existence of Congress as an institution but believe that it has never done anything useful or "good." If a person with these beliefs attributes the failures to the members of Congress, as opposed to the institution, he or she is exhibiting diffuse support for the institution absent and apart from specific support (*see* **Congressional Approval**).

Some scholars have argued that it is improper to discuss diffuse support for a particular institution (such as Congress, the presidency, or the military), as opposed to the system as a whole. Easton was writing mainly about governmental systems, but in the contemporary political world—especially in the United States—many individuals are scarcely aware that they might choose some governmental system other than their own. That is, many simply accept the inevitability of the political structure under which they live. To the extent that is true (and it is by no means universal), it is useful to conceptualize diffuse support to include narrower levels of confidence in political institutions within those existing structures.

While we would all like to think that we come to hold such attitudes by weighing information from multiple perspectives and coming to a rational decision, the reality is much more complicated. Information that comes to us is processed in a variety of ways. Cognitive psychologists write about schemas that we use to store and organize information. Each person's life experiences and socialization impacts the way he or she filters information. When the information is retrieved (for instance, when someone is asked his or her attitude on a survey), certain schemata may be activated while others are not. This process greatly affects attitude formation, persistence and behavior. By understanding a person's political socialization, we can understand (and possibly predict) attitudes and behaviors.

Socialization research took off in political science during the 1950s and 1960s. As scholars from a number of fields scrambled to explain how the Nazi regime in Germany was able to effectively convince so many people to comply with policies that would lead to genocide, political learning came to the forefront of many research agendas. While this specific question led to a variety of important studies of political learning in the 1980s, it was early work by Stanley Milgram and Herbert Hyman that was responsible for bridging the gap between psychology and political science. The idea of studying the transmission of political ideas was more broadly embraced by scholars such as Fred Greenstein.

Greenstein conducted studies of fourth through eighth grade children in New Haven, Connecticut, in 1958. He wanted to know how children felt about political authority, how their orientations developed, and how this differed on a range of socioeconomic indicators. In the most comprehensive analysis of this project, he found that "children's views of political leaders are substantially more favorable than those of their elders." This idea came to be referred to as the "benevolent leader" hypothesis.

Milgram is perhaps most famous for his work on obedience to authority. Working from his offices at Yale University in the 1960s, Milgram summoned several men and women individually to his laboratory for what they thought was an experiment about teaching and learning. The experiment was fixed so that the respondent was always designated as the "teacher," and the research assistant was always the "learner." The learner was taken to a back room and strapped to a machine that was ostensibly capable of administering electric shock to the learner. In fact, no shocks were being administered, but the teacher was misled until the experiment was complete. The teacher read a series of pairs of words, and then asked the learner to respond with the match when the first word in the pair was read a second time. If the learner was correct, the teacher would indicate that with a verbal response of positive reinforcement ("That's good."). If the learner was incorrect, the teacher would administer an electric shock from the board, increasing the voltage with each incorrect answer. At certain points in the experiment, the learner would yell out in pain, claim that he had a heart condition, and demand to be let out of the room. Teachers' responses ranged from refusal to continue, to reluctance, to obedience. The researcher in the room consistently urged that the teacher "must continue" and that "the experiment requires" the teacher to continue. Some refused, but the majority (about 60 percent) administered (what they believed to be) shocks of high voltages long after the learner stopped protesting.

While this was not an experiment about learning in the way the subjects originally understood, it was very much an experiment about how political learning happens in a society. The subjects who were willing to continue to administer high voltage shocks did so because an authority figure—the researcher—was encouraging them to follow the directions, and promised to take responsibility for the consequences. That combination led what we would presume to be otherwise compassionate people to act cruelly toward a total stranger. The learning that occurred was that which the so-called teacher in the experiment got through his or her socialization. This is a powerful reminder that the convenient finger-pointing of individuals who commit atrocities throughout history is an insufficient explanation to the behavior. The complexities of political socialization (and political learning broadly) are, at least arguably, at the root of compliance with human rights abuses, as well as more benign political behavior (such as voting behavior).

Research on political socialization has tapered off considerably since the 1970s. This is largely because of findings suggesting that learning does, indeed, continue into adulthood. With the increase in quantity of media, the opportunities for changes to early socialization become greater, so studying that process becomes less important for predicting adult attitudes and behaviors. Still, it has been argued that early and adolescent socialization are still quite important predictors of adult attitudes on issues that are less visible (such as support for the U.S. Supreme Court). Socialization in adulthood also continues to be a topic of discussion among social scientists. Further, as suggested above, the inquiries into this process occur in many cultural contexts. Much of the early work was done by American social scientists, but we can only understand how political socialization works if we understand it more universally.

Further Reading

Dennis, Jack, ed. *Socialization to Politics: A Reader*. New York: John Wiley, 1973.
Easton, David. *A Systems Analysis of Political Life*. New York: John Wiley, 1965.
Greenstein, Fred I. *Children and Politics*. New Haven, CT: Yale University Press, 1965.
Hyman, Herbert H. *Political Socialization: A Study in the Psychology of Political Behavior*. New York: The Free Press, 1959.
Milgram, Stanley. *Obedience to Authority: An Experimental View*. New York: Harper & Row, 1974.

Stephen Maynard Caliendo

Standardized Interviewing

Standardized interviewing is an approach to data collection in which respondents are asked the same questions in the same manner by interviewers. The goal is to ensure that different answers truly reflect different respondent circumstances (primarily their behaviors and opinions) and not differences in the question— where "differences in the question" has come to mean differences in how it is asked. Thus standardized interviewers are typically required to read each question exactly as worded and to limit their other statements to a small set of *neutral* or *nondirective* probes, that is, scripted utterances designed to elicit additional information without biasing the respondent. Examples include "Let me repeat the question." "Is that a 'yes' or a 'no'?" "Whatever it means to you." By standardizing the stimulus the goal is to make the interviewers interchangeable so that, ideally, any two interviewers would collect the same answers from a given respondent. In statistical terms, the goal is to minimize the amount of response variance due to interviewers.

This approach has recently been called into question on the grounds that different respondents can interpret the same question wording differently and so the meaning of the question is not standardized. In addition, it has been pointed out that some respondents may not know how to answer a question without obtaining clarification from the interviewer and may answer inaccurately if clarification is withheld. Finally, detailed analyses of what interviewers and respondents say to each other in standardized interviews have suggested that the restrictions of standardization may lead to clumsy and redundant interactions. Yet, despite recent skepticism about the virtues of standardized interviewing, the practice—or at least belief in the theory of standardized wording—is still nearly universal in the survey industry.

Survey researchers have not always subscribed to the principles of standardization. In the 1930s the introduction of interviewer-administered questionnaires to academic survey research was considered an improvement over self-administration because interviewers could interact with respondents and help them understand the questions. In addition, it was believed that interviewers developed rapport with respondents that led them to persevere at the response task and give more candid answers. In fact when standardized interviewing was introduced in the 1940s and 1950s, it was the threat to rapport more than respondent comprehension that generated the most criticism of standardized interviewing. Over time it became apparent that rapport—to the extent that the concept could be measured—was not related to the structure of the interview and did not affect the quality of survey data. Perhaps a more important factor in the near universal adoption of standardized interviewing was its relatively low cost. Standardized interviews are fast by comparison to less structured methods and interviewers require less training than they do for other techniques.

The practice of standardizing wording extends well beyond survey research, throughout the social sciences and beyond. Practitioners advocate some version of standardized wording in intelligence and personality testing, personnel selection, experimental psychology, educational testing, physician training, police line-ups, police interviews, and user interface design, among others. In each of these cases, standardization is seen as an important improvement over earlier less consistent methods. But in each of these fields, as in survey research, standardized wording has been challenged on the grounds that the same words may be interpreted differently by different participants and even by the same participant on different occasions.

Within the survey industry, there is widespread variation in how organizations translate the concept of standardization into their training procedures and documentation. For example, suppose a respondent says, "definitely agree" but the agreement options provided with the question are "strongly agree" and "somewhat agree." Some organizations allow interviewers to code the response as the option that they believe the respondent intended but others require the interviewer to probe (e.g., "would that be 'strongly agree' or 'somewhat agree'?") until the respondent selects one of the options provided with the question. In addition to variation across organizations, interviewers within individual organizations may not implement the approach identically. Despite completing the same training, some interviewers provide substantive, unscripted answers to respondent's inquiries about the meaning of words in the question while others provide only neutral probes, such as repeating the question.

This variation in practice is a concern to the extent that it affects the quality of survey responses. The picture emerging from recent studies is that some departure from uniform wording can improve the accuracy of respondents' answers. In particular, when that departure helps respondents understand the meaning intended by the author(s) of a question, respondents answer more accurately. Consider a respondent in a labor force survey who baby-sits for several families and is asked whether she has more than one job. Without knowing the definition of "more than one job," she would not know how to answer. Is she simply a baby sitter (i.e., just one job), or does she have as many jobs as employers (i.e., several jobs)? To try and resolve this confusion she might ask the interviewer, "What do you mean by 'more than one job'?" If the interviewer adheres to strict standardization, she will administer a neutral probe such as, "Whatever it means to you." This approach ensures that no respondents receive more (i.e., definitional) information than others and so maintains uniform question wording, but it relinquishes control over how respondents interpret the question; if the phrase means something different to different respondents then this approach actually introduces variation in interpretation compared with an approach that permits clarification.

Allowing the kind of clarification that this respondent has requested has come to be called "conversational interviewing." The name refers to the central role of this kind of clarification in understanding ordinary conversation. The version of the technique that has been most widely evaluated requires interviewers to initially read the question exactly as worded and then to say what is necessary to assure respondents understand as intended. The evidence to date suggests that conversational interviewing leads to greater response accuracy relative to strictly standardized interviews when respondents are not sure how to classify their circumstances in the terms provided by the question. The advantage is evident even when the burden is on respondents to request clarification, but it is greater when interviewers can both respond to such requests and voluntarily clarify concepts if they believe respondents have misunderstood a question but do not realize it. The improvement is greatest when interviewers can both volunteer and paraphrase definitions.

The main cost that has been reported for this approach is that clarification takes time. Depending on how much clarification is necessary—this is usually unknown ahead of time—conversational interviews can take considerably longer than standardized interviews to administer. The exact relationship between time and accuracy is almost certain to vary with survey topic and the interviewers' knowledge of the relevant concepts, but in one study this was estimated at a 7 percent increase in accuracy for each additional minute spent interviewing.

A limit to the conversational approach is that some misconceptions may go uncorrected when (1) respondents do not suspect they misunderstand and so do not ask for clarification, and (2) interviewers do not anticipate the misunderstanding so do not offer clarification. Of course, these misconceptions would also be overlooked in standardized interviews, but conversational interviewing at least holds the promise of correcting them if detected. Another limit to conversational interviewing is that it cannot be used unless the survey sponsors have carefully defined the key survey concepts, which is not nearly as frequent as one would hope. Once definitions for concepts are developed, they must be taught to interviewers. Of course concepts should be clearly defined and interviewers trained on their content irrespective of the interviewing technique.

While pretesting and refining survey questions before they are fielded can eliminate the need for some clarification, the diversity of many populations makes it hard to anticipate and reduce all ambiguities of this kind. What about reading the definition to all respondents? This could clarify potentially ambiguous survey concepts for many respondents without forsaking standardized wording. Because the definitions can be quite long to cover the list of possible confusions and because much of the content of definitions is relevant to only a small proportion of respondents, this approach makes interviews unnecessarily burdensome, possibly harming completion rates. Allowing respondents and interviewers to determine when they need to discuss the meaning of the question may be the best compromise.

Standardized wording was introduced to improve the measurement of opinions at least as much as the measurement of facts and behaviors. If it is even possible to quantify the accuracy of responses about opinions, it is certainly harder to do so than it is for responses about facts and behaviors. The well-known impact of question context on respondents' reported opinions underscores the need for consistent measurement processes. Nonetheless, the words in opinion questions are no less variably interpreted than the words in other sorts of questions. For this reason, some methodologists have cautiously advocated allowing interviewers to clarify the words about which opinions have been solicited, for example, what is meant by "abortion." In fact, this may be one way to help reduce the impact of question context. However, in other opinion measurement situations, researchers may intend to capture variation in how respondents interpret the concept about which their opinion is being solicited, for example, "Now generally speaking, would you say that things in the country are going in the right direction or have they pretty seriously gotten off on the wrong track?" If a respondent were to ask what was meant by "heading in the right direction" it might be consistent with the goals of the survey for the interviewer to respond "whatever it means to you."

Further Reading

Beatty, P. "Understanding the Standardized/Non-Standardized Interviewing Controversy." *Journal of Official Statistics* 11 (1995): 147–60.

Conrad, F. G., and M. F. Schober. "Clarifying Question Meaning in a Household Telephone Survey." *Public Opinion Quarterly* 64 (2000): 1–28.

Fowler, Floyd J., and Thomas W. Mangione. *Standardized Survey Interviewing: Minimizing Interviewer-Related Error.* Newbury Park, CA: Sage Publications, 1990.

Fred Conrad

State of the Union Addresses

Every year the president delivers his State of the Union Address to a join session of Congress, which is also broadcast to the nation. The State of the Union Address is the most important speech that presidents make during the year. Presidents use the State of the Union Address to detail their accomplishments over the past year, to outline the condition of the nation, and to make a case for new policies and programs to address pressing problems. It is also a tool of public leadership.

Ever since Theodore Roosevelt coined the term "bully pulpit" a century ago, presidents have spent a considerable amount of their time and energy trying to lead public opinion. As the public expects presidents to lead the nation and for-

mulate policies to address important issues, presidents have sought political resources, such as public support for themselves and their policies.

Given our system of checks and balances and separation of powers, presidents
are unable to force Congress to act on their policy initiatives. But with public
backing, presidents figure that congressional willingness to enact their policies
will increase. With an eye on upcoming elections, members of Congress are often
highly attuned to the public mood and look for any sign of how the public will
vote in the upcoming election. If the public supports the president, members of
Congress calculate that it would be politically dangerous to oppose the president
and politically beneficial to support him.

Presidents use several techniques to rally public support. They seek positive
coverage in the news, for instance. But since presidents have little ability to control the way that journalists write their stories, presidents also use more direct
methods to reach the public. In the age of electronic mass communications
media, such as radio and television, presidents also address the public directly.
By directly speaking to the nation, presidents have complete control over the
message that reaches the public. They do not have to worry that journalists may
alter the intention of their speech by, for instance, de-emphasizing some aspects
of the speech that the president deemed important.

A second lure of the major national address is that such speeches give presidents access to the entire nation. Major national addresses are those aired in
prime time and where the major networks pre-empt their usual broadcast for the
president's address. The fact that the broadcast networks pre-empt their programming for the president's address also signal to the public that the president
is going to talk about something serious and important. Such signaling helps
focus public attention on the president and likely heightens the impact of the
speech on public opinion.

But presidents cannot go to the public in major national addresses too frequently. To do so would undercut the value of each address in the public's eyes.
Since the advent of radio in the late 1920s, when the means for a national address became available, presidents have on average directly addressed the nation
only four to five times a year. Some presidents, like Herbert Hoover, rarely addressed the nation this way. He did so, on average, only about twice a year. Richard Nixon, in contrast, publicly addressed the nation in major speeches more
often. During this second term in office, he did so, on average, eight times a year.

Moreover, Nixon frequently asked the networks for prime time access to the
nation. This led the networks to begin denying some presidential requests, fear-
ing the loss of advertising revenues when they pre-empted popular entertainment
programs with a presidential address. Since Nixon, presidents have had to convince network executives that they had something important to say before the
networks would pre-empt their usual programming.

However, there are some occasions in which the networks never refuse the
president prime-time access. Two such occasions stand out: the Inaugural address and the State of the Union Address. The Inaugural address is rarely used
to promote policies. Rather it is a moment of high ceremony where the new president is sworn in and the nation is reunited after the presidential election contest.

In contrast, the State of the Union Address is a common occasion for presidents to promote their policies and to see public support. The use of the State of the Union Address as a policy document dates to the beginning of the republic. Article II, Section 3 of the Constitution reads, "He [the president] shall from time to time give to the Congress Information of the State of the Union, and recommend to their Consideration such Measures as he shall judge necessary and expedient." From this constitutional responsibility the annual State of the Union Address evolved.

George Washington began the practice of annually addressing Congress with a State of the Union Address. In those addresses he requested that the legislature take action on certain issues. All subsequent presidents used the State of the Union Address similarly. However, where Washington and his successor, John Adams, presented their State of the Union Addresses in person, Thomas Jefferson ended that practice. Instead, he submitted his Addresses in writing, a sign of his strong belief in the separation of powers.

It was not until Woodrow Wilson became president in 1913 that a president would personally deliver the Address before a joint session of Congress again. Since Wilson, every president has presented the Address in person to a joint session of Congress, with members of both the House and Senate attending. Wilson's intention in presenting the Address in person was to lower the wall of separation between the two branches of government, in effect, converting the president into a more active participant in the legislative process. Moreover, Wilson wanted to attract greater public attention, arguing that public backing would be indispensable for the president in his dealings with Congress.

In the 1920s when Calvin Coolidge was president, radio allowed the Address to also be broadcast live to a national audience. Eisenhower, in the early 1950s, began the practice of having his Address to Congress broadcast on television. By using the electronic media, presidents were attempting to reach the nation directly. Thus, the modern State of the Union Addresses possess two target audiences: Congress and the public.

Deciding what to mention in a State of the Union Address is a complex affair. Presidents have to juggle several, often competing considerations. First, his two major audiences, Congress and the public, may hold different ideas or concerns about policies and issues. Second, the Address has become the centerpiece of the presidents' legislative program. Merely mentioning an issue in the Address catapults it to a high-level presidential policy priority; items not mentioned are thought to be of lesser status. Hence, there is strong competition within the administration, as well as among outside advocates, over what will be mentioned in the Address.

The formal process of building the Address begins with a survey of all government departments. Each is asked to prepare a list of items to include in the Address, as well as justifications for their inclusion. The process of boiling down this large compilation of policy suggestions to those that finally make it onto the Address can take several weeks or more. Along the way, top-level administration personnel and other advisers to the president may negotiate intensely over what to include and what to exclude. Moreover, the Address goes through several drafts, where not only the content but also the language and wording to be used are debated. It matters not only whether an issue is mentioned but also how the president mentions it. Since the Address will identify and define the administration for the next year, extreme care is taken in its preparation.

With regard to the public, presidents look to the Address to affect public opinion in three ways. Presidents want to increase public support for themselves as a leader. Second, they also want to affect the public's agenda, that is, the public's list of policy priorities. Third, presidents want to mobilize public support for their policy solutions. While evidence suggests that the Address can affect the public's agenda, it is not entirely clear that the State of the Union Address can boost presidential support in the public or increase public support for the president's policy solutions to pressing issues.

One might expect **presidential approval** to rise after a State of the Union Address. The Address brings the president before the nation. The ceremonial aspects of the Address also help the incumbent look presidential—the nation's leader, rather than a party or factional leader. Yet research on whether State of the Union Addresses uplift presidential standing with the public is equivocal.

Some studies find that major presidential speeches, including State of the Union Addresses, as well as other prime-time addresses, stimulate increases in presidential approval, but the increases tend to be small: around 3 percent. Moreover, after a State of the Union Address, declines in approval are as common as increases. Of the twenty-two State of the Union Addresses from 1978 to 2003, in eleven instances approval after the Address dropped when compared with presidential approval before the Address. In several cases, these declines were substantial. George H. Bush saw a seven point drop after his 1990 Address, and Ronald Reagan polls dropped five points after his 1987 Address. Of the remaining eleven Addresses, only nine led to poll increases, while two (1982, 1999) showed no change. Generally, increases in approval after the Address are quite small. Of the nine increases, seven were of four points or less. Only two are larger. In 1996 Clinton saw his polls rise by six points and in 1998 Clinton's polls rose a massive ten points.

Several factors may help explain why State of the Union Addresses fail to uniformly or greatly increase presidential standing with the public. First, those in the public most susceptible to such effects do not watch the president's Address. Those who do watch the Address are more likely to be politically informed, and thus, their opinion about the president is set. Of those who already dislike the president, watching the Address may merely reinforce those negative attitudes.

Furthermore, although presidents aim to boost their approval with the Address, the Address is used for other purposes that might undermine that goal. Presidents also used the State of the Union Address in their campaign for reelection, especially in the last Address before the presidential election. When used this way, presidents may look highly partisan; this may undercut their appeal to voters who identify with the other party.

The public agenda consists of the problems and issues over which the public expresses the greatest level of concern. Research suggests that as presidents talk more about an issue or problem in their State of the Union Addresses, the number of people who cite the issue or problem as being important also increases. For instance, if presidents highlight defense in their State of the Union Address, we can expect an increase in the percentage of people who also consider defense to be an important issue. However, if presidents suggest that progress is being made on a problem, then public concern with that problem will tend to recede. But why are presidents able to affect the public's agenda but not their own popularity levels through the State of the Union Address?

The public views the president as being a credible source when it comes to singling out a policy or issue as being important. Presidents sit atop the federal bureaucracy and thus have access to the vast resources of government, including information and the expertise of thousands of bureaucrats.

But presidents do not merely bring issues to the public's attention. In building their State of the Union Addresses, presidents also pay particular attention to what is on the public's mind. When polls and other information indicate that the public is concerned about a problem or concern, presidents tend to talk about it in their Address. This responsiveness of the president to the public increases the president's credibility with the public and the sense that the president is in tune with the nation. Thus, when presidents point to a problem to which the public has not given much attention, the public is likely to follow the president's lead and increase its level of concern with that problem.

However, if a president appears out of touch with the nation, he may undermine any ability to influence the public with his State of the Union Address, or any speech. For instance, in the early 1990s, as the economy worsened and public anxiety over the economy rose, the public felt that President Bush was more concerned with foreign affairs than the economy. This hurt Bush's credibility with the public and eventually had a part to play in his re-election defeat in 1992.

However, even when the public follows the president's lead in identifying important issues and problems the public does not necessarily accept the president's policy solution. Recent research suggests that State of the Union Addresses do not lead to increases in the percentage of people who agree with the president's solution to a problem.

To understand why presidential State of the Union Addresses are not more effective in rallying support for the president's policy solutions, we have to understand something about the audience for the president's Address. Generally, the audience is composed mostly of people who are politically interested and knowledgeable—and identify with one party or the other. Such people tend to possess preferences about what type of policy solution to follow to deal with a specific problem. For instance, in the case of Democrats, the favored solution will lean in a liberal direction or one that prominent Democrats have been advocating. If the president is a Republican, he is unlikely to convert these Democrats to his side, and Republicans in the audience are already likely to agree with him.

In contrast, people who are less knowledgeable and interested in politics and those who identify with neither party are the least likely to possess policy solution preferences. Presidents would seem to have a greater likelihood of mobilizing these types of people to accept their policy solutions, but these types of people are the least likely to watch the televised speech. Thus, the audience for the president's speech contains few of the people most open to presidential persuasion.

As discussed above, the composition of the audience for the State of the Union Address and other presidential speeches plays a large part in understanding the potential effect of a presidential speech on public opinion. Changes in the mass media over the past two decades have had important implications for the composition of the audience for presidential speeches. Perhaps the most important of these changes is the rise of cable television.

Cable television became available to the public in the late 1970s. By the end of the twentieth century, about two-thirds to three-quarters of households subscribed to cable television. Cable television altered people's television viewing habits. In the days before cable television, the three major networks, ABC, CBS, and NBC, held a virtual monopoly over television programming. Most television markets were served only by the local affiliates of the three networks. When a presidential speech was being broadcast during prime time, it was broadcast on all three networks simultaneously. If a person wanted to watch television during this era, that person had no choice but to watch the president's speech. Consequently, in the heyday of network television—from the late 1950s to the middle 1970s—the audience ratings of presidential speeches was comparatively large.

In contrast, cable offers people many viewing choices. One is no longer restricted to the programming of the three networks. As a result, the size of the audience for presidential speeches has declined. In fact, the audience for all network programming has declined. Not only has the size of the audience for the president's speech shrunk, but the composition of the audience has also changed. In the age of network dominance, many people who were less interested and knowledgeable about politics still watched the president's speech, because that was all that was being broadcast at the time. When cable became available, instead of watching the president's address, the less interested were likely to turn the channel and watch something else. Thus, where the audience for a presidential speech in the age of network dominance contained both those who were interested and those who were not interested in politics, the percentage of the audience that was not interested declined sharply once cable became available.

The changing composition of the audience for a presidential speech has important implications for presidential leadership of public opinion. First, as the audience is smaller, presidents in the cable age have a harder time reaching the whole nation than did presidents in the age of network dominance. Second, that audience is composed of people who on average are more interested and knowledgeable about politics—and more likely to identify with one of the parties. These people are more likely to possess relatively well-defined and considered opinions about politics and issues. Consequently, they will be relatively resistant to presidential persuasion effects compared with people who lack such well-developed opinions. Thus, presidents find that they have a harder time rallying the public behind them when addressing the nation in a major speech, like the State of the Union Address.

Further Reading

Cohen, Jeffrey E. *Presidential Responsiveness and Public Policy Making: The Public and the Policies that Presidents Make.* Ann Arbor: University of Michigan Press, 1997. Discusses how public opinion affects presidential speeches and how presidential speeches affect public opinion.

Edwards, George C., III. *On Deaf Ears: The Limits of the Bully Pulpit.* New Haven, CT: Yale University Press, 2003. Discusses the limitations to presidential attempts to influence public opinion.

Kernell, Samuel. *Going Public: New Strategies of Presidential Leadership*. 3rd ed. Washington, DC: CQ Press, 1997. A classic study of why and how presidents use public activities and appearances to influence public opinion.

Web Sites

The American Presidency Project is a Web site maintained by John Woolley and Gerhard Peters, of the Department of Political Science, the University of California-Santa Barbara. It offers valuable information about the presidency, including presidential speeches and public opinion polls, and is available at http://www.presidency.ucsb.edu.

PollingReport.com (http://www.pollingreport.com/) compiles polls on public opinion about the president, other political leaders, election races, and major public issues. Very complete and up to date.

U. S. Presidency Links, available at http://cstl-cla.semo.edu/renka/PresidencyLinks.htm is a page of hyperlinks to many resources about the presidency, it is maintained by Professor Russell D. Renka, of the Department of Political Science, Philosophy and Religion, at Southeast Missouri State University.

Jeffrey E. Cohen

Statistical Matching

Statistical matching is a procedure used to merge information in two or more survey data files, allowing combined analyses of the variables contained in the input files. The goal is to create one or more synthetic files that allow multivariate analyses to be done on the merged set of variables, even though they were not all collected together in one survey.

A typical scenario for statistical matching is that data on a vector of variables (**X,Y**) are collected in Survey A, and data on a vector of variables (**X,Z**) are collected in Survey B. Statistical matching procedures usually match on some function of the common vector of variables **X** (e.g., minimum **X** distance), to produce a synthetic file with values of **X**, **Y**, and **Z** on each record. No assumption is made that Survey A and Survey B interviewed the same persons; this is the critical distinction between statistical matching and *record linkage*, where the goal is to link information from different sources for the same entities.

Statistical matching could be viewed as a procedure to impute *missing data*, that is, missing **Z** from Survey A, and/or missing **Y** from Survey B. However, these data are "missing" by design; **Z** was not collected in Survey A, and **Y** was not collected in Survey B.

Statistical matching strategies can be grouped into two general categories: "unconstrained" matching and "constrained" matching. An unconstrained match allows pairing of the "closest" records, as defined by the match criteria. However, this strategy can result in some records being matched multiple times, while others are not matched at all. A constrained match requires that all records be matched. Constrained matching usually requires more computational effort than unconstrained matching; often the "closest" records are not always paired as the trade-off for requiring that all records be paired.

Rodgers provides an excellent overview of statistical matching, which includes a detailed example that showed the outcome of an unconstrained match and a constrained match. A summary of Rodgers's example follows. File A, containing eight records, is treated as the base file, and File B, containing six records,

Table 1. Two Hypothetical Datasets Eligible for Matching

File A Records				
Case #	Sex	Age	Y	Weight
A1	M	42	9.156	3
A2	M	35	9.149	3
A3	F	63	9.287	3
A4	M	55	9.512	3
A5	F	28	8.494	3
A6	F	53	8.891	3
A7	F	22	8.425	3
A8	M	25	8.867	3

Average age: 40.38
S (age): 15.32
Average Z: 8.97
S (Z): 0.38

File B Records				
Case #	Sex	Age	Z	Weight
B1	F	33	6.932	4
B2	M	52	5.524	4
B3	M	28	4.223	4
B4	F	59	6.147	4
B5	M	41	7.243	4
B6	F	45	3.230	4

Average age: 43.00
S (age): 11.76
Average Z: 5.55
S (Z): 1.57

Note: File A has eight records and File B has six records, but the sum of the weights is the same (24) for the two files.

is the supplemental or donor file. The common vector of variables **X** are sex and age. File B is statistically matched to File A using the **X** variables. Records must match on sex, and the distance function between two records eligible for matching is defined as the absolute value of the difference of the age variables in the two records.

In the summary statistics shown in Table 1, S(.) is the unweighted standard deviation, using (n-1) in the denominator. (Or, equivalently, S(.) can be computed using the weights, followed by a degrees of freedom adjustment.)

To illustrate the unconstrained matching process, consider record A1 in File A. The eligible records in File B are B2, B3, and B5, because of the requirement of a match on sex. The distance function values are 10, 14, and 1, for B2, B3, and B5, respectively; hence, record B5 is matched to record A1. The unconstrained match result is shown in Table 2. Because File A is the base file, the

Table 2. Outcome of Unconstrained Statistical Matching

Matched Case #'s	Sex	Age File A	Age File B	Y	Z	Weight
A1,B5	M	42	41	9.156	7.243	3
A2,B5	M	35	41	9.149	7.243	3
A3,B4	F	63	59	9.287	6.147	3
A4,B2	M	55	52	9.512	5.524	3
A5,B1	F	28	33	8.494	6.932	3
A6,B4	F	53	59	8.891	6.147	3
A7,B1	F	22	33	8.425	6.932	3
A8,B3	M	25	28	8.867	4.223	3

mean and S for Age-File A and Y are the same as before. For the variables appended from File B, the mean and S are as follows:

Average Age-File B: 43.25

S(Age-File B):   12.103718

Average Z: 6.298875

S(Z):   1.0378727

Comparing these statistics to those computed from File B, it is clear from this example that the means and standard deviations for Age-File B and Z can change when unconstrained matching occurs. Also, one of the records in File B (B6) does not appear in the merged file in this example.

A constrained match requires that all of the records in the supplemental file are used. When weights are present, the requirement is that the weight of each record in the supplemental file must be "used up" during the match (*see* **Weighting**).This requirement implies that the sum of the weights in the two files must be equal, both overall and within any subgroups that matching is done (in Rodgers's example, by sex). Typically, in practice, some "universe adjustments" must be done to satisfy these requirements.

For constrained matching, the requirement of matching the closest records is replaced by a global minimization requirement. The set of w_{ij}, the weights assigned for combining record i in

$$\text{stack } \{\{n\}\#\{SUM\}\#\{i = 1\}\} \sim \text{stack } \{\{m\}\#\{SUM\}\#\{j = 1\}\} \ (d\,\text{sub}\{ij\} \sim^* \sim w\,\text{sub}\{ij\})$$

File A with record j in File B, are chosen to minimize the objective function where d_{ij} is the value of the distance function between record i of File A and record j of File B. The w_{ij} must be nonnegative. For each fixed i, the sum across j of the w_{ij} must equal the original weight for record i in File A, and for each fixed j, the sum across i of the w_{ij} must equal the original weight for record j in File B.

The values of w_{ij} that minimize this objective function can be found by solving a linear programming problem, specifically, a "transportation problem." Rodgers reported a solution that minimizes the objective function (see Table 3).

Table 3. Outcome of Constrained Statistical Matching

Matched Case #'s	Sex	Age File A	Age File B	Y	Z	Weight
A1,B2	M	42	52	9.156	5.524	1
A1,B5	M	42	41	9.156	7.243	2
A2,B3	M	35	28	9.149	4.223	1
A2,B5	M	35	41	9.149	7.243	2
A3,B4	F	63	59	9.287	6.147	3
A4,B2	M	55	52	9.512	5.524	3
A5,B1	F	28	33	8.494	6.932	3
A6,B4	F	53	59	8.891	6.147	1
A6,B6	F	53	45	8.891	3.230	2
A7,B1	F	22	33	8.425	6.932	1
A7,B6	F	22	45	8.425	3.230	2
A8,B3	M	25	28	8.867	4.223	3

Note: In this example, the minimizing solution is not unique. There is another combination, not given here, that gives the same minimum value for the objective function.

As with the unconstrained match, the means of Age-File A and Y are the same as in File A. Unlike the unconstrained match, the means of Age-File B and Z are the same as in File B. The standard deviations for the variables in File A and File B can be obtained from the merged file if records in the merged file are restructured to resemble File A or File B and an unweighted analysis is performed, or if a weighted analysis followed by an adjustment for degrees of freedom is carried out. This is a general result: constrained matching preserves means and standard deviations.

Rodgers's example illustrates the advantages and disadvantages of unconstrained and constrained matching. Unconstrained matching allows the association of the "closest" records, as measured by the distance function metric. Unconstrained matching may not "use" all of the records in the supplemental file, and hence is not guaranteed to preserve the distributions present in the supplemental file. For this reason, unconstrained matching is not a symmetric process between the base file and the supplemental file; the results can differ, according to which file is designated as the "base" file. Constrained matching uses all of the records in the supplemental file and preserves the marginal distributions present in the supplemental file. Hence, constrained matching is a symmetric process; the same result is obtained, regardless of which file is designated as the "base" file. However, constrained matching may not allow the association of the "closest" records. Typically, constrained matching leads to the creation of a synthetic file with "split" records. Also, although efficient algorithms are available to solve the "transportation" linear programming problem, constrained matching generally requires more computation than unconstrained matching.

Neither unconstrained matching nor constrained matching, when applied as in Rodgers's example, can address a fundamental limitation of statistical matching. In general, it is not possible to accurately construct the true (X,Y,Z) distribution using information about (X,Y) from one source and information about (X,Z) from another source; what is lacking is information about the relationship between **Y** and **Z**. Usually, little or no auxiliary information about the (**Y**,**Z**) relationship is available, and the observed (**X**,**Y**) and (**X**,**Z**) relationships usually do not provide much constraint on the possibilities for the (**Y**,**Z**) relationship (e.g., no correlation, positive correlation, negative correlation).

Almost all of the statistical matching strategies described in the literature have assumed that records with similar values for **X**, the vector of variables common to the base file and the supplemental file, are good candidates for pairing of the vector **Y** of variables that appear only in the base file with the vector **Z** of variables that appear only in the supplemental file. As pointed out initially by Sims, this assumption is tantamount to an assumption of *conditional independence* of **Y** and **Z**, given **X**. It can be shown that this assumption always leads to the construction of a plausible (i.e., nonsingular) distribution for (**X**,**Y**,**Z**) in the synthetic file created by statistical matching; it also can be shown that many other assumptions besides the conditional independence of **Y** and **Z**, given **X**, also lead to a plausible (**X**,**Y**,**Z**) distribution.

An approach to address this issue is to allow a variety of assumptions to be made about the (**Y**,**Z**) relationship that are consistent with the observed (**X**,**Y**) and (**X**,**Z**) relationships, carry out statistical matching to create a dataset corresponding to each assumption, and then assess the variation in estimates made from the group of data sets created by this procedure. This approach exhibits the amount of uncertainty in estimates due to the statistical matching procedure. Several articles in the literature by Kadane and Rubin discussed such an approach, and outlined procedures to do so. A common feature of the approaches outlined by Kadane and Rubin was to use the assumed (**Y**,**Z**) relationship in regressions to estimate missing **Z** from **X** and **Y** in the Survey A file and missing **Y** from **X** and **Z** in the Survey B file, and use the regression estimates in the matching process; this feature allows **Y** and **Z** to play a role in the formation of the synthetic files that are created.

However, as Moriarity and Scheuren point out, the algorithms described by these authors required innovations to work correctly. For the simplest case of (**X**,**Y**,**Z**) having a trivariate normal distribution, an effective statistical matching procedure is to postulate an assumption about the (**Y**,**Z**) relationship that is consistent with the observed data, and carry out regressions that use the postulated value to estimate missing **Z** for Survey A and missing **Y** for Survey B, as outlined by Kadane and Rubin. Then, residuals are imputed to the regression estimates to add back variability lost during the regression process. After residual imputation, a constrained match on (**Y**,**Z**) is applied. Kadane recommended constrained matching, but he suggested matching on (**X**,**Y**,**Z**) rather than on (**Y**,**Z**). A match on (**Y**,**Z**) still is influenced by **X**, because **X** is used to construct the regression estimates. However, a match on (**Y**,**Z**) can be expected to be more effective in preserving the (**Y**,**Z**) relationship than matching on (**X**,**Y**,**Z**).

Following Kadane's formulation, once two records are matched, the **Z** regression estimate (with residual) for Survey A is replaced by the observed value of **Z** from the matched record from Survey B, and the **Y** regression estimate (with residual) for Survey B is replaced by the observed value of **Y** from the matched record from Survey A, yielding two files with the same (**Y**,**Z**) pairs linked to the **X** values from the two surveys. Simulations were carried out using initial files of size 1000 selected by simple random sampling; the simulations demonstrated that this procedure reliably creates synthetic files containing observed data values that retain the postulated (Y,Z) relationship and all observed relationships in the data. These findings indicate that when information about the (Y,Z) relationship is known from an auxiliary source, the procedure is capable of producing a synthetic file that retains all observed relationships.

Recent research by Moriarity and Scheuren has shown that this procedure extends well to multivariate normal $(X_1,X_2,Y_1,Y_2,Z_1,Z_2)$ for files of size 1000, and the algorithm is now expressed in general terms to extend to (X,Y,Z) of any dimension. Additional research is needed to assess how well the procedure works when the (X,Y,Z) variables do not have distributions that are normal, which corresponds to most applications of statistical matching, and also to specify recommended minimum sample sizes. As sample sizes get smaller, regression estimates become more variable, impairing the ability to retain observed and postulated relationships in the final synthetic files. Practitioners need guidelines for sample sizes that are "too small" versus "adequate."

A recent publication by Rassler outlines a procedure for statistical matching that explores the effect of alternative assumptions on the (Y,Z) relationship by creating synthetic datasets using Markov chain Monte Carlo methods and hierarchical models. Rassler's procedure does not produce synthetic datasets consisting of (X,Y,Z) values created by assignment of observed values to replace modeled values. The statistical matches described in the literature prior to this publication usually, if not always, include a final step of matching to assign observed values (sometimes, to replace modeled values). In at least some instances (e.g., Kadane's method), the method worked very well prior to this final step, but the final step introduced distortion into the end product. As Rassler's method does not carry out this final step, it is not possible to directly compare Rassler's procedure to other statistical matching methods.

In summary, statistical matching is a procedure initially developed more than thirty years ago on an ad hoc basis out of necessity (a desire to conduct analyses of variables not jointly observed in a single survey dataset). A theoretical structure to support the procedure was not developed until much later, and once developed, it became clear that limitations existed. Most statistical matches that have occurred have assumed, implicitly or explicitly, conditional independence of Y and Z, given X. While it has been shown that this always is a plausible assumption, it also has been shown that other assumptions also are plausible. In the absence of auxiliary information about the (Y,Z) relationship, there is no defensible reason, a priori, to prefer one plausible assumption over another. Thus, inferences made from analyses of synthetic files created by statistical matching may be faulty, to the extent that alternative plausible assumptions would lead to large changes in the outcome of the subsequent analyses of the synthetic files created. Research to address this potential liability has made progress, but more research needs to be done to develop procedures that rest on a sound theoretical basis, can be implemented without excessive burden, and have been shown to have robust performance in a variety of simulated situations, including when the (X,Y,Z) variables do not have distributions that are normal.

No statistical matching procedure can be expected to reproduce the true values of unknown variables at the level of individual observations; this would amount to creation of information. The best possible outcome that can be expected is the creation of one or more synthetic files that retain all observed univariate distributions (**X,Y,Z**), all observed bivariate relationships ((**X,Z**), (**X,Y**)), and the (**Y,Z**) relationship that either is postulated or inferred from an auxiliary source. The observed distributions of **X**, **Y**, and **Z** are preserved if constrained matching is used. Given the increasing availability of inexpensive and powerful computational resources, the additional computing effort that usually is required for constrained matching is available. Thus, it is difficult to justify the continued use of unconstrained matching methods. Retaining observed and postulated bivariate relationships has been a more difficult problem, but recent research has produced good results for the multivariate normal case; there may also be robust performance in the more general setting.

Further Reading

Kadane, Joseph B. "Some Statistical Problems in Merging Data Files." *1978 Compendium of Tax Research*, U.S. Department of the Treasury (1978): 159–71; *Journal of Official Statistics* 17 (reprinted 2001): 423–33. The first reference in the statistical matching literature that outlined a statistical matching procedure for assessing the effect of alternative plausible assumptions about the (**Y,Z**) relationship.

Moriarity, Chris, and Fritz Scheuren. "Statistical Matching: A Paradigm for Assessing the Uncertainty in the Procedure." *Journal of Official Statistics* 17 (2001): 407–22. A complete description of the method described in this article for reliably creating synthetic files containing observed data values that retain the postulated (**Y,Z**) relationship and all observed relationships in the data for the trivariate normal case.

Rassler, Susanne. *Statistical Matching: A Frequentist Theory, Practical Applications, and Alternative Bayesian Approaches*. Lecture Notes in Statistics No. 168. New York: Springer-Verlag, 2002. A recent publication that discusses the result of using matching methods that assume conditional independence, and proposes a method akin to statistical matching that explores the effect of alternative assumptions on the (**Y,Z**) relationship by creating synthetic datasets using Markov chain Monte Carlo methods and hierarchical models.

Rodgers, Willard L. "An Evaluation of Statistical Matching." *Journal of Business and Economic Statistics* 2 (1984): 91–102. An often-cited reference in the statistical matching literature that provided an excellent overview of the subject and the current state of development as of the date of its publication.

Rubin, Donald B. "Statistical Matching Using File Concatenation with Adjusted Weights and Multiple Imputations." *Journal of Business and Economic Statistics* 4 (1986): 87–94. An often-cited reference in the statistical matching literature that was an early example of Rubin's multiple imputation method.

Chris Moriarity

Stereotypes

Stereotypes are sets of beliefs about the personal qualities of individual members of a group based on expectations about the group in general. Members of any group can be subject to stereotypes, including older people, women, men, blacks, whites, Hispanics, the poor, and the wealthy. Stereotypes can be negative or positive in content. Stereotypes are almost always a gross oversimplification when applied to individual group members, but they are not necessarily inaccurate at the group level. They can lead to an accurate appraisal of someone who fits the typical group profile but can produce an erroneous assessment of some-

one who is atypical or holds a mixture of typical and atypical group characteristics. Stereotypes are often studied because they influence the assessment of an
individual group member, but they are also of interest to political scientists because they can shape political beliefs more broadly.

Public opinion is influenced by group stereotypes in two key ways. First,
stereotypes flavor public assessments of politicians, leaders, and other highly visible individuals by depicting them as typical of their race, class, gender, or political party regardless of their personal qualities. The tendency to stereotype
political leaders has broad ramifications for the assessment of their leadership
skills, political positions, and areas of policy competence. Second, stereotypes
color the formation of attitudes toward key public policies, such as affirmative
action, welfare, and Social Security, by depicting policy recipients as more or less
deserving, and more or less in need of government assistance.

Research on the political impact of social stereotypes fits within the broader
study of political reasoning and information processing. One of the key insights
of contemporary information-processing approaches is the mind's remarkable
ability to efficiently process information without expending enormous cognitive
resources on any given mental task. Stereotypes serve these goals admirably. They
are a tremendously powerful tool that augments existing, and perhaps minimal,
information with a rich set of associations that produce complex impressions of
a person or a group of people. In that sense, stereotypes are a remarkably efficient mental tool. But they are also costly. They can result in obvious inferential
errors when applied to an atypical individual and are highly resistant to new information. Atypical individuals are typically dismissed as aberrant, minimizing
the ability of diverse group members to alter the group's image, and there is a
tendency to pay greater attention and better recall information that is consistent
with an existing stereotype than that which is inconsistent.

Stereotype content varies across groups and can contain a kernel of truth
linked, for example, to group members' socioeconomic status or typical occupational and family roles. A group's history and culture can also influence stereotype content. A detailed analysis of stereotype content is beyond the scope of
this entry. But there are two groups for whom stereotypes and their content have
special relevance within the study of American public opinion. Racial stereotypes
have been investigated most fully by public opinion researchers because of their
enduring influence on assessments of political figures and reactions to racial policy, and gender stereotypes have received research attention because of their influence on assessments of women politicians.

The influence of gender stereotypes on reactions to men and women politicians has received considerable research attention within political science. Interest in the topic has been sparked by the glaring absence of women from national
politics in the United States and almost any western-style democracy, with the
exception of Scandinavian countries. In the United States, a country seen as at
the forefront of the modern women's movement, women represent a mere 13.6
percent of all congressional districts and constitute 14 percent of all senators in
2004. These numbers raise concerns about the extent to which voters' gender
stereotypes that depict women as warm, gentle, kind, and passive are at odds
with the expectations of a typical political leader, who is expected to fit a more
masculine profile as tough, aggressive, and assertive. The burning question is

whether such stereotypes result in less support for women who run for political office. The reality turns out to be complex, but it suggests that gender stereotypes can influence public support for women and men politicians. These effects, however, can be both positive and negative.

Gender stereotypes are remarkably constant across different cultures and typically portray women as more nurturing, caring, and emotional than men, whereas men are seen as more rational, assertive, and aggressive. Social psychologist Alice Eagly has argued that gender stereotypes arise from women's gender roles as mothers and caregivers. These expectations can be reversed by specific information about a woman's occupational and social roles, although it is difficult to reverse standing expectations about the personality traits and qualities of women in general.

Typical female traits are not regarded as highly desirable for politicians. For example, presidential popularity is based to a large degree on the extent to which presidents possess typically masculine leadership traits, such as strength, determination, and confidence. The perceived importance of masculine qualities extends beyond the presidency to include legislative positions, and state and local offices. Typical female personality traits, such as warmth and caring, are considered less crucial—especially for higher levels of office, such as the presidency. Overall, gender stereotypes typically boost the electoral chances of a male candidate but can worsen those of a woman, conveying potentially bad news for women candidates.

The situation for women candidates is not, however, as bleak as suggested by this assessment. Research studies provide compelling evidence that voters use gender stereotypes to assess a male and female politician's respective areas of issue expertise. Women are typically seen as better able to handle "compassion" issues, such as **education, health policy**, and poverty (*see* **Welfare**), but are seen as less able to deal with big business, the military, and defense issues. Moreover, these differences are due to gender stereotypes. Candidates with feminine personality traits are rated as more competent to handle compassion issues regardless of their gender, and candidates with masculine personality traits are seen as more competent to handle the military, **crime**, and law enforcement. This can be an advantage for women running for office in elections dominated by "compassion" issues but prove disadvantageous in elections dominated by war or military concerns. Political scientist Kim Kahn's work on women running for political office in the late 1980s and early 1990s demonstrates that women gubernatorial candidates were at a significant electoral advantage over women running for the Senate because gubernatorial races were dominated at that time by education, health care, and social services whereas the military and foreign policy were at the forefront of the Senate contests.

Stereotypes are often based on group members' perceived personality characteristics. But when it comes to politics, group stereotypes also include assumptions about a politician's broad political beliefs and ideology. This holds true for women politicians who are seen as more liberal and Democratic than their male colleagues of the same party (*see* **Liberalism and Conservatism**). In fact, in one study women members of the House of Representatives were seen as more liberal than men, especially by voters who knew little about them. In another study, female Republican and Democratic Senate candidates were rated by citizens as more liberal than indicated by their actual voting record. The impact of stereotypes that paint women as more liberal and Democratic than men may be helpful in a liberal electorate but quite damaging to women candidates in an electoral district dominated by conservative voters. From this perspective, gender stereotypes can have both positive and negative electoral consequences.

One of the reasons that gender stereotypes are not more harmful to the electoral prospects of women running for office is that women candidates anticipate their impact and act to minimize it. Women who have run for highly visible state or national elected office over the past several decades have waged increasingly combative campaigns in which they stress their toughness and aggressiveness in an attempt to soften the negative impact of gender stereotypes. Women politicians attempt to combat voters' stereotypes through the use of carefully designed campaign slogans, visual imagery, and specific issue positions that portray them as in possession of desirable masculine qualities (*see* **Gender and Campaigns**). This strategy can succeed to some degree, especially among voters who attend closely to political matters (*see* **Political Knowledge**).

One issue that continues to engage stereotype researchers is the extent to which an individual such as a visible politician is immune from stereotypes once someone has formed an impression of them as a distinct individual. Some social psychologists, such as Susan Fiske, argue that once an individual is viewed in this differentiated way stereotypes have no impact on future impressions of that person. In contrast, recent evidence suggests a less sanguine view of a leader's ability to evade stereotypes. From this vantage point, even a highly visible politician, such as Hillary Clinton, who may be seen as competent and ambitious (atypical female traits) can also be viewed as volatile and emotional (typical female traits) when placed in a situation—such as an instance of spousal infidelity—that is likely to evoke gender stereotypes. The lingering impact of stereotypes helps to explain their enduring political power and suggests an ongoing problem for women politicians who face the ever-present threat of being stereotyped as typical weak, emotional, and insufficiently assertive women. When extended to politics, this implies that a woman candidate who is individuated as tough and aggressive in one instance can still be seen through the prism of voter gender stereotypes as weak and powerless in a future scenario.

In addition to shaping views of individual politicians, stereotypes powerfully influence policy opinions, a link most closely explored in the realm of racial policies. Sadly, a sizable minority of whites in the United States continue to view most blacks as lazy and complaining, and a near majority view them as violent. Evidence of whites' negative racial stereotypes, drawn from the 2000 **General Social Survey** (GSS), is presented in Table 1. This table makes clear that a substantial minority of whites view blacks as more lazy than hardworking (37 percent), and almost a half of all whites regard blacks as more violent than not. Fewer whites, however, believe that blacks are unintelligent. Moreover, individuals who endorse such negative racial stereotypes are most likely to oppose government spending on programs to help blacks or guarantee their fair treatment in the workforce, and believe that blacks prefer government assistance to working.

Some of the most politically powerful racial stereotypes center on the view that blacks are unwilling to work hard and, therefore, do not deserve any form

Table 1. Stereotypes of Blacks Among White Respondents (2000 General Social Survey)

Response Choices	Percent
Rich > Poor (1–3)	7.7
Neither (4)	25.3
Poor > Rich (5–7)	67.0
Nonviolent > Violent (5–7)	15.0
Neither (4)	37.5
Violent > Nonviolent (1–3)	47.5
Hardworking > Lazy (1–3)	18.6
Neither (4)	44.3
Lazy > Hardworking (5–7)	36.9
Intelligent > Unintelligent (5–7)	26.7
Neither (4)	49.9
Unintelligent > Intelligent (1–3)	23.4

Note: Responses are based on the following question stem: "Now I have some questions about different groups in our society. I'm going to show you a seven-point scale on which the characteristics of people in a group can be rated. In the first statement a score of 1 means that you think almost all of the people in that group are 'rich.' A score of 7 means that you think almost everyone in the group [is] 'poor.' A score of 4 means you think that the group is not towards one end or another, and of course you may choose any number in between that comes closest to where you think people in the group stand." Respondents were also asked to rate blacks using the same scale for "hard working or lazy," "intelligent or unintelligent," and "violence-prone or not violence-prone."

of government assistance. Unlike gender stereotypes that have remarkably similar content across different cultural settings, the content of racial stereotypes is linked to prevailing social and political conditions, and has changed over time. Prior to the American **civil rights** movement many whites viewed blacks as inherently inferior with less inborn ability and intelligence than whites. This perception declined through the 1960s and was replaced by another stereotype of blacks as lazy, immoral, and unwilling to help themselves. This perception increased in the late 1960s and early 1970s with claims that political changes in response to the civil rights movement had provided blacks with opportunities that they had failed to capitalize on.

The considerations brought by citizens to discussions of racial policy changed in tandem with this shift in policy climate. Instead of debating blacks' innate ability and intelligence, racial policy elicited concerns about black deservingness and explanations for persistent black poverty. This brought stereotypic views about blacks' willingness to work to the forefront of the debate. Numerous studies demonstrate that endorsement of such negative racial stereotypes increase opposition to government racial policies. Whites who endorse negative racial stereotypes also oppose government policies designed to increase black economic opportunity consistent with their belief that blacks lack ambition, violate the work ethic, and are responsible for their own failures.

Racial stereotypes that depict blacks as unwilling to work hard are not the only group stereotype that influence public policy attitudes. Stereotypes that depict older people as poor lead to greater support of government old-age programs, such as Social Security and Medicare. Anglos who view Hispanics as stereotypically lazy are more likely to oppose bilingual education programs. And racial stereotypes that depict blacks as aggressive increase support for the more punitive treatment of criminals. Since many public policies are linked to or targeted for specific groups of beneficiaries, stereotypes clearly have broad power to shape public support or opposition to a range of government policies.

One of the pressing issues in recent stereotype research is the extent to which stereotypic thinking can be avoided. Researchers focus on two phases of stereotype use: their activation and their application to an individual or individuals once activated. Social psychologist Patricia Devine's seminal study suggested that stereotypes arise automatically outside of conscious awareness but can be consciously overridden by someone with sufficient time and motivation. From this perspective, it is impossible to avoid the emergence of culturally pervasive stereotypes, regardless of one's level of prejudice, but it is possible for nonprejudiced individuals to reject their use. Subsequent research has further challenged the notion that stereotype use is inevitable, finding that stereotypes are automatically activated among prejudiced but not among nonprejudiced individuals, and that individuals can be trained to prevent their automatic activation. Stereotype activation may be even more selective, according to evidence accumulated by Ziva Kunda and her colleagues, who find that stereotype activation can also be suppressed by prejudiced individuals who are motivated to think highly of a group member. Overall, the resounding conclusion of recent research is that stereotypes are common but far from inevitable. They are most likely to surface in situations in which someone is prejudiced, has little time to think about the basis for his or her judgment, and is not strongly motivated to counteract stereotypic thoughts.

While it is possible to avoid stereotypes, doing so requires effort and motivation. In many situations stereotypes are activated automatically, even for nonprejudiced individuals. Social psychologists have developed several ingenious methods to study this, and these methods are beginning to appear in laboratory studies of public opinion. One of the most popular methods is called the Implicit Attitudes Test (IAT), developed by social psychologists Anthony Greenwald and Mahzarin Banaji, in which the existence of stereotypes is examined by assessing the speed with which someone associates stereotypic characteristics, such as caring or family-oriented, with a group label, in this case women. A large number of people have taken this test online, and it provides a sobering reminder of how difficult stereotypes are to counteract under tight time pressure. Other implicit tests include lexical decision tasks in which a racial word is primed outside conscious awareness and is followed by a reaction-time task in which the research participant decides that a stereotypic or nonstereotypic group of letters is a word.

Evidence that stereotypes can be counteracted by conscious thought and effort highlights the important role of the media and political elites in exposing the use of racial, gender, and other stereotypes within political messages. Political scientist Tali Mendelberg argues that the media and political elites effectively played this role in connection to the Willy Horton campaign commercials in the 1988 presidential campaign. In that campaign, Republican George H. Bush portrayed his Democratic challenger, Michael Dukakis, as being soft on crime through the use of negative racial imagery. When the explicit racial nature of the ad was made publicly salient, racial attitudes had much less impact on assessment of Dukakis effectively counteracting the influence of racial stereotypes. Making such associations salient helps individuals to detect their stereotypic content and reject the application of negative group stereotypes.

Overall, stereotypes are politically pervasive but far from inevitable. Future research on the political impact of group stereotypes is likely to delve more deeply into the circumstances under which stereotypes operate and the extent to which they can be successfully counteracted by political elites. This research is likely to tackle a number of politically important questions. For example, what is the likely success of efforts, such as media "ad watch" stories, to "out" the use of stereotypes in election ads? Do such efforts equally negate both subtle and blatant attempts to evoke group stereotypes? How successful are politicians' efforts to portray themselves as nonstereotypic of their race, gender, or political party? Can politicians effectively use stereotypes to their advantage while avoiding their negative consequences?

There is also growing research interest in the type of individuals who are most susceptible to stereotypic thinking. Psychological research demonstrates that some individuals resist stereotype activation at both a conscious and preconscious level. Can these individuals be successfully identified in political studies that rely on survey data? At present, stereotype endorsement is assessed with a series of overt questions about the extent to which a particular group is either lazy or hard working, intelligent or unintelligent, and other polar opposite traits (see Table 1). But there are a number of individuals who feel uncomfortable answering such questions, potentially contaminating the assessment of stereotypic thinking with concerns about social desirability. Psychologists have developed more subtle means to assess the activation and application of stereotypes, and political scientists are beginning to develop comparable measures for inclusion within surveys. The use of survey experiments and other less blatant survey approaches are needed to ensure that political scientists obtain an accurate assessment of an individual's endorsement and application of stereotypes.

Finally, policy researchers have considered public policies that target individuals based on their socioeconomic need—not race, gender, or other group characteristics—to remove such considerations from political judgments. From this perspective, policies would be more publicly palatable if they focused on recipient need rather than contentious issues linked to race and gender. This approach has been championed as an alternative to affirmative action programs and has the presumed added benefit of evading public reactions based on negative group stereotypes. But is it really possible to remove group considerations from public policy discussions? It is incredibly difficult, for example, to take race out of the debate surrounding social welfare policy. The media tends to link race and welfare programs by portraying welfare recipients as disproportionately black. College admission programs aimed at students who come from disadvantaged and lower socioeconomic households have been offered as an alternative to affirmative action. But even these programs have been visibly and publicly evaluated in terms of how well they increase college admissions among racial minorities. The same problem extends to assessments of women politicians. The media is more likely to discuss women's clothing and other gender-linked characteristics for female than male politicians. It is clearly difficult to formulate policies or to present political candidates in ways that are devoid of any group reference. In the end, it may be easier to counteract the influence of group stereotypes by highlighting their political uses and abuses than to eradicate group references from political life.

Further Reading

Eagly, Alice H., and Steven J. Karau. "Role Congruity Theory of Prejudice Toward Female Leaders." *Psychological Review* 109, no. 3 (2002): 573–98. Discusses the discrepancy between women's gender roles and leadership roles, and the consequences for the development of prejudice against women leaders.

Fiske, Susan T. "Stereotyping, Prejudice and Discrimination." In *The Handbook of Social Psychology*, 4th ed., edited by D. Gilbert, S.T. Fiske, and G. Lindzey. New York: Random House, 1998, pp. 357–411. A thorough overview of social psychological research on stereotypes and other aspects of prejudice.

Huddy, Leonie, and Theresa Capelos. "The Impact of Gender Stereotypes on Voters' Assessment of Women Candidates." In *Social Psychological Applications to Social Issues: Developments in Political Psychology*, vol. 5., edited by Victor Ottati. New York: Kluwer Academic/Plenum, 2002, pp. 29–53. An overview of the complex role played by gender stereotypes in shaping voters' reactions to women candidates.

Hurwitz, Jon, and Mark Peffley, eds. *Perception and Prejudice: Race and Politics in the United States*. New Haven, CT: Yale University Press, 1998. A good collection of articles on the varied political impact of racial stereotypes.

Web Sites

The Web site of the American **National Election Studies,** a survey of American citizens conducted during each congressional and presidential election, includes questions that assess racial stereotypes in 1992, 1996, and 2000. It can be found at http://www.umich.edu/~nes/.

The Web site of the General Social Survey (GSS) contains a series of questions about racial stereotypes between 1990 and 2000. The codebook and basic tabulations can be obtained from the following site: http://www.icpsr.umich.edu:8080/GSS/homepage.htm.

A demonstration copy of the Implicit Attitude Test (IAT) can be found at the following Web site: http://implicit.harvard.edu/implicit/. The test can be taken at this site, providing a first-hand demonstration of the difficulty in avoiding the use of various group stereotypes in making judgments under time pressure.

Leonie Huddy

Stratified Sampling

Stratified sampling is a probabilistic sampling method in which the population is initially divided into nonoverlapping subgroups or strata and then units are chosen randomly from each stratum. The strata are based on a predetermined factor, such as the size of the units or a demographic characteristic. It is typically used when there is concern that certain sub-populations may be underrepresented if **simple random sampling** is used to select a sample.

For example, consider a study of all hospital beds in a particular geographic region. A simple random sampling could lead to a sample that is not representative of the population of hospitals. For example, by chance alone, the large hospitals (or mid-sized or small) could be totally missed, oversampled, or undersampled. Stratified random sampling would avoid such a problem by selecting a sample from the large hospitals, a sample from the mid-sized hospitals, and a sample from the small hospitals.

A *stratum* is defined as a sub-population of the original population. The entire set of strata consists of nonoverlapping groups that comprise the population. The strata are formed on the basis of some known characteristic about the population that is believed to be related to the variable of interest. The goal is to create strata that contain elements that are homogeneous within each stratum, but heterogeneous between strata. In the hospital example, strata of hospitals may be formed based on number of beds, number of physicians, and so forth.

In stratified random sampling, the population is broken down into mutually exclusive and exhaustive strata. Then, a random sample from each of the strata is taken. The total number of possible samples taken with a stratified design is smaller than the total under simple random sampling. With simple random sampling the number of possible samples is $\binom{N}{n}$, which is less than the number with stratified random sampling, $\binom{N_1}{n_1} \times \Lambda \times \binom{N_L}{n_L}$. Suppose that 25 population elements are split into two strata with sizes 12 and 13. Now, the 5 sample elements will be taken from each stratum (2 from stratum 1 and 3 from stratum 2). This means that there are a total of $\binom{12}{2} \times \binom{13}{3} = 66 \times 286 = 18{,}876$, which is less than the 53,130 samples possible with simple random sampling.

The data from these within-stratum random samples are combined to form estimates of the population parameters. The population parameters and standard errors are estimated using the following formulae:

$$\bar{x}_h = \frac{\sum_{i=1}^{n_h} x_{h,i}}{n_h} \qquad \bar{x}_{str} = \frac{\sum_{h=1}^{L} N_h \bar{x}_h}{N} \qquad \hat{SE}(\bar{x}_{str}) = \sqrt{\sum_{h=1}^{L} \frac{N_h^2}{N^2} \frac{s_h^2}{n_h} \left(\frac{N_h - n_h}{N_h} \right)}$$

$$p_h = \frac{\sum_{i=1}^{n_h} y_{h,i}}{n_h} \qquad p_{str} = \frac{\sum_{h=1}^{L} N_h p_h}{N} \qquad \hat{SE}(p_{str}) = \sqrt{\sum_{h=1}^{L} \frac{N_h^2}{N^2} \frac{p_h(1 - p_h)}{n_h - 1} \left(\frac{N_h - n_h}{N_h} \right)},$$

where $h = 1, \ldots, L$ denote the strata, $\bar{x}_h$ is the within-stratum mean, $\bar{x}_{str}$ is the combined mean from stratified sampling, p_h is the within-stratum proportion and p_{str} is the combined proportion. Notice the combined stratified sampling estimates are just weighted averages of the within-stratum estimates, with weights proportional to the size of the stratum. Similarly, the standard error is a linear combination of the within-stratum standard error estimates. If the strata are homogeneous within and heterogeneous between, then each possible sample taken within each stratum will result in a similar estimate of the population parameter. Therefore, the variability will be lower within each stratum than it would be if simple random sampling were used. That is, taking simple random samples of size n from a heterogeneous population would yield some estimates that are quite small (for samples with mainly small values for the outcome) and some that are quite large (for samples with predominantly large outcome values), which will inflate the variance. Because creating homogeneous strata will lower the within-stratum variability and because the overall standard error is a linear combination of the within-stratum estimates, stratified sampling will often lead to estimates with lower standard errors compared to simple random sampling.

Once it is decided to use stratified random sampling, a decision must be reached as to how many elements are to be selected from each stratum. This is known as allocation of the sample. The simplest allocation scheme involves selecting an equal number of observations from each stratum. That is, $n_h = n/L$, where L is the total number of strata, and n_h is the number of elements selected from stratum h.

The most commonly utilized allocation scheme is proportional allocation. In this scheme, the sampling fraction, n_h/N_h, is specified to be the same for each stratum. That is, the number of elements taken from the hth stratum is given by

$n_h = N_h\left(\dfrac{n}{N}\right)$. When proportional allocation is used, estimates of the population

mean and proportion are *self-weighting*. This means that when estimating the population mean, proportion or total, each sample element is multiplied by the same constant, $1/n$, irrespective of the stratum to which the element belongs.

A third scheme is known as optimal allocation. This method results in estimated means and proportions that have minimum variance because the sample units are allocated to strata in a manner that is proportional to the within-stratum

variance. The sample size for each stratum is calculated as $n_h = \left(\dfrac{N_h\sigma_{hx}}{\sum_{h=1}^{L}N_h\sigma_{hx}}\right)(n)$.

Thus, strata with larger variance estimates will have more units sampled compared to strata with smaller variance estimates. Intuitively, this makes sense because if the elements within a stratum are homogeneous, then fewer have to be sampled to obtain a precise estimate of the parameter. In contrast, a stratum that is more heterogeneous will need to have a larger sample taken for a precise estimate of the parameter. Optimal allocation with respect to cost is another way to allocate the sample. This is particularly useful if the cost associated with sampling units differs among the strata, but the overall costs are fixed (which is usually the case with sample surveys). If the cost is fixed, the allocation that will yield an es-

timate with the smallest variance is given by $n_h = \left(\dfrac{N_h\sigma_{hx}\,/\,\sqrt{C_h}}{\sum_{h=1}^{L}N_h\sigma_{hx}\sqrt{C_h}}\right)\times C$ where

C is the overall cost for the survey and C_h is the cost of sampling a unit within stratum h.

There are several advantages to using stratified random sampling designs. First, a stratified random sample may provide increased precision (i.e., narrower confidence intervals) over that which is possible with a simple random sample of the same size. This is particularly true if the strata are chosen to be relatively homogeneous with respect to the variable under investigation (as mentioned above). A second advantage is that within-stratum estimates are easily obtainable. Thus, with a stratified design not only can you make inference to the entire population, but to each stratum as well. Finally, for either administrative or logistical reasons, it may be easier to select a stratified sample than a simple random sample.

The major disadvantage of stratified sampling is, however, that it is no less expensive than simple random sampling since detailed frames must be constructed for each stratum prior to sampling. For this reason, despite the high level of precision possible with stratified sampling, the most commonly employed sampling method in survey research is **cluster sampling**.

Example. A mid-sized manufacturing company is considering building a gym for its employees. However, prior to making the final decision, the top executives want to estimate the proportion of employees who will use the gym at least three days per week. They know that there may be differences between the males and females, and between the production line employees and management/professional staff. Therefore, they decide to use a stratified random sampling design to ensure that all groups are represented in the overall estimate. Suppose the stratum sizes are the following: 557 male production line employees, 175 female production line employees, 322 male management/professional staff employees, and 142 female management/professional staff employees. Using a proportional allocation scheme, how many individuals would be assigned to each stratum if the total sample size for the survey is 210?

The solution uses the proportional allocation $n_h = N_h \left(\dfrac{n}{N} \right)$. Thus, the sample sizes needed for each stratum are the following:

Male production line employees: $n_h = N_h \left(\dfrac{n}{N} \right) = 557 \left(\dfrac{210}{1196} \right) = 97.8$, or, 98

Female production line employees: $n_h = N_h \left(\dfrac{n}{N} \right) = 175 \left(\dfrac{210}{1196} \right) = 30.7$, or, 31

Male management/professional staff: $n_h = N_h \left(\dfrac{n}{N} \right) = 322 \left(\dfrac{210}{1196} \right) = 56.5$, or, 56

Female management/professional staff: $n_h = N_h \left(\dfrac{n}{N} \right) = 142 \left(\dfrac{210}{1196} \right) = 24.9$, or, 25

Now, suppose the survey is conducted and the data indicate that 13 percent of the male production line employees, 10 percent of the female production line employees, 34 percent of the male management/professional staff employees, and 28 percent of the female management/professional staff employees would use a worksite gym at least three times per week. What are the combined proportion and standard error from this survey? The solution uses the formulae presented above to derive the following estimates:

$$p_{str} = \frac{\sum_{b=1}^{L} N_b p_b}{N} = \frac{(557 \times 0.13) + (175 \times 0.10) + (322 \times 0.34) + (142 \times 0.28)}{1196}$$

$$= \frac{72.41 + 17.5 + 109.48 + 39.76}{1196} = 0.1999, \text{ or, } 20 \text{ percent}$$

$$\hat{SE}(p_{str}) = \sqrt{\sum_{b=1}^{L} \frac{N_b^2}{N^2} \frac{p_b(1 - p_b)}{n_b - 1} \left(\frac{N_b - n_b}{N_b}\right)}$$

$$= \sqrt{\left(\frac{557^2}{1196^2} \frac{0.1131}{97} \frac{459}{557}\right) + \left(\frac{175^2}{1196^2} \frac{0.09}{30} \frac{144}{175}\right) + \left(\frac{322^2}{1196^2} \frac{0.2244}{55} \frac{266}{322}\right)}$$
$$+ \left(\frac{142^2}{1196^2} \frac{0.2016}{24} \frac{117}{142}\right)$$

Further Reading

Levy, Paul S., and Stanley Lemeshow. *Sampling of Populations: Methods and Applications*. New York: John Wiley, 1999. An accessible guide to sampling methods that offers extensive coverage of systematic sampling.

Stanley Lemeshow and Amy Ferketich

Structural Equation Modeling (SEM)

Structural Equation Modeling (SEM) is a broadly applied confirmatory statistical technique to test proposed models of relationships among variables. The statistical tests are conducted based on the structural properties of a covariance matrix computed from a set of empirically observed or measured variables. Hence, this technique is also known as Covariance Structure Analysis (CSA). The models in SEM typically include latent factors that are indicated by observed variables and the relationships among the latent factors. Thus these models, which are referred to as measurement models, incorporate the main features of factor analysis. SEM models also include relationships among the latent factors in terms of paths of direct influence from independent to dependent variables or factors. In addition, SEM may also include reciprocal influence between variables or factors in the form of bidirectional paths of influence. Models that include directional or bidirectional paths of influence are referred to as structural models.

The analyses of structural models with paths of direct influence of some factors (or variables) on others provide the same type of information that is obtained from multiple regression analysis, that is, information regarding the degree of predictive accuracy or influence of specified independent variables on a dependent one. Whereas regression analysis is limited to only one dependent variable, SEM usually involves the simultaneous analysis of several dependent variables. SEM application can therefore be regarded as a type of a broad integration of factor analysis with multiple regression technique.

SEM also provides additional features and analytic options for comparing models across groups, handling dichotomized variables (e.g., dummy variables), ordinal variables, and data with missing values. Other analytic options of SEM include the capability of conducting sensitivity analyses that determine how results change with modifications in various parameters of the model, and simulation studies that determine the stability of results with repeated analyses using randomly drawn sub-samples.

In structural equation models latent factors are hypothetical constructs. They are not being observed directly but are inferred from observed variables or indicators. (The terms *factors*, *latent factors*, and *latent variables* are often used interchangeably.) In contrast to latent factors, observed variables consist of empirical data in the form of responses to questions in an interview or questionnaire, records of structured observations of various phenomena by observers or instruments, as well as archived administrative and statistical data. Typically, structural equation models also include correlations among factors and hypothesized paths of influence from some latent factors to others or to observed variables. The results of SEM analysis include both overall measures of goodness-of-fit that permit the evaluation of how well the model fit the data. They also include the estimated values for the correlations, the directional paths of influence on factors and indicators (i.e., factor loadings), and the estimated variance accounted for in the dependent variables and factors.

To perform SEM, the researcher must specify in advance all the relationships of observed variables to latent factors as well as the relationships among the factors. These relationships must be specified in the form of correlations or paths of direct influence. Thus, unlike the exploratory technique of factor analysis, SEM is a confirmatory analytic technique. The results of SEM, particularly those involving measures of goodness-of-fit, are used as evidence to reject or to provide support for the hypothesized model.

Contemporary SEM evolved from Sewall Wright's work on path analysis in the 1920s. The methodology of path analysis was promulgated and used in the mid-1960s and early 1970s by a number of sociologists. By the early 1980s, with the publication of the Linear Structural Relations (LISREL) model, by Karl Jöreskog, SEM replaced path analysis as a more general analytic method. Finally, with the introduction of LISREL, EQS, AMOS, and other computer software to perform SEM analyses, the dissemination of the method has accelerated throughout the social and behavioral sciences. Already early on, path analysis utilized graphic presentation of models similar to charts that depicted the flow of influence from key independent variables to mediating and other dependent variables. In these models, the following graphical conventions are followed: observed variables are depicted as rectangular shapes, paths of direct influence as unidirectional arrows and correlations as curved lines with double-head arrows. Most

SEM applications continue to use such graphic presentations including latent factors depicted by round or oval shapes. The representation of models in a graphic flowchart-like form is instrumental in displaying and communicating the results of even complex models in an efficient way.

In structural models an important distinction is made between latent factors that are inferred from, or reflected by, the observed variables and those latent factors that are caused or formed by the observed variables. In the former case the latent variable is referred to as reflective because the observed variables reflect the underlying condition that actually is the cause of the observed variables. Here, the observed variables are literally indicators or symptoms of an underlying condition such as a disease. For example, the psychological state of depression is a latent factor that is not observed directly but is inferred based on the appearance of clinical manifestations in the form of observations by the clinician or via verbal reports of the individual. Thus, the observed indicators of an underlying construct serve the same function for the statistician as clinical symptoms do for the physician who diagnoses an underlying disease before it is confirmed by additional laboratory or other tests. In the latter, causal case, the latent variable is referred to as a formative latent variable because it is formed or caused by the observed variables. Here it is the observed variables that give rise to the underlying condition. For example, a democratic system of government is a latent condition that is formed by free elections, representative legislatures, free independent judiciary, free press, and so forth. In the same vein, psychological stress is an underlying condition that is formed by various observed variables, including such undesirable life events as, for example, illness, divorce, bankruptcy, and job loss. The events do not indicate a condition of stress and they are not symptoms of stress; rather, they create it and precede its manifestations.

One of the unique features of SEM analysis is that it provides disattenuated estimates, that is, estimates that are adjusted upward by the relative unreliability of the measures. More specifically, the resulting estimates are adjusted to what they would be if the measures were assessed without measurement error, that is, with perfect reliability. It has long been recognized that measurement error that reduces the reliability of a measure also reduces its correlation with other measures. The lower the reliability of measured variables, the lower will be the degree to which the independent variables can predict dependent variables. This is akin to the degradation in the performance of a sharpshooter who is standing on a vibrating platform, or having to shoot at a target that moves erratically. The standard statistical analyses proceed with the implicit and false assumption that variables are measured with no error. Consequently an unknown number of conclusions in the literature may be completely false or misleading. If these conclusions are based on comparisons of relative size of correlations, or the relative impact of variables on an outcome as reflected in regression coefficients, they ignore the role of unreliability. It may be the relative unreliability of the measures that made one parameter appear greater than the other, rather than the true impact of the one variable compared to the other, as stated in the conclusion of the study. In contrast to conventional regression analyses, SEM analysis provides results that allow comparisons of parameters such as correlations and paths unconfounded by measurement error. As SEM analysis eliminates the effects of measurement error, its results serve the needs of basic research better than those of standard statistical analyses. While the use of results that are plagued by measurement error may be suitable in many applied settings, it does confound the pure nature of relationships among theoretical constructs.

SEM analysis proceeds along five major steps. Model specification is the first step in which the researcher builds what is called a measurement model by specifying which observed variables are the indicators of which reflective factors, and which are causal indicators of formative factors. Later the relationships among the latent factors in terms of paths of direct influence are added to form a "structural model." The second step is known as model identification. The goal of this step is to determine whether the specified model including its structural part is formally identified. That is, here the analysis determines whether the estimation of the model can provide a unique solution to the set of equations derived from the variances and covariances of the observed variables. Model estimation is the third step. It involves the application of a statistical procedure to estimate the model's parameters in such a way that minimizes the discrepancy between the parameters of the specified or implied model and those based on of the empirical data set. The fourth step, known as model evaluation, is undertaken to determine how well the results fit the data. Various goodness-of-fit measures and other information guide the researcher as to whether to accept or reject the model. Usually the evaluation process proceeds to examining more specific questions of which particular paths demonstrate statistically significant influence on hypothesized latent factors, and how much of the factor variance is accounted for by the independent factors or variables. The evaluation of the model may also include inspection of results that suggest modification or re-specification to achieve a better fitting model. The fifth step is the re-specification of a new model based on information supplied as part of the estimation and evaluation process regarding possible improvement in the model's fit.

The most important issue with regard to the interpretation of results from SEM analysis is the issue of the causal status of paths of direct influence. Fundamentally, the results of SEM are based on analysis of the covariances of all the observed variables. It has been argued that analysis of co-variation cannot serve to inform us of causal relationships unless additional information is available regarding, for example, which variables preceded others in time, and thus may be regarded as causes rather than effects. Even when such information is available, it may be deemed insufficient for concluding that a causal relationship exists between the variables because of unspecified third variables. That is, other variables that do not appear in the model may be causing both variables to be related, rather than being a causal connection between the two. Furthermore, it has been shown that for nearly all models, there are sets of alternative models that fit the data equally well and the values of the paths in these alternative models are often quite different from each other. It is therefore important to consider good fitting models and their parameters as providing support for the hypothesized model and its implied hypotheses rather than providing a proof or confirmation of the model validity.

Thus, the prevailing wisdom is to exercise a great deal of caution in the application of causal interpretation to SEM results, and in particular, when the results are based on cross-sectional designs where the data were collected at the same time point. With this caution notwithstanding, in the past few years an emerging new and exciting line of research has provided new tools to identify specific models or paths as causal ones solely on the basis of the SEM analysis. This work on causality in SEM was pioneered by Judea Pearl, of the University of California at Los Angeles, and is only now becoming recognized by leading SEM researchers who attempt to make it more accessible to practitioners. Early in their developments, path and SEM analysis were expected to become methods of choice for providing causal analysis for observational data. With the new line of research developed by Pearl, the potential of SEM for meeting this expectation takes a significant leap forward.

Because of the general nature of the linear structural relation model, and the availability of excellent software for conducting SEM analysis, the technique is being used in ever increasing number of fields, as well as in studies with complex methodologies and designs. For example, there is increasing use of SEM for analysis of studies using randomized experimental designs (*see* **Experiment**). The critical analysis in a study based on experimental design centers upon the question of whether the experimental manipulation or variation has a significant impact on the intended outcome. The conventional analysis of variance approach is quite effective in answering this key question. However, frequently experimental studies are also concerned with mediation processes: that is, the extent to which the ultimate effect on a distal outcome is mediated by a proximal one that serves as a mediator. SEM is an efficient form of analysis for investigating mediation processes, including in experimental studies, for it provides a unified model with all the direct and mediating links from the hypothesized causes to the final outcomes. In addition to providing estimates for direct effects, SEM also provides estimates of indirect and total effects of every independent variable in the model. It thus provides a more comprehensive and detailed set of results borne out of a simultaneous estimation procedure rather than of fragmentary sets of analyses using other techniques.

Social survey researchers and public opinion pollsters develop and apply methodologies to collect unbiased information using scientific sampling techniques (*see* **Sampling Process**). In the same vein, their efforts should also include appropriate methodologies for the analysis and interpretation of data. Much of the information that is collected with various survey and polling instruments serves to provide assessment of various latent conditions, such as, for example, the public's confidence in the **economy**, the public's **trust in government**, or attitudes toward policy issues. Other analytic issues touch upon the socioeconomic or ideological characteristics of respondents as determinants of their trust or attitudes toward the issues. The information that is collected in these surveys consists of verbal responses to questions that are the observed indicators of these latent factors. As such, they also must be considered for what they are: fallibly measured indicators with varying degrees of reliability. SEM analysis that adjusts for the unreliability of the measures provides another scientific tool to improve the validity of interpretation based on the information collected in these public opinion polls.

Further Reading

Bollen, K. A. *Structural Equations with Latent Variables*. New York: John Wiley, 1989. Provides a comprehensive treatment of SEM with its mathematical and statistical foundations.

Kline, R.B. *Principles and Practice of Structural Equation Modeling.* New York: Guilford Press, 1998. Provides accessible presentation of SEM methodology and practice.

Pearl, J. *Causality: Models, Reasoning, and Inference.* Cambridge: Cambridge University Press, 2000.

Web Sites

For more information about SEM, go to http://www.gsu.edu/~mkteer/semnet.html. As stated on the Web site, "SEMNET is an open forum for ideas and questions about the methodology that includes analysis of covariance structures, path analysis, and confirmatory factor analysis. SEMNET bridges the gaps between users, between disciplines, and between conferences . . . [It] is for sharing ideas about this methodology with other interested researchers. SEMNET is also for researchers who are just learning (or re-learning) about structural equation modeling, or who are facing problems in applying these techniques to their own research."

Amiram D. Vinokur

Survey Error

Survey error refers to the error that is associated with any individual survey or any survey statistic. There are two fundamental types of error in a survey: variable error and systematic error. Variable error refers to the variability of results that might be found during different administrations of the same survey design and procedures. Systematic error or bias, in contrast, refers to cases where survey designs, methods, or procedures consistently measure something different from the true value of a particular statistic or measure.

The most common discussions of survey error are those where a survey is reported with a "margin of error," which typically refers to the sampling error generated under certain circumstances for a survey with the equivalent number of interviews. Although sampling error is one source of error in a survey, the concept of a total survey error reflects both the impact of sampling error and the impact of non-sampling errors. Although non-sampling errors may have a greater impact on public opinion survey data than sampling errors, the potential magnitude of non-sampling errors is significantly more difficult to measure than sampling error.

Survey methodology typically assumes that there exists a "true" value for each statistic that is imperfectly measured in a survey. If a given survey methodology is employed consistently over a number of occasions, survey researchers expect that different estimates of the value of a statistic will be produced. How widespread these estimates are is typically understood as the variance of a given measure, and researchers understand that different survey designs will produce different levels of variance for any statistic.

In a basic sense, survey research views any particular survey as one trial or replication of a potentially infinite number of administrations of a survey that might have occurred. For example, the final pre-election poll of a major media organization can be understood to include a random sample of respondents; under a slightly different set of circumstances, different respondents would have been selected and the survey likely would have found slightly different results for survey questions.

Under ideal circumstances, the different values observed from different surveys should vary randomly around the true but unobserved value of a survey statistic, which is the variation that occurs with all random samples. For example, if exactly 50 percent of all voters will vote for Candidate X, then different surveys should be equally likely to find more than 50 percent or less than 50 percent of voters voting for Candidate X. Any particular survey might produce an estimate with Candidate X receiving more or less than 50 percent of the vote. But researchers expect that these variable errors will be in different directions from the true value of the statistic and cancel each other out. With variable error, different administrations of the survey should produce, on average, an accurate estimate of the true proportion of voters who plan to vote for X.

Systematic error or bias comes about when variable errors are not centered on the true value of the statistic, and consequently do not entirely cancel each other. Even though different administrations of the survey will yield different results, and some of these survey results may be extremely accurate, with systematic error the results of multiple administrations of the same survey methodology do not, on average, balance each other or center on the true value of the statistic. In contrast, with systematic error different replications of a survey method will on average produce an estimate for a statistic that is different than the true value of that statistic.

For example, if exactly 50 percent all voters will vote for Candidate X but we employ a survey method that consistently and systematically excludes 10 percent of Candidate X's supporters while excluding none of those who do not support X, then surveys using that method would produce biased results. Random variation would cause different administrations of a survey with this biased methodology to produce different results; random variation even makes it possible that a survey with this method would produce an estimate that was exactly correct. However, on average, surveys with this biased method would estimate Candidate X receiving 45 percent of the vote, or 10 percent less than the true value of this statistic. Although there will still be variability in the results of surveys, the variability would center on a biased value of 45 percent of the vote, rather than the accurate value of 50 percent.

Bias in surveys, as well as variation, can come from a number of sources. Survey methodologists typically think of survey error in two ways: as Total Survey Error and as Mean Squared Error (MSE). Both of these concepts take into account the commonly discussed sampling error and myriad other possible sources of error introduced into survey estimates through the survey research process. Total Survey Error is the difference between the estimate for a statistic measured in a particular survey and the true value of that statistic. The Mean Squared Error takes into account not only error associated with the variability of survey statistics but also systematic bias.

The MSE is a concept and measure commonly used to encompass both the systematic error or bias in a survey and the variable error or variance in a survey. The MSE is typically measured as the sum of the squared bias in a survey and the variance. Thus, in cases where there is no bias, the MSE is equal to the variance. The MSE applies to any specific statistic measured in a survey, and might be different for different survey questions contained in the same public opinion poll. Since survey researchers can rarely know the true value of a statistic, and rarely know the bias involved in a given method, the MSE cannot typically be calculated or reported.

A variety of sources can influence both bias and variance in a survey. Typically, these include both sampling error and non-sampling error. Biemer and Lyberg delineate different potential sources of survey error and their potential impact on both variable error and systematic error. Specification error, frame error, and nonresponse error all have a relatively small impact on the measured variability of survey results but have a potentially high risk for producing systematic bias. In contrast, sampling error has minimal risk of bias but has a potentially high influence on variability. Measurement error and data processing error have a potentially high impact on both variable error and systematic bias. Under this formulation, the MSE formula can be expanded to read MSE = $(B_{SPEC} + B_{NR} + B_{MEAS} + B_{DP})^2 + VAR_{SAMP} + VAR_{MEAS} + VAR_{DP}$.

One extremely useful typology for understanding survey errors is presented by Groves and partitions survey error into two categories: errors of nonobservation and observational errors. Errors of nonobservation primarily impact coverage, sampling, and response. Observational errors principally involve errors of the interviewer, respondent, questionnaire, measure, or survey instrument.

Errors of Nonobservation

Errors of nonobservation occur when a survey fails to observe or include members of the target or inferential population for a survey. This primarily occurs due to sampling errors and to problems with coverage and nonresponse.

Sampling errors are the most commonly reported errors in public opinion surveys. Sampling errors are measures of variability that arise from data generated from a sample rather than a whole population. Since public opinion surveys are fundamentally based on samples, the sampling error associated with a given survey design can be calculated with reasonable precision and be reported as a quantifiable measure of the potential quality of a survey.

Sampling errors for public opinion polls are often reported as a "margin of error." News organizations that take more care typically refer to a margin of sampling error. When an explanation is given, it is typically worded similarly to the following description from a New York Times poll: "In theory, in 19 cases out of 20, overall results based on such samples will differ by no more than 3 percentage points in either direction from what would have been obtained by seeking out all residents of New York City. For smaller sub-groups the margin of sample error is larger. As an example, for registered voters it is plus or minus 4 points" (*New York Times*, February 16, 2005).

The sampling error reported for public opinion polls is typically a simple random sample drawn with replacement. A typical calculation of this would be specified as: $\sqrt{\dfrac{(p^* (1 - p))}{n}} * 1.96$ where n = the number of respondents contacted in

survey, p = the proportion of respondents who provided a given response, and 1.96 is the standard value from a statistical table to provide a two-tailed confidence interval at the 95 percent level of confidence.

This statistic will actually vary depending on the proportion of respondents answering a question (p). The sampling error is greatest when p = 50 percent;

when the proportion of respondents answering a question is larger or smaller, the sampling error is less. A careful reader might calculate a specific sample error for each question asked in a survey, based on the survey response, the number of respondents who answered the particular question, and the confidence interval that mattered most to the reader. The typical convention among publicly reported public opinion polls, however, is to report an overall sampling error at the 95 percent confidence interval, based on the maximum error obtained in this calculation, where $p = .5$ or where 50 percent of respondents provided a specific answer.

In cases of very small populations or very large samples, where the survey sample is a significant percentage of the population, sampling statisticians typically modify the formula above to include a finite population correction. This factor, which multiplies the calculated sample error by $1 - \sqrt{\dfrac{n}{N}}$ where n is the **sample size** and N is the size of the total population. Since the samples for public opinion polls are typically substantially less than 1 percent of a population, this factor can be ignored. However, an analyst might include a finite population correction in a calculation of sample error when the sample is 5 percent or more of the population being studied.

The sampling error measured for a given survey or given survey questions can also vary according to other factors of a survey design. If samples are stratified unequally, or certain groups are over-sampled, then the sample must be adjusted (e.g., weighted) to reflect their true proportion in the population. More complicated sample designs, such as clustered samples or multistage designs, also impact the variability of a sample in complex ways. Although complex sampling errors are rarely reported with the results of public opinion polls, analysts can take sample weights and more complex survey designs into account using readily available software packages such as SUDAAN or STATA.

Coverage errors result when the **sample frame** or frame population for a survey does not correspond to the target population for a survey. The most problematic type of coverage error for surveys is generally noncoverage, which occurs when the sample frame population and the target population for a survey do not correspond. The extent of the bias introduced by noncoverage error depends on both the magnitude of the noncoverage and the differences between respondents included in the sample frame on the particular statistics involved in any analysis.

Noncoverage is very similar to nonresponse. In both cases, bias may result when members of the target population of a survey are systematically excluded from the survey population. In the case of coverage error, members of the target population are excluded from the sample frame. Nonresponse, in contrast, comes about when members of a sample frame do not respond to the survey.

Noncoverage bias can be expressed by the formula:

$$B_{NC} = \frac{N_{nc}}{N}(Y_c - Y_{nc})$$

In words, this says that the level of noncoverage bias is equal to the proportion of the population excluded from a sample frame multiplied by the difference between the value of the statistic for cases covered in the survey and those not covered. In cases where the bias is positive, the value of the statistic is larger for the covered population, while a negative bias indicates the value of the statistic is greater in target population members excluded from the sample frame.

From this formula, it can be seen that the magnitude of coverage error in a survey depends both on the proportion of the target population omitted from the frame and the differences between the covered and noncovered populations. In cases where only a small proportion of a population is excluded from a sample frame, coverage error is likely to be small unless there are large differences between the covered and noncovered populations. In contrast, if there are minimal differences between covered and noncovered populations, a sample frame can omit a large portion of a population without producing substantial coverage error.

Estimating the magnitude of coverage error is usually difficult in public opinion surveys because the difference between covered and omitted populations on survey statistics is usually not known. Analysts can often estimate the magnitude of coverage error based on information such as comparison between a sample frame and known population characteristics. However, except in very special cases, analysts do not know how omitted members of the sample frame may have responded to survey questions and cannot estimate the impact of this factor on coverage error.

Nonresponse errors result when individuals are not interviewed but are included in the sample for a survey. Item nonresponse occurs when data is missing from a particular question or measure in a survey, while **unit nonresponse** occurs when a member of the sample does not produce any usable data for a survey. In a typical public opinion poll, item nonresponse occurs when respondents refuse to answer a particular survey question, whereas unit nonresponse occurs when respondents do not answer any questions in a poll or survey.

Nonresponse bias is conceptually quite similar to coverage bias, and the formulae to measure these biases are also similar. The formula to measure nonresponse bias can be written as:

$$B_{NR} = \frac{N_{nr}}{N} (Y_r - Y_{nr})$$

In words, this says that the level of nonresponse bias is equal to the proportion of the population who do not respond to the survey multiplied by the difference between the value of the statistic for cases who do respond compared to those who do not respond.

The two principal causes of unit nonresponse are **refusal** by an individual to be interviewed and failing to make contact with an individual who is included in the sample. Both can impact the ability to make inferences from the survey data. If the reasons for nonresponse are random, or are not correlated with the variables of interest in a survey, then the impact of even large levels of nonresponse may be minimal. In contrast, however, if the reasons for survey nonresponse are related to questions being asked in the survey, then the impact of nonresponse may be substantial.

Traditionally, the survey **response rate** has been taken as a proxy for nonresponse bias. In cases where the response rate is high, the level of possible response bias is necessarily limited, and a high response rate can be taken as a sign of low response bias. However, public opinion surveys in developed countries are increasingly obtaining response rates that are quite low by traditional norms. Although some take this as a sign that nonresponse bias is exceptionally high, this is not necessarily the case. Since the level of nonresponse bias depends both on response rates and on differences between respondents and nonrespondents, researchers increasingly need to consider both levels of response and nonresponse and differences between respondents and nonrespondents.

The principal methods to counter nonresponse are prevention and adjustment. Preventive measures aim to increase response rates, while nonresponse adjustments attempt to adjust the data of existing survey respondents to account for nonresponse.

Preventive measures attempt to remedy the unavailability of respondents to participate in a survey or poll and the unwillingness of sampled members of a population to become survey respondents. Survey methodologists design research protocols to maximize the ability to reach a respondent and to reduce the proportion of members of a sample who are unavailable to be interviewed. Survey researchers typically attempt to reach a household or a respondent multiple times to contact respondents who may be home infrequently. For example, protocols may specify that sample records be calls at different times of the day, different days of the week, weekends, and so forth. Additionally, field protocols may schedule **callbacks** at times that are convenient for a respondent. Surveys that obtain high response rates typically require long **field periods**.

Reducing refusals is accomplished through refusal avoidance and refusal conversion. Refusal avoidance involves training interviewers to have courteous voices, to learn how to "read" a respondent's mood, and to otherwise entice a prospective respondent to complete a survey. Refusal conversion involves calling respondents who have initially refused to do an interview and asking them to reconsider. Surveys that obtain low refusal levels typically include refusal reduction methods such as mailings to supplement telephone or personal contact. Incentives, both symbolic and monetary, are increasingly used to persuade respondents to complete surveys.

Survey data can also be statistically adjusted to compensate for nonresponse. One standard method is to apply post-stratification weights to the survey data based on responses to key variables (*see* **Weighting**). For example, data may be weighted so that the final survey data set that is analyzed mirrors population estimates for key characteristics such as age, gender, race, income, and level of educational attainment. These weights adjust for nonresponse to the extent that the differences between respondents and nonrespondents are correlated with these variables. However, in cases where nonresponse is correlated partially with demographic characteristics and partially with other non-estimable characteristics, weighting can provide only a partial solution to nonresponse.

Observational Errors

Observational errors principally involve errors of the interviewer, respondent, and instrument. While errors of nonobservation typically affect the generalizability or external validity of a survey, observational errors can have a more complex impact on survey data. In particular, observational errors can lead to both increased variability and bias in ways that are more complex than those encountered in errors arising from sampling, coverage, and nonresponse. Moreover, interactions between questionnaire items, interviewers, and respondents may occur in ways that make it difficult to specify the exact source of an observational error. For example, a poorly designed survey question might lead to a greater propensity of interviewer error, and this might be compounded by the way a respondent interacts with the interviewer, leading to a wide range of potential variability and bias.

Interviewer errors can occur when interviewers make data entry errors, when they fail to administer the survey instrument in a standardized manner, when they fail to probe, and so forth (*see* **Interviewing Effects**). An additional type of interviewer-related error occurs when survey responses are affected by demographic or personal characteristics of interviewers, such as gender or race. Interviewer errors can also occur if interviewers fail to accurately record or transcribe the results of a survey interview. When interacting with respondents, different interviewers may probe questions or interpret responses in different ways.

Interviewer errors lead to both variable and systematic errors. In cases where interviewer errors are random, interviewer effects primarily serve to increase the variability of survey data. Kish describes $\square_{int}$, or the intra-interviewer correlation coefficient, as a measure which taps the proportion of the total variability of a question that is due to interviewer variability. In some cases, however, systematic interviewer errors can cause bias in survey data as well.

The principal methods of avoiding interviewer error involve extensive training, monitoring of interviewers, and developing work environments that encourage the correct reporting of data. Also, standardized field administration procedures and practices, such as centralized administration of survey interviews, can serve to minimize and standardize this error. One technique used to reduce correlated interviewer bias in clustered or face-to-face surveys is the use of interpenetrated interviewer assignments, which randomly assign interviewers to different records in a given sample unit or cluster. In this case, interviewer bias, if present, is randomized among respondents in a given set of the sample. Telephone survey methods, which are increasingly used for public opinion research, make random assignment of interviewers across different parts of the sample exceedingly simple.

Interviewers can also be trained differently to reduce interviewer variation or systematic bias. Traditionally, survey interviewers have been trained to operate in an extremely standardized and neutral manner, reading survey questions to a respondent verbatim, using a neutral tone of voice, and to provide standard probes to questions with no additional interpretation. Survey interviewers trained in this manner become accustomed to answering respondent requests for clarification on questionnaire items with "whatever it means to you." These methods serve to minimize the differences between the bias that might be introduced by one interviewer compared to another.

An alternative method of training, however, encourages interviewers to adopt a more conversational tone and, in some cases, to use customized or ad hoc probes to attempt to elicit a response from a respondent. Proponents of this interviewing style argue that respondents who are more engaged in a conversation with an interviewer are more likely to respond to a survey, and more likely to pay attention to survey questions. Additionally, this method can provide enhanced data quality when interviewers can use clues provided by respondents to probe questions differently or offer more clarification. In cases where survey questions are attempting to obtain factual information, such as a level of education, household composition, income, and so forth, highly skilled and well-trained interviewers can often utilize this less restrictive interviewing method to reduce both bias and variation in survey responses.

In practice, most survey organizations train interviewers to adopt some parts of each of these methods. Friendly and personable interviewers who are capable of addressing respondent concerns about an interview typically have higher response rates and more engaged respondents. However, most public opinion survey interviewers are also trained to provide neutral probes to questions, and to interpret questions only within narrow parameters as provided by the authors of a survey.

Respondent errors occur because of respondent memory problems, hearing problems, unwillingness to provide accurate information, and so forth. Disinterest in the interview is another cause of errors. Respondent errors are similar to interviewer errors in producing both variability and bias in survey data.

In many cases, survey interviewing techniques are designed to attempt to reduce respondent errors. In cases where questions have factual answers, interviewers may be trained to use their judgment to probe or clarify responses. Specialized survey instrument designs can be used to increase the accuracy of responses. Interviews that attempt to elicit information about past events in a respondent's life, for example, may first encourage the respondent to think of significant life events such as marriages and birth of children, and then ask the respondent to date other events in relation to these. Questions about income, for example, can be broken down into components: weekly wages, overtime, tips, and so forth.

Attitude and opinion surveys can be particularly susceptible to problems with respondent effects. Political scientist Philip Converse pointedly critiqued the ability of general respondents to coherently respond to survey questions. Converse discussed several problems with survey responses, including the lack of a coherent or constrained ideological structure in many individuals and the existence of "non-attitudes" in responses to survey questions. These critiques fundamentally point to difficulties with the reliability of survey responses or with the ability of survey questions to produce consistent results.

Common observers of public opinion data often note surveys on seemingly similar topics that produce widely different results based on subtle differences in question wording. In addition to problems with respondent attention or attitudes, researchers have also pointed out problems in questions about public policy that often tap different underlying value structures. When presented with questions about the specifics of different public policy issues, slight differences in question wording or impact often cause respondents to tap different underlying sets of values to develop survey responses. An alternative view to the strict notion that respondents hold "non-attitudes" is a more flexible one that understands that genuine ambivalence often occurs in survey respondents on a number of issues.

Political scientists have devoted particular attention to the problems of reliability and constraint in answers to questions about ideology and policy. Levels of general political knowledge, cognitive sophistication, and educational attainment have all been found to correlate with respondent errors. In addition, respondent information about the specific topic of a survey question has been found to play a crucial role in the stability or reliability of survey responses. Although respondents generally have more stable opinions about issues on which they have high levels of information, the impact of information as presented through the news media is somewhat less clear and more complex. In some cases, attitude instability in respondents can be induced by media exposure, particularly in respondents with low general levels of political knowledge and sophistication.

Researchers have also focused on the impact of respondent engagement in determining the quality of a survey response. Krosnik and colleagues discuss respondent "**satisficing,**" as a response process where respondents engage minimal cognitive and memory processes to give an answer to a survey. In this case, encouraging engaging interviewers and engaging questionnaires are two possible solutions for researchers to minimize the impact of respondent satisficing on responses.

Psychologists who study survey responses typically focus on different aspects of errors introduced by response processes. One problem is the possibility of a social desirability effect, or a tendency of respondents to provide responses that they perceive will be acceptable either to an interviewer or to other members of the general public. The impact of social desirability can be particularly acute in topics such as racism, sexism, or sexual practices where respondents might think their personal opinions are dramatically outside of a social norm. These effects can be particularly strong when interacting with interviewer effects. Responses to questions about some matters of racial policy and politics are different, for example, depending on whether the interviewer is perceived to be of the same race of the respondent or a different race.

A different set of research studies on respondent errors focuses on acquiescence effects, or the tendency of respondents to answer questions affirmatively. In a battery of questions that ask a respondent to respond yes or no, respondents are sometimes more likely to respond with the affirmative "yes" response when controlling for other factors.

Instrument errors refer to problems with the survey questionnaire or measures included in a survey. Examples of this include specification error, **question-wording effects**, and **question-order effects**.

Specification error can occur when a survey question or measure is poorly designed and measures something different than the researcher intends. For example, a survey question that asks respondents their income may elicit different responses depending on whether respondents think the item refers to personal income or household income. A public opinion survey analysis of "Democrats" may mean different things depending on whether a question measures party registration, party identification, or recent votes. To minimize specification error in a survey questionnaire, terms should be properly defined and easily and consistently interpretable.

The wording of a survey question can also produce survey error. Response categories for a survey question, for example, must be mutually exclusive and collectively exhaustive. Questions should use clear, generally nontechnical words that are likely to be understandable to all respondents. One example of a very common question wording problem is a "double-barreled" question, or one that asks a respondent to discuss more than one attribute. For example, if a survey question asks whether a public figure is "friendly and caring," respondents who believe the official is caring but unfriendly may have difficulty responding.

Question-order effects refer to the possible effect of previous questions on any given survey question. For example, responses to a survey question may be influenced by a previous question. In the context of a political poll, for example, a question measuring presidential job approval might elicit different responses if included after a question on the respondent's economic security than it would if included after a question on the respondent's feeling of safety in the event of terrorist attacks.

Future Directions

Survey methodology is devoted to measuring and understanding survey errors, and will continue to come to a better understanding of numerous sources of bias and variability in surveys. However, the two most pressing trends impacting errors in public opinion surveys in the coming decades will be declining response rates and increasing problems with coverage in telephone surveys due to new technologies. Although research continues to be done to develop methods of reducing nonresponse and maximizing coverage in telephone surveys, it is unlikely that these techniques alone will minimize total survey error. Consequently, researchers will need to develop better means of understanding differences between those who are included in survey data sets and those that are not, and will need to develop better methods for adjusting survey data to account for these differences.

Further Reading

Biemer, Paul P., and Lars E. Lyberg. *Introduction to Survey Quality*. New York: John Wiley, 2003, pp. 63–80.

Groves, Robert M. *Survey Errors and Survey Costs*. New York: John Wiley, 1989, pp. 81–131.

Lessler, Judith T., and William D. Kalsbeek. *Nonsampling Error in Surveys*. New York: John Wiley, pp. 40–102.

Chase H. Harrison

Survey Ethics

Survey ethics are agreed-upon rules of professional practice in the conduct of public opinion research. They inform survey researchers of their obligations to survey participants, survey sponsors, and the public when designing, conducting, and reporting on opinion research. When followed, they are intended to engender public trust in the research process as well as the poll results produced by it.

There are a number of trade and professional organizations, such as the American Association for Public Opinion Research (AAPOR), the Council of American Survey Research Organizations (CASRO), the National Council on Public Polls (NCPP), and the Survey Research Methods Section (SRMS) of the American Statistical Association (ASA), that have adopted a code of standards and conduct relating to the practice of survey research. These codes typically address such issues as:

- How will consent be obtained for survey participation, and who can give consent?
- What type and how much information is appropriate to collect in a survey?
- How will the survey be conducted, and what will be done to protect respondents' privacy?
- How will the survey data be analyzed and reported?

Although the codes of conduct are not identical among the various organizations, they rest on similar principles.

Issues Related to Obtaining Survey Cooperation. Survey research depends on the willingness of persons to participate in surveys. This reservoir of cooperation must be viewed as a precious resource and should not be consciously or inadvertently abused or contaminated when obtaining consent for or conducting surveys. Ethical codes in the survey profession evince a common concern for the welfare of survey respondents. How much and what information must be provided to potential survey respondents, at what age can someone give their consent, and can consent be verbal or must it be in writing—these concerns exemplify issues related to obtaining survey cooperation.

Survey Introductions. Survey introductions provide varying amounts of information to potential respondents; in most surveys, individuals give their consent by verbally agreeing to participate at the beginning of the interview or by returning a completed questionnaire. Survey introductions usually provide some indication of the population being surveyed (or how the respondent was selected) and the subject matter (or types of questions that will be asked). However, they do not always provide the name of the sponsoring organization or detailed information about the purpose of the survey because of the possibility of biasing respondents' answers. For example, in advertising or public relations studies, disclosing the sponsors' names in the introduction to an interview might evoke positive or negative feelings that could influence or contaminate the studies' results.

Irrespective of the length of the survey introduction, interviewers in their recruitment efforts should honestly identify their research firm or affiliation and not knowingly misrepresent the length of the interview or make other factually incorrect statements. Interviewers should not imply that survey participation is mandatory; if the survey sponsor is identified and perceived to have authority over the potential respondent (as in the case of an employee survey), the survey introduction should be explicit about the voluntary nature of participation. If electronic equipment is used to monitor or tape interviews, it should be done only with the knowledge, understanding, and consent of respondents.

Surveys of Children. There does not appear to be a consensus among research professionals concerning the minimum age for giving consent to survey participation, and this may vary depending on the survey topic (e.g., a survey about preferences for different toys versus a survey about use of controlled substances). Regardless of the topic, normally permission is obtained from a parent or guardian before interviewing a young child. When parental consent is verbal, interviewers usually record the identity of the person giving permission for the child to be interviewed. To ensure safety, whenever possible a parent or other responsible adult should be present when conducting personal interviews of young children, and interviewers of young children may require additional background screening, qualifications, and training. When collecting information on extremely personal or controversial topics that could be embarrassing or cause uneasiness, it is customary to obtain permission from a parent or guardian for all persons under age eighteen. Some survey sponsors and organizations require parental permission before interviewing anyone under age eighteen, regardless of the type of information being collected (unless the consent process itself will endanger the child, such as for a study of abuse).

Verbal Versus Written Consent. Most surveys merely ask questions about opinions, attitudes, values, and behavior or collect demographic or other factual information from survey participants. Unlike medical experiments, they generally do not involve assignment to different treatment groups or any type of physical intervention and pose little risk to participants. Consequently, it is generally considered sufficient to obtain verbal (rather than written) permission before administering a survey provided there are no perceived risks associated with survey participation and the person giving consent is an adult.

Avoidance of Harassment. To maximize survey participation and minimize the potential for nonresponse bias, interviewers often make repeated attempts to contact or persuade a potential respondent to participate in a survey. This may involve recontacting persons in households or businesses who previously have refused their cooperation. When doing this, interviewers need to avoid practices that could be interpreted as harassment (e.g., attempting to contact respondents numerous times within a short time period; intentionally making contact attempts at inconvenient times; knowingly leaving messages on answering machines that might be perceived as annoying). If refusal conversion efforts are anticipated, interviewers should record whether the person who refused is the designated respondent or someone else (e.g., another household member, a company receptionist), and the reasons for refusing participation (to the extent that this information is known). Interviewers sometimes are asked to make judgments as to whether the refusal is a "soft" one (someone likely to become a survey participant) or a "hard" one (someone unlikely to become a survey participant); and only to recontact persons classified as soft refusals. To minimize the potential for harassment, sometimes specially trained interviewers are assigned the responsibility of recontacting people who initially refused to obtain their cooperation for a particular study.

Appropriate Subject Matter for Surveys. In addition to issues relating to obtaining consent for survey participation, researchers must concern themselves with other issues such as what types and how much information is appropriate to collect in a survey. Most surveys are expensive to conduct, and respondents rarely are paid for their participation (except for an occasional courtesy payment). Therefore, researchers owe it to both research sponsors and survey respondents to have specific information goals for a survey, to consider alternatives for obtaining the desired information, and to not employ research methods that are either unsuited to the research problem or likely to yield misleading conclusions.

Assuming a survey is appropriate, researchers should collect only as much information as necessary to address the specific research objectives and not intentionally ask biased questions. Fishing expeditions (collecting information that serves no particular purpose or is not necessary for the research) unnecessarily burden survey respondents. However, there is no consensus as to the maximum allowable length for a survey, and this may vary depending on the population being surveyed, their interest in the topic, and the perceived importance of the survey.

Given the intrusiveness of collecting extremely personal information or information on controversial subjects in a survey, the reasons for doing so need to be evaluated in terms of both the potential burden to respondents and the benefits of the research. When it is necessary to collect such information, the researcher should use techniques to minimize the possible discomfort of survey respondents and should be explicit about the respondents' right to refuse to answer specific questions or to stop the interview. Researchers should respect the right of respondents to decline to cooperate at any time during a study.

Prevention of Interviewer Falsification. During the administration of a survey, researchers are responsible for ensuring that the data are collected in accordance with their instructions and that interviewers accurately and completely record respondents' answers. One area of concern is interviewer falsification, particularly for door-to-door surveys and other surveys that are not conducted from a central location where it is relatively easy to monitor interviewer performance. Interviewer falsification is sometimes referred to as cheating or "curbstoning," a reference to when errant interviewers made-up interviews while sitting on a curbstone rather than knocking on the door or ringing the bell of a designated household and then attempting to complete an interview. Interviewer falsification takes different forms and may include fabricating all or part of an interview or intentionally engaging in one or more of the following activities: misclassifying answers to one or more questions (e.g., to avoid having to ask certain questions and shorten the length of the interview), interviewing a person not in the survey sample (e.g., because the designated respondent is not available), misreporting the results of efforts to contact a sample member (e.g., to conceal the number of refusals), or departing from any other data collection guidelines or instructions for administering a survey (e.g., for reasons of convenience).

Researchers are obliged to use methods that will discourage and detect instances of interviewer falsification. Motivations for interviewer falsification vary, and this type of activity is more likely to occur when interviewers are unqualified or are not properly trained or supervised. It may also occur when researchers place unrealistic demands on interviewers (e.g., require them to complete a large number of interviews with a low incidence or difficult population in a short time period) or compensate interviewers based on the number of completed interviews or give production bonuses. Interviewer falsification can be prevented through careful selection and training of interviewers, ongoing monitoring and supervision of all data collection activities, and by not compensating interviewers on a piecework basis. If interviewer falsification occurs, survey practitioners are obliged to inform the sponsors of the research of this and the steps they have taken to correct any contamination of the data.

Protection of Respondent Confidentiality. Researchers and all other persons involved in collecting, processing, and analyzing data for a survey share an ethical obligation to ensure respondent confidentiality and to protect the names of individual respondents or other identifying information from disclosure to third parties (e.g., the sponsor of the research, the public). The emphasis on confidentiality in ethical codes adopted by associations in the survey industry reflects the fact that many individuals will not agree to take part in a survey if they believe they will be identified or their responses will be used for nonresearch purposes. Moreover, even if some individuals participate in surveys without being guaranteed confidentiality, they may not be representative of the entire population being sampled (i.e., they may differ in important ways from those who are unwilling to participate). Thus, confidentiality not only helps to ensure representative survey samples but also encourages accurate responses (i.e., survey respondents are more likely to answer truthfully if they are assured confidentiality).

To protect confidentiality, researchers may separate all identifier information (name, address, telephone number) from the interview itself immediately after the interview has been completed or verified, or they may actually destroy identifier information. If retained, information that would enable someone to connect respondents with their answers should be stored securely. In some instances, protection of respondent confidentiality necessitates additional efforts or special measures to ensure that respondents cannot be identified through analysis of the data file alone (e.g., a respondent to an employee survey may be recognized by their job title even if their name and telephone number have been removed from the data file).

Sometimes researchers retain personal information about survey respondents after a survey is completed so that they can conduct another survey in the future on the same or similar topic and merge the data obtained from the different surveys (as in panel studies). However, respondents to a survey should not be contacted for another study based on their participation in a previous one or be automatically enrolled in a panel study without their permission.

Analysis and Reporting of Survey Results. After interviews for a survey have been completed, researchers must decide how to analyze and report the survey results. When analyzing results, researchers are responsible for ensuring that questionnaire information is processed accurately and appropriately (e.g., editing, coding, and entry of data on a computer are completed according to instructions and analysis programs work properly). When survey results are reported, researchers should provide sufficient information regarding the survey methods and the basis for their findings to enable the research sponsor or audience (including the general population if the data are publicly released) to evaluate their reliability and validity. Researchers should not knowingly misrepresent the results of a survey, or suggest interpretations or conclusions inconsistent with the survey data.

The format of a research report and the amount of information included depends on the research sponsor or the audience for which the report is intended (e.g., whether it is a press release for journalists, a top-line report for business executives, a report to a government agency, or an article intended for publication in an academic journal). While the amount of detail provided in a research report about the manner in which a survey was conducted varies, most survey associations require that the following information be made available: the name of the organization for whom the study was conducted (i.e., the research sponsor), the name of the organization that conducted the study, the dates of interviewing, the method of obtaining interviews (e.g., in-person, telephone, mail, or Internet), the population that the survey was intended to represent, the **sample frame** or method used to sample from this population, the number of completed interviews overall and for subgroups for which data are reported, the complete wording of questions upon which the analysis is based, the use of statistical weights (if any), and the basis for reported percentages or other statistical analyses.

Researchers also are encouraged to make available information about the number of persons, households, businesses, or other sample members they attempted to contact that did not result in a completed interview as well as the reasons for this (if this information is known). Professional associations in the survey industry advocate the use of a standard set of disposition codes for summarizing the results of data collection efforts (e.g., number of completed interviews, partial interviews, refusals, non-contacts) and/or the use of specific formulas for reporting response rates, cooperation rates, or other types of rates summarizing data collection outcomes. In practice, there remains considerable variation in the survey industry concerning the reporting of data collection outcomes. Consequently, if a **response rate**, cooperation rate, or other type of **outcome rate** summarizing the results of data collection is reported, the basis for calculating this rate should be described as well.

When survey results are based on a probability sample, it is customary to report estimates of sampling error. However, when estimates of sampling error are reported, researchers should not imply that this is the only possible source of error or even the largest potential source of error.

Unrepresentative Measurements of Public Opinion. Professional associations in the survey industry have expressed concern about the use of the term "poll" or "survey" to describe unscientific or unrepresentative measurements of public opinion, such as call-in polls conducted by television and radio stations or magazine polls that invite anyone to mail in a questionnaire. Respondents for these types of solicitations are self-selected, and usually there is nothing that prevents them from completing as many interviews or questionnaires as they choose. Therefore, there is no way to determine whose opinions are being collected or what the results of these inquiries represent.

Internet Polls. Some associations have issued statements condemning **Internet survey methods** that claim to be representative of the general population even though they make no attempt to scientifically or systematically select respondents and merely allow anyone who is interested to visit a Web site and take a survey. Such polls exclude persons not on the Internet, do not randomly sample from all persons on the Internet, and often overrepresent heavy Internet users. Because of the ease and low cost of conducting research over the Internet with large samples, professional associations in the survey industry also are concerned about the creation of enormous databases for the distribution of hundreds of thousands or even millions of questionnaires over the Internet. Extremely large survey samples are not needed to address most types of research problems. More importantly, the accuracy of survey results depends not only on sample size but also on how the sample for the survey was chosen and the representativeness of those who participated in the survey.

Even though some Internet polls (especially those that claim to represent the general public) have been the subject of criticism, professional associations in the survey industry recognize that the Internet can be a useful tool for conducting certain types of research (particularly list-based research for a population that has access to the Internet, such as college professors). For this reason, some associations in the survey industry have developed codes specifically relating to conduct of research over the Internet. These associations forbid engaging in deceptive practices or subterfuge in obtaining email addresses of potential respondents and bar the use of false or misleading return email addresses when conducting surveys.

Distinction Between Research and Nonresearch Activities. To enhance respect for survey research, associations in the industry seek to promote a separation of research from nonresearch activities by condemning individuals who misrepresent sales calls or canvassing of voters as legitimate surveys. For example, telemarketers sometimes claim to be interviewers conducting an opinion survey when they are really salespersons promoting a product or service or soliciting for a particular cause. Often these inquiries begin by asking respondents whether they are satisfied with their current service provider (e.g., their long-distance carrier, their insurance provider) or whether they care about a particular cause or issue (e.g., cost of prescription drugs, reforming the public schools). Based on the answers to these questions, the salesperson then attempts to get the respondent to buy something or asks them to contribute money to a candidate, political party, advocacy group, or other organization. Selling under the guise of interviewing and fund-raising under the guise of interviewing are sometimes referred to as "sugging" and "frugging."

Like salespersons, political candidates and their consultants also sometimes attempt to disguise negative campaigns as legitimate survey research. Legitimate political polls endeavor to measure existing opinion about political candidates, office holders, and various social and public policy issues among representative samples of the public and voters. However, sometimes politicians contact large numbers of voters under the guise of doing a poll to affect voter opinions by distorting candidate characteristics and feeding negative statements about candidates to potential voters. This type of activity is sometimes called a **push poll** because its aim is to push potential voters away from one candidate and toward another candidate. However, despite the reference to polling, these are not really legitimate surveys but rather a pernicious form of negative campaigning.

To summarize, codes of conduct published by trade and professional associations in the survey industry require that researchers not knowingly do any of the following: seriously mislead respondents when attempting to interview them, use biased methods for conducting research, fabricate data, misrepresent their survey methods, or distort their results. These codes also encourage researchers to take other steps to promote confidence in the survey process, including pointing out and correcting misstatements or misuse of their survey results and publicizing nonresearch activities disguised as surveys when they become known.

Web Sites

American Association for Public Opinion Research (AAPOR): Code of Professional Ethics and Practices, Statement for Institutional Review Boards, Statement on Web-based Surveys and 2003 Statement on Push Polls at http://www.aapor.org.

American Statistical Association Survey Research Methods Section (SRMS): Committee on Privacy and Confidentiality, Surveys and Privacy at http://www.amstat.org/sections/srms/brochures/privacy.

Council of American Survey Research Organizations (CASRO): Code of Standards and Ethics for Survey Research at http://www.casro.org/codeofstandards.

European Society for Marketing and Opinion Research (ESOMAR): Guide to Opinion Polls, Guideline on Interviewing Children and Young People, Guideline on Conducting Marketing and Opinion Research Using the Internet, and Guideline on Maintaining the Distinction between Marketing Research and Direct Marketing at http://www.esomar.org/guidelines.

National Council on Public Polls (NCPP): Statement of Disclosure, Statement about Internet Polls, and Press Warning from the National Council on Public Polls at http://www.ncpp.org.

World Association for Public Opinion Research (WAPOR): Code of Professional Ethics and Practices at http://www.unl.edu/wapor/ethics.

E. Deborah Jay

Survey Introductions

Survey introductions are the initial contact between interviewers and respondents during which participation for a study is solicited. Introductions are critical to achieving high response rates and limiting the costs of a survey. Effective survey introductions depend on (1) identifying elements that can motivate participation in a given survey, (2) using the elements to craft a script, and (3) adapting the script to the particular survey mode being employed.

Motivating Participation

Motivating respondents to participate in a poll is the primary objective of a survey introduction. Three aspects of survey participation have been shown to increase **response rates**: personal benefits, societal benefits, and survey attributes. The challenge for researchers is identifying which mix of these attributes appeals to the greatest number of respondents.

Personal Benefits. Messages in the introduction can connect with the respondent on a personal level in two different ways: by describing a topic that is of special interest or particularly salient to the respondent and by offering a **financial incentive**. For example, an introduction to a poll that mentions it is about the cost of prescription drugs is more likely to be of interest to a person who is 65 years old or older than to a person who is 20 years old, and one that introduces the topic of public school education will be more salient to parents than non-parents. While some research has shown that saliency tops the list of reasons why people participate in polls, researcher may not be able to take advantage of saliency to motivate participation because the poll topics are not of equal interest to all people. Offering a financial incentive is a more universal approach. A financial incentive is a direct benefit to the person, and it has the added psychological effect of both thanking the person and paying him or her for the time it will take to participate.

Societal Benefits. An introduction that appeals to a person's social responsibility may be successful with some types of respondents. For example, a study that is being conducted by a health organization can use the introduction to connect participation with the development of policies that will result in better health services for all of society. Another approach is to remind the respondent that only a small number of people are being asked to participate and he or she is needed to make sure the poll responses represent "people like you." The societal benefits approach is most successful when the respondent recognizes the poll sponsor and has a high level of trust for the person or organization. Some research suggests that a poll request from a college or a university can increase the rate of participation. Also, polling organizations such as the Gallup Poll are recognized by respondents, and they are more willing to cooperate with a known entity.

Survey Attributes. Some respondents, in particular those who have never been asked to participate in a poll, may respond to an introduction if it simply informs them about the survey process. A message that appeals to this type of respondent would include information about the length of time it will take to complete the questionnaire, gives the respondent a general summary of the topics that will be covered, and reassures him or her that this is not a test. For example, the introduction text might say "it will only take fifteen minutes" or "I'm not trying to sell you anything—I just want to ask you a few questions about the upcoming election" or "there are not any right or wrong answers—I just want your opinions."

Crafting the Introduction

While crafting the introduction a researcher has to translate elements that motivate respondents to participate into text that can be delivered to them. In the development of the text both the content of what will be communicated to the respondent and the method used for the communication have to be considered. The content of what is included in the introduction can be classified into two broad areas: requirements to meet professional standards, and strategies to promote response.

Requirements to Meet Professional Standards. When crafting survey introductions, professional standards oblige survey researchers to follow the guidelines for best practices and meet the demands of the Institutional Review Board (IRB) or the federal Office of Management and Budget (OMB) overseeing the study. Organizations such as the American Association for Public Opinion Research (AAPOR), the **National Council on Public Polls** (NCPP), and the Council of American Survey Research Organizations (CASRO) mandate that survey introductions be truthful, provide information about the survey process, and describe how responses will be kept confidential. Moreover, most IRBs and the OMB insist that survey introductions meet as many as fifteen different conditions, including describing the purpose of the research, the risks and benefits of participation, the time requirement, and the rights of the respondent.

Strategies to Promote Response. Multiple strategies can be used to promote response, and they often vary depending on the specific attributes of a study—such as the research topic, sample population, and method of data collection. From a strategic perspective, the introduction has the duel purpose of accentuating the benefits and of overcoming potential barriers to participation. To accentuate the benefits the introduction will describe the purpose of the study, the sponsor of the research, the topics that will be included, the respondent's role and confidentiality rights, and the amount of the incentive, if one is being given.

These positive benefits are presented in a way to connect with the respondent and to establish a trusting relationship. While the introduction itself would be too long if it included text that responded to the various barriers people have to participation, knowing what these barriers are can be useful in crafting the introduction or in providing succinct responses to overcome these barriers if they are raised. The following are some of the most common barriers to participation: (1) not having enough time, (2) concerns about privacy, (3) not seeing any benefit to participation, (4) concerns that the contact will result in a sales attempt, and (5) uncertainty about the polling process and what is expected from them as a respondent.

Method of Communication

The text developed for an introduction may be communicated by various methods, such as a letter, a telephone call, an in-person visit from an interviewer knocking on the door, or an e-mail message. Each of these modes requires unique considerations when crafting the introduction.

Letter of Introduction. A letter to the respondent can be used in different ways to gain respondent participation. An introductory letter can be used to detail the timing when a follow-up contact soliciting participation will occur, to describe the research and provide information about how to participate (e.g., through a toll-free number or Internet Web site), or to persuade the respondent to participate (e.g., when it is included in a mail packet with a questionnaire). Whatever the reason for the introductory letter, similar elements have to be considered when designing it.

The introduction begins with the outside envelope that encloses the letter. The researcher's goal is to have the sampled respondent open the envelope and review the content. Two key decisions to be made about the outside envelope are the type of postage used and its visual appearance.

The researcher has the choice of using regular mail with either a metered or a postage stamp. Some research suggests a postage stamp is more likely to attract attention because it appears more personal than metered postage. An alternative is to use priority or overnight mail that arrives in a package that suggests immediacy and importance. While the fees for a priority or overnight letter delivery exceeds the postage required for regular mail, current polling experience suggests that this type of packaging will get the respondent's attention and increase the probability that the enclosed letter will be read.

If the introductory letter is sent via regular mail, the visual appearance of the envelope can also be important. The outside of the envelope can adopt a standard appearance (nonthreatening), look official (authoritarian), or employ an attention-getting commercial design (marketing). Research suggests that an official-looking envelope, especially when the request is from a government agency, can increase participation. An envelope that is too commercial looking may be tossed aside as "junk" mail.

The next challenge is the design of the letter that the respondent sees when the envelope is opened. Decisions have to be made about the verbal and the visual appeal of the letter. General guidelines for the visual presentation are to make the letter attractive by having lots of space and by minimizing the amount and density of the text. The verbal appeal needs to provide a message that quickly and succinctly gives the respondent the type of information she or he needs to make a decision to participate, and to overcome any potential objections. While a personalized salutation is desirable, this technique can add additional cost to the production of the letter. Moreover, great care must be taken to ensure that the personal introduction is accurate in the presentation of both the individual's title and the spelling of the person's name.

Research has focused on three styles that can be used to guide the construction of the content of an introductory letter. An altruistic style is used to appeal to the social aspects of the research and to gain assistance for the sponsor of the poll; the egotistic approach describes what the person will gain and can include information about monetary or other incentives; and the authoritarian style (generally used with government research) targets the official reasons why a person should participate. Once the tone of the letter has been decided, the amount of information included in the body of the letter needs to be determined. Too much information can discourage a respondent from reading the letter. The goal for the researcher is to use the letter to connect with the respondent and to get across a message to motivate participation. A useful approach is to keep the text of the letter itself brief and focused and to include an opportunity to gain more detailed information by providing a toll-free telephone number and Web site the respondent can contact for more information or enclosing a page of Frequently Asked Questions.

The person who signs the letter, who is viewed by the respondent as making the request, should also be carefully considered. A simple rule is there should be an individual person identified so the appeal to participate is viewed as a social contract between two people. The introductory letter should also have an actual signature to reinforce the personal appeal. Now that polls are being conducted electronically via the Internet, similar considerations are needed about the visual and verbal appeal of e-mail messages that are sent to encourage participation.

Telephone Introductions. One of the major challenges of a telephone contact is the ability to deliver the introduction. While a researcher may carefully plan the content of the messages in a telephone introduction, technology, legal restrictions, and the behavior of the respondent can prevent an interviewer from delivering the introductory message. Telecommunication features such as Caller ID and answering machines are used to screen calls so respondents can determine what calls to accept (*see* **Call Screening**). While the calling restrictions of the Do Not Call legislation do not apply to calls made for polls, respondents may not make the distinction between research contacts and marketing calls. Even when personal contact is made and an interviewer can begin an introduction, people will hang up. This action happens so frequently that a term, "HUDI" (Hung Up During Introduction), has been developed to describe this experience. While the percentage of HUDIs may differ depending on a particular study, they can be up to 40 percent of the contacts. Estimates of how long an interviewer has before a HUDI takes place is about 10 to 15 seconds. Therefore, when contact is made it is critical that the introduction capture the respondent's attention. The telephone interviewer will have a formal introduction that will present the respondent with the required study information. However, a skilled interviewer will use the initial few seconds to build rapport with the respondent so he or she feels a social commitment to cooperate with the interviewer. While there are multiple positive messages to transmit to the respondent, sometimes it is what the call is not that can be the most important message. Interviewers can begin their introductions by saying, "This is not a sales call," or, "I'm not trying to sell you anything." For telephone introductions, the two most effective characteristics to focus on are: brevity and unambiguous identification as a public opinion survey—not a marketing call.

In-Person Introduction. During an in-person introduction, the interviewer is literally attempting to get his or her "foot in the door." The structure of an in-person introduction is anchored in the informal, acceptable social behavior that occurs when two people meet for the first time. While there is a formal introduction that will present the respondent with the required study information, a skilled in-person interviewer, similar to the telephone interviewer, will use the initial moments to build rapport with the respondent so he or she feels a social commitment to cooperate with the interviewer. These first few seconds provide the opportunity to stress that the study was important enough to send a person to the house to conduct the interview. The interviewer can also describe how he or she has conducted interviews at other people's home to build legitimacy, trust, and social norming—others have done this so it is acceptable for me to do it. Similar to HUDIs in the telephone scenario, the respondent may not open the door or permit the interviewer to get a chance to provide any type of introduction or to describe his or her reason for being there. Moreover, with an in-person contact the physical appearance of the interviewer is an additional "introduction" to the respondent that needs to be taken into consideration. The respondent not only has the text of the introduction to use as cues in making the decision about participation, the visual appearance of the interviewer can also contribute to the success or failure of the introduction to gain cooperation. The dress and appearance should make the respondent feel comfortable and secure.

Introductory Text

How can these general guidelines about introductions be used to craft text to motivate participation? Table 1 summarizes specific text that can be used to address different types of motivational attributes. The examples used to illustrate the development of text for the introduction are for telephone communications and should be adapted for a letter or for in-person introductions.

In addition to the positive motivational messages, an introduction can also include text to overcome barriers to participation. Table 2 shows typical barriers to participation and how they can be addressed in a telephone or in-person interview.

Introductions are critical to conducting polls. Without the participation of selected respondents, information cannot be collected. Knowing the key elements that motivate participation and using these elements to craft a successful introduction can be effective. Unfortunately, getting a "foot in the door" is becoming increasingly difficult. The technical and perceived legal barriers to making contact with respondents increase the challenge of being able to deliver that introduction.

Table 1. Examples of Introduction Messages and Related Motivational Elements

Introduction Element	Possible Messages	Motivational Attribute
Name of interviewer	"Hello, my name is (give name)."	Personal: interviewer likeability
Name of sponsor	"I'm calling from XYZ for ABC."	Personal: saliency Societal: authority
Topic of research	"I'd like to ask you some questions about (name topic)."	Personal: saliency Societal: individual responsibility
What is not being done	"I'm not trying to sell you anything."	Survey: process
Representation	"Only xx people will be included in this study."	Societal: individual responsibility
Identification of respondent	• "I'd like to speak to XX." • "I'd like to speak to the person in the household who had the last birthday." • "I'd like to speak with the oldest/youngest male/female in the household."	Societal: altruistic
Confidentiality pledge	"All of your answers will be completely confidential. The results will only be presented in the aggregate."	Personal: trust
Time it will take	"It will only take about xx minutes."	Societal: altruistic Survey: process
Monetary incentive	"As a token of our appreciation you will receive xx dollars for answering our questions."	Personal: monetary
Informational incentive	"The results of this poll will be reported in xx newspaper. If you would like, we will send you a copy of the results."	Personal: saliency
Informed consent	IRB text.	Personal: trust Survey: protection

Further Reading

Dijkstra, Wil, and Johannes H. Smit. "Persuading Reluctant Recipients in Telephone Surveys." In *Survey Nonresponse*, edited by Robert M. Groves, Don A. Dillman, John L. Eltinge, and Roderick J. A. Little. New York: John Wiley, 2002. This chapter describes the diverse elements of the survey process that researchers should heed when developing survey introductions.

Dillman, Don A. *Mail and Internet Surveys*. New York: John Wiley, 2000. Dillman describes the costs and benefits of different content and visuals used in survey introductions.

Groves, Robert, Stanley Presser, and Sarah Dipko. "The Role of Topic Interest in Survey

Table 2. Examples of Barriers and Messages for Addressing Them

Barrier	Text to Address Barrier
"I don't have time."	"I can call you back at a better time. What's most convenient for you?"
"I don't want to buy anything."	"I am not asking for money or any kind of donation. I am calling from [name of sponsor] to ask you some questions about [name of topic]."
"I'm not interested."	"Other people I've interviewed really enjoyed having a chance to give their opinion about x."
"How did you get my number?"	"Your name was randomly selected. You were selected from a listing of x."
"How do I know you are legitimate/who you say you are?"	"You can call [give a toll-free number] to learn more about this poll."

Participation Decisions." *Public Opinion Quarterly* 68 (Spring 2004): 2–31. The authors conduct an experiment to test the impact of including different types of information about topics and incentives when respondents are asked to participate in surveys.

Janice Ballou

Survey Response Behaviors

Response behaviors comprise the options available to prospective survey participants. Understanding response behaviors, particularly nonresponse, is important because the unknown characteristics and attitudes of nonrespondents may cause inaccuracies in the results of the study in question. Historically, researchers differentiated between three possible behaviors: unit nonresponse (i.e., the complete loss of a survey unit), item nonresponse (i.e., missing responses to individual questions), and complete response. Recent innovations in **Internet survey methods** have revealed a much broader typology of responses, more fully able to explain the potential variations in participation.

Classifying Response Patterns. The response process can be deconstructed as long as three conditions are met: (1) each question is presented separately, (2) participants are not forced to provide an answer to one question before being allowed to move to the next one, and (3) responses are independently recorded for each question. If these conditions are fulfilled, the resulting data set of response behaviors can be used to classify participants. Figure 1 illustrates the typical response patterns that can be differentiated.

In Figure 1, the number of separately displayed questions (abscissa in Figure 1) is set in relation to the number of questions actually answered (ordinate in Figure 1). This graphical representation of observable response patterns allows for a differentiation between the following seven processing types: (1) Complete Responders, (2) Unit Nonresponders, (3) Answering Drop-Outs, (4) Lurkers, (5)

Figure 1. Types of Survey Response Behaviors

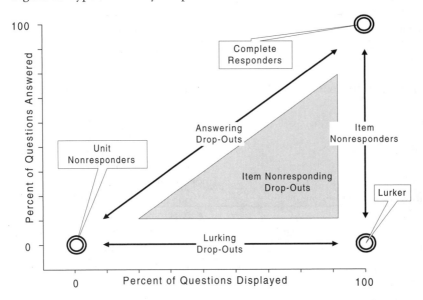

Lurking Drop-Outs, (6) Item Nonresponders, and (7) Item Nonresponding Drop-Outs. Each pattern is described below.

Complete Responders (Segment 1) are those respondents who are presented every question and answer every question. *Unit Nonresponders* (Segment 2) are those individuals who do not participate in the survey. There are two possible variations to the Unit Nonresponder. Such an individual may be technically hampered from participating, or he or she may purposefully withdraw from the survey prior to viewing any questions. *Answering Drop-Outs* (Segment 3) consist of individuals who provide answers to those questions presented, but quit prior to completing the survey. *Lurkers* (Segment 4) are presented all of the questions in the survey but do not answer any of the questions. *Lurking Drop-Outs* (Segment 5) represent a combination of segments 3 and 4. Such a participant is presented some of the questions without answering them, but also quits the survey prior to reaching its end. *Item Nonresponders* (Segment 6) are presented the entire questionnaire, but only answer some of the questions. *Item Nonresponding Drop-Outs* (Segment 7) represent a mixture of segments 3 and 6. They are presented a subset of questions, answer some but not all of those presented, and quit prior to the end of the survey.

This typology of response patterns is a more accurate depiction of actual decisions in opinions than the relatively basic categorization of complete participation, unit nonresponse, or item nonresponse. Using the traditional categorization of possible response behaviors, some behaviors would be mistakenly categorized. Specifically, Lurkers (Segment 4) and Lurking Drop-Outs (Segment 5) would be classified as Unit Nonresponders (Segment 2). Answering Drop-Outs (Segment 3) and Item Nonresponding Drop-Outs (Segment 7) would be classified the same as Item Nonresponders (Segment 6). Only Segment 1, Complete Responders, remains unaffected by the classification system used. The variations among the segments represent significant differences, particularly when one seeks to understand and possibly change response behaviors.

Dual process theories of persuasion established the importance of motivation, opportunity, and ability in processing messages fully. An individual's motivation to respond (possibly due to an interest in the topic or the desire to comply with a request) explains the difference between someone who views and proceeds through the survey and someone who chooses not to address the survey. However, motivated respondents could still behave in any category except Unit Nonresponder. It is the three variables of motivation, opportunity, and ability that differentiate between the remaining six categories. That is, respondents may be motivated (and have the opportunity and ability) and so behave as Complete Responders. They may be motivated to view the survey but not to actually answer (Lurkers). They may be Lurkers experiencing difficulties (Lurking Drop-Out). Such difficulties could be technical in nature (such as an improperly functioning computer or a lack of technical skills). They may be motivated but experience difficulties (Answering Drop-Out). They may be motivated but feel protective of sensitive information and so leave those questions blank (Item Nonresponder). They may be motivated and protective and experience difficulties and so behave as an Item Nonresponding Drop-Out.

Unit Nonresponders are commonly thought of as people who refused to answer (lack of motivation) or are hindered from answering due to a lack of opportunity or ability. Lurkers and Lurking Drop-Outs, however, are able to respond and are interested enough in the topic to peruse the questions. Yet, they refuse to answer.

Item Nonresponders are commonly thought of as people who were not comfortable answering certain questions but otherwise completed the survey. We do not tend to assume that Item Nonresponders lack motivation to respond, but rather that the question(s) influenced their response, or lack thereof. Answering Drop-Outs, however, begin the survey process much like a Complete Responder but they drop out prior to completion. These participants may drop out due to technical difficulties or because they purposefully decide to drop out. Item Nonresponding Drop-Outs begin the survey process like Item Nonresponders but also quit prior to the end of the survey. This responder type may be more similar to a Unit Nonresponder than to an Item Nonresponder.

In segments 2, 3, 5, and 7 (nonresponse and drop-outs), there is always the possibility of both volitional and nonvolitional behaviors. With volitionally controlled, or intentional nonresponse types, the (potential) respondent decides for himself or herself to which extent he or she will or will not participate in a survey. Technical artifacts, or other external obstacles cause nonvolitional nonresponse. In principle, these two classes of causes must be taken into consideration as an explanation in all drop-out types, as well as for Unit Nonresponse. In segments 1, 4, and 6, one can assume that all actions are volitionally controlled due to the evidence that the participants view all questions in the survey.

An Example. Web surveys offer a good setting for demonstrating how response behaviors can be differentiated. They can be easily designed to meet the aforementioned necessary conditions: (1) each question can be presented on a separate screen, (2) participants can be permitted to continue without answering a given question, and (3) each question can be transmitted separately to a server. The resulting log file and data set distinguishes between different types of participants.

We conducted a Web-based survey on the roles of men and women in family and work life. The survey questions were arranged according to the design guidelines described above. Participants were invited to the survey through advertising placed on search engines and Web catalogs (e.g., Yahoo, Altavista, etc.). Because the goal was to investigate response patterns, no incentive for participation was offered.

In total, 1,469 people participated in the study. Of those answering demographic questions, 35.4 percent were male and 64.6 percent were female. The mean age in this group was 27.6 years (SD = 8.4 years) and most of the participants were employed (46.5 percent) or students (34.8 percent). It is important to note, though, that not all participants are represented in the demographic descriptions. For instance, Lurkers viewed the questions, but did not answer them.

Participants were classified into the appropriate segments by analyzing data from both the automatically generated log file and data set. Specifically, we tracked the questions viewed and answered for each participant. As anticipated, seven specific response types were identifiable.

In this study, 25.3 percent of the participants were Complete Responders, 10.2 percent were Unit Nonresponders, and 4.3 percent were Answering Drop-Outs. Of all the respondents, 6.9 percent were Lurkers, while 13.3 percent were Lurking Drop-Outs. Of all the participants, 36 percent were Item Nonresponders, and 4 percent were Item Nonresponding Drop-Outs.

Analysis of the log file and data set confirmed the existence of the seven response types proposed in the model. The existence of these specific types is of particular importance to those seeking to increase response and to minimize nonresponse bias.

Using the traditional categories of Complete Response, Unit Nonresponse, and Item Nonresponse, the study would have reported Nonresponse at 30.4 percent with a response rate somewhere between 25.3 and 44.3 percent (depending upon the degree of unanswered questions in each case). As discussed previously, if using only three response types, Lurkers and Lurking Drop-Outs would have been grouped with Unit Nonresponders. While Unit Nonresponders and Lurking Drop-Outs may have experienced technical difficulties, which prevented further participation, it is likely that the three groups differ significantly from each other. If one seeks to minimize nonresponse by encouraging those individuals who are likely to refuse to respond, these differences must be better understood. For instance, given that Lurkers do not experience technical problems and willingly choose to view the entire survey, perhaps it is not lack of interest nor motivation, which prevents response but some other attitude.

Similarly, using only Item Nonresponse, Unit Nonresponse, and Complete Response as categories, Item Nonresponse would have been estimated at 44.3 percent of returned surveys. Using the response typology, we see that 8.3 percent of the participants answered some questions but dropped out prior to completing the survey. This is an important distinction. The 36 percent who finished the survey but left missing answers to some questions maintained enough involvement in the survey to complete the activity and did not experience problems completing the survey. However, the Answering Drop-Outs and Item Nonresponding Drop-Outs either chose to quit or possibly experienced some problem that interrupted the session. If the drop-out was volitionally controlled, we must learn what variables may have affected that decision. This is especially important for Answering Drop-Outs, as this segment represents individuals who answered all questions up until the decision to quit. Answering Drop-Outs may be easily converted into Complete Responders if we develop an understanding of the reasons behind the choice to end participation.

Much more research needs to be conducted before the nature of response behaviors are fully understood. In particular, researchers need to assess how conclusions derived from the simple distinction between Unit Nonresponses, Item Nonresponses, and Completions are altered in light of the more detailed typology outlined here. For example, they need to re-analyze how techniques designed to increase response rates impact each of the seven available response behaviors. They need to reconsider how the techniques for estimating and correcting nonresponse bias are affected by a more extensive typology. They also need to re-examine the underlying psychology of the survey response in light of the greater number of options actually available to prospective participants.

Further Reading

Cook, C., F. Heath, and R. L. Thompson. "A Meta-Analysis of Response Rates in Web- or Internet-Based Surveys." *Educational and Psychological Measurement* 60, no. 6 (2000): 821–36. Research synthesis on the factors affecting response rates in Internet-based surveys.

Dillman, Don A. *Mail and Internet Surveys—The Tailored Design Method.* New York: John Wiley, 2000. Comprehensive overview of the Tailored Design Method (TDM), the most prominent procedure to improve response rates in self-administered surveys.

Groves, Robert M., and Mick P. Couper. *Nonresponse in Household Interview Surveys.* New York: John Wiley, 1998. "Must have" book on nonresponse theory and research.

Tuten, T., D. Urban, and M. Bosnjak. "Internet Surveys and Data Quality: A Review." In *Online Social Sciences*, edited by B. Batinic, U.-D. Reips, and M. Bosnjak. Seattle: Hogrefe & Huber, 2002. Narrative review of the factors affecting response rates and data quality in Internet-based surveys.

Web Sites

Scientific papers by Michael Bosnjak and Tracy L. Tuten on classifying response behaviors in Web-based surveys can be found at http://www.ascusc.org/jcmc/vol6/issue3/boznjak.html and http://www.gesis.org/Publikationen/Zeitschriften/ZUMA_Nachrichten/documents/pdfs/zn48_05-band_bosnj.pdf.

Michael Bosnjak and Tracy L. Tuten

Surveying Children

Children constitute a special population and those between 7 and 18 years old require special instruments to be surveyed. Below the age of 7 children do not have sufficient cognitive skills to be effectively and systematically questioned. The age of 7 is a major developmental point in the cognitive and social maturation of children, and with care children can be interviewed with structured questionnaires or complete self-reports from 7 years onward. At the age of 18, adolescents are generally treated as adults in surveys, as is reflected in definitions of adult populations for many surveys.

Designing any survey requires a careful decision process, but when designing surveys for the young, several survey design issues warrant extra attention. An important issue is when to use proxy reports instead of self-reports. Children older than 7 can be surveyed directly, and the older the child, the more reliable the answer will be. A good rule is to collect information directly from children on topics for which they are the best informant, such as their feelings, and other subjective phenomena. Children are also the best respondents on factual or general questions that are outside the scope of parents' knowledge. A good example is food intake and eating habits, as children often do not eat the food taken with them to school. Till adolescence, a well-informed adult **proxy respondent** will likely provide better data in all other cases. For example, on facts about schooling, family, and many health related issues, such as visits to the doctor and vaccinations, an informed parent will have more accurate knowledge. Below the age of 7, direct questionnaire research of children is not feasible. In many cases, an informed parent or daily caretaker can serve as a proxy respondent and provide information on daily activities, health issues, or other topics of interest.

A related issue is the choice of mode of data collection. Data on very young children are usually collected through observational and assessment studies performed by specially trained interviewers, and through interviews with caretakers. From 4 to 6 years of age, children can be interviewed, but not with structured questionnaires. For this age group, an interview should resemble a qualitative open interview with a topic list, instead of a survey interview. The form is play and talk, and much attention should be given to nonverbal communication and explanation of the rules of an interview. For older children structured questionnaires may be used either during a survey interview or through self-completion. Which particular mode is chosen depends on design constraints, such as research topic and budget, and on the literacy of the intended population. From the age of 7–8 years onward, educational researchers start to use simple self-administered questionnaires in the classroom. When literacy is a problem, a combination of methods is often used, with an instructor reading the questions aloud and the pupils recording their responses on a simple self-administered form. Also, in individual or household surveys, a combination of methods can be used when asking sensitive questions of young respondents. For instance, a combination of a Walkman with prerecorded questions on tape and an anonymous self-completion questionnaire. If the budget allows, computer assisted self-administrative methods have advantages both in school surveys and in household surveys of young respondents. Children and adolescents are good respondents in computer-assisted surveys, and ordinary school children as young as 8 years can successfully complete electronic questionnaires and enjoy the process.

An extremely important point in surveying the young concerns obtaining informed consent for a study. ESOMAR, the world association for research professionals in opinion polling and market research, gives explicit guidelines. ESOMAR states that first of all a researcher should conform to any relevant definitions in any national code of conduct and/or in national legislation, and second that in the case of children under 14 explicit permission should be asked of a parent, guardian, or other person to whom the parent has conferred responsibility. Of course, national legislations may differ regarding the age at which children can legally give their consent. For instance, in the United Kingdom this is

16, and as a consequence the British Market Research Society prescribes that consent of a parent or responsible adult must be obtained with children under 16. In the United States, parental consent is needed until the age of 18. However, permission of a parent or guardian is not enough. Professional research organizations like the Society for Research in Child Development require that researchers inform the child about the study and obtain permission of the child in addition to the consent of the legal guardian. This implies that the information presented to the child should be given in clear language and at a level that the child can understand. To verify this, a **pretest** of the wording and phrasing of the consent statement should take place for the relevant age groups.

Young respondents between the age of 7 and 18 are a far from homogenous group. As children grow from infancy to adulthood, their thinking becomes more logical, and their reasoning skills develop more and more. At the same time memory and language develop and social skills are acquired. These are important prerequisites for the understanding of survey tasks and questions, and designers of children surveys should tailor a survey according to the cognitive and social development of the intended age group.

In middle childhood (7–12) language and reading skills are sufficiently developed to use individual or group semi-structured interviews, structured interviews, self-administered group tests, or even computer-assisted self-interviews. Children of this age can answer well-designed questions with some consistency. But, as reading and language skills are still developing in middle childhood, the understanding of words has to be checked very carefully for this group. Questions using logical operators such as "or" (e.g., does your father or mother . . .) or negations are not yet understood correctly. Extra attention should be paid to complexity of wording. As children in this age group can be very literal, depersonalized or indirect questions should be checked very carefully. When preparing the questionnaire, one should take care that both questions and instructions are simple—and that the **question wording** is clear and unambiguous.

Memory and processing time is a second important issue. In middle childhood (7 to 12) both memory capacity and memory speed is still developing. Therefore, complexity of the question and number of response categories should be carefully examined. If possible, one should use visual stimuli and response cards, to make the task more concrete and interesting. Response cards are very helpful, as young children tend to forget even a limited set of response options and have difficulties with more than two to three verbal response categories. Retrospective questions may pose extra problems, and young children are prone to construct scripts of familiar routines if they do not clearly recollect events.

In early adolescence (12 to 16) cognitive functioning is already well developed, and logical operators and negations are understood. It is possible to use standardized questionnaires similar to questionnaires for adults, but one should guard extra against ambiguity of question wording. Memory capacity is now full-grown, but memory speed is not. Even in this older age group ample time for answering questions should be allowed.

Besides cognitive development, the emotional and social development of the intended age group should be taken into account. In younger children suggestibility is an important item. In early middle childhood (7 to 10) children have a tendency to please and are afraid of doing something wrong. This may result in more superficial answers through satisficing and in an inclination toward social desirability. In late middle childhood (10 to 12) children become less suggestible, but start to compare themselves with others, and peer pressure and self-presentation are becoming important.

From the age of 12, peers become increasingly important, making adolescents increasingly sensitive to peer pressure and group norms. As a result, sensitivity of topic and privacy of interview situation become important. Both the nearness of schoolmates or siblings and parents can influence the answers dramatically. Confidential methods, such as self-completed questionnaires and computer assisted self-interviewing can help to obtain better answers. Again, both audio and visual presentation of the questions (e.g., questionnaire plus walkman, audio-CASI) may be useful to keep the respondent's attention and to avoid literacy problems with special groups. But above all, one should keep this group motivated and guard against flippancy and boredom.

From 16 years onward, adolescents can be regarded as adults with respect to cognitive development and information processing. But resistance to peer pressure is still very low, and older adolescents have their own group norms and social norms. The social context of the survey (e.g., classroom, presence of siblings or friends, type and age of interviewer) remains extremely important, especially in interaction with special topics (e.g., health, social networks).

Special care should be given to the construction of questionnaires for children and adolescents. In addition, pretesting of the questionnaire is necessary to examine the adequacy of question wording and response options for different age groups. To ensure a high-quality survey of children, one should go one step further and pretest other aspects of the questionnaire and of the survey design. For example, do children in the relevant age group clearly understand general instructions and introductions to questions? Do they understand the task that is being asked of them? Do they understand the request for informed consent? Is the topic sensitive to a particular age group? Is the setting increasing the risk of social desirability bias? Only specially designed pretests can answer these questions.

Further Reading

Borgers, Natacha, Edith de Leeuw, and Joop Hox. "Children as Respondents in Survey Research: Cognitive Development and Response Quality." *Bulletin de Methodologie Sociologique (BMS)* 66 (2000): 60–75. A literature review focusing on the quality of the data obtained when surveying children and adolescents. Findings are grouped according to age categories and cognitive development, that is ages 4–7, 8–11, 11–15, 16+.

Leeuw, Edith de Natacha Borgers, and Astrid Smits. "Pretesting Questionnaires for Children and Adolescents." In *Methods for Testing and Evaluating Survey Questionnaires*, edited by S. Presser, J. Rothgeb, M.P. Couper, J.T. Lessler, E. Martin, J. Martin, and E. Singer. New York: John Wiley, 2004. Discusses effective methods for pretesting questionnaires for respondents between 7 and 18 years old. Contains a summary of empirical studies of the young as respondents and the resulting implications for designing surveys.

Scott, Jacqueline. "Children as Respondents: Methods for Improving Data Quality." In *Survey Measurement and Process Quality*, edited by L. Lyberg, P. Biemer, M.

Collins, E. de Leeuw, C. Dippo, N. Schwarz, and D. Trewin. New York: Wiley, 1997, pp. 331–50. An introduction to using children as respondents. It contains an extended example describing the methods used in the British Household Young People's Survey (11–15 years).

Web Sites

A helpful guideline on ethics and codes when interviewing children and young people can be found on the home page of the world association of market research ESOMAR, available at http://www.esomar.org.

Edith Desiree de Leeuw

Symbolic Politics

Political symbols represent something about politics beyond the manifest content of the symbol. Symbols evoke (sometimes unconsciously) an attitude, an impression, or a historical occurrence that is associated in a meaningful way with the symbol. Symbols are thus highly efficient forms of communication in that they associate a wealth of information and feeling with a single attitude object. They consequently are among the most important elements in shaping and affecting public opinion.

Flags are perhaps the most intuitively appealing example of a political symbol. The Confederate flag symbolizes something very different for large numbers of whites on one hand, and African Americans on the other. Some southern whites see it as the symbol of Old South and southern culture. Many blacks see the Confederate flag as the symbol of oppression and slavery. The power of symbols can be seen in the intense and bitter fights that have occurred in many southern states over the removal of the stars and bars that were at one time, or remain, incorporated into their state flags.

A political candidate in the draped in Confederate flag is making a statement about his or her political convictions that does not require verbalization. The same is true for a liberal candidate in the northeast who prominently displays a peace symbol at his or her political rally. These symbols, and what politically they stand for, are immediately recognized by almost everyone.

It is sometimes politically advantageous for politicians to communicate with citizens via symbols rather than speaking to them directly. Perhaps the classic example is the notorious "Willie Horton" campaign ad used by George H. Bush against Michael Dukakis in the 1988 presidential campaign. Willie Horton was an African American and convicted murder who, during a furlough from a Massachusetts prison (Dukakis's home state), raped a white women. "Willie Horton" became a symbol for Michael Dukakis being soft on crime, particularly in the case of sexually aggressive, violent, black males. By tying Dukakis to the symbol "Willie Horton," Bush did not have to say anything distasteful in linking blacks to violent crime. The symbol made it clear that George Bush would take a hard line on these sorts of criminals while implying Michael Dukakis would not.

In the field of mass politics, the term "symbolic politics" was first popularized by the political scientist Murray Edelman in his book *The Symbolic Use of Pol-*

itics (1964). Edelman is a mass society theorist. His primary interest is in the relationship between the individual and the polity—and how symbolic activities (such as voting) cement ties between citizens and the state. He saw the public as politically uninformed and unsophisticated, but anxious and threatened by its surroundings. He thus saw symbolic politics as a method by which government can both reassure the public and manipulate it. Children are socialized to see the president and other figures of authority as benevolent symbols of the state; "outgroups" are in turn symbolically demonized (the Soviet Union as the "Evil Empire" or Iran, Iraq, and North Korea as the "Axis of Evil") to promote national unity and citizen compliance with governmental ideology. Perhaps Edelman's most lasting contribution was his distinction between self-interested politics and symbolic politics. Politics, according to Edelman, appears to be about citizen behavior designed to achieve tangible material benefits. However, real politics is symbolic. Thus, the Bush campaign succeeded in convincing the public to vote Republican in 1988, not by arguing that Bush was the candidate most likely to promote the voter's personal self-interest, but because Bush could best protect the public from the abstract dangers symbolized by Willie Horton.

The current research on symbolic politics has evolved from the mass society paradigm used by Edelman. Rather than being a critique of society focusing on dangers posed by mob psychology and the potential for symbolic manipulation, the focus is now primarily on how political symbols structure everyday public opinion. The recurring theme of the symbolic politics literature is that personal self-interest matters only rarely for political opinions. It is symbolic predispositions that most effectively form and condition public opinion. The most important of symbolic predispositions in the public opinion literature are party identification, liberal-conservative ideology, abstract racial predispositions, attitudes toward social groups, and nationalism.

Several defining features distinguish symbolic predispositions from other political attitudes. First, they tend to be learned at an early age through the **socialization** process. Oftentimes, children will identify with a symbol before they fully understand the manifest content of the symbol. A good example is party identification. Children as early as the fourth grade are able to identify themselves as "Democrats" or "Republicans," even though they may have only the vaguest notions of what those labels mean. Rather, they first come to understand that "we" are associated with one party and "they" are associated with the other party.

Second, symbolic predispositions come with strong emotional charges. Associated with the symbol is a keenly felt good-bad, like-dislike evaluative dimension. During socialization, children may learn that Democrats are good, Republicans are bad. The term "political symbol" refers to that part of an attitude that is charged with "affect" (i.e., with emotion).

Third, symbolic predispositions are among the most stable of attitudes and predispositions over time. Using panel data, where the same person is reinterviewed one or more times, symbolic attitudes tend to show less fluctuation over time than more specific policy opinions (*see* **Ideology**). In particular, party identification, ideology orientations, attitudes toward social groups, and racial attitudes have been shown to be significantly more stable than focused policy issues. The importance of this attitude stability is that it supports the contention that symbolic predispositions have been etched more or less permanently into a person's psychological makeup.

Fourth, symbolic predispositions influence how political issues, objects, and personalities are evaluated. Symbolic predispositions are more abstract than ordinary political issues. They influence how issues are analyzed, not the reverse. Symbolic attachments are particularly powerful in shaping reactions to new issues that appear on the political agenda. These attachments can provide necessary cues for how to respond to new circumstances or new issues, so that people do not have to rethink their positions every time they encounter a new political event. A good example comes from a "natural experiment" that occurred during the 1956 campaign for president. Unexpectedly, in mid-campaign, Democratic presidential candidate Adlai Stevenson announced that he favored a cessation of nuclear testing. His opponent, Dwight Eisenhower, immediately announced his strong support for continued nuclear testing. Previously, there had been no difference between the views of Democrats and Republicans on the issue of nuclear testing. However, following the announcement, citizens identifying as Democrats moved sharply in opposition to continued testing, while citizens identifying as Republicans moved in the opposite direction. Few citizens had the background to make an informed judgment about nuclear policy. Rather, they based their opinions on their symbolic attachment to one or the other political parties, and the cues they received from the presidential nominee of their party.

Symbolic predispositions as a source of public opinion are sometimes contrasted with altruism, cognitive heuristics (taking cognitive shortcuts such as aligning ones views with a favored interest group such as the Sierra Club), or rational choice. However, the most frequent comparison is between symbolic predispositions and primitive self-interest (*see* **Self-Interest and Altruism**). When it comes to politics, what is human nature? Is the source of public opinion mostly rooted in reasoned calculations to promote personal gain, or is it mostly rooted in emotion and irrational psychological needs?

The history of western thought would lead one to conclude that the drive for personal gain is the most important of life's motives. As the English philosopher David Hume noted, "Avarice, or the desire for gain, is a universal passion which operates at all times, in all places and upon persons." We might, therefore, expect that people act in the political arena as they act in the realm of economics—seeking to maximize their material gain. A self-interested approach to public opinion implies that **opinion formation** and change is primarily motivated by economic and other personal gains or losses that might reasonably benefit citizens in a short-to-medium-term time frame. Thus, self-interest is aligned with the common economic understanding of the term as involving the pursuit of "selfish" ends. By this narrow definition, hypotheses about self-interest are falsifiable, as nonmaterial goals such as spiritual well-being, the satisfaction derived from doing good deeds, or the search for a heavenly afterlife are excluded from the definition. Mother Theresa's good works among the poor are, therefore, not indicators of a self-interest motive, even though some may feel her primary motivation was a reward in the heavenly kingdom.

For many years the American **National Election Studies** have asked citizens if "the government in Washington should provide fewer services, even in such areas as health and education, to reduce spending . . . or is it more important for the government to provide many more services even if it means an increase in spending." Based on self-interest motive, one would expect that family income would be a strong predictor of the answer to this question. Among whites in the 2000 election study, we do in fact see a tendency for those in lower income brackets to say "provide more services and increase spending." However, the symbolic predisposition of **partisanship** clearly overwhelms any self-interest calculation. For example, among those Republicans making $75,000 a year or more only 8 percent said "provide more services and increase spending" while among Democrats making over $75,000 a year 76 percent offered this opinion. We see the same pattern when it comes to support for national health insurance (*see* **Health Policy**). There is only a trivial self-interest effect in that those without health insurance are barely more likely to favor a national health program than those who have health insurance. In one study, party identification and liberal-conservative ideology were four times as strong a predictor of attitudes toward national health insurance than either self-interest or demographic variables, and almost twice as strong as an index consisting of other domestic policy attitudes.

Rather than being an interesting exception, the data reported above show the typical pattern when symbolic predispositions are juxtaposed against personal self-interest. Symbolic predispositions are generally more effective in shaping public opinion than is self-interest. The literature on the subject is replete with examples. In the 1980 ANES, women were no more likely to favor the Equal Rights Amendment than were men (*see also* **Gender Differences in Public Opinion**). However, 88 percent of liberals favored the ERA versus 12 percent of conservatives; 61 percent of Democrats favored it compared with 38 percent of Republicans, and 84 percent who positively rated feminists (*see* **Feminism**) favored it versus 5 percent who negatively rated feminists. Symbolic predispositions carried much more weight than did self-interested calculations.

We see a similar pattern in support for **abortion**. Over the years, men have sometimes been more supportive than women, sometimes not, but the differences tend to be small (in the 2000 ANES women were 3 percent more likely than men to say that "by law women should always be able to obtain an abortion as a matter of choice"). In contrast, the same data show liberals, Democrats, and feminists to be most likely to support the pro-choice position. For example, liberals are 40 percent more likely to be pro-choice than self-identified conservatives. A final gender-relevant example shows that support for government spending on child care is only weakly predicted by a self-interested mix of gender, parental status, age of children, income, and martial status while the symbolic predispositions of ideology, partisanship, and feminism ideology are much more successful in accounting for variation in support for government programs to defray the cost of child care.

Opinions on war also seem more driven by symbolic predispositions than by self-interest. Take the Vietnam War as an example. Just before the 1968 election, over half of the electorate cited the war as the most important problem facing the United States. Almost 30 percent of the public had friends or relatives who were serving in Vietnam and were very much in harm's way. Based on the principles of personal self-interest, we might expect those citizens with close friends or relatives in Vietnam would be more likely to oppose the war than those without. In fact, they were slightly more likely to support the war—contrary to the self-interest hypotheses. Symbolic predispositions, such as liberal-conservative ideology and abstract anticommunism, were much stronger predictors of opinion about the war, even with extensive controls for demographic factors. The same pattern was true for antiwar protestors. The most intense opposition to the Vietnam War tended to come from young men and women at the nation's most elite colleges and universities—those least likely to be drafted. However, their socialization led them to reject the symbolic values of anticommunism and militarism, which were more likely to be embraced by young men and women from working class families, who also accounted for the majority of the casualties in Vietnam.

Finally, several studies have shown that attitudes about "English as the official language" and attitudes about bilingual education are strongly grounded in symbolic predispositions, such as national identity and group worth, and only weakly, if at all, grounded in personal self-interest. One study showed that white parents whose children were affected by bilingual education programs were no more or less likely than other whites to oppose such programs. Another study, using an index of items indicating support for English as the official state language, found Hispanics and Asians tended to support bilingualism, but support and opposition among whites and blacks was not related to personal self-interest, as measured by the percentage of Hispanics and Asians in the county or the growth rate within the county of these two groups. Rather, a measure of national identify (what makes someone a "true American") proved to be a statistically and substantively significant predictor of English as the official state language.

Why is self-interest so relatively ineffective in structuring political opinions? One reason is a lack of sufficient information on the part of the public necessary to make a self-interest calculation. An important advantage that symbolic processing has over self-interested processing is that symbolic processing is based on easily accessible emotions. Self-interested processing is a more intellectually demanding task for the average person. Most people simply lack the necessary information to make a rational self-interested calculation in forming and changing their political opinions. They are unaware, in any meaningful sense, of the costs and benefits associated with alternative policies. We would expect, however, that when costs and benefits are pointedly clear, self-interest will play a more prominent role in opinion formation and opinion change. Ideal conditions for self-interest effects are when the personal consequences of choice are visible, large, certain, and immediate. Under these circumstances, the influence of self-interest can overwhelm the influence of symbolic predispositions on political opinions.

One of the more thoroughly studied political conflicts involved California's Proposition 13, designed to cap property taxes. The proposition, accompanied by a well-financed and hotly contested campaign, offered homeowners a very significant and immediate tax reduction, while at the same time threatening large spending cuts on public services and public employees. Among homeowners, there was a large and statistically significant effect. They scored high on a "tax rebel" index. There was an equally sizable effect among public employees in the opposite direction. However, there was no effect among those receiving government assistance or those with children in the public schools—those likely to bear the brunt of the service cuts. One reason is that the consequences to this latter group were not as clear or immediate as they were to homeowners and public employees.

The fact that those receiving state services seemed not to evidence any self-interested calculation points up a fundamental distinction between self-interest as it operates in economic markets and self-interest as it operates in the political world. In the market, benefits are mostly allocated individually. In politics, they are usually allocated collectively. It is a good deal easier to make a self-interested calculation on an individual basis ("should I work 20 hours of overtime next month?") as opposed to "will a cap on property taxes mean the school my child attends will deteriorate in quality?"

As self-interest becomes self-obvious, strong relationships have been found: for example, on the issue of rent control. Homeowners are far more likely to oppose rent control than are non-homeowners. While this may strike one as completely unsurprising, it needs to be placed in the context noted above of overwhelming evidence that self-interest is usually unrelated or weakly related to policy preferences. Symbolic predispositions were also significant, most notably partisanship. However, the direct effects of self-interest significantly exceeded symbolic predispositions.

Two other areas where strong self-interest effects have been documented are those financing the public schools (*see* **School Choice**) and the regulation of tobacco. Citizens over the age of sixty-five are generally a good deal less supportive of school revenue bonds than are parents with school-age children. Symbolic predispositions are still important, but generally a variety of self-interest measures show a stronger relationship to school bond issues. Studies have also shown a clear self-interest effect on attitudes toward smoking restrictions. Opinion polls show smokers clearly opposed to smoking restrictions while nonsmokers favor them. A 1987 Gallup Poll showed 69 percent of nonsmokers, but only 25 percent of smokers favored a complete ban on smoking in public places. On this issue, symbolic predispositions seemed irrelevant. Democrats were no more likely than Republicans to support such restrictions; liberals were no more likely than conservatives. An important point to take from this latter study is that the influence of symbolic versus self-interest processing on political opinions will vary from issue to issue. It is not impossible that opinions could be formed or changed wholly based on self-interested calculations.

The mode by which information is processed for opinion formation also has important implications for democratic theory. The symbolic politics process capitalizes on uninformed citizens (*see* **Political Knowledge**), who react in an unthinking, reflexive, and emotional manner to distant attitude objects, rather than reacting with a calculated appraisal of their own self-interest. Among twentieth-century political theorists, self-interested politics is seen as civic virtue. Self-interested politics is qualitatively superior to symbolic politics because in a pluralistic society self-interests can be articulated, aggregated, and reconciled within the usual give and take of everyday politics. Symbolic politics, in contrast, is uniquely unsuited to pluralist politics. When politics focuses on emotionally charged out groups, there is little opportunity to frame the political debate in terms of real costs and benefits associated with policy choice. Rather, symbols are used to arouse mass emotions, and reasoned discourse falls by the wayside. A good example is in the case of **welfare**—a symbol with meaning that goes beyond its dictionary definition of "receiving aid from the government because of need." In 1998 the **General Social Survey** asked a random half of a national sample if spending for "welfare" should be increased, decreased, or stay the same. The other half of the sample was asked if "assistance to the poor" should be increased, decreased, or stay the same. Sixty-three percent said spending on "assistance to the poor" should be increased, but only 16 percent said spending on "welfare" should be increased. One reason for the power of this symbol is its association with an abstract and even more powerful symbol—that of race. It is one reason that some conservative politicians sprinkle their rhetoric with the word "welfare" rather than "helping the less fortunate."

Along with partisanship and political ideology, race is the most important symbol among white Americans for structuring public opinion. By race is meant the symbolic content associated with being African American. Like partisanship and ideology, racial predispositions are learned early in life and are relatively stable over time. According to the symbolic politics school, the reason for the lack of support for "welfare" among whites is because they identify most recipients as black and undeserving. The same is true of affirmative action and busing. As we shall see, primitive self-interest considerations are mostly irrelevant for opinions about affirmative action and busing. What is crucial are symbolic racial predispositions.

A pervasive strain of racism runs through America's past. This "old fashioned racism" is a belief that blacks are biologically inferior to whites, plus an opposition to the principle of equal treatment for African Americans. By the 1960s, however, polls showed these beliefs were largely rejected by white Americans, but many critics found it hard to believe that racial prejudice among whites had truly disappeared.

Whites overwhelming support racial integration in principle. By 1970, 75 percent agreed that black and white children should attend the same school, and by 1985 it had risen to 93 percent. There is, however, a good deal less support for specific government policies designed to achieve racial equality—most notable busing in the 1970s and 1980s and affirmative action in the 1980s and following. If whites overwhelmingly accepted the general principle of formal equality, why do they continue to resist changes intended to promote it?

The answer from a number of scholars led by psychologist David Sears is that racism had reinvented itself in the modern era. Because it had become politically incorrect and socially unacceptable to publicly express opposition to the principle of racial equality, white racial resentment needed a new and different outlet. In 1971 (along with Donald Kinder) Sears proposed the concept of "symbolic racism" (sometimes called "new racism," "modern racism," or "racial resentment"), which was defined as a blend of anti-black affect and a belief in the traditional American values of individualism and self-reliance. The term "symbolic" is used because Sears and his associates concluded that the predisposition (1) originated in negative stereotypes about blacks learned in childhood socialization that have left a reservoir of racial resentment, and (2) was devoid of any self-interest calculation (such as having one's children bused for school integration), and (3) invokes a denial of continuing race discrimination, focusing instead on abstract beliefs that blacks violate basic American values, such as the Protestant work ethic, traditional morality, and respect for authority.

Among the items commonly used to measure symbolic racism are the following agree-disagree statements: "Irish, Italian, Jewish, and many other minorities overcame prejudice and worked their way up. Blacks should do the same without any special favors," and "It's really a matter of some people not trying hard enough; if blacks would only try harder, they could be just as well off as whites." Thus, "symbolic racism" is an amalgam of anti-black affect and the time-honored American principle of individualism. According to one widely published author in the field, "[T]oday racial prejudice is expressed primarily in the language of individualism." The symbolic racism approach has generated a voluminous amount of research, which generally concludes that opposition among whites to specific policies designed to promote racial equality does not have its source in the direct effect on a individual's material self-interest, but in deep-seated resentments against African Americans because of their unwillingness to "play by the rules."

The concept of symbolic racism has been most prominently used to explain white opposition to busing and to affirmative action. In one study, self-interest was defined by an index composed of (1) living in neighborhoods that were vulnerable to busing, (2) having school age children who might be bused, and (3) the racial composition of the neighborhood school. The study also included an index measuring symbolic racism, as well as party identification, liberal-conservative ideology, and demographics. The dependent variable was support or opposition to busing to integrate the public schools. About a quarter of the sample had a self-interest in busing, but the self-interest scale was completely unrelated to support or opposition to school busing. The strongest predictor was symbolic racism, followed by liberal-conservative ideology and a small, but significant, coefficient for age. The research on affirmative action shows a somewhat similar pattern. Depending on the study, there are sometimes significant self-interest effects. These are, however, overshadowed by symbolic predispositions—particularly symbolic racism—which often shows a coefficient three or four times larger than shown for self-interest effects.

The research on busing and affirmative action have important implications for how these controversies can be resolved. If opposition to race-targeted programs are based on a rational calculation of self-interest, then it becomes simply a matter of using the normal political processes to ameliorate costs associated with these policies. Integrated schools can receive enhanced resources, or students graduating in the top 5 percent of their high school class can be guaranteed a place in their state's best schools. However, if opposition to race-targeted programs is based on resentment and emotions, and subject to symbolic manipulation, the solutions to these problems will be more difficult because the source of opposition is based on reasoned analysis.

The literature on symbolic racism has generated some of the most heated controversy in the field of public opinion. The symbolic racism school tends to be championed by psychologists who stress the irrational, emotional determinants. Critics are mostly political scientists whom stress political explanations for white opposition to race-targeted programs. The political critique holds that opinion on racial policies, such as affirmative action, is not predominantly driven by an emotional reaction to blacks as a symbol, but by conventional political considerations. Among them is political ideology. Liberal and conservatives differ about the proper role of government in solving social problems. It should be no surprise that conservatives oppose heavy-handed government intrusion. These critics note that measures of symbolic racism are double barreled. They reference both anti-black affect and conservative principles. The political critique holds that whites are mostly responding to the political ideology barrel of these questions, not the race barrel.

A second political critique holds that whites are willing to endorse special measures to help blacks so long as they do not violate fundamental principles of fairness and equal treatment. The problem with affirmative action is, in the name of achieving equal opportunity, policies are proposed and implemented that systematically violate that principle. There is an inescapable conflict between the principle of equal opportunity and the way it is practiced in race conscious public policies. It is this conflict which primarily drives white opposition—not an irrational response to emotion-laden political symbols.

A different critique calls into question the distinction between the "new" or symbolic racism and old-fashioned racism. In other words, there is nothing new about the "new" racism. Critics note a high correlation between measures of symbolic racism and old-fashioned racism. The new concept is simply new wine in an old bottle. Others claim measures of symbolic racism and race-targeted dependent variables are not empirically separate. Rather, they are simply different ways of measuring the same thing—race-based policy attitudes. Because the same theoretical domain is being measured by the symbolic racism questions and race-targeted policies, there is naturally going to be a high correlation among them.

The symbolic politics school of thought has made important contributions to understanding the potential sources and changes in public opinion. While we have mostly juxtaposed symbolic predispositions with self-interest, these are not the only influences on political opinions. There are also core values, such as individualism and equalitarianism; personality traits, such as authoritarianism; or realistic group political conflict. There are, in fact, many—far to many to review in this essay. Sorting through their impact will undoubtedly occupy scholars for years to come.

Further Reading

Edelman, Murray. *The Symbolic Use of Politics*. Urbana: University of Illinois Press, 1964. A classic work from the mass society perspective showing how governments and political leaders use symbols to manipulate the public.

Sears, David O. "Symbolic Politics." In *Explorations in Political Psychology*, edited by Shanto Iyengar and William McGuire. Durham, NC: Duke University Press, 1993. A review of the symbolic politics approach by one of the leading figures in the field.

Sniderman, Paul, and Edward Carmines. *Reaching Beyond Race*. Cambridge, MA: Harvard University Press, 1997. Two political scientists criticize the symbolic politics approach and offer a political explanation for white opposition to race-targeted public policies.

Tedin, Kent L. "Self-Interest, Symbolic Values, and the Financial Equalization of the Public Schools." *Journal of Politics* 56 (1994): 628–49. An empirical study where self-interest and symbolic values are contrasted in the context of the financial equalization of the public schools.

Web Sites

The Web site of the American National Elections Study archives the bi-annual survey of American citizens during each election since 1952 and lists papers written from these data. Go to http://www.umich.edu/~nes and where it reads "Search the NES site" enter "symbolic racism."

Kent L. Tedin

Systematic Sampling

Systematic sampling is a sampling method in which the first case is selected at random from a list of population members and subsequent cases are selected at prescribed intervals. As long as the list does not contain a hidden pattern, this method is as good as **simple random sampling**. However, it can save much time and effort and is more efficient in some situations than simple random sampling.

Suppose, for example, that for a study on nutritional intake the medical records of a sample of n patients treated during the past year at a local health clinic are to be selected. With systematic sampling, this is accomplished by creating n zones in the files of size $k = N/n$ records each. Within the first zone, a random number between 1 and k is selected, representing the first chosen record. Subsequent records are identified by successively adding the constant k to the starting random number i. Thus, the sample of size n is composed of the ith, $[i + k]^{th}, \ldots, [i + (n - 1)k]^{th}$ records in the filing cabinet.

There are several advantages to using systematic sampling rather than simple random sampling. First, it may be possible to select a systematic sample in situations where a simple random sample cannot be selected. For example, suppose an audit of hospital records is required on an ongoing basis. In this situation, a simple random sample is not possible since N is not known in advance. However, if N can be approximated and if we know what size n is required, a "1 in k" sample can be selected where $k = N/n$. Second, using systematic sampling the selected sampling units are likely to be more uniformly spread over the whole population and may therefore be more representative than a simple random sample. Finally, under most conditions, simple random sampling formulae for parameter and variance estimates can be used with systematic sampling.

Unfortunately, there are some situations where selection of a systematic sample is ill-advised. For example, if the list or frame is arranged in a cyclical fashion and k is the length of the cycle, a highly biased estimate will result. For example, suppose a study of visits to a hospital emergency room is planned. If the emergency room has Sundays as the busiest day of the week while Wednesdays are the least busy, then the cycle is of length 7. If zones of length 7 are established, very unfortunate results may arise, as seen in the following diagram:

S M T W T F S / S M T W T F S / . . . / S M T W T F S

↓ 1　　↓ 2　　↓ k

Here, selecting a random number between 1 and 7 resulted in a 4, identifying Wednesday. Then, repeatedly adding 7 to this random start results in the selection of successive Wednesdays—the least busy day of the week. Estimates produced from this sample will certainly not be representative of the emergency room's experience. Establishing a zone size that differs from the cycle size effectively eliminates this problem.

Even when cycles do not exist, systematic sampling is often not the method of choice for actual field surveys. This is due to the fact that many of the problems listed previously with simple random sampling apply to systematic sampling as well, and it is possible to get better precision at lower cost with other methods than is possible with systematic sampling.

Example. Suppose now that the HMO in the previous example wants to assess satisfaction with services rendered among its members in an ongoing manner. They know that they will need to sample 1,200 claims per year (out of approximately 120,000 claims per year) to obtain a precise estimate. How would the HMO obtain a systematic random sample of claims?

Solution. They would first select a random number between 1 and $k =$ 120,000/1,200 = 100. Suppose this number is 4. Then, the 4th, 104th, 204th, etc. claim would be selected for the survey.

After the first year of the survey, the HMO has data from the satisfaction survey. They received 1,150 surveys back from the 1,200 that were sent out. The satisfaction instrument measures satisfaction on a scale of 1 to 100. The average score was 85, and the standard deviation was 10. What is the standard error of this estimate?

Solution. Using the standard deviation formula for simple random sampling, the standard error estimate for the satisfaction score is the following:

$$\hat{SE}(\bar{x}) = \sqrt{\frac{N-n}{N}}\left(\frac{s}{\sqrt{n}}\right) = \sqrt{\frac{120,000 - 1,150}{120,000}}\left(\frac{10}{\sqrt{1,150}}\right)$$
$$= 0.995 \times 0.295 = 0.294$$

Systematic Sampling in Practice

The American Community Survey (ACS) is an annual survey conducted by the U.S. Census Bureau. The ACS captures demographic, housing, social, and economic data. These data can be used to compare individuals across states, communities, and population groups. The ACS will eventually replace the census long form and thus allow the decennial census to focus on counting the population. Since 1996 the Census Bureau has been pilot testing the survey. Eventually, data will be gathered on all states, as well as on all cities, counties, metropolitan areas and population groups of 65,000 or more people.

When the ACS is fully operational, the Census Bureau will select a systematic sample of addresses from the Master Address File each month in every county. The U.S. Census Bureau created the MAF prior to the 2000 Census using addresses from the 1990 Census and information from the U.S. Postal Service. The ACS sample will be representative of every county in the United States.

Further Reading

Levy, Paul S., and Stanley Lemeshow. *Sampling of Populations: Methods and Applications.* New York: John Wiley, 1999. An accessible guide to sampling methods that offers extensive coverage of systematic sampling.

Stanley Lemeshow and Amy Ferketich

T

Taxes. *See* Budget, Taxes, and Deficits

Third-Person Effect

The third-person effect refers to the tendency of individuals to perceive that mass media have greater effects on other people than on themselves, and to the behavioral consequences of those perceptions (such as endorsing censorship). Sociologist W. Phillips Davison first introduced the concept in 1983. Resulting research has been interdisciplinary, concentrated in communication, social psychology, and sociology. Third-person effect research is part of a growing body of literature about individual perceptions of public opinion, and the influence that those perceptions can have on our collective social and political life. Studies have either attempted to verify the existence of the effect in different domains, tried to understand the conditions that limit or magnify the effect, and/or sought an explanation for the origins of the effect.

The perceptual component of the third-person effect has been well documented across many different content types, including news programming, television violence, pornography, hate speech, defamatory speech (libel and slander), rap music, and advertising. Typically, respondents are asked to estimate the amount of influence that a particular form of media content will have on themselves, and on other people. The gap between the effects on others and effects on self is reflective of the third-person perception.

Although findings of third-person perceptions have been prevalent, the size of the effect has varied across studies. The content of the media message under study is one factor that moderates the size of third-person perceptions. Media messages perceived as undesirable have almost uniformly produced a third-person perception. Furthermore, recent research has demonstrated that the third-person gap is especially large for particularly antisocial outcomes. For example, a respondent is more likely to perceive a wide gap in the tendency for violent content to cause aggressive behavior in others as opposed to themselves. The gap lessens, though, when the same respondents are asked to estimate the likelihood of themselves and others becoming more fearful as a result of viewing media violence.

The third-person perception is attenuated, for media messages that individuals consider are socially desirable and by which they do not object to be influenced. For example, children report that they are less likely than their peers to be influenced by cigarette advertising, but more likely than their peers to be influenced by antismoking public service announcements. Similarly, in an adult sample persuasive messages containing weak arguments produced a third-person perception. By contrast, effects on self were seen as greater when messages contained strong persuasive messages.

Another factor that influences the magnitude of third-person perceptions is the particular "other" for which respondents are asked to estimate effects. The further removed the other is from self, the greater the third-person perception. Every study that has examined this "social distance corollary," has supported this tenet. The common explanation is one of psychological distance from the comparison group. Other researchers have found that the increased size of more distant comparison groups makes an independent contribution to increasing the magnitude of the third-person perception. Still other research suggests that respondents have stereotypes about the media-use patterns of other groups, and these stereotypes factor in to estimates of media effects for particular groups of "others."

A 2000 meta-analysis by Bryant Paul and his associates also found that nonrandom samples produced greater third-person perceptions than did random samples. Similarly, college student respondents exhibited larger third-person perceptions than did non-college student subjects. Many of the nonrandom samples are college student samples, and it has been posited that college students may perceive themselves to be better educated than other comparison groups—and therefore less likely to be influenced by media than are other, less educated people. This question deserves further exploration, as alternative explanations may raise serious methodological and substantive challenges for third-person research.

Findings about the behavioral component of the third-person effect have been more limited, but are growing. Generally, researchers have examined whether or not there is a positive relationship between third-person perceptions and a willingness to endorse restrictions on the content in question. Most of these studies have used regression analysis, where third-person perception is one of several possible predictors for endorsement of censorship. It has been a robust predictor for many different kinds of content, although not usually for news programming. Paul and his associates noted in their meta-analysis that due to the way these findings have been presented, they are not amenable to current meta-analytic techniques. Also, because the analyses are correlational in nature, it is unclear if third-person perceptions precede a willingness to censor or vice versa.

Recent research has focused on explaining the origins of the perceptual bias. The prevailing theory is that third-person perceptions result from a desire for ego-enhancement. In other words, individuals feel superior to others in the form of less vulnerability to negative media effects. This is a parsimonious explanation that can account for the distinction between messages perceived to be desirable and those perceived as undesirable. It would enhance one's ego equally well to believe oneself to be more influenced by messages that are socially desirable as it would to believe that one is better able to counteract undesirable media effects. It also accounts for the social distance corollary, where comparison groups who are more different from self are perceived to be more strongly impacted by media content.

Future research in this area needs to explore aspects of message desirability—what characteristics of media messages and/or their perceived effects influence the magnitude of third-person perceptions? In many studies to date, the desirability of the message has been assumed a priori, rather than incorporated as a measured variable. Further specification is necessary. Additionally, more research is needed on the individual and group characteristics of those who exhibit strong third-person perceptions versus those who do not. Finally, methodological questions about the influence of nonrandom and college student samples on measurement of the effect must be addressed.

Further Reading

Davison, W. Phillips. "The Third-Person Effect in Communication." *Public Opinion Quarterly* 47 (1983): 1–13. The seminal article introducing the concept of the third-person effect.

Paul, Bryant, Michael B. Salwen, and Michel Dupagne. "The Third-Person Effect: A Meta-Analysis of the Perceptual Hypothesis." *Mass Communication and Society* 3, no. 1 (2000): 57–85. Summarizes the findings about the perceptual hypothesis of the third-person effect, indicating which variables have impacted effect size.

Perloff, Richard M. "The Third-Person Effect." In *Media Effects: Advances in Theory and Research*, edited by J. Bryant and D. Zillman. Mahwah, NJ: Lawrence Erlbaum, 2002, pp. 489–506. A thorough review of the conceptual and operational challenges facing researchers interested in the third-person effect.

Jennifer L. Lambe

Three-Step Test Interview (TSTI)

The Three-Step Test Interview (TSTI) is an instrument for **pretesting** a self-completion questionnaire by observing actual instances of interaction between the instrument and the respondents. Because this process consists primarily of cognitive processing and is therefore hidden from the observer, thinking aloud is used as a technique for making the thought process observable. The TSTI consists of the following three steps:

1. Concurrent thinking aloud aimed at collecting observational data.
2. Focused interview aimed at remedying gaps in observational data.
3. Semi-structured interview aimed at eliciting experiences and opinions.

Steps 1 and 2 are distinctive for the TSTI. Step 3 is similar to other types of in-depth and **cognitive interviewing**.

Measurement error poses numerous challenges for data collection. Problems may arise at any step in the completion of a questionnaire, resulting in data errors. **Cognitive interviewing** has been developed as an instrument for identifying such problems in the response process, their localization (both in the response process model and in the questionnaire), their effects (in terms of data error), and their causes.

In current pretesting practice, the term "cognitive interviewing" refers to two main techniques: think aloud and probing. These two techniques are very different in terms of their aims and methodological status. Think aloud was developed and is used by (cognitive) psychologists as a technique for producing data about the process of thinking. Its aim is to make this process, which is usually hidden, observable by asking subjects to verbalize their thoughts concurrently: that is, at the very moment they think them. It is debatable whether this can be done at all without changing the process of thinking and these thoughts themselves. But it is of the utmost importance to recognize that it is the aim of the think-aloud technique to make the thinking process itself observable. Probing, in contrast, is a technique for eliciting reports from respondents about their thinking. As soon as probing starts, the nature of the data is changed from observations to self-reports. This is an important difference, considering that probing is the technique most favored by cognitive researchers.

In the pretesting literature the distinction between observational data (i.e., the actual thinking process of the respondent, made observable through thinking aloud) and self-report data (i.e., the respondents' accounts of this process) is not (or insufficiently) acknowledged. Reports on cognitive pretesting research only rarely mention insights that are gained from observing what respondents in the research actually did when they responded to the test questionnaire: that is, based on concurrent think-aloud protocols. Instead, reported results of cognitive pretesting are usually based on data produced by respondents when probed to perform tasks other than responding to the questionnaire, such as paraphrasing questions, explaining definitions of terms, and expressing preferences regarding wordings, layouts, and so forth. However, such reports about interpretations and preferences, produced in pretesting, have a questionable relationship to the actual response process, which occurs when the same respondents complete the questionnaire.

The emphasis in the current practice of cognitive pretesting on the exploration of ideas (definitions, etc.) through probing also has the effect that important differences between the two main modes of questionnaire administration (interview and self-completion) are neglected. Probing tests the wording of questions outside of their context (a questionnaire), not the live questionnaire as encountered and experienced by the respondent. It does not test how the question is understood in its actually intended form when it is delivered (for hearing) by a specific interviewer in a specific interview context or provided (for reading) in a specific textual format for self-completion. To assess and improve the actual performance of the instrument in the field (i.e., in the chosen mode), the response process must be observed in action.

Because responding in an interview is very different from self-completing a written questionnaire, the appropriate techniques for observation should also be different. The appropriate technique of observing the response process in an interview is observing (i.e., audio- or videotaping) the interaction in the interview. This type of observation is known as **behavior coding.**

The methodological issues associated with assessing respondents' behavior during self-completion are very similar to the issues encountered by psychologists when they study the process of thinking. Whereas a questionnaire for an interview survey seems most adequately to be tested by means of behavior coding (followed by both interviewer and respondent debriefing), a self-completion questionnaire should be tested by means of a think-aloud technique. This implies that the questions for the think-aloud session should be offered to the respondent in a written format (as would be the case in the real-life questionnaire).

The TSTI method is designed to do just this, assessing the quality of a self-administered questionnaire by observing actual instances of interaction between the instrument and a respondent (see **Response Process**). Concurrent thinking aloud is used as a technique for making the thought process observable. Applying the TSTI to different measuring instruments produces "new" data on the performance of these instruments (data that are not produced with other methods for pretesting questionnaires), as well as the data produced with other extant methods.

The aim of the TSTI is to produce observational data on actual response behavior of respondents who respond to a self-completion questionnaire. Because much of this behavior consists of thinking and is therefore hidden from the observer, the (concurrent) thinking-aloud technique is used for making it observable. Therefore, the first and main step of the TSTI is concurrent thinking aloud, aimed at collecting observational data regarding the respondent's response behavior. These data consist of two types: (1) observations of respondent behavior (such as skipping questions; correction of the chosen response category; hesitation; distress; etc.) and (2) think-aloud data. Obviously, respondents must produce the required behavior for observation. For that purpose, respondents are instructed to complete the questionnaire as they would do at home or otherwise when they would be asked to complete the questionnaire with the additional task to concurrently verbalize what they think.

Ideally, both types of observational data—actions and verbalizations—are recorded and kept on audio- and videotape for later analysis. But the researcher also makes real-time notes of observed behaviors and of verbalized thoughts that seem to be indicative of problems in the response process. These real-time notes are made for immediate use in the following steps of the interview. The strictly observational nature of this first and essential step of the TSTI must not be compromised by any intervention—such as a question, comment, probe—by the researcher that might suggest that a self-report from the respondent be required.

Two additional steps follow upon this think-aloud step: (1) a focused interview and (2) a semi-structured interview. The focused interview is aimed at remedying the gaps in observational data. After the first step, researcher and respondent might further reconstruct a number of actions (or thoughts) of the respondent during the completion process on which the observational data collected in the first step appears incomplete. The assessment of this incompleteness is difficult because it must be made in real-time based on the researcher's observations during the first step.

The third and final step—the semi-structured interview—is the first and only one in the TSTI in which the respondent is allowed and even stimulated to add secondary data—accounts and reports of, for example, feelings, explanations, and preferences—to the primary, observational ones. The third step can take different forms depending on the kind of questionnaire tested. Respondents might comment on specific problems encountered in responding to the questionnaire, indicating what they thought the nature of the problem was and/or why they behaved as they did. Respondents might be asked to paraphrase questions and to comment on their definitions of terms (such as might be done in cognitive interviewing). Or, respondents might be probed about the substantive issues that are covered by the questionnaire that is tested, asked to explain their attitudes in their own words. Regardless, it is important to recognize that the comments provided constitute opinions of the causes of the problems detected in steps 1 and 2, not facts. Ultimately, researchers must make their own analysis of problems associated with the questionnaire (based on observations in all interviews of the pretest).

As yet, the TSTI has only been tested in pilot studies. In one of them, the quality of a set of questions about alcohol consumption was assessed. The TSTI proved to be particularly good at identifying problems that result from a mismatch between the theory underlying the questions and features of a respondent's actual behavior and biography. In another pilot study, Dutch and Norwegian versions of an attitude scale, the 20-item Illegal Aliens Scale, were validated. The TSTI appeared to be uniquely productive in identifying problems resulting from different response strategies. This suggests that, for self-completion questionnaires, the TSTI might eventually replace the other pretest methods without a significant loss of useful information.

Further Reading

Hak, T., H. Jansen, and K. van der Veer. *Manual for the Three-Step Test-Interview (TSTI)*. Rotterdam: ERIM, 2003. Available at http://www.fbk.eur.nl/ERIM/welcome.html.

Presser, J., and J. Blair. "Survey Pretesting: Do Different Methods Produce Different Results?" In *Sociological Methodology*, vol. 24, edited by P. V. Marsden. Washington, DC: American Sociological Association, 1994, pp. 73–104.

Van der Veer, K., R. Ommundsen, T. Hak, and K. S. Larsen. "Meaning Shift of Items in Different Language Versions: A Cross-National Validation Study of the Illegal Aliens Scale." *Quality and Quantity* 37 (2003): 193–206. An example of the application of the TSTI in validating a questionnaire concerning attitudes toward immigrants.

Kees van der Veer

Tolerance. *See* Political Tolerance

Trust in Government

The concept of trust in government is commonly defined as an affective or evaluative orientation toward government. It is, at least conceptually, an indicator of diffuse support (e.g., support for a political system or regime) rather than an indicator of specific support (e.g., support for an incumbent administration). Feelings of trust in government are grounded in one's assessment of how well government is satisfying normative expectations for government performance. Understanding trust in government thus requires some understanding of citizens' normative expectations. Two such expectations are thought to be particularly important. The first is an expectation of competence. Citizens expect government officials to possess the technical competence needed to develop and implement sound public policy. The second is an expectation of public obligation and responsibility. Citizens expect public officials to place the public interest ahead of their own personal or partisan interests. A third, often unspoken expectation, is that of integrity. Citizens expect public officials to behave honestly. Levels of trust in government are thought to fluctuate according to the perceived fulfillment of these expectations. To trust a government is to express confidence and faith that it will meet the public's normative expectations.

For more than four decades, the measurement of trust in government has been heavily influenced by a battery of trust-in-government instruments developed by the Center for Political Studies (CPS) and currently maintained by the **National Election Studies** (NES) at the University of Michigan. In 1958 the CPS made its first attempt to measure public trust in government. Specifically, survey respondents were asked: How much of the time do you think you can trust the government in Washington to do what is right—just about always, most of the time, or only some of the time? By 1964 the CPS had added four additional instruments designed to measure trust in government: (1) Would you say the government is pretty much run by a few big interests looking out for themselves or that it is run for the benefit of all the people? (2) Do you think that people in the government waste *a lot* of money we pay in taxes, waste some of it, or don't waste very much of it? (3) Do you feel that almost all of the people running the government are smart people who usually know what they are doing, or do you think that quite a few of them don't seem to know what they are doing? (4) Do you think that quite of few of the people running the government are a little crooked, not very many are, or do you think hardly any of them are crooked at all? Since the early 1960s, political trust has most commonly been measured by using the original question introduced in 1958 or by using some combination of the five questions in the expanded NES battery.

While trust in government is a concept whose meaning is widely shared, its measurement has been the subject of considerable scholarly concern and debate. First, scholars have noted ambiguities and inconsistencies in the attitude objects embedded in the various trust instruments. While some questions make reference to such institutions as "the government" or "the government in Washington," others make reference to such individuals as "the people in government" or "the people running the government." Second, beginning with a prominent exchange in the 1970s, scholars have debated the validity of the NES instruments. At principal issue in this debate has been the question of whether these measures truly capture attitudes toward the political system in general (diffuse support) or whether they really tap attitudes toward the incumbent authorities that happen to be in power (specific support). More recently, scholars have begun to question the theoretical interpretation of the NES trust measures. Do these measures, for example, really represent a scale than runs from active trust to active distrust (i.e., cynicism), or do they simply reflect a scale that runs from active trust to the mere absence of trust (i.e., skepticism)? The answers to the questions raised above have direct implications for how one interprets changing levels of trust in government.

The study of trust in government was first motivated by a desire to understand and explain declining levels of political trust in the United States and to consider the implications of this decline for American democracy. In 1964, 78 percent of Americans believed they could trust the government in Washington to do what is right at least most of the time. From its height in 1964, political trust began a period of steep decline that would continue uninterrupted for sixteen years. By 1980, only 26 percent of Americans felt they could trust government most of the time. Levels of trust in government experienced a brief rebound during the first term of the Reagan administration, peaking at 45 percent in 1984. After this temporary recovery, however, political trust entered a ten-year period of almost continuous decline. By 1994, trust in government had fallen below 22 percent, a level that remains the lowest on record. Since that record low, levels of trust in government have experienced a modest but consistent rise. Trust in government has increased every year since 1994 and, in the wake of September 11, 2001, actually surpassed the 50 percent mark in the 2002 NES. While trust in government has trended upward in recent years, its overall pattern across the past four decades has been one of steady, though not monotonic, decline.

Although few challenge the assertion that levels of trust in government are much lower today than they once were, the normative implications of this decline in political trust have been a source of some dispute. Most scholars agree that diffuse support is important because it helps to preserve the legitimacy of a political system or regime. At issue, though, is whether traditional measures of trust in government are really gauging diffuse support for the political system or whether they are simply tapping specific support for the performance of the incumbent administration. If it is the former, then steep declines in political trust may, over time, threaten the perceived legitimacy of a regime. If it is the latter, then fluctuations in political trust are likely to be more ephemeral and thus less politically consequential. Recent work has emphasized the need for a balanced perspective, arguing that trust indexes often capture both kinds of support.

Using a diverse array of research designs and estimation techniques, scholars have repeatedly sought to identify and explain the determinants of trust in government. Collectively, these studies have informed our understanding of the causal factors that shape political trust. For example, demographic factors, such as education, race, education, income, and sex, have been found to be relatively unimportant. While some studies report that trust is lower among women and African Americans, the effects of demographic characteristics on political trust have, in the main, been rather weak and inconsistent. The effects of other individual-level attributes, such as party and ideological identification, are somewhat mixed. Some have argued that Republicans and conservatives, particularly those who hold a traditional worldview, are less trusting of the federal government than Democrats and self-identified liberals. Others argue that the effects of party and ideology are conditional upon who is in political power at the time. Recent work suggests that party and ideology have strong indirect effects on trust by shaping both presidential and congressional evaluations, which, in turn, are involved in a reciprocal causal relationship with trust in government.

Numerous studies report that citizens' level of trust in government is linked to various indicators of government performance. First, trust is shaped by citizens' degree of policy satisfaction. The closer government policies are to a citizen's issue preferences along an ideological continuum, the more trusting of government that citizen is likely to be. Second, trust is influenced by perceptions of government responsiveness. Citizens are more likely to trust government if they believe that the government is doing an effective job of handling current problems. Third, both cross-sectional and time-series analyses have consistently found that trust in government is a function of the public's economic perceptions (*see* **Economy**). When perceptions of economic conditions are more positive, the government is the recipient of greater public trust. Implicit in this relationship is the assumption that government bears some responsibility for macroeconomic performance. Finally, trust in government is inversely related to perceptions of crime. When crime is perceived to be an important problem facing the nation, trust in government declines.

Since the concept of trust involves an element of integrity, it is not surprising that declines in political trust have often been associated with periods of political corruption and scandal. Indeed, the largest two-year drop in political trust occurred between 1972 and 1974, a change that no doubt reflects the influence of Watergate. Research also indicates that congressional scandals, such as the Keating Five scandal and the House Banking scandal, result in lower levels of trust. While there is little evidence that political corruption is on the rise, there is some evidence that it has become the subject of increased media focus. Finally, research suggests that trust is shaped by international events and perceptions of external threat. One study reports that trust in government rises as the percentage of Americans naming foreign policy or defense as the most important problem facing the nation increases. This observation provides one plausible account for the spike in trust that occurred after September 11. It may also help to explain why trust tends to be higher among citizens who believe the president is a strong leader. In sum, trust in government is a complex phenomenon that is driven by a diverse set of individual-level and contextual factors.

A growing body of literature argues that, apart from any effects it may have on the perceived legitimacy of a regime, trust in government has important political consequences. Political scientists have shown that political trust increases the likelihood of compliance with government demands, such as paying one's taxes and serving in the military. Trust has also been shown to affect citizens' attitudes concerning the balance of power between national and subnational governments. Individuals who voice less trust in the federal government prefer a greater devolution of power to subnational governments. Researchers have also uncovered a link between trust in government and attitudes toward term limits. Specifically, those who distrust government express greater support for limiting the terms of federal and state legislators.

Recent work demonstrates that trust in government also has implications for voting behavior. In two-candidate presidential elections, political distrust has been found to benefit challengers at the expense of incumbents. In three-way contests, political distrust benefits third-party candidates at the expense of major-party candidates. Scholars have also discovered a connection between political trust and public policy mood. The nature of this relationship is such that increases in trust lead to increased support for domestic policy liberalism. This finding has profound implications for the direction of public policy in the United

States. When trust in government spirals downward, so too does public support for progressive public policy.

While the literature is likely to retain its interest in the measurement and movement of trust in government, the study of trust in government is also likely to expand in new directions. One recent trend, which is likely to continue, is the analysis of trust in government from a comparative perspective. Through both cross-national and subnational analysis, scholars are increasingly broadening their focus beyond the federal government in the United States. Using survey data from nine different countries, one recent study analyzed the determinants of political trust in post-communist Europe. Another recent advance in the study of trust in government is the use of multilevel analysis. Multilevel or hierarchical models allow researchers to simultaneously account for both individual-level and contextual determinants of trust. Multilevel models have been used to partition individual-level and country-level variance in citizens' trust in civil servants across sixteen democratic nations. Multilevel models have also been used to explain trust in local government within the United States. One recent study reports that trust in local government is a function not only of citizens' individual-level beliefs and characteristics but also of city-level factors, such as income inequality, ideological polarization, ethnic fractionalization, and institutional structure. Given recent theoretical and methodological advances, the study of trust in government is likely to have a promising future, as evidenced by its contribution to our understanding of **social capital** and **international trust**.

Further Reading

Chanley, Virginia A., Thomas J. Rudolph, and Wendy M. Rahn. "The Origins and Consequences of Public Trust in Government: A Time-Series Analysis." *Public Opinion Quarterly* 64, no. 3 (2000): 239–56. An aggregate-level time-series analysis of the causes and consequences of trust in government.

Citrin, Jack. "Comment: The Political Relevance of Trust in Government." *American Political Science Review* 68, no. 3 (1974): 973–88. A classic statement of the position that trust measures gauge specific rather than diffuse support.

Hetherington, Marc J. *Why Trust Matters: Declining Political Trust and the Demise of American Liberalism.* Princeton, NJ: Princeton University Press, 2004. An analysis of the decline in political trust and its implications for public policy.

Hibbing, John R., and Elizabeth Theiss-Morse, eds. *What Is It About Government that Americans Dislike?* Cambridge: Cambridge University Press, 2001. An edited volume featuring current research by leading scholars in the field.

Thomas J. Rudolph

TSTI. *See* **Three-Step Test Interview**

U

Unit Nonresponse

Unit nonresponse refers to cases where members of the sample cannot be found or do not respond to a survey. In a typical public opinion survey, unit nonresponse occurs when sampled individuals or households are unreachable, unavailable, unable, or unwilling to complete a survey. Unit nonresponse, where no responses are obtained from a person, is distinguished from item nonresponse, in which only some survey questions are not answered.

Unit nonresponse is typically measured in a survey **response rate**. The response rate measures the proportion of eligible members of the sample that responded to the survey. As a corollary to this, the nonresponse rate would be (1-RR) where RR is the response rate.

Whether unit nonresponse introduces bias in a survey depends on both the magnitude of the nonresponse and the degree of difference between survey respondents and nonrespondents. If nonresponse is random then its impact on survey estimates is negligible. If nonrespondents differ systematically from survey responders, however, there is potential bias in results from a survey or public opinion poll.

Suppose we are estimating p, the proportion of the population with a certain opinion. Every step of the research process that eliminates members of the population introduces an error. Errors from random sampling, however, can be made as small as we want by increasing the sampling rate, and the size of that error is easily calculated using statistical theory. However, in addition to the easily calculable sampling error, each nonrandom step causes an additional potentially systematic error.

Systematic error can be measured by the following formula:

$$\text{systematic error} = (\text{proportion eliminated}) * (\text{p\_retained} - \text{p\_eliminated})$$

where p_retained and p_eliminated are the proportions of the retained and eliminated people with the opinion in question.

More specifically, for nonresponse:

$$\text{nonresponse error} = (1\text{-RR}) * (P_r - P_{nr})$$

where RR is the response rate, P_r is the value of a survey statistic for responders, and P_{nr} is the value of the survey statistic for nonresponders.

From this formula, it follows that although the level of unit nonresponse may be the same for any questions asked in a given survey, the impact of the error introduced by this can vary from question to question. Thus the unit nonresponse for any given survey might provide relatively little impact for some questions, while having a greater impact on other questions asked in the same survey.

It should also be noted that an accurate estimate of the impact of nonresponse error in a survey requires knowing both the response rate and the value of relevant statistics both in survey respondents and in nonresponders. Typically, the response rate is easy to calculate according to several standard formulae, and survey response rates are often reported in methodology reports. The value of a survey statistic for nonresponders is much more difficult to determine. In some cases, for example where high response rate surveys have obtained comparable measures, it is possible to estimate these differences. In most cases, however, such data is not available and survey researchers must either develop specialized methods to estimate this, or simply make rough guesses and estimates of the likely difference or range of differences that might apply.

Considerations for Nonresponse for Public Opinion Surveys. Although any source of systematic error in a survey may be cause for concern, nonresponse is a special concern in public opinion surveys because it is almost always present in contemporary public opinion results. Although public opinion polls utilize different sampling and research methods to reach different target populations, there are limits to a survey researcher's ability to encourage cooperation from people who do not want to participate in a survey. Except when a population is sampled directly, such as an **exit poll** which draws its sample directly from people who are leaving a polling place, there is also likely to be nonresponse in a survey because some people in the sample cannot be located.

Unit nonresponse is also of concern because in surveys that use **random digit dialing**—the most common tool for measuring public opinion in the United States—other sources of error have been reduced. **Coverage error** in telephone surveys has been largely reduced as the proportion of households reachable by telephone has increased. Sampling error has been reduced and quantified by implicit agreement about standards for reporting **sample size**; public scrutiny of sample sizes and their associated errors has motivated survey organizations to use reasonable sample sizes.

The success in reducing coverage and sample error has left nonresponse as one of the least controlled sources of selection errors. Although some researchers encourage the reporting of response rates for public opinion polls, the relationship between the rate of nonresponse and bias or error introduced by nonresponse is complex, can vary among different survey questions and statistics, and is not typically known. Unlike the simple relation between sample size and margin of error, nonresponse error cannot be reduced indefinitely by spending more money.

One important characteristic of nonresponse that makes evaluating the quality of surveys based on response rates difficult is the loose relation between nonresponse rates and nonresponse error. The nonresponse rate limits the possible error, but in most opinion surveys the limits are too large to be useful.

For example, suppose respondents are evenly split on a Yes/No question, and nonresponse is 50 percent. Since nonresponse error is measured by $(1-RR)$ * $(P_r - P_{nr})$, $(1-RR)$ is 50 percent, and P_r is 50 percent, the possible bias in this question will be found by examining the boundaries of the equation: $(50\% * (50\% - P_{nr}))$. Since the nonrespondents' opinions on this question could range from 0 to 100 percent, the nonresponse error can range from -25 to $+25$ percent, meaning that the true opinions of all members of the sample might range from 25 to 75 percent. However, these extremes would only occur if nonrespondent opinion is unanimous one way or the other, which is very unlikely for most opinions.

Nonresponse error depends on differences in opinion between two groups: respondents and nonrespondents. Although significant research remains to be done to understand this in detail, many studies have found that differences in opinions between groups are usually moderate unless the grouping is obviously related to the opinion being measured.

Differences between respondents and nonrespondents can also be understood to be less dramatic if one understands that nonrespondents are not a completely distinct group from respondents. A person who is a non-contact in one survey because of a vacation trip during the survey period, might be a respondent in a survey conducted at a different time of year. Some **refusals** are similarly a matter of chance, rather than a permanent policy of not cooperating with surveys. This reduces the differences between respondents and nonrespondents.

Types of Nonresponse. Nonresponse is not a single phenomenon. Households or individuals might be nonresponders because they are unreachable, unavailable, unable, or unwilling to complete a survey. The causes and correlates of each of these are different, and it is likely that there is as much variation between individuals who do not respond to a survey for different reasons as there is between respondents and nonresponders. This makes understanding the reasons for nonresponse more useful than simply understanding a simple response rate.

Detailed reports of sample outcomes or dispositions typically separate different components of nonresponse. For example, many methodologists look at differences between non-contacts, non-cooperators, and refusers.

A common reason for non-contact is that no one is home when the contact attempts are made. This includes several groups, whose opinions may differ: people who happened not to be home at those times, people who are never home during survey hours because of a fixed schedule, and people away from home during the survey period (vacation, business trip, jail, etc.). Others are not contacted because of a gatekeeper, human or otherwise, such as answering machines in telephone surveys or doormen in face-to-face interviews.

Some of these non-contacts could be more accurately described as running out of time. Some interviews are completed during the first visit or phone call, but selecting a household member and finding a convenient time for the survey may take several attempts spread over many days. For some willing participants, the survey may end before this process does. In contrast, some non-contacts who seem to be taking a long time to find a satisfactory time for an interview may be "polite refusals"—respondents who have no intention of completing an interview but do not want to say no. Instead they ask to be called later.

A refusal may be a conscious long-term decision not to participate in surveys, or because the potential recipient misidentifies a call as telemarketing (or a door-to-door visit as a robber).

Nonresponse can also come about in a survey when an interviewer and a willing respondent are unable to communicate sufficiently to complete a survey interview. For example, a respondent may be deaf or hard-of-hearing and therefore unable to complete a survey interview under conventional circumstances. Some people contacted for a survey may speak a language other than English, and consequently unable to complete a survey interview unless a translated questionnaire and appropriate non-English language interviewer are provided in field procedures.

Response Rate Standards. The need to separate nonresponse rates into components without ambiguity led two American survey research associations to publish standards for reporting response rates: the Council of American Survey Research Organizations in 1982 and the American Association for Public Opinion Research (AAPOR) eighteen years later. The AAPOR Standards, which are currently undergoing a series of revisions and expansions to account for different types of surveys, provide multiple methods of calculating rates to measure response, cooperation, and contact.

AAPOR response rate calculations also allow for different assumptions about cases of unknown survey eligibility. In many cases where no contact can be made with a sample record, it is not clear whether the record leads to a valid respondent. For example, in a telephone survey of households, a sampled telephone number may continually ring and not be answered despite multiple attempts. This might result from a household where the phone is not being answered, but it also might be a nonresidential telephone number that would not be eligible for a survey. Different AAPOR response rates make different assumptions about these cases, including assuming all are eligible, assuming all are ineligible, or attempting to estimate eligibility.

Although the reporting of response rates is not a universal or even common practice, when reported in full detail a full set of standardized response, cooperation, and contact rates can provide a useful measure for comparing different surveys and for estimating the potential impact of nonresponse on different survey measures.

Measures to Reduce Nonresponse. The most typical measures to reduce nonresponse are those designed to increase response rates. Careful design and preparation of a **sample frame** can decrease the number of respondents who are unreachable. Surveys with longer **field periods** can reduce the proportion of sampled respondents who are unavailable to complete an interview. Including special considerations for respondents who speak different languages can reduce the percentage of sample contacts that are unable to complete an interview. Refusals can be reduced through careful training of interviewers and employing specialists to recontact prospective respondents who have initially refused to complete an interview.

Care must be taken, however, when employing methods designed to increase response rates to ensure that these measures do not exacerbate the differences between respondents and nonrespondents. This is sometimes used as an argument against **financial incentives,** or supplementing a telephone survey with letters that only reach nonrespondents whose address can be found.

Survey data can also be adjusted to reduce the potential impact of nonresponse. In these cases, demographic or other correlates are used to minimize the impact of nonresponse on survey statistics. Post-stratification weights are a common method of this type of adjustment. In this type of **weighting,** survey data is often adjusted to known population parameters based on demographic groups that are believed or known to have different response rates and different opinions. Gender, age, level of educational attainment, marital status, and income are all demographic characteristics that are typically used to adjust for nonresponse. An advantage of this type of weighting is that it also adjusts for other errors in surveys, such as coverage error, that may have omitted respondents.

Whether demographic or other correlates are used to improve estimates, each group must have enough respondents for accurate estimates within the group. Thus the ideal correlate has some association with response rate, but not so much that the low-response group has too few respondents. The most dangerous correlates are those that may be unknown or overlooked by the researcher. That includes not only characteristics that correlate so well with nonresponse that members of the groups cannot be interviewed but also characteristics that cannot be measured—or those where the researcher cannot determine into which group a respondent belongs. The notorious *Literary Digest* presidential poll of 1936 incorrectly predicted a victory for candidate Alf Landon instead of the landslide victory of Franklin Delano Roosevelt because of an unmeasured correlate. The rich were both more likely to be sampled and more likely to vote for Alf Landon.

The decrease in response rates seems to be a long-term trend. In telephone surveys, survey response rates have been observed in recent years to be in particularly steep decline. Among the plausible explanations are a decrease in contact rates because of answering machines and other privacy devices, and an increase in refusals because of competition for the respondent's time from telemarketers and even other surveys. Response rates are also decreasing in Europe and for nontelephone surveys, probably for similar reasons.

In the long run, the principles of sampling and statistics will remain valid; however, many factors that correlate with survey response are currently in flux. Telephonic technologies and customs are changing in ways that may reduce the ability of telephone surveys to adequately contact random samples of respondents. Social norms about the importance of completing surveys are changing as respondents feel overburdened by numerous requests for surveys and other information-gathering exercises. Social and workforce customs are changing in ways that lead to people being at home less frequently and at different hours than in the past. Researchers need to be open to changes in methods to minimize response error, whether through small modifications or completely different strategies.

Further Reading

American Association for Public Opinion Research. *Standard Definitions: Final Dispositions of Case Codes and Outcome Rates for Surveys.* Ann Arbor, MI: AAPOR, 2000. Provides not only response rates but also a rational system of case definition codes, fundamental to process control in a survey operation. Includes formulas for calculating the response rates from the codes.

Council of American Survey Research Organizations. *On the Definition of Response Rates.* N.p., 1982. An early, simple, and widely used definition of response rates.

Groves, R. M., et al., eds. *Survey Nonresponse.* New York: John Wiley, 2002. A collection of in-depth articles on specific topics involving item and unit nonresponse. The extensive references are a good entry into the literature.

Keeter, Scott, Carol Miller, Andrew Kohut, Robert M. Groves, and Stanley Presser. "Consequences of Reducing Nonresponse in a National Telephone Survey." *Public Opinion Quarterly* 64 (Summer 2000): 125–48. Experimental investigation of the relation between nonresponse rate and nonresponse error.

Web Sites

The American Association for Public Opinion Research keeps the latest edition of *Standard Definitions: Final Dispositions of Case Codes and Outcome Rates for Surveys* on its Web site, which is available at http://www.aapor.org; see Standards and Best Practices under Survey Methods. The Response Rate Calculator, also under Survey Methods, is an Excel spreadsheet that you can use to calculate the response rates defined in Standard Definitions.

Similarly, the Council of American Survey Research Organizations keeps its publication *On the Definition of Response Rates* on its Web site at http://www.casro.org/resprates.cfm. You can get to it from http://www.casro.org through Publications.

Michael Butterworth and Chase H. Harrison

U.S. Supreme Court and Public Opinion, The

The U.S. Supreme Court is often believed to differ from the other institutions of government, such as Congress, in its supposed neutrality regarding public opinion. The realities are quite different, as an illustrated by the 1954 landmark case *Brown v. Board of Education*, which declared unconstitutional the "separate but equal" doctrine. While most people are familiar with this ruling, many do not realize that the case arrived on the Court's docket in 1951. The reason for the delay is nicely explained by a conversation between Justice Frankfurter and his law clerk, as documented by David O'Brien in his 2003 book *Storm Center.* When asked why the Court did not rule on the case earlier, Frankfurter commented, "Well, we're holding it for the election," since 1952 was a presidential election year. The clerk responded in disbelief, "You're holding it for the election? I thought the Supreme Court was supposed to decide cases without regard to elections." Justice Frankfurter continued, "When you have a major social political issue of this magnitude," timing and public reactions are important considerations. For precisely these kinds of reasons, scholars have devoted considerable attention to understanding the importance of public opinion to the Court.

In approaching the public's attitudes toward the Supreme Court, the most basic questions we face are those of support, legitimacy, and confidence. Most institutions depend on a certain degree of legitimacy to operate effectively. The concept of legitimacy plays a central role within the judiciary, since the courts possess 'neither the purse nor the sword.' That is, judges do not possess enforcement mechanisms to compel adherence to their decisions and therefore must rely on institutional legitimacy to impact society. Scholars generally agree that legitimacy is a normative concept involving whether an institution possesses the authority to take a specific action.

At an initial level, legitimacy involves determining whether the public supports an institution. Support can be defined as whether a political object is viewed favorably or unfavorably. Since the courts possess 'neither the purse nor the sword,' the efficacy of their actions relies upon institutional support. However, support can involve both short-term and long-term effects. Thus, scholars traditionally divide this concept into two component manifestations: specific support and diffuse support. Specific support depends on an institution fulfilling demands for particular policies. Diffuse support refers to favorable attitudes or good will that allow citizens to accept decisions or outcomes that they oppose. For the judiciary, specific support therefore involves short-term responses to particular decisions, whereas diffuse support captures long-term sentiments toward institutional authority.

Distinguishing between specific support and diffuse support seems to work well at a conceptual level. Yet, when one attempts to measure these two concepts, difficulties ensue. Some scholars argue that specific and diffuse support, while distinct theoretically, are empirically indistinguishable: that is, we lack the tools to tell one kind of support from the other with survey data. Hence, attention has turned to alternative approaches.

One notable method involves measuring peoples' confidence in judicial institutions. The annual **General Social Survey** (GSS) routinely asks questions regarding levels of confidence for political institutions, including the U.S. Supreme Court. Specifically, individuals are asked whether they have confidence in the people running the institutions. However, with regard to the Supreme Court, who exactly are the "people running" this institution? Are respondents supposed to base their opinions on the actions of the Supreme Court justices, or are the administrative personnel responsible for running the Court? Does a question pertaining to confidence in individuals accurately measure the legitimacy of an institution? Gibson, Caldeira, and Spence discover that questions about confidence in the leaders of the Supreme Court picks up both short-term satisfaction with the performance of the Court (i.e., specific support) as well as long-term attachments to the institution (i.e., diffuse support). They caution scholars by claiming that "those who analyze confidence to learn something about legitimacy of the Supreme Court ought to be sensitive to these findings that confidence reflects a blend of short-term and long-term judgments of the institution." Thus, it is not entirely appropriate to equate confidence in an institution as a measure of either diffuse support or legitimacy. As an alternative, they suggest incorporating a measure that focuses on whether individuals would agree to either the elimination of the Court or a fundamental restructuring of jurisdiction. This strategy, they claim, provides a more reliable and valid measure of diffuse support or legitimacy than the measure of confidence employed by the GSS.

Given the various definitions and concepts surrounding support, confidence, and legitimacy, an appropriate question to ask is whether the Supreme Court can influence public opinion. The next section focuses on whether public sentiments change due to Supreme Court rulings and highlights the problems associated with media coverage of the Court.

In 1989 the *Washington Post* reported the results of a poll taken on the Supreme Court. Less than 10 percent of the public could name the Chief Justice, but almost three times as many individuals could identify Judge Wapner, from the television program "The People's Court." This example illustrates a major obstacle in determining the Court's influence on public opinion; namely, the institution is barely recognized by the public. Given this lack of saliency, can the Supreme Court influence public opinion? If so, does this influence exist throughout the country, or are the effects more pronounced at a local level? How does media coverage of the Supreme Court and its decisions impact this influence?

At a fundamental level, the Supreme Court operates as though it can influence the public mood. An examination of any opinion uncovers language designed to educate the populace about the rationale behind the decision. This language is targeted not simply to the legal community but also to the general public, and the justices behave as if this public education is extremely important. Therefore, it is somewhat ironic that few empirical analyses exist about the Court's ability to change public opinion. As Gregory Caldeira notes, studies of the Supreme Court and public opinion come in three basic varieties. First, several analyses attempt to define the connection between specific Court decisions and aggregate shifts in public opinion via historical narration, without multivariate analysis. Second, some analyses incorporate multivariate techniques to identify relationships between opinion polls and Supreme Court decisions. Finally, recent examinations are relying on experimental and quasi-experimental (*see* **Experiments**) techniques to study changes in individuals in reference to specific Court decisions. One obstacle encountered by national analyses involves the public's knowledge about the Court (*see* **Political Knowledge**). Most individuals in the United States receive political information through mass media, especially television. However, journalists covering the Court, while highly professional themselves, may see their reporting limited or restricted by the commercial pressures of the news "industry." Consequently, the American public is underinformed and occasionally misinformed about the actions of the Supreme Court. Yet, regardless of the mode of analysis and the concern about media attention, it is probably unreasonable to expect the Supreme Court to stimulate significant changes in public opinion nationally in relatively short periods of time. Therefore, analyses of the Court's impact in this area may need to rely on an alternative area of focus.

One such alternative involves focusing on the Court's ability to foster change in local public opinion. Looking at changes on a local level is important for a number of reasons. First, if one assumes that only landmark Court cases influence public opinion then, by implication, one must assume that the remaining cases (a large portion of the Court's work) are inconsequential. Consequently, national opinion data of Court opinions may provide systematic evidence for the impact of monumental decisions, but the more routine cases may not offer similar conclusions. Additionally, if one assumes that citizens learn about Court decisions based on salient and available information then a uniform national approach is not appropriate. Instead, one must focus on local public opinion to control for idiosyncratic information effects. The final reason for examining local opinion is that Court decisions often require active implementation by local officials. This implementation in turn affects local sentiment about the Court, making a systematic analysis of opinion change possible.

One recent examination of the Court's influence on local public opinion was conducted by Valerie Hoekstra. Using a two-wave panel study to examine changes in local sentiment surrounding a Supreme Court case originating within the community, she discovers several interesting findings. First, in a comparison of media coverage between local newspapers and the *New York Times*, Hoekstra notices that the national paper did not perform better than local media. Local papers devoted more space to the case and started coverage earlier in the process (including deliberations in the lower courts). Therefore, focusing on local reactions to Supreme Court cases avoids the media-neglect obstacle that examinations of national public opinion encounter. Second, her analyses of four separate communities reveals only limited evidence that the Court shapes public opinion. In two of the studies some evidence exists of opinion change in the direction of the Court's decision; this change, however, is difficult to explain and not systematic. The lack of systematic influence contradicts previous theoretical expectations about the Court being a persuasive institution (i.e., being able to convince the public to conform to the Court's view).

In sum, analyses of Supreme Court influence on national public opinion provide mixed conclusions about the Court's impact. These somewhat contradictory results are possibly caused by the lack of media attention on the Supreme Court. Therefore, alternative analyses examine the Court's impact on local public opinion. The recent example by Hoekstra indicates that the Court possesses a limited ability to change opinions at the local level, contrary to previous theoretical expectations about Court persuasiveness.

Perhaps a more important question is whether justices of the Supreme Court are influenced by public opinion. Some posit that the Supreme Court, over the long run, takes on the views of the governing coalition. The implications of this statement are that the Court is sensitive to public opinion and over a period of time responds to public sentiment. Other scholars contend that the Court is a counter-majoritarian institution, insolated from the public's influence. Do expressions of public sentiment factor into the decisions of the Court, or is it a stoic counter-majoritarian institution?

Mishler and Sheehan empirically test the majoritarian hypothesis, using a time-series analysis of Supreme Court decisions from 1956 to 1989. They note that while the relationship between public opinion and the Court is often subtle and complex, since 1956 the Court has been responsive to changes in public sentiment. Though the decisions of the justices are not influenced by relevant opinion polls seen in the morning paper, a more gradual relationship exists. The authors note the effects of public opinion take, on average, five years to register with the Court, and this "probably reflects both the time it takes for a change in public opinion to be reflected in presidential elections and the time required before a newly elected president has a Court vacancy." Thus, public opinion affects the Supreme Court in a somewhat indirect fashion, working through the appointment process after presidential regime changes. Even where the Court adjusts its decisions absent membership change, it is likely to take several years for the justices to perceive, interpret and react to changes in the public mood.

Some other scholars take exception to Mishler and Sheehan's claim of a five-year lag between changes in public opinion and changes in Court decisions. Still, despite the controversy over the specific period of time, it is apparent that the Supreme Court is gradually affected by public opinion. The justices alter their decisions, in accordance with public sentiment, after a period of several years.

The future relationship between the Court and public opinion is difficult to discern. While continuity in the patterns discussed above is likely, the increasing polarization of American politics has the potential to affect dramatically the public's confidence in the Court to the extent that the Court is seen as behaving as a conventional political actor. The Court's intervention in the 2000 presidential election, for instance, was seen by many as potentially damaging the long-term credibility of the judiciary.

Further Reading

Caldeira, Gregory A. "Neither the Purse Nor the Sword: Dynamics of Public Confidence in the Supreme Court." *American Political Science Review* 80 (December 1986): 1209–26.

Gibson, James L., Gregory A. Caldeira, and Lester Kenyatta Spence. "Measuring Attitudes toward the United States Supreme Court." *American Journal of Political Science* 47 (April 2004): 354–67.

Hoekstra, Valerie J. *Public Reaction to Supreme Court Decisions*. Cambridge: Cambridge University Press, 2003.

Mishler, William, and Reginald S. Sheehan. "The Supreme Court as a Countermajoritarian Institution? The Impact of Public Opinion on Supreme Court Decisions." *American Political Science Review* 87 (March 1993): 87–101.

Norpoth, Helmut, and Jeffrey A. Segal. "Popular Influence on Supreme Court Decisions: Comment on Mishler and Sheehan (1993)." *American Political Science Review* 88 (September 1994): 711–16.

O'Brien, David M. *Storm Center: The Supreme Court in American Politics*. 6th ed. New York: W. W. Norton, 2003.

Kirk A. Randazzo and Reginald S. Sheehan

V

Vague Responses

A vague response is an answer to a survey question that does not provide enough information for the coder—the person whose job it is to count and score all responses—to determine the meaning of the response or the category to which it belongs. Vague responses are generally answers that result in coder disagreement: that is, different coders interpret the same answer differently. Because open-ended questions—those that do not provide a list of acceptable answers— offer the greatest leeway, they tend to produce more vague responses than do closed-ended questions. It should not be assumed, though, that closed-ended questions (which provide response alternatives) are immune to vague responses. Such questions often include an "other" category that allows respondents to offer their own responses if the alternatives provided prove insufficient.

Vague responses typically take two forms. They occur when respondents omit seemingly irrelevant information. For example, a person asked to provide her occupation might respond with "school teacher's aide." This response could be insufficient for survey needs, which might require a more precise title (e.g., "after-school teacher's aide" or "elementary school teacher's aide"). The respondent's failure to include "after" or "elementary" would leave the coder uncertain whether the respondent provides in-school care during school hours or after-school care at another facility.

Alternatively, vague responses occur when respondents provide lengthy answers. Long answers to open-ended questions can actually decrease clarity, because respondents have a greater likelihood of providing a word or phrase that results in greater coder disagreement.

Although respondents are typically the source of vague responses, survey procedures themselves can also cause them to occur. If survey **question wording** is unclear, it is likely that responses also will be unclear. Open-ended questions are particularly vulnerable to this situation because respondents have little guidance about the nature of usable responses. In contrast, closed-ended questions offer a list of possible responses that enable respondents to identify the desired type of response, even if one does not come immediately to mind. Moreover, poor interviewer training can result in vague responses. Interviewers represent a potential first line of defense against vague responses as they usually have the opportunity to ask for immediate clarification if necessary, and those interviewers who are not familiar with the survey goals or the issue of vague responses in general may fail in this role. This last issue does not arise in the case of self-administered surveys.

Vague responses are problematic because they can result in increased costs and measurement error. Vague responses escalate costs when coders attempt to clarify them. If a coder is unable to classify a particular response, it may require additional coders to classify the answer. In some instances, coders may even have to re-contact respondents for clarification. Such tactics not only expand coders' workloads but also increase project expenses.

Second, vague responses may increase measurement error. If coders are unable to place responses into pre-existing categories, they may develop their own idiosyncratic rules for classifying these responses into the classification system. As a result, two different coders may classify the same response differently. This can lead to misleading conclusions about the distribution of responses. Worse, coders may choose to discard vague responses simply because of the difficulty in finding an appropriate category. Such discarding may lead to systematic biases in the data if the discarded respondents answer differently than included ones.

Proposed solutions to the problem of vague responses generally focus on proactive rather reactive approaches. Interviewers can be trained more thoroughly or provided with computer programs specifically designed to respond to vague responses by prompting the interviewers to ask for clarification. Surveys can be designed more carefully to convey to the respondents the purpose of the questions. Replacing open-ended questions with closed questions or partially closed questions (which provide a list of possible responses but also include an "other" response option) can help. Even in the latter case, the respondent may draw a helpful inference from the response options that are provided. Finally, surveys can be pretested with small groups to identify potential sources of ambiguity. In other words, before the survey is given to a large number of respondents, a smaller group can be administered the survey solely to determine whether and where vagueness might arise.

Further Reading

Cantor, D., and J. Esposito. "Evaluating Interviewer Style for Collecting Industry and Occupation Information." *Proceedings of the Section on Survey Research Methods.* American Statistical Association. (1992): 661–66. A good example of how poor interviewer probes and recordings can affect data quality.

Conrad, F. G., and M. P. Couper. "Classifying Open-Ended Reports: Coding Occupation in the Current Population Survey." Paper presented at the Federal Committee on Statistical Methodology (FCSM) Research Conference, Arlington, VA, November 2001. A good example of how response length and word difficulty can produce coder difficulty.

Dashen, M., and S. Fricker. "Understanding the Cognitive Processes of Open-Ended Categorical Questions and Their Effects on Data Quality." *Journal of Official Statistics* 17, no. 4 (2001): 457–77. A good example of how interpret open-ended questions.

Monica Dashen

Voting Report Bias

Voting report bias is the discrepancy between a respondent's self-report of the act of voting and actual voting records. The earliest surveys of political behavior found that more respondents consistently report voting than official records indicate—a finding that has been subsequently reaffirmed numerous times. Voting report bias is a serious challenge to researchers since it may confound observed associations between survey questions, thereby leading to erroneous conclusions.

There are two ways to check the validity of voting reports: by examining aggregate voting statistics and by checking the voting records of individuals. The first method involves comparing the percentage of individuals who claimed they voted with the percent of the population that actually voted in an election. A careful approach matches the **sample frame** of the survey with the aggregate statistics for the universe of voters selected in the sample frame. Groups in the population used to generate voting statistics but not included in many political surveys—most notably noncitizens—have grown at substantial rates over time, thereby confounding comparisons. Failure to adequately match the two universes can result in erroneous conclusions about trends in overreporting bias over time.

Two well-known studies of political behavior—the **National Election Study** (NES) and the Current Population Survey (CPS), Voter Supplement File—can be used to demonstrate this method. Figure 1 plots the self-reported turnout rates in presidential elections of the NES and CPS surveys against a slightly modified voting-eligible population (VEP) turnout rate that is congruent with these survey's sample frames. The series starts with the first survey conducted: 1948 for the NES and 1964 for the CPS.

Figure 1 presents rather conclusive evidence of vote overreporting on these surveys. Although survey sampling error could explain one deviant result, the consistency of the degree of overreporting on the two surveys is striking. So too, is the consistent way in which the NES has a higher turnout rate than does the CPS. In the aggregate, vote overreporting appears to be a real phenomenon.

Another method of ascertaining voting report bias is to check a respondent's answer against actual voting records available at local election board offices. Voter behavior studies as early as 1948 found that some individuals reported voting in the presidential election when records indicated otherwise, a pattern that has been continuously established in subsequent vote validation efforts. The most comprehensive undertaking of vote validation has been performed by the National Election Study, which found 9 to 12 percent of respondents who self-reported voting in presidential elections did not vote. Moreover, people reported not voting in presidential elections—albeit at much smaller rates—when they actually did.

Vote validation is not a costless or straightforward enterprise. Interviewers must visit local election board offices and locate voting records of respondents.

Figure 1. A Comparison of Turnout Rates: National Election Study (NES), Current Population Survey (CPS), and the Voting-Eligible Population (VEP)

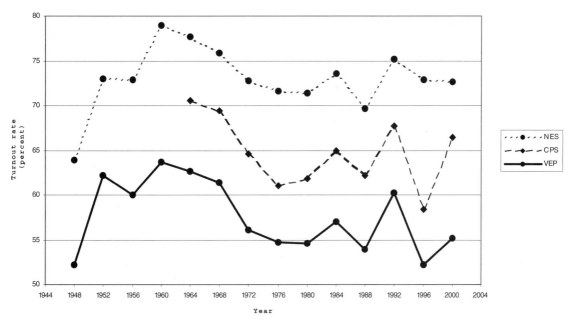

Some 12 to 14 percent of self-reported voters simply do not have a record: some people give the interviewer an incorrect name or live outside the interviewing area and thus voting records cannot be checked by the interviewer. An increasing reliance on phone interviews makes validation difficult if not impossible. The difficulty in validation also lies with the improper recording of voting records, a problem more prevalent in poor and minority communities. This results in the overestimate of vote overreporting bias among African Americans by some researchers.

In 1990 NES re-validated the 1988 vote validation and found that only 87 percent of the voting records were consistent. Some records could no longer be found, missing records were now available, some people were recorded as not voting but now had a record of voting, and some the reverse. The authors of the 1990 NES technical report caution that "validation attempts employing administrative records should be treated with some care."

Given the problems with the reliability and the additional cost associated with conducting vote validation, the National Election Study discontinued validation efforts after 1990. Still, despite the reliability of the vote validation, the method consistently demonstrated that a significant percentage of respondents claimed to have voted when official records indicated otherwise. At the individual level, vote overreporting bias is a real phenomenon.

Aggregate and individual-level studies of voting indicate that report bias is a serious issue on political surveys. Naturally, then, a number of researchers have investigated the causes of vote overreporting, and have sought ways to reduce the bias. The causes of vote reporting bias can be classified into two general areas: issues surrounding the methodology of the surveys and issues regarding the behavior of individual respondents.

Two survey methodological features—non response and pre-election stimulus—have been identified as potentially responsible for voting report bias. Low **response rates** can substantially bias survey results if those who participate in surveys are substantially different than those who refuse participation. For voting, nonresponse may be particularly troublesome since the same motivation that induces a respondent to participate in a survey may also induce a respondent to participate in an election.

The demographic characteristics of those who refuse to participate can be inferred by comparing a poll with information from a source like the census of population. **Weighting** schemes have been developed to adjust the demographic distribution of a poll with the census. Unfortunately, the propensities to vote and other opinions or behaviors of those who choose not to participate in a survey are unknown. Examination of the voting propensities of those who might drop out of **panel surveys** or those respondents who required extraordinary cajoling to participate in a survey indicates that nonrespondents are less likely to vote than respondents.

Despite growing nonresponse on the NES, there has not been a commiserate increase in the overreporting bias when the NES turnout rate is compared with the aggregate voting-eligible rate (see Figure 1). The CPS provides another cut at this issue. The CPS is an important government survey used primarily for labor statistics, and once every two years an additional battery of voting questions are asked. The U.S. Census Bureau expends considerable resources to maintain a high response rate to the CPS survey. The NES and CPS turnout rates track with one another, so the nonresponse bias present on the NES but not as prevalent on the CPS, while a potential concern, cannot explain vote overreporting bias by itself.

A second potential source of report bias generated by survey methodology is the effect of pre-election surveys on stimulating respondents to participate. Consider Figure 1, which shows that the NES consistently uncovers higher levels of overreporting bias than the CPS. A significant difference between these two surveys is that the NES has a pre-election and postelection interview component, while the CPS is only a postelection survey. Thus, the pre-election component of the NES—a long survey of political attitudes and behaviors—may induce low participatory respondents to think about politics and voting more than they would otherwise.

Many academic studies have shown that receiving a face-to-face political message from a campaign or other organization stimulates participation. Researchers have found a stimulus effect of pre-election surveys but do not find that pre-election surveys affect two factors that influence participation: a reduction of a sense of **political alienation** or an increase in a sense of **political efficacy** by the respondent. Thus, pre-election surveys appear to affect voting propensities directly, rather than indirectly by changing other political attitudes.

Although nonresponse and pre-election stimulus offer compelling explanations for voting report bias, neither is sufficient to solely explain the phenomenon. Nonresponse cannot be the lone explanation since vote validation indicated overreporting among those who respond to a survey. Pre-election stimulus cannot be the lone explanation since the CPS—which has no pre-election component—exhibits overreporting bias at the aggregate level.

Further explanations of overreporting bias focus on the behavior of the respondents. Two lines of research explore whether voting report bias is an unintentional memory error or an intentional falsehood given by the respondent to appear socially correct.

The first line of research investigates if respondents do not accurately remember the act of voting. Psychologists note the behavior of source confusion when memories of similar imagined and real events become intermingled. When memory of the real event fades, people tend to rely on the memory of the imagined event. In the context of voting, source confusion seems to be a real issue. Respondents who report in pre-election surveys as intending to vote are more likely to overreport than are those who do not, suggesting that those intending to vote have constructed an imagined act of voting in the future that some people do not carry out.

Attempts have been made to reduce source confusion by seeking to improve memory recall by drawing out memories of the event of voting, such as the weather on Election Day or the location of the polling place. Consistent with a degrading memory, these sorts of question designs are more successful in reducing overreporting bias the longer the time between the election and asking the voting question, both for those who misreport voting but did not vote, and those who report not voting but did vote. Although studies on memory-induced errors are intriguing, these studies still find overreporting bias in early waves of a survey, immediately following an election.

A second and perhaps more intuitive explanation is that vote overreporting is caused by social desirability bias—the desire of respondents to give the socially acceptable answer to a question. Voting is expected of good citizens, so perhaps some respondents desire to portray themselves in a favorable light to interviewers. Habitual misreporting respondents may also misreport on other survey items, which is why misreporters appear to resemble actual voters in terms of education and civic values.

A group of people perhaps likely to exhibit overreporting bias is habitual voters who happened to miss the last election. Misreporting by these individuals may be either through memory error, conflating past participation with current participation as discussed above, or a desire to portray themselves as the habitual voters they tend to be. Suggestively, respondents with a participatory history of voting tend to misreport voting more than those that do not frequently vote.

To reduce the social desirability of those highly participatory respondents who may tell a little white lie about missing the last election, experimental questions have been framed first as a question of lifetime of voting, followed by a probe about a specific election. Unfortunately, these experimental questions do not successfully reduce vote overreporting bias. In another unsuccessful attempt to reduce social desirability pressures, the voting question was reworded to reverse the normal pressure to respond in the affirmative, by changing the question to be about missing voting, rather than voting. Ironically, the most intuitive explanation of vote overreporting bias has the least amount of empirical evidence to support it.

Vote report bias is a real phenomenon that threatens the validity of political surveys and what we can learn from them. Competing theories concerning a real threat naturally invite further study, which is why voting report bias continues as an active sub-field of survey research.

Further Reading

Abelson, Robert P., Elizabeth F. Loftus, and Anthony G. Greenwald. "Attempts to Improve the Accuracy of Self-Reports of Voting." In *Questions About Questions*, edited by Judith M. Tanur. New York: Russell Sage Foundation, 1992. Explores alternative question wordings designed to reduce vote overreporting.

McDonald, Michael P. "On the Over-Report Bias of the National Election Study." *Political Analysis* 11, no. 2 (Spring 2003): 180–86. Steps through the surprisingly tricky matching of turnout rates of the NES sample universe with aggregate voting statistics.

Presser, Stanley, and Michael Traugott. "Little White Lies and Social Science Models: Correlated Response Errors in a Panel Study of Voting." *Public Opinion Quarterly* 56, no. 1 (Spring 1992): 77–86. Shows, through examination of an NES panel study, that there is a "type" of person who is likely to misreport voting, and suggests that these people are likely to misreport answers on other questions, too.

Michael P. McDonald

W

Weighting

Weighting is a technique for reducing potential **unit nonresponse** bias in sample estimates. Unit nonresponse is a serious problem that occurs in virtually all sample surveys. If some of the sampled units are not measured, the resulting survey estimates will be inexact if the unmeasured units possess different characteristics than the measured ones. In cases where nonresponse rate is extensive, it can lead researchers to make false inferences about the target population. Unfortunately, the magnitude of the nonresponse bias is unknown and must be estimated. Weighting methods represent efforts to generate such estimates, which under certain assumptions can eliminate, or at least reduce, the potential nonresponse bias in our estimates.

To demonstrate the principles of nonresponse weighting, some notation must first be introduced. Consider a population of N individuals. The values of the target variable for these individuals are denoted $y_1, y_2, \ldots, y_N$. The purpose of the survey is to estimate the population mean:

$$\overline{Y} = \frac{1}{N} \sum_{i=1}^{N} y_i \tag{1}$$

A sample of size n is selected from the population with probability π_i for individual i to be included in the sample. Let $y_1, y_2, \ldots, y_n$ denote the values of the target variable for the n selected individuals. If data is collected from all individuals in the sample, an unbiased estimator of $\overline{Y}$ is

$$\hat{\overline{Y}} = \frac{1}{N} \sum_{i=1}^{n} \frac{y_i}{\pi_i} = \frac{1}{N} \sum_{i=1}^{n} w_i y_i \tag{2}$$

We can call w_i the sample weight for individual i in the sample. The sample weight can be interpreted as the number of people individual i represents in the population. If, for example, the sampling procedure is **simple random sampling** without replacement, all $w_i = \dfrac{N}{n}$ and $\hat{\overline{Y}}$ simplifies to the sample arithmetic mean.

If nonresponse occurs, the resulting estimator of $\overline{Y}$, based on data for the $m < n$ respondents only, might be

$$\hat{\overline{Y}}_r = \frac{1}{N} \sum_{i=1}^{m} w_i y_i \tag{3}$$

This estimator is, however, apparently biased and not appropriate for estimating $\overline{Y}$. In the presence of nonresponse, each respondent has to represent more people in the population than was intended when the sample was designed. Thus, to adjust or compensate for this bias we need to enlarge the sample weights w_i for the respondents by some factor. How do we do this? To discuss this further, we need to introduce a model for how nonresponse is generated.

A Model for Nonresponse

A widely accepted model for the generation of nonresponse is the response probability model. In this model, individual i in the population of study is assumed to respond with a probability p_i. If this probability were known for each of the m respondents in the sample, the estimator

$$\hat{\overline{Y}}_p = \frac{1}{N} \sum_{i=1}^{m} \frac{w_i y_i}{p_i} = \frac{1}{N} \sum w_i^* w_i y_i \tag{4}$$

would be an unbiased estimator of $\overline{Y}$. Here, $w_i^* = 1/p_i$ is the factor by which we enlarge the w_i:s. Unfortunately, the p_i:s are never known in practice. What we can do in practice is to calculate rough estimates of the p_i:s. Attempts to estimate the p_i:s are usually based on a partitioning of the sample into groups within which all p_i:s are supposed to be the same and different groups have different response probabilities. These groups have been called weighting classes or response homogeneity groups.

Response Homogeneity Groups

The model, or assumption, behind the construction of response homogeneity groups is that the response probabilities may depend on auxiliary variables x, such as age, gender, and race, but not on the target variable y. If the assumption holds and relevant x-variables are known for the entire sample, the x-variables may be used to partition the sample into response homogeneity groups. Also, since the p_i:s are assumed independent of y, the respondents and the nonrespondents are regarded similar with respect to y, that is, under these assumptions, the estimator (4) adjusts the nonresponse bias of estimator (3). Estimator (4) can be rewritten as

$$\hat{\overline{Y}}_p = \frac{1}{N} \sum_{i=1}^{m} \frac{w_i y_i}{p_i} = \frac{1}{N} \sum_{c=1}^{C} \sum_{i=1}^{m_c} \hat{w}_c^* w_i y_i \tag{5}$$

where $\hat{w}_c^*$ is an estimator of the weight factor w_c^* common to all m_c respondents in group c (the estimator (5) has a small bias, negligible in practice if the sample size is large enough).

Discussed below are two principal types of adjustment methods based on response homogeneity groups, sample weighting adjustment, and population weighting adjustment. It should be noted that the assumptions behind the use of response homogeneity groups are very strong and seldom possible to verify. In practice, the models never describe the true state of affairs. A realistic motivation for using response homogeneity groups is that the nonresponse bias may be somewhat reduced rather than completely eliminated.

Sample Weighting Adjustment

In sample weighting adjustment, the weight factors $\hat{w}_c^*$ for the response homogeneity groups are made proportional to the inverses of the response rates in the groups. To compute these response rates, the numbers of respondents and nonrespondents in the groups must be determined. It is therefore necessary to know to which group each respondent and nonrespondent belongs. As pointed out by Kalton and Kasprzyk, very little information about the nonrespondents is usually available, and the choice of weighting class is therefore very restricted. The choice is often limited to general sample design variables (e.g., primary sampling units and strata), characteristics of those variables (e.g., urban/rural, geographical region). Auxiliary variables may also be available in the **sample frame**, and, on occasion, it may be possible to collect information on one or two variables for the nonrespondents, for instance by interviewer observation.

Formally, in sample weighting the weight factors $\hat{w}_c^*$ are in group c defined by the reciprocal of the group response probability estimate: $\hat{w}_c^* = $ (sum of sample weights w_i for the entire sample in group c) / (sum of sample weights w_i for all m_c respondents in group c).

Consider an example. Suppose the sampling design is simple random sampling without replacement. Then all $w_i = \dfrac{N}{n}$ and $w_c^* = \dfrac{n_c}{m_c}$. Estimator (5) now takes the form

$$\hat{\overline{Y}}_{p,sample} = \sum_{c=1}^{C} \frac{n_c}{n} \overline{y}_{cr} \tag{6}$$

A reader familiar with sampling theory may note that sample weighting adjustment resembles two-phase sampling. The first phase sample is the total sample of respondents and nonrespondents; the second phase sample is the sub-sample of respondents, selected with different fractions (response rates) in different strata (weighting classes).

Population Weighting Adjustment (or Poststratification). Population weighting adjustment is probably more widely known as poststratification. However, as pointed out by Kalton and Kasprzyk, poststratification was originally a method to reduce variance in an ideal survey situation when no nonresponse is present and thus not aimed at reducing nonresponse bias. We therefore prefer the term "population weighting," suggested by Kalton and Kasprzyk.

Population weighting adjustment differ from sample weighting adjustment in the use of auxiliary information. While sample weight adjustment use only data internal to the sample and require information about the nonrespondents, population weight adjustment is based on external data and no information about the sample nonrespondents is needed.

The auxiliary information used in making population weighting adjustments is the distribution of the population over one or more variables, such as the population distribution by age, sex and race available from standard population estimates. The response homogeneity groups are defined by the available auxiliary information.

Formally, the weight factor $\hat{w}_c^*$ in group c is defined by $\hat{w}_c^* = N_c$ / (sum of sample weights w_i for all m_c respondents in group c), where N_c is the population count in group c, taken from an external data source. (This factor may be regarded as the reciprocal of the estimator of the response probability in class c, adjusted by auxiliary population information.)

Consider a second example. Suppose again that a simple random sample without replacement is taken. Then all $w_i = \dfrac{N}{n}$ and $\hat{w}_c^* = \dfrac{N_c}{\dfrac{N}{n}m_c}$, and estimator (5) takes the simple form:

$$\hat{\bar{Y}}_{p,population} = \sum_{c=1}^{C} \frac{N_c}{N} \bar{y}_{cr} \qquad (7)$$

where $\bar{y}_{cr}$ is the arithmetic mean of the respondents y-values in group c.

Note the similarity between estimators (6) and (7); the only difference is that in population weighting the N_c are known, whereas in sample weighting the N_c are unknown and estimated by Nn_c / n. Moreover, population-weighting adjustment as opposed to sample weighting may correct for coverage bias as well as nonresponse bias.

Raking Methods

Raking ratio adjustment is, in its original sense, a population weighting method that is used when population counts are available for a number of variables but not for the cross-classified cells formed by these variables. The principle of raking is to adjust the sample survey cell counts first to one of the known population margins, then to another known margin, and so on. When the cell counts have been adjusted to the last auxiliary variable margin, the procedure continues with the first selected variable margin, and so on until the cells changes are ignorable. The procedure can be described as a post-stratification method with the response probabilities defined by the marginal distributions.

Raking can also be performed as a sample weighting method. For example, when adjusting for nonresponse in sample surveys, register information may be known for the nonrespondents in the sample but not for the entire population. In this case, the raking is performed toward known full sample margins.

Raking may also be seen as a method to deal with the problem of too many weighting classes. This may occur if it is possible and desirable to use many auxiliary variables and to take the full cross-classification of them. Even if auxiliary information is available for the cross-classified cells, the **sample size** in each cell may be small and lead to instability in the **response rates**, thus resulting in a loss of precision in the survey estimates. Therefore, in such situations, an alternative may be to use only auxiliary information of the margins, perform raking ratio adjustment, and thus overlook auxiliary information for the cross-classified cells.

The above presented weighting techniques—sample weighting, population weighting, and raking—may be described as special cases of a general family of weighting techniques, called calibration. The calibration approach provides a unified treatment of auxiliary information in surveys with nonresponse. Thus, in recent years, "calibration" has become a standard concept for nonresponse weighting, in particular in large-scale surveys conducted by statistical bureaus.

The Politz-Simmons Method

In a procedure suggested by Politz and Simmons, the response probabilities p(i) are estimated from a question asked at the interview. Suppose that calls are made during the evening on the six weeknights. Each respondent is asked whether she was at home, at about the time of the interview, on each of the five preceding evenings. If respondent i answers that she was at home at k_i nights, the p_i : s are estimated by $\hat{p}_i = (k_i + 1) / 6$ and the estimator of the population mean is

$$\hat{\bar{y}}_{PL} = \frac{\sum\limits_{i=1}^{m} \dfrac{w_i y_i}{\hat{p}_i}}{\sum\limits_{i=1}^{m} \dfrac{w_i}{\hat{p}_i}} \tag{8}$$

If there is no answer, no call-backs are made in the original procedure. However, the procedure can be combined with call-backs. The method is theoretically appealing and simple to use. However, an important limitation is that it does not deal with **refusals** or those who are away from home all six days.

Regression Modeling

When a lot of variables are known for both the respondents and the nonrespondents, we may estimate response probabilities by regressing response status on these variables. Defining the stochastic indicator variable z = 1 for respondents and 0 for nonrespondents, we can define p_i as the probability that $z_i = 1$ and model this probability with a logistic or probit regression model. The predicted values for the respondents are then taken to be their response probabilities. A concern about this method is that the predicted response probabilities may vary a lot and thus generate estimates with high variance.

As pointed out by Kalton and Kasprzyk, regression modeling of response probabilities may be more useful in the case when the predictor variables are dummy variables that identify a set of classes. The predicted response probabilities are then the class response rates, and the method reduces to sample weighting adjustment. In this case, regression modeling of response probabilities can be seen as a method to form appropriate weighting classes.

The situation described here coincides with one application of propensity score weighting for survey nonresponse. Since some attention recently has been drawn to this technique we describe it below a little more in detail.

Propensity Score Weighting for Nonresponse

Propensity score adjustment was originally developed to reduce selection bias in observational studies, or quasi-random experiments (see Rosenbaum and Rubin). Typical for such studies is the comparison of treatment effects between two subpopulations, such as smokers and nonsmokers. When propensity score weighting is used for survey nonresponse adjustment, the "treatments" corresponds to response (z = 1) and nonresponse (z = 0). Assume that we have a number of auxiliary variables or covariates, $\underline{x}$. The propensity score, often denoted $e(\underline{x})$, is the probability of response, that is, $e_i(\underline{x}) = p_i = \Pr(z_i = 1)$, for individual i in the sample, given the covariates. It can be estimated using a logistic or probit model as described in the section of regression modeling above. An important assumption is that, given covariates $\underline{x}$, the indicator variable z and the variable of study, y, are independent (called the assumption of "strong ignorability").

If we restrict here, for simplicity, the discussion of propensity score theory to the case when the $\underline{x}$-variables are categorical (dummy variables), the situation coincides with weighting class adjustment. The assumption of strong ignorability may look very optimistic, but we can note that this assumption is inherently made in any weighting class adjustment method.

An important result by Rosenbaum and Rubin (1983) implies that, if the assumption of strong ignorability holds given propensity score, the assumption still holds when classes with the same propensity score are collapsed. This result can be used in an approximate way in that classes with similar propensity scores are collapsed into a small number of, say, five weighting classes. Strong ignorability is assumed to hold approximately in these five larger classes and sample weighting can be performed.

Propensity score weighting for nonresponse can only be used when a good deal of information is available for both the respondents and the nonrespondents. This can be the case when auxiliary information is available in the frame or if the nonrespondents are losses in the second or later waves of a panel survey. In such situations the covariates may define a very large number of weighting classes. By using the Rosenbaum and Rubin theorem, the information in those weighting classes is reduced to one dimension (the propensity score values), which simplifies the weighting procedure enormously.

Propensity Score Weighting Using a Control Survey

In recent years, an application of propensity score adjustment that uses a parallel control survey and allows for an arbitrary number of covariates has been suggested by Harris Interactive. This application of propensity score weighting was originally developed for adjusting for selection bias in volunteer Web panels. However, it may also be used to compensate for nonresponse bias in panels recruited from probability samples. In this application, a parallel probability sample based survey is conducted for reference, and the propensity score is defined for the respondents of the Web (treatment 1: z = 1) and the control samples (treatment 2: z = 0) only. The propensity score in a cell defined by the covariates (assumed categorical here) is here the proportion of Web users in the merged group of Web and control survey respondents. This approach admits the use of an arbitrary large number of covariates (measured in both surveys) but relies heavily on the control sample being "perfect." In principle, no nonresponse should be allowed in the control survey since the propensity score is defined for the respondents only in the two surveys—the weighting "lifts" the Web panel data to the control survey level, which needs to be close to the population level.

In practice, of course, the control survey will not be conducted each time the Web panel survey is performed. The method is designed for situations when the Web panel is, for example, a daily omnibus survey. Then the control survey, typically a telephone survey, may be preformed once a month or so.

Sub-Sampling Among the Nonrespondents: A Mixed-Mode Approach

In case a superior data collection method exists, the nonresponse bias problem can—theoretically but seldom in practice—be solved: A sub-sample of the nonrespondents is measured by the superior method and a weighted estimator of the population mean $\overline{Y}$ is constructed by the respondent means in the original sample and the sub-sample. For illustration, assume the following deterministic response model. The population consists of two nonoverlapping parts, a response stratum and a nonresponse stratum. Every individual in the response stratum is assumed to respond with certainty if selected for the sample, and every individual in the nonresponse stratum has probability zero to respond. Assume a simple random sample of n with m respondents and a simple random sample of n' from the n-m nonrespondents. The method can be regarded as an application of the technique of two-phase sampling. If we denote the first phase (respondent) mean with $\overline{y}_r$ and the second phase (sub-sample) mean with $\overline{y}'_{nr}$, an estimator of $\overline{Y}$ is

$$\hat{\overline{Y}}_{subsampling} = \frac{m}{n}\,\overline{y}_r + \frac{n-m}{n}\,\overline{y}'_{nr} \tag{9}$$

If no nonresponse appears in the sub-sample, the estimator (9) is unbiased and the only price for nonresponse is a variance increase (compared with the case when all respondents answer in the original sample). Usually, however, there is nonresponse in the sub-sample. Then, estimator (9) is biased but the sub-sampling may have reduced the nonresponse bias substantially compared with the bias of $\overline{y}_r$.

Further Reading

Kalton, G., and D. Kasprzyk. "The Treatment of Missing Survey Data." *Survey Methodology* 12 (1986): 159–67. A general, nontechnical review of nonresponse weighting methods.

Little, R., and D. Rubin. *Statistical Analysis with Missing Data*. New York: John Wiley, 1986. Deals with the analysis of incomplete data in general. Three chapters on survey nonresponse remedies, including propensity score weighting and model-based approaches to survey nonresponse. Technically demanding.

Lundström, S., and C.-E. Särndal. *Estimation in the Presence of Nonresponse and Frame Imperfections*. Stockholm: Statistics Sweden, 2001. A comprehensive review of the calibration technique for nonresponse. Technically demanding.

Politz, A. N., and M. P. Simmons. "An Attempt to Get the Not-at-Homes into the Sample Without Callbacks." *Journal of the American Statistical Association* 44 (1949, 1950): 9–31; 45; 136–37. Each author introduces the Politz-Simmons method.

Särndal, C., B. Swensson, and J. Wretman. *Model Assisted Survey Sampling*. New York: Springer, 1991. Includes a comprehensive review of weighting methods for survey nonresponse.

Gösta Forsman

Welfare

The history of American public opinion on "welfare" and the actual provision of income assistance have been marked by conflicting attitudes or ambivalence: the public has distinguished those recipients who seem more deserving of help from those who appear less so. While this distinction has been blurred at times in government policies, it has continued to influence American public opinion toward various types of people who have sought government aid.

Racial stereotypes also have been associated with these attitudes, increasingly apparent since the 1960s, in ways that reflect both factual misunderstandings and other misperceptions about racial differences in experiences with welfare. Efforts to overcome the stigma of race in American society and politics by improving the economic conditions and opportunities of African Americans had unintended consequences, evoking the image that African Americans had become dependent on welfare and a drain on the nation. Very likely due to distortions in media coverage, many Americans had exaggerated perceptions of racial minorities receiving public assistance. The implications of racially tinged opinions toward welfare are significant.

Another key to understanding opinions toward welfare is how their measurement is colored by **question-wording effects**. Because the terms often used in survey questions tend to evoke powerful presuppositions among respondents, question-wording effects exert particularly strong influences in **framing** issues in this area.

Americans have supported welfare provision, though typically with reservations about how much help and to whom it should be available. Data from the first Gallup Poll in 1935 ("Do you think expenditures by the Government for relief and recovery are too little, too great, or just about right?" Sixty percent said "too great.") through the present indicate that majorities have supported reductions in welfare spending, especially when survey questions have framed the issue in terms of "welfare" or "relief." This majority sentiment does not extend to calls for welfare's elimination, however. The underlying support may be best understood in terms of a humanitarian (*see* **Humanitarianism**) tendency in American public opinion. The distinction between humanitarianism and egalitarianism is important in understanding why antipoverty efforts in the United States historically have operated at the margins and have not sought a fundamental redistribution of wealth. Ideological conservatives have tried to curtail the scope and generosity of welfare while maintaining enough of a safety net to prevent starvation and minimize what they consider the inevitable disincentives to work. Liberals have sought to expand the scope and generosity of welfare in an effort to grant fuller opportunities, indeed broader citizenship rights, to society's poorer members (*see* **Liberalism and Conservatism**). The resulting compromise has continued assistance for the poor without a broad, egalitarian-oriented redistribution of wealth.

Explanations of poverty in the United States have tended to fall into one of two broad categories: individual shortcomings and structural problems in the market. Substantial evidence suggests that Americans more strongly endorse explanations of poverty that attribute economic failures to personal short-comings than structural explanations that capitalism inevitably produces poverty as well as wealth. Thus, substantial numbers of Americans long have believed that welfare has a corrosive effect on individuals' work effort. Allowing for the possibility that both explanations have a place in poverty discussions, Reverend Charles Burroughs of Portsmouth, New Hampshire, declared in 1834, "In speaking of poverty, let us never forget that there is a distinction between this and pauperism. The former is an unavoidable evil, to which many are brought from necessity. . . . It is the result, not of our faults, but of our misfortunes. . . . Pauperism is the consequence of willful error, of shameful indolence, of vicious habits. It is a misery of human creation, the pernicious work of many, the lamentable consequence of bad principles and morals" (quoted in David Rothman, *The Jacksonians on the Poor*, 1971).

Even among such important figures in the development of the American welfare state as President Franklin Roosevelt, deep concerns about the unintended ill effects of welfare provision are pervasive. In the 1930s, as Aid to Dependent Children, the federal government's first nationwide cash assistance program for poor children was being created as part of the Social Security Act of 1935, Roosevelt lamented what he saw as welfare's double-edged effect. The program would help children trapped in poverty due to no fault of their own, but "relief," as it was then called, "induces a spiritual and moral disintegration fundamentally destructive to the national fiber." This concern over the possible effect of welfare provision has been a recurring theme in social science literature as well as in popular attitudes.

In cross-national perspective, the United States historically has lagged behind Western Europe in its adoption of various social insurance and welfare programs. This lag has been attributed to various factors, including the early emulation in America of England's 1601 Elizabethan Poor Law, which prescribed some public responsibility but also many punitive aspects to antipoverty measures; the unique immigration patterns that populated the United States, which fostered individualistic attitudes among many of its citizens; and a federalist structure, which has discouraged some, though not all, centralized responses on the part of the national government—leaving many of these potential responses to the fiscally less able state governments. Despite sharing the advanced economic development of other industrialized nations, most of which have extensive welfare states, and notwithstanding significant development of mothers' pensions by the American states, the United States only slowly and belatedly adopted widespread public assistance programs. American public opinion has consistently expressed less enthusiasm for public assistance than public opinion in other western industrialized nations.

A number of considerations and concerns, then, are important in understanding American public opinion on welfare. These include the trade-off between equality and individualism, the impact of survey question wording, trends in aggregate opinion toward welfare, the determinants of individuals' opinions toward welfare, race and support for welfare, and support for welfare versus other social insurance programs.

American public opinion on welfare can be understood through the tension involving the public's values concerning democracy, equality and fairness, on one hand, and its simultaneous and strong belief in individualism and self-reliance on the other. McClosky and Zaller in their important book, *The American Ethos*, document the ways in which Americans balance between these two conflicting ideas, moderating each to accommodate some degree of the other. Numerous commentators, from Alexis de Tocqueville forward, have noted the strong sense of individualism characterizing Americans' opinions. This expressed itself as Calvinism and the Protestant work ethic in the 1800s to rugged individualism at the turn of the twentieth century to entrepreneurship later that century. According to this notion, economic opportunities are available to those willing to seize them. Under this perspective, poverty is more a function of personal moral failure than of structural problems in the economic market.

Americans also have long cherished a notion of collective responsibility and humanitarianism. As Feldman and Steenbergen illustrate, what most Americans support is largely humanitarianism, not chiefly egalitarianism. Most Americans embrace the need to help those in a crisis, but the majority of the public does not support an equalization of economic outcomes. However awkwardly, most Americans strike a balance between these two values, recognizing a need for individual effort but also expecting at least a modicum of sustenance for those who work hard. In line with this qualified view of public aid provision, antipoverty spending in the United States only modestly reduces poverty. As of 1997 antipoverty spending in the United States reduced poverty by 29 percent, compared with rates of poverty reduction of 50 percent and greater in many European nations.

The tensions that many people experience in balancing their conflicting beliefs about poverty and welfare often lead them to waver in their opinions when they are asked about welfare. These conflicting perceptions and attitudes have been apparent in studies that have utilized evidence from intensive interviews, and they can be found in more in-depth survey studies that can detect wavering opinions and how respondents deal with conflicting considerations that come to mind as they respond to survey questions. Thus the picture of public opinion toward welfare that emerges is one of considerable ambivalence. This ambivalence is not unique to welfare issues but it is often more pronounced in this case compared to others.

Question-Wording Effects

While question-wording effects are well known in public opinion research, they are especially important in the case of social welfare issues (*see also* **Priming**). Measuring support for welfare programs is complicated by sometimes powerful question-wording effects. To the extent words or phrases in a question, or even an earlier question in an interview, raise the importance of one consid-

Figure 1. Percent of Respondents Saying Current Spending Is "Too Little" on Various Programs

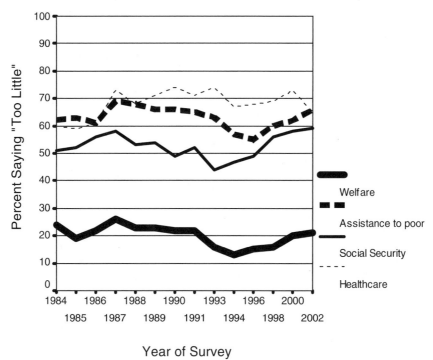

Year of Survey

Source: NORC General Social Surveys.

eration over others, questions can effectively re-frame how survey respondents form an answer. Prompting a respondent to think about needy children or, alternatively, chronically unemployed, able-bodied adults and their respective need for public assistance leads to very different levels of support as measured by surveys. Even subtle question wording variations can produce large differences in marginal response rates. In a 1987 article in *Public Opinion Quarterly*, Tom Smith reported differences of thirty to forty percentage points between questions asking about support for spending on "welfare" versus spending on "aid to the poor." Figure 1, showing data from the **General Social Survey** (GSS) from 1984 through 2002, illustrates this point. That survey has included questions on various federal spending items, including "welfare," "assistance to the poor," "health care," and "Social Security." While the trends through time resemble each other, the percentage of respondents who think "too little" is being spent on these programs varies greatly.

Similarly, soliciting respondents' affect toward "poor people" versus "people on welfare" finds large gaps. The **National Election Studies** (NES) have included a battery of feeling thermometers gauging the warmth or coolness of respondents' feelings toward various social groups. Higher numbers on these 0–100 scales indicate warmer feelings. This battery has included "poor people" and "people on welfare" as target groups since 1976. Figure 2 shows the mean re-

Figure 2. Thermometer Ratings for "Poor People" and "People on Welfare"

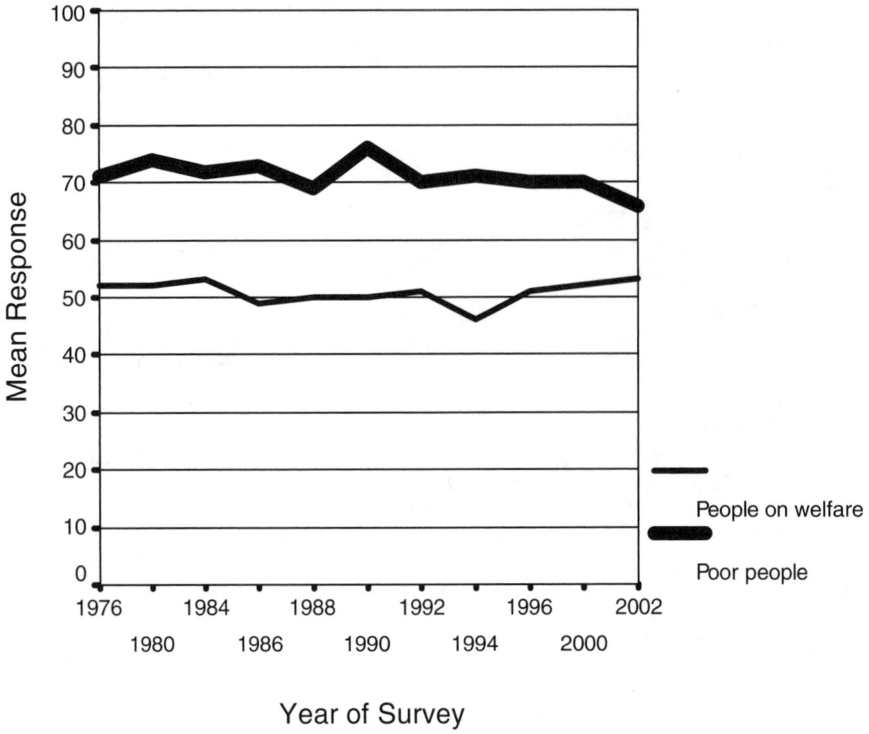

Year of Survey

Source: American National Election Studies.

sponses from 1976 through 2002. Only minor changes appear through time on these two measures. However, the average rating for "people on welfare," in the fifty-point range, consistently lies some twenty points below the rating for "poor people," in the seventy-point range (though note some slight shrinking of this gap in 2002).

In his analysis of varying questions on welfare and the poor, Smith found significant correlations between respondents' fiscal conservatism and their responses to questions about "welfare" funding. This was not the case when they were asked about spending on "help for the poor," suggesting that "welfare" more strongly triggers concerns about wasteful or unnecessary spending than does the other version of the question. Concerns of wasteful spending on public assistance programs are indeed widespread. Survey elicited estimations of the proportion of welfare dollars spent on administrative costs, for instance, run much higher than actual costs.

Since the 1970s American public opinion has experienced change on some issues related to welfare while remaining largely stable on others. Through the 1990s the public remained about evenly divided on whether a lack of effort or circumstances beyond the control of poor people was more to blame for poverty. To the extent that this question poses a false dichotomy it misses the subtlety of the finer contours of public opinion, but it still illustrates an important point about how welfare sharply divides Americans. Throughout the 1990s large majorities—70 percent or more—believed there were jobs available for welfare recipients who really wanted them, but weaker majorities also thought that most of those jobs do not pay enough to support a family. A related question in various CBS/*New York Times* polls from 1976 through 1994 asked Americans if most people on welfare really need the help or if they could get by without it. To this, bare majorities have tended to say public aid is not necessary. Use of this question by other survey organizations in more recent years produced similar findings. Related to this trend, through the 1990s a growing percentage of Americans came to believe that the poor are willing to seek employment. In 1994 more than twice as many respondents (63 percent compared with 27 percent) said that poor people do not want to work. By 2001 the public became nearly evenly split on this question (44 percent saying the poor do not want to work compared with 47 percent saying they do).

Public opinion on preferred levels of welfare spending has experienced more dramatic change over the past two decades. Most of the available poll data on welfare spending show a drop in support for public assistance funding during the early to mid-1990s and movement back in the liberal direction through the late 1990s and the first few years of the twenty-first century. When framed as a trade-off between helping needy people versus having the government going deeper in debt there was only a relatively brief decline in public support for spending during 1993 and 1994, when the majority of the public was disinclined to support additional spending.

The early to mid-1990s in particular saw public opinion shift in the conservative direction, but it returned approximately to its previous position by the end of that decade. This period illustrates a case of a thermostat-like relationship between public opinion and policy. Welfare caseloads nationally grew dramatically during the early 1990s, feeding a growing call for spending cuts. Following the passage of important welfare legislation in 1996, however, which substantially shifted responsibility for welfare to the states, caseloads fell by just over half through the end of the decade, a fact that was highly publicized, and a concurrent shift in opinion occurred in a liberal direction concerning spending. What was also striking here is that there was, apparently, a change in the short-term in the relationship between economic conditions and public opinion toward welfare. Historically, opposition to welfare spending has varied with economic growth, so during difficult economic times opposition to welfare typically declines. This likely occurs because, for many people, rising poverty is readily attributed to a depressed economy, not so much to personal shortcomings among those negatively affected. In contrast, declining opposition to welfare spending after the enactment of welfare reform in 1996 occurred during a period of economic growth and very good times, which suggests that welfare reform may have begun to produce a change in how the public thinks about assistance to the poor.

Still, public opinion on a number of more general questions about aid recipients themselves remained largely stable through the 1990s. Enduring skepticism and concern persist regarding the potential moral hazards of welfare dependency and various negative perceptions of the lifestyles of the poor, including fertility issues and lagging workforce participation. Through the 1990s Americans remained about evenly split on the question of whether welfare recipients' lives are "easy" or "hard," as revealed in a series of polls by Princeton Survey Research Associates. According to this version of the question, by 2003 a bare majority of Americans thought welfare recipients have hard lives compared with 35 percent who called their lives easy.

To the extent public opinion moved somewhat in a liberal direction after 1996, the public may have perceived that the nation made progress against poverty during that time. Survey results are consistent with this claim. With steep welfare caseload declines and widely publicized restrictive provisions in place, it seems that Americans became more accepting of welfare spending as these programs engaged recipients of public assistance more assertively than before. The opinion data indicate a readiness to prioritize programs to help those who still remained on public assistance, even though doing so had begun costing states more than in the mid- to late 1990s. The evidence also shows, however, that large minorities of the public lack specific knowledge of recent welfare reforms, so the certainty that welfare programs are working as majority public opinion would have them should not be overstated. Public ignorance on this issue, as on many others, has, by various scholars' accounts, left substantial room for elite leadership of policy (*see* **Political Knowledge**).

A dramatic shift occurred between 1990 and 2001 in perceptions of how difficult it is to work one's way out of poverty. When asked for a subjective estimation of whether working one's way out of poverty has become easier or more difficult, 18 percent of respondents to a *New York Times* survey in 1990 said it had become easier. By 2001 fully 44 percent said it had become easier.

The mid- to late 1990s saw the implementation of a variety of restrictive provisions on welfare receipt. Individual states and later the federal government imposed time limits, work requirements in exchange for cash assistance, limits on eligibility for minors who become mothers, and provisions to refuse cash grant enlargements with the birth of additional children while on welfare. Once these proposals became part of the debate over congressional welfare reform in 1994, they began appearing in polls. Among the results was strong and modestly growing support for time limits (75 percent support in a 1997 *Los Angeles Times* survey), strong support for mandatory birth control for welfare mothers (62 percent support in a 2001 Zogby poll), and mandatory drug testing for aid recipients (68 support in a 1999 Opinion Dynamics poll). Majority support developed around most, though not all, of the major provisions of the new welfare program. Work requirements for mothers of very young children marked a case of distinctly mixed public opinion.

Polls from the 1990s show that when asked if the amount of cash aid given to welfare recipients should be cut, approximately two-thirds said no. However, when asked if welfare spending overall should be reduced, a plurality of Americans typically say it should. What seems to be at work is a belief that too many undeserving people receive cash assistance and that welfare program resources should be more narrowly focused on the truly needy, harkening back to the distinction between the reputedly worthy and unworthy poor and to Americans' embrace of humanitarianism over egalitarianism.

Despite some of these qualifications, historically there has remained an underlying support for government assistance to the poor. A 1939 Roper poll found

69 percent support for the idea of government obligation to those "without any other means of support." A 1964 Gallup poll found 72 percent of respondents agreeing that "doing away with poverty" should be "a government responsibility." More recently, a pair of polls by Princeton Survey Research Associates in 1997 and 1999 found that just over 60 percent of respondents agree (either "completely" or "mostly") that "government should provide every citizen enough to eat and a place to sleep." Numerous other poll results unambiguously support the conclusion that Americans strongly support at least a minimal governmental role in poverty relief. The evidence concerning whether government should do more to equalize income differences is distinctively more mixed and tends to vary over time. A useful indicator of this comes from the General Social Survey's question about whether government should do more to "reduce income differences between rich and poor." On this item's seven-point scale, respondents tend to disperse widely, but the plurality of just over 20 percent typically chooses the middle position. Data through the 1990s show a noticeable tendency toward the "government should do more" end of the scale. Public opinion trend data on welfare and other issues have regularly been presented in the "Poll Trends" section of *Public Opinion Quarterly*.

Cross-group differences in affect toward people on welfare are and have been significant. Table 1 breaks down some of the NES data from Figure 1 and displays thermometer ratings for "people on welfare" by respondent group for 1980, 1986, 1994 and 2000. Democrats have, on average, offered ratings eight to ten degrees warmer than have Republicans. Political independents typically fall about mid-way between self-identified partisans. Across most of this period, age made little difference in affect toward people on welfare. During the 1980s younger people reported slightly cooler feelings toward people on welfare than did older people, though the differences were marginal and virtually disappeared during the 1990s. Women tend to offer slightly higher ratings on this question than do men. This gender gap has been of only a few percentage points over the past two decades. This approximate parity across gender persists despite welfare caseloads consisting overwhelmingly of single-mother families. Center city residents have tended to report slightly warmer feelings toward those on welfare than have suburbanites or rural residents, though this difference was not evident in the 2000 survey.

The largest cross-group differences appear on race and income, two dimensions along which welfare recipients on the whole dramatically differ from the larger population. During the 1980s whites offered significantly lower ratings to people on welfare than did blacks, by better than twenty points (*see* **Racial Differences in Public Opinion**). Hispanics fell about midway in between (*see* **Hispanic Public Opinion**). During the 1990s, however, the gap between whites' and blacks' scores on this question was diminished by about half. This was mainly, but not entirely, accounted for by a cooling of scores offered by blacks across this time, despite the growing percentage of the nation's welfare caseload consisting of African Americans during the 1990s. Lastly, the responses of individuals in the top and bottom income brackets have become more similar over the past twenty years on this question. In 1980 an eighteen-point gap separated those in the bottom sixteen percentiles from those in the top five. By 2000 that gap stood at two points. People of high and low income moved toward the center of the scale during the past two decades.

Table 1. Average Thermometer Rating for "People on Welfare" by Group: 1980, 1986, 1994, 2000

	1980	1986	1994	2000
Democrats (including leaners)	57	52	50	55
Independents	49	50	44	49
Republicans (including leaners)	46	45	40	48
17–24 years old	52	46	47	52
25–34 years old	50	48	44	51
35–44 years old	49	49	45	50
45–54 years old	52	49	46	51
55–64 years old	54	51	45	54
65–74 years old	58	52	45	51
Whites	49	47	44	51
African Americans	71	59	58	59
Hispanics	58	54	50	51
Men	50	48	44	50
Women	54	50	47	53
Center cities	58	50	48	53
Suburbs	49	50	46	50
Rural/small towns	51	48	43	53
Income in 1st–16th percentile	62	57	54	56
Income in 17th–33rd percentile	55	51	48	53
Income in 34th–67th percentile	51	48	44	50
Income in 68th–95th percentile	46	44	40	50
Income in 96th–100th percentile	44	47	42	54

Source: American National Election Studies surveys.

Entries are average thermometer readings on a 0–100 "cold" to "warm" scale, in which high scores represent more positive feelings toward "people on welfare."

Both material self-interest and symbolic concerns contribute to opinion formation on welfare. Americans' resistance to welfare spending only partially involves a concern about waste of fiscal resources. Those who believe welfare is fiscally wasteful have been found to oppose welfare spending only slightly more than those who do not think welfare particularly wasteful. However, analysis of General Social Survey data from the 1980s found that resistance to welfare spending was significantly higher among those who thought their taxes were too high. Opposition to welfare spending was consistently lower among those respondents who thought their financial situations were getting worse (as opposed to remaining stable or getting better) and among those who thought they were doing financially less well than others (as compared to those who thought themselves to be about average or better than average). These findings suggest that economic self-interest or empathy has some impact on opinions toward welfare opinion, though other research has also found significant influence of political ideology, independent of objective self-interest, in welfare opinion formation.

Measured differently, investigators have found a somewhat stronger relationship between welfare spending and income. In his analysis of nationwide survey data Martin Gilens reports that controlling for one's own experience with welfare reduces the impact of household income as an explanatory variable on welfare spending preferences by more than one-half. Other investigators have reported similar findings, supporting the claim that personal experience with welfare goes a particularly long way toward explaining individual-level support for it.

Given what is known about the strong link between racialized thinking and welfare, it is difficult to discuss Americans' opinions on welfare without also discussing their opinions toward people of historically disadvantaged racial minorities. While old-fashioned racism among whites is less often seen at the beginning of the twenty-first century than a generation or two earlier, a more subtle form of more subtle or symbolic racism has taken its place (see also Symbolic Politics). Under this racism, objections to persons of different races are blunted, being cloaked in language of objections to those people based on supposed violations of symbolically important tenets such as the work ethic, equal treatment and individualism. With this, whites object to government aid to blacks not because they are black per se but rather because of resistance to government assistance for a special class of people (involving arguments about a level playing field) or to persons who fail to pursue self-help (involving also arguments about an overly intrusive government).

Through this perspective it becomes understandable that the single most powerful predictor of whites' support for welfare spending is the degree to which they view African Americans as either hard working or lazy. Working from the incorrect assumption that the welfare roles are overwhelmingly populated by blacks, whites use their estimation of blacks' work ethic as a filter through which to judge an aid program that seems mostly to help black people. To the extent the news media tend strongly to portray the poor as overwhelmingly African American, whites' beliefs about welfare recipients as overwhelmingly black, lazy, and thus undeserving are reinforced.

Similar findings come from earlier research as well. Analysis of data from the General Social Survey from the 1970s and the 1980s revealed that those with more tolerant racial attitudes more strongly supported spending on public assistance. This corroborates Gilens's more recent in-depth study of survey data from the 1990s.

Whites' antagonism toward government help for blacks extends to some interesting outcomes. Paul Sniderman and his colleagues in a 1991 *American Journal of Political Science* article reported the standard finding that whites supported assistance less for hypothetical black recipients than for hypothetical white recipients. However, when the hypothetical black recipient was portrayed as hard working, support for assistance rose above that expressed for a hypothetical white recipient. The explanation is that whites see such African Americans as so exceptional that whites exaggerate their endorsement of this deservingness. The finding that whites see blacks as less hard working than whites fits with a historical pattern among respondents to the National Election Studies who consider blacks, more than any other named group, as more likely to want to rely on welfare rather than to work to earn a living.

Aggregate level support for welfare rose somewhat during the late 1990s despite a growing percentage of the national welfare caseload being African American during the same time. This paradox is likely explained by other factors, chiefly dramatic caseload declines and a sense that welfare is less permissive than it was before. While race is a powerful factor in explaining support for welfare, it does not trump all other explanations at the aggregate level.

Public support for cash welfare consistently lags below that for other programs, whether in-kind programs, such as health care assistance; or means-tested programs, such as food stamps or housing assistance; or universal social insurance programs, such as Social Security retirement benefits. Figure 1 shows the persistent high level of public support from increasing spending on Social Security and healthcare (as well as "assistance to the poor," phrased this way). The significant distinctions the public makes between welfare and other programs derives from several differences across those programs. Welfare is not universal but is instead targeted at a clearly identifiable (out) group. It goes mainly to those who work less than full time. Cash benefits potentially can be spent in ways that the majority public would think frivolous. Last, unlike Social Security and unemployment insurance, welfare eligibility does not depend on one's history of contributions. In the eyes of the public, the noncontributory nature of welfare lessens the sense of a right of receivership attached to it.

A number of questions about public opinion toward welfare remain. One concerns the role of ambivalence in survey response. Given the strongly conflicting demands of such ideas as equal opportunity to participate meaningfully in society and the economy, a fundamental right to enjoy a full measure of the fruits of one's labor and talent, and the right to some minimum level of sustenance, especially for children, most people enter conversations about welfare with a built-in tension over how much government should intervene to ease poverty. The ambivalence inherent in opinions on welfare not only makes survey responses more subject to context and question-wording effects but also invites more wavering in people's responses than seen in other areas. Another area bearing further inquiry is how major welfare policy changes can affect public support for those programs. The extent to which Americans relate considerations about a changed welfare contract to their thinking about support for public assistance is not well understood. Some evidence exists that public opinion responded to the 1996 federal legislation by becoming more supportive for welfare spending, but a similar pattern was not seen during the spread of state-initiated policy changes during the early 1990s, which also tended to shift welfare in a conservative direction. This shift in policy, however, was evidently not widely visible and debated nationally, in contrast to national welfare reform legislation in 1996. Little is known, moreover, about how the public connects and responds to such events as terrorism, war, or budget deficits in its level of support for welfare spending. Difficult economic times have historically seen stronger support for welfare, given the apparently greater perceived need for such benefits. While this pattern was altered during the prosperity of the late-1990s, as Americans seemed to consider welfare policy changes as an important part of the new welfare contract, it remains to be seen how the classic guns-butter trade-off will play out in the future of welfare policy making.

Last, historical comparisons of the United States with European and other welfare states have emphasized the latter's greater largesse in protecting its citizens from poverty and how the United States might learn from these countries' experiences. The future, however, has begun to look different. European nations have had to adjust to new domestic and global economic trends, raising the question of how they will deal with racial and ethnic diversity, aging populations, and economic uncertainties. This suggests that the experiences of the United States and Europe will become more like each other; what effect this has on European public opinion will be interesting to see.

Further Reading

Cook, Fay Lomax, and Edith Barrett. *Support for the American Welfare State: The Views of Congress and the Public.* New York: Columbia University Press, 1992. Offers a thorough treatment of congressional and popular opinions on welfare.

Feldman, Stanley, and Marco Steenbergen. "The Humanitarian Foundation of Public Support for Social Welfare." *American Journal of Political Science* 45 (July 2001): 658–77. A corrective to the well-worn investigation of egalitarianism as an explanation of Americans' support for welfare. Highlights how humanitarianism is probably a better description of what most Americans really support.

Gilens, Martin. *Why Americans Hate Welfare: Race, Media, and the Politics of Antipoverty Policy.* Chicago: University of Chicago Press, 1999. Examines the relationship between attitudes on race and opposition to welfare spending.

Hochschild, Jennifer. *What's Fair? American Beliefs About Distributive Justice.* Cambridge, MA: Harvard University Press, 1981. Presents findings from a series of in-depth interviews with a cross-section of Americans talking about their beliefs regarding economic distribution.

McClosky, Herbert, and John Zaller. *The American Ethos: Public Attitudes Toward Capitalism and Democracy.* Cambridge, MA: Harvard University Press, 1984. Offers a comprehensive treatment of the balancing act that Americans do regarding individualism and equality.

Page, Benjamin, and Robert Y. Shapiro. *The Rational Public: Fifty Years of Trends in Americans' Policy Preferences.* Chicago: University of Chicago Press, 1992. Makes an argument about the value of considering aggregate public opinion over individual-level opinion and presents policy-relevant public opinion trend data on numerous topics.

Schiltz, Michael. *Public Attitudes Toward Social Security, 1935–1965.* Social Security Administration (Research Report no. 33). Washington, DC: U.S. Department of Health, Education and Welfare, 1970. Provides a wealth of longitudinal public opinion data on Social Security, welfare, and related programs.

Web Sites

The definitive online archive of American public opinion is maintained by the Roper Center for Public Opinion Research in Storrs, Connecticut. The Roper Center's POLL database, iPOLL, is an excellent resource for public opinion data. Much of the data cited here came from this archive. The Web site is available at http://www.ropercenter.uconn.edu/ipoll.html.

The Institute for Research in the Social Sciences at the University of North Carolina, Chapel Hill, maintains an online archive of state and national polls, including Harris polls. This database is available at http://www.irss.unc.edu/data_archive/home.asp.

The Pew Center for the People and the Press provides public opinion data and analysis online at http://people-press.org.

Greg M. Shaw and Robert Y. Shapiro

Professional Organizations, Archives, and Polling Centers

PROFESSIONAL ORGANIZATIONS

American Association of Public Opinion Research (AAPOR)
Address: PO Box 14263, Lenexa, KS 66285-4263
Internet: http://www.aapor.org

The Council of American Survey Research Organizations (CASRO)
Address: 170 North Country Rd., Suite 4, Port Jefferson, NY 11777
Internet: http://www.casro.org

Marketing Research Association (MRA)
Address: 1344 Silas Deane Hwy., Suite 306, Rocky Hill, CT 06067-1342
Internet: http://www.mra-net.org

The National Council on Public Polls (NCPP)
Address: Marist College, Poughkeepsie, NY 12603
Internet: http://www.ncpp.org

DATA ARCHIVES

Inter-University Consortium for Political and Social Research
Address: University of Michigan, Institute for Social Research, PO Box 1248, Ann Arbor, MI 48106-1248
Internet: http://www.icpsr.umich.edu

National Election Studies
Address: Center for Political Studies, PO Box 1248, Ann Arbor, MI 48106-1248
Internet: http://www.umich.edu/~nes/

The Odum Institute
Address: Manning Hall, CB#3355, UNC-CH, Chapel Hill, NC 27599
Internet: http://www.irss.unc.edu/data_archive/home.asp

National Journal Hotline
Internet: http://www.nationaljournal.com/pubs/hotline

Pew Research Center for the People and the Press
Address: 1150 18th St., NW, Suite 975, Washington, DC 20036
Internet: http://www.people-press.org

PollingReport.com
Internet: http://www.pollingreport.com

The Roper Center for Public Opinion
Address: 341 Mansfield Rd., U-164, Storrs, CT 06269-1164
Internet: http://www.ropercenter.uconn.edu

COMMERCIAL SURVEY CENTERS

The Gallup Organization
Address: 901 F Street, NW, Washington, DC 20004
Internet: http://www.gallup.com

Harris Interactive
Address: 111 5th Ave., New York, NY 10003
Internet: http://www.harrisinteractive.com

International Communications Research
Address: 605 West State St., Media, PA 19063
Internet: http://www.icrsurvey.com

Mason-Dixon Polling & Research
Address: 2121 K Street NW, Suite 800, Washington, DC 20037
Internet: http://www.mason-dixon.com

Opinion Dynamics
Address: 1030 Massachusetts Ave., Cambridge, MA 02138
Internet: http://www.opiniondynamics.com

Princeton Survey Research Associates
Address: 911 Commons Way, Princeton, NJ 08540
Internet: http://www.psra.com

Yankelovich Partners
Address: 101 Merritt, 7 Corporate Park, Norwalk, CT 06851
Internet: http://www.yankelovich.com

Zogby International
Address: 1600 K Street, Suite 600, Washington, DC 20006
Internet: http://www.zogby.com

ACADEMIC SURVEY CENTERS

Alabama

Institute for Communication Research, University of Alabama
Address: PO Box 870172, Tuscaloosa, AL 35487-0172
Internet: http://www.icr.ua.edu

Alaska

Institute of Social and Economic Research, University of Alaska
Address: 3211 Providence Dr., Anchorage, AK 99508
Internet: http://www.iser.uaa.alaska.edu/

Arizona

Social Research Laboratory, Northern Arizona University
Address: PO Box 15301, Flagstaff, AZ 86011-5301
Internet: http://www4.nau.edu/srl/

California

Survey Research Center, University of California-Berkeley
Address: 2538 Channing Way, Berkeley, CA 94720-5100
Internet: http://srcweb.berkeley.edu/

Survey Research Center, University of California-Los Angeles
Address: 4250 Public Policy Bldg., Los Angeles, CA 90095-1484
Internet: http://www.sscnet.ucla.edu/issr/src/

Social Science Research Laboratory, San Diego State
Address: 5500 Campanile Dr., San Diego, CA 92182
Internet: http://ssrl.sdsu.edu/

Colorado

Social Science Data Laboratory, University of Colorado
Address: Ketchum 3, University of Colorado at Boulder, UCB 333, Boulder, CO 80309-0333
Internet: http://socsci.colorado.edu/LAB/

Connecticut

Center for Survey Research and Analysis, University of Connecticut
Address: 341 Mansfield Rd., Unit 1032, Storrs, CT 06269-1032
Internet: http://www.csra.uconn.edu/

The Polling Institute, Quinnipiac University
Address: 275 Mount Carmel Ave., Hamden, CT 06518
Internet: http://www.quinnipiac.edu/x11358.xml

Social Science Statistical Laboratory, Yale University
Address: 100 Urban Hall, New Haven, CT 06520
Internet: http://statlab.stat.yale.edu/

Florida

Florida International University's Public Opinion Center
Address: Biscayne Bay Campus, HM246, 3000 NE 151st St., North Miami, FL 33181
Internet: http://www.fiu.edu/orgs/ipor/

Survey Research Laboratory, Florida State University
Address: College of Social Sciences, FSU, Tallahassee, FL 32306-2221
Internet: http://www.fsu.edu/~survey/

Georgia

Survey Research Center, University of Georgia
Address: 238 McWhorter Hall, Athens, GA 30602
Internet: http://www.src.uga.edu/

Illinois

National Opinion Research Center
Address: 1155 E. 60th St., Chicago, IL 60632
Internet: http://www.norc.uchicago.edu

Indiana

Indiana University's Center for Survey Research
Address: Eigenmann Hall, 2 South, 1900 E. 10th St., Bloomington, IN 47406-7512
Internet: http://www.indiana.edu/~csr/

The Public Opinion Laboratory at Indiana University, Purdue University
Address: Madame Walker Plaza, 719 Indiana Ave., Suite 260, Indianapolis, IN 46202
Internet: http://polecat.iupui.edu/

Iowa

Survey Section of the Statistical Lab, Iowa State University
Address: 216 Snedecor Hall, Ames, IA 50011
Internet: http://www.statlab.iastate.edu/survey/

Kansas

Docking Institute of Public Affairs, Fort Hays State University
Address: 600 Park St., Hays, KS 67601-4099
Internet: http://www.fhsu.edu/docking/index.shtml

Policy Research Institute, University of Kansas
Address: 607 Blake Hall, 1541 Lilac Lane, Lawrence, KS 66044-3177
Internet: http://www.ku.edu/pri/

Kentucky

Survey Research Unit, Urban Studies Institute, University of Louisville
Address: University of Louisville, Louisville, KY 40208
Internet: http://www.louisville.edu/cbpa/sru/

Louisiana

Louisiana Population Data Center, Louisiana State University
Address: 126 Stubbs Hall, Baton Rouge, LA 70803
Internet: http://lapop.lsu.edu/

Michigan

The Survey Research Center, University of Michigan
Address: 1355 ISR Bldg., PO Box 1248, Ann Arbor, MI 48106
Internet: http://www.isr.umich.edu/src/

Mississippi

The Social Science Research Center, Mississippi State University
Address: PO Box 5287, 103 Research Park, MS 39762-5287
Internet: http://www.ssrc.msstate.edu

Missouri

Public Policy Research Centers, University of Missouri-St. Louis
Address: 362 Social Science Business Bldg., One University Boulevard, St. Louis, MO 63121
Internet: http://pprc.umsl.edu/

Nebraska

Gallup Research Center, University of Nebraska-Lincoln
Address: 200 N. 11th St., Lincoln, NE 68588-0241
Internet: http://sram.unl.edu/grc/GRC.htm

New Hampshire

The Survey Center, University of New Hampshire
Address: Thompson Hall, Rm. G16, 105 Main St., Durham, NH 03824
Internet: http://www.unh.edu/ipssr/survey-center/

New Jersey

The Survey Research Center, Princeton University
Address: 169 Nassau St., Princeton, NJ 08540
Internet: http://www.wws.princeton.edu/~psrc/

Center for Public Interest Polling, Rutgers University
Address: 185 Ryders Lane, New Brunswick, NJ 08901
Internet: http://www.rci.rutgers.edu/~eaglepol/

New Mexico

The Institute for Public Policy, University of New Mexico
Address: MSC02 1660, Albuquerque, NM 87131-0001
Internet: http://www.unm.edu/~instpp/

New York

Center for the Social Sciences, Columbia University
Address: International Affairs Bldg., 8th floor, 420 W. 118th St., Mail Code 3355, New York, NY 10027
Internet: http://www.columbia.edu/cu/iserp/index.html

Center for Survey Research, SUNY, Stony Brook
Address: Social and Behavioral Sciences Bldg., 7th Floor, Rm. no. S-758, Stony Brook, NY 11794-4392
Internet: http://ws.cc.stonybrook.edu/surveys/

Institute for Social and Economic Research, Cornell University
Address: 391 Pine Tree Rd., Ithaca, NY 14850-1365
Internet: http://www.ciser.cornell.edu/

Marist Institute for Public Opinion, Marist College
Address: Fontaine Hall, 3399 North Rd., Poughkeepsie, NY 12601
Internet: http://www.maristpoll.marist.edu/

North Carolina

Institute for Research in Social Science, University of North Carolina
Address: Manning Hall, CB#3355, University of North Carolina at Chapel Hill, Chapel Hill, NC 27599-3355
Internet: http://www2.irss.unc.edu/irss/home.asp

Survey Research Center at Research Triangle Institute
Address: PO Box, 12194 Research Triangle Park, NC 27709-2194
Internet: http://www.rti.org/index.cfm

Ohio

Center for Policy Studies, The University of Akron
Address: 225 South Main St., Akron, OH 44325-1911
Internet: http://www.uakron.edu/centers/cps/

The Center for Survey Research, The Ohio State University
Address: College of Social and Behavioral Sciences, 154 N. Oval Mall,
Derby Hall, Rm. 3045, Columbus, OH 43210-1330
Internet: http://www.csr.ohio-state.edu/

The Center for Urban and Public Affairs, Wright State University
Address: 225 Millett Hall, 3640 Colonel Glenn Hwy., Dayton, OH 45435
Internet: http://www.wright.edu/cupa/

The Institute for Policy Research Survey Research Center, University of Cincinnati
Address: 3110 One Edwards Center, Cincinnati, OH 45221-0132
Internet: http://www.ipr.uc.edu/Home/Home.cfm

Oklahoma

The Center for Economic & Management Research, University of Oklahoma
Address: 302 West Brooks, Adams Hall, Rm. 4, Norman, OK 73019
Internet: http://cemr.ou.edu/cemr/index.asp

Oregon

Oregon Survey Research Laboratory, University of Oregon
Address: 5245 University of Oregon, 97403-5245
Internet: http://osrl.uoregon.edu/

Survey Research Center, Oregon State University
Address: 312 Kerr Administration Bldg., Corvallis, OR 97331
Internet: http://oregonstate.edu/research/

Pennsylvania

University of Pittsburgh, University Center for Social and Urban Research
Address: 121 University Place, Pittsburgh, PA 15260
Internet: http://www.ucsur.pitt.edu

Rhode Island

Public Opinion Laboratory, Brown University
Address: 67 George St., Box 1977, Providence, RI 02912
Internet: http://brown.edu/Departments/Taubman_Center/taubman/pubopin.html

Virginia

Survey Research Laboratory, Virginia Commonwealth University
Address: Kearney House, 921 W. Franklin St., PO Box 843016, Richmond, VA 23284-3016
Internet: http://www.vcu.edu/srl/

University of Virginia's Survey Research Center
Address: 2400 Old Ivy Rd., Suite 223, Charlottesville, VA 22903
Internet: http://www.virginia.edu/surveys/

The Virginia Tech Center for Survey Research
Address: 207 W. Roanoke St. (0543), Blacksburg, VA 24061
Internet: http://www.csr.vt.edu/

Washington

Social and Economic Sciences Research Center, Washington State University
Address: PO Box 644014, Washington State University, Pullman, WA 99164-4014
Internet: http://www.sesrc.wsu.edu/sesrcsite/

Wisconsin

Social Science Research Facility, University of Wisconsin–Milwaukee
Address: Bolton Hall, Rm. 874, 3210 N. Maryland Ave., Milwaukee, WI 53211
Internet: http://www.uwm.edu/Dept/ISPR//

University of Wisconsin, Madison Survey Center
Address: 1800 University Ave., Rm. 102, Madison, WI 53726
Internet: http://www.wisc.edu/uwsc/

Wyoming

Survey Research Center, University of Wyoming
Address: Laramie Plains Civic Center, 710 E. Garfield St., Suite 320, Laramie, WY 82070
Internet: http://www.uwyo.edu/src/

Index

About the Editors and Contributors

SAMUEL J. BEST is director of the Center for Survey Research and Analysis and associate professor of public policy at the University of Connecticut, Storrs, Connecticut. He is the author of numerous articles on public opinion and survey methods. His latest book, *Internet Data Collection*, describes how to perform each stage of the data collection process on the Internet, including sampling, instrument design, and administration. He holds a Ph.D. in political science from the State University of New York at Stony Brook.

BENJAMIN RADCLIFF received his Ph.D. in political science from the University of Illinois at Urbana in 1991. He has spent most of his academic career at the University of Notre Dame, Indiana, where he is presently professor of political science and director of graduate studies. Radcliff has published extensively in the major peer reviewed journals within the discipline, including the *American Political Science Review*, the *American Journal of Political Science*, the *Journal of Politics*, and the *British Journal of Political Science*, among others. His research focuses primarily on democratic theory and political behavior, with particular emphasis on electoral participation and public opinion. His current research agenda, "On the Political Economy of Human Happiness," examines the relationship between electoral outcomes and the quality of life that citizens experience.

MAHALLEY D. ALLEN, J.D., is a doctoral candidate in political science at the University of Kansas, Lawrence, Kansas.

MOLLY W. ANDOLINA, Ph.D., is assistant professor of political science at DePaul University, Chicago, Illinois.

JAMES M. AVERY is assistant professor of political science at Southern Illinois University, Carbondale, Illinois.

NEIL BAER is a graduate student in the Department of Political Science at San Diego State University, San Diego, California.

JANICE BALLOU is vice president and deputy director of survey and information services at Mathematica Policy Research, Princeton, New Jersey.

JASON BARABAS, Ph.D., is assistant professor of political science in the Department of Political Science at Southern Illinois University, Carbondale, Illinois.

GORDON G. BECHTEL, Ph.D., is professor emeritus of marketing at the Warrington College of Business Administration, University of Florida, Gainesville, and a research scientist at the Florida Research Institute, Gainesville.

ROBERT BELLI is professor of psychology and associate director of the Gallup Center's Survey Research Methodology Program at the University of Nebraska, Lincoln, Nebraska.

JOHN M. BENSON, M.A., is managing director of the Harvard Opinion Research Program at the Harvard School of Public Health, Boston, Massachusetts.

GEORGE BISHOP is professor of political science and director of the Graduate Certificate Program in Public Opinion and Survey Research at the University of Cincinnati, Cincinnati, Ohio.

GEORGE Y. BIZER is assistant professor of psychology in the Psychology Department at Eastern Illinois University, Charleston, Illinois.

ROBERT J. BLENDON, Sc.D., is professor of health policy and political analysis at the Harvard School of Public Health in Boston, Massachusetts, and the John F. Kennedy School of Government, Cambridge, Massachusetts.

MICHAEL BOSNJAK, Ph.D., is assistant professor of consumer psychology at the University of Mannheim (Germany), Department of Psychology II, and director of research at SurveyHoo Web-based Marketing Research Company, Richmond, Virginia.

KARLYN BOWMAN is a resident scholar at the American Enterprise Institute, Washington, D.C.

RICHARD BRAUNSTEIN, Ph.D., is assistant professor of political science at the University of South Dakota, Vermillion, South Dakota.

PAUL R. BREWER, Ph.D., is assistant professor of journalism and mass communications at the University of Wisconsin-Milwaukee, Milwaukee, Wisconsin.

MOLLYANN BRODIE is vice president and director for public opinion and media research at the Kaiser Family Foundation in Menlo Park, California.

NANCY BURNS is professor of political science and co-principal investigator, American National Election Study.

CHRISTOPHER K. BUTLER, Ph.D., is assistant professor of political science at the University of New Mexico, Albuquerque, New Mexico.

MICHAEL BUTTERWORTH, M.S., is information systems director for the Election and Survey unit of CBS News, New York, New York.

STEPHEN MAYNARD CALIENDO, Ph.D., is assistant professor of political science at Avila University, Kansas City, Missouri.

DAVID E. CAMPBELL is assistant professor of political science at the University of Notre Dame, Notre Dame, Indiana.

DAVID CANTOR, Ph.D., is an associate director at Westat, a social science research firm in Rockville, Maryland.

ALBERT H. CANTRIL is an independent scholar based in Washington, D.C.

THERESA CAPELOS is assistant professor of political science at Leiden University, Leiden, The Netherlands.

LISA R. CARLEY-BAXTER, M.A., is survey director and methodologist in the Program for Research in Survey Methodology, Survey Research Division, at RTI International, Research Triangle Park, North Carolina.

DIANA B. CARLIN is dean of the graduate school and international programs and professor of communication studies at the University of Kansas, Lawrence, Kansas.

EDWARD G. CARMINES is Rudy Professor and Warren O. Chapman Professor of Political Science at Indiana University, Bloomington, Indiana.

RYAN L. CLAASSEN is a doctoral candidate in the Department of Political Science at the University of California, Davis, California.

MICHELE CLAIBOURN, Ph.D., is assistant professor of political science at the University of Oklahoma, Norman, Oklahoma.

RICH CLARK is administrator of research and data services for the Vinson Institute at the University of Georgia, Athens, Georgia, and director of its Peach State Poll.

HAROLD D. CLARKE, Ph.D., is Ashbel Smith Professor, School of Social Sciences, University of Texas at Dallas, Dallas, Texas.

TIMOTHY C. COBURN is professor of statistics in the Department of Management Science at Abilene Christian University, Abilene, Texas.

JEFFREY E. COHEN is professor of political science at Fordham University, Bronx, New York.

FRED CONRAD is associate research scientist at the Institute for Social Research at the University of Michigan and research associate professor in the Joint Program for Survey Methodology at the University of Maryland, College Park, Maryland.

MIKE COOKE is senior analyst at the National Opinion Research Center, the University of Chicago, Chicago, Illinois.

ROSALYN COOPERMAN, Ph.D., is assistant professor of political science in the Department of Political Science and International Affairs at Mary Washington College, Fredericksburg, Virginia.

J. KEVIN CORDER, Ph.D., is associate professor of political science at Western Michigan University, Kalamazoo, Michigan.

THOMAS CRAEMER received his doctorate from the University of Tuebingen, Germany, in 2001 and is presently pursuing a Ph.D. in political psychology at the Department of Political Science at Stony Brook University, Stony Brook, New York.

CHRISTIAN S. CRANDALL is associate professor of psychology at the University of Kansas, Lawrence, Kansas.

MONICA DASHEN, Ph.D., is a research psychologist at the Bureau of Labor Statistics, Washington, D.C.

ROBERT P. DAVES is director of strategic and news research at the *Star Tribune* (Minneapolis–St. Paul, Minnesota), where he directs the Minnesota Poll.

CLARISSA DAVID, M.A., is a doctoral candidate of the Annenberg School of Communication at the University of Pennsylvania, Philadelphia, Pennsylvania.

ROBERT DAVIDSON is a graduate student at the University of Notre Dame, Notre Dame, Indiana.

MARK A. DAVIES teaches at Heriot-Watt University in Edinburgh, United Kingdom.

MATTHEW DeBELL, Ph.D., is a research analyst at the Education Statistics Services Institute, American Institutes for Research, Washington, D.C.

BENJAMIN DEUFEL is a doctoral candidate in the Department of Government at Harvard University, Cambridge, Massachusetts.

MARC DEUTSCHMANN is a survey methodologist at the Social Survey Research Center of the University of Duisburg-Essen, Germany.

WIL DIJKSTRA, Ph.D., is professor of methods of data collection in the social sciences at the Free University of Amsterdam, the Netherlands.

DON A. DILLMAN is Regents' Professor and the Thomas S. Foley Distinguished Professor of Government and Public Policy in the Departments of Sociology and Community and Rural Sociology, and deputy director of the Social and Economic Sciences Research Center at Washington State University, Pullman, Washington.

LINDA L. DIMITROPOULOS, Ph.D., is a social psychologist currently working as a survey director in the Health Services Program within the Survey Research Division at RTI International, Chicago, Illinois.

VESNA DOLNICAR is a Ph.D. student of communications and researcher at the Center of Methodology and Informatics, Faculty of Social Sciences, University of Ljubljana, Slovenia.

TODD DONOVAN, Ph.D., is professor of political science at Western Washington University, Bellingham, Washington.

LISA J. DOTTERWEICH is a doctoral candidate in political science at Kent State University, Kent, Ohio.

KATHRYN DOWNEY-SARGENT, Ph.D., is a research psychologist at the U.S. Bureau of Labor Statistics, Office of Survey Methods Research, Washington, D.C.

STASJA DRAISMA, Ph.D., is assistant professor of social research methodology at the Department of Social Research Methodology, Vrije University, Amsterdam, The Netherlands.

JAMES N. DRUCKMAN, Ph.D., is assistant professor of political science at the University of Minnesota, Minneapolis, Minnesota.

CLAIRE DURAND is associate professor of quantitative methodology and survey methods in the Department of Sociology, University of Montreal, Montreal, Quebec, Canada.

W. SHERMAN EDWARDS, MBA, is a vice president at Westat, a social science research firm in Rockville, Maryland.

NATHANIEL EHRLICH is a survey research specialist for the Office of Survey Research in the Institute for Public Policy and Social Research at Michigan State University,

MICHELLE ERNST is a developmental psychologist and a survey director at the National Opinion Research Center, the University of Chicago, Chicago, Illnois.

DAVID P. FAN is professor in the Department of Genetics, Cell Biology, and Development at the University of Minnesota,

BARBARA C. FARHAR is adjunct professor at the University of Colorado, Boulder, Colorado.

JAMES FARR is professor of political science at the University of Minnesota, Minneapolis-St. Paul, Minnesota.

AMY FERKETICH is assistant professor in the Division of Epidemiology and Biostatistics of the School of Public Heath at Ohio State University.

GLENN FIREBAUGH is professor of sociology and demography, head of the Department of Sociology, and senior scientist at the Population Research Institute at Penn State University.

GÖSTA FORSMAN is a professor in the Department of Mathematics at Linkoping University in Linkoping, Sweden.

JOHN F. FREIE, Ph.D., is professor of political science and acting director of the Honors Program at LeMoyne College, Syracuse, New York.

ANDREW S. FULLERTON, M.A., is a doctoral candidate in the Department of Sociology at the University of Connecticut in Storrs, Connecticut.

PATRICIA M. GALLAGHER, Ph.D., is a senior research fellow at the Center for Survey Research, University of Massachusetts, Boston, Massachusetts.

PHILIP GENDALL, Ph.D., is professor of marketing and head of the Department of Marketing at Massey University, Palmerston North, New Zealand.

JOSEPH D. GIAMMO is a graduate student in the Government Department at the University of Texas at Austin, Austin, Texas.

EWA A. GOLEBIOWSKA, Ph.D., is associate professor of political science at Wayne State University, Detroit, Michigan.

TOM GOUGEON, Ph.D., is associate professor in the Faculty of Education at the University of Calgary, Calgary, Alberta, Canada.

ARTHUR C. GRAESSER, Ph.D., is professor of psychology and computer science at the University of Memphis, Memphis, Tennessee. Dr. Graesser is director of the Center for Applied Psychological Research and co-director of the Institute for Intelligent Systems.

DONALD P. GREEN is the A. Whitney Griswold Professor of Political Science and director of the Institution for Social and Policy Studies at Yale University, New Haven, Connecticut.

KATHY E. GREEN, Ph.D., is professor of educational psychology, College of Education, University of Denver, Denver, Colorado.

SID GROENEMAN, Ph.D., is founder and president of Groeneman Research and Consulting in Bethesda, Maryland, which provides survey and marketing research services to a wide range of client organizations.

TRACEY HAGERTY-HELLER, M.S., is a senior research analyst at Westat, a social science research firm in Rockville, Maryland.

CATHERINE HAGGERTY is a senior survey director at the National Opinion Research Center, the University of Chicago, Chicago, Illinois.

CHASE H. HARRISON is chief methodologist for the Center for Survey Research and Analysis at the University of Connecticut, Storrs, Connecticut.

ANDREW F. HAYES, Ph.D., is assistant professor in the School of Journalism and Communication at Ohio State University, Columbus, Ohio.

DIANE J. HEITH, Ph.D., is assistant professor in the Department of Government and Politics at St. John's University, Jamaica, New York.

C. RICHARD HOFSTETTER is professor of political science and adjunct professor in the Graduate School of Public Health at San Diego State University, San Diego, California.

ALLYSON L. HOLBROOK, Ph.D., is assistant professor of public administration and psychology at the Survey Research Laboratory at the University of Illinois at Chicago, Chicago, Illinois.

ROBERT HUCKFELDT is professor of political science at the University of California at Davis.

LEONIE HUDDY is professor of political science at Stony Brook University, Stony Brook, New York.

GRAHAM HUEBER is a senior research associate at the Opinion Research Corporation, Princeton, New Jersey.

KRISTEN HUGHES conducts research at the Center for Survey Methods Research in the Statistical Research Division of the U.S. Census Bureau, Washington, D.C.

JENNIFER E. HUNTER, M.S., is a survey methodology researcher in the Center for Survey Methods Research in the Statistical Research Division of the U.S. Census Bureau, Washington, D.C.

JON HURWITZ is professor of political science at the University of Pittsburgh, Pittsburgh, Pennsylvania.

WILLIAM G. JACOBY is professor of political science at Michigan State University, East Lansing, Michigan.

MATTHEW JANS is an assistant study director at the Center for Survey Research at the University of Massachusetts, Boston, Massachusetts.

E. DEBORAH JAY, Ph.D., is president/CEO of Field Research Corporation, the San Francisco-based public opinion and marketing research firm founded by Mervin Field in 1945.

TED G. JELEN, Ph.D., is professor of political science at the University of Nevada, Las Vegas, Nevada.

KRISTA JENKINS, Ph.D., is assistant professor of political science at Fairleigh Dickinson University, Teaneck, New Jersey.

JENNIFER JERIT, Ph.D., is assistant professor of political science in the Department of Political Science at Southern Illinois University, Carbondale, Illinois.

LISA V. JOHN, M.S.W., is a project director at Battelle Centers for Public Health Research and Evaluation in St. Louis, Missouri.

RENÉE J. JOHNSON, Ph.D., is assistant professor of political science in the Department of Political Science at the University of Florida, Gainesville, Florida.

TIMOTHY P. JOHNSON, Ph.D., is director of the Survey Research Laboratory at the University of Illinois at Chicago, Chicago, Illinois.

EMILY W. KANE, Ph.D., is professor of sociology and chair of the Department of Sociology at Bates College, Lewiston, Maine.

DONALD R. KINDER is Philip E. Converse Collegiate Professor of Psychology at the University of Michigan, Ann Arbor, Michigan, and co-principal investigator, American National Election Study.

PATRICK KISER is a senior study leader at Battelle Centers for Public Health Research and Evaluation in St. Louis, Missouri.

BÄRBEL KNÄUPER, Ph.D., is assistant professor of psychology in the Department of Psychology at McGill University, Montreal, Canada.

PARVATI KRISHNAMURTY, Ph.D., is a survey economist in the Statistics and Methodology Department, National Opinion Research Center, the University of Chicago, Chicago, Illinois.

BRIAN KRUEGER is assistant professor of political science at the University of Rhode Island, Kingston, Rhode Island.

THOMAS LAMATSCH is director of the Cannon Center for Survey Research at the University of Nevada, Las Vegas, and an assistant professor in residence at the University's Department of Political Science.

JENNIFER L. LAMBE, Ph.D., is assistant professor in the Department of Communication at the University of Delaware, Newark, Delaware.

SUNGHEE LEE is a doctoral candidate in the Joint Program in Survey Methodology at the University of Maryland, College Park, Maryland.

DAVID C. LEEGE is professor emeritus of political science at the University of Notre Dame, Notre Dame, Indiana.

EDITH DESIREE DE LEEUW, Ph.D., is associate professor of survey methodology at the Department of Methodology and Statistics at Utrecht University, The Netherlands.

STANLEY LEMESHOW is the dean of the School of Public Health and the Director of the Center of Biostatistics, Ohio State University, Columbus, Ohio.

HUGH ANTHONY LEVINE, Esq., is a trial lawyer in San Francisco with more than thirty years of courtroom experience.

JAIME LIESMANN, M.S., R.D., is a study leader at Battelle Centers for Public Health Research and Evaluation in St. Louis, Missouri.

MICHAEL W. LINK, Ph.D., is a senior survey methodologist for the Centers for Disease Control and Prevention.

MARY E. LOSCH is associate professor of psychology and assistant director of the Center for Social and Behavioral Research at the University of Northern Iowa.

ERIC MacGILVRAY, Ph.D., is assistant professor of political science at the University of Wisconsin, Madison.

KATJA LOZAR MANFREDA, Ph.D., is assistant professor of statistics and social informatics at the Faculty of Social Sciences, University of Ljubljana, Slovenia.

CHRISTOPHER B. MANN, M.A., is a research fellow at the Institution for Social and Policy Studies at Yale University in New Haven, Connecticut.

KRISZTINA MARTON is a doctoral candidate and graduate research associate at the Center for Survey Research, Ohio State University, Columbus, Ohio.

FRANCO MATTEI is associate professor of political science at the University at Buffalo, State University of New York, Buffalo, New York.

MAXWELL McCOMBS, Ph.D., holds the Jesse H. Jones Centennial Chair in Communication in the School of Journalism at the University of Texas at Austin, Austin, Texas.

MONIKA L. McDERMOTT is assistant professor of public policy at the University of Connecticut, Storrs, Connecticut, and director of the Masters of Survey Research Program.

MICHAEL P. McDONALD, Ph.D., is assistant professor of government and politics at George Mason University, Fairfax, Virginia.

CHARLTON D. McILWAIN, Ph.D., is assistant professor of culture and communication at New York University, New York, New York.

LINDSAY McLAREN, Ph.D., is a Canadian Institutes of Health Research/Alberta Heritage Foundation for Medical Research Postdoctoral Fellow in the Health and Society Research Program, Department of Community Health Sciences, University of Calgary, Alberta, Canada.

STEPHANIE McLEAN is assistant professor of political science at the University of Pittsburgh, Pittsburgh, Pennsylvania.

RAMONA S. McNEAL is a doctoral candidate in political science at Kent State University, Kent, Ohio.

MATTHEW MENDELSOHN, Ph.D., is associate professor in the Department of Political Studies and director of the Canadian Opinion Research Archive at Queen's University, Kingston, Ontario.

JOANNE M. MILLER is assistant professor of political science at the University of Minnesota, Minneapolis, Minnesota.

YOUNG MIN, Ph.D., is assistant professor in the Department of Communication at Kyung Hee University, Seoul, Korea.

LEE M. MIRINGOFF is president of the Nation Council on Public Polls (NCPP), Hackensack, New Jersey.

WARREN J. MITOFSKY is president of Mitofsky International and a trustee of the National Council on Public Polls (NCPP), Hackensack, New Jersey.

ALAN D. MONROE is professor emeritus of political science at Illinois State University, Normal, Illinois.

DAVID MORGAN is University Professor of Interdisciplinary Studies at Portland State University in Portland, Oregon.

CHRIS MORIARITY, Ph.D., is a senior mathematical statistician with the U.S. government in Washington, D.C.

MICHAEL E. MORRELL is assistant professor of political science at the University of Connecticut, Storrs, Connecticut.

WHITNEY MURPHY, M.S., is a senior survey statistician at the National Opinion Research Center, the University of Chicago, Chicago, Illinois.

RICHARD G. NIEMI is Don Alonzo Watson Professor of political science at the University of Rochester, Rochester, New York.

HELMUT NORPOTH is professor of political science at the State University of New York at Stony Brook, Stony Brook, New York.

COLM O'MUIRCHEARTAIGH, Ph.D., is a vice president in statistics and methodology at the National Opinion Research Center at the University of Chicago, and a professor at the Irving B. Harris Graduate School of Public Policy Studies at the University of Chicago, Chicago, Illinois.

NORMAN ORNSTEIN is a resident scholar at the American Enterprise Institute, Washington, D.C.

LINDA K. OWENS, Ph.D., is assistant director for research planning at the Survey Research Laboratory at the University of Illinois at Chicago.

MICHAEL PARKIN is a graduate student in political science at the University of Minnesota.

ROBERT H. PATCHEN is vice president for research standards at Arbitron Inc., Columbia, Maryland.

MARK PEFFLEY is professor of political science at the University of Kentucky, Lexington, Kentucky.

SUSAN H. PINKUS is director of the Los Angeles Times Poll, a trustee on the National Council on Public Polls, and a member of the board of directors at the Roper Center.

S. JAMES PRESS, Ph.D., is distinguished professor in the Department of Statistics at the University of California at Riverside, Riverside, California.

MELVIN PRINCE is associate professor in marketing at Southern Connecticut State University, New Haven, Connecticut.

KIRK A. RANDAZZO, Ph.D., is assistant professor of political science at the University of Kentucky, Lexington, Kentucky.

KENNETH A. RASINSKI is principal research scientist at the National Opinion Research Center and adjunct professor at the Harris School of Public Policy Studies, the University of Chicago, Chicago, Illinois.

BRYCE B. REEVE, Ph.D., is a psychometrician at the Outcomes Research Branch, National Cancer Institute, Bethesda, Maryland.

HOWARD RIDDICK, Ph.D., is chief of the Survey Planning and Development Branch of the Division of Health Interview Statistics at the National Center for Health Statistics, Hyattsville, Maryland.

TERRY ROBERTSON is chair of the Department of Communication Studies at the University of South Dakota, Vermillion, South Dakota.

RICHARD ROCKWELL is executive director of the Roper Center for Public Opinion Research, the University of Connecticut, Storrs, Connecticut.

CHRIS RODGERS is a doctoral candidate in political economy at the School of Social Sciences, the University of Texas at Dallas.

THOMAS J. RUDOLPH, Ph.D., is assistant professor of political science at the University of Illinois at Urbana-Champaign.

MONICA C. SCHNEIDER is a graduate student of political science at the University of Minnesota, Minneapolis, Minnesota.

SID J. SCHNEIDER, Ph.D., is a senior study director at Westat, a social science research firm in Rockville, Maryland.

NORBERT SCHWARZ is professor of psychology at the University of Michigan, professor of marketing at the University of Michigan Business School, and senior research scientist at Michigan's Institute for Social Research.

ROBERT Y. SHAPIRO, Ph.D., is professor of political science at Columbia University, New York, New York.

GREG M. SHAW, Ph.D., is associate professor of political science at Illinois Wesleyan University, Bloomington, Illinois.

REGINALD S. SHEEHAN, Ph.D., is professor of political science at Michigan State University, East Lansing, Michigan.

IRIS SHIMIZU, Ph.D., is a mathematical statistician in the Office of Research and Methodology, National Center for Health Statistics at Hyattsville, Maryland.

LEO SIMONETTA is a research associate at the Art and Science Group, a consulting firm specializing in higher education and the nonprofit sector, where he oversees research for *studentPoll*, the firm's quarterly omnibus survey.

MONROE SIRKEN, Ph.D., is a mathematical statistician in the Office of the Director, National Center for Health Statistics at Hyattsville, Maryland.

ELIZABETH THEISS SMITH, Ph.D., is assistant professor of political science at the University of South Dakota in Vermillion, where she also serves as associate director of the Farber Center for Civic Leadership.

TOM W. SMITH is director of the General Social Survey, National Opinion Research Center, the University of Chicago, Chicago, Illinois.

GER J.M.E. SNIJKERS, Ph.D., is a senior researcher in survey methodology, at Statistics Netherlands, Heerlen, and the Utrecht University, Utrecht, The Netherlands.

PEVERILL SQUIRE, Ph.D., is professor of political science at the University of Iowa, Iowa City, Iowa.

CHARLOTTE STEEH is associate research professor in the Department of Public Administration and Urban Studies at Georgia State University, Atlanta, Georgia.

MARCO R. STEENBERGEN is associate professor of political science at the University of North Carolina, Chapel Hill, North Carolina.

MARIANNE C. STEWART is professor in the School of Social Sciences, the University of Texas at Dallas, Dallas, Texas.

CHRISTINE STICH is research associate and lecturer for statistics in the Department of Psychology, Free University of Berlin, Germany.

NATHANIEL STONE, M.A., IMBA, is a senior researcher at the Research Branch of Communication Canada, an agency of the Government of Canada, in Ottawa, Ontario, Canada.

BARBARA J. STUSSMAN is a survey statistician at the National Center for Health Statistics, Hyattsville, Maryland.

CHARLES S. TABER is associate professor of political science at the State University of New York at Stony Brook, Stony Brook, New York.

JUDITH M. TANUR, Ph.D., is distinguished teaching professor in the Department of Sociology, the State University of New York at Stony Brook, Stony Brook, New York.

BETH L. TAYLOR is a survey statistician at the National Center for Health Statistics, Hyattsville, Maryland.

KENT L. TEDIN is professor of political science at the University of Houston in Houston, Texas.

PAUL TESKE, Ph.D., is professor of public affairs at the University of Colorado's Graduate School of Public Affairs in Denver, Colorado.

ALVIN B. TILLERY, JR., is assistant professor of political science at the University of Notre Dame, Notre Dame, Indiana.

ROGER TOURANGEAU, Ph.D., is director of the Joint Program in Survey Methodology at the University of Maryland, College Park, Maryland.

ALEX R. TROUTEAUD is a doctoral candidate in applied sociology at Baylor University, Waco, Texas.

TRACY L. TUTEN, Ph.D., is assistant professor of advertising research at Virginia Commonwealth University in Richmond, Virginia.

KEES VAN DER VEER, Ph.D., is associate professor of social research methodology at the Faculty of Social Sciences, Vrije University, Amsterdam, The Netherlands.

JOHANNES VAN DER ZOUWEN, Ph.D., is professor of social research methodology, Faculty of Social Sciences, Vrije University in Amsterdam, The Netherlands.

VASJA VEHOVAR, Ph.D., is associate professor of statistics at the Faculty of Social Sciences, the University of Ljubljana, Slovenia.

AMIRAM D. VINOKUR, Ph.D., is a senior research scientist at the Institute for Social Research, the University of Michigan, Ann Arbor, Michigan.

PENNY S. VISSER is associate professor of social psychology at the University of Chicago, Chicago, Illinois.

MICHAEL W. WAGNER is a doctoral candidate in political science at Indiana University in Bloomington, Indiana.

DROR WALK is a doctoral candidate in the Psychology Department of Bar-Ilan University in Ramat Gan, Israel, a researcher at the JDC-Brookdale Institute, Jerusalem, and an associate editor of *Megamot*, a Hebrew-language journal on the behavioral sciences.

RUTH WARNER is a Melik Fellow of Psychology at the University of Kansas, Lawrence, Kansas.

CLYDE WILCOX is professor of government at Georgetown University in Washington, D.C.

AIMEE WILLIAMSON is a doctoral candidate in public affairs at the University of Colorado at Denver and an instructor in political science at the Community College of Aurora, Aurora, Colorado.

GORDON WILLIS, Ph.D., is cognitive psychologist at the National Cancer Institute, National Institutes of Health, Rockville, Maryland.

ED WINGENBACH is associate professor of political science at the University of the Redlands, Redlands, California.

CHRISTINA WOLBRECHT is Packey J. Dee Associate Professor of Political Science at the University of Notre Dame, Notre Dame, Indiana. She is author of *The Politics of Women's Rights* (2000) and numerous articles on political parties, interest groups, mass behavior, and gender politics.

CATHERINE WORTHINGTON, Ph.D., is assistant professor of social work at the Faculty of Social Work, University of Calgary, Calgary, Canada; and Research Associate at the HIV Social, Behavioural, and Epidemiological Studies Unit, Faculty of Medicine, University of Toronto, Toronto, Canada.

MARIA ZAGATSKY is a graduate student in the Department of Social Psychology at the University of Chicago, Chicago, Illinois.

JEREMY ZELL is a research assistant at the University of South Dakota, Vermillion, South Dakota. His research interests include law and social policy, political participation, and social capital in the United States.